Bon[illegible]

August 1984.

THE AIR DEFENCE OF BRITAIN 1914–1918

Capt G. H. Hackwill (*left*) inspecting the wreckage of Gotha G V/938/16 which he and another No.44 Squadron Camel pilot, 2nd Lieut C. C. Banks, shot down at Wickford, Essex, on 28/29 January, 1918. This was the first Gotha to fall on British soil. The other officer, sometimes wrongly described as Banks, is unidentified.

THE AIR DEFENCE OF BRITAIN

1914–1918

CHRISTOPHER COLE
and
E. F. CHEESMAN

PUTNAM
AN IMPRINT OF THE BODLEY HEAD
LONDON

BY CHRISTOPHER COLE

McCudden V.C.
But Not in Anger (with Roderick Grant)

British Library Cataloguing
in Publication Data
Cole, Christopher
The air defence of Britain 1914–1918
(Putnam aeronautical).
1. Great Britain. *Royal Flying Corps* – History
2. Great Britain, *Royal Naval Air Service* – History
3. World War, 1914–1918 – Aerial operations, British
I. Title
II. Cheesman, E. F.
III. Series
940.4′4941 D602
ISBN 0-370-30538-8

Printed in Great Britain for
The Bodley Head Ltd
9 Bow Street, London WC2E 7AL
by Thomson Litho Ltd, East Kilbride
First published 1984

Contents

Introduction and Acknowledgments

To most people there is only one Battle of Britain—the historic struggle in the summer of 1940 between the Hurricanes and Spitfires of the Royal Air Force and the Messerschmitts, Heinkels and Dorniers of Goering's Luftwaffe.

That memorable event has been described from every angle in scores of books and articles, in films and in radio and television programmes.

But there was an earlier, now almost forgotten, air battle over Britain during the First World War, when B.Es, Pups, Camels, Bristols and other aeroplanes sought to destroy the raiding Zeppelins, Gothas and Giants of the German navy and army air services. Little has been written about that conflict except for a handful of books written principally from the enemy viewpoint, and perennial feature articles describing the more spectacular victories over the airships.

The chief reason for this omission is that although the dramatic new dimension of air power in the 1914–18 conflict first brought modern warfare to the home front—with reactions from the raided areas comparable with those generated by the bombing of the Second World War—everything was overshadowed by the grim struggle in France, where a single day's fighting could inflict casualties far exceeding the 4,830 killed and injured in four years of air raids on Britain. Also, despite the brief adulation heaped on the first pilots to destroy airships over England, home defence flying lacked the ingredients of 'glamour' surrounding air fighting on the Western Front, with the popular notion of individual 'aces' joined in chivalrous combat high above the squalor of the trenches.

Nevertheless the story of Britain's efforts to defeat the early air raiders is a fascinating one, which this book for the first time records in detail. It covers the progressive phases of the enemy offensive—the initial hit-and-run forays, the hated Zeppelin attacks, the daylight assault and the nagging night raids of 1917–18. It traces the counter-measures taken, from the first interception attempts by airmen armed with rifles and hand-held bombs to the ultimate organization employing the best contemporary fighters under rudimentary ground control.

This book deals principally with the work of the aircraft defences—the aeroplanes used, the pilots, their squadrons, and the aerodromes from which they flew. The story is set against the politico-military background, with the insatiable demands for men and aircraft for the Western Front, and the remarkable, prolonged wrangling between the Admiralty and War Office over air defence, temporarily halted by an uneasy truce following the formation of the Royal Air Force in April 1918.

Ancillary services—the guns, searchlights and the observer organization—and detailed effects of the bombing are dealt with only briefly. This is for reasons of space and because those matters are well covered in other publications, notably that essential reference work, *The War in the Air*, by H. A. Jones, generally regarded as the official history. Detailed accounts of the raids from the German viewpoint are provided in those admirable definitive works, *The Zeppelin in Combat* by Douglas H. Robinson, *The First Battle of Britain* by Raymond H. Fredette and *The German Giants* by G. W. Haddow and Peter M. Grosz.

The First World War air defence story is one of frustration and inspiration, failure and success, tragedy and humour. Hindsight can evoke some exasperation with the authorities for what sometimes appears as a pig-headed refusal to perceive the obvious—but it must be remembered that with British military aviation only three years old when the war started, the realities of air combat could be learned only from experience, trial and error.

In the early days before even the basic process of flying could be taken for granted the experts reasonably concluded that to perform military tasks, and especially to operate safely by night, the aeroplane must be a fully stable vehicle—though it emerged later that the doctrine of inherent stability in fact militated against the emergence of effective fighting aircraft. Likewise the apparently simplest method of destroying an airship, by bombing from above, was seemingly confirmed by an early success—but this inevitably delayed development of the surer and easier method of close machine-gun attack with incendiary and explosive bullets.

Most problems arose from the very novelty and wide potential of the air weapon, which few were able to grasp until one side or the other actually demonstrated some new application. The German formation daylight raids provide a good example. Although this form of attack had been foreseen for many months, the first such raiding force, in 1917, flew over England for an hour without once being intercepted. Some blame should perhaps rest with the intelligence organization, which at times seemed to regard the acquisition of enemy information as an end in itself. There were several examples of inordinate delay in passing down to the operational units important facts about German developments, which delayed the evolvement of suitable tactics and countermeasures.

Progress was understandably slow in the early months when all flying activities were in the development stage. After eighteen months of hostilities the home defence responsibility was transferred from the Admiralty to the War Office, and, with the stimulus of the daylight raids, notable advances were made towards building a defence force which presented a real threat to day and night raiders. The basic principles remained in being during the inter-war years, but some important techniques were apparently forgotten—notably the use of upward-angled guns by night fighters, which had proved their value in action.

For a generation conditioned to jet aircraft performance it may be difficult to appreciate that even by 1918 the home defence fighters had a performance below that of the basic club and training aircraft of the 1970s and '80s. Another factor to remember is that the fighters operated without any radio aids—apart from a few equipped with primitive radio telephony during the last aeroplane raid of the war.

This book results fundamentally from the study of more than a thousand files in the Public Record Office, which contained much important detail, naturally withheld from contemporary publication, but also absent from subsequent accounts. Critical analysis of all the available information—including the numerous pilots' reports—and correction of some simple but long perpetuated errors of fact, has resulted in rather different, but more accurate, versions of some actions than have appeared hitherto.

For reasons of space and because they are easily accessible elsewhere, full verbatim reports by pilots who shot down airships have not been quoted. However, their essential facts have been correlated with reports by other airborne pilots and with additional relevant details to present a wider overall picture of those actions.

An unexpected by-product of the research was the emergence of important facts about some of the famous squadrons and aerodromes which are absent from any published RAF unit histories. For example, No.7 Squadron, best remembered as a leading Second World War bomber unit, made the first fighter interception of an aeroplane raider over England and shortly followed this with the first anti-Zeppelin sorties. And that from that most celebrated of aerodromes, Biggin Hill, night fighter operations began several months earlier than previously recorded.

So far as surviving records can provide, every home defence sortie of the First World War has been listed. Unfortunately there are a few gaps in the information, usually in the earlier years but also on several later occasions where complete details of important actions are inexplicably missing. Where official records themselves show conflicting versions of basic facts—such as sortie times—those which relate most closely to any other available information have been used.

Squadrons and other units are given the designations in use at the time of the operations described. These may sometimes conflict with titles apparently promulgated earlier, but instructions were not uncommonly issued retrospectively, and there was some delay before they were followed by all units.

Service serial numbers where available are quoted since these can be a useful aid to further research—for example in identifying unit photographs.

Every effort has been made to record names correctly, and especial thanks are due to the Ministry of Defence RAF Officers' Records section, which showed a remarkable ability to check basic details about individuals who left the Services more than 60 years ago. Even so it has not been possible to record the initials of some, and due apologies are extended to their families.

We are deeply indebted to Mr A. E. Ferko, who generously contributed from his extensive researches into German air operations of the First World War, and made it possible to identify units which conducted most of the early hit-and-run attacks, hitherto only loosely or wrongly attributed. Also to Mr Donald Chidson, for the extract from his father's log book relating to the first air engagement over England; and to Mrs Margaret Castle, for providing access to the log book of her father, Captain C. C. Banks, which disclosed important facts concerning No.44 Squadron activities.

Former officers of the RNAS and RFC who have supplied valuable background information and photographs include Air Commodore Sir Vernon Brown (Orfordness), Group Captain H. A. Buss (Dover and Westgate), Mr E. F. Haselden (Nos.38 and 141 Squadrons), Group Captain G. E. Livock (Yarmouth), Mr F. L. Luxmoore (No.78 Squadron), and Sir Lawrence Wackett (Orfordness). Sadly, others have died since research was begun: these include Air Vice-Marshal A. J. Capel (No.50 Squadron), Wing Commander N. H. Dimmock (Nos.46, 78 and 141 Squadrons), Captain G. W. R. Fane (Yarmouth), Mr L. Latham (Nos.36 and 77 Squadrons), Mr T. A. Lloyd (No.39 Squadron), and Mr A. B. Yuille (No.112 Squadron).

Grateful acknowledgment is made for assistance from the Air Historical Branch of the Ministry of Defence, the Imperial War Museum, the Royal Air Force Museum, the Fleet Air Arm Museum, the Trinity House Corporation, and Albright and Wilson Ltd (for information on the armaments work of Sir Richard Threlfall). Among individuals who have helped in various ways special mention must be made of Mr D. B. Robertson, Mr Errol Martyn, and Mr Geoffrey Williams, while translations by Mr K. Moroniewicz greatly clarified aspects of some German operations.

Sopwith Camel N6812 flown by Lieut S. D. Culley, displayed in the Imperial War Museum.

Original sources of many illustrations are obscure, but we are deeply indebted to people who took much trouble to produce previously unpublished photographs from family albums—and in particular to Mrs M. F. Sadler, of Brockville, Ontario (for photographs by her father, Mr G. Fred Hollington, Nos.37 and 75 Squadrons), Mr L. B. Latham (for items from the collection of his father, Mr Leslie Latham, Nos.36 and 77 Squadrons), Mrs C. Alexander (for photographs by her nephew, Captain A. A. C. Garnons-Williams, Nos.37 and 112 Squadrons), Mrs Phyllis Fane, Mr C. J. E. Saint, Miss H. Sowrey, and Mrs C. A. Ridley. Photographs have also been kindly provided by Mr R. C. Bowyer, Mr Peter W. Brooks, Mr D. G. Collyer, Mr P. J. R. Moyes, Mr H. J. Nowarra, Mr L. Pilkington, Dr Douglas H. Robinson, the J. M. Bruce/G. S. Leslie Collection, and from Mr Peter Liddle's 1914–18 Personal Experience Archives, presently housed within Sunderland Polytechnic.

To avoid confusion the 24-hr clock is used throughout.

Times are given in British Time, namely Greenwich Mean Time until the introduction of British Summer Time on 21 May, 1916—when clocks were advanced one hour—which was used between March and October thereafter.

Sorties: to avoid arbitrary decisions on what constituted an effective home defence patrol, and to assist in comparing the scale of effort against various enemy attacks, every take-off has been recorded as a sortie.

Ranks and Abbreviations

Navy

German rank	Abbreviation	British equivalent	Abbreviation
Fregattenkapitän	—	Captain	Capt
Korvettenkapitän	Kvtkpt	Commander	Cdr
Kapitänleutnant	Kptlt	Lieutenant-Commander	Lieut-Cdr
Oberleutnant-zur-See	Oblt-z-S	Lieutenant	Lieut
Leutnant-zur-See	Lt-z-S	Sub-Lieutenant	Sub-Lieut
Fähnrich-zur-See	—	Midshipman	—
Flugmeister	—		
Deck Offizier	—		

Army

German rank	Abbreviation	British equivalent	Abbreviation
Oberst	—	Colonel	Col
Oberstleutnant	—	Lieutenant-Colonel	Lieut-Col
Major	Maj	Major	Maj
Hauptmann	Hptmn	Captain	Capt
Oberleutnant	Oblt	Lieutenant	Lieut
Leutnant	Leut	2nd Lieutenant	2nd Lieut
Offizierstellvertreter	—	Probationary officer	
Feldwebel	—	Sergeant Major	Sgt Maj
Vizefeldwebel	—	Sergeant	Sgt
Unteroffizier	—	Corporal	Cpl
Gefreiter	—	Lance Corporal	L.Cpl
Gemeiner	—	Private	Pte

Other British Ranks and Abbreviations

RNAS

Wing Commander	Wing Cdr
Squadron Commander	Sqn Cdr
Flight Commander	Flt Cdr
Flight Lieutenant	Flt Lieut
Observer Lieutenant	Obs Lieut
Flight Sub-Lieutenant	Flt Sub-Lieut
Observer Sub-Lieutenant	Obs Sub-Lieut
Petty Officer	PO
Leading Mechanic	LM

Army and RFC

Quartermaster Sergeant	QMSgt
1st Class Air Mechanic	1st AM
2nd Class Air Mechanic	2nd AM
Air Mechanic	AM

Chapter I

The New Air Menace to Britain

During the winter of 1912–13 a wave of Zeppelin mania swept through Britain. It began with reports that a German airship had flown over Sheerness on 13 October, 1912, and substance was added to alleged eye-witness accounts when the date was later found to coincide with the 30-hr endurance trial of the German navy's first Zeppelin, the L1.

The following February, Winston Churchill, First Lord of the Admiralty, assured the Committee of Imperial Defence that the stories were well-founded, though Count Ferdinand von Zeppelin himself denied that the airship had flown near Sheerness.

'Phantom airship' stories proliferated. The master of the *City of Leeds* sailing from Grimsby to Hamburg claimed to have seen a large airship heading towards the Humber on the night of 22 February, 1913, and a few weeks later the passenger airship *Hansa*, flown by a military crew, was said to have passed over the eastern counties. These stories were never substantiated.

Zeppelins had already existed for more than a decade. Von Zeppelin's original aerial express-train project—a powered unit towing separate freight or passenger sections—was abandoned in 1894, but his LZ1 of 1900 showed promise. Although its two 15 hp engines gave the 420-ft monster a speed of only 16 mph, the inventor was sufficiently encouraged to continue, and the eight-hour flight achieved by the LZ3 of 1907 prompted the German army to specify a vessel capable of flying 24 hours nonstop. The LZ5 of 1909 achieved this and was duly purchased. Further military orders came only slowly, and von Zeppelin turned to civil operations. His LZ10 *Schwaben* of 1911 was a great success, carrying 1,500 passengers in its twelve months' lifetime.

The German navy, requiring larger and faster airships of longer range, adopted a more cautious attitude, and their L1 (LZ14) was not ordered until April 1912. She was just over 518 ft long, powered by three 170 hp engines, and attained 47 mph on trials.

The possibility of bombardment from the air had exercised statesmen and their military advisers for some years. A Hague Conference decision of 1899 had barred combatants from delivering projectiles or explosives from balloons or other aerial vessels, and a second conference in 1907 prohibited the bombing of undefended places—without specifically defining them. In 1908 the British Government instructed the Committee of Imperial Defence (hereinafter abbreviated as the CID) to examine both the threat posed by airships and aeroplanes and the advantages which Britain herself might derive from their use.

In January 1909, just six months before Blériot's historic cross-Channel flight, a CID sub-committee reported that in addition to reconnaissance and the transport of small raiding parties to attack special objectives, airships might also bomb ships and dockyards, against which the defences were of doubtful adequacy. The offensive powers of aeroplanes would be limited by their small carrying capacity, and their endurance restricted by 'the physical strain on the driver'.

> 'It has also been suggested', added the report, 'that in the future aeroplanes might be utilised for attacking dirigible balloons, their superior speed and handiness enabling them to gain the upper position, from which they could assail the gas-bags of the dirigibles with hand grenades, bombs, machine guns and revolvers. Until these machines have proved their ability to ascend to great heights—a point concerning which expert opinion appears divided—this method of employing them must remain in the region of speculation. It is worthy of note that aeroplanes should be peculiarly difficult to destroy in flight.'

Despite the view of its only witness with practical flying experience, the Hon Charles S. Rolls, that aeroplanes would expose London and other places to attack, the sub-committee concluded that they were scarcely out of the experimental stage, and recommended spending £35,000 on a naval rigid airship, since the enemy threat could not be definitely assessed until Britain owned a comparable craft. This led to the construction of the R1 *Mayfly*, which unfortunately broke its back during mooring trials in September 1911 before the first flight.

More deliberations on air defence followed major strategic implications which emerged from the Paris International Conference on Aerial Navigation of May–June 1910. The General Staff believed that any German civil airship operations over British air space would be of great military value, and, since peacetime regulations would go by the board in war, that Britain must develop

Winston Churchill in the rear seat of Short S.38 No.2 at RNAS Eastchurch, probably photographed on 30 November, 1913, after a 45-min flying lesson from Capt G. V. Wildman-Lushington, RMA (in front seat). On 2 December Wildman-Lushington crashed to his death in this aircraft when approaching to land at Eastchurch. (*Imperial War Museum*)

guns and other appliances capable of destroying airships. The Admiralty was in general agreement, and regarded the major task of all aircraft in war as reconnaissance, with bombing more likely to produce panic among the public than any direct military gain.

During 1911 the navy and the army each formed the nucleus of an air service with heavier-than-air machines, but Britain lagged behind some other nations in this field. With a view to rectifying the position the CID recommended the formation of a unified air service, with naval and military wings. This bold and imaginative idea inevitably presented difficulties, and soon after the formation of the Royal Flying Corps in May 1912 it became apparent that the two Services had very different ideas and philosophies. The technically-minded navy, in which successful action could often depend on personal initiative, had more money to spend on aviation than had the army, which tended to become bogged down by rules and regulations. During the next two years the navy ordered a variety of aircraft from the emerging British industry while the army, tempering its early enthusiasm for French machines, became largely reliant on the products of the Government Royal Aircraft Factory at Farnborough.

The Factory was particularly concerned with developing the aeroplane as an aid to reconnaissance. This led to something of an obsession over inherent stability, desirable in some respects as witnessed by the feat of a B.E.2c pilot in June 1914 who wrote a reconnaissance report while flying 'hands off' between Farnborough and Upavon, but later recognized as a handicap in combat, when survival could depend on rapid manoeuvrability.

Meanwhile the Zeppelin menace continued to exercise the CID, which reported in July 1912:

> 'It is possible that aeroplanes, owing to their superior mobility, may be found capable of destroying airships, but this has yet to be proved. Having regard to the great speed of modern airships (47 miles per hour), to the great rapidity with which they can rise, to their independence of weather conditions as compared with aeroplanes, to the fact that they can carry guns and firearms for purposes of defence, and to the difficulty of destroying them by shells or explosives, it is by no means proved that aeroplanes are likely to have the better of an encounter, though they can travel faster and ultimately rise higher than the present type of airship, which is some compensation for the greater time taken in rising.
>
> 'It appears probable that, for the immediate present, the surest method of attacking airships would be by a superior force of armed airships.'

The traditional principle that defence against an enemy on British soil was a War Office responsibility was extended to include incursions into British air space, and in August 1912 the RFC Military Wing was tasked with providing the aircraft to defend ports and other key objectives. In fact, while the War Office sadly failed to produce any air defence scheme, the Admiralty did start to establish a chain of coastal aerodromes, primarily for working with ships at sea, which clearly possessed air defence value. In November 1913 it was further agreed that while the War Office retained responsibility for air superiority over Britain, Naval Wing aircraft should protect important naval targets close to their bases. Among naval air requirements listed by Churchill was a home service fighting aeroplane to repel enemy aircraft.

In June 1914, further consideration of the home defence situation by the CID disclosed that the availability of army aircraft was subject to many provisos, quite apart from their small numbers limited by financial restrictions. The outcome was a formal request for the War Office to define its position—and the answer again to return the home defence question to the melting pot. The General Staff claimed that the entire responsibility, including the defence of naval key points, was a War Office one, and that any conveniently available navy aircraft should operate under army control. But the War Office did not then possess even a paper home defence organization, and its existing squadrons were committed to any British Expeditionary Force despatched to the Continent. It was not until 27 July, 1914, that a draft scheme proposed six new squadrons—two in Scotland, one in the Humber area and one each at Orfordness, Dover and Gosport—totalling 162 aircraft.

Regardless of much goodwill and co-operation between navy and army aviators at working level, the early hopes of a unified air service had largely evaporated. On 1 July, 1914, the RFC Naval Wing was reorganized as the Royal Naval Air Service, with its own constitution and under Admiralty administration. This meant that there were now virtually two separate air services, despite Churchill's remark to the CID less than a week before—that he had always looked on the naval and military wings as branches of one great Service. On paper the RNAS remained the Naval Wing of the RFC until 1 August, 1915, but it is more convenient to anticipate events and use the terms RNAS and RFC to denote that there were in effect already two separately controlled organizations.

Although the 1914–18 War was not preceded by the long period of mounting inevitability which characterized the rise of Nazi power in the 1930s, German airship development was something which could not be ignored. Churchill became much enamoured of the airship, and eventually the Admiralty resumed its building programme, abandoned after the *Mayfly* fiasco. Research was undertaken into one obvious shortcoming—the airship's vulnerability to attack, but this was rather superficial, producing the answers its protagonists wanted to hear. The false belief—held until the middle of 1915—that Zeppelins were protected from fire by a layer of engine exhaust or some other inert gas piped between the hydrogen cells and the outer envelope stemmed from 1913 experiments by the Admiralty Air Department.

Churchill was then deep in controversy with Admiral Sir Arthur Wilson, a former First Sea Lord and a member of the CID, who had little faith in the airship's long-term future. Wilson commented:

> 'The governing idea in carrying out these experiments has apparently been to save the airships, while what we want is to find means to destroy them. We want to establish a feud between the aviators and the airship men.'

Churchill argued that airships were probably safe from aeroplane attack by night, or Germany would hardly have spent so much on them—though a few months later he conceded that they might be vulnerable to dive bombing from above.

The years 1912–14 saw considerable research into various aspects of military aviation within the limits of the money available. It was beyond reasonable expectation that by the outbreak of war squadrons should be fully trained and equipped to perform the multifarious operational tasks which emerged only after months of conflict, but a lot of basic ground was covered.

Initially concentrated at the Central Flying School and the Royal Aircraft Factory, much research concerned purely aerodynamic and piloting matters, though some was relevant to home defence. The Military Wing, conscious of its prime role as the eyes of the army, sought to perfect the aeroplane as a reconnaissance platform, while the navy gave more consideration to its development as an armed weapon of war. In 1913 squadron experimental officers were appointed to work with Farnborough, and a year later a headquarters flight was formed, with responsibilities including the co-ordination of research.

On 16 April, 1913, Lieut R. Cholmondeley, No.3 Squadron, flew a Maurice Farman by moonlight from Larkhill to Upavon and back—the first night flight by the Military Wing—and in June, Lieut G. I. Carmichael took off and landed with the aid of petrol flares on the ground. In July, No.4 Squadron was tasked (in Experiment No.34) to test electric landing lights, and Lieut K. P. Atkinson flew Maurice Farman No.306 fitted with a 60 candlepower Blériot lamp. Results were unimpressive and the light did not pick out the ground until the aircraft had descended to about 25 ft. Although it assisted touchdown on a familiar aerodrome, it was not sufficient to locate a landing place in unknown country on a dark night. More promising was the apparatus devised by H. S. Holt, of Adare, County Limerick. This comprised a pyrotechnic flare attached to a parachute which could be used for landing or night reconnaissance. A similar type produced by Louis Muller was also evaluated.

No.3 Squadron experimented with various machine-guns for use in aircraft, concluding that the Lewis offered greatest promise. At Eastchurch the Naval Wing made some preliminary trials with Farnborough's fearsome Fiery Grapnel. Resembling a gigantic fish-hook, this was designed to be lowered from an aircraft by cable and entangle with an airship's structure or envelope, whereupon an explosive charge would ignite leaking hydrogen.

There were experiments to assess the effects of rifle and machine-gun fire on aircraft, while shooting was practised against small balloons released from aircraft and kites towed by a railway locomotive at Shoeburyness. Early in 1914, RNAS armaments specialist Lieut R. H. Clark-Hall recommended that all main aerodromes should maintain at least two aircraft armed with machine-guns for dealing with raiders.

During the tense weeks between the assassination of Archduke Franz Ferdinand on 28 June, 1914, and Britain's declaration of war on 4 August various precautionary measures were taken. Eastchurch, the main RNAS base, with nearby water areas for floatplane operations, had already flown air defence exercises against a simulated enemy, and its aircraft, dispersed on a training and prestige tour after their Fleet Review flypast on 22 July, were recalled to base. On 29 July Churchill ruled that naval aircraft must regard defence against aerial attack as their prime responsibility, and next day the Army Council temporarily relieved No.4 Squadron of Expeditionary Force commitments in order to reinforce the air defences. A and B Flights accordingly went to Eastchurch and C Flight to Dover.

Official and public expectations were for air raids on key points from the beginning of the war. Churchill recorded his own belief, in *The World Crisis* (1923), that 'at any moment half a dozen Zeppelins might arrive to bomb London, or what was more serious, Chatham, Woolwich or Portsmouth'. The War Office, however, did not expect London itself to be an early target.

Precisely what action could be taken against raiders was not clearly defined. With virtually all but second-line machines committed to Expeditionary Force squadrons, the army retained for home defence only a handful of Farman pushers, Blériots and early version B.E.2s, barely capable of 70 mph. All were unarmed apart from any personal weapons carried by their crews. Maj Charles Burke, CO of No.2 Squadron, told his pilots that if they failed to shoot down a

Zeppelin they should take other measures—meaning to ram it.

The navy had a wider assortment of aircraft with generally greater development potential, and one of these could be considered a fighter. This was a solitary Vickers Gunbus, powered by a notoriously unreliable 100 hp Gnome Monosoupape rotary engine, and based at Eastchurch. It was a pusher type and the observer in the front cockpit had a Vickers machine-gun. It had been under development since 1912, and both Services began to receive a few production models during the early months of the war. Also at Eastchurch was a Short S.28 seaplane previously used for machine-gun experiments, plus a loaned Lewis gun which could be mounted on aircraft at the station commander's discretion.

The first RNAS Vickers Gunbus at Eastchurch in the late summer of 1914.

From the outset it was apparent that War Office resources were utterly inadequate to provide any viable defence organization, and regardless of tradition or army pride, this vital responsibility must necessarily devolve upon the RNAS. On 4 August the Admiralty arranged to position three anti-aircraft guns to defend major government buildings in Whitehall and asked the War Office to provide a defence flight of four RFC aircraft to operate from, say, Hyde Park. The Office of Works quickly provided the gun sites—on the Admiralty Arch and the roofs of the Foreign Office and Crown Agents building—and after some deliberation as to whether this could categorize London as a 'fortified town' the guns were operational by 8 August, discreetly screened from public gaze to avoid creating alarm and despondency.

The War Office told the Admiralty on 6 August that it hoped to find some defence aircraft shortly. However, the Army Council believed that:

> '. . . the aeroplane would not be a suitable form of defence for use over London, and that action in such an area would be almost certain to result in heavy casualties to pilots and aeroplanes, which would be unjustifiable having due regard to the limitations of the present resources and to the improbability of the form of attack which it is desired to provide against.
>
> 'It is considered that the stationing of aeroplanes on the east coast with a view to the interception of dirigibles is a more desirable method of defence' continued the War Office letter. ' . . . if it should be decided to use aeroplanes in the manner suggested, Hendon would be a more suitable place to station the flight than Hyde Park, although the latter could be made use of if it were found desirable.'

The Admiralty had on 5 August promulgated Churchill's directive that the priority RNAS task was to counter enemy aircraft attacks, and on the 7th followed up the War Office suggestion and began to activate Hendon. On that date Flt Lieut E. Bentley Beauman delivered from Eastchurch an unarmed 70 hp Caudron, which for several days remained the sole aircraft deployed for the direct defence of the capital. It was soon joined by various others, including some impressed into naval service from civil ownership, and the Hendon CO, Lieut-Cdr J. C. Porte, exhorted pilots in terms similar to those used by Burke—failing other means of stopping a Zeppelin heading for London they must sacrifice themselves and aircraft and ram it at the utmost speed. On 8 August the Admiralty ordered coastal patrols from the Moray Firth to Dungeness, with the RFC covering the northern and southern extremities.

After discussions between Churchill and Lord Kitchener, Secretary of State for War, the Cabinet agreed that the Admiralty should formally assume responsibility for home defence from 3 September. Two days later the main theme of Churchill's policy statement was that, attack being the best form of defence, a squadron operating from Dunkirk would aim to engage enemy aircraft as near as possible to their departure points, and also raid their bases. Interception aircraft would be based along the east coast of Britain, and gun defences concentrated at military key points rather than for the protection of towns. He considered the three existing guns as sufficient protection for the Whitehall area, and that to avoid their fire airships would be obliged to fly too high for accurate bombing. The Third Sea Lord, Rear-Admiral F. C. T. Tudor, assumed overall command of gunnery matters and also headed a committee to formulate an air defence plan.

The expected Zeppelin raids did not materialize because Germany had insufficient resources for any immediate onslaught, nor were bombs available until October. At the outbreak of war she possessed eleven rigid airships—ten belonging to the army and one to the navy—all Zeppelin products except for one army Schütte-Lanz. Like the British, the German military commanders gave priority to reconnaissance, and during August three army airships were lost to Allied gunfire while attempting relatively low-level daylight missions on the Continent. The solitary naval Zeppelin was fully employed on spotting for the fleet. But those who regarded the airship as the ideal long-range bomber were biding their time.

There were several early false alarms. On 14 August a Short seaplane was ordered to readiness at Grain following a reported airship sighting off the coast. On the night of 5/6 September, Claude Grahame-White, the celebrated aviation pioneer, with Richard Gates, his former general manager, both holding RNAS commissions, were airborne from Hendon for more than an hour in a Farman after a nebulous alert from the Admiralty. This was the first night patrol over London. The following night a Deperdussin from Hendon was ordered up to seek another non-existent raider, and at dawn Albatros B II biplane No.890 from Grain patrolled for 30 min with the same object.

While aircraft recognition remained virtually a closed book to the Services and civilians alike, there appeared no reason why this rugged and reliable German aircraft, bought privately before the war and impressed into RNAS service, should not be used for home defence—though it did create a minor contretemps several months later. In 1914, and for the next two or three years, any German aircraft was a 'Taube' to the public at large. The Taube (dove), named from the birdlike shape of its monoplane wing, was designed by an Austrian, Igo Etrich, in 1910 and built under licence by Rumpler and other German manufacturers.

Albatros B II impressed into RNAS service and employed on home defence until the end of May 1915.

Because of its widespread early use and characteristic appearance it was one of the few enemy aeroplanes known to the popular Press, and anglicized as 'Torb' the very name had a sinister ring.

Apart from these 'official' false alarms, reports flowed from the public about mysterious night intruders over various parts of the country, but none was found to have factual basis. One persistent rumour of a Zeppelin operating from a clandestine base near Grasmere was dispelled only after Lieut B. C. Hucks—a highly experienced prewar civil pilot—had searched the Lake District from a Blériot monoplane.

The lack of German activity provided useful breathing space during which home defence responsibilities were more clearly defined and plans formulated. On 16 October a joint Admiralty-War Office conference agreed that while the primary duty of home-based army aeroplanes was to assist ground forces in opposing attempted enemy landings, any surplus machines could co-operate with the RNAS in air defence. The Admiralty was confirmed in the responsibility for the defence of London—aeroplanes, guns and searchlights—temporarily assisted by RFC aircraft from Joyce Green and Hounslow, of other large undefended towns and for dealing with enemy aircraft crossing the coast. The War Office controlled the guns and searchlights, 'protecting', Woolwich Arsenal, defended ports and certain other vulnerable points.

On 22 October Churchill told the Cabinet that no attempt could be made to protect London's residential areas, adding:

> 'I do not consider that aerial attack can yet produce decisive military results, but I cannot feel that our arrangements to cope with it are yet in a satisfactory state. Loss and injury, followed by much public outcry, will probably be incurred in the near future. In these circumstances, while the naval air service is ready to undertake to make the best use of the resources available, there are obvious limits to our responsibility.'

At lower levels various practical steps were being taken to meet the expected Zeppelin raids. The prospect of aeroplane or seaplane attack was considered remote, and gunners were instructed not to molest such aircraft.

The initial RFC deployment was promulgated by the War Office Directorate of Military Aeronautics to Eastern Command on 14 October in these ponderous terms:

> 'I am commanded by the Army Council to inform you that with a view to undertaking an offensive by night against an aerial attack on London two aeroplanes with a detachment of two officers and a few mechanics will be stationed at the Heath Cottage, Hounslow, in the vicinity of the RAMC huts near the Staines–London road. A Piggott tent is being erected on this site to house the aeroplanes.'

This detachment was administered by No.1 Squadron, then working up at Brooklands after changing from airships to aeroplanes, and a few days later the CO received more specific informal instructions from RFC Military Wing HQ, which also covered use of the Vickers aerodrome at Joyce Green:

> 'Hounslow'. Two BEs with grapnels or bomb-boxes, at any rate one with grapnels, at Hounslow. The BEs will be sent you shortly. Captain Burdett will be posted to you. You will send with these BEs eight men and a NCO, who will be accommodated under the arrangements already made at Hounslow.
>
> 'Joyce Green. Two Henri Farman machines. It will be necessary to send two machines to Joyce Green to stop the night there, returning in the morning if the weather is suitable. No mechanics will be necessary at Joyce Green, as Vickers will arrange to have the machines there at night, but two good mechanics should go as passengers and should take with them rifles, grenades, flaming bullets with Martini carbines, and a few hand grenades with rope tails. The two officers and two mechanics will sleep at Joyce Green at night. A supply of flares is being arranged by the War Office, fourteen for Joyce Green and fourteen for Hounslow.'

Aircraft at Farnborough and Brooklands were also to be available for anti-Zeppelin work, and on 29 October arrangements were made to deploy RFC flights as necessary to Tunbridge Wells, Bury St Edmunds and Chelmsford—provided by the Central Flying School (Upavon), Netheravon and Farnborough respectively. These aircraft were primarily for anti-invasion duties, to operate under local army commanders.

The Admiralty arranged for the Office of Works to provide emergency landing areas in Kensington Gardens, Regents Park, Battersea Park and in the grounds of Buckingham Palace. Outlined by red acetylene lamps pointing upwards, these were for aircraft from the regular aerodromes in any difficulties over central London. The Kensington and Battersea emergency landing areas were shortly replaced by two in Hyde Park—near Marble Arch and Rotten Row. Regular naval aerodromes were lit by car headlamps and small searchlights.

A captive observation balloon for Zeppelin spotting was installed at Hendon and later moved to Crystal Palace. In those pre-radio and -radar days this facility had obvious merit, and could operate in fog or low cloud.

Aircraft production was getting under way and by the end of the year the navy had ordered more than 400 additional machines of various types. In the same period the RFC took 50 new aircraft into service and placed even larger orders than the navy. Because of the great benefits claimed for its inherent stability, the B.E.2c was selected for largescale production—a decision which later received widespread condemnation, but produced a successful Zeppelin fighter almost by accident.

The RFC began to form Reserve Aeroplane Squadrons for the elementary training of pilots and ground tradesmen, who then split off to create new active service squadrons. Flying instructors were available for home defence duties. By the end of 1914, Nos.1, 2 and 3 RASs had formed at Farnborough, Brooklands and Shoreham. RAS numbers did not necessarily relate to regular squadron numbers; for example, No.1 RAS was then training the nucleus of No.15 (regular) Squadron. The RNAS strengthened its coastal patrols, and a detachment of Bristol T.B.8 two-seaters was sent from Gosport for the defence of Tyneside.

Nothing had been done about producing an effectively armed aircraft for home defence, and the RNAS considered that the hand-held ·45-in Martini-Henry carbine, firing a new Woolwich incendiary bullet and ball ammunition, would supersede all other methods of attacking airships. The Admiralty was so convinced in this belief as to order RNAS Grain to cease anti-Zeppelin armament experiments and discourage inventors suggesting other methods of attack. Among those sent about their business following this edict was Capt F. V. Holt of the RFC, later to become a leading figure on the home defence scene.

However, the Admiralty did suggest that Hale grenades offered an alternative should the 'flaming bullets' prove ineffective in practice, and various bombs were also available. The rifle grenade designed by F. Marten Hale was regarded as a potential anti-airship weapon in its own right, and could also be hand-launched, minus its stick, with strips of fabric or a rope tail to stabilize its fall. Hale's 20 lb HE bomb was being produced by the Cotton Powder Company, and the Royal Laboratory at Woolwich had developed 10 lb and 20 lb bombs. Other weapons available were the two-gallon and ¾-gallon tin and copper canister petrol bombs invented by Flt Lieut C. R. Finch-Noyes of the Admiralty Air Department. By the end of the year 10 lb and 20 lb bombs filled with incendiary composition were produced, and another 20 lb type filled with petrol and TNT, ignited with a Very cartridge.

Night navigation and the assistance which Zeppelins might obtain from ground illuminations received considerable study. On the night of 22/23 September—chosen because of the foggy conditions—Wing Cdr E. M. Maitland and Flt Lieut R. G. Lock flew over London in the airship *Beta* to see whether Zeppelins could locate targets in such weather. Results were inconclusive, for having left Wormwood Scrubs at 21.30 hr, they lost the landing ground lights at 200 ft and shortly afterwards lost themselves. Eventually, at 23.05 hr, they found a gap and came low enough to make out the illuminated nameboard of Golders Green underground station. Heading south they located Piccadilly Circus and soon afterwards landed safely at base, despite having seen none of the rockets and flares fired to assist them.

The following night Wing Cdr R. M. Groves made a two-hour balloon flight from Battersea to Colney Heath, in Hertfordshire, and concluded that the enemy could only locate central London targets on dark nights by flying compass courses from easily distinguished suburban points, or by following a main road or the Thames. On the 24th, Wing Cdr N. F. Usborne made a 4½-hr trip in Airship No.3 from Kingsnorth, Kent, and readily identified places from 1,000 ft—though he regarded accurate bombing as impossible from even that modest height.

There was regrettably little Service co-operation and the War Office asked for an RFC assessment. On the clear moonlit night of 30 October, Maj C. A. H. Longcroft, CO of No.1 Squadron, flew Farman Longhorn 478 from Brooklands to Hounslow and back. He found main roads easy to follow and picked up the Thames without difficulty, while parks were distinguishable by their lack of lights. He saw the Brooklands petrol flares from six miles, and blamed their heat for his exceptionally bumpy final descent. Longcroft added:

> 'Given a reliable engine I see no reason why, with practice (at any rate on moonlit nights) one should not be able to find one's way across country at night with nearly as much certainty as by day—provided that the destination landing ground is made very distinct.'

It should be remembered, however, that Longcroft was probably the RFC's outstanding navigator, who had won the 1913 Britannia Trophy for his 7½-hr, 650-mile nonstop flight in a B.E.2 from Montrose to Farnborough.

The RFC did not intend to be caught napping over Christmas, so two aircraft and crews were ordered to stand by at Farnborough, Brooklands and Hounslow from 19 December, and others were nominated for duty at non-regular aerodromes. No.1 RAS was instructed to detach Farman Shorthorn 370 (Sgt W. Watts and 2nd Lieut Woodiwiss) and Longhorn 610 (Lieut A. E. Morgan and 2nd Lieut Davies) for duty at Joyce Green—flying reconnaissances at first and last light—and B.E.2b 709 (Lieuts G. J. Malcolm and R. G. H. Murray) and Longhorn 360 (Sgt R. Chambers and Lieut L. V. S. Blacker) to Chelmsford. Shorthorn 343 (Lieuts A. M. Read and C. R. Rowden) was positioned at Lydd to operate under No.2 RAS. On 22 December two No.7 Squadron C Flight Gunbuses were transferred from Netheravon to Joyce Green.

Armament requirements for each pair of aircraft were listed as three carbines, 50 flaming bullets, ten petrol bombs, ten HE bombs and (for the No.1 RAS flights only) a Fiery Grapnel. The RNAS made standby arrangements at coastal aerodromes.

Chapter II

Preliminary Probes

The German air offensive against Britain opened in low key and subsequently fell into broad phases.

These brought progressive changes in defence deployments. Air policy was much affected by political and military factors, but there was slow and steady technical progress with aircraft and armaments. Rather than record details of these developments strictly chronologically as they occurred between operations, they will be discussed before each phase to provide the necessary background to the operational narrative.

Against all expectations, the first attacks came not from airships but from small floatplanes of the German navy's first seaplane squadron, See Flieger Abteilung 1, which became operational at Zeebrugge early in December 1914. However, Count von Zeppelin was indirectly involved because the 120 hp FF 29s employed were made by the Friedrichshafen company with which he was associated. Daylight sorties were flown against Dover on the 21st and 24th, followed on Christmas Day by an audacious attempt to reach London. The small bombs caused only trifling damage. After the first two attacks the RNAS concentrated resources in the Dover area and were understandably aggrieved when the Christmas Day intruder switched targets and was engaged by an RFC aircraft sent to Joyce Green for the holiday standby.

On 27 December the Admiralty introduced a larger and more detailed air defence scheme for the London area. This aimed to position a screen of aircraft between Grimsby and London to intercept airships flying from northern Germany, and between Dungeness and London to cope with aeroplanes from Belgian bases. Stations were instructed to maintain landplanes at readiness on the following scale:—Eastchurch—maximum possible, Hendon—at least four, Dover and Joyce Green*—four, Felixstowe, Yarmouth and Killingholme—three. So-called branch stations were nominated at Chingford, Burnham-on-Crouch, Chelmsford, Maidstone and Ramsgate, the first with four aircraft and the others with two each.

As regards seaplanes, Grain was to maintain the maximum possible at readiness, Felixstowe, Yarmouth and Killingholme four each, and Dover, Westgate and Clacton two each.

Aircraft were allotted predetermined patrol lines, the hope being that those closest to London would have climbed high enough to intercept raiders nearing their targets, while those from coastal stations would attack on the enemy's homeward flights. Direct telephone links were established between the air stations, the Admiralty, anti-aircraft batteries and police, and there was provision for advanced reporting of British aircraft movements in areas likely to be attacked. Certain aerodromes were designated examination grounds, where

* In the event Joyce Green remained a War Office responsibility.

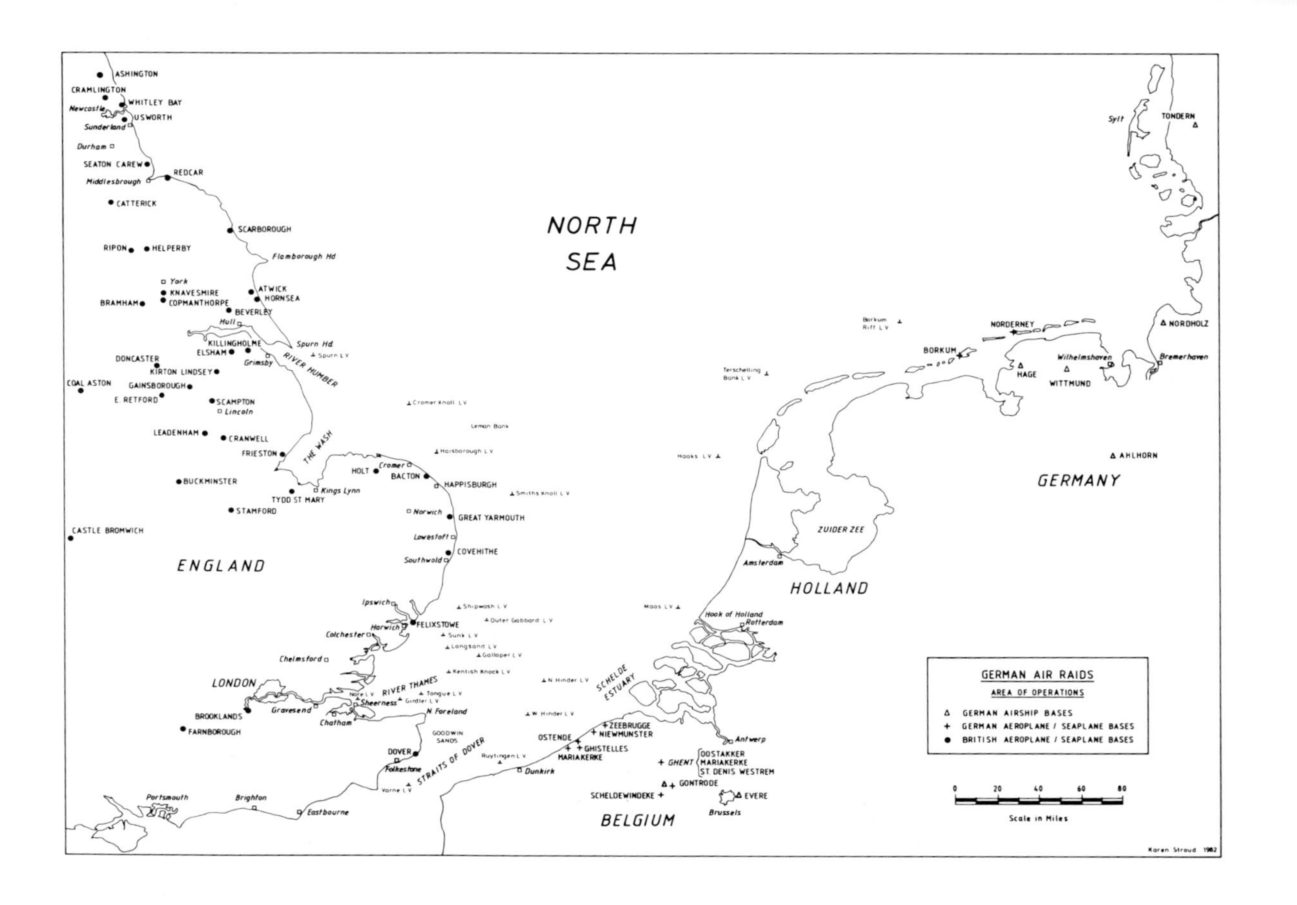
GERMAN AIR RAIDS
AREA OF OPERATIONS
GERMAN AIRSHIP BASES
GERMAN AEROPLANE / SEAPLANE BASES
BRITISH AEROPLANE / SEAPLANE BASES
0
20
40
60
80
Scale in Miles
Karen Stroud 1982
NORTH SEA
ENGLAND
HOLLAND
GERMANY
BELGIUM
ZUIDER ZEE
SCHELDE ESTUARY
STRAITS OF DOVER
RIVER THAMES
RIVER HUMBER
THE WASH
ASHINGTON
CRAMLINGTON
WHITLEY BAY
Newcastle
USWORTH
Sunderland
Durham
SEATON CAREW
REDCAR
Middlesbrough
CATTERICK
SCARBOROUGH
RIPON
HELPERBY
Flamborough Hd
York
KNAVESMIRE
COPMANTHORPE
BRAMHAM
ATWICK
HORNSEA
BEVERLEY
Hull
KILLINGHOLME
ELSHAM
Spurn Hd
Spurn L V
DONCASTER
KIRTON LINDSEY
Grimsby
COAL ASTON
GAINSBOROUGH
E. RETFORD
SCAMPTON
Lincoln
LEADENHAM
CRANWELL
FRIESTON
BUCKMINSTER
Kings Lynn
TYDD ST MARY
STAMFORD
CASTLE BROMWICH
HOLT
Cromer
BACTON
HAPPISBURGH
Norwich
GREAT YARMOUTH
Lowestoft
COVEHITHE
Southwold
Cromer Knoll L V
Leman Bank
Haisborough L V
Smiths Knoll L V
Ipswich
Harwich
FELIXSTOWE
Colchester
Chelmsford
LONDON
BROOKLANDS
FARNBOROUGH
Gravesend
Chatham
Sheerness
Nore L V
Girdler L V
Tongue L V
N Foreland
GOODWIN SANDS
DOVER
Folkestone
Varne L V
Portsmouth
Brighton
Eastbourne
Shipwash L V
Outer Gabbard L V
Sunk L V
Longsand L V
Galloper L V
Kentish Knock L V
N Hinder L V
W Hinder L V
Ruytingen L V
Dunkirk
OSTENDE
MARIAKERKE
GHISTELLES
ZEEBRUGGE
NIEWMUNSTER
GHENT
OOSTAKKER
MARIAKERKE
ST DENIS WESTREM
GONTRODE
SCHELDEWINDEKE
EVERE
Brussels
Antwerp
Hook of Holland
Rotterdam
Maas L V
Amsterdam
Haaks L V
Terschelling Bank L V
Borkum Riff L V
BORKUM
NORDERNEY
HAGE
WITTMUND
Wilhelmshaven
Bremerhaven
NORDHOLZ
AHLHORN
Sylt
TONDERN

aircraft flying towards London and other key points were required to check in.

The Admiralty's Inspecting Captain of Aircraft, Capt F. R. Scarlett, had meanwhile assessed some of the machines available for home defence. One was the Bristol T.B.8 two-seater, powered by an 80 hp Gnome engine and capable of 75 mph—a tidy-looking biplane apart from its clumsy four-wheeled undercarriage. Scarlett found that the deep, narrow fuselage made it almost impossible for the observer to deliver accurate rifle fire anywhere except downwards through a small aperture in the fuselage floor. This offered a very limited field of view, and incendiary bullets could only be aimed at an airship flying directly beneath, since attempts to use a rifle in any other position at night risked damage to the attacking aircraft. He suggested that it might be more effectively operated as a single-seater, carrying small petrol or HE bombs to be dropped by the pilot.

Scarlett's note on fighting tactics circulated at the end of December underlined the elementary state of the art at that time:

> 'The effect of gunfire against German aircraft up to the present has been to force him to climb: it also worries him and distracts his attention from his objective and forces him to drop his bombs from so great a height that he will probably miss his target by a large margin.
>
> 'The effect of being pursued by an aeroplane of superior speed and climbing power is to force the enemy to lose height because he dips the nose of his machine to get more speed to escape. Taking these two effects it appears that our aircraft should pursue the enemy and attempt to destroy him, at the same time forcing him down before reaching his objective, which would presumably be protected by anti-aircraft guns.'

There were other reasons prompting a closer scrutiny of the defences. On Christmas Eve the Home Secretary had asked the Cabinet to reconsider the policy of leaving the civil population to take its chance of death or injury from enemy aircraft. Considerable casualties had been caused by the German navy's shelling of the northeast coast on 16 December, and a Zeppelin attack on densely-populated areas would probably inflict far higher losses. The Home Secretary felt that these would be deeply resented by the population whatever their purely military significance, and wanted adequate guns and searchlights to protect a circle radiating six miles from Charing Cross.

This became of more than academic interest when the Admiralty received reports portending imminent raids. On 1 January, 1915, Churchill warned the War Council about a planned night attack on London by up to twenty airships—which the navy was powerless to prevent. This greatly disturbed the 73-year-old First Sea Lord, Admiral of the Fleet Lord Fisher, who feared that it would cause a terrible massacre. He believed that the only defence would be to announce that if bombs were dropped, German prisoners would be shot in reprisal. Since this had not been done, the Admiralty would be held responsible, and he wrote privately to Churchill asking to be relieved of his post. Churchill persuaded him to withdraw the request, and a week later Fisher told the council that this combined naval and military raid would probably be preceded by a smaller naval airship attack on the east coast.

Churchill outlined the London defence arrangements and claimed that within the London–Sheerness–Dover triangle about sixty aeroplanes, armed with rifles firing incendiary bullets, were always ready, while some pilots were prepared to charge Zeppelins. The Admiralty's responsibility for the London air defences, with some assistance from the War Office, was reaffirmed.

These warnings clearly suggest that naval intelligence had acquired the gist of a signal sent by the German Chief of Naval Staff to his Fleet C-in-C on Christmas Day advocating such raids. Their estimate of enemy airship strength, however, was wildly inflated, since the navy then possessed only six Zeppelins and the army two, plus a Schütte-Lanz. The army's ZIX had been destroyed in its shed at Düsseldorf on 8 October and the navy's L7 had narrowly escaped damage on 21 November at the Friedrichshafen Zeppelin works in daring attacks by the RNAS. In fact it was not until 9 January, 1915, that the navy received the Kaiser's approval to raid Britain, with coastal areas, and docks and military establishments in the lower Thames area classed as legitimate targets—but *not* central London.

The commander of the German Naval Airship Division was eager for action. Korvettenkapitän Peter Strasser, appointed at the end of 1913, was an officer of outstanding drive and ability, determined never to become merely a chairborne leader. He accompanied the first raid against England on 19 January by two M-class Zeppelins. These 518-ft vessels, each powered by three 210 hp Maybach engines, had a top speed of 52 mph, and with a 1,100–1,430 lb bomb load could reach about 5,000 ft.

Damage was estimated at £7,740 compared with £40 caused by the few bombs dropped from aeroplanes up to that time, and there were four fatal casualties—the first caused by air raids. The defences were unable to make any effective intervention.

February and March brought a few small aeroplane attacks against coastal shipping and one night penetration over Essex. These early incursions introduced one problem which was never satisfactorily solved—the difficulty of providing adequate early warning for the coastal air stations.

During the first winter of war, Britain experienced, albeit on very small scale, virtually every permutation of air attack likely to be employed by the enemy. There had been daylight hit-and-run forays against coastal targets and London, a night aeroplane raid and, most important, the Zeppelin threat had become a reality.

The result was a further sharpening of the defences, the RNAS forming a mobile anti-aircraft force and reminding coastal aerodromes that three standby aircraft must always be ready for immediate take-off. The War Office increased gun and searchlight defences at ports and other key points and on 25 January directed that all RFC stations east of Farnborough would be warned of any night raids and required to produce two aircraft ready for instant action. Those closest to any developing threat would be given the latest information, and the senior officer would order pilots into the air according to his judgement of the situation.

> 'It must be recognised, however, that it will usually be difficult for an aeroplane to find an airship in the dark' added the War Office instruction, 'and therefore pilots should not be ordered to fly unless it seems very likely that the enemy can be found and engaged.'

At the same time, units were notified that any aircraft approaching the Royal residence at Sandringham would be fired on. This resulted from L4's passage over the area on 19 January—which prompted Queen Alexandra, the Queen Mother, to urge Fisher to provide 'a lot of rockets with spikes or hooks' to defend the Norfolk coast.

Increased efforts were made to achieve greater operational efficiency. The Admiralty circulated a report on night-flying trials by No.1 Squadron, RNAS, mostly with 80 hp Avros. One aircraft carried a 50-watt searchlight mounted in the undercarriage and lit by a 12-volt battery in the fuselage. Small wingtip lights were fitted to help the pilot maintain lateral balance in the air. In practice the nose of the Avro was found to block the pilot's view, and the problem was solved by offsetting the beam. Various downward angles were tried, and patches of light-coloured material—newspapers, fabric, and so on—strewn about the landing area considerably assisted judgement of height when landing.

The overall conclusions were more fundamental—that successful night flying depended on a pilot's knowledge of his aircraft and the aerodrome; that instruments should be carefully grouped together under subdued lighting (to be switched off when landing); that a low-reading altimeter was of great value; and that a proper system of aerodrome beacons was necessary.

An RNAS 80 hp Gnome-engined Avro 504B, as used in early night-flying trials.

The War Office pinned its faith on the Holt flare, and on 3 March, after encouraging trials, the Central Flying School placed the first production order for 750 with the Yorkshire Steel Company, at £1–6s–6d each, with discharge tubes.

Provision was made for more night emergency landing grounds in the London area, and the War Office selected sites at Northolt, Wimbledon Common, Beddington (Croydon), Eynsford, Blackheath Common, Enfield and Woodcock Field (East Horndon, Essex). The Admiralty picked sites at Chingford, Chelmsford and Maidstone.

German army plans for a major aeroplane bombing offensive had been frustrated by the failure of their land drive to the Channel ports. A force of single-engined bombers had assembled at Ghistelles, near Ostende, with the intention of moving to Calais and thus bringing a wide selection of targets within range. It was given the cover name of Brieftauben Abteilung Ostende—the Ostende Carrier Pigeon Section. Since the German forces did not reach Calais the bombers were obliged to restrict attacks to Continental targets, and in due course they moved to another operational area.

A German publicity photograph of Leutnants Karl Caspar and Roos after their claimed attack against Dover on 25 October, 1914—not recorded in any British reports.

During October another army unit—Feldflieger Abteilung 9——had attempted the first of what were virtually private enterprise sorties against England flown at sporadic intervals throughout the war. On the 25th two Gotha-built Tauben set off to attack Dover, one turning back because of poor visibility before it reached the Channel. The crew of the second, Leutnants Karl Caspar (pilot) and Roos (observer) claimed to have bombed the port and their feat was hailed in the German Press. Although British records show no enemy incursions on that date, the incident is sometimes cited as the first bombing attack on Britain.

A Friedrichshafen FF 29 at Zeebrugge.

Chapter III

Operations—December 1914 to March 1915

Basic details about defence sorties are listed in the order—aircraft type, serial number, crew, take-off and landing times. Sorties terminated before their planned duration are annotated as returned early and, where known, reasons are given.

21 December, 1914 (Daylight)

Target: Dover.
Enemy force: One Friedrichshafen FF 29.
Results: No casualties or damage.
Defence sorties: None.

This solitary raider was Friedrichshafen FF 29 floatplane No.203 of the German navy's See Flieger Abteilung 1 (Seaplane Unit No.1), Zeebrugge. It appeared off Dover at 13.00 hr and dropped two bombs in the sea near Admiralty Pier. By the time the facts of the incident had registered the intruder was almost out of sight and any attempt at pursuit was judged useless.

24 December, 1914 (Daylight)

Target: Dover.
Enemy force: One Friedrichshafen FF 29.
Results: No casualties, £40 damage.
Defence sorties: Two.

RNAS
Dover: Wight seaplane 171 took off 10.30 hr; Bristol T.B.8 1224 (Flt Lieut H. A. Buss, AM Makin) 11.20–11.45 hr.

To meet Dover's air defence shortcomings the Admiralty ordered the transfer of two Bristol T.B.8s from Eastchurch for the Christmas period, but did not move quite fast enough.

Bristols 1223 and 1224 left Eastchurch at 10.15 hr but 15 min later, while they were still en route, Dover observers spotted a pale brown-coloured seaplane approaching from the sea at about 5,000 ft between patches of low cloud. The Wight seaplane, airborne immediately from the East Promenade base, was a poor climber and long before it was remotely within range the enemy had dropped a single 22 lb bomb and departed.

This first enemy bomb on British soil—from FF 29 No.204 of SFA 1—fell at 10.45 hr, forming a crater ten feet across and four feet deep in the garden of

Bristol T.B.8 1224 flown by Flt Lieut Harold A. Buss on 24 December, 1914.

Flt Lieut Harold A. Buss (*centre*) who flew one of the RNAS Dover sorties on 24 December, 1914. On the left is Flt Lieut G. E. Hervey, who shared in the destruction of a Gotha in August 1917. The photograph was taken at Imbros during the Dardanelles campaign. Flt Lieut A. C. Teesdale (*right*) was not engaged in home-defence operations.

Thomas A. Terson, an auctioneer and valuer living near the castle. There was little damage beyond broken windows.

At 11.10 hr, as the Wight was about to abandon its vain attempt to climb above the clouds, the two Bristols from Eastchurch arrived at the RNAS Dover Guston Road aerodrome. Although there was now small prospect of catching the enemy, Harold Buss was airborne at 11.20 hr and flew out to sea, gradually climbing to 4,500 ft. He saw nothing and returned after 25 min.

25 December, 1914 (Daylight)

Target: London dock area.
Enemy force: One Friedrichshafen FF 29.
Results: No casualties or damage.
Defence sorties: Six.

RNAS
Dover: Bristol T.B.8 1224 (Flt Lieut H.A. Buss, AM Andrews) 13.15–14.00 hr.
Eastchurch: One sortie, details not known.
Grain: Albatros B II 890 13.05–14.05 hr.

RFC
Joyce Green: Vickers F.B.4 664 (2nd Lieut M. R. Chidson, Cpl Martin) 12.35–14.00 hr (Eastchurch).
Farnborough and Brooklands: One sortie each, details not known.

Against the possibility that the initial hit-and-run raids might presage some weightier Christmas attack, RNAS Dover launched standing patrols from 08.00 hr on 25 December, flying the Eastchurch Bristols on alternate two-hour shifts at 5,000 ft along the coast to Deal. The half-expected raider duly arrived—but made landfall 30 miles northwest of the patrol line.

Short Folder floatplane No.121 which stood by at Grain on 25 December, 1914.

2nd Lieut M. R. Chidson, No.7 Squadron, RFC (*left*); and William Henry Charles Mansfield—a late war portrait after he had commanded No.20 Squadron for fifteen months on the Western Front. He became a lieutenant-colonel in the RAF, but in 1919 returned to his regiment, the King's Shropshire Light Infantry.

At 12.20 hr an unfamiliar engine sound was heard from the Bartons Point (Sheerness) anti-aircraft battery, and five minutes later an enemy floatplane was spotted at about 7,000 ft. It was greeted by fire from several gun sites, the Beacon Hill (Sheppey) gunners shooting away their own telephone wires in their enthusiasm. Unbothered, the enemy flew on north of Grain, then turned west.

This raider was FF 29 No.203 making its second sortie against England, piloted by Oberleutnant-zur-See Stephan Prondzynski, with Fähnrich-zur-See von Frankenburg as observer. Both were awarded the Iron Cross on 26 December.

Surviving British reports on subsequent events are fragmentary and conflicting, but a general picture emerges. By 12.30 hr three landplanes from Eastchurch and two machines from Grain—Short S.41 landplane No.21 and Short seaplane No.121—were put on emergency standby, but only one aircraft from each station was actually airborne. At Grain it was in fact Albatros No.890, which eventually took off at 13.05 hr after some difficulty in starting the engine. It is not known what aircraft was airborne from Eastchurch. The War Office ordered single machines up from Joyce Green, Farnborough and Brooklands.

Meanwhile the Friedrichshafen had descended to 4,000 ft and was proceeding serenely up the Thames, being reported from Gravesend, Tilbury and Dartford. At 13.15 hr over Erith it was intercepted by the RFC Vickers Gunbus from Joyce Green, crewed by Chidson and Martin.

Montagu Chidson, of No.7 Squadron and formerly of the Royal Garrison Artillery, had qualified as a pilot at the Bristol School on Salisbury Plain on 30 April, 1913, and his Central Flying School graduation report of 19 October, 1914, described him as 'a very keen and reliable officer with very good judgement'. His aircraft, a prototype Vickers Gunbus, had been with No.7 Squadron since early December and carried a Vickers-built Maxim machine-gun.

Whatever target Prondzynski had in mind, he turned on seeing the Gunbus and retreated down the Thames, Martin firing several bursts as the chase proceeded over Purfleet and Tilbury. The enemy started to climb, crossed the river, and at 13.35 hr unloaded two bombs in a field near Cliffe railway station. The pilot later claimed to have attacked oil storage tanks at Sheerness. At about this time Martin's gun jammed and he was unable to clear the stoppage because his hands were numb with cold, having forgotten his gloves in the rush to take off. Also the engine was running badly, so after keeping up the pursuit beyond Sheerness, Chidson landed at Eastchurch at 14.00 hr.

The British crew were confident that their Maxim had scored some hits. They also found splintering on the Gunbus undercarriage, caused by an enemy bullet—or perhaps a shell fragment, since the Purfleet gunners had fired with splendid disregard for friend or foe. The same gun, which later attacked the Gunbus during its return to Joyce Green, was inexplicably not listed in the Thames and Medway defence scheme and therefore not warned of the flight.

Vickers F.B.4 Gunbus 664 minus its machine-gun.

As the Gunbus was abandoning the chase, Bristol 1224 arrived over Herne Bay, having left Dover hoping to head off the enemy. It was again piloted by Buss, who had flown a 90-min standing patrol during the morning. He spotted the enemy a long way off but the Bristol's 75 mph top speed was not good enough, and after losing sight of his quarry beyond the North Foreland he returned to Dover.

According to the C-in-C Nore's report neither the Eastchurch nor Grain aircraft joined combat, and there is no record of the RFC Farnborough and Brooklands machines. A Press communiqué gave only sketchy details of the affair, and with no PR organization to provide details—but plenty of willing eye-witnesses—it is little wonder that the newspapers carried some imaginative accounts. The sight of an aeroplane was rare enough, and the first 'air battle' over Britain was big news. This is an extract from *The Times* Southend correspondent's report:—

'Meanwhile three biplanes started in pursuit, and a wonderful aerial

RECORDS OF FLIGHTS.

Date.		Machine.		Passenger.	Time in Air.		Course.	Height.	Distance.	Weather.	Remarks.
					Hours.	Minutes.					
1914.									Miles.		
December	16th	V.F.B.	704.	Self	-	7.	Beeches Barn Ranges.	800'.	7.	Breeze.	With Capt. Rees firing Lewis gun.
..	..	..	704.	..	-	7.	.. .. ..	1000'.	7.	..	.. ..
..	..	..	649.	–	-	26.	Aerodrome.	4100'.	30.	Stiff Breeze.	
..	17th.	..	649.	1st A.M. Shields.	-	10.	Bulford.	900'.	11.	.. ..	Landed owing to engine failure.
..	..	..	649.	.. .. ..	-	7.	Bulford to Netheravon.	1000'.	7.	.. ..	Returned from above flight.
..	21st.	..	649.	Self.	-	35.	Farnborough.	4500'.	45.	Breeze.	With Capt. Mansfield: ran into trees landing.
..	~~22nd~~										
"C". Flight, No: 7 Squadron R.F.C. Joyce Green.											
December	22nd	V.F.B.	664.	—	-	5.	Aerodrome.	400'.	6.	Breeze.	Very misty: broke skid landing.
..	25th.	..	664.	Gl. Martin.	1	55.	Eastchurch via the Nore.	5400'.	120.	Breeze.	Chasing German sea-plane: fog on aerodrome.
..	..	..	664.	.. ..	-	40.	Eastchurch to Joyce Green.	3200'.	48.	..	Very misty: buckled wheel landing.
..	27th.	..	1617.	Self.	-	45.	Farnborough to Joyce Green.	3000'.	50.	..	Passenger to Major Board.
1915.											
January	4th	V.F.B.	863.	1st A.M. Perrott.	-	10.	Aerodrome at Yarmouth.	1200'.	12.	Breeze.	Intended to go to Joyce Green, engine missed badly.
..	6th	..	863.	—	2	20	Yarmouth to Chelmsford.	4300'.	100.	Very windy.	Head wind, very misty, forced landing at Chelmsford
..	8th	..	863.	—	-	40.	Chelmsford to Joyce Green.	1200'.	30.	Windy.	Head wind, misty.

2nd Lieut M. R. Chidson's log-book record of the first air combat over England. V.F.B in the Machine column denotes Vickers Fighting Biplane.

combat followed. The German attempted to rise completely out of range. Two of the British machines at once sought to head him off. Here the intrepid enemy had three foes to contend with. Two of our aircraft rose above him, while the third, mounted with a quick-firing gun, assailed him with high-angle fire.

'All four of the combatants were well over the centre of the river and the firing of the fort was somewhat restricted on account of the risk of injuring our own men. The enemy and his passenger kept firing in return, but it was evident that their main idea was to escape as quickly as possible. The manoeuvring was of a most remarkable character. The enemy obviously was an airman of quite exceptional skill, and he so piloted his machine as to place it in such a position that while minimising in every way the chance of being hit, he made it difficult for his foes to fire without the risk of injuring each other.'

Although the intruder escaped, the defences generally made a creditable showing. The element of chance which directed the Friedrichshafen into the path of the sole aircraft with any fighter pretensions perhaps gave the enemy an exaggerated impression of Britain's defence readiness. At all events there were no serious attempts to penetrate any distance inland by day for a long time to come.

Several curiously vague Press reports in early February described the finding by a fishing boat somewhere off Southend of a German aviator's body with a bullet wound in the right lung. No date was given for this incident, and although the reports doubtless had no more basis than other odd wartime rumours, they were inevitably linked with the Christmas Day action.

German accounts admitted that the Friedrichshafen's floats and fuselage received damage—attributed to shrapnel but more probably caused by Martin's machine-gun fire. The observer was reported as wounded in the elbow, by fire from an Allied post on the Flanders coast when the Germans put down near the shore to check their position.

The subsequent flying careers of both pilots were brief. Chidson went to France in February, and with his observer, 2nd Lieut D. W. C. Sanders, was taken prisoner on 1 March after their Gunbus (No.1621) of No.16 Squadron, was forced down with its propeller shattered by anti-aircraft fire. During captivity he devised various ingenious methods of smuggling information out of Germany and after the war resumed his career as a Regular Army officer. Prondzynski was taken prisoner on 21 February after a forced alighting, described later.

19/20 January, 1915 (Night)

Targets: Humber, Thames.
Enemy forces: Navy Zeppelins L3 (Kptlt Hans Fritz), L4 (Kptlt Magnus von Platen-Hallermund); L6 (Oblt-z-S Horst von Buttlar) returned early with engine trouble.
Results: Four killed, 16 injured, £7,740 damage.
Defence sorties: Two.

RFC

Joyce Green: Vickers F.B.5 1617 (Capt W. H. C. Mansfield, QMSgt H. E. Chaney) 21.17–22.35 hr; unknown F.B.5 (2nd Lieut R. M. Pike, 1st AM Shaw) 21.15–22.25 hr. Both aircraft forced landed.

Strasser wasted no time in organizing airship raids against England, and although his first attempt—on 13 January, only three days after receiving the Kaiser's authorization—was frustrated by bad weather, there was a good forecast for the three Zeppelins which set off on the 19th.

L3 and L4 from Fuhlsbüttel (now Hamburg Airport) planned to attack the Humber area while L6 from Nordholz, with Strasser on board, was bound for the Thames estuary. However an engine failure caused L6 to turn back when still 90 miles from the English coast.

L3, one of the early M-class Zeppelins, which raided Yarmouth on 19/20 January, 1915.

Fritz in L3 was carried far south of his intended landfall and decided to raid Great Yarmouth, which he reached at 20.20 hr. He released a parachute flare and began his attack from 5,000 ft five minutes later, dropping six HE and seven incendiary bombs. L4 crossed the coast nearby, became hopelessly lost, and eventually her commander decided that he was north of his target. He claimed to have attacked fortified places between the Tyne and Humber, receiving heavy artillery fire from one 'big city'. In reality he had bombed sundry Norfolk villages and deposited the bulk of his load on the small town of King's Lynn—which had no gun defences—passing over Sandringham en route.

It was a dark, squally night offering defending aircraft minimal prospects of finding their quarry. However, the attempt was made—a shining example of the courage and high sense of duty shown by aircrews ready to face the unknown realm of night combat with ludicrously inadequate equipment and facilities. The night's events also exposed the muddle and confusion existing in the embryo air defence organization.

These first night sorties against enemy raiders over England have been ignored by earlier historians. This curious omission of a major event in military aviation history may be because the relevant GHQ Great Britain intelligence report baldly stated: 'No anti-aircraft action was taken either by guns or aeroplanes'. This document was, however, compiled in 1918 without the benefit of some essential facts which appear to have been wrongly filed.

Naval headquarters at Lowestoft received the first report of an airship approaching the coast at 19.40 hr, followed 15 min later by news that it had reached land. There was some unexplained delay in passing the information to RNAS Yarmouth, which was not notified until L3 had bombed and was on its way home. By that time a second Zeppelin was reported flying south from Cromer. The station commander, Flt Cdr de Courcy W. P. Ireland, held back his three available aircraft for this raider, but when no further movement reports arrived, decided, realistically, that attempts by his low-performance machines to seek out raiders in pitch-black weather would be fruitless and dangerous.

Twenty minutes after the first bombs fell on Yarmouth a badly briefed Admiralty duty officer telephoned the aerodrome at Joyce Green, saying that Zeppelins—possibly bound for London—were over eastern England. He asserted that all standby naval aircraft were taking off, and asked how many were available at Joyce Green. No general take-off had in fact been ordered and Joyce Green operations were an army responsibility. Its two No.7 Squadron Vickers Gunbuses were under the charge of the C Flight commander, Capt Mansfield, who promptly sought instructions from the War Office. Orders were given for the aircraft to patrol the southern outskirts of London.

Mansfield and Chaney—a mature and well qualified crew by contemporary standards—took off at 21.17 hr, their Gunbus arousing the fleeting curiosity of the Woolwich searchlight as it slowly climbed over the aerodrome.

William Mansfield, 27, of the Shropshire Light Infanty, had learned to fly in January 1914 and from August spent several eventful months with the original RFC contingent in France. Chaney, 32, had been instructing for eleven years at the School of Musketry, taken part in the prewar experiments using machine-guns from aircraft and was in effect machine-gun adviser to the RFC.

For all his experience Chaney was somewhat daunted by the variegated armament stowed in the front cockpit of the Gunbus. As well as a Lewis gun plus seven drums of ammunition, he had a Martini-Henry carbine with incendiary bullets—and two loose petrol bombs. An earlier Maxim mounting had been modified to accommodate the Lewis, but in the restrained words of Chaney's report:

> 'The disadvantage was that I had to hold the gun during the whole of the flight as there was no means of clamping it. This was extremely awkward as I was hampered by the presence of the bombs in my arms.'

The Gunbus entered cloud at 2,000 ft, broke clear over London and continued climbing, still meeting occasional cloud patches so thick as to make it impossible to read the sketchy cockpit instruments with an electric torch. By the time Mansfield reached 3,500 ft he was lost, and his troubles were aggravated by one cylinder cutting out, which reduced the Gnome engine's revolutions from 1,200 to 1,000. He turned north and without warning fell into a 'spinning nose dive'. Although the recovery technique had been known for about three years, the spin was still regarded as fraught with peril, even in daylight, and practical instruction on the subject formed no part of pilot training. It is a tribute to Mansfield's cool expertise that he managed to extricate the aircraft after it had spun down to 600 ft. The mind boggles at the picture of Chaney trying to control his arsenal during those terrifying moments. Shortly afterwards another cylinder went, reducing engine revolutions to 950 and the Vickers' air speed to 52 mph.

Unable to maintain height, Mansfield steered towards a dark area between house lights visible below. Suddenly, with his altimeter still showing 400 ft, he saw

A mobile navy anti-aircraft unit of 1915–16. Early operations of this force were conducted on an ad hoc basis, and it was a less sophisticated vehicle which followed Gunbus 1617 on 19/20 January, 1915.

trees 30 yards ahead against the skyline, turned sharply to the right but almost immediately hit the ground. His seat belt held and he received only a cut above one knee. Chaney was thrown out, and escaped with a sprained finger and extensive bruising. What happened to the carefully nursed petrol bombs is not recorded.

The 78-min flight had abruptly terminated in a sloping field at Salters Heath Farm, Chevening, near Sevenoaks, and the only damage was one broken wheel. During the last stages of the descent the Vickers was under machine-gun and rifle fire from the ground, one bullet grazing the left elbow of Chaney's leather coat. Sporadic shots were also heard immediately after the forced landing. Shortly afterwards a navy armoured car arrived with a flourish, and its commander proudly announced that he had been following the Gunbus for some distance. Suspicions that the machine-gun fire came from this vehicle could not be verified, nor was the identity established of the local soldiery who also let fly.

To protect details of Britain's latest fighter from prying eyes and cameras it was covered with sheeting and cordoned by soldiers. In the absence of reliable information the *Sevenoaks Chronicle*'s explanation of the 'rather premature descent' showed no appreciation of Mansfield's skilful handling—'the aviator was under the impression that the machine was at least 2,000 feet above the ground. Unfortunately this was not so . . .'

Airborne from Joyce Green two minutes before Mansfield in another Gunbus, Maxwell Pike and Shaw had fared no better. At 1,200 ft their engine cut and refused to pick up until they had descended to 600 ft, but they climbed again, eventually lost sight of the aerodrome flares and turned west. Thirty minutes later over New Cross at 3,200 ft the engine again started cutting, revolutions dropped to 600 and once more the Gunbus began to lose height. Turning east in the hope of finding Joyce Green, they passed through patches of cloud, and at 800 ft the engine stopped completely.

With no aerodrome visible they glided towards the darkest stretch ahead, hoping for flat ground, but unfortunately hit a dyke. The aircraft somersaulted, leaving Pike hanging by his safety belt while Shaw received the classic comedy treatment, catapulting into a ditch full of icy water. They found themselves half a mile from Tilbury Fort, where Shaw remained to dry out while Pike was driven back to Joyce Green, ready to fly another sortie if required. He learned from a policeman that local soldiers were gleefully claiming that their rifle fire had brought the 'enemy' down.

After their own eventful night the RFC crews were surprised to learn that no RNAS machines had flown during the raid, the only activity being two patrols from Yarmouth at first light, long after the raiders had departed. Despite the mishaps their valiant effort had demonstrated that the War Office did not intend to be a sleeping partner in home defence, and No.7 Squadron gained the unique distinction of following the first contact with an enemy day raider with these first anti-Zeppelin sorties by night.

Mansfield's report queried the wisdom of despatching patrols long before airships over Norfolk could hope to reach London. It also suggested that all aerodromes be illuminated as a navigation aid and for emergency use, and stressed the need for proper bomb fittings and cockpit lighting. The War Office tartly questioned the propriety of the Admiralty's direct approach to Joyce Green, and started an inquiry into the identity of the trigger-happy individuals who had fired on their aircraft. They were not traced, but the Admiralty quickly issued instructions that fire must be held until a target was positively identified as hostile.

Mansfield later commanded No.39, then No.20 Squadron, and although awarded a permanent RAF commission after the war, returned to his army regiment. Chaney was commissioned in March, rose rapidly to command the School of Aerial Gunnery for two years and reached the rank of lieutenant-colonel. He died in 1919.

21/22 February, 1915 (Night)

Target: Not known.
Enemy force: One Friedrichshafen FF 29.
Results: No casualties, £30 damage.
Defence sorties: None.

This was another enterprising sortie by Stephan Prondzynski of SFA 1, with Fähnrich-zur-See Heym as observer. The intended target is not known.

Friedrichshafen No.203—the same aircraft used for the 21 and 25 December raids—passed over Clacton at 19.45 hr and penetrated 25 miles inland to Braintree, where it released two incendiary bombs. On the return flight it dropped a small HE bomb in a field near Coggeshall, and at 20.45 hr another near a Colchester barracks which slightly damaged buildings.

No defence action was taken because of initial doubts as to whether it was an enemy, followed by confusion over the regulations for engaging hostile aeroplanes at night. Nobody was prepared to identify by sound, and the rule was that they should not be attacked until they had performed a hostile act.

Probably because of engine trouble, the Friedrichshafen alighted some distance off the English coast, damaging its floats. The crew was picked up 36 hr later when it was almost sinking. Details of the rescue by a British ship have not been traced, but two captured German airmen were reported as being landed at Lowestoft on 26 February by the tug *New Boy*.

22 February, 1915 (Day)

Target: Coastal shipping.
Enemy forces: Two Friedrichshafen FF 29s.
Results: No casualties or damage.
Defence sorties: None.

At about 10.25 hr, two FF 29s of SFA 1 flying towards Lowestoft dropped a few bombs near the Gabbard lightship. They were homeward bound before any defence action could be taken.

26 February, 1915 (Day)

Target: Coastal shipping.
Enemy forces: Two Friedrichshafen FF 29s.
Results: No casualties or damage.
Defence sorties: Two.

RNAS
Felixstowe: Short 830 No.821; Voisin floatplane 551; details not known.

At 10.30 hr two FF 29s of SFA 1 attacked the steamer *Cordoba* two miles west of the Sunk lightship, scoring no hits. Two Felixstowe aircraft covered possible tracks of the departing raiders, north and south, but saw nothing.

This line-up of See Flieger Abteilung 1 aircraft at Zeebrugge includes Oertz FB 3 No.46 and Friedrichshafen FF 29 No.407, which took part in the shipping attack of 20 March, 1915. Friedrichshafen 204 made the 24 December raid on Dover, and 208 and 407 the shipping attacks of 22 and 26 February. (*H. J. Nowarra*)

20 March, 1915 (Daylight)

Target: Coastal shipping.
Enemy forces: Three Friedrichshafen FF 29s, one Oertz FB 3 flying-boat.
Results: No casualties or damage.
Defence sorties: Four.

RNAS
Dover: Curtiss flying-boat (Flt Cdr S. D. A. Grey); White & Thompson No.3 1197 (Flt Lieut C. A. Eyre); details not known.

Service not recorded
Vickers F.B.5; two sorties; details not known.

At 10.30 hr four enemy aircraft were seen flying towards Dover, and after conflictingly reported movements, one unsuccessfully aimed six bombs at a small coaster in the Downs at 11.05 hr.

SFA 1 claimed that this force of three FF 29s and Oertz flying-boat No.46 dropped altogether 25 bombs. No sightings were made from the four British aircraft which took off.

Despite first assumptions that the Vickers Gunbuses as well as the two flying-boats were from RNAS Dover, later events suggest that at least one may have been an RFC aircraft.

At 11.25 hr an unidentified biplane appearing out of the mist over Thameshaven was promptly attacked by a six-pounder anti-aircraft gun and brought down with a damaged wing.

The gunners' jubilation at this first 'success' by the British ground defences was abruptly silenced by the discovery that the victim was RFC Gunbus No.1629. The two officers on board were unhurt. The filing of a note on this incident with the scrappy raid reports suggests that the Vickers was flying a defence sortie, though it is described only as having become lost after departure from base—unnamed, but probably Joyce Green.

Chapter IV

Zeppelins Ascendant—and the Whitehall War

Airship deliveries to the German navy and army gathered momentum during the second quarter of 1915 and both Services were anxious to extend activities over Britain.

Weather and other factors frustrated several attempts, but more exasperating to the military chiefs was the Kaiser's vacillation over raiding London. Having on 12 February authorized attacks against the docks he changed his mind a month later. On 5 May he sanctioned bombing east of the Tower, but this was not promulgated to the Services until the end of the month. On 20 July he finally approved unrestricted raids provided that historic buildings were spared.

By this time establishment of army airship bases in Belgium had shortened the distance to England, and London was first raided on the night of 31 May/1 June. Between April and October there were nineteen airship attacks, some of the most effective being made by the army, and 1915 could be called the year of the Zeppelin.

In the same period there were only four aeroplane raids, very minor hit-and-run attacks—including the first flown by an army unit.

L12, third of the P-class Zeppelins for the German navy, commissioned in June 1915.

Zeppelin design progressed, and four-engined craft of more than a million cubic-ft capacity superseded the earlier three-engined types. The German army received the first of the new P-class, LZ38, in April, while the navy commissioned the equivalent L10 in May. Altogether twenty-two were built, twelve for the army and ten (L10-19) for the navy. With a length of 536 ft 5 in, the P-class had a speed of 57–60 mph and a bomb load of 4–5,000 lb. Cruising height ranged from 8,000 to 10,500 ft. From September the 210 hp Maybach C-X engines in the first models were replaced by the 240 hp HSLu version, which slightly improved overall performance.

Little real progress was made towards creating an effective air defence organization, and paradoxically, successes by No.1 (RNAS) Squadron against two army airships over Belgium proved a delaying factor. On 16/17 May LZ39 was badly damaged by Flt Lieut A. W. Bigsworth, and on 6/7 June LZ37 was destroyed by Flt Sub-Lieut R. A. J. Warneford. The weapons used in both cases were 20 lb bombs.

After the first incident Wing Cdr Arthur Longmore, the squadron commander, reported to the Admiralty that the chances of successfully attacking Zeppelins approaching their bases at dawn were better than interception at night near their targets. He maintained that there should be no great difficulty in bombing once the pilot was well positioned above, and a variety of missiles offered the best chance of destruction—10 lb Hale's, Zeppelin bombs and perhaps a petrol bomb or 'fusée arrow'. The object was to tear the airship's inner and outer skins with the bombs and ignite the escaping gas with incendiaries. A fast-climbing single-seat aeroplane was required to carry several of each weapon and release them consecutively. A bomb combining both functions should be developed. Longmore's memorandum added that 'flaming bullets' appeared ineffective, since it seemed necessary to tear the envelope before a good escape of gas could be ignited.

Commodore Murray Sueter, Director of the Admiralty Air Department, noted on 29 May:

> 'It was very disappointing not to be able to fire the airship with the incendiary ammunition and bombs provided. Probably the exhaust gases from the motors are turned into the ring space. If this is so, the matter of igniting the hydrogen is one of great difficulty.'

The War Office had notified RFC units the previous day that 'it has been found that flaming bullets are useless against Zeppelins. They can, however, be usefully employed as tracer bullets against aeroplanes.'

Warneford's success so soon afterwards tacitly confirmed that Zeppelins were best attacked from above and that the bomb was the most suitable weapon. However, this assumption overlooked a well-handled airship's ability to gain height much faster than contemporary aeroplanes. Despite lack of further successes, belief in bombing dominated air defence thinking for about a year—more so in the RNAS than the RFC—though some in both Services had an inner conviction that the true answer lay with the machine-gun, which allowed a more flexible attack pattern.

One early success was achieved by naval intelligence. The coastal wireless direction-finding stations installed to pick up transmissions from enemy submarines also proved capable of intercepting messages from Zeppelins. By the third raid, intelligence had discovered the significance of a cryptic phrase in signals transmitted soon after the Zeppelins had left their bases. When these included the words 'only HVB on board' the indication was that the airship was bound for Britain and not merely on a routine North Sea reconnaissance. 'HVB' was an abbreviation for Handelsschiffsverkehrsbuch, the German navy code book for signalling merchant ships. This was known to be compromised and thus of no security significance. When raiding Britain, crews were forbidden to carry the more highly classified naval code publications.

Politics were much to the fore in the 1915 air defence scene, and the Admiralty and War Office found great difficulty in agreeing about anything—beyond the fundamental truths that Zeppelins were difficult to find in the dark and that night flying was fraught with problems. While the aircrews, with their inadequate machines and facilities, valiantly strove to confront the enemy, another war was being waged in Whitehall—a remarkable and long drawn out inter-departmental struggle over the responsibility for Britain's air defence.

It is unlikely that this unseemly wrangle significantly delayed the development of a sound and co-ordinated air defence scheme, since experience alone could produce any really effective counter to the raids, and this was conspicuously lacking. A few early experiments had pointed the way, but regular night flying and interception were utterly new spheres of activity beset by numerous special problems and hazards, and it may be that the element of competition resulting from navy and army pilots tackling these independently ultimately provided a wider pool of knowledge.

The Admiralty maintained that they were guarding Britain's skies only until the army was equipped to resume its traditional responsibility for home defence. And the War Office, despite preoccupations with the Expeditionary Force, believed at heart that aviation—certainly over dry land—was no activity for sailors. Both the navy and army were woefully short of experienced pilots and effective aircraft for the new air defence techniques.

Arthur Balfour, who became First Lord of the Admiralty on 27 May, 1915, lacked Churchill's enthusiasm for aviation and felt that the navy should not have become involved with the defence of London. On 18 June the Admiralty formally requested the War Office to resume this duty but at a joint conference on 19 July were nevertheless startled by War Office insistence on a full takeover of all the guns, aircraft and pilots. A second meeting two days later saw a more realistic and conciliatory attitude, with the War Office forecasting their ability to meet the home defence commitment by about January 1916—provided that there were no more demands on the RFC, and the navy gave some temporary assistance. The Admiralty agreed to submit firm proposals.

Outside Whitehall senior elements of the army seldom missed an opportunity to belittle naval air activities. The failure of Killingholme's aircraft to take off during an attack on Hull (6/7 June) prompted Maj-Gen H. M. Lawson, GOC-in-C Northern Command, to send a highly critical letter to the War Office. Killingholme, with only two effective aircraft, was notoriously prone to fog, he wrote on 14 June, and landing conditions at night were bad. Better results might be achieved from an aerodrome north or south of Hull in a fog-free area.

> 'As aeroplane attack appears to be the true method of defence' wrote Lawson, 'it is, I consider, unfortunate that the action of the Flying Corps is not under my control while the responsibility for all other land measures of defence rests with me. I think more aeroplanes should be made available.'

After an attack on Tyneside (15/16 June) the garrison commander advised Lawson that naval aircraft at Whitley Bay were too few and too slow, and that a military air station at Gosforth would be an advantage.

The temptation to criticize the navy over-rode attempts to understand the practical flying problems. On 16 June Lieut-Col R. H. James of the Directorate of Home Defence minuted his Director, General L. E. Kiggell, about the two recent raids. Naval co-operation in the Humber defences was evidently faulty, he wrote. Seaplanes were of little use against Zeppelins as they could not rise quickly enough, and landplanes should not wait on the ground until the enemy arrived.

> 'Ample warning of attack was received' he declared, 'yet no attempt was made to send up aeroplanes, which would soon have been above the mist.
>
> 'A similar lack of co-operation was shown by naval aircraft on the Tyne last night, as they did not attempt to go up until within a few minutes of the

first bombs being dropped. The aeroplanes should have gone up an hour or more before the Zeppelin was expected. They would then have been at sufficient height not only to see, but also attack the raider.

'Landing at night is difficult but not impossible with the system of illumination adopted by the Military Wing of the RFC. Of course the landing grounds must be sufficient in number and provided with the proper lighting facilities. As long as the navy are responsible for the defence by aircraft we can do nothing in the matter, and they apparently are not willing to do very much.

'I would suggest that the attention of the Admiralty be drawn to the conspicuous lack of success attendant upon the efforts of their aircraft to fulfil the responsibilities they have undertaken.'

Kiggell passed the papers to the Chief of the Imperial General Staff, General Sir Archibald Murray, next day, commenting that although aircraft appeared to offer better prospects of destroying Zeppelins, night operations would probably prove costly in pilots and aircraft. On the wider issue he wrote:

> 'The present system of divided control does not seem to give very satisfactory results and I submit that it is now necessary to consider the advisability of arranging for the attack on these airships to be controlled entirely by the Army Council while the ships are over the land, and for pursuit when they are over the sea to be taken up by the naval seaplanes.'

On 18 June, apparently unaware that the Admiralty had that day seized the initiative, the CIGS authorized an approach on those lines.

General L. E. (later Sir Launcelot) Kiggell, Director of Home Defence at the War Office in 1915 (*left*); and Sir David Henderson as a brigadier-general, before he qualified for his pilot's 'wings' in June 1911. Henderson, Director-General of Military Aviation at the War Office in 1915–17, died in 1921, and remains one of the most under-rated figures in the early development of British air power. (*Imperial War Museum, left-hand photograph*)

The Martinsyde S.1 scout, which failed to meet expectations as an early home-defence aircraft.

The RFC had flown only four home defence sorties since April and their resources to back up the RNAS were slender in the extreme. On 6 May the War Office had instructed Farnborough, Brooklands, Hounslow, Northolt, Joyce Green, Dover and Shoreham to maintain at least one aircraft always at readiness for the defence of London. Martinsyde S.1 scouts were recommended for anti-Zeppelin work, and their weapon load was specified as six carcass bombs with launching tubes, three powder bombs and carriers, twelve Hale's grenades and 150 incendiary darts. 'It is not considered that any advantage will be gained by equipping the machines with rifles' added the War Office instruction. No front-line operational aircraft could be spared for meeting attacks by enemy aeroplanes, but there were a few Lewis-armed Vickers Gunbuses at Joyce Green, and ·45-in Winchester rifles for other available machines.

At Farnborough, where pilots were rightly sceptical about the sluggish Martinsyde's capabilities when carrying such a burden, Maj G. I. Carmichael of No.4 RAS test-climbed one on 24 May with the specified bomb load, plus carbines and flaming bullets of equivalent weight to the grenades and incendiary darts, which were not available. Even when exceeding recommended engine revolutions he took 21½ min to reach 6,000 ft. However, it was not until 29 October that the War Office declared the Martinsyde unsuitable for the role.

Lieut-Col J. M. Salmond, commanding the RFC Administrative Wing at Farnborough, told the War Office that only fast climbing two-seaters were suitable for home defence and each station should have two RAF-engined B.E.2cs fitted for carcass bombs, Lewis guns and Fiery Grapnels. Older B.Es being adapted for the grapnel lacked the speed and climb to attack airships.

Contemporary returns to the War Office show the RFC order of battle for the defence of London as: Brooklands and Farnborough—two Martinsydes with incendiary bombs; Dover—two Martinsydes with incendiary bombs and two B.E.2cs being fitted for Fiery Grapnel; Hounslow—B.E.2cs 1692 and 1693 with bomb racks and incendiary launching tubes and one Martinsyde with launching tubes; Joyce Green—two Vickers Gunbuses with Lewis guns, one Martinsyde with incendiary bombs and one Bristol Scout; Northolt—two Martinsydes with incendiary bombs and Lewis guns; Shoreham—one Martinsyde with incendiary bombs; Gosport—B.E.2cs 1664 and 1690 with bomb racks and incendiary launching tubes.

Additional to this puny twenty-strong air defence fleet, No.6 Wing offered three Farman Shorthorns, two Blériots, two B.E.2cs and a Martinsyde—if these could be made combat-ready and provided with pilots. The No.6 Wing armoury contained a dozen different stores for home defence—three types of rifles or carbines with ·303 and ·45 ammunition; powder, incendiary, smoke and petrol bombs; flaming bullets; rifle grenades and rockets. Farnborough held three Fiery Grapnels, and Northolt two.

The carcass incendiary bomb, in 10 lb and the 14½ lb Mk II sizes, was a quaint device delivered via an RL (Royal Laboratory) tube fixed externally to the aircraft fuselage or internally to project through the floor. The tube lining incorporated battery-powered electrical contact strips which completed a circuit with matching strips on the bomb casing, to ignite the carcass powder 20 seconds after the bomb had cleared the tube. The bomb also had, at each end, cables bearing three-pointed hooks, freed during the fall, and intended to engage an airship's envelope.

On 19 June, 1915, nearly three weeks after the first London attack, the War Office Directorate of Military Aeronautics recapitulated procedures and listed aerodromes likely to be operating in any future raids, including Hyde Park and Regent's Park among emergency landing grounds. As soon as hostile airships had been located, naval aircraft would ascend to attack them, wrote the War Office, adding:

> 'Military aircraft will co-operate whenever possible but at night it is not considered desirable to take to the air unless the airship can actually be seen or heard.'

This cautious line was diametrically opposed to the Home Defence Directorate's 'press-on' advice for naval aircraft, and typifies the confusion and conflicting views then bedevilling the home defence scene.

The directive noted the collision risk, reminding stations that it was impossible to brief pilots before take-off about subsequent departures, or warn them of aircraft from naval aerodromes or RFC Dover which might follow Zeppelins to London.

Meanwhile the Admiralty went into hibernation over the transfer question, probably because of preoccupation with the fundamental reorganization of the RNAS, which established it as an integral part of the navy from 1 August. Air stations were placed under appropriate commanders-in-chief or area senior officers—though Hendon and Chingford remained under direct Admiralty control—and a new post of Director of Air Services was created. The officer appointed, Rear-Admiral Charles L. Vaughan-Lee, was not an aviator, and generally the changes suggested a desire to keep an ambitious new offshoot of the traditional sea-going navy in its place.

Vaughan-Lee took office on 8 September, and his first recorded minute, on the same date, struck a gloomy note:

> 'The many accidents resulting in considerable loss of life and material which have occurred to aircraft flying at night in Zeppelin raids raise the question as to whether the results obtained justify the continuation thereof. Experience in France has shown that this work can be done in safety provided the necessary clear and illuminated landing grounds of sufficient

area and at no great distance apart are provided, and that only pilots who have been trained in night flying go up. At present most of our pilots who have been trained in night flying have gone abroad.'

Before these views could receive consideration, air defence became a priority issue following strong Press criticism of the organization which allowed airships to raid London with impunity on two successive nights—7/8 and 8/9 September.

On 10 September the Admiralty decided that the first task was to strengthen and reorganize the anti-aircraft guns under one officer, and two days later gave the job to Admiral Sir Percy Scott. Retired since 1909, Scott was a leading gunnery expert, a shrewd thinker and a renowned enemy of red tape, whose vigorous and unconventional methods soon transformed the situation. One of his first moves—asserting that 'we have invasion on the brain'—was to withdraw many coastal defence guns and convert them for anti-aircraft use. Nevertheless, he also had more faith than most senior officers in the aeroplane which, he declared, would eventually become the Zeppelins' worst enemy. In November he told Balfour that Britain could establish a fleet of 100 aircraft, armed with Davis shell guns and flown by well-trained pilots—if rapid action were taken. He ended on a typical note, questioning the wisdom of posting all the best pilots overseas—'this policy should be reconsidered before Woolwich Arsenal is destroyed, and not afterwards'.

The Admiralty told Scott that the relinquishment of the entire home defence commitment was under consideration, but when the War Office again raised the matter there was another long silence.

On 15 September a new Admiralty aeroplane defence sub-committee, which included three experienced pilots, recommended study of the French system of standing patrols over Paris during Zeppelin activity, aware that this would involve reversing the 'concealment' policy since it required beacons and more illuminated landing grounds. Pending further information about the French organization, any effective defence system for London was estimated to require forty aircraft and twenty-four pilots, and additional aerodromes spaced five miles apart. The sub-committee considered that guns and searchlights would still provide the main defences, with patrolling aeroplanes playing a supplementary role. Aircraft would achieve nothing unless they were in the air and at about the same height as the Zeppelins. Regardless of the outcome, such a scheme would be good for public morale.

Scott was pessimistic, believing that more illuminated landing grounds might assist the enemy to locate London targets, and that guns could not easily combine with aeroplane operations at night. Also, bombs from the defending aircraft which missed Zeppelins would fall on London. He felt that the answer lay with skilled night pilots flying from more remote bases in areas which the airships must cross en route for the capital.

Towards the end of September, after studying a report on the Paris defences from Sqn Cdr J. T. Babington, the Admiralty perversely decided that despite employing thirty aircraft in co-operation with guns, searchlights and observer posts, the French system confirmed their own view that aircraft occupied a subordinate role. Overseas units would therefore retain their prior claim on trained pilots and home commitments be met by those of lesser experience. The aerodrome situation could be resolved by improving the existing sites.

At that time there were only sixteen night-trained RNAS pilots at stations concerned with London defence, disposed as follows: Hendon two, Chingford two, Chelmsford one, Eastchurch two, Grain two, Westgate one, Felixstowe three and Yarmouth three. Other young and inexperienced pilots were prepared to fly night sorties in emergency.

The London raids also precipitated urgent action in the War Office. Lord Kitchener, Secretary of State for War, summoned the Director-General of Military Aeronautics and overall Commander of the RFC, Maj-Gen Sir David Henderson, and peremptorily demanded 'what are you going to do about these airship raids?' Though familiar with Kitchener's style, Henderson was nevertheless taken aback and protested that this was strictly for the RNAS. Kitchener retorted that he did not care whose job it was—if the RFC made no attempt to meet the next attack he would hold Henderson personally responsible.

Such a remark from Kitchener was an order, and Henderson immediately instructed No.5 Wing to position a B.E.2c with pilot at Writtle, near Chelmsford, and another at Joyce Green. This was done on 9 September.

Meteorological Office experts forecast that the favourable period for the next major raid would be 5–12 October, which allowed Henderson time to plan the most effective deployment for his slender available resources.

The attack eventually came on 13/14 October and was the biggest and costliest to date. It was opposed by six RFC sorties—but not one from the RNAS—and although only one sighting was made, valuable knowledge was gained about the very real problems facing the pilots.

Reporting on the night's activities, the No.5 Wing CO, Lieut-Col W. G. H. Salmond, suggested that gaps in the patrol pattern caused by retaining each station's second aircraft on the ground until the first had landed could be closed by extending sortie time from 90 minutes to two hours, with the second aircraft taking off 30 minutes before the first was due to land. Collision risks could be minimized by restricting the two machines to opposite sides of the aerodrome during the overlap period.

To help locate Zeppelins he suggested that some aircraft be adapted as flare-droppers, and a special searchlight-carrier developed. There should be stricter control of searchlights and more research into aerodrome flares, which were difficult to see through mist except from directly overhead, producing a tendency for pilots to touchdown on top of the mist itself. He recommended formation of a special defence squadron with detachments at five aerodromes near London, manned by pilots screened from overseas postings and thus able to acquire some expertise in night flying.

In a rather lukewarm comment the No.2 Brigade commander, Brig-Gen J. F. A. Higgins, protested that the plan for one aircraft per station to patrol for an hour at 8,000 ft would have worked had not two Zeppelins inconsiderately lost their way. He did not think it advisable for two machines from one aerodrome to be airborne simultaneously. There was little early prospect of specialized searchlight aircraft being built, and provision of an exclusively home defence squadron was a matter for the Admiralty. Higgins confidently forecast more efficient arrangements when the War Office took charge.

The Admiralty/War Office collaboration on this improved defence plan had clearly failed to produce any common operating criteria for the two flying Services, and after learning that no RNAS aircraft had been airborne Kiggell commented that 'we must be self-supporting'. The Admiralty's embarrassment was little abated by the uncompromising reply from the C-in-C Nore, Admiral Sir George Callaghan, when asked the reason:

> 'From experience gained in night flying since the commencement of the

war it has been found quite useless to send machines up unless Zeppelins are actually sighted.'

From the newspapers and MPs came the inevitable taunts about the missing 'swarm of formidable hornets' which Churchill, in March 1914, had promised Parliament would rise to meet raiders.

On 26 October the Admiralty wrote to appropriate senior officers demanding that every effort (the original draft said 'greater effort') in future should be made to intercept and destroy Zeppelins—which was one of the reasons why executive control of air operations had been transferred from Whitehall. Where resources permitted, regular patrols should be flown at last light, and all stations must maintain aircraft at immediate readiness on evenings when conditions favoured raids.

The Admiral of Patrols, Rear-Admiral G. A. Ballard, retorted that at least seventeen additional B.E.2cs, or aircraft of comparable performance, would be required to maintain an effective patrol system—though since the Zeppelins usually made landfall after dark, twilight patrols were of doubtful value. In darkness airships were almost impossible to see, and to date night patrols had only produced extensive casualties to pilots and aircraft without achieving useful results.

Since the start of raiding the RNAS had attempted interceptions with various aircraft possessing reasonable capabilities for their day but patently lacking the performance for the task. One such was the 69 mph Sopwith Two-Seater Scout, irreverently known as the 'Spinning Jenny' because of its proneness to enter the dreaded spin. It was a rather nondescript machine of similar category to the Bristol T.B.8, but of lower performance, ordered for military use before specific roles had evolved. Its offensive capability was limited to what might be achieved by the observer with a rifle, though since its 80 hp Gnome engine could not lift it higher than about 3,000 ft, Zeppelins were at little risk. Some stations modified it to carry small bombs.

A newly-completed Avro 504C, before installation of its Lewis gun.

Similarly powered but of rather better performance was the Avro 504B, capable of about 80 mph. Built as a two-seater, it was usually operated with a pilot only, carrying personal weapons plus a few bombs, and little better equipped to deal with airships. It was followed by the 504C constructed as a single-seater, with greater endurance and performance and armed with a Lewis gun.

Of the various RNAS floatplanes only the single-seat Sopwith Schneider—developed from the winner of the 1914 Schneider Trophy race—had the

Sopwith Schneider 3794, photographed on the Thames in 1915, was still in service two years later, at Felixstowe, and was among the miscellaneous types airborne against the 13 June, 1917, raiders.

performance to offer any threat, but it was armed in makeshift fashion with a Lewis gun angled to fire clear of the propeller.

Ballard's riposte ended with a valuable suggestion, which was duly acted upon. He recommended that several ships be fitted to carry seaplanes and deployed 50–60 miles from the coast an hour before sunset in favourable attack weather so that Zeppelins could be intercepted in daylight. The paddle steamers *Brocklesby* and *Killingholme* adapted to carry two Sopwith seaplanes each became operational in the spring of 1916.

On 3 November the Admiralty at last replied to the War Office on the transfer

HMS *Killingholme*, with a Sopwith Baby on board, showing damage possibly caused by a mine. (*Imperial War Museum*)

question—but only to suggest another deferment for further consideration by a joint conference in December. They pleaded that having modified their earlier opinion that aircraft were indispensable for the defence of London, they could not propose any definite transfer arrangements without further experience.

The effect produced in the War Office by this blatant stone-walling may be gauged from Henderson's comments. A veteran of the South African campaigns, Henderson had learned to fly in 1911 at the age of 49, and, as Director of Military Training, had been a most active supporter of aviation. While commanding the RFC in the field during the opening twelve months of the war he had been the first to advocate the formation of special fighter squadrons, and probably possessed greater understanding of the air potential than any of his contemporaries. After his death Trenchard described him as 'the true father of the Royal Air Force'. Of normally mild temperament, he rarely expressed himself so bluntly as in his minute of 5 November to the Director of Home Defence:

> 'I am of the opinion that aeroplanes are an invaluable adjunct to the defence of any locality against air raids provided that they are efficiently organised.
>
> 'The question of the responsibility for the defence of London has been shelved by the Admiralty since last July, and I think we should be putting ourselves in a very false position if we did not press strongly for an immediate decision, instead of allowing the matter to be continually postponed. I therefore suggest that a conference should be called at once: we should ask the Admiralty definitely:—
>
> (a) whether they consider that aeroplanes are [or are not] essential for the defence of London;
>
> (b) whether they do or do not intend to organise a sufficient aerial defence. If they do not, then I am prepared to make arrangements to carry it out.'

In passing this minute on to Kiggell, the irrepressible Lieut-Col James could not resist this complacent addition:

> 'The Admiralty's view that aeroplanes are not indispensable is, I think, based on the fact that their aviators are not well enough trained to fly at night, whilst Sir David's aviators are.'

The conference was held on 10 November, chaired by Vice-Admiral Sir Frederick Hamilton, Second Sea Lord. Vaughan-Lee said that aeroplanes were of little or no value against Zeppelins at night, and in any case should be employed at some distance from the enemy's objective. Henderson gently pointed out that while the airships could use many different lines of approach they must eventually converge on the target, thus providing good opportunities for attack near the objective. It was essential, he added, that guns and aircraft were under the same command. Hamilton proposed that the navy should defend the coast and a belt 20 miles inland, and the army protect the rest of the country.

This was formally put to the Army Council two days later, with several further points for consideration:—that aeroplanes had so far proved ineffective in defending London at night, their only value being to satisfy public opinion and possibly hasten the movement of Zeppelins over the metropolis; that aircraft could not operate successfully over a large city unless an extensive area was illuminated by powerful searchlights; and that there were perhaps better prospects of attacking the airships as they approached or passed the coast—for which arrangements were being elaborated by the Admiralty.

Clearly the introduction of an invisible 20-mile demarcation line presented formidable operating difficulties, and on 26 November the Army Council came back with Kiggell's proposal of 17 June—that the navy deal with enemy aircraft approaching the coast and the army take over when they had crossed our shores.

This was agreed, and the First Lord of the Admiralty put the scheme to the Cabinet War Policy Committee three days later. With Kitchener absent in the Dardanelles, the committee took note that the two Departments had agreed the transfer in principle, and on 3 December various fundamentals were discussed at yet another Admiralty conference, attended by representatives of the War Office and the new Home Forces Command. All now seemed set fair for the transfer, apart from a few distant rumblings—one from the Master General of the Ordnance, who questioned the wisdom of taking over an incomplete and unsatisfactory organization and thus exposing the War Office to obloquy should it be found wanting.

The bombshell burst when the plan was put to Kitchener on his return. The Admiralty's procrastinations paled to insignificance when the War Secretary virtually repudiated the agreement which his staff had reached after wearisome months. A formal letter from the Army Council on 18 January, 1916, told the Admiralty that they were averse from making a further important change of this sort during hostilities, more especially as the arrangements for the air defence of the United Kingdom were still in a very incomplete state.

Henderson, so recently charged by Kitchener to 'do something' about the Zeppelins, was perhaps more shaken than even the Admiralty—which, on 21 January, expressed its surprise and regret, and urged the Army Council to honour the transfer arrangements 'decided some six months ago'.

The question was resolved at the 26 January meeting of the War Policy Committee, Balfour claiming that the transfer had been settled between the two Departments in September and should take place as soon as possible. The main difficulty, he said, was the shortage of guns, which British and French experts agreed were better than aeroplanes for dealing with Zeppelins at night.

Kitchener declared that the controversy had started with Churchill's insistence that the defence of London was an Admiralty duty. Despite their opposite view, the War Office had given every possible assistance to the navy. Now the question was reversed, and the War Office felt that with the system of defence not yet elaborated and the supply of aircraft not completed, the present was not the time to change. With increased requirements from the Front the army had no aircraft to spare, he argued, and there would be demands for large numbers of anti-aircraft guns which they did not possess. However, the War Office would take over and do their best.

Next day Balfour and Kitchener blandly assured a deputation of London MPs that great improvements in gun and aeroplane defences had been effected since the October raid and the two Services had worked harmoniously together—but unity of control was desirable, and the transfer of the defences to War Office control was planned to take effect within the next three weeks.

The formal agreement endorsed by the War Committee on 10 February provided for:—

> '(a) The navy to undertake to deal with all hostile aircraft attempting to reach this country, whilst the army undertake to deal with all such aircraft which reach these shores.

'(b) All defence arrangements on land to be undertaken by the army, which will also provide the aeroplanes required to work with the home defence troops and to protect garrisons and vulnerable areas and the flying stations required to enable their aircraft to undertake these duties.'

Woolwich was given special priority in view of its vital munitions production. Generally the two Services were urged to co-operate to avoid unnecessary duplication.

The Commander-in-Chief Home Forces assumed responsibility for the defence of London at 12 noon on Wednesday, 16 February, 1916, and for the rest of the country on the 22nd. This post was held by Field Marshal Lord French, who, on 19 December, 1915, had been superseded as C-in-C British Expeditionary Force by Douglas Haig, one of his subordinates, while Robertson, his former deputy, had become Chief of the Imperial General Staff. French's peerage was small consolation for this relegation to a backwater, and his irascible temperament was apparent from subsequent correspondence with higher authority, in which his often legitimate demands for better equipment were sometimes couched in the terms of an old-fashioned school teacher lecturing a tiresome class.

Service staffs had begun transfer planning immediately after the 3 December meeting, and the War Office adopted, with provision for expansion, the comprehensive gunnery scheme in preparation by Sir Percy Scott. It also decided to deploy some searchlights outside the London area specifically to help fighter pilots locate their quarry. These were termed 'aeroplane lights'. The ad hoc

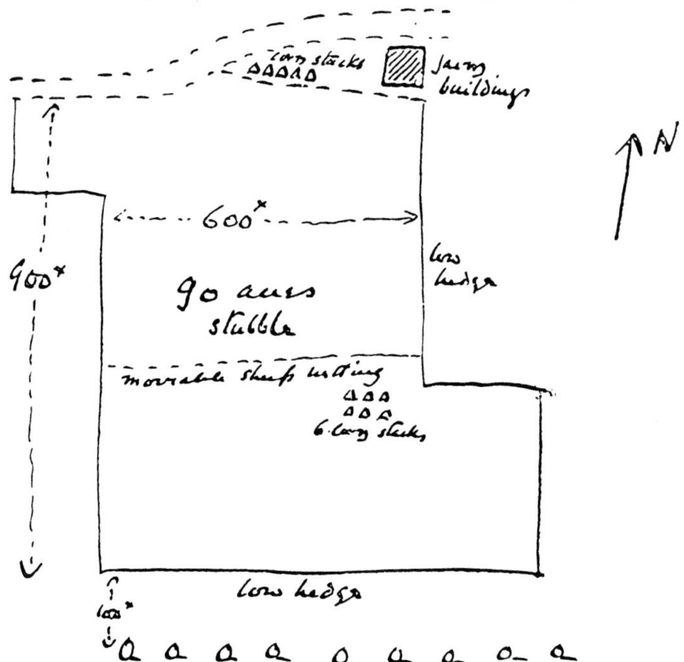

The original sketch map of Landing Ground No.II—Suttons Farm, Rainham. The ground was the property of Mr T. Crawford. (*Public Record Office*)

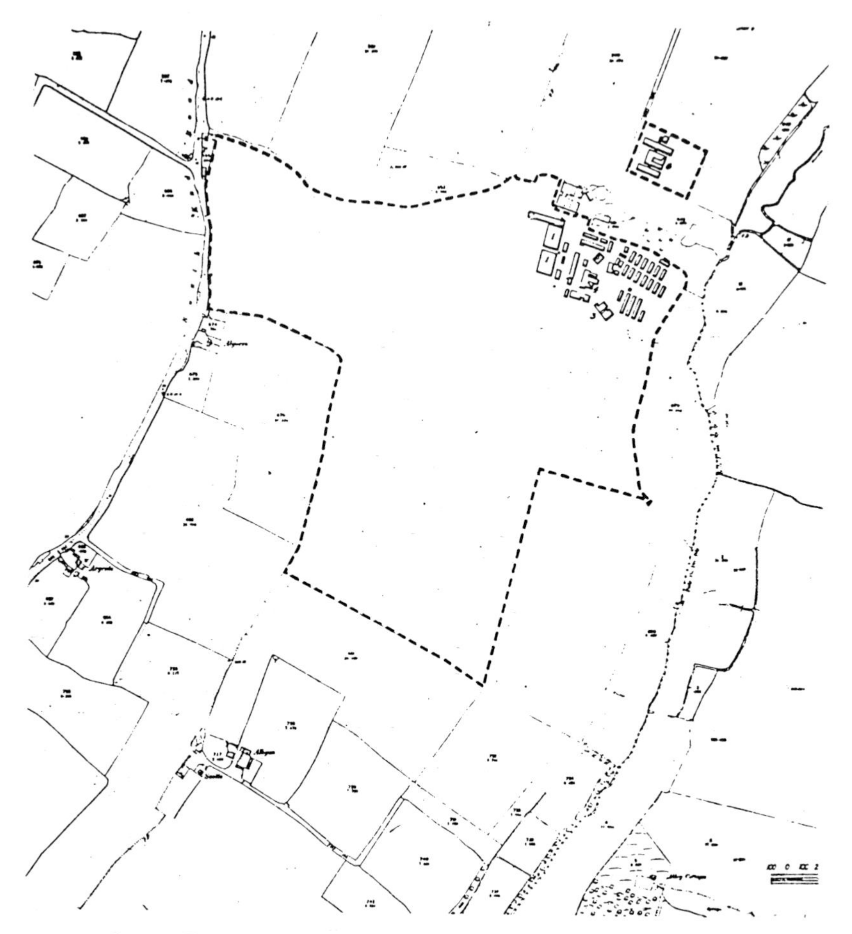

Suttons Farm as depicted in the official aerodromes publication of 1918.
(*Public Record Office*)

aircraft arrangements made in October were extended, and the War Office undertook to provide B.E.2cs with night-trained pilots from reserve aeroplane squadrons to operate from Croydon, Farningham, Hainault, Hounslow, Joyce Green, Northolt, Suttons Farm, and Wimbledon Common. Two aeroplanes were to operate from each place. RNAS aircraft from Chingford and Hendon were to assist until the formal takeover, after which the latter station would house an RFC night fighting element.

The patrol system was unchanged, with pilots operating within visual range of their bases, hopefully to deal with any airships which crossed their paths. Plans were also made to meet attacks against other major cities, and by earlier agreement the RFC had on 1 December positioned three B.E.2cs at Cramlington for the defence of Tyneside.

Throughout 1915 research into night flying continued, and on 5 August the Admiralty Air Department produced a report summarising RNAS experience.

This emphasised the need to fly precisely, avoiding steep inadvertent sideslips, which were difficult to correct at night, and to keep plenty of power in hand during the landing approach. It recommended daylight practice of straight-and-level flying and turning by instruments, without using the horizon as a guide; gliding and landing slowly; making gentle sideslips and quick recoveries; noting indicated air speeds and identifying them with the sound of the bracing wires under various conditions.

Lighting which could be varied in intensity to suit the pilot's preference had been developed for the B.E.2c instrument panel, and Eastchurch produced landing lights comprising two 5⅜-in diameter headlamps fitted to the outer interplane struts. The installation weighed only 16 lb, and best results were obtained by setting the two beams to converge on the ground 30 yards ahead when the aircraft was in normal landing attitude. The station also invented a plummet device trailing on a 30-ft line behind an aircraft which activated a red cockpit warning light when the machine was 15 ft above the ground. The RFC Administrative Wing recommended that the RNAS cockpit and landing light systems should be evaluated for army aircraft.

The Central Flying School fully endorsed the RNAS handling observations and maintained that at least half the night-flying difficulties were solved by using an inherently stable aircraft fitted with an oleo undercarriage. A stationary engine capable of being throttled down—as opposed to the rotary with its 'on/off' control—lifted another load from the pilot's mind. The Commandant, Capt Godfrey M. Paine, RN, had strong views on the subject, and on 22 August wrote:

> 'It is criminal to send pilots out at night without previous experience or on machines which are strange to them, even if they are of the same type they are used to flying. They will effect no good and will probably cause the loss of the machine and pilot. Pusher machines should be avoided at night if possible, as the sense of control in this type even in daytime is far less than in a tractor machine, and they have usually considerably less inherent stability, and in the event of a mistake occurring when landing the result will in all probability be more serious.'

An aeroplanes' sub-committee of the Board of Inventions and Research reported on 14 September that the prime cause of night accidents was the lack of proper navigation and landing facilities. Provided pilots could find an adequate aerodrome—such as Eastchurch—and given reasonable freedom from engine failure, there was little more difficulty in flying on clear nights than by day.

Since night raids by large enemy aeroplanes could become a reality within a few months, Britain should prepare to meet them by becoming thoroughly experienced in night flying, and if necessary develop specialized aircraft for the purpose. But it was impossible to take even the first steps until adequate landing and navigation facilities were available.

The sub-committee noted that in 89 sample RNAS night flights in England, some twenty aircraft had been 'wholly or partly wrecked', three pilots killed and eight 'more or less seriously injured'. These broad categorizations of damage and casualties gave an exaggerated impression and evidently included training flights. Operational returns suggest that probably no more than ten aircraft received major damage on defence sorties—about half being repairable—and that only two of the crash survivors sustained more than minor injuries. All considered it is remarkable that the accident rate was not very much higher.

No system of notifying accident damage by defined categories was then in use and squadron reports varied. It was common practice to describe as 'wrecked'—and implying written off—badly damaged aircraft which were subsequently repaired or rebuilt. Some reports did, however, itemize damage and indicate whether an aircraft had been destroyed, *eg* by fire.

On 16 November the War Office Directorate of Military Aeronautics instructed No.2 Brigade to increase night training in anticipation of the imminent demands, adding:

> 'It is realised that there are considerable risks attendant on flying at night, but these risks are minimised when pilots practice over their own aerodromes. At the same time, the officers selected for this duty should be very carefully chosen. Only stable machines are to be used for this purpose.'

It was notified that more Renault-engined B.E.2cs would be issued for night training as they became available.

The stability fetish was now well established, and only a few bold spirits dared challenge it. One such was Capt E. F. Unwin of No.4 RAS, transferred from Farnborough to Northolt, who sought permission to use Avros and Maurice Farmans for training on clear nights. This was rather grudgingly given on 30 November, provided they were restricted to flying within the aerodrome area.

> 'At such times the use of a stable machine is not essential, as the pilot has a horizon and lights to assist him' wrote the War Office. 'No pilot is, however, to be permitted to leave the aerodrome, or to fly at any great height, in other than stable machines.'

During the year Mr Holt's flares were developed into an essential aid for the pilot facing a forced landing at night. Central Flying School report No.138 of 9 September said that the parachute flare, normally released at 2–3,000 ft, burned for two to two-and-a-half minutes with a brilliant light enabling a pilot to select a suitable landing area. During a trial over Larkhill from 5,000 ft, roads, buildings and even a wire fence were discernable. Fixed wingtip flares activated by an electric push-button when the aircraft was at about 300 ft (a later instruction gave 100–150 ft) burned for one minute. A metal shield above the flame protected the pilot from glare, and for the CFS trials the lower wing undersurface was covered with silvered black silk cloth and the rear of the propeller lamp-blacked. Pilots were advised to look out on the side opposite to the flare being used but not to employ them on misty nights, when the effect could be very dazzling.

Parachute flares were issued to several units for testing them as a means of illuminating Zeppelins from above, but there is no record of this having been attempted.

Other means of locating Zeppelins were being studied. Professor T. Mather and J. T. Irving of the City & Guilds Engineering College devised a sound locator in the form of a 16-ft diameter paraboloid reflector cut into the face of a chalk quarry at Bimbury Manor Farm, at Detling in Kent. Tests with Eastchurch aircraft during July 1915 showed that the sound of a Renault B.E.2c could be picked up by the reflector from half a minute to two-and-a-half minutes before it was heard by the unaided ear, and that the device could double the period during which the aircraft was audible.

On one occasion the reflector picked up a B.E.2c flying at 4,500 ft between Sheerness and Grain, 10½ miles away. Mather claimed that these promising results

Holt flare and navigation light fitted to the lower wing of a B.E.12. The metal shields for the flares were largely discarded after operational experience.

could be improved with a movable concrete mirror positioned away from trees, and that it should be possible to hear a Zeppelin 20 miles away. The RNAS was not particularly impressed, and after trials with smaller mirrors at Farnborough and the CFS, the War Office likewise told Mather that performance was not quite good enough to justify their adoption. One of Mather's equipments was at Capel in 1916, but it is not known whether he was concerned with the later developments in this field.

Chapter V

Operations—April to October 1915

14/15 April, 1915 (Night)

Target: Tyneside.
Enemy force: Navy Zeppelin L9 (Kptlt Heinrich Mathy).
Results: None killed, two injured, £55 damage.
Defence sorties: One.

RNAS
Whitley Bay: Bristol T.B.8 1217 (Flt Sub-Lieut P. Legh, LM H. J. L. Hinkler) 20.25–21.50 hr.

This raid was launched on an opportunity basis. The L9 was engaged on a long North Sea reconnaissance, but when Mathy found himself within striking distance of the English coast, in good weather and carrying a substantial bomb load, he obtained wireless authorization to attack a land target at his discretion.

At 19.45 hr he reached the coast at Blyth—which he mistook for Tynemouth—but with navigation hampered by new lighting restrictions, most of his bombs fell in open country. A few incendiaries caused minor damage in Wallsend.

RNAS Whitley Bay, opened six weeks earlier for such a contingency, received the raid warning at 20.00 hr. Although officially operational, the station equipment left much to be desired. The armoury contained 209 incendiary bullets for use with its few ·45-in carbines, 24 Hale grenades without the ·303-in rifles to fire them, and 20 Hale bombs—but only one set of dropping gear. The best aircraft, B.E.2c No.1099, was unserviceable and, of the two available machines, Farman No.1454 broke a valve spring while running up.

A Bristol T.B.8 was held pending further news of the raider's movements. Its pilot, Peter Legh, had passed out of the RNAS flying school on 10 March and had never flown at night. In the front seat, armed with carbine and incendiary bullets, was the young Australian, Bert Hinkler, who had joined the navy from the Sopwith firm.*

After reports that the Zeppelin had turned south, the Bristol took off and headed west, hoping to intercept before it reached the likely target of Newcastle. Gradually attaining 5,000 ft, Legh patrolled over the town for an hour—blindly, since there were no searchlights to indicate the general whereabouts of the enemy. Returning over the dark countryside he was becoming acutely anxious about ever finding the aerodrome when Hinkler spotted Very lights being fired

* In 1918 Hinkler became a pilot, and flew Sopwith Camels on the Italian front. He is best remembered for the first ever England–Australia solo flight in 1928 and later record-breaking performances.

from the ground. They arrived overhead, and at a prearranged signal 'Imperial lights'* and petrol flares were lit and a safe landing achieved.

This was a creditable performance for a first night flight in exceptionally dark conditions, and the Whitley Bay CO, Flt Cdr C. E. Robinson, urged the Admiralty to issue a Press statement describing the attempted interception.

> 'My officers and men feel slightly hurt that even the Newcastle papers (though they must have known) made no mention of anyone trying to beat off the attack' he wrote, 'though long and exhaustive accounts of the Zeppelin's course are given as though the enemy was allowed completely to have his own way without any effort being made to stop him.'

Preserved home defence files contain vague references to an aircraft from RFC Cramlington also having been airborne.

15/16 April, 1915 (Night)

Target: Humber area.
Enemy forces: Navy Zeppelins L5 (Kptlt Alois Böcker), L6 (Oblt-z-S H. von Buttlar), L7 (Oblt-z-S Werner Peterson).
Results: None killed, one injured, £6,498 damage.
Defence sorties: Two.

RNAS
Yarmouth: Sopwith seaplane 880 (Flt Cdr de C. W. P. Ireland, LM C. Notley) 00.55–01.50 hr; Sopwith Two-seater Scout 1053 (Flt Sub-Lieut V. Nicholl, PO Lytton) took off 04.30 hr.

Navigation difficulties, aggravated by high winds and British lighting restrictions, prevented this raiding force from reaching the intended targets in the Humber area. The operation was commanded by Strasser, flying in L7. The airship captains later admitted that they were not sure where they had been.

* So far it has not proved possible to find a description of Imperial lights.

Sopwith Two-seater Scout 1053 at RNAS Yarmouth. This aircraft flew five fruitless anti-airship sorties during the spring and summer of 1915. (*RAF Museum*)

L5 was first reported off Southwold at 21.40 hr and after some obscure movements bombed Lowestoft about two hours later. L6 made landfall off the Naze at 23.30 hr and bombed Maldon. L7 spent an hour skirting the coast from Hunstanton to Yarmouth, then at 02.40 hr headed back to Germany without bombing. The greatest damage was to a timber yard at Lowestoft.

RNAS Yarmouth had been warned of an impending raid as early as 18.00 hr, thanks to an intercepted 'HVB' message, and a Spinning Jenny flew a precautionary patrol from 18.15 hr until dark.

At 00.15 hr engine sounds were reported from Kessingland, followed 25 minutes later by news that a Zeppelin was over Southwold. As Ireland was about to take off there came a report that the intruder—the L5—was heading out to sea. Sopwith No.880 was not a sprightly performer, and plunging through the darkness struck a sandbank as it was reaching flying speed. Ireland decided that examination for possible damage could wait until after the sortie. A search of nearly an hour yielded nothing, and fortunately the damaged float held together for a safe alighting.

RNAS Felixstowe also heard L5 and started up Curtiss H-4 flying-boat No.951. When it was ready for take-off Zeppelin sounds had faded, so guidance was sought from the Admiralty—which ruled that aircraft should not be despatched unless the airship was visible.

16 April, 1915 (Daylight)

Target: North Kent.
Enemy force: One Albatros B II.
Results: No casualties or damage.
Defence sorties: 14.

RNAS

Dover: Blériot Parasols 1541 and 1542, Vickers F.B.5 747; took off about 12.30 hr, further details not known.

Eastchurch: Eight sorties, details not known.

Westgate: Avro 504Bs 1011 and 1013, details not known; 1011 second sortie (Flt Lieut H. A. Buss, AM Gardner) 12.32–12.57 hr.

This was the first sortie against England by a German army aeroplane—from Feldflieger Abteilung (Field Aviation Unit) No.41, with the Albatros B II.

The raider—variously described as a monoplane, a biplane and a seaplane—crossed the coast near Kingsdown at 11.40 hr and flew at 8–9,000 ft over broken cloud to Sittingbourne, dropping four small HE bombs at 12.20 hr and shortly afterwards another which fell in the Swale. It returned via Faversham—where it released five incendiaries—and Canterbury, finally leaving north of Deal at 12.50 hr.

Newspaper accounts which mention pursuit by a British aircraft must refer to an Eastchurch machine, but no official reports from that station have been traced.

Two Avros, probably flown by Flt Lieut A. F. Bettington and Flt Sub-Lieut R. H. Mulock, were airborne from Westgate within two minutes of receiving the warning and narrowly missed the enemy over Whitstable. Following a later ground sighting report, Buss patrolled between Westgate and Eastchurch, and the Dover aircraft were ordered up when the intruder was homeward bound from Faversham, but nothing was seen.

This minor raid was notable for the confusion caused by the Albatros stationed at Eastchurch. Neighbouring gun sites had been warned that a machine 'of German type' would be flying locally, and at 12.10 hr when an aircraft appeared high up from the east, the Faversham gunners were in a quandary. They recognized it as German, but felt obliged to delay fire until it was almost overhead and their telescopic sight revealed the black cross wing markings. They traversed right round and managed five shots. At 12.30 hr the aircraft returned, and again the gunners dutifully waited until they could see the German markings before firing 18 rounds at gradually lengthening range.

29/30 April, 1915 (Night)

Target: East Anglia.
Enemy force: Army Zeppelin LZ38 (Hptmn Erich Linnarz).
Results: No casualties, £9,010 damage.
Defence sorties: Four.

RNAS
Yarmouth: Sopwith Two-seater Scouts 1052 (Flt Sub-Lieut C. H. C. Smith, AM Collier) 04.25–06.10 hr; 1053 (Flt Lieut V. Nicholl, AM Harrison) 04.25–06.05 hr; 1056 (Flt Lieut F. M. Barr, AM Latta) 04.37–05.32 hr; Henry Farman seaplane 97 (Flt Cdr de C. W. P. Ireland, LM C. Notley) 04.40–05.32 hr.

Flt Sub-Lieut C. H. Chichester Smith in Sopwith Two-seater Scout 1052 at RNAS Yarmouth in 1915. Chichester Smith flew nine home-defence sorties in 1915–16, two of them in this 'Spinning Jenny'. (*RAF Museum*)

This was the first raid on England by an army Zeppelin—the new four-engined, one million cubic feet capacity LZ38. Linnarz crossed the coast north of Felixstowe at about midnight and sought opportunity targets. He bombed Ipswich ten minutes later, Bury St Edmunds at 01.00 hr and flew out over Aldeburgh at 02.00 hr.

Thick mist prevented take-offs by defence aircraft while LZ38 was within reach, and the four Yarmouth sorties were flown later in case she was still loitering close to the coast.

Henry Farman floatplane 97 at RNAS Yarmouth. (*J. M. Bruce/G. S. Leslie collection*)

9/10 May, 1915 (Night)

Target: Southend.
Enemy force: Army Zeppelin LZ38 (Hptmn Erich Linnarz).
Results: One killed, two injured, £5,301 damage.
Defence sorties: 11.

RNAS

Chingford: Avro 500 939 (Flt Lieut E. B. Beauman); Avro 504 876 (Flt Lieut H. Rosher); details not known.

Eastchurch: Three sorties, details not known.

Felixstowe: Curtiss H-4 951 (Flt Cdr W. R. Crocker, Flt Sub-Lieut E. R. Moon) 04.55–06.00 hr.

Westgate: Avro 504B, three sorties (flown by Flt Lieut A. F. Bettington, Flt Sub-Lieut R. H. Mulock and one other), details not known.

Yarmouth: Sopwith Two-seater Scouts 1053 (Flt Lieut V. Nicholl, AM Latta) 04.55–07.20 hr; 1052 (Flt Sub-Lieut C. H. C. Smith, LM Caple) 05.05–07.00 hr.

The planned target for this raid was London, but shortly before departure belated doubts concerning the Kaiser's current ruling on the subject caused a less controversial objective to be selected. Linnarz attacked Southend, first at 02.50 hr, then crossed the Thames estuary and returned for a second run.

Avro 500 No.939 taking off at RNAS Chingford. Piloted by Flt Lieut E. Bentley Beauman, it patrolled when LZ38 attacked Southend on 9/10 May, 1915.

Incendiaries formed the bulk of the bomb load.

Little is recorded about the defence activities and there were no sightings. From Westgate, Mulock patrolled at 11,000 ft and had some difficulty in finding the aerodrome on his return because of patchy cloud. Bettington came down near Colchester for some unstated reason.

LZ38's meandering homeward course placed her ten miles off Harwich at about 04.30 hr but she was not seen by aircraft sent out from Felixstowe and Yarmouth. Nicholl put down at Bawdsey during his patrol to fix a broken oil pipe. No Chingford or Eastchurch reports have come to light.

On 13 May the *Southend Standard* published an 18-page supplement illustrating damage and describing the raid in much detail. This greatly annoyed the Government, already well aware that airship commanders were often uncertain of the results achieved, and breached the mildly-worded Defence Notice D206 of 5 May requesting editors not to publish material disclosing useful information.

LZ38, commanded by Hptmn Erich Linnarz, the army's most successful airship, flew on five operations against England in April–May 1915 (including the first raid on London) before being destroyed at Evère (Brussels) by RNAS bombing. Two crew members can be seen standing on the hull-top gun platform. (*Dr Douglas H. Robinson*)

16/17 May, 1915 (Night)

Target: Kent coast.
Enemy force: Army Zeppelin LZ38 (Hptmn E. Linnarz).
Results: Two killed, one injured, £1,600 damage.
Defence sorties: Five.

RNAS

Dover: Vickers F.B.5 862 (Flt Sub-Lieut R. Lord, CPO Gott) took off 02.50 hr; Sopwith 860 seaplane 859 (Flt Sub-Lieut T. V. Lister) took off 03.30 hr.

Westgate: Avro 504B 1013 (Flt Sub-Lieut R. H. Mulock) 01.40–03.25 hr; 504Bs 1011 and 1018 took off at 02.55 and 03.00 hr, details not known.

LZ38 crossed the coast near Margate at 01.35 hr on 17 May and shortly afterwards dropped about twenty bombs on Ramsgate. She then flew out to sea and approached Dover at 02.25 hr. After being picked up by searchlights and fired on by anti-aircraft guns she dropped thirty-three bombs northeast of the town and made off towards the Goodwins.

This was the first searchlight illumination of a Zeppelin over Britain and also the first time that a defending pilot actually saw one.

Redford Mulock, a Canadian from Winnipeg, was airborne five minutes after RNAS Westgate lookouts spotted the airship crossing the coast at a mere 1,500–2,000 ft. The official sortie report gives his armament as two incendiary bombs, two hand grenades and a revolver—not a Lewis gun as described in some accounts. On reaching 500 ft Mulock saw LZ38 flying southeast, about 1,500 ft above him. He was climbing at 50 mph and was probably seen from the airship, which also started to climb.

At this point Mulock's account conflicts with the plotted movements of the Zeppelin, and in his anxiety to retain sight of his quarry he may have briefly lost his bearings. He eventually got quite close over what he said was Ramsgate, but was more probably Dover, for while he was still trying to reach a bombing position above, the airship headed out to sea. Mulock said it was 'climbing at a great rate' and did not again fly inland. He could not match its climb and gradually fell behind, losing it in cloud at about 7,000 ft between the West Hinder and Ruytingen lightships.

Mulock could now see the Belgian coast and continued to climb for a short time before turning back. He drifted south of his intended course and approached Dover at 8,500 ft, mistaking it initially for Ramsgate, then, blissfully unaware that he was triggering off a new series of raid alarms, flew up the coast to await the first glimmer of daylight before landing. Despite the lack of success, this long chase on a dark night was an encouraging performance.

Following the now standard practice, the Admiralty had notified the RNAS in France of the raid, and nine assorted aircraft of No.1 Squadron from Dunkirk and Furnes took off to intercept the airship on its homeward journey.

Several pilots found instead the LZ39 returning from an abortive raid on Calais, and at 03.55 hr Sqn Cdr Spenser Grey and Flt Sub-Lieut R. A. J. Warneford, both flying Nieuports, made spirited attacks. Grey had a Lewis gun, but Warneford's gunner, Leading Mechanic G. E. Meddis, made do with a ·45-in rifle and 'flaming bullets'—two scoring possible hits while the other three failed to flame.

At 04.05 hr Flt Lieut A. W. Bigsworth, flying Avro 504B No.1009, managed to get above the Zeppelin at 10,000 ft over Ostende and dropped four 20 lb bombs along its back. Smoke emerged, and hits were later confirmed via naval intelligence sources. One crew man was killed and several injured, five gas cells ruptured and the rear starboard propeller lost.

Although not strictly a home defence sortie, this was the first time that British airmen had come to grips with a Zeppelin—in an engagement which had an important influence on future defence tactics.

23 May, 1915 (Daylight)

Target: Coastal shipping.
Enemy force: One Albatros floatplane.
Results: No casualties or damage.
Defence sorties: Four.

RNAS

Eastchurch: Sopwith Tabloids 1209 and 1211 took off at 10.02 and 10.15 hr, details not known.

Westgate: Avro 504Bs 1013 and 1018, details not known.

At 09.30 hr a single Albatros floatplane of SFA 1 dropped several bombs near

Albatros W 1 floatplane of the type which attempted shipping raids on 23 May and 3 July, 1915. (*H. J. Nowarra*)

ships in the Goodwins area, and was later sighted off Westgate. None of the defence aircraft made contact.

This was the first time the Sopwith Tabloid was used on home defence duties. Although powered by a modest 80 hp Gnome rotary engine, the single-seat Tabloid was a clean design capable of 92 mph. Its earlier wartime functions were 'scouting'—or unarmed reconnaissance—and bombing. The home defence version probably carried a Lewis gun mounted to fire clear of the propeller blades.

During the afternoon another enemy aircraft was reported near Dover but no defence sorties were flown.

26/27 May, 1915 (Night)

Target: Southend.
Enemy force: Army Zeppelin LZ38 (Hptmn E. Linnarz).
Results: Three killed, three injured, £987 damage.
Defence sorties: Five.

RNAS

Eastchurch: Sopwith Tabloid 1210, 23.20–00.29 hr; Blériot Parasol 1546, 23.20–23.59 hr; one unspecified aircraft, details not known.

Grain: Albatros B II 890 (Flt Sub-Lieut E. de C. Hallifax, AM Bunn) 23.22–23.50 hr; Short 830 1337 (Flt Lieut B. F. Fowler, AM Barrett) 23.28–00.05 hr.

This second attack on Southend by Linnarz was conducted with textbook efficiency. LZ38 came in over the Blackwater estuary at 22.45 hr, flew direct to Southend, bombed at 23.15 hr and crossed the Blackwater outbound at 23.45 hr.

Information about the defence effort is minimal. Linnarz was clearly well on his homeward flight before any defenders could reach combat altitude and there were no sightings. The impressed Albatros had now moved to Grain, which saw no objection to using it against night raids when it presented no identification problems.

The Eastchurch Blériot and the unspecified aircraft which flew the station's third sortie were both damaged on landing.

31 May/1 June, 1915 (Night)

Target: London.
Enemy forces: Army Zeppelins LZ38 (Hptmn E. Linnarz), LZ37 (Commander not known).
Results: Seven killed, 35 injured, £18,596 damage.
Defence sorties: 15.

RNAS

Chingford: B.E.2a 47 (Flt Cdr W. G. Sitwell) 50 min; B.E.2c 966 (Flt Lieut C. W. H. Pulford) 90 min; Deperdussin 1377 (Flt Lieut F. W. Merriam) 90 min.

Dover: One floatplane and three landplane sorties, airborne by 22.44 hr.

Eastchurch: Avro 504B 1010 (Flt Lieut P. A. Johnston) 21.50–22.58 hr; Blériot Parasol 1538 (Flt Lieut G. G. Dawson) took off 22.00 hr; B.E.2c 988 (Flt Cdr J. R. W. Smyth-Pigott) 00.50–01.30 hr; Sopwith Tabloid 1210 (Flt Lieut S. Pickles) took off 00.55.

Hendon: Sopwith Gunbus 802 (Flt Lieut D. M. Barnes, Flt Sub-Lieut B. Travers), crashed, pilot killed.

Rochford: Blériot Parasol 1546 (Flt Sub-Lieut A. W. Robertson) took off 22.20 hr.

Westgate: Sopwith Tabloid 1212 (Flt Sub-Lieut R. H. Mulock) 22.03–23.55 hr; Avro 504B 1018 (Flt Lieut A. F. Bettington) took off 22.44 hr.

The Kaiser's authority to attack London east of the Tower had now been formally promulgated, and this raid was a fitting climax to a remarkable and intensive spell of operations by LZ38 under Linnarz, Germany's ablest bomber airship commander.

Hptmn Erich Linnarz (*front row, centre*) with crew members, by the LZ38's control car, before leaving on a raid. (*Dr Douglas H. Robinson*)

Linnarz came in over Margate at 21.42 hr, flew northwest to Shoeburyness and then made for London. The attack started on Stoke Newington at 23.20 hr and altogether thirty small HE bombs and ninety incendiaries were scattered on a curving line south to Stepney, then northeast to Leytonstone. The airship made her exit north of Foulness. The violent indignation of some London East End residents found release in assaults on premises owned by people of supposedly German origin. One victim was a Scottish baker's shop in Shoreditch, where a woman employee took refuge in a workhouse until auxiliary police arrived in a taxi.

LZ37 was briefly over the north Kent coast, having been unsuccessfully sought by ten RNAS aircraft from Dunkirk, but dropped no bombs.

Mindful of Press treatment of the Southend raid, the Government issued D-Notice 217 in the early hours of 1 June, stating that in the public interest, and to prevent publication of information useful to the enemy, 'nothing must appear in the Press in regard to raids by enemy aircraft except the official statements issued by the Government'. This ruling caused a bitter row between Press and Government two years later.

A Blériot Parasol with Lewis gun fitted to fire over the propeller. (*P. H. Liddle*)

The RNAS produced its biggest effort to date, using at least seven different types of aircraft with a single common factor—none was adequately equipped to fight a Zeppelin. Despite much enthusiasm the general outcome was an unco-ordinated shambles, marred by a fatal accident—inevitable sooner or later.

LZ38 flew high, its movements were only vaguely notified and it was not picked up by searchlights. Confusion was increased by mysterious reports of an RFC 'Caudron type' aircraft flying over the Chatham area.

The only sighting was by Robertson from Rochford (the aerodrome, now Southend Airport, was then called Eastwood) who struggled up to 6,000 ft, spotting the Zeppelin ahead and still above him. He was forced by engine failure to abandon the chase and landed safely on the mud at Leigh-on-Sea at about 01.00 hr. What weaponry he carried is not recorded. The other Blériot airborne, from Eastchurch, probably had a 12-bore mounted on the wing to fire clear of the propeller, for its pilot, Grahame Dawson, was experimenting with such a weapon. It fired chain-shot cartridges containing steel cable linked to lead balls, and required two hands to load—a delicate operation in an unstable aircraft.

A Sopwith Gunbus at Hendon—similar to that flown by Flt Lieut Barnes and Flt Sub-Lieut Travers on 31 May/1 June, 1915.

Victim of the fatal accident was Douglas Barnes, from Hendon. Apparently lost, he crashed his Sopwith Gunbus while trying to land at Theobalds Park in Hertfordshire. In the absence of another serviceable aircraft, Ben Travers, a pilot, had volunteered to fly as Barnes' gunner. Some instinct made him defy the rules and unfasten his seat belt during the descent, and the impact projected him clear of the front cockpit. He recovered from his injuries to do much more flying—and to delight future generations of theatregoers.

Conway Pulford, from Chingford, also had a narrow escape. Towards the end of an uneventful patrol at 6,000 ft he lost the aerodrome, so dropped his petrol bomb to act as a marker. When this failed to ignite he continued his blind descent and hit the top of a tree—but was able to walk out of the wrecked B.E.2c.

Another lucky pilot was Warren Merriam, accompanied by an observer armed with a rifle and grenades. After roaring around central London for more than an

Flt Sub-Lieut Ben Travers, who survived a serious crash on 31 May/1 June, 1915.

hour his instrument lights failed. He then lost his goggles, and altogether was not happily situated in an aircraft notoriously difficult to land well even in daylight. However, Merriam was one of Britain's most skilled civil pilots before joining the RNAS, and, almost blinded by castor oil from the engine and unable to see any flares, he pancaked the Deperdussin with no more damage than a bent axle.

Mulock flew a long sortie in Westgate's recently-acquired Sopwith Tabloid, scorning semi-jocular remarks that in the dark he would 'not be able to keep it right side up'. Despite its low stalling speed of 40 mph, some pilots seemed to regard the Tabloid as a 'hot ship'—and indeed it was perhaps less forgiving than the Avro and not well suited for night flying from the small and awkward Westgate aerodrome. Mulock patrolled at 10,000 ft between the Essex coast and Dover, and his 60 mph touchdown, mentioned in a family letter, suggests that he may have experienced some difficulty during the approach.

4/5 June, 1915 (Night)

Targets: London, Humber area.
Enemy forces: Navy Zeppelin L10 (Kptlt Klaus Hirsch), Navy Schütte-Lanz SL3 (Kptlt Fritz Boemack).
Results: None killed, eight injured, £8,740 damage.
Defence sorties: Nine.

RNAS

Eastchurch: B.E.2c 988 took off 00.01 hr; Avro 504B 1010 (Flt Lieut P. A. Johnston) took off at 01.30 and 02.14 hr; Bristol T.B.8 1223 (Flt Lieut F. Besson) took off 03.00 hr.

Grain: Bristol Scout C 1243 (Flt Sub-Lieut W. G. Moore) 02.47–04.05 hr.

RFC

Joyce Green: Two sorties.
Northolt: Two sorties.

The German naval airship bombing offensive was resumed after a spell of priority fleet reconnaissance work, but navigation was hampered by strong winds and poor visibility over the British coast.

Hirsch in L10 mistook Shoeburyness for Lowestoft, and believing that he was too far away to reach London, eventually bombed what he reported as Harwich; in fact it was Gravesend.

Boemack's sortie was the first over England by one of the wooden-framed Schütte-Lanz airships. Although of generally inferior performance, they incorporated some features in advance of the Zeppelins and were popular with crews because of their roomier accommodation. SL3 crossed the coast ten miles south of Bridlington, then flew north to Flamborough Head and set course for Hull at 00.30 hr. Progress against strong headwinds was slow, and after dropping a few bombs in open country Boemack abandoned the raid.

Fog at the aerodromes is the likely reason for the absence of sorties flown against SL3 and the slow reaction to the L10 raid. L10 came in midway between Grain and Eastchurch at 23.00 hr and remained in the neighbourhood for another 30 minutes, yet it was an hour before any defending aeroplane was airborne. Grain's solitary sortie was launched 72 minutes after the Zeppelin had crossed the coast near Southwold on the way home.

No reports of RFC activities have been found.

Flt Sub-Lieut W. G. Moore in Bristol Scout C No.1243 at RNAS Grain. He patrolled in this aircraft on 4/5 June and 9/10 August, 1915, during raids on Gravesend and Eastchurch respectively. (*RAF Museum*)

6/7 June, 1915 (Night)

Targets: Hull, London.
Enemy forces: Navy Zeppelin L9 (Kptlt H. Mathy). Army Zeppelins LZ37 (Oblt van der Haegen), LZ38 (Hptmn E. Linnarz), LZ39.
Results: 24 killed, 40 injured, £44,795 damage.
Defence sorties: Three.

RNAS
Killingholme: Sopwith Two-seater Scout 1055 (Flt Sub-Lieut J. C. Brooke, AM Bager) took off 05.10 hr.
Yarmouth: B.E.2c 977 (Flt Lieut V. Nicholl, LM J. S. Philp) 20.20–22.10 hr; Sopwith Two-seater Scout 1053 (Flt Sub-Lieut C. H. C. Smith, PO Lytton) 02.25–04.30 hr.

This raid caused the heaviest casualties to date and further emphasized the shortcomings of the defences.

Public indignation was heightened by what seemed an attempt to minimize the extent of casualties in Hull. There was an unfortunate delay in correcting the first official Press release, based on provisional figures, which reported only five killed and 40 injured. Serious rioting broke out, with attacks on supposedly German shops.

Some consolation came from the destruction of LZ37 over Belgium by Flt Sub-Lieut R. A. J. Warneford, who was awarded the Victoria Cross for this first aerial victory over a Zeppelin. Sadly, he was killed ten days later in a flying accident.

Mathy in L9 decided soon after departure that conditions made it more prudent to attack Hull rather than London. He reached the coast near Cromer at 20.00 hr, crossed the Wash to appear briefly over Mablethorpe and established his position off Bridlington at 23.10 hr. He set course for Hull, where he arrived at 00.50 hr and dropped ten HE and fifty incendiary bombs. The only opposition came from the guns of HMS *Adventure.*

Preliminary warning of a likely raid had been received at 17.30 hr. Nearly three hours later, only minutes after a firm sighting report from the Haisbrough lightship, Nicholl was airborne from Yarmouth. After a 30 min search he landed at the new satellite aerodrome at Bacton, farther up the coast, and learned that the Zeppelin was flying westwards from Cromer. He searched for another hour without result. A Spinning Jenny despatched later in the hope of finding the enemy on the return journey was also unsuccessful.

Athough generally the night was calm and clear, Killingholme was blanketed by fog and no take-offs were possible until long after Mathy had departed. Nevertheless a Spinning Jenny went out on a precautionary patrol.

None of the army airships reached England. LZ38 developed engine trouble and returned to her shed at Evère, near Brussels, and LZ37 and LZ39 abandoned their missions because of navigation problems.

Flt Sub-Lieut R. A. J. Warneford, RNAS, (*right*) who destroyed LZ37 on 6/7 June, 1915, seen with other No.1 Wing pilots also engaged on anti-Zeppelin operations from France: from left; Flt Sub-Lieut J. S. Mills, Flt Lieuts A. W. Bigsworth and J. P. Wilson. On 25/26 September, 1916, Bigsworth fruitlessly chased L31 near Portsmouth.

When No.1 (RNAS) Squadron in France received news of the enemy activity it was already involved in a planned raid on the Belgian airship sheds. Flt Lieut J. P. Wilson and Flt Sub-Lieut J. S. Mills flying Henry Farmans scored direct hits on the Evère hangar and destroyed LZ38, just docked after her abortive sortie.

Meanwhile, Reginald Warneford, flying Morane Parasol No.3253 to attack the Berchem St Agathe shed, had spotted LZ37 over Ostende and begun a careful, hour-long chase. Despite its spindly, ungainly appearance the Morane Type L was a good performer, and Warneford gradually coaxed it to 11,000 ft—some 4,000 ft above the Zeppelin—coming under fire every time he moved within range.

At 02.25 hr, over Ghent, he glided to about 150 ft above his quarry and released six 20 lb bombs in quick succession. As the last was still falling the

Morane-Saulnier Type L Parasol No.3253 flown by Flt Sub-Lieut Warneford.

Zeppelin exploded. The blast hurled the Morane on its back and subjected it to some alarming involuntary manoeuvres before Warneford could regain control.

Shortly afterwards a broken petrol pipe forced him to land, and he spent 35 min in enemy territory making repairs. After some difficulty in starting up single-handed, he was airborne again at 03.15 hr, became lost in the fog and finally put down safely near Cap Gris Nez.

Further emphasising that truth is stranger than fiction, one of LZ37's ten crew members survived the holocaust. The wreckage fell on and around a convent, and helmsman Alfred Muhler's one-and-a-half-mile free fall in the forward gondola ended abruptly when it crashed through the roof—and precipitated him on to a bed.

15/16 June, 1915 (Night)

Target: Tyneside.
Enemy forces: Navy Zeppelins L10 (Kptlt E. Hirsch); L11 (Oblt-z-S H. von Buttlar), returned early with engine trouble.
Results: 18 killed, 72 injured, £41,760 damage.
Defence sorties: Five.

RNAS

Killingholme: Sopwith Two-seater Scouts 1070 (Flt Lieut Adams) 19.00–20.30 hr; 1071 (Flt Sub-Lieut W. H. Elliott) 19.00–21.15 hr.

Whitley Bay: B.E.2cs 1101 (Flt Cdr C. E. Robinson, LM H. J. L. Hinkler) 23.39–00.30 hr; 1099 (Flt Sub-Lieut K. S. Savory) 23.50–00.15 hr.

Yarmouth: Sopwith Two-seater Scout 1055 (Flt Lieut E. J. Cooper, AM Martin) 19.05–20.30 hr.

After an unexpectedly fast North Sea crossing it was still daylight when L10 neared the English coast at 20.45 hr, so Hirsch cruised offshore and eventually came inland north of Blyth at 23.45 hr. The Zeppelin then turned south and for 30 min rained 3,500 lb of bombs on Wallsend, Jarrow and South Shields. Many factories were brightly lit, having received no raid warning, no searchlights were in action and there were still very few anti-aircraft guns.

The Spinning Jenny patrols from Killingholme and Yarmouth indicate that L10's presence off the coast was detected well before she penetrated inland. A lookout from the airship reported seeing a British aircraft at 20.25 hr—probably Elliott's—but none of the pilots mentioned an airship sighting.

With the raid well in progress, the first take-off from Whitley Bay was nearly a disaster. Robinson's B.E. swung slightly, and as it climbed away the undercarriage struck the aerodrome rifle butts and lost two of its port struts. Despite the substantial load of two 20 lb Hale and four petrol bombs, plus the observer and his two rifles for Hale grenades and incendiary bullets, the aircraft still flew well enough and Robinson pressed on, climbing through broken cloud to 2,000 ft in the hope of intercepting the Zeppelin before it reached Newcastle. He saw nothing, became lost for a time, then glided down to 800 ft and picked up his bearings north of Sunderland.

Knowing that his undercarriage must be badly damaged, Robinson exerted every ounce of concentration to achieve the gentlest possible touchdown, but inevitably the remains of the chassis collapsed, and his aircraft was described as 'wrecked'. Neither occupant was injured.

Savory also headed towards Newcastle and likewise saw nothing. He found similar difficulty in navigating above the patchy cloud, and returned to base when his engine began to show symptoms of imminent failure.

3 July, 1915 (Daylight)

Target: Harwich.
Enemy forces: One Albatros floatplane, one Gotha WD 2 floatplane.
Results: No casualties or damage.
Defence sorties: Nine.

RNAS
Chelmsford: Caudron G.3 1594 (Flt Sub-Lieut E. V. Reid) 12.05–12.45 hr.
Dover: B.E.2c 1105 (Flt Sub-Lieut R. C. Hardstaff, AM Robson); Vickers F.B.5 3595 (Flt Cdr C. M. Murphy, LM Marsden).
Eastchurch: Morane—details not known.

Gotha WD 2 No.257 of SFA 1 which accompanied an Albatros on an abortive attack near Landguard Point on 3 July, 1915. (*Airphotos*)

Felixstowe: Curtiss H-4 950 (Flt Lieut P. E. H. Wakely, Flt Sub-Lieut L. P. Openshaw) 11.40–14.20 hr; Deperdussin 1379 (Flt Lieut R. J. Hope Vere) took off 11.45 hr.
Westgate: Avro 504Bs 1018 and 1027—details not known.

RFC
Joyce Green: One sortie—no details available.

At 11.20 hr two high-flying seaplanes were sighted by the Inner Gabbard light vessel and 20 min later one dropped four bombs in the sea near the Landguard Point signals station opposite Harwich. The aircraft were fired on by naval vessels and departed, one turning north and the other south.

Defending aircraft from Felixstowe were airborne smartly, but not in time to overhaul the enemy—from SFA 1, Zeebrugge. The Deperdussin returned early with engine trouble.

Despite the remote likelihood of any useful contribution from the Chelmsford Caudron, with its top speed of under 70 mph, Reid plodded along to St Osyth, where he landed to up-date himself. He flew out to sea to investigate some officially reported 'suspicious movements on the horizon', then to Felixstowe, where he landed on the golf course, and eventually back to Chelmsford.

Aircraft from the southerly stations saw nothing of the enemy supposedly heading in their direction—which probably joined its companion after a brief reconnaissance.

9/10 August, 1915 (Night)

Targets: London, Humber area.
Enemy forces: Navy Zeppelins L9 (Kptlt Odo Loewe), L10 (Oblt-z-S Friedrich Wenke), L11 (Oblt-z-S H. von Buttlar), L12 (Oblt-z-S W. Peterson), L13 (Kptlt H. Mathy).
Results: 17 killed, 21 injured, £11,992 damage.
Defence sorties: 21.

RNAS
Atwick: Bristol T.B.8 1217 (Flt Cdr C. Draper, Flt Sub-Lieut A. S. Goodwin) took off 20.20 hr and later airborne 21.10–22.00 hr; Blériot XI 3228 (Flt Sub-Lieut R. G. Mack) took off 20.20 hr, crashed landing.
Dover: Avro 504B 1016 (Flt Sub-Lieut C. E. Brisley) 00.25–01.10 hr; Sopwith Schneider 1562 (Flt Sub-Lieut J. B. P. Ferrand) 04.16–05.00 hr.
Eastchurch: B.E.2cs 1103 (Flt Cdr R. J. Bone) 00.01–01.35 hr; 1124 (Flt Cdr R. E. C. Peirse) 00.01–01.33 hr.
Felixstowe: Sopwith Schneider 3717 (Flt Sub-Lieut J. d'A. Levy) took off 05.30 hr; Curtiss H-4 950 (Flt Lieut E. R. Moon) took off 05.30 hr.
Grain: Bristol Scout C 1243 (Flt Sub-Lieut W. G. Moore) took off 19.45 hr; Avro 504B 1026 (Flt Sub-Lieut E. de C. Hallifax) 03.45–05.15 hr; Short 184 844 (Flt Lieut B. F. Fowler) 03.49–06.35 hr.
Redcar: B.E.2cs 1112 (Flt Lieut C. B. Dalison) 19.45–21.10 hr; 1149 (Flt Cdr C. E. H. Rathborne) took off 20.00 hr.
Scarborough: Caudron G.3 3867 (Flt Sub-Lieut J. F. Roche) 04.40–05.00 hr.
Westgate: Sopwith Tabloid 1212 (Flt Sub-Lieut R. Lord) took off 22.51 hr; crashed landing, pilot killed.
Whitley Bay: B.E.2cs, serials not recorded, (Flt Lieut R. E. Nicholl) took off

20.10 hr and (Flt Lieut K. S. Savory) at 04.00 hr.

Yarmouth: B.E.2c 977 (Sqn Cdr de C. W. P. Ireland) 22.31–23.35 hr, damaged landing; Sopwith Two-seater Scouts 1053 (Flt Sub-Lieut E. Cadbury) took off 03.30 hr; 1056 (Flt Sub-Lieut E. J. Cooper) 06.00 hr.

This intended major bombardment of London by four of the navy's newest four-engined Zeppelins was a dismal failure, degenerating into a series of scattered minor attacks, with no bomb falling on the capital.

The raiding fleet assembled north of Borkum, and Strasser, flying in L10, ordered the old L9 to find a suitable target in the Humber area. She appeared off Flamborough Head at 20.15 hr and tentatively nosed over the coast twice before finally crossing six miles south of Hornsea at 23.15 hr. She then flew on to bomb Goole, which Loewe thought was Hull.

B.E.2c 977 damaged in a heavy landing by Sqn Cdr de Courcy Ireland, RNAS Yarmouth, after seeking L9 on 9/10 August, 1915. This aircraft was flying again shortly afterwards and made at least four anti-Zeppelin sorties. (*B. J. Lowe*)

The main force fared worse, and only L10 got within 35 miles of central London. She made landfall near Aldeburgh at 21.40 hr and reached Shoeburyness about two hours later. Wenke believed that he was much farther up the Thames and claimed to have hit shipping. Apart from a neat stick of twelve bombs which struck Eastchurch aerodrome, his main bomb load fell into the estuary.

L11 arrived over Lowestoft at 22.18 hr—but most of her bombs dropped in the sea—and made off without delay. Von Buttlar thought he was over Harwich, and considered it more profitable to attack that busy port than try to reach London in indifferent weather.

L12 went most badly astray. At 22.48 hr she reached Westgate, followed the coast to Dover and bombed at 00.30 hr, causing minor damage. Peterson thought that he had made landfall north of Yarmouth, and also claimed Harwich as his target. L13 turned back with engine trouble within sight of the coast.

There had been provisional warning of a raid and several RNAS stations flew precautionary patrols in the early evening. Pilots at the newly-opened Atwick aerodrome on the racecourse north of Hornsea, awaiting news of L9 after an initial sighting, were rapidly enlightened when she was spotted looming through the twilight towards their station. Chris Draper, the CO, was first airborne in a

Bristol T.B.8, and as he slowly climbed to 3,000 ft the airship turned about and was lost in the haze. Mack's experience in a Blériot was similar, though he crashed while landing in the declining visibility.

At 21.10 hr the L9 made a second attempt and Draper again took off, despite the thickening mist. As he coaxed the Bristol up to 4,000 ft, L9 again retreated, and he chased her for 35 min until she once more faded from view. She was heard shortly after her third crossing of the coast, but visibility was then too bad for take-offs.

For unrecorded reasons RNAS Yarmouth received no warning of L11's proximity until bombs were falling on Lowestoft. Ireland then took off in heavy mist and spent nearly an hour at 5,000 ft, patrolling down to Southwold before abandoning the search. The fog had thickened when he returned and he struck the ground heavily, wiping off his B.E's undercarriage, though mercifully the bombs did not go off. He vetoed further sorties until the weather improved.

From Eastchurch, Peirse and Bone were already airborne when L10—apparently spotting a worthwhile opportunity target—began showering bombs along the flarepath. The Zeppelin was not picked up by searchlights and neither pilot saw her. On return Peirse noticed the bomb craters and landed well to the side of the flarepath proper. Bone had not seen them, but fortunately decided to do likewise.

L12 approached Westgate from a westerly direction, then turned northeast and became lost to view. It is doubtful whether Lord, who took off in pursuit, saw the airship, and when he was heard returning the flarepath and a searchlight were lit for his landing. The Tabloid seemed to be approaching normally, then dipped suddenly to hit the ground 50 yards short of the first flare, turned over twice and was completely wrecked. Grievously injured, Lord died soon after admission to Margate Cottage Hospital.

This was the same Tabloid which had prompted earlier Westgate comment about its night-flying suitability.

B.E.2c 992 which came to grief when Flt Lieut Vincent Nicholl, returning with a failing engine on 12/13 August, 1915, tried to land with no flarepath lighting at RNAS Yarmouth. (*RAF Museum*)

Arriving at Dover, L12 was caught by searchlights and briskly engaged by the AA guns. Brisley was airborne promptly and urged his Avro up to 6,000 ft, only to see the Zeppelin gradually fade from view above cloud. He patrolled for another 20 minutes and came back to a text-book landing.

Coastal fog began to clear towards dawn and several stations flew patrols to look for any late departing Zeppelins.

The Dover gunners' belief that they had damaged L12 was well founded. Two gas cells were badly holed and hydrogen loss forced her down off Zeebrugge, whence she was towed to Ostende and partially salvaged. Eight RNAS aircraft from Dunkirk and one from Dover tried unsuccessfully to bomb the ditched airship. Flt Lieut D. K. Johnston flying a Farman from Dunkirk was shot down and killed.

12/13 August, 1915 (Night)

Target: London.
Enemy forces: Navy Zeppelins L10 (Oblt-z-S F. Wenke), L9 (Kptlt O. Loewe), L11 (Oblt-z-S H. von Buttlar), and L13 (Kptlt H. Mathy).
Results: Seven killed, 23 injured, £3,649 damage.
Defence sorties: Four.

RNAS

Yarmouth: Sopwith Two-seater Scout 1056 (Flt Lieut C. H. C. Smith) 19.20–20.00 hr, returned due to weather; B.E.2cs 990 (Flt Sub-Lieut G. W. Hilliard) 20.30–21.20 hr; 992 (Flt Lieut V. Nicholl) 21.25–21.45 hr; 991 (Flt Cdr de C. W. P. Ireland) 21.50–22.30 hr. All B.E.2cs returned with engine trouble.

Another attempt to raid London in some strength was frustrated by mechanical troubles, which caused L9 and L13 to turn back, while L11 also abandoned the mission. She was reported ten miles off Harwich at about 21.00 hr, then flew south to cross Thanet twice and finally departed over Deal just before 01.00 hr. No bombs were dropped, and the reason for von Buttlar's return are not known.

Wenke in L10 arrived south of Lowestoft at 21.25 hr and decided to attack Harwich rather than attempt the 70-mile flight to London against headwinds. Bombs were dropped at various places in the Harwich area.

Yarmouth had an unfortunate night and its four sorties were all abandoned early. Chichester Smith returned from a routine last-light patrol after 40 min, when heavy rain and mist drastically reduced visibility. Hilliard was airborne when L10 was first reported out to sea, but came back with falling oil pressure and slightly damaged his B.E.2c on landing. Nicholl, who relieved him, also returned with engine trouble and wiped off his undercarriage when attempting to land with the flarepath unlit.

For the second time on successive operational sorties Ireland had an unpleasant experience. The 70 hp Renault engine of his B.E. broke an inlet valve, lost power and showed signs of catching fire, so he put down hastily on rough ground short of the aerodrome. The aircraft was damaged but he was unhurt.

During the night Felixstowe held its Deperdussin at readiness for a Zeppelin sighting, but it did not take off on the reported grounds that the pilot might be so dazzled by searchlights as to lose control of the aircraft.

No reasons are recorded for Westgate and Dover's lack of response to L11's proximity during the night.

17/18 August, 1915 (Night)

Target: London.
Enemy forces: Navy Zeppelins L10 (Oblt-z-S F. Wenke); L11 (Oblt-z-S H. von Buttlar); L13 (Kptlt H. Mathy), returned early; L14 (Kptlt A. Bocker), returned early.
Results: 10 killed, 48 injured, £30,750 damage.
Defence sorties: Six.

RNAS

Chelmsford: Caudron G.3s 1593 (Flt Sub-Lieut H. H. Square) 22.45–01.15 hr, crashed landing; 1596 (Flt Sub-Lieut C. D. Morrison) 22.45–23.55 hr, crashed landing.

Yarmouth: Sopwith Two-seater Scout 1056 (Flt Sub-Lieut E. Cadbury) 19.15–19.50 hr; B.E.2cs 990 (Flt Sub-Lieut G. W. Hilliard) 20.50–22.25 hr; 977 (Sqn Cdr de C. W. P. Ireland) 22.55–00.20 hr.

Holt: One sortie, details not known.

The German Naval Airship Service persevered in its attempt to achieve a major raid on London, and this time one Zeppelin did reach the northeastern outskirts. Mathy's L13 was again turned back by engine trouble, and the new L14 spent three hours circling off the Norfolk coast before her crew gave up hope of rectifying two ailing engines.

L11 came in over Herne Bay at 21.30 hr, flew south to bomb Ashford and nearby villages then departed, again over Herne Bay, at 23.45 hr. Von Buttlar filed a glowing account of his attack on 'Woolwich'.

Wenke, in L10, one of the ablest airship navigators, crossed the coast north of Bawdsey at 20.55 hr, flew a direct course to London and bombed the Walthamstow–Leyton–Wanstead area at 22.30–22.45 hr, causing heavy damage and some casualties. A puzzling discrepancy in an otherwise good operational performance was his claim to have attacked central London, six miles to the south.

Caudron G.3 No.3865 of an unidentified unit—possibly RNAS Redcar. (*C. P. O. Bartlett*)

Sufficient preliminary warning of this raid was received to attempt a new defence technique. The Lowestoft trawler, *Kingfisher*, adapted to carry a seaplane, put to sea in the hope of spotting approaching Zeppelins in the late evening. The aircraft would then be lowered and, sea state permitting, take off to intercept. On this occasion Chichester Smith in Sopwith Schneider No.3710 was embarked, but there were no sightings.

The Caudrons from Chelmsford were not airborne until 45 min after L10 had passed almost overhead en route for London. This unexplained lapse was fortuitously redeemed, since although Wenke was then 20 miles away, he was starting a homeward flight that would again take him over Chelmsford. Reports vary as to whether Morrison saw the Zeppelin, but at all events he came back after 70 min to a heavy landing which detonated three of his four Hale bombs. The flimsy Caudron was blown to pieces, Morrison being badly burned about the face and arms and injured in a foot.

Meanwhile Square had seen L10 and given chase, though he could make no headway in his sluggish birdcage masquerading as a Zeppelin fighter. He, too, came to grief in a landing crash, of which no details are recorded beyond the fact that his Caudron was also destroyed. Square's injuries put him into hospital for a long time and he was invalided out of the RNAS in early 1917, but rejoined in November to fly again in Handley Page bombers of No.7A Squadron.

No sorties were flown against the L11, for reasons which again are not recorded.

7/8 September, 1915 (Night)

Target: London.
Enemy forces: Army Zeppelins LZ74 (Hptmn Friedrich George), LZ77 (Hptmn Alfred Horn), Army Schütte-Lanz SL2 (Hptmn Richard von Wobeser).
Results: 18 killed, 28 injured, £9,616 damage.
Defence sorties: Three.

RNAS

Felixstowe: B.E.2c 1132 (Flt Cdr R. J. Hope Vere) 02.30–03.30 hr, forced landed.

Yarmouth: B.E.2c 1147 (Flt Sub-Lieut C. E. Wood) 02.15–04.10 hr; Sopwith Two-seater Scout 1052 (Flt Lieut E. J. Cooper) 04.45–06.00 hr.

Recovered from some early summer losses, the German Army Airship Service resumed its campaign against London.

The SL2 was most successful, coming in over Foulness at 22.50 hr, bombing between Southwark and Woolwich around midnight and departing over Harwich at 02.15 hr. LZ74 made landfall over Bradwell at 22.55 hr and, apparently mistaking the big Lea valley glasshouse complex for a more deserving target, unloaded her bombs on Cheshunt at midnight. Continuing south, she dropped a single incendiary on Fenchurch Street, then flew northwest to depart with the SL2 over Harwich.

LZ77 became hopelessly lost. Making landfall at Clacton at 22.40 hr, she flew inland nearly to Bishops Stortford, then wandered northeastwards to drop a few bombs near Saxmundham and finally departed over Lowestoft at 02.20 hr, dropping several more bombs out to sea.

Misty weather probably limited activities from the east coast aerodromes. The B.E.2c, making Felixstowe's sole and unsuccessful attempt to find the departing

SL2 and LZ74, suffered engine failure and was badly damaged in a forced landing near Trimley. There was again some debate about the possibility of searchlights dazzling the pilot, and in the event they were not used. Apparently Felixstowe did not accept the prevailing view that without the lights to indicate the position of targets, a night search was a forlorn hope.

From Yarmouth, Wood patrolled a 15-mile stretch of coast when LZ77 was reported approaching the area, but saw nothing. Remembering the recent Chelmsford accident, he jettisoned his bombs at sea before landing.

8/9 September, 1915 (Night)

Targets: London, Skinningrove.
Enemy forces: Navy Zeppelins L9 (Kptlt O. Loewe), L13 (Kptlt H. Mathy), L14 (Kptlt A. Böcker).
Results: 26 killed, 94 injured, £534,287 damage.
Defence sorties: Seven.

RNAS

Redcar: Caudron G.3 3870 (Flt Sub-Lieut A. J. Jacob) 21.35–22.17 hr; B.E.2cs 1135 (Flt Sub-Lieut Johnston) 21.45–23.25 hr; 1109 (Sqn Cdr C. E. H. Rathborne) 21.55–22.13 hr.

Yarmouth: B.E.2cs 977 (Sqn Cdr de C. W. P. Ireland) 19.45–19.53 hr, returned early with engine trouble; 991 (Flt Lieut J. M. R. Cripps) 19.50–21.00 hr, forced landed; 990 (Flt Sub-Lieut G. W. Hilliard) 20.12–22.10 hr, crashed, pilot killed.

Kingfisher: Sopwith Schneider 3723 (Flt Lieut V. Nicholl).

The L13 and L14, both intending to attack London, made landfall over the Norfolk coast, while the old L9 went for a shorter-range target in the northeast.

L14 developed engine trouble soon after turning inland near Cromer at 20.10 hr, unloaded her bombs around East Dereham in mistake for Norwich, and departed at about 22.00 hr.

L13, a P-class Zeppelin, commanded by Kptlt Heinrich Mathy, reached England on its fourth attempted raid, the earlier sorties having been abandoned because of mechanical troubles. L13 made in all 158 operational flights, more than any other naval airship.

After his long spell of misfortune in L13, Mathy had a trouble-free run. He made landfall near Wells at 19.35 hr, skirted the Wash to King's Lynn, then maintained a straight course for London. At 22.40 hr a sighting stick of bombs was dropped on Golders Green, then the main load—including the first 660 lb (300 kg) bomb—fell along a line from Euston to Liverpool Street, causing substantial damage and casualties. Mathy followed a more easterly track outwards and departed over Yarmouth at 02.00 hr.

Early warning of the raid enabled *Kingfisher* to position about 40 miles off Yarmouth, but Nicholl saw nothing during a brief patrol flown at last light. The three sorties from Yarmouth in search of L13 and L14 were also negative, one ending in disaster.

Attempting to land at Bacton after patrolling between Cromer and Lowestoft, Hilliard misjudged his approach and touched down heavily in an adjoining field. The B.E's undercarriage collapsed, the bombs exploded and Hilliard was killed instantly. After this incident the carriage of bombs at night was suspended until a full investigation had been made. This showed that while the bombs were theoretically safe until they had fallen for 200 ft, in a crash they were liable to fracture at the neck where the detonator was fitted.

Cripps had a remarkable escape when his engine spluttered to a stop halfway through his patrol. He could see no suitable landing place in the darkness and mist, and uppermost in his mind was the fear of his bombs exploding in a crash. Blessing the inherent stability of the B.E.2c he descended to 100 ft, climbed on to the lower wing and leaned over the cockpit to reach the control column. He managed to hold the aircraft in a gentle glide, then after six seconds, jumped. He came down on his shoulders on soft ground, unhurt, and the aircraft landed itself a little way ahead with only minor damage. They were on Caister marshes, and when a station Talbot transport arrived two hours later a red-faced Cripps confessed that the engine stoppage was due to his failure to pump petrol to the gravity tank.

Ireland's patrol was cut short when four of his engine cylinder heads cracked. No sorties were flown against the departing L14, probably because of bad visibility.

L9's attack on Skinningrove was made with great accuracy but to small effect since the bombs caused little damage. She came in a few miles north of Whitby at 21.15 hr, bombed at 21.35 hr and left ten minutes later.

The first Redcar aircraft was airborne just as Loewe was starting his bombing run and so had no chance of catching the raider. The other two had equally poor prospects, though Johnston earned his CO's praise for a diligent search down the coast to Whitby.

A vague note on the files suggests that an RFC sortie from Norwich may have been flown against this raid.

11/12 September, 1915 (Night)

Target: London.
Enemy force: Army Zeppelin LZ77 (Hptmn A. Horn).
Results: No casualties or damage.
Defence sorties: Three.

RNAS

Chelmsford: Caudron G.3s 1594 (Flt Sub-Lieut R. M. Blake) took off 01.25 hr; 1597, details not known.

RFC

Writtle: B.E.2c (Lieut Morison) 60-min sortie.

Surviving records indicate some confusion on this night. RNAS Killingholme at 21.40 hr and Redcar an hour later both launched sorties apparently based on false alarms, and next day the army Central Forces and Eastern Command complained about wild and conflicting naval reports concerning up to six airships. This raises the possibility of some undocumented enemy movements.

The only raider identified was LZ77, which crossed the coast north of the Crouch at 23.15 hr and became lost on the way to London. She ineffectually bombed the North Weald area, and departed over Yarmouth at 02.05 hr. The RNAS Chelmsford patrol for which a time is recorded stood little chance of intercepting.

The RFC B.E.2c had been positioned at Writtle, near Chelmsford, since 9 September by urgent order of the War Office. Its pilot reported that unless illuminated by searchlights, airships would be found only by sheer accident.

12/13 September, 1915 (Night)

Target: London.
Enemy force: Army Zeppelin LZ74 (Hptmn F. George).
Results: No damage or casualties.
Defence sorties: One.

RNAS

Eastchurch: B.E.2c 983 (Flt Sub-Lieut F. T. Digby) 22.55–23.47 hr.

For the second successive night an army Zeppelin became lost over England. LZ74 crossed the coast near Walton-on-the-Naze at 22.45 hr, penetrated almost to Halstead, then scattered bombs over the East Anglian countryside. She left near Southwold at 00.18 hr.

Though airborne in good time, the Eastchurch B.E.2c clearly had no prospect of finding the airship some 35 miles away to the north.

13 September, 1915 (Daylight)

Target: Margate.
Enemy force: One floatplane, type not known.
Results: Two killed, six injured, £500 damage.
Defence sorties: Two.

RNAS

Westgate: B.E.2cs 980 and 982, 17.45–19.30 hr.

This was the first coastal hit-and-run attack to cause casualties. The enemy seaplane from SFA 1, type not recorded, was spotted at 17.40 hr when still some six miles out to sea west of the Tongue light vesel. It crossed Cliftonville and dropped ten bombs, then continued south over the Channel. The two B.E.2cs kept the enemy in sight for a time, but it eventually drew away.

13/14 September, 1915 (Night)

Target: London.

Enemy forces: Navy Zeppelins L11 (Oblt-z-S H. von Buttlar), L13 (Kptlt H. Mathy), L14 (Kptlt A. Böcker).
Results: No casualties, £2 damage.
Defence sorties: Two.

RNAS
Dover: B.E.2c 994 (Flt Lieut L. D. McKean) 05.35–07.10 hr; Bristol Scout C 1254 (Flt Sub-Lieut R. F. S. Leslie) 05.35–07.35 hr (landed at Eastchurch).

A substantial raid planned for London collapsed when L11 and L14 turned back because of headwinds and thunderstorms. Mathy pressed on but, at about midnight, damage from an anti-aircraft shell over the Harwich area forced him to jettison his bombs and also return.

Although officially listed with the night's defence operations, the Dover sorties have no apparent connection with L13's activities. The two aircraft covered an area from 45 miles northeast of the North Foreland to the French coast, and may have been alerted by some unrecorded movements of the other two airships.

13/14 October, 1915 (Night)

Target: London.
Enemy forces: Navy Zeppelins L11 (Oblt-z-S H. von Buttlar), L13 (Kptlt H. Mathy), L14 (Kptlt A. Böcker), L15 (Kptlt Joachim Breithaupt), L16 (Oblt-z-S W. Peterson).
Results: 71 killed, 128 injured, £80,020 damage.
Defence sorties: Six.

RFC
Joyce Green: B.E.2c 2049 (Lieut R. S. Tipton) 20.20–21.35 hr and 22.37–23.22 hr; unidentified B.E.2c (Capt L. da C. Penn-Gaskell) 21.40–22.15 hr.
Hainault Farm: B.E.2cs 2051 (2nd Lieut F. H. Jenkins) 20.00–21.30 hr; 4078 (2nd Lieut C. E. Wardle) 21.50–23.20 hr.
Suttons Farm: Unidentified B.E.2c (2nd Lieut J. C. Slessor) 21.40–23.15 hr.

This was the most ambitious raid yet launched against London, and the costliest in casualties. Following growing Government pressure, there was for the first

L11, commanded by Oblt-z-S H. von Buttlar, which bombed the Norfolk countryside on the 13/14 October, 1915, raid. L11 ended its service as a training airship.

time an organized attempt to intercept the raiders as they approached the capital, but resources and techniques proved inadequate to the task.

L11 came in over Bacton at 20.30 hr and, after being fired on by a mobile AA section, jettisoned bombs in open country around Coltishall and departed over Yarmouth at 21.15 hr. Von Buttlar described this short and futile trip over England as a significant attack on West Ham and Woolwich.

The other airships crossed in the same area between 18.15 and 18.45 hr, and thereafter their tracks diverged. Mathy in L13 strangely decided to attack the Hampton water works before visiting London, and during this westward deviation he became lost and actually bombed near Guildford. He then turned northeast and dropped the rest of his bombs at Woolwich shortly before midnight.

L14 went badly astray and flew south after crossing the Thames estuary to reach the coast at Hythe. Four bombs on a military camp at Shorncliffe killed fifteen soldiers. On the return flight the airship dropped more bombs near Tunbridge Wells and at Croydon, crossed southeast London and departed over Aldeburgh at 01.45 hr.

Breithaupt in L15, the first of the more powerful Zeppelins with the new 240 hp Maybach HSLu engines, making his own first raid on England, achieved the most competent performance of the night. He reached central London at 21.25 hr, dropped thirty bombs between the Strand and Limehouse, then flew out, also over Aldeburgh, at 23.55 hr.

Peterson in L16—another new craft—flew a good course to within 20 miles of London but apparently mistook the River Lea for the Thames, and at 22.00 hr bombed Hertford; not industrial and railway targets in east London as he reported. He flew out north of Bacton shortly after midnight.

Appropriate RFC stations were alerted at 17.00 hr when intercepted wireless messages revealed that a raid was under way. At 19.55 hr came observers' reports that Zeppelins were over the Thetford area, heading south, and during the next ten minutes the War Office ordered Hainault, Joyce Green, Suttons Farm and Northolt each to send up one B.E.2c, weather permitting. Ground mist delayed some take-offs and added to the inherent hazards of night flying. Northolt remained unfit for flying throughout, with visibility so bad that the flare party lost themselves on the aerodrome.

Jenkins, detached to Hainault from No.14 Squadron forming at Gosport for overseas service, was first off, and after a diversion north towards what he reported as heavy gunfire, flew a wide orbit between Hainault and London at 8–9,000 ft. He continued for more than an hour, and was returning to base just as L15 began bombing and therefore saw nothing. With visibility so bad that he could hardly discern the flarepath from 100 ft, he touched down short, arriving on the aerodrome via a hedge and a barbed-wire fence, which broke his propeller and ripped the lower wing fabric.

Fifteen minutes later L15 passed almost overhead, and Wardle took off. He climbed to the east, where a gun was firing, but saw nothing of the Zeppelin, then continued a fruitless patrol for another 75 min. He also lost the flarepath at 100 ft as he approached Hainault, stalled, and damaged his propeller, starboard lower wing and undercarriage.

Tipton, of No.14 Squadron, who had been at Joyce Green since 9 September, found that, having cleared the ground mist and reached 8,000 ft, visibility over London was good. At about 21.25 hr, just as he fleetingly glimpsed a possible Zeppelin below and some distance away, failing engine pressure demanded a prompt return to base.

Penn-Gaskell had barely started the Joyce Green relief patrol when he too was obliged to turn back with engine trouble. Meanwhile, Tipton's engine had been rectified, so he took over and climbed to 9,000 ft over Deptford, seeing nothing except gun flashes on the ground. Shortly after he had returned and the aircraft put away for the night, pilots and mechanics were presented with the spectacle of L13 and L14 serenely flying north of the aerodrome. Tipton had his B.E. wheeled out and the engine run up, but Penn-Gaskell vetoed take-off since the chances of overtaking were nil and the aircraft's presence would confuse the AA gunners.

Slessor*, detached from No.17 Squadron to Suttons Farm, was the only pilot to positively see a Zeppelin from the air. He was at 2,500 ft and still climbing when he spotted L15 held by a searchlight to the east. He kept her in view for three or four minutes while his B.E. laboured upwards, then he met a layer of cloud. When he emerged the Zeppelin was no longer visible, and he continued to search in vain. The mist had thickened when he descended to land, making it difficult to pick up the Suttons Farm flares, but he was approaching satisfactorily until the well-meaning local searchlight operator switched the beam in his direction. Temporarily blinded, Slessor touched down in a root field at the end of the aerodrome, tipping his aircraft on to its nose and damaging a wingtip and the undercarriage.

Then Suttons Farm suffered the same experience as Joyce Green as L13 and L14 became visible on their homeward flight, the former passing overhead. Despite prior planning, the second B.E.2c was not fully armed for combat and did not take off.

The raiders noticed the defence improvements and Breithaupt's crew claimed four aeroplane sightings over London—which probably came from some duplication rather than spotting four separate B.E.2cs.

The defences were unlucky in that when L15 was well illuminated over central London the B.Es happened to be about ten miles away, descending to land, and that aircraft were held on the ground when Zeppelins appeared virtually overhead. But that situation was almost inevitable, since the War Office had committed all the first wave aircraft when Zeppelins were still over an hour's flying time from the capital, with no provision for overlapping patrols during the alert period.

Generally the searchlights enjoyed little success in illuminating Zeppelins, and none of the pilots saw any of the pre-arranged signal rockets. Despite the minor aircraft damage, the pilots did well in difficult circumstances, and the GOC No.2 Brigade formally expressed his appreciation, individually naming them. By some administrative error he left out Slessor, whose name was added in a hasty amendment letter.

The absence of a single RNAS sortie against this first raid to be faced with organized RFC defence participation was curious, and during the inevitable recriminations, the official naval view that it was useless to attempt the interception of Zeppelins not actually seen was vigorously reiterated. There were considerable enemy comings and goings near the RNAS coastal aerodromes, and faced with similar situations in the past, many naval pilots had readily taken off to search for airships regardless of whether they were illuminated.

* Later Marshal of the RAF Sir John Slessor, Chief of the Air Staff, 1950–52.

Bristol Scout Cs in the elegantly camouflaged D shed at RNAS Yarmouth in 1916. This artistic piece of deception was of short duration since it did not reflect seasonal variations. (*RAF Museum*)

Chapter VI

Under New Management

Planning for an improved home defence organization continued during the early weeks of 1916 and the War Office clearly hoped that some positive signs would be visible by the take-over dates—16 February for London and 22 February for the rest of the country.

Home Forces Command estimated the long-term requirement as ten home defence squadrons, but resources for such a programme would not be available for some months. However, interim improvements were effected, some clearly based on Geoffrey Salmond's suggestions after the October 1915 raid—despite their initially cool reception.

On 1 February operating efficiency of the London aircraft defences was significantly improved by placing the various detachments under a single commander. They remained at their existing locations but became elements of the newly-formed No.19 Reserve Aeroplane Squadron under Maj T. C. R. Higgins, with squadron headquarters at Hounslow.

Charles Higgins, who had transferred to the RFC the previous summer at the mature age of 34, had enjoyed a remarkably varied Service career. Educated in HMS *Britannia*—the ancestor of Dartmouth—he spent three more years in the navy, then in 1900 joined the King's Own Royal Regiment and served in the Boer War. In 1911 he was among the first 25 army officers to obtain flying certificates, but when he applied to join the RFC some months after its formation the officer complement was over-subscribed. Wounded in France early in the fighting, he eventually achieved the transfer in May 1915 and served in Nos.7 and 9 Squadrons. Higgins made no claim to be a widely-experienced pilot, but he was a very able administrator, well-enough versed in Service procedures to know the short cuts and when to turn a blind eye to the more esoteric Whitehall pronouncements.

Although No.19 RAS retained its function as a training unit, it was clearly not practicable for the pilots manning the small night-flying detachments to combine productive instructional work with regular night standbys and operations, so their duties became solely home defence.

For units outside the London area responsibilities were less clear, and among queries to the War Office was one from the meticulous Maj H. C. T. Dowding*, CO of No.7 Wing, Gosport, as to what anti-Zeppelin action he was supposed to take while he had no suitable aircraft for repelling raids, nor any guarantee that his training aircraft would be serviceable. The reply was hardly helpful:

> 'If the raid takes place over Portsmouth garrison and stable machines are available, such action as is deemed advisable will be taken by OC 7 Wing; if the raid is in another area, he will be telephoned instructions by the War Office.'

HQ 6 Brigade then protested that their promised 70 hp Renault-engined B.E.2cs would be ineffective against Zeppelins—to which the War Office replied that Gosport was getting the 80 hp version, as good as the RAF-engined model for home defence work.

Naval air stations also had their problems, and on 21 February Sqn Cdr C. E. H. Rathborne, at Redcar, complained to the Director of Air Services that his aircraft were so worn out and unreliable that daytime forced landings were commonplace, and that RAF-engined B.E.2cs were essential for night operations. His plea evidently fell on deaf ears, for Redcar was still using the old Renault B.Es on anti-Zeppelin sorties in November.

On 31 January/1 February German naval airships made their biggest raid to date. The main attack was on the Midlands, but early movement reports were vague and the War Office had to assume that London was the intended target. The night was a disaster for the defences, producing the highest proportion of aircraft losses, casualties, and accidents per sortie, for any home defence action of the entire war. Of the twenty-two aircraft which took off six were either burned out or listed as wrecked and seven damaged in lesser degree. Only six landed intact on their own aerodromes. Two pilots were fatally injured.

Six days earlier Kitchener had grudgingly agreed that the RFC would accept the air defence responsibility, and although the formal take-over date was still a few weeks away, the War Office was clearly anxious to present its interim arrangements in good light. In extremely bad flying conditions the RFC pilots demonstrated a determination to frustrate the raiders which, with hindsight, appears to have exceeded the bounds of prudence.

This time there was no question of RNAS aircraft waiting on the ground for positive Zeppelin sightings, and their performance was marginally better. Thus any naïve beliefs lurking in sections of the War Office about the inherently

* Air Chief Marshal Sir Hugh Dowding, AOC-in-C Fighter Command, 1936–40.

superior night-flying abilities of army pilots were rudely shattered. The sorry tale was redeemed by some examples of skilled flying, several lucky escapes and a high rate of survival from the crashes.

Two of the participating Zeppelins—L20 and L21—were of the new interim Q type, in effect a P-class with extra gas cells increasing the length to 585 ft 5 in. The change brought a slight increase in ceiling and bomb load.

As well as emphasizing the shortcomings of the warning system, this raid generated an epidemic of spurious Zeppelin sightings and false alarms, spreading as far west as Gloucester and Bath. Only one, on 10 February, stimulated any defence reaction, when two Bristol Scouts and two B.E.2cs from RNAS Redcar spent three hours patrolling Teesside and the coast following reports of a Zeppelin off Scarborough. More important than such minor diversions of the defence effort was the loss of war production caused by false alarms, and GHQ Home Forces was instructed by the Cabinet to devise some efficient warning system without delay. An interim arrangement instituted on 14 February established military centres in London, York, and Edinburgh for handling information on enemy aircraft, and during the next three months much time was devoted to producing a comprehensive warning system.

The early weeks of 1916 witnessed fairly brisk hit-and-run activity against Kent coastal targets. Most of the attacks were made by See Flieger Abteilung 1 using Friedrichshafen FF 33 and Hansa-Brandenburg NW floatplanes, both good straightforward designs, cleaner and probably more efficient than the various Short machines which were their British counterparts.

The FF 33 was built for various roles in different versions, some with two- and others with three-bay biplane wings spanning from 43 to 55 ft. The engine was a 150 hp Benz or 160 hp Maybach. The Brandenbrug NW was of broadly similar characteristics. Speeds were only around 70–85 mph, but arriving without warning at 7,000–10,000 ft they could bomb or photograph and be well on their homeward flights before the available fighters could hope to reach them from a standing start. Some sorties were probably flown by L.V.G. landplanes of Marine Feld Flieger Abteilung 1, whose records have not been traced.

RNAS coastal stations launched any aircraft which happened to be available against these raiders, though a few main types did most of the work.

An FBA flying-boat of the type flown from RNAS Dover and Grain in 1916. This example, N1059, was probably a trainer at Calshot.

Sopwith Schneiders and Babies of the RNAS Grain war flight in early 1916. Baby 8118 (third from left) was the first built and retained the 100 hp Gnome engine and cowling of the earlier Schneider. (*J. M. Bruce/G. S. Leslie collection*)

Among the more widely-used landplanes was the Bristol Scout, developed from the neat sporting biplane which had been the sensation of the 1914 Aero Show at Olympia. Most of the first production version, the C, were powered by the 80 hp Gnome engine—though some had the Le Rhône—while the later D models had various minor improvements and provision for more powerful engines. The C had a top speed of 92½ mph at ground level and 86½ mph at 10,000 ft—a height reached in 21 minutes. The D was a little faster, with a better rate of climb. The Scout's design was ahead of armament development and early versions carried various makeshift equipment, though latterly most of them had a machine-gun.

The French-designed Nieuport 10 and 12 were also employed. Though built as two-seaters these were mostly flown with a pilot only, and armed with a Lewis gun firing over the top wing. Performance was very similar to the Scout's.

RNAS Dover operated several FBA (Franco-British Aviation) flying-boats. These were side-by-side two-seaters in which the observer operated a Lewis gun, though their performance was inadequate to deal with raiders except in the most favourable circumstances.

The Sopwith Schneider floatplane was superseded by a development, the Baby, powered by a 110 or 130 hp Clerget engine which gave a sea level speed of 92–100 mph. Various armament permutations were used, and some later aircraft had two Lewis guns above the top wing. They were manoeuvrable and easy to fly, but climb was poor and ceiling only 13,000 ft.

Station commanders were understandably anxious to obtain some of the better contemporary fighters capable of inflicting casualties, but since the raids were of little more than nuisance value the British authorities wisely resisted the probable enemy motive of diverting a big defence build-up to the area.

On 22 February Capt C. L. Lambe, commanding RNAS Dover, had notified the Director of Air Services that his 'war flight' of six landplanes plus a few low-performance seaplanes patrolling the Downs was quite inadequate. However, he conceded that even given a force of ten new Bristol Scouts and ten Baby seaplanes it would still be extremely difficult to counter the enemy intrusions.

Nor was the situation at RNAS Westgate any more satisfactory. On 29 March

A double fixed Lewis gun installation on a Sopwith Baby.

Wing Cdr H. P. Smyth-Osbourne the Divisional Commander of Air Stations, Nore, advised his C-in-C of the need for fifteen fast landplane fighters able to get airborne in 30 seconds against the five minutes required by his seaplanes. He considered B.E.2cs of no practical value where the notice of attack was so short, and since Westgate was too small for faster fighters, he recommended that the larger new aerodrome at Manston be used. A few Bristol Scouts began operating there in July.

The War Office was at first more inclined to supply better fighters and on 22 March allotted three new D.H.2s to RFC Dover. But it, too, came to the view that such a move would be playing the enemy's game, and Dover's query six weeks later about the non-arrival of the fighters was met with vague excuses about interference with the wider training programme.

As for the ubiquitous B.E.2c, it was accepted that it had little value as a day fighter, though it had now become the standard anti-Zeppelin aircraft for both Services.

Bristol Scouts, Nieuports and B.E.2cs of the RNAS Dover war flight. Nieuports 3165, 3967 and 3968 are recorded as making in all nine sorties against hit-and-run raiders.

Chapter VII

Operations—January to February 1916

9 January, 1916 (Daylight)

Target: Dover.
Enemy force: One floatplane, type not known.
Results: No casualties or damage.
Defence sorties: Seven.

RNAS
Dover: Nieuport 10s 3967 (Flt Lieut H. Rosher); 3173 (Flt Sub-Lieut C. H. Potts); Bristol Scout Cs 1254 (Flt Lieut F. G. Andreae); 1258 (Flt Lieut B. L. Huskisson); no times available.
Eastchurch: Nieuport 10s 3176 (Flt Lieut C. T. MacLaren); 3964 (Flt Sub-Lieut A. D. W. Allen); no times available.

RFC
Dover: One sortie—details not known.

At 14.13 hr a floatplane of SFA 1, type not recorded, was spotted by the Dover Castle AA battery approaching the harbour at 6–7,000 ft. It was attacked by the guns, and, after flying towards the RNAS aerodrome, it turned out to sea having completed its reconnaissance mission.

Of the defence pilots airborne, only Huskisson saw the intruder, but he made little headway and lost it in cloud about ten miles off Dunkirk.

22/23 January, 1916 (Night)

Target: Dover.
Enemy force: One Friedrichshafen FF 33b.
Results: One killed, six injured, £1,591 damage.
Defence sorties: None.

In bright moonlight a Friedrichshafen floatplane of SFA 1 dropped eight HE and one incendiary bomb near the Dover garrison headquarters. Bombing began at 00.47 hr, and the enemy was seen flying out to sea near St Margaret's at 01.03 hr. There was no advance warning, and no attempt was made to overtake this first hit-and-run night raider to appear for nearly a year.

23 January, 1916 (Daylight)

Targets: Folkestone, Dover.
Enemy forces: One Friedrichshafen FF 33b, one Hansa-Brandenburg NW.
Results: No casualties or damage.
Defence sorties: Six.

RNAS
Dover: FBA flying-boat 3208 (Flt Lieut T. F. N. Gerrard, Flt Sub-Lieut G. G. Hodge) 13.30–14.30 hr.
Yarmouth: Avro 504C 8591 (Flt Sub-Lieut J. A. Page) 14.20–15.45 hr.

RFC
Dover: Four sorties—details not known.

Information on this Sunday lunchtime sortie is sparse and conflicting. British records state that one of the two floatplanes which attacked Dover at 12.52 hr flew on to Capel, near Folkestone, and dropped five bombs close to the RNAS airship hangars 30 min later.

The German account says that two aircraft from SFA 1 first dropped seventeen bombs at Capel—starting a fire in a hangar—and then released the remaining two on Dover. One British report briefly mentions bombs falling at St Margaret's at 14.14 hr, long after the enemy should have cleared the area.

Some of the RFC aircraft sighted the enemy but were unable to overtake. The RNAS FBA flying-boat, airborne much too late to intervene, was fired on in error by the AA guns. The Lewis-armed Avro from Yarmouth patrolled southwards to Aldeburgh against the remote possibility of the intruders returning along a northerly course.

24 January, 1916 (Daylight)

Targets: Folkestone, Dover.
Enemy force: One floatplane, type not known.
Results: No casualties or damage.
Defence sorties: Six.

RNAS
Dover: Curtiss JN-3 3414 (Flt Sub-Lieut J. R. Potts); Bristol Scout C 1260 (Flt Sub-Lieut R. F. S. Leslie); Morane Parasol 3248 (Flt Lieut H. L. Wood); FBA flying-boat 3208 (Flt Lieut T. F. N. Gerrard, Flt Sub-Lieut A. T. Cowley); no timings available.

RFC
Dover: Two sorties—details not known

This intruder dropped no bombs and was to all appearances photographing the results of the previous day's raid.

British observers described it as a seaplane, but since SFA 1 recorded no such operation it is presumed to have been flown by some other unit. However, SFA 1 did list a Dover area reconnaissance by an FF 33b on 25 January—possibly an incorrectly dated entry.

The aircraft appeared over the Capel airship sheds at 15.45 hr, then turned northeast and was seen over Dover 16 minutes later. Two RNAS aircraft—

believed to be the Bristol and the Morane—were already on patrol after a telephoned warning from Dunkirk that an enemy had been seen heading for the English coast. One closed to 300 yards and the unidentified pilot attacked with his Lewis gun until it jammed. The enemy had disappeared into cloud before he could see whether it had been damaged.

31 January/1 February, 1916 (Night)

Target: Liverpool.
Enemy forces: Navy Zeppelins L11 (Kptlt H. von Buttlar), L13 (Kptlt H. Mathy), L14 (Kptlt A. Böcker), L15 (Kptlt J. Breithaupt), L16 (Oblt-z-S W. Peterson), L17 (Kptlt Herbert Ehrlich), L19 (Kptlt O. Loewe), L20 (Kptlt Franz Stabbert), L21 (Kptlt Max Dietrich).
Results: 70 killed, 113 injured, £53,832 damage.
Defence sorties: 22.

RNAS

Chingford: B.E.2c 1122 (Flt Sub-Lieut H. McClelland) 19.55–21.40 hr (Joyce Green), slightly damaged.

Hendon: B.E.2c 1142 (Flt Sub-Lieut F. P. Reeves) 20.30–20.50 hr, damaged.

Rochford: B.E.2c 1189 (Flt Sub-Lieut J. E. Morgan) took off 20.43 hr, forced landed Thameshaven.

Yarmouth: B.E.2cs 1155 (Flt Lieut V. Nicholl) 17.00–17.50 hr (Bacton); 1167 (Flt Cdr de C. W. P. Ireland) 17.07–17.35 hr, returned early due to weather; 1150 (Flt Lieut C. E. Wood) 17.15–19.00 hr, crashed Spixworth; 1151 (Flt Cdr de C. W. P. Ireland) 23.40–00.01 hr; unidentified B.E.2c (Flt Lieut C. H. C. Smith) took off 19.00 hr.

RFC

No. 5 R. A. Squadron, Castle Bromwich: R.E.7 2363 (Maj A. B. Burdett, 2nd Lieut R. A. Cresswell) 20.20–21.50 hr, forced landed.

No.10 R.A. Squadron, Farningham: B.E.2c 1776 (2nd Lieut W. J. Y. Guilfoyle) crashed on take-off at 19.45 hr.

No.10 R.A. Squadron, Joyce Green: B.E.2cs 4700 (Maj E. F. Unwin) 19.35–19.50 hr, crashed, pilot fatally injured; 4147 (2nd Lieut C. A. Ridley) 20.15–23.15 hr, crashed near Reigate.

No.11 R.A. Squadron, Northolt: B.E.2c 2091 (Maj L. da C. Penn-Gaskell), crashed on take-off at 19.35 hr, pilot fatally injured.

No.17 R.A. Squadron, Croydon: B.E.2c 2574 (Lieut P. Rader) 19.35–20.25 hr, slightly damaged; unidentified B.E.2c (Lieut C. T. Black) 22.02–22.15 hr, returned early due to weather.

No.17 R.A. Squadron, Hainault: B.E.2cs 2087 (Lieut R. S. Maxwell) 19.40–21.35 hr, crashed on landing; 2085 (Lieut W. P. Cort) crashed on take-off at 21.00 hr.

No.17 R.A. Squadron, Hendon: B.E.2c 2110 (Lieut Jowett) 20.05–21.50 hr (Hainault).

No.17 R.A. Squadron, Suttons Farm: B.E.2c 2089 (Lieut Steele) took off at 19.35 hr, damaged landing.

No.17 R.A. Squadron, Wimbledon Common: B.E.2c 2107 (2nd Lieut H. Tomlinson), crashed on take-off at 19.40 hr.

No.24 Squadron, Hounslow: Two sorties, details not known.

This factory-fresh B.E.2c, 2574, initially flown on anti-Zeppelin operations by No.17 Reserve Aeroplane Squadron from Croydon in January–April 1916, later went to No.39 Squadron at North Weald. It was airborne on 2/3 September, 1916, the night SL11 was shot down. 'Central Argentine Railway Aeroplane' appears beneath the cockpits. (*R. C. Bowyer*)

During the break in bombing caused primarily by bad weather the German navy acquired five new Zeppelins, all with the more powerful 240 hp engines—though one (L18) was destroyed in a fire ten days after commissioning.

Germany had decided to extend attacks to all major industrial centres in Britain within Zeppelin range, and for this biggest raid to date Liverpool was the primary target, with London as the weather alternative. The airships encountered heavy rain and icing over the North Sea, and made landfall at various points between The Wash and Happisburgh from 16.50 hr to 19.10 hr.

They were frequently lost, generally drifting farther south than their captains realised, and ranged over an area bounded by Scunthorpe, Burslem, Shrewsbury, Bewdley and Huntingdon. It was impossible to track with accuracy their individual paths. Captains claimed to have bombed Liverpool, Manchester, Sheffield, Nottingham, Goole and Immingham, but the places actually hit were Loughborough, Ilkeston, Scunthorpe, Derby, Burton-on-Trent and the Tipton–Wednesbury–Walsall area.

B.E.2c 2089 enjoyed a long operational career. It was first recorded at Suttons Farm on the disastrous night of 31 January/1 February, 1916, and finally at North Weald on 25 May, 1917. This photograph was taken during the later stage of its career.

Engine teething troubles hampered four of the Zeppelins and contributed to the loss of L19. She did not clear the coast until 05.25 hr, was further delayed over the North Sea and then holed by Dutch rifle fire from the Friesian Islands. Some time afterwards three of the four engines failed and she came down at sea with the loss of all on board.

Strasser flew in L11, and after penetrating to the Buxton area without locating what he regarded as a legitimate target, he authorized von Buttlar to return without bombing.

From the 205 HE and 174 incendiary bombs dropped casualties were relatively light; of greater impact was the demonstration that enemy airships could wander at will over the country for 12 hours.

If the raid was disappointing to the Germans it was a disaster for the defences, with six aircraft destroyed or listed as 'wrecked' and two squadron commanders fatally injured. As one of the biggest fiascos in British air defence history it merits description in some detail.

Enemy signals intercepted soon after midday warned of a raid in strength, and RNAS Yarmouth aircraft were airborne shortly after L13 and L21 had been reported off Cromer. Visibility was poor, causing Ireland to return early and Nicholl to put down at Bacton. Wood had a remarkable escape. Meeting heavy snow at 5,000 ft he became progressively more lost in the atrocious visibility, and while vainly searching for friendly flares his engine stopped. He glided down, praying for smooth ground ahead, and hit surprisingly gently. But this was a brief prelude to some rending crashes and a sudden deceleration. The unharmed but shaken pilot found that he had landed in an avenue of trees at Spixworth, Norwich, which had neatly sheared off the B.E's wings.

Chichester Smith searched for some of the later arrivals over the coast, and Ireland sought the departing L21 shortly before midnight. None of the Yarmouth pilots saw anything of the enemy.

By 19.00 hr seven Zeppelins had crossed the coast, and with no clear attack pattern emerging the War Office had to assume that London was the objective, with the raiders due at about 20.15 hr. To eliminate any risk of being caught napping, first patrols were ordered 65 min before that time. In the event fog ruled out immediate take-offs, and, apart from a few short-lived clearances, visibility at ground level remained near the limits and was the principal cause of the high accident rate. No Zeppelin was plotted within 60 miles of London, nor, with the exception of a solitary pom-pom, did the guns open fire. Flashes on the ground which pilots reported as bomb bursts or gunfire were caused by trains and trams.

At Northolt visibility was still minimal when Leslie Penn-Gaskell, CO of No. 11 RAS and a skilled pilot of four years' standing, took off at 19.35 hr to investigate conditions before allowing less experienced officers to fly. His B.E.2c disappeared into the murk and seconds later struck an elm tree at the western end of the aerodrome, plunged to the ground and caught fire. Two corporals from a nearby flight shed were quickly on the scene and lifted the pilot from the wreck before the bombs exploded, but he was badly injured and died five days later.

At precisely the same time, 27 miles southeast, Ernest Unwin took off from Joyce Green, also in fog and with the same object of assessing fitness for flying. Unwin too had been a pilot since 1912, and only that morning had taken command of No.10 RAS. His aircraft, the first of a small batch of B.E.2cs built as single-seaters for home defence work, was immediately lost to sight and its engine sound gradually faded as it climbed away. Exactly what went wrong is not known, but he was probably trying to find the aerodrome having failed to break into clear weather. At 19.50 hr the aircraft hit trees on Erith Marshes, south of the Thames Ammunition Works, and caught fire. Although thrown clear, Unwin was seriously injured and died on 23 March.

Within five minutes of each other, two more B.Es had crashed in similar circumstances, though both pilots escaped with minor injuries. At Wimbledon Common, Hugh Tomlinson was flying the first—and only—operational sortie from that location. It achieved in drama what it lacked in duration, for seconds after becoming airborne this B.E. also hit a tree, then cannoned off a house into a field, scattering six of its bombs. Two which remained in their carriers exploded and set fire to the wreckage, but Tomlinson, slightly cut and bruised, scrambled out before the flames took hold.

At Farningham, Guilfoyle came to grief three miles from take-off point and was taken to Dartford Cottage Hospital suffering from shock, abrasions and a sprained ankle. Details of the crash which wrecked his B.E. are not recorded.

Although Unwin had crashed across the River Darenth less than a mile distant, Joyce Green knew nothing of the accident until police telephoned at 20.10 hr, when the fog had cleared sufficiently for Ridley to get away. Claude Ridley, 19, had recently recovered from a foot wound received in France, when his No.3 Squadron Morane was attacked by three Fokkers. James McCudden, then a sergeant observer and later to become a leading fighter 'ace', flew with Ridley before that episode and commented '. . . I did not enjoy it much for the pilot was one of the most dashing and enterprising kind. Such flying is all very fine for the pilot but not always for the passenger.' However, these remarks need not be

Bert Hinkler as a petty officer observer before he became a pilot; and (*right*) Claude Ridley in 1917 as a captain. He was awarded the MC in April 1916 for anti-Zeppelin work, and the DSO with No.60 Squadron in August after evading capture for two months when forced down in enemy-occupied French territory while carrying an Allied agent. In 1917–18 he was again on home-defence operations.

taken as any serious reflection on Ridley's piloting skill, as will become apparent later in the home defence story.

Ridley climbed slowly through several cloud layers, and after emerging over London at 9,000 ft he spotted a moving light. On turning to investigate he entered dense cloud, lost control and spun down to 3,000 ft. He laboured back into the clear and patrolled for nearly three hours, with occasional glimpses of the ground but no sign of an enemy, so decided to land.

Bumping down through the darkness and mist until his altimeter showed 1,000 ft he could still see nothing below and was levelling out to drop a parachute flare when his port wingtips struck the ground. The aircraft was instantly reduced to wreckage but, miraculously, Ridley emerged unscathed. The time was 23.15 hr, and he was further shaken to find that he had wandered 25 miles southwest from base, his let-down having terminated not over the flat reaches of the Thames estuary—for which his altimeter was correctly set—but at a point more than 600 ft above sea level on the North Downs near Reigate.

The light which Ridley had chased was in fact from the B.E. flown by Stuart Maxwell, who had left Hainault Farm about 35 min earlier and also saw Ridley—though neither pilot realized that his quarrry was another B.E. Maxwell had broken cloud at 8,000 ft, and through a gap he saw flashes on the ground which he assumed to be bomb bursts or AA fire. He climbed to 10,000 ft and then followed Ridley's light northeastwards until it vanished in cloud. At this point Maxwell could see five flarepaths, but after flying south again for some minutes these disappeared—though the Thames and the lights of London remained visible through intermittent breaks.

At about 21.15 hr, concluding that any raiders must have departed, he turned northeast and ten minutes later spotted flares so decided to land. He made a good approach down to 250 ft, but on levelling out his engine was slow to pick up and he hit a small rise which wiped off his undercarriage and smashed his propeller. Fortunately the bombs did not explode and Maxwell was unhurt. By some inspired piece of navigation he had arrived at Hainault. His altimeter, correctly set before take-off, read 200 ft at the time of impact.

From Croydon, Rader took off in thick mist, climbed to 5,000 ft without breaking clear, then went down to 3,000 ft. After 40 minutes during which he saw nothing of the ground and at times could barely distinguish his wingtip lights, he decided that such activity held little future and came down. By great skill or good luck he located the Croydon flares through the mist and incurred no more damage than a broken aileron king-post. On Croydon's second patrol, Black climbed to 3,000 ft, but visibility was so bad that he wisely came straight back.

Flying Hainault's second sortie, Cort lost his instrument lights just as he became airborne. While still fumbling for his torch the engine started missing badly and the B.E. began to lose height. Its starboard wings struck a haystack, then it hit the ground and trundled along to nose over against a wire fence. Petrol leaking on to the exhaust pipe started a fire, but Cort was unhurt and managed to smother the flames with his flying coat before they gained a hold.

Steele from Suttons Farm reached 12,500 ft, patrolled without seeing anything, then, despite an unserviceable altimeter, achieved a good landing approach. However, he then hit a fence, breaking the tip of a propeller blade.

Naval pilots operating in the southeast fared little better than their RFC brethren. At Hendon, Fabian Reeves gave up after 20 minutes of groping around in the mist and was fortunate to find the aerodrome again—though his abrupt arrival on the ground removed the B.E's undercarriage and damaged the propeller and lower wings. There was some anxiety about Jowett, an RFC pilot who had taken off earlier, until he eventually arrived at Hainault.

From Chingford, McClelland climbed to his ceiling height of 9,400 ft, cruised over London for an hour, then put down on the first landing ground seen after descending through substantial cloud layers. This happened to be Joyce Green, and he broke his starboard undercarriage skid in a heavy landing. He reported numerous gun flashes on the ground and also claimed to have seen a Zeppelin held briefly in a searchlight beam at 21.00 hr. It vanished as he closed the distance.

Eric Morgan, from Rochford, reported a close sighting near Southend which was dismissed as another 'phantom airship' story. However, he was a level-headed young officer, praised for his overall performance that night, and may indeed have seen an airship. There was great confusion over enemy movements, and Peterson's L16, departing with engine trouble at the time of the incident, could have been much farther south than was generally believed.

Morgan was patrolling between Rochford and Southend, and at 21.00 hr he saw above him to starboard and about 35 yards ahead 'a row of lighted windows . . . something like a railway carriage with the blinds down.' He was at 6,400 ft and unable to climb higher because of a misfiring engine, so he loosed off several rounds from his service revolver. The lights then rose so rapidly that his B.E. seemed to be diving—but a glance at his instruments confirmed that he was maintaining altitude. Having now lost the object and his own bearings, he began descending to the west and fired off a Very light (seen from Southend pier) hoping for acknowledgment from some nearby aerodrome.

At 3,000 ft he saw a blur of light through a break in the cloud and, descending to 300 ft, found a large steamer. He circled three times, signalling in morse for a bearing to Southend. There was no response from the ship—which was Dutch—but a burst of pom-pom fire from a position nearby. This was later traced to a Thameshaven battery, which had not been warned of any friendly air activity.

While wondering whether to alight near these signs of civilization Morgan glimpsed a stretch of coastline in a sweeping searchlight beam. Gingerly letting down in the darkness he flared out at the precise moment to achieve a perfect touchdown, which unfortunately ended in a muddy watercourse. He fired his pistol to attract attention and soon discovered that he was on the marshes at Thameshaven. The following afternoon he flew the undamaged B.E. back to Rochford.

In the Midlands, which saw most of the enemy activity, the only defence aircraft available was a solitary Lewis-armed R.E.7 at Castle Bromwich. Burdett, CO of No.5 RAS, took off shortly after L21 began her attack on Tipton, but having arranged to inspect Birmingham's partial black-out, flew towards the city centre and thus saw nothing of the bombing in progress ten miles to the northwest.

Burdett found that while central Birmingham was adequately darkened, the suburbs and linking roads remained easily visible. Unfortunately this did not apply to the Castle Bromwich flarepath, which at the end of the sortie was hidden by mist, and the R.E.7 was wrecked in a forced landing. The crew, unhurt, had faced additional difficulty during the patrol because the R.E. had no cockpit lighting.

To acquaint higher authority with some of the problems surrounding night interception, McClelland's rather verbose report of his flight over London was forwarded to the Admiralty, ultimately reaching the desk of the Third Sea Lord, Rear-Admiral F. C. T. Tudor. He was not very impressed, and having established that there were no Zeppelins or gunfire in the London area had this to say:

> 'Night flying must be most difficult and dangerous, and require considerable nerve and pluck, but this airman seems to have been gifted with a more than usually vivid imagination'

It is perhaps as well that Their Lordships did not have a sight of Morgan's report.

Ten RNAS Nieuports from Dunkirk, patrolling off the Belgian coast to intercept any airships returning along a southerly course, also encountered weather problems. They took off 90 min before sunrise, and had Zeppelins been in the area they would have been easily spotted in the clear dawn light. Rising mist obscured the ground when the fighters returned, and only two pilots found their way back to base—one being Red Mulock, who had earlier distinguished himself at Westgate. The others came down more or less successfully on the sands—with the exception of one, hopelessly lost, who was fortunate to be picked up after ditching in the Channel nearly 100 miles southwest of Dunkirk.

9 February, 1916 (Daylight)

Targets: Broadstairs, Ramsgate.
Enemy forces: One Friedrichshafen FF 33e, one Hansa-Brandenburg NW.
Results: None killed, three injured, £305 damage.
Defence sorties: 24.

RNAS

Dover: Bristol Scout Cs 1254 (Flt Lieut F. G. Andreae) 30 min; 1260 (Flt Sub-Lieut R. F. S. Leslie) 35 min; 3039 (Flt Cdr S. V. Sippe) 30 min; 3043 (Flt Lieut H. Rosher) 60 min; Nieuport 10 3967 (Flt Lieut H. L. Wood) 95 min; FBA flying-boat 3208 (Flt Lieut T. F. N. Gerrard, Obs Sub-Lieut R. M. Inge); Short 184 8038 (Flt Sub-Lieut A. T. Cowley, AM Smith).

A W/T-equipped Friedrichshafen FF 33e, similar to those which took part in some of the early 1916 hit-and-run attacks.

Grain: Bristol Scout C 1248 took off 15.50 hr; Avro 504B 1026; Sopwith Schneider 3753 (Flt Lieut E. de C. Hallifax) 16.07–16.35 hr; FBA flying-boat 3201 (Flt Lieut B. F. Fowler, LM Temple) 16.20–17.20 hr.

Eastchurch: Nieuport 10 3964 (Flt Lieut R. G. A. Baudry) took off 15.48 hr; R. E. P. Parasol 8459 (Flt Sub-Lieut R. E. Greensmith) took off 15.48 hr.

Westgate: Bristol Scout Cs 3023 (Flt Lieut R. Y. Bush); 3027 (Flt Sub-Lieut J. A. Carr); B.E.2cs 1157 (Flt Sub-Lieut H. V. Worrall, AM Somerville); 1188 (Flt Sub-Lieut W. H. Oakey, AM H. Phipps); Short 827 3071 (Flt Sub-Lieut B. A. Millard); Sopwith Baby 8121 (Flt Sub-Lieut E. J. Burling). All airborne between 15.57 hr and 16.17 hr.

RFC

Dover: Five sorties—details not known.

Coastal defence efficiency had been questioned in Parliament following the indifferent response to the enemy's January intrusions, and reactions to this attack did little to enhance the image.

The two floatplanes—from SFA 1—approaching the North Foreland were sighted by the North Goodwin lightship at about 15.40 hr, and although reports quote conflicting times, flying stations were evidently not notified for nearly ten minutes. Dover protested that this effectively ruled out any hope of interception.

Reports also differ as to whether the aircraft remained together or divided to drop eight bombs on Ramsgate at 15.50 hr, narrowly missing a tramcar, and twelve on Broadstairs at 16.05 hr damaging a girls' school.

Brandenburg No.487 was flown by Leut Friedrich Christiansen, who ended the war as one of Germany's oustanding maritime pilots.

The official Press communiqué explained the lack of even remote contact with the enemy in these ponderous terms:

> 'Within a few minutes of the sighting of the hostile aircraft, naval and military aeroplanes went up in pursuit, but were unable to overtake them owing to the precipitous nature of their flight.'

Four fighters sent up from RNAS Dunkirk likewise saw nothing of the enemy.

20 February, 1916 (Daylight)

Targets: Lowestoft, Walmer and Channel shipping.
Enemy forces: Two Friedrichshafen FF 33es, one Hansa-Brandenburg NW.
Results: One killed, one injured, £1,168 damage.
Defence sorties: 29.

RNAS

Dover: Bristol Scout Cs 3043 (Flt Sub-Lieut R. F. S. Leslie) 10.41–12.11 hr; 3039 (Flt Lieut H. Rosher) 11.28–11.43 hr and 12.10–12.50 hr; 3045 (Flt Lieut F. G. Andreae) 11.28–12.18 hr; Nieuport 10s 3967 (Flt Lieut G. R. H. Talbot) 12.10–12.40 hr; 3165 (Flt Lieut H. L. Wood) 20 min; FBA flying-boats 3200 (Flt Sub-Lieut A. T. Cowley, AM Clarke) 11.29–12.39 hr; 3208 (Flt Sub-Lieut B. C. Tooke, AM Peagram) 11.29–11.35 hr (Ramsgate, with engine trouble).

Eastchurch: Bristol Scout C 3015 (Flt Cdr F. Fowler); Nieuport 10 3964 (Flt Sub-Lieut A. D. W. Allen); R. E. P. Parasols 8457 (Flt Sub-Lieut Wood); 8459 (Flt Sub-Lieut H. G. Brackley, AM Peachey); B.E.2c 986 (Flt Sub-Lieut

Nieuport 10 No.3165 was among the seven aircraft from RNAS Dover which unsuccessfully sought enemy raiders attacking shipping on 20 February, 1916. The pilot is unidentified.

Birkbeck, AM Briggs); Caudron G.4 3334 (Flt Sub-Lieut H. G. Henley, AM Turner). Airborne from 11.35 hr, details not known.

Grain: Bristol Scout C 1248 (Flt Lieut Walmsley) 11.30–12.40 hr; FBA flying-boat 3201 (Flt Lieut B. F. Fowler, Cpl Grant) 11.38–12.40 hr; Short 827s 3064 (Flt Lieut A. R. Arnold, PO Hodgson) 11.35–11.45 hr, returned with engine trouble; 3063 (Flt Lieut Arnold, PO Hodgson) 12.25–12.37 hr, returned with engine trouble; Sopwith Baby 8145 (Flt Lieut Arnold) 13.05–13.30 hr.

Yarmouth: Bristol Scout C 1253 (Flt Lieut V. Nicholl) took off 11.05 hr; Avro 504Cs 1467 (Flt Lieut F. G. Hards) took off 11.06 hr; 8576 (Flt Lieut C. H. C. Smith) took off 11.18 hr; 8581 (Flt Sub-Lieut E. Cadbury) took off 11.23 hr; unspecified aircraft (Flt Sub-Lieut G. W. R. Fane).

RFC

Dover: Unspecified Bristol Scout (Capt R. Balcombe-Brown) took off 11.45 hr; B.E.2cs 2577 (Capt A. S. Barratt, Lieut Young) 11.50–12.50 hr; 2582 (Lieut Turner, 2nd Lieut E. de L. le Sauvage) 11.55–12.40 hr; unspecified Martinsyde G.100s (Capt W. J. Cairns) 12.15–13.30 hr; (Maj S. Smith) 1300–14.30 hr.

Lewis-armed Avro 504C single-seater 8581 at RNAS Yarmouth, flown by Flt Sub-Lieut E. Cadbury in a belated attempt to find the enemy aircraft which bombed Lowestoft on 20 February, 1916.

The twin-engined Caudron G.4, No.3334, which operated from RNAS Eastchurch. (*RAF Museum*)

German hit-and-run raiding by the SFA 1 floatplanes assumed a more sophisticated form with these attacks on two widely-separated areas within a short space of time.

Sunday morning may have been chosen in the belief that defences would be less alert, and although the pattern of take-off times does give some support to that assumption, the total air defence response was the largest to date.

Enemy W/T transmissions—probably from a participating Friedrichshafen, No.472—intercepted by the Caister wireless station at 10.30 hr gave first indication of unusual activity, but before their significance could be assessed two floatplanes appeared over Lowestoft, at 10.55 hr, dropping nineteen bombs from 5–6,000 ft.

Five aircraft from Yarmouth—the first not airborne until ten minutes later—patrolled between Cromer and Southwold. They saw nothing, but attracted brisk fire from the AA guns on their return.

There was no warning of the Friedrichshafen which dropped six bombs on Walmer at 11.20 hr, causing the day's single death. Shortly afterwards three more bombs fell near ships south of the Kentish Knock. It was assumed that these were from a second aircraft, but the SFA 1 records show only one operating along the Kent coast that morning.

Leslie, already airborne in an RNAS Dover Bristol Scout on a routine patrol, was too far west to have any chance of intercepting. Other RNAS aircraft took off in reasonable time, but not quickly enough to see anything.

RFC Dover received no warning until 11.35 hr, with no prospects of achieving anything useful, and some of its aircraft returning from abortive searches were misreported as hostile—which in turn started stories of an aerial engagement over Deal. Altogether the confusion which prevailed until about 13.00 hr would have delighted the German planners.

The two Martinsyde Elephants which joined the search were from No.27 Squadron, then working up at Dover for transfer to the Western Front.

Chapter VIII

The Defence Awakening

Although the War Office had allowed six months for planning and preparation after provisionally agreeing to take over home defence, Kitchener's last-minute misgivings proved not entirely baseless.

Any illusions remaining after the salutary experience of 31 January, 1916, that RFC pilots could somehow succeed where the RNAS had failed were dispelled by the dismal performance against the 17 Zeppelin raids and nine hit-and-run aeroplane attacks mounted during the first six months of the new regime. One Zeppelin fell to anti-aircraft gunfire and one seaplane was shot down by an RNAS aircraft. It became clear that plans were of little avail without practical operating experience, the right weapons, and adequate fighter aircraft—for which the ever-pressing demands of the Western Front retained priority.

The Admiralty further hardened its pessimistic view about night flying against Zeppelins—apart from its cosmetic value—and the position was frankly defined by Vaughan-Lee in a memorandum of 3 March:

> '. . . everything that can possibly be done to meet the Zeppelin should be carried out so long as undue risks to personnel and material are not incurred. Moreover, as the Military are undertaking this work on a large scale, it is considered that for public opinion alone the Navy should do a certain amount.'

Nevertheless it was a period of consolidation during which useful lessons were learned. New techniques gradually emerged and, despite the seemingly endless disappointments, squadrons held to the belief that success would eventually come their way.

For the definitive long-term air defence plan GHQ Home Forces envisaged ten squadrons, each of twelve aircraft, suitably based for the defence (in priority order) of London (two squadrons), Newcastle, Leeds/Sheffield, Birmingham, Hull, Harwich/East Anglia (two squadrons), Chatham/Dover and Portsmouth/Newhaven.

An interim scheme laid down in a War Office directive of 1 March allotted additional B.E.2cs to existing units—six to No.5 RAS, Castle Bromwich (of which three, with mechanics, were to be based at Lilbourne to defend Coventry), and three each to No.9 RAS, Norwich, No.15 RAS, Doncaster, No.20 RAS, Dover and No.35 Squadron, Thetford. Although training remained the first responsibility of these units, the additional aircraft were not to be used for instruction. Two were to be regarded as 'active' (the third being a reserve) though only one might be employed on cross-country training flights. The 'active' aircraft were restricted to essential air test flights. On receipt of raid warnings, competent night pilots would be warned for duty.

The War Office accepted that operating aircraft against airships on dark nights, unassisted by searchlights, was not practical, but with lights or in clear moonlight there was some prospect of success. The B.Es were not to be employed at night against hostile aeroplanes—presumably to eliminate the risk of accidental combat between friendly machines.

Normal drill on receipt of a warning required one aircraft to take off for a two-hour patrol over its aerodrome at 8–10,000 ft. The merits of continuity advanced by Geoffrey Salmond were now accepted, and the second aircraft was to leave 90 min after the first. Sufficient warning was necessary for the defenders to reach at least 8,000 ft so that they were higher than the raiders on their arrival.

Where possible, fighters were to be employed outside anti-aircraft gun defence zones. Searchlights should not be lit until an airship was heard, and searchlight crews were to include an RFC mechanic able to distinguish between the sounds of airship and aeroplane engines. A Zeppelin caught in the beam was to be held despite the risk of dazzling any nearby fighter.

The directive reiterated that the senior RFC officer on the aerodrome, as the best judge of local conditions, would be responsible for ordering machines airborne. While every opportunity should be taken to attack airships, discretion must be exercised when the weather might prejudice successful action or prove unduly costly in lives and aircraft.

Brig-Gen John Salmond, brother of Geoffrey Salmond and OC No.5 Brigade at Birmingham, immediately queried one detail which indicated a lack of operational knowhow in those responsible for the drafting. Why, he asked, should pilots for the aircraft hangared at Lilbourne drive from Castle Bromwich if a Coventry raid threatened? Was it not more sensible for these aircraft also to operate from Castle Bromwich and use Lilbourne only as an emergency landing ground? Pilots could then be over Coventry at 9,000 ft ready for action instead of just arriving at Lilbourne after a 30-mile road journey. His suggestion was agreed forthwith.

Formation of definitive home defence squadrons—at least on paper—began surprisingly quickly. The first, No.36, had formed at Cramlington, Newcastle upon Tyne, on 1 February under the command of Capt R. O. Abercromby, from the B.E.2c detachment responsible for Tyneside defence since December 1915. It was formally designated a home defence squadron on 18 March, 1916. On the same date, No.33 Squadron at Filton, Bristol, was similarly nominated, moving to York on 6 April and taking over two flights of No.47 Squadron, which had operated from Beverley since 1 March. No.47 retained a home-defence commitment for several months thereafter, and No.33 later had detachments flying from a number of aerodromes in Yorkshire and Lincolnshire.

The London defences were again reorganized and placed under the new No.18 Wing, formed on 25 March with headquarters in Albermarle Street and commanded by Lieut-Col Fenton Vesey Holt, an Old Etonian aged 30. Holt had been flying since 1912 and, while with No.4 Squadron in January 1915, had helped to shoot down an Albatros near Dunkirk with rifle fire from a Maurice Farman Shorthorn.

On 15 April No.19 RAS became No.39 (Home Defence) Squadron, remaining under Higgins' command, and soon afterwards its scattered aircraft detachments were concentrated at Suttons Farm and Hainault Farm, with the headquarters flight staying at Hounslow. Defence of the Birmingham area remained the responsibility of No.5 RAS until No.54 Squadron took over on 15 May.

Despite their official home-defence designation, these squadrons still belonged to No.6 (Training) Brigade and were in effect under the direct operational control of the War Office. They retained certain pilot training obligations, and there was some relaxation of the recent embargo on using operational aircraft for this purpose.

The short nights of early summer caused a temporary halt in Zeppelin raiding from early May, which coincided with a reduction in coastal aeroplane attacks. This perhaps strengthened the Cabinet view that greater priority must be given to the Western Front and the planned home-defence force of ten squadrons was cut to eight. On 5 June the order of battle was:

Sqn	Base	Aircraft establishment	Strength
28	Gosport	4	2 B.E.12
	Newhaven	4	0
33	Bramham Moor	4	4 B.E.2c
	Coal Aston	4	0
	Beverley	10 (includes 2 scouts)	1 B.E.12
	Doncaster	0	1 B.E.12
36	Cramlington	10 (includes 2 scouts)	11 (3 B.E.12, 6 B.E.2c, 2 Bristol Scout)
	Turnhouse	4	0
	Seaton Carew	6	0
39	Hounslow*	0	11 (3 B.E.12, 6 B.E.2c, 2 Bristol Scout)
	Hainault Farm	8 (includes 2 scouts)	7 (2 B.E.12, 4 B.E.2c, 1 Bristol Scout)
	Suttons Farm	8 ,, ,, ,,	6 (1 B.E.12, 4 B.E.2c, 1 Bristol Scout)
	North Weald	8	0
50	Dover	6 (includes 4 scouts)	5 (3 B.E.12, 2 B.E.2c)
	Wye	6 ,, ,, ,,	0
51	Thetford	4	0
	Norwich	4	3 B.E.2c
	Narborough	4	0
52	Hounslow	0	5 (2 B.E.12, 3 B.E.2c)
	Goldhanger	8 (includes 4 scouts)	0
	Rochford	16 ,, ,, ,,	0
54	Castle Bromwich	4	4 B.E.2c
	Lilbourne	4	0
	Papplewick	4	0
	Waddington	4	0
	Total	134	Total 60

* The Hounslow flight of No.39 Squadron was scheduled to move to North Weald during August.

On the same date 271 anti-aircraft guns and 258 searchlights were available for the defence of vulnerable points, against a planned requirement of 487 and 490 respectively.

With total aircraft strength less than half the establishment, it was perhaps with some idea of compensating for the deficiency that several units were given early production models of the new B.E.12 single-seater developed from the well-tried B.E.2c. With its 150 hp RAF engine it was some 20 mph faster than the 2c, achieving 91 mph at 10,000 ft, and taking 35–40 min to reach that height—about half the time required by the older machine. It was, however, an undistinguished aircraft, sluggish in manoeuvre, and the powerful engine torque produced a marked swing to port which could involve inexperienced pilots in take-off accidents. Initially the B.E.12 carried a Lewis gun on a bracket mounting, but by mid-June the Vickers gun with interrupter gear to permit firing through the propeller arc was being fitted.

B.E.12 No.6158 of No.38 Squadron, Stamford, with full night-flying equipment. The RL tube can be seen below the pilot's cockpit.

The War Office was anxious to perpetuate the system whereby half the squadron aircraft were used for the final stages of pilot training, but on 3 June Holt reported that No.39 Squadron had been obliged to abandon this because:

> '. . . officers under instruction ill-treated the engines and upset the true-ing of the machines so that it was impossible to expect pilots to fly at night in the machines which had been used for instructional purposes by day, even though they were still serviceable.'

On 13 June Higgins handed over No.39 Squadron to Maj W. H. C. Mansfield and became Inspector of Home Defence. On 25 June the squadrons were placed under a new Home Defence Wing, with Holt still in command but divorced from No.6 (Training) Brigade and relieved of instructional duties. Formed as No.16 Wing, with headquarters at Adastral House on the Victoria Embankment in London, the number was dropped on 29 July.

Meanwhile the Army Council had decided that growing overseas demands made it impossible at that time to proceed with more than six home-defence squadrons. Formally promulgated to GHQ Home Forces on 11 July, this further reduction removed Nos.28 and 52 Squadrons from the earlier order of battle, though it was agreed that Nos.37, 75, 76 and 77 Squadrons due to emerge later in the year would be allocated for home defence. No.38 Squadron began to form at Castle Bromwich under Capt A. T. Harris to take the place of No.54.

The lack of success during the spring had shaken Henderson's faith in aeroplanes to the extent of admitting to the Air Board that their value at night was somewhat problematical. He had, however, always envisaged a more flexible defence system, with fighters patrolling the Zeppelins' probable lines of approach, and welcomed what he felt was only a temporary respite from night raiding as a breathing space in which to mould his slender resources into a more effective organization. The principal architect was Brig-Gen W. Sefton Brancker, Director of Air Organization, ably assisted by Holt and the GHQ Home Forces operations staff.

Old notions dating from the early raids were thrown overboard and a new scheme produced taking advantage of the improved aircraft and accumulated experience now available. It received War Office blessing and was approved at a GHQ Home Forces/War Office conference on 14 July.

In the belief that navigation difficulties and the forced landing risk must limit pilots to patrolling the base of an inverted cone centred over their own aerodromes, and that chasing Zeppelins at night was impossible, fighters had hitherto been disposed for the close protection of vulnerable areas. Several aerodromes proved unsuitable because of terrain or local weather problems, and the scheme was wasteful since the aircraft were employed only against an immediate threat to a particular area. Some were based so far west as to enjoy little action, and there were gaps in the cover provided.

It was now realized—as claimed by far-sighted officers from the beginning—that night navigation held no particular terrors, and pilots were landing successfully on quite unfamiliar aerodromes. There were now 96 night landing grounds available. Without searchlight assistance airships were certainly difficult to locate, but once found and the range closed to about 2,000 ft they could be chased—and attacked.

The conference report included one confident technical prediction which remained unfulfilled—'it is certain that within six months chasing machines will carry powerful searchlights and should then be independent of ground searchlights'.

The new scheme proposed a 'barrage line' of night-flying bases and searchlights situated approximately 30 miles inside the coastal observer cordon so that fighters could attain at least 5,000 ft in readiness to intercept airships flying inland. All flights would thus be more fully occupied, and in reasonable weather might prevent the enemy from crossing the line. Fighters would also be better placed to intercept aeroplane raids, regarded as a certainty in the near future. The first step was to redeploy further east the existing flights near Birmingham, Leeds and

B.E.12 with synchronized Vickers gun. (*J. M. Bruce/G. S. Leslie collection*)

Sheffield. It was appreciated that the complete scheme would be costly, and in fact it was never fully implemented.

The B.E.2cs were intended for night operations against airships, leaving a handful of Bristol Scouts scattered among the squadrons as the main defence against day raiders. The B.E.12 was regarded as a day and night fighter, and squadron commanders had discretion to switch aircraft roles in emergency—'provided that none but stable machines are flown at night'. Units were again reminded that no attempt should be made to attack hostile aeroplanes during darkness.

Minuting a memorandum on the new scheme to the Air Board, its assistant secretary, Wing Cdr R. M. Groves, commented with devastating frankness—'the majority of the aeroplanes would be of little use in the case of a day attack by heavier-than-air craft, but the B.E.12s and the Scouts could put up a good fight'.

During 1916 several ingenious naval anti-Zeppelin projects emerged. The A.P.1 'Airship-Plane', a B.E.2c slung beneath an SS-type airship envelope, was devised by Wing Cdr N. F. Usborne and Flt Cdr de Courcy W. P. Ireland. The intention was that the airship element would sustain the aeroplane aloft in the Zeppelin approach lanes. On sighting the enemy the B.E. would cast off and make its attack. Initial tests in August 1915 showed a need for some modifications, but the first release trial on 21 February, 1916, at Kingsnorth ended in disaster. The B.E. released prematurely and crashed, killing Usborne and Ireland.

Another bold idea for carrying a fighter into the Zeppelin lanes far beyond its normal range was the attachment of a Bristol Scout to the upper wing of a three-engined Porte Baby flying-boat. A trial launching off Felixstowe on 17 May, 1916, with Flt Lieut M. J. Day flying the Bristol, was completely successful, but the project was not developed further, possibly because surface aircraft carriers held greater promise.

Academic aspects were explored in a second night-flying report by the Board of Inventions and Research aeroplanes sub-committee, published on 13 July. This included contributions from Sqn Cdr John Babington and Frederick W. Lanchester, a leading aerodynamicist. Babington listed essential requirements

The Bristol Scout/Porte Baby combination at RNAS Felixstowe.

for night-flying aircraft as:– inherent stability, durability, engine reliability, good vision for the crew, slow landing speed, fast rate of climb, silence, and a rugged undercarriage—preferably of the four-wheeled type. Of existing aircraft he favoured the B.E.2c because of its stability, though it suffered the disadvantage of a tractor propeller and rather restricted view.

Lanchester expounded the virtues of inherent stability thus:

> 'It is well known by night pilots that once vision of terrestial objects is lost it is extremely difficult and requires much undivided attention . . . to maintain a constant course, either in the vertical plane or in the horizontal plane. Thus it has been a frequent experience of pilots (even in day time) emerging from clouds to find that they are flying nearly vertically downwards, when they imagined they were flying on an ordinary course. An inherently stable machine has a sense of its own as to its direction in the vertical plane of flight which no pilot, however expert, has ever been able to attain.'

This report prompted an apprehensive minute from Lord Sydenham, a member of the Air Board, who foresaw demands for specialized night-flying aircraft with consequent expense and complication. But he ended on a self-comforting note—'air fighting at night is never likely to assume real importance'.

Sydenham's anxieties were unfounded, for although the report contained some wisdom it did not impress the home-defence squadron commanders. Maj H. Wyllie, No.51 Squadron, vigorously rebutted Lanchester's dictum on disorientation. 'This is not the case' he wrote. 'Your engine, your rigging and your compass are all trying to tell you what is wrong.' Wyllie considered the conventional V undercarriage quite adequate if the pilot was of average ability—'if he isn't and lands ten feet above the ground, or flies straight into it, the result will be the same irrespective of the type of undercarriage' he declared.

Wyllie claimed that a properly rigged F.E.2b was more stable than a B.E.2c and did not require the rudder bar pressure which was necessary in most tractor aircraft. The unconscious relaxation of this pressure in the absence of any horizon was a likely cause of night accidents, he suggested. Furthermore when pusher aircraft did crash the occupants were, with luck, thrown clear, and in five recent F.E.2b accidents pilots had escaped with a shaking.

The CO of No.50 Squadron, Maj M. G. Christie, thought that inherent stability was unnecessary on clear nights with a quarter or more of moon. Flight commander Capt John Sowrey considered it more important to design an aircraft which was directionally stable with engine on as well as off. It was, he said, a well-known property of the B.E.2c—and even more marked in the B.E.12—to gradually swing round to the left if the feet were removed from the rudder bar. Sowrey also advocated the development of air-brakes to permit a steep descent without gaining excessive speed.

Malcolm Christie was responsible for the first specialized colour scheme for night fighters. During August he black-doped all his B.Es, explaining to the Dover Garrison Commander that this was partly for invisibility but mainly to prevent pilots from being blinded when using their wingtip landing flares. To help identify these sinister black aircraft as friendly during day training flights, white rings the same size as the outer blue of the national roundels were painted on the upper and lower wing surfaces. GHQ Home Forces approved the scheme and promulgated it for adoption by all 'black-winged night flying machines' on 29

The skull and crossbones device adopted by No.50 Squadron was a natural follow-up of the black colour scheme. It is shown here on a crashed B.E.2e at Detling in 1917.

August. Many months passed before it was appreciated that the white circles did much to destroy the desired invisibility.

A major problem facing the defending pilots was actual location of the enemy—whose broad movements could normally be plotted from the ground by the engine sounds. Searchlights were of small value on cloudy nights, and in bright moonlight the operators had difficulty in pin-pointing airships. Henderson hoped that wireless telegraphy could help solve the problem, but the sorry tale of the 1916 trials is told in a later chapter.

In the absence of wireless some visual ground signalling system was essential. As early as January 1915, Lieut H. Ingram, First Lieutenant at RNAS Westgate, devised a practical method using cloth strips but this was apparently ignored or pigeon-holed by higher authority, for six months later Capt Murray Sueter at the Admiralty Air Department was advocating adoption of a more primitive French system using a gigantic arrow, 200 yards long and 50 yards wide made up of fabric strips, to point in the direction of the enemy. As more up-to-date information was received, the arrow's bearing was laboriously altered.

In July 1916 direction signals based on the clock face, with the hour hand pointing to the reported direction of enemy aircraft, were in use near the North Foreland lighthouse.

During the summer the versatile and simple Ingram system was adopted by the RNAS, and on 25 November by the RFC for home-defence aerodromes. The central feature of each message was the letter T, its head measuring 20 ft by 4 ft and the tail 40 ft by 4 ft. Up to three 8-ft diameter discs could be placed adjacently in 40 different positions, each conveying a specific message. For example there were patterns instructing pilots to search for enemy aircraft in 25 defined locations in southeast England and adjacent sea areas. The signals were designed to be legible from heights up to 14,000 ft, but in exceptionally clear weather they could be read from about 17,000 ft.

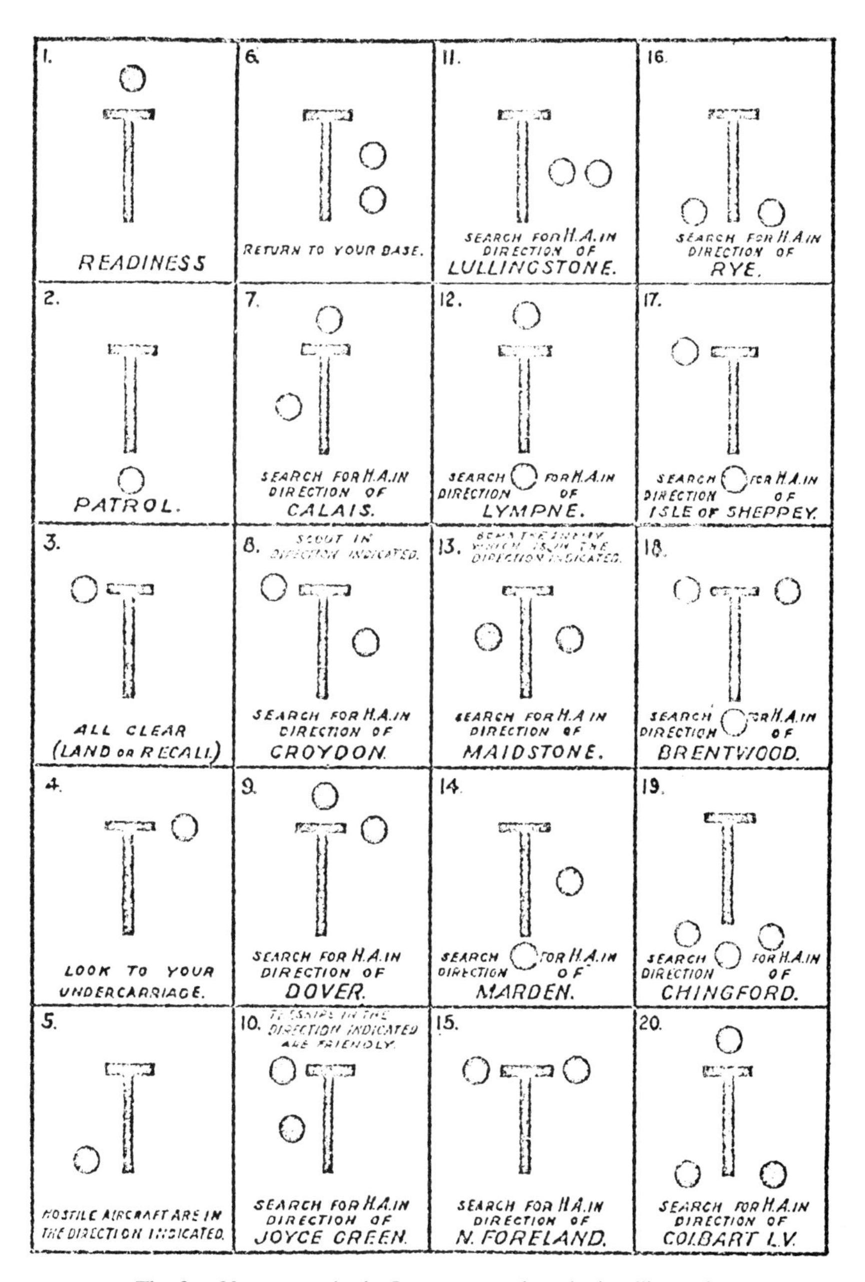

The first 20 messages in the Ingram ground-to-air signalling code.

To assist pilots at night, GHQ Home Forces asked the War Office in March 1916 for star shells, as used by French gunners to indicate the position of—and it was claimed, illuminate—enemy airships. The War Office possessed none, but after six months of prodding persuaded the Ministry of Munitions to start a design. There is no evidence that French assistance was sought and it was not until early 1918, after numerous delays and failures, that a production star shell was issued. It contained a small parachute flare which gave a brilliant light for 10–20 seconds, and, although no enemy target was ever thus illuminated, it was useful for indicating the whereabouts of the enemy and as a recall signal.

Meanwhile research continued into the fundamental matter of destroying the Zeppelin once the fighter had made contact. On the basis that so vast a target was most easily attacked from above, one promising weapon ordered for general use was the Ranken dart, an ingenious device which never really fulfilled the hopes of its inventor, Engineer Lieutenant Francis Ranken. Weighing about 1 lb, it was an iron-pointed metal tube containing high explosive and black powder. The tail unit embodied spring-loaded vanes which opened and locked into position when they engaged the airship's envelope, after the head had penetrated inside, and at the same time activated a detonator rod. The sparks produced by the black powder were intended to assist the high explosive in igniting hydrogen released from the ruptured gas cells.

Several problems emerged during trials—in particular the darts toppled badly on release—and various fin patterns, parachute devices and launching methods were tried. Eventually the protective rubber tail cap was adapted to serve as a stabilizing parachute, and the best launching method was found to be from a box angled at 40–45 deg to the rear. This normally held 24 darts, which could be released together or in small groups, from 150–700 ft above the target, preferably from the middle of the range. Chances of a hit were improved by flying at an angle of about 20 deg to the fore and aft axis of the airship.

Initially an RNAS weapon, first reported in action on 1 February, 1916, the Ranken dart was also adopted by the RFC. A 5 lb version and a purely incendiary model were developed but not adopted for service.

The principal alternative armament for home-defence aircraft remained the small bomb—the 20 lb Hale and the 16 lb incendiary designed at the Royal Laboratory, Woolwich.

Surprisingly the Fiery Grapnel—now in a Mk 2 version—was still on the armament inventory. A two-grapnel installation was found to reduce a B.E.2c's speed by only one mph and climb by some 40 ft a minute—though another 1½ mph was lost when the right-hand grapnel was lowered for engagement. After successful trials at the Central Flying School against a balloon, the attack method recommended was to approach the Zeppelin from right angles at 85 mph—with the grapnel trailing 140 ft below and 190 ft behind—until reaching close quarters, then to leap over the intended victim and allow the weapon to engage. During May 1916 the offer of two pairs of grapnels for use on the Western Front was gracefully declined by RFC Headquarters.

The Admiralty had much faith in the Davis gun, invented in 1911 by Cdr Cleland Davis, United States Navy. Its attraction as an aircraft weapon was the lack of recoil, allowing a large-calibre shell to be fired without damage to the aircraft structure. The recoil was absorbed by a quantity of lead shot discharged from the rear of the gun. By 1915, 2 lb, 6 lb and 12 lb versions were in production, and the first British test firing of a six-pounder was made from a Short S.81 seaplane on 13 April. After further trials a substantial number was ordered, and

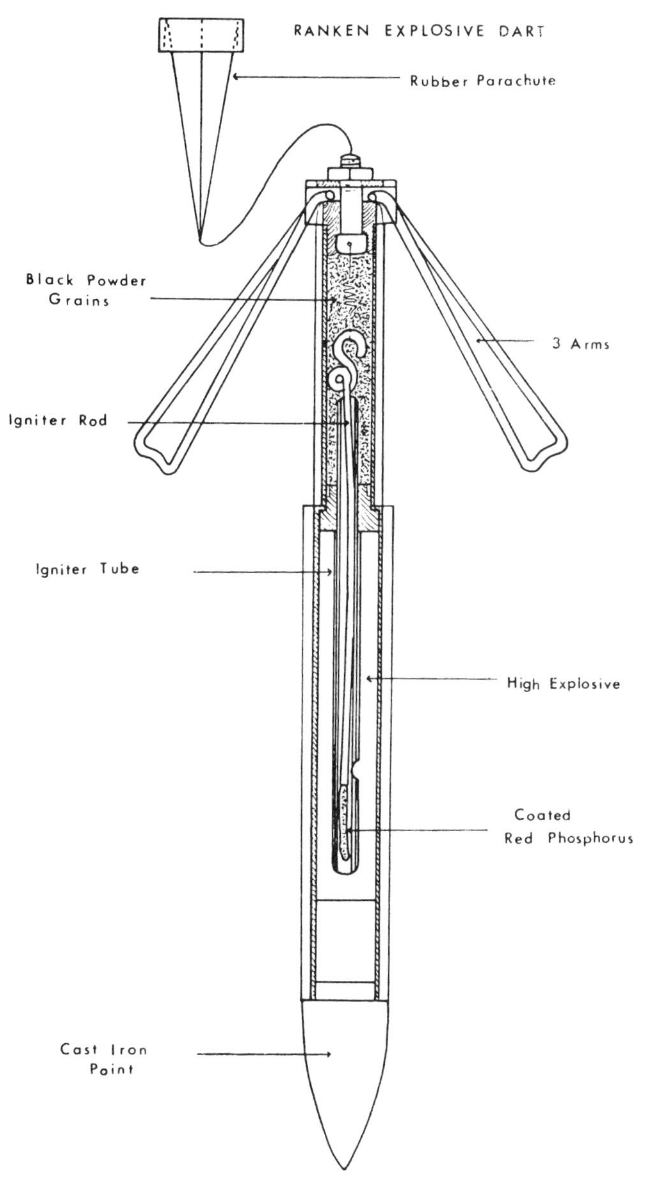

Cross-section diagram of the Ranken dart. (*Cross & Cockade GB*)

on 3 February, 1916, an Admiralty technical committee decided that the weapon was sufficiently promising to justify development of a special anti-Zeppelin aircraft to carry it. The committee felt that with machine-guns being 'practically useless' until suitable ammunition was perfected, the Davis would be more effective than anything else in prospect.

A few weeks later armament expert Flt Cdr C. R. Finch-Noyes proposed to the Admiralty that the 35 guns already available to the RNAS be fitted in Short 225 seaplanes to maintain standing patrols over airship approach routes. He claimed that the guns could be mounted and the scheme made fully operational ten days from the go-ahead order. There is no evidence that this proposal was taken very seriously. Although the Davis was claimed to be very accurate up to ranges of 2,000 yards, the prospect of the cumbersome Shorts attaining striking distance of Zeppelins was clearly remote.

The War Office began to show interest in early 1916 when trials were sufficiently encouraging to justify the order of experimental mountings from several aircraft manufacturers. However, eventual success with the machine-gun made the Davis superfluous in the anti-Zeppelin role, and none of the specialist aircraft progressed beyond the prototype stage.

Up to this time the machine-gun had been regarded essentially as a weapon capable of causing such hydrogen losses from punctured gas cells as to gravely prejudice an airship's chances of safely returning to base, while bombs and darts were thought more likely to inflict immediately crippling damage and destruction. It had become increasingly clear, however, that well-handled airships easily outclimbed the British fighters, which were therefore seldom able to position for attack from above. In any case the Zeppelins were much more difficult to distinguish against the darkened countryside than silhouetted in the sky above.

Fiery Grapnel fitted to a B.E.2c at the Royal Aircraft Factory, Farnborough. (*RAE*)

The Robey-Peters RRF 25, one of the prototypes built to meet Admiralty requirements for an anti-Zeppelin aircraft armed with the Davis gun. Development of such machines was shelved after it had been demonstrated that conventional aircraft using improved ·303 machine-gun ammunition could destroy airships. (*J. M. Bruce/G. S. Leslie collection*)

This rather belated recognition of the logic in machine-gun attack from below stimulated work on specialized anti-airship ammunition, which had made only desultory progress since the start of the war, possibly because of doubts whether it would be acceptable under the terms of the Hague Convention. However, on 12 April, 1916, a War Office letter to No.6 Brigade contained a significant item—' . . . it is proposed to issue shortly an explosive bullet for use against Zeppelins'.

John Pomeroy, of Invercargill, New Zealand, had invented an explosive bullet which he demonstrated to armament specialists of HMS *Encounter*, which visited Auckland in August 1908. But nothing transpired, nor was any serious interest apparent when he formally offered his bullet to the British Government in 1914. After the start of the Zeppelin raids he visited England to try again, travelling via America, where a demonstration at Fort Ben Harrison resulted in a recommendation for its adoption by the US Chief of Ordnance.

Demonstrations at Fort Grange (Gosport) and Upavon in June 1915 failed to convince the British authorities, and according to Pomeroy's postwar account, it was only after he had written to Lloyd George in January 1916 that the Munitions Inventions Department agreed to sponsor development.

Eventually, after RFC trials at the Machine Gun School, Hythe, on 20 May, 1916, an initial batch was ordered. Although early specimens tended to burst prematurely, a 500,000-round order for a development version was placed in August.

A homely touch to the story was Pomeroy's claim that the first 5,000 bullets for the RFC were made by his wife in a top floor room at Home Defence Wing headquarters, Adastral House in London.

As well as old aeroplane wings the test targets included Zeppelinettes, which were double cubes of rubberised fabric. The outer 8-ft cube enclosed an inner one of about 6 ft containing hydrogen. The space between cubes was filled with petrol engine exhaust gas, simulating the fire protection which British authorities had since prewar days stubbornly and wrongly believed was incorporated in Zeppelin construction.

The Admiralty had displayed more interest in an explosive bullet—initially known as the BIK—designed early in 1915 by Flt Lieut F. A. Brock, of the famous fireworks firm, who was serving in naval intelligence. (He was killed during the historic Zeebrugge operation in April 1918, seeking information about a new German rangefinder.)

Trials against a balloon in October 1915 were encouraging. The range of the bullet was increased to 800 yards, and after further tests on 14 February, 1916—during which a Zeppelinette protected by exhaust gas was ignited by the seventh Brock bullet fired from a Lewis gun—the Admiralty placed an order. RFC trials on 29 April, while less convincing, were good enough to justify the placing of a 500,000-round order on 15 May. Some rounds from a trials batch had already been issued, and the first were reported in use by No.39 Squadron on 25 April.

Work on a phosphorus incendiary bullet was initiated by a Coventry engineer, J. F. Buckingham. In April 1915 he demonstrated to the RNAS a ·45-inch bullet which ignited a balloon from 400 yards, and in October the performance of a ·303 trials version led to an Admiralty production order, first deliveries being made in December. It was tested, with the Brock, by the RFC in April 1916, and while it failed to ignite a Zeppelinette protected with exhaust gas it was nevertheless judged worthy of an initial production order. Further orders followed after modifications had improved performance.

All these bullets were somewhat erratic in behaviour, and no single type promised the immediate destruction of a Zeppelin. But their combined effects seemed likely to inflict very considerable damage.

The Ministry of Munitions also revived research on tracer bullets, which had lapsed after the unsuccessful performance of an example designed by the Royal Laboratory early in the war. Work was resumed in the factory of Messrs Aerators (who made the Sparklet soda water syphon) and in June 1916 an effective bullet was evolved. Formally designated the SPK, it was inevitably known as the Sparklet.

Early in June GHQ Home Forces issued this recommended scale of armament for home defence aircraft:

B.E.2c flown as a single-seater. 4 HE bombs or 1 box of Ranken darts, 1 Lewis gun mounted to fire upwards through the top-wing trailing edge cut-out and 3–5 drums of ammunition.

B.E.12 1 box of Ranken darts, 1 Lewis gun with 3–5 drums of ammunition, 10 Le Prieur rockets.

F.E.2b two-seater (entering service in No.51 Squadron). 4 HE bombs or 1 box of Ranken darts, 1 Lewis gun for the observer with at least 7 drums of ammunition.

Le Prieur rockets, a French invention, were mounted on the outer interplane struts and fired electrically. They proved effective against observation balloons on the Western Front but were never actually fired on home-defence operations. All aircraft were to be equipped with wingtip landing flares, compass light, navigation lights and luminous instruments. Parachute flares were an optional extra, and a footnote advised that landing searchlights, one per aircraft, would be issued shortly.

A significant change resulted from a Home Defence Wing conference attended by squadron commanders on 29 June. After considering encouraging progress reports on the new ammunition it was agreed that bombs might be discarded, and reliance placed on the machine-gun, Ranken darts and Le Prieur rockets.

The resumption of airship raiding on 28/29 July after the early summer lull saw the introduction of the larger and more powerful R-class Zeppelin. Nearly 650 ft long and with a capacity of 1,949,600 cu ft, it was powered by six 240 hp HSLu engines. Maximum bomb load was 9,250 lb, but on operations the average was

B.E.12 with Lewis gun and Le Prieur rocket rails. The mouth of the internally installed RL tube can just be seen protruding beneath the fuselage in line with the position of the pilot's feet.

about 6,600 lb. Despite increased power and better streamlining, speed was only 62–63 mph, and with an operating height of 11,500—13,000 ft—little greater than the earlier types—the so-called 'super Zeppelins' in fact presented no additional difficulties for the defences. Von Buttlar had taken over the first, L30, on 30 May and Mathy the L31 on 14 July.

During the next eleven days there were four raids involving 29 Zeppelin incursions but only three abortive attacks by defence aircraft—one being an RNAS Bristol Scout from HMS *Vindex* on 2 August. *Vindex*, converted from the 2,900-ton passenger vessel *Viking*, was the first aircraft carrier with a flying-off deck, from which the initial successful ascent had been achieved in November 1915. She could accommodate two Bristol Scouts—whose pilots were obliged to ditch their aircraft after missions—and five seaplanes. Since commissioning she had taken part in various North Sea operations, and from the end of July was on anti-Zeppelin standby at Harwich.

On 9 August the Third Sea Lord, Rear-Admiral Tudor, minuted the Director of Air Services about the lack of effective anti-Zeppelin aircraft and rather unfairly criticized station commanders for failing to employ what they did possess to the best advantage. It was hardly surprising, he wrote, that a B.E.2c loaded with machine-gun, darts, and bombs, could not get above a Zeppelin, and the

L30, first of the R-class 'super Zeppelins'.

need was for a machine, armed with a one- or two-pounder gun, which could outclimb and outpace the airships.

On 11 August he chaired an Admiralty conference to review the position and a week later held a further meeting attended by RNAS officers with recent first-hand home-defence experience. Discussion ranged over every aspect, and no two pilots present could agree on the best armament up to a practical weight limit of 100 lb. They felt that more experience of all weapons was needed. Trials of Le Prieur rockets had been disappointing (it was suspected that the test batch was damp) and their installation imposed a serious performance penalty—a loss of 6–7 knots on a Sopwith Baby seaplane. It was reported that a B.E.2c was being experimentally fitted with a 2 lb Davis gun, while a 6 lb revolver-barrelled gun was under development by the Elswick Ordnance Company.

The naval thinking on home defence seemed lacking in clarity and sense of purpose, and the conclusion reached at this gathering contrasted with the more realistic views of the RFC. The Admiralty felt that existing aircraft could be most effectively armed by light bombs, rockets and darts. They still believed that the bomb offered the best prospects of success—as demonstrated by Warneford and Bigsworth in 1915—and also advocated development of a downward-firing gun. The RFC in contrast had already abandoned the bomb and switched its faith to the machine-gun—firing upwards since airships were most easily attacked from underneath.

There were two more raids towards the end of August, producing five airship sightings and one unsuccessful attack, and on 1 September in a mood of near desperation the Air Board discussed the apparently insuperable difficulties in destroying a fragile and highly inflammable object, nearly as big as the *Lusitania*, arrogantly cruising at 60 mph two or three miles above Britain.

There was gloomy talk about the 'failure' of the new ammunition, and it was suggested that the Brock and Buckingham bullets were being extinguished by the sheer volume of hydrogen pouring from airships' gas cells torn by hits. It emerged that the RNAS preferred the Brock while the RFC favoured the Pomeroy—though the ·303 calibre was considered too small and its explosive properties possibly affected by the low temperatures around 10,000 ft. It was proposed to test ·45 Pomeroy bullets in old-pattern Maxim guns, ten of which were ready for

The aircraft carrier HMS *Vindex*, with a Bristol Scout on the flying-off platform forward of the masts and a Sopwith Schneider aft of the hangar. (*J. M. Bruce/G. S. Leslie collection*)

An F.E.2b modified to carry the Vickers 1 lb 'pom-pom' and a CFS landing searchlight. Five F.Es thus armed were reported to be with No.51 Squadron in March 1917, but their serial numbers are not known. The gun was of 1·59-in calibre, fed by a 40-round belt.

installation in F.E.2bs. Five other F.Es were to be fitted with 1 lb Vickers guns, and the firm was also producing an improved breech mechanism for the Davis gun to make it operable by the pilot instead of the hitherto necessary passenger. It was planned to develop an improved 5 lb Ranken dart, carried in boxes of six, to replace the so far unsuccessful 1 lb model.

Not discussed at this meeting was a dramatic proposal received a few days earlier, which indicated the desperate remedies being considered against the seemingly invulnerable airships. E. R. Calthrop, the pioneer parachute designer, suggested that a fighter pilot should aim his aircraft directly at the Zeppelin and jump with a parachute just before the moment of impact. Capt Sir Bryan Leighton, RFC, was ready to attempt this and had made a preparatory training jump. Calthrop was well known to the War Office for what some considered his eccentric proposal that all aircrew should have parachutes to escape from crippled aircraft, and predictably this more bizarre idea was turned down.

Henderson stoutly resisted the growing air of pessimism which greeted the approach of autumn, and rightly felt that Holt's organization required more time and experience before being condemned as ineffectual. Squadron morale remained high, and in their increasing exasperation over the feeble climbing capabilities of the B.E.2c the pilots began to evolve their own methods to meet the situation.

Chapter IX

Operations—March to August 1916

1 March, 1916 (Daylight)

Target: Margate.
Enemy force: One Friedrichshafen FF 29.
Results: One killed, none injured, £497 damage.
Defence sorties: None.

This attack resulted in the loss of one of SFA 1's oldest FF 29s—No.201—which dropped seven bombs in the Kingsgate–Cliftonville area between 18.10 and 18.22 hr.

The CO of RNAS Westgate decided that pursuit in the gathering darkness would be fruitless, but as the floatplane flew home across the North Sea it was damaged by fire from patrol boats and came down near the Middelkerk Bank. The observer was drowned and the pilot taken prisoner.

5/6 March, 1916 (Night)

Targets: Tyne/Tees, Rosyth.
Enemy forces: Navy Zeppelins L11 (Kvtkpt Viktor Schütze), L13 (Kptlt H. Mathy), L14 (Kptlt A. Böcker).
Results: 18 killed, 52 injured, £25,005 damage.
Defence sorties: One.

RNAS
Eastchurch: B.E.2c 987 (Flt Sub-Lieut C. C. Wyllie) 01.47–02.32 hr.

With the latest Zeppelins temporarily out of service for modifications to improve the reliability of their new HSLu engines, this intended raid against British naval installations by three older airships was planned to co-ordinate with German fleet operations.

In the event the airships were delayed by unforecast northwesterly winds of up to 50 mph, with heavy snowfalls, and by 17.00 hr their commanders abandoned ideas of reaching Rosyth and headed for more southerly targets.

L14 made landfall north of Flamborough Head at 22.30 hr, and after dropping six bombs near Beverley, eventually located the Humber and bombed Hull soon after midnight. L11 crossed near Withernsea at 21.45 hr and wandered over Yorkshire and Lincolnshire, lost in heavy snowstorms, until a clearance revealed the unfortunate city of Hull, which was bombed at 01.00 hr.

Despite an engine failure over the North Sea, Mathy in L13 made good time and crossed the Humber at 21.15 hr. The airship was flying blind through snowstorms, and strong winds made navigation a nightmare. He pressed on to Newark, then southeastwards, dropping bombs at intervals until 01.10 hr, when a break revealed a substantial estuary. Mathy was astonished to discover that this was the Thames, placing him some 150 miles south of his estimated position. L13 was attacked by the Sheerness guns and made three unsuccessful attempts to find targets for the remaining bombs, eventually flying south to depart at 02.20 hr.

Most of the night's casualties were in Hull, where the continued absence of anti-aircraft guns caused bitter indignation. Bad weather ruled out operations from northern aerodromes, though in any case No.47 Squadron, nominally formed at Beverley four days earlier, is unlikely to have been ready for effective action.

London area aerodromes went on standby at 00.50 hr as L13 flew south, but all except Eastchurch were affected by heavy snowfalls—and that station received no warning until the Zeppelin was almost overhead and under AA fire. Wyllie climbed his B.E. to 7,000 ft, following the shell bursts, but L13 was not picked up by searchlights and he failed to find her. At Dover, which had 15 minutes' warning, conditions were unfit for flying.

19 March, 1916 (Daylight)

Targets: Dover, Deal, Ramsgate.
Enemy forces: Four Friedrichshafen FF 33b-f, one Hansa-Brandenburg NW, one Gotha Ursinus W.D.
Results: 14 killed, 26 injured, £3,809 damage.
Defence sorties: 30.

RNAS

Dover: Bristol Scout Cs 3039 (Flt Lieut G. R. H. Talbot) 13.52–14.02 hr, forced landed; 3043 (Flt Sub-Lieut R. F. S. Leslie) 13.53–15.25 hr (Dunkirk); Nieuport 10s 3968 (Flt Sub-Lieut F. C. C. Calder) 13.55–14.56 hr; 3967 (Flt Sub-Lieut C. A. Eyre) 14.09–14.26 hr; B.E.2c 998 (Flt Sub-Lieut J. P. Coleman)

Friedrichshafen FF 33fs were in the mixed force attacking Kent coastal towns on 19 March, 1916.

Gotha Ursinus WD No.120 which took part in the 19 March raid. Despite its unconventional design, it was apparently unnoticed by any of the British pilots airborne that afternoon. (*H. J. Nowarra*)

14.05–14.52 hr; Breguet 1394 (Flt Sub-Lieut S. Cotton, Flt Sub-Lieut R. Soar), 14.02–14.12 hr, returned with engine trouble; FBA flying-boats 3204 (Flt Lieut J. B. P. Ferrand, AM Fanshawe) took off 13.55 hr, forced alighted with engine trouble, towed to Westgate; 3208 (Flt Sub-Lieut G. G. Hodge, AM Manning) 14.05–14.50 hr and 14.55–16.30 hr; Short 830 1335 (Flt Sub-Lieut F. J. Bailey, AM Smith) 14.15–17.10 hr.

Eastchurch: Bristol Scout C 3015 (Flt Sub-Lieut C. Perrett); Caudron G.4 3334 (Flt Lieut F. T. Digby, PO Smale); R. E. P. Parasol 8457 (Flt Sub-Lieut R. J. O. Compston); no times available.

Grain: Bristol Scout C 1248 (Flt Lieut P. Legh) 14.30–15.30 hr; Avro 504B 1026 (Flt Lieut E. de C. Hallifax, Cpl Grant) 14.55–15.20 hr; Sopwith Baby 8143 (Flt Cdr H. M. Cave-Browne-Cave)14.25–15.15 hr; FBA flying-boat 3206 (Flt Lieut B. F. Fowler, Lieut West) 15.00–15.45 hr.

RNAS Westgate B.E.2c No.1159, flown by Flt Lieut H. A. Buss during the attack of 19 March, 1916. The Lewis gun was fixed, accepting the risk of some bullets striking the propeller.

Westgate: Bristol Scout Cs 3023 (Flt Sub-Lieut J. S. Browne) 14.10–14.40 hr; unspecified (Flt Sub-Lieut J. A. Carr) 14.10–14.40 hr; B.E.2cs 1157 (Flt Sub-Lieut E. E. Deans, LM R. Frater) 13.55–14.40 hr; 1159 (Flt Lieut H. A. Buss, AM Speck) 13.55–14.35 hr; 1159 (Flt Sub-Lieut Deans. AM H. Phipps); 1188 (Flt Lieut F. M. L. Barr, LM Frater) times not known; Sopwith Schneider 3761 (Flt Sub-Lieut B. A. Millard) times not known; Short 827 3068 (Flt Sub-Lieut Millard, CPO Boyle) 17.30–18.40 hr; Detling aircraft: Nieuport 10 3964 (Flt Cdr R. J. Bone) 14.10–15.30 hr.

RFC

Dover: B.E.2b 2888 took off 14.05 hr; B.E.2cs 2577 and 2582 took off 14.00 hr.

Lympne: F.E.2b, unspecified (2nd Lieut R. Collis, Flt Sgt A. C. Emery) took off 13.30 hr, landed in France.

Bristol Scout C 3015 before delivery to the RNAS. In more warlike condition it was flown by Flt Sub-Lieut C. Perrett, from Eastchurch, during the 19 March 'air battle'.

This biggest hit-and-run coastal raid to date, mounted on a Sunday like three lesser attacks earlier in the year, suggests that after eighteen months of war See Flieger Abteilung 1 still believed that weekend operations were less susceptible to British interference.

However, the pattern had not gone unnoticed and there was sharp reaction to a two-pronged attack planned and led by the Zeebrugge station commander, Oberleutnant-zur-See von Tschirschky und Bogendorff. Temporarily prevented from piloting for medical reasons, he flew in Christiansen's Hansa-Brandenburg NW, No.521, as observer. His machine and another were forced down at sea after combats, both narrowly escaping destruction. With the skies full of aircraft, hostile and friendly, this first action to merit the popular description of an 'air battle' offered excellent Sunday afternoon entertainment for residents and holidaymakers, who gathered at the best vantage points regardless of possible danger.

At 13.50 hr three enemy floatplanes approached Dover at 5–6,000 ft and bombed the town for five minutes before flying northeast to attack Deal. Twenty-four bombs were plotted in Dover and nine in Deal—though the Germans claimed to have dropped over twice that number. At 14.10 hr three more raiders came in to drop fifteen bombs on Ramsgate and Margate.

From RNAS Dover three fighters were airborne within five minutes of the warning, though Talbot's Bristol Scout suffered engine failure shortly after take-off and was badly damaged in a forced landing. Leslie in another Scout gradually overhauled a raider returning across the Channel, but it was still 2,000 ft higher and outside the field covered by his fixed Lewis gun. He eventually managed to zoom up and fire a six-round burst, which caused no damage. Short of fuel, he landed at Dunkirk.

Eyre's Nieuport was in a meadow at St Margaret's, where fitters were completing engine repairs after a forced landing the previous day. The pilot rushed from Dover in a car, ran across adjacent fields and was airborne 19 min after the alarm. Coleman struggled along behind one raider for 20 min, but it outpaced his B.E.2c and he abandoned pursuit at 6,600 ft. Hodge in an FBA flying-boat also gave up his hopeless chase of another. There was a touch of farce in the attempt by Sidney Cotton and Reg Soar to bring their cumbersome 225 hp Breguet de Chasse into action. Only after their third forced landing in less than ten minutes did they give up.

None of the aircraft from RFC Dover even saw the enemy. The station received no warning and its first intimation of a raid was the sound of bombs exploding in the town.

Short 830 No.1335 was among the aircraft despatched by RNAS Dover against the 19 March attacks.

The Westgate CO, Sqn Cdr R. Peel Ross, despatched two B.E.2cs to patrol on learning of the Dover attack, but held his faster aircraft to await developments. At 14.10 hr the Margate raid warning was telephoned simultaneously with the station's own sighting, and two Bristols and a Nieuport took off immediately.

This Nieuport was strictly a poacher, but since its pilot was Flt Cdr Bone, CO of RNAS Detling 30 miles to the west, Peel Ross took a charitable view. Reginald Bone, a former submariner who had been flying since 1913, predicted with uncanny accuracy that the Germans would choose to disturb the post-prandial calm of this particular Sunday, so, armed with coffee, sandwiches and a full load of ammunition, he had flown off to picnic at Westgate.

Bone spotted one of the enemy soon after he was airborne and followed it towards the Belgian coast, gradually closing the distance. After a concentrated 40-min chase he reached 9,000 ft—about 2,000 ft above the seaplane—and made a diving attack from the rear, being greeted by a spirited burst from the observer. He banked steeply and made a second pass, apparently wounding the observer, then closed to 20 ft firing several six-round bursts which sent the machine into a steep dive, with propeller stopped and engine smoking.

Nieuport 10 No.3964, flown by Flt Cdr Bone. The pilot in this photograph is not identified. (*RAF Museum*)

Bone estimated the position as about 30 miles east-northeast of the North Foreland. He saw his victim alight successfully, then watched another enemy machine apparently put down nearby but, being short of petrol, returned to Westgate. A Short seaplane detailed to bomb the disabled enemy failed to get airborne, and when one eventually took off two hours later it found nothing.

The forced-down machine was FF 33 No.537, crewed by Flugmeister Ponater and Leut Herrenknecht, which had attacked Deal. The crew received minor injuries and the damaged aircraft was later towed to Zeebrugge.

Flt Cdr R. J. Bone, awarded the DSO for forcing down a Friedrichshafen on 19 March, 1916; and (*right*) Flt Lieut B. P. H. de Roeper, RNAS Redcar, whose several determined anti-Zeppelin sorties during the summer and autumn of 1916 were frustrated by the inadequacies of his elderly B.E.2c. (*Left-hand photograph Mrs R. J. Bone*)

The combat with Christiansen's Brandenburg followed the keen observation and intelligent anticipation of an RFC crew, Reginald Collis and Alfred Emery, who had left Lympne at about 13.30 hr delivering a new F.E.2b to France.

Collis was more experienced than his modest 2nd Lieut rank and mundane job as a Southern Aircraft Depot ferry pilot might suggest. After a motor engineering apprenticeship he enlisted in the RFC, aged 19, a month after its formation, receiving the Service number 109. Under the initial plan that half the RFC pilots should be NCOs, Collis was the sixth of some 50 promising airmen and NCOs to receive flying training before the war, qualifying on 22 January, 1913. However because of indecisive policy about NCO pilots it was not until he was commissioned in June 1915 and joined No.6 Squadron in France that he began operational flying. He flew many sorties over the lines and survived several brushes with the famous Fokker monoplanes.

Having reached 8,000 ft Collis noticed one of the enemy under fire from the Dover guns and immediately gave chase, making little progress. He then saw another seaplane flying towards Deal and, rather than attempt pursuit, continued climbing up-Channel, hoping to cut it off as it returned.

He kept it in sight until it headed for home, when he was well-positioned for attack some 4,000 ft above. He throttled back and dived until 150 yards directly behind, apparently unnoticed by the German crew, for there was no return fire or evasive action as Emery opened up with his Lewis. He fired a complete drum, causing the seaplane to plunge into a steep right-hand spiral, with its engine spouting steam. It had made no attempt to level out down to 1,5000 ft, when the F.E's crew was distracted by a problem with their own fuel system. When they searched a few minutes later there was no sign of it.

According to German records Collis' F.E.2b—it was described as a Caudron—attacked Brandenburg No.521 at 14.10 hr, at about 7,850 ft. The apparent lack of return fire is understandable, since von Tschirschky in the front seat was armed only with a Mauser automatic rifle. Emery's burst damaged the cooling system, put one cylinder out of action and wounded the observer in the shoulder, making an early forced alighting almost inevitable.

However, as the Brandenburg slowly circled down, von Tschirschky heroically climbed out on the wing and managed to repair the damaged radiator with his handkerchief and insulating tape. This enabled them to remain airborne for another 70 min, and they eventually came down about 20 miles from Ostende. After taxying for a time the engine developed a new lease of life and Christiansen got airborne again to reach Zeebrugge at 17.20 hr.

No timings are recorded for the Eastchurch sorties, but, like those from Grain, they were probably precautionary patrols against further incursions rather than belated attempts to catch the Thanet raiders.

Hallifax flying the Grain Avro 504B took off with the recommended full quota of armaments—two boxes of Ranken darts and three drums of ammunition for the observer's Lewis—and demonstrated that operating with such a load was a patently academic exercise. He was unable to coax the heavily burdened aircraft above 3,000 ft.

It is remarkable that no ground observers or pilots appear to have noticed the unusual Gotha Ursinus W.D. (Wasser Doppeldecker—sea biplane) No.120, which German reports state was the first aircraft to reach Dover, dropping 32 bombs. This was a twin-engined machine with its upper wing unconventionally in line with the top of the fuselage, similar to the much later Handley Page Heyford. In the Gotha Ursinus, however, the engines were placed closely inboard on the lower wing instead of below the upper plane. Only one was built.

Press release B1244 describing events was a staid document, making no concessions to news values. Bone's success was relegated to the final paragraph and Collis' combat not mentioned, since it had not then been reported from France.

Bone was awarded an immediate DSO, though the War Office, with its more rigid policy, turned down the RFC recommendation for an MC and DCM for Collis and Emery respectively because there was no corroboration of their claim.

Collis later became an instructor in Canada, and after the war Emery received a consolation prize quite unconnected with this combat. He was awarded the Meritorious Service Medal in the 1919 Birthday Honours.

Air activity was renewed at 20.45 hr following a major false alarm reporting several Zeppelins off the east coast between Lowestoft and Dover. This led to a dozen sorties from seven RNAS aerodromes, lasting until after midnight.

31 March/1 April, 1916 (Night)

Targets: London (navy), East Anglia (army).
Enemy forces: Navy Zeppelins L13 (Kptlt H. Mathy), L14 (Kptlt A. Böcker), L15 (Kptlt J. Breithaupt), L16 (Oblt-z-S W. Peterson), L22 (Kptlt Martin Dietrich); L9 and L11 returned with mechanical troubles. Army Zeppelins LZ90; LZ 88 and LZ92 returned because of bad weather.
Results: 48 killed, 64 injured, £19,431 damage.
Defence sorties: 24

RNAS

Eastchurch: B.E.2cs 8609 (Flt Sub-Lieut C. C. Wyllie) 22.00–00.42 hr; 8609 (Flt Cdr R. E. C. Peirse) 01.32–02.40 hr; 987 (Flt Sub-Lieut N. S. Douglas).

Redcar: B.E.2c 1139 (Flt Sub-Lieut B. P. H. de Roeper) took off 01.20 hr, forced landed with engine trouble.

Rochford: B.E.2cs 1164 (Flt Sub-Lieut G. L. F. Stevens) landed 02.41 hr; 1189 (Flt Sub-Lieut E. P. Hicks) took off 21.40 hr.

Yarmouth: B.E.2cs 1194 (Flt Sub-Lieut F. P. Reeves) 21.07–21.50 hr; 991 (Flt Sub-Lieut H. G. Hall) 05.05–06.13 hr and 06.33–07.15 hr; Sopwith Baby 8163 (Flt Lieut C. E. Wood) 05.22–06.32 hr.

Covehithe: B.E.2c 1161 (Flt Sub-Lieut E. L. Pulling) 21.55–22.30 hr.

RFC

No.19 R.A. Squadron, Croydon: B.E.2cs 2584 (Capt F. G. Dunn) 21.55–22.56 hr; 2574 (Lieut P. Rader) 23.55–01.00 hr.

No.19 R.A. Squadron, Hainault: Unspecified B.E.2c (2nd Lieut A. de B. Brandon) 21.25–23.10 hr (Farningham); unspecified B.E.2c took off at 22.00 hr.

No. 19 R.A. Squadron, Hendon: Two B.E.2c sorties, one at 21.05–23.35 hr.

No.19 R.A. Squadron, Hounslow: Unspecified B.E.2cs (2nd Lieut G. H. Birley) 21.45–23.55 hr (Suttons Farm); one took off at 22.00 hr.

No.19 R.A. Squadron, Joyce Green: Unspecified B.E.2cs (2nd Lieut C. A. Ridley) 21.30–23.40 hr; (2nd Lieut C. S. Ross) 21.50–01.10 hr.

No.19 R.A. Squadron, Northolt: Unspecified B.E.2c (Lieut J. W. Bailey) took off at 21.05 hr, crashed, pilot killed.

No.19 R.A. Squadron, Suttons Farm: Unspecified B.E.2c (2nd Lieut H. S. Powell) 21.15–23.25 hr.

No.9 R.A. Squadron, Norwich: One sortie at 22.45 hr, details not known.

Although both German airship services took part in this night's operations there was no co-ordination, the naval Zeppelins being briefed for London while the army chose to attack in East Anglia.

Navy Zeppelins no longer transmitted standard departure signals, having learned that these were intercepted, but British Intelligence still received ample early warning of raids by other means. In this instance it was soon known that seven raiders had departed. There was no advance information about the army airships, but only one (LZ90) came inland, penetrating to Ipswich, and dropped no bombs.

British anti-aircraft gunners achieved their first success, bringing down L15, and two defence pilots managed to attain attacking range. A Northolt pilot was killed in a take-off crash.

L15 crossed the coast at Dunwich at 19.45 hr, with L13 following some 15 min later. Soon afterwards, to gain safer altitude for attacking London, Mathy lightened L13 by dropping a dozen bombs on an explosives factory at Stowmarket. They missed, but AA fire damaged the Zeppelin amidships, piercing two gas cells. This was confirmed when the signal reporting Mathy's return to base, blown overboard after transmission, was found next morning. L13 departed north of Southwold at 22.20 hr after dropping her remaining bombs in open country.

Meanwhile, Breithaupt in L15 had flown a good course to London, and at about 21.40 hr he came under heavy gunfire from the Purfleet–Erith–Plumstead area. He dropped his bombs at Rainham, and at 21.45 hr received a direct hit from the Purfleet gun. There was great confusion aboard for some minutes while her crew established that two gas cells were virtually empty and others damaged. The ship became nose heavy, and despite jettisoning everything movable, including guns and all but enough fuel to reach Belgium, eventually broke its back and ditched 15 miles north of Margate just after 23.00 hr. The crew, less one member who drowned, was picked up by a British destroyer.

The only other Zeppelin to penetrate within 20 miles of central London was L14, with Strasser on board. She crossed the Norfolk coast near Palling at 21.05 hr, flew steadily southwestwards dropping a few bombs at Sudbury and Braintree, then at 23.40 hr a dozen more around Brentwood. Böcker then

The tail of Zeppelin L15 visible during salvage operations after she ditched as the result of AA gun damage during the raid of 31 March/1 April, 1916.

inexplicably diverted 45 miles northwards before continuing south to drop fourteen bombs on Thameshaven at 01.30 hr, and finally departed off Aldeburgh at 02.50 hr. He claimed to have bombed near the Tower Bridge.

Unrecorded difficulties—probably navigational—affected L16's performance. Crossing the coast north of Yarmouth at 22.10 hr, Peterson claimed to have bombed Hornsey, when in fact he hit Bury St Edmunds. A solitary bomb was dropped on Lowestoft before departure at 01.15 hr.

L22 was delayed by engine troubles and made for Grimsby. Bombs were dropped at Humberston and Cleethorpes, which suffered the night's most serious incident when a chapel used as a Service billet was hit, killing 29 soldiers and injuring 53.

Because of gale damage to telephone lines, RNAS Yarmouth received no warning of the incoming Zeppelins, and apart from one sortie by Reeves during a quiet period, activities were confined to early morning patrols to check for stragglers. Pulling was airborne from Covehithe in an attempt to find L13 on her outward flight. De Roeper from Redcar took off on receiving news of L22's activities to the south, but he crashed when trying to land after engine failure. Naval aerodromes in the southeast despatched aircraft to search for L14 and L15.

With much detail about the RFC effort missing, it is not possible to amplify the No.18 Wing report that three of its thirteen aircraft were completely wrecked and two partially so. However, some facts are available.

The first B.E.2cs of No.19 RAS were airborne at 21.05–21.25 hr with orders to patrol the outer London perimeter at 6,000 ft. They were followed by a second wave covering east and central London at 10,000 ft, and this pattern was repeated later. It was hoped that airships eluding the outer patrols would be picked up by the inner high flyers as they bombed.

First to see a Zeppelin was Claude Ridley from Joyce Green, none the worse for his Reigate crash. At 21.36 hr he spotted L15 in the searchlights, well ahead and several thousand feet higher up. He gave chase and fired 20 optimistic rounds from his Lewis at extreme range before the airship disappeared out of the searchlight beams. He patrolled for another two hours at 9,000 ft but saw nothing.

Another pilot equally frustrated when the searchlights lost L15 was Alfred de Bathe Brandon, from New Zealand. Recently qualified, and a member of No.19 RAS for just over a week, he had taken off from Hainault a little earlier and reached 6,000 ft when he spotted the airship to his right and only about 600 ft higher. He had her in sight just long enough to estimate her course, and began climbing in the direction which would place him above.

It was at this moment—at 21.45 hr—that L15 received the direct hit from the Purfleet gun, and ten minutes elapsed before Brandon found her again over Ingatestone. He carefully positioned 3–400 ft above and dropped a first clutch of three Ranken darts. Above the noise of his engine and machine-gun fire from the airship's top platform, Brandon thought he heard three reports denoting hits—but later learned that his darts straddled the hull.

He then noticed that his navigation lights were still on and hastily switched off before positioning for another attack. Circling round, he decided to try an incendiary bomb and throttled back to place it in the launching tube. While thus occupied and temporarily unsighted he nearly overshot his target, so held the bomb in his lap and released two more groups of darts. Brandon was disconcerted by the speed with which he was overshooting and concluded that he must have inadvertently positioned for a head-on attack. However, it is more likely that the severely damaged L15 was moving very slowly in an abnormal flying attitude. He turned to launch a third attack but lost his quarry, which had swung to the east and was attempting to struggle home.

Brandon's engagement had lasted ten minutes and he cruised around for another hour without seeing anything. By this time mist was obscuring some of the aerodromes, so he landed at the first he spotted, Farningham, breaking a wing skid and flare bracket in the process. Despite his forgetful self-illumination, his B.E. bore only three bullet holes—one in the starboard aileron and two in the tail surfaces.

Powell from Suttons Farm, flying at 6,000 ft about a mile to the north, had witnessed Brandon's attack on L15 and joined the chase. He got within 500 yards but was still well below the airship when it disappeared from view.

The other pilots saw nothing except occasional bursts of AA fire. Dunn from Croydon flew back and forth across the Thames several times, reaching 11,700 ft, and returned to base having been unable to transfer petrol into his service tank. Rader followed a similar pattern at 9,500 ft. Birley from Hounslow cruised over northeast London at 9,800 ft, lost sight of base and decided to land at an aerodrome visible below—Suttons Farm—but had difficulty in judging his height through mist patches. He approached too fast, overshot and ran through hurdles into a pond, damaging his propeller and lower wing leading edge.

At Northolt there was slight haze when Bailey took off. He had reached about

B.E.2c 2584 of No.19 Reserve Aeroplane Squadron, Croydon, flown by Capt F. G. Dunn on 31 March/1 April, 1916. 'Baroda' appears beneath the front cockpit. (*J. M. Bruce/G. S. Leslie collection*)

20 ft, climbing normally when he passed the last flare, then his B.E. crashed 200 yards farther on. It appeared to have side-slipped into the ground, nose first, with no indications of engine trouble. It was assumed that Bailey—who was killed instantly—lost control in a patch of mist.

All considered, it was a promising start for the reorganized air defences, and the pilots' sense of purpose was enhanced by the general debriefing session held next day by Holt, the CO of No.18 Wing. One point to emerge was that some aerodromes were displaying over-complicated flare patterns which caused confusion. Many pilots complained of being attacked by AA guns, and some felt that they would achieve better results if they could concentrate on the flying and carry an observer to look for the enemy. There was general agreement about the difficulty of spotting airships from above, and at least one pilot apparently missed one almost directly below him.

Ridley and Brandon were awarded the Military Cross for their endeavours.

B.E.2c 1114, from RNAS Whitley Bay, was flown by Flt Sub-Lieut G. A. Gooderham in an unsuccessful search for L11 on 1/2 April, 1916.

1/2 April, 1916 (Night)

Target: Northern England.
Enemy forces: Navy Zeppelins L11 (Kvtkpt V. Schütze), L17 (Kptlt H. Ehrlich).
Results: 22 killed, 130 injured, £25,568 damage.
Defence sorties: Seven.

RNAS

Redcar: B.E.2c 1145 (Flt Sub-Lieut H. C. Vereker) 00.20–01.20 hr.

Scarborough: Bristol Scout C 3030 (Flt Cdr C. Draper); Avro 504C 8601 (Flt Sub-Lieut J. F. Roche) forced landed Speeton; times not known.

Whitley Bay: B.E.2c 1114 (Flt Sub-Lieut G. A. Gooderham) 23.35–00.30 hr.

RFC

No.36 Squadron, Cramlington: Two B.E.2c sorties—details not known.
No.47 Squadron, Beverley: One B.E.2c sortie—details not known.

Having set off to bomb London, L11 and L17 diverted to northern targets for weather reasons.

It was still dusk when L17 arrived ten miles off Flamborough Head, so Ehrlich cruised offshore until dark. About an hour later, ten miles southeast of Hornsea, the airship suffered a major engine failure and returned home after jettisoning the bombs at sea.

L11 came in over Seaham Harbour at 23.05 hr, dropped 27 bombs in and around Sunderland, flew south to deliver a smaller attack on the Middlesbrough area and then departed over Saltburn at 00.30 hr. Most of the casualties were in Sunderland.

Subsequent analysis of the night's activities showed that Chris Draper, CO of RNAS Scarborough, narrowly missed intercepting L17 off Flamborough Head. Following vague reports of Zeppelin activity he flew a last-light patrol down the coast, landing back in the dark. Had he been a few minutes later he must inevitably have seen the airship. Roche, flying one of the single-seat Avro 504C Scouts on a similar mission forced landed at Speeton, ten miles south of Scarborough, severely damaging the aircraft.

Gooderham from RNAS Whitley Bay patrolled the coast at 8,000 ft down to Seaham in an abortive search for L11, and Vereker from Redcar likewise saw nothing.

A B.E.2c of No.47 Squadron RFC, Beverley, crashed following engine failure but details are not recorded. No reports from No.36 Squadron, Cramlington, have been traced.

2/3 April, 1916 (Night)

Targets: Forth area (navy), London (army).
Enemy forces: Navy Zeppelins L14 (Kptlt A. Böcker), L16 (Oblt-z-S W. Peterson), L22 (Kptlt Martin Dietrich); L13 (Kptlt H. Mathy) returned with engine trouble. Army Zeppelins LZ88 (Hptmn Falck), LZ90 (Oblt Ernst Lehmann).
Results: 13 killed, 24 injured, £73,113 damage.
Defence sorties: 14.

RNAS

Covehithe: B.E.2c 1161 (Flt Sub-Lieut E. L. Pulling) 03.25–04.10 hr.
Dundee: Wight seaplanes; two sorties, details not known.
East Fortune: Avro 504C 8588 (Flt Sub-Lieut G. A. Cox) took off 21.40 hr, crashed landing.
Rochford: B.E.2c 1164 took off 23.58 hr.

RFC

No.36 Squadron, Cramlington: B.E.2c, two sorties, one crashed landing.
No.19 R.A. Squadron, Croydon: B.E.2c, one sortie. Details not known.
No.19 R.A. Squadron, Hainault: B.E.2c, two sorties. Details not known.
No.19 R.A. Squadron, Hounslow: B.E.2c, two sorties. Details not known.
No. 19 R.A. Squadron, Suttons Farm: B.E.2c, two sorties. Details not known.

This was another example of attacks by German naval and army airships on the same night without any co-ordination. The primary target for the navy was the Rosyth Royal Navy base and the Forth railway bridge, while the army airships planned to raid London.

L14 made landfall off St Abbs Head and remained well out to sea before turning up the Forth. Böcker failed to locate the bridge or Rosyth, and bombed Leith and Edinburgh between 23.30 and 00.15 hr, then departed south of Dunbar at 01.00. L22 was farther south and from 21.15 to 21.45 hr unloaded most of her bombs in fields around Berwick-upon-Tweed, claiming to have attacked factories near Newcastle. She then followed the coast and eventually released the few remaining bombs on Edinburgh at 23.50 hr. L16, making less allowance for the northerly winds, came in eight miles north of Blyth at 23.00 hr, meandered south and departed 90 min later near her entry point. Her bombs fell in open country, some on the Cramlington aerodrome.

LZ90 made landfall at Mersea Island and, skirting Chelmsford at 23.30 hr, steered for London. At 23.55 hr she was attacked by the Waltham Abbey guns and unloaded 90 bombs, causing minimal damage, and then returned along a more northerly course to depart over Clacton at 01.00 hr. LZ88 flew in south of Orfordness at about 23.00 hr and because of unfavourable winds abandoned London as a target. She reached Ipswich, then retreated to drop her bombs near the mouth of the Deben—apparently in mistake for Harwich—and flew out at 01.20 hr.

Again only scrappy information about the defence effort has survived. Cox was injured when his Avro was badly damaged in a landing crash at East Fortune. Reports vary as to whether the two Wight seaplanes actually became airborne at Dundee or failed in the attempt.

One Cramlington B.E. hit a ditch on landing, caught fire and was blown up by its bombs—the pilot escaping unhurt. Seven No.19 RAS aircraft despatched to look for LZ90 were airborne by midnight, and one pilot (unidentified) claimed a sighting. No.18 Wing reported the night's flying operations as totalling 13 hr 20 min, with one aircraft wrecked and two slightly damaged.

3/4 April, 1916 (Night)

Target: London.
Enemy forces: Navy Zeppelins L11 (Kvtkpt V. Schütze), L17 (Kptlt H. Ehrlich).
Results: No casualties or damage.
Defence sorties: Four.

RNAS

Yarmouth: B.E.2cs 1167 (Flt Lieut F. G. D. Hards) 04.21–06.05 hr; 1169 (Flt Lieut C. E. Wood) 04.45–05.55 hr.

Covehithe: B.E.2c 1161 (Flt Sub-Lieut E. L. Pulling) 03.25–06.30 hr, forced landed.

RFC

No.15 R.A. Squadron, Doncaster: B.E.2c 2620 (Capt A. A. B. Thomson) 23.00–01.40 hr, crashed, Tealby.

Strong headwinds frustrated this intended attack on London, and apparently caused L17 to abandon the mission when about ten miles off the Norfolk coast.

L11 came in near Cromer at 01.30 hr and was unable to find the alternative targets of Norwich, Yarmouth or Lowestoft. A few bombs were dropped in open country, and others in the sea after the airship had departed north of Yarmouth at 03.00 hr.

Heavy mist prevented take-offs from the Norfolk coastal aerodromes when L11 was in the area, though it lifted sufficiently for Pulling to get airborne from Covehithe 25 min after the airship had cleared the coast. Conditions worsened and he strayed inland, eventually putting down near Norwich short of petrol, having seen nothing. The Yarmouth weather also improved later and two sorties were flown, but L11 was then safe from pursuit.

The early movements of the airships are not recorded, but some threat of attack further north clearly prompted Thomson to take off from Doncaster, carrying four 16 lb HE bombs and four incendiaries. At 23.30 hr when at 9,000 ft north of Hull he thought he saw a Zeppelin well to the east, and he followed it for 30 min out to sea without gaining.

Visibility was deteriorating, so he turned back and eventually became lost. At 01.25 hr, short of fuel, he descended to 1,000 ft over snow-patched countryside and spotted a field which looked suitable for landing. As he approached he managed to avoid one tree which loomed ahead but hit a second and crashed. He had flown into a 600 ft hill at Tealby, near Market Rasen, misled by his altimeter which was set for Doncaster at much lower altitude 35 miles to the west. Although Thomson's sighting was generally regarded as a 'phantom airship', the presence of L11 or L17 in the area cannot be categorically dismissed.

Arthur Ashford Benjamin Thomson (known as 'Ack Ack Beer' from his initials in the contemporary phonetic alphabet) who had celebrated his 21st birthday the previous day, emerged from this major crash with trifling injuries only to lose his life in a ground accident 23 years later. He became one of the more dynamic home-defence squadron commanders, then had charge of a wing and progressed rapidly to air commodore rank in the postwar RAF. On 28 August, 1939, when AOC No.3 Bomber Group and captaining a No.115 Squadron Wellington engaged in bomb trials, he landed at Boscombe Down to investigate a release failure. While inspecting the bomb bay he stepped back into an idling propeller and received fatal injuries.

5/6 April, 1916 (Night)

Target: Northern England.
Enemy forces: Navy Zeppelins L11 (Kvtkpt V. Schütze), L16 (Oblt-z-S W. Peterson); L13 (Kptlt H. Mathy), returned early with engine trouble.
Results: One killed, nine injured, £7,983 damage.
Defence sorties: Five.

RNAS

Scarborough: B.E.2c 1144 (Sqn Cdr C. Draper) 21.30–23.40 hr.

RFC

No.36 Squadron, Cramlington: Unspecified B.E.2cs, two sorties, both crashed on landing, one pilot (Capt J. Nichol) killed.

No.47 Squadron, Beverley: B.E.2c 2720 (Lieut N. H. Bottomley) 22.00–23.10 hr; unspecified B.E.2c (Capt F. G. Small), details not known.

L11 crossed the coast at Hornsea at 21.05 hr and 15 min later was greeted by heavy AA fire on approaching Hull. After dropping four bombs Schütze retreated out to sea, intending to return inland over a different course, but an engine failure and the wind state made him decide to make for Hartlepool. At about 02.15 hr, off Skinningrove, he suffered another engine failure, so turned inland and bombed the iron works.

L16 came in north of Hartlepool at 23.30 hr and bombed colliery buildings west of Bishop Auckland shortly after midnight. She flew out over Seaham Harbour at 01.15 hr.

Despite generally fine weather, fog badly affected RNAS coastal aerodromes except at Scarborough, where Draper took off for a lengthy patrol down the coast to Spurn Head and over Hull without sighting the enemy. He considered landing at Beverley to check the latest news of airship movements but was confused by the flare pattern and changed his mind. He met much low cloud on the return flight, and eventually spotted rockets from Scarborough, landing with 15 min petrol in his tank.

B.E.2c 8410 of RNAS Dover, flown by Flt Cdr Geoffrey Bromet on 23 April, 1916.

No.36 Squadron suffered another bad night, with two B.E. landing crashes. Nichol struck a house and was killed when his bombs exploded. The other machine hit a hedge but the pilot was unhurt.

Norman Bottomley, No.47 Squadron, had an exciting landing at Beverley after a vain search for L11 over Hull and the Humber. His throttle would not close completely, but he managed to put the B.E. down with only minor damage.

A complaint from Sir Joseph Walton, MP for Barnsley, about inadequate protection for Skinningrove prompted an acid minute from the Admiralty Director of Air Services to the First Lord: '. . . if these gentlemen who write and talk so glibly about night flying were made to do a flight at night as a passenger, we should not have to waste time in answering letters of this sort.'

23 April, 1916 (Daylight)

Target: Dover.
Enemy force: One aircraft, type not known.
Results: No casualties or damage.
Defence sorties: Seven.

RNAS

Dover: Bristol Scout C 3045 (Flt Sub-Lieut G. Preen) 30 min; B.E.2c 8410 (Flt Cdr G. R. Bromet) 65 min; Nieuport 10 3967 (Flt Lieut G. R. H. Talbot) 90 min.

RFC

Dover: Four sorties—details not known.

A high-flying reconnaissance aircraft was seen over Dover at 12.28 hr, departing two minutes later. No reports have been traced of the sorties flown in the forlorn hope of catching this intruder.

24 April, 1916 (Daylight)

Target: Dover.
Enemy force: One aircraft, type not known.
Results: No casualties or damage.
Defence sorties: 16.

RNAS

Dover: Bristol Scout Cs 1254 (Flt Sub-Lieut C. D. Booker) 11.37–12.47 hr; 3043 (Flt Sub-Lieut E. R. Grange) 11.37—12.52 hr; Nieuport 10s 3165 (Flt Lieut F. J. E. Feeny) 11.36–12.16 hr; 3967 (Flt Lieut G. R. H. Talbot) 11.38–12.45 hr; Sopwith Schneider 1573 (Flt Lieut J. B. P. Ferrand) 11.40–12.50 hr; FBA flying-boat 3208 (Flt Lieut J. C. Brooke, AM Fanshawe) 11.55–13.20 hr.

Grain: Sopwith Baby 8151 (Flt Lieut E. de C. Hallifax) 12.18–13.05 hr.

Westgate: Bristol Scout Cs 3049 (Flt Cdr C. H. Butler) 30 min; 3054 (Flt Sub-Lieut J. A. Carr) 30 min, damaged landing; B.E.2cs 1156 (Flt Sub-Lieut E. S. Boynton) 60 min; 1188 (Flt Sub-Lieut C. W. Greig, LM Frater) 50 min; 8413 (Flt Cdr H. A. Buss, Sgt Davis) 46 min.

RFC

Dover: Bristol Scout Cs unspecified (Capt P. Babington) 11.40–12.30 hr; 4681 (Maj A. S. Barratt) 11.42–11.50 hr, returned with engine trouble; B.E.2cs 2577 (Capt Edgar, Sgt Rogers) 11.45–12.50 hr; 2747 (Lieut Murray, Sgt Davis) 11.40–13.20 hr.

This reconnaissance closely resembled that of the previous day, with a single aircraft, type not recorded, emerging from cloud at 11.35 hr and circling Dover at 8–9,000 ft. It was captained by Leut Walther Ilges, of Marine Landflieger Abteilung 1.

Despite prompt and substantial reaction from the defences, the intruder had ample altitude to provide immunity from interception. RNAS Dover despatched four aircraft within three minutes, but no pilot even saw the enemy. The Westgate aircraft, some already airborne at the time of the warning, were equally unsuccessful.

Both the RFC B.E.2cs sighted the intruder, but as they staggered off in pursuit, eventually reaching 9,000 ft, it steadily pulled ahead. Babington circled his Bristol at 9,000 ft over the aerodrome ready to deal with any further incursions, unaware that Barratt, who intended to chase the first, had precipitately landed with engine failure.

24/25 April, 1916 (Night)

Target: London.
Enemy forces: Navy Zeppelins L11 (Kvtkpt V. Schütze), L13 (Kptlt E. Prölss), L16 (Oblt-z-S W. Peterson), L17 (Kptlt H. Ehrlich), L21 (Kptlt Max Dietrich), L23 (Kptlt Otto von Schubert).
Results: One killed, one injured, £6,412 damage.
Defence sorties: 22.

RNAS

Eastbourne: Bristol Scout C 3060 (Flt Lieut M. S. Marsden) took off 04.25 hr, forced landed Lympne; B.E.2c 1183 (Flt Lieut Jones, Flt Sub-Lieut A. Durstan) 04.25–05.55 hr; Maurice Farman S.11 1846 (Flt Sub-Lieut R. J. McMinnies, Flt Sub-Lieut Walker) 04.25–06.00 hr.

Felixstowe: Short S.38 8438 (Flt Sub-Lieut C. J. Galpin, AM Pinn); Short 184 8351 (Flt Sub-Lieut F. D. Till, AM Ayling). Times not known.

Yarmouth: Bristol Scout Cs 1257 (Flt Lieut C. H. C. Smith) 03.52–04.45 hr; 1256 (Flt Lieut B. D. Kilner) 04.00–05.05 hr; 1252 (Flt Lieut C. E. Wood) 04.02–04.45 hr; B.E.2cs 1155 (Flt Sub-Lieut S. R. Watkins) 22.35–00.01 hr (Sedgeford); 1167 (Flt Sub-Lieut G. W. R. Fane) 22.46–23.50 (Holt); 1161 (Flt Sub-Lieut S. Kemball) 23.22–00.57 hr (Covehithe); 1166 (Flt Sub-Lieut E. L. Pulling) 23.50–01.20 hr, crashed at Bacton; 1100 (Flt Sub-Lieut B. S. Wemp) 03.10–04.20 hr; 8493 (Flt Cdr V. Nicholl) 03.43–05.40 hr; 8326 (Flt Lieut F. G. D. Hards) 03.44–05.35 hr; Short 827 3105 (Flt Sub-Lieut E. Cadbury, Flt Sub-Lieut A. H. Sandwell) 03.40–07.25 hr; Sopwith Baby 8140 (Flt Sub-Lieut S. G. Beare) took off 04.00 hr.

Bacton: B.E.2c 1194 (Flt Sub-Lieut F. P. Reeves) 22.55–00.05 hr.

Westgate: Short 184 8032—details not known.

RFC

Dover: Two sorties, at 03.43 and 04.00 hr—details not known.

No.35 Squadron, Thetford: One sortie, 00.01–02.40 hr—details not known.

Planned as a substantial raid on London, combining reconnaissance assistance for warships bombarding Lowestoft, this operation was rendered largely ineffective by the weather.

Bristol Scout C 1257 flown by Flt Lieut C. H. Chichester Smith, RNAS Yarmouth, during the Zeppelin activity of 24/25 April, 1916. (*Mrs P. Fane*)

L16 crossed the coast at 22.15 hr, to be followed five minutes later by L13, both coming in near Cromer. At 23.10 hr L21 made landfall five miles south of Lowestoft, at 23.50 hr L23 crossed north of Yarmouth and at 00.30 hr L11 arrived over Bacton. L17 made a belated appearance north of Skegness at 01.40 hr, flew briefly inland and departed 25 min later.

On reaching England the commanders realized that headwinds ruled out any successful attack on London, and their search for suitable opportunity targets in East Anglia was hampered by low cloud. L21 reached Stowmarket at 00.15 hr, and L16 was over Newmarket 15 min later. The remainder travelled only short distances inland and flew out between 23.30 and 01.45 hrs over a 15-mile stretch of coast between Sheringham and Happisburgh. Some did not bomb.

RNAS Yarmouth aircraft had been standing by since 21.50 hr, and shortly after L13 and L16 crossed the coast, Watkins and Fane were airborne in B.E.2cs. They were joined by Reeves from Bacton, but no sightings were made. After belated news of L21's crossing farther south, Kemball took off and was equally unsuccessful. A little later Pulling was luckier, at least getting a glimpse of L23 some 2,000 ft above him. He was unable to gain close quarters, and after eventually losing sight of the Zeppelin decided to land at Bacton. He crashed after hitting telephone wires on the approach, but although his B.E. was badly damaged he was not seriously hurt.

Zeppelin movements which caused the renewed activity from about 03.00 hr are obscure, but L21 after making contact with her seaborne comrades approaching Lowestoft, evidently turned about and reconnoitred ahead of the ships towards the Norfolk coast. The three Yarmouth Bristol Scouts all sighted this airship and pursued for 50 miles until it was lost in cloud.

Meanwhile there was a bonus for Nicholl and Hards who had taken off a little earlier, for at 04.38 hr in the faint morning light, 40 miles east of Lowestoft, they came upon the old L9 which had been engaged on close fleet reconnaissance throughout the night. L9 was flying at only 2,600 ft, and the two B.Es armed with 16 lb bombs and Ranken darts, had the height advantage. During a 25-mile chase both pilots attacked, and Hards thought his darts had struck—though in fact they

Short 827 No.3105 was one of RNAS Yarmouth's aircraft which was Zeppelin hunting in the early hours of 25 April, 1916. (*P. Wright*)

B.E.2c 1183 from RNAS Eastbourne is officially listed as having flown a home-defence sortie on 24/25 April, 1916, but the object is obscure.

narrowly missed. L9 escaped thanks to highly skilled handling, with her executive officer on the upper gun platform directing the coxswain by voice tube when to turn as, one after the other, the B.Es entered their bombing runs.

The RFC contribution to the night's effort was a single sortie by an unspecified aircraft of No.35 Squadron when L16 was in the Thetford area.

The six-minute bombardment of Lowestoft duly took place shortly after 04.00 hr, causing severe damage but relatively light casualties.

Patrols flown from Eastbourne, Westgate and Dover listed with the night's air raid records were presumably in response to a false alarm.

25/26 April, 1916 (Night)

Target: London.
Enemy forces: Army Zeppelins LZ87 (Oblt Barth), LZ88 (Hptmn Falck), LZ93 (Hptmn Wilhelm Schramm), LZ97 (Hptmn E. Linnarz); LZ26 returned early.
Results: None killed, one injured, £568 damage.
Defence sorties: 16.

RNAS

Eastchurch: B.E.2c 983 (Flt Sub-Lieut D. G. Fleming) 23.26–00.37 hr; unspecified B.E.2c 00.35–01.45 hr; Avro 504B 1011 (Sqn Cdr C. Draper) 31 min.

Rochford: B.E.2c 8610 (Flt Sub-Lieut E. P. Hicks) took off 23.00 hr.

Westgate: B.E.2cs 8413 (Flt Lieut H. A. Buss) 22.10–23.00 hr; 8497 (Flt Cdr C. H. Butler) 01.35–02.25 hr (Manston).

RFC

Dover: B.E.2cs 2577 (Maj A. S. Barratt) 22.00–23.45 hr; 2747 (Capt P. Babington) 01.50–02.40 hr.

No.39 Squadron, Hounslow: B.E.2c 7324 (Lieut R. C. L. Holme) 22.45–23.45 hr (Chingford); unspecified B.E.2cs (2nd Lieut G. H. Birley) 22.45–00.10 hr (Joyce Green); (Lieut M. S. Stewart) 23.49–01.30 hr (Suttons Farm).

No.39 Squadron, Suttons Farm: B.E.2c 4112 (Capt A. T. Harris) 22.30–00.50 hr; unspecified B.E.2c (2nd Lieut W. L. Robinson) 22.45–01.15 hr; a third B.E.2c took off at 23.47 hr.

No.39 Squadron, Hainault: B.E.2c 2583 (2nd Lieut A. de B. Brandon) 22.50–00.35 hr; unspecified B.E.2c (2nd Lieut C. T. Black) 22.45–00.25 hr.

This was an ineffectual attempt by German army airships to mount a major attack on London after a spell of operations over continental Europe had brought substantial losses.

Only LZ97, commanded by the redoubtable Linnarz, came anywhere near the capital, but because of navigation errors her bombs fell in the Ongar–Barkingside area, between 22.45 and 23.15 hr, instead of on central London. Linnarz came in over the Blackwater at 22.00 hr and departed north of Clacton at 00.35 hr.

LZ87 dropped a few bombs in Deal harbour at 21.55 and, after heavy shelling from Walmer, skirted the coast to Ramsgate before turning homewards. LZ88 was more venturesome, flying in between Herne Bay and Whitstable at 00.30 hr, proceeding south beyond Canterbury, then turning northeast to scatter bombs in open country before departing near Westgate at 01.35 hr. LZ93 was inland for only 15 min, bombing indiscriminately near Harwich at 22.30–22.45 hr. The veteran LZ26, in service since 1914, was trailing by several hours and abandoned the mission after being further delayed in avoiding a French aircraft over the sea.

Neither of the Westgate pilots—Harold Buss seeking LZ87 or Charles Butler the LZ88—made sightings, nor was the unidentified Eastchurch pilot looking for the latter airship any more successful. Eastchurch and Rochford patrols during LZ97's homeward flight were too far south to see anything.

No.39 Squadron, RFC, just created from the redeployed aircraft and pilots of No.19 RAS, made an encouraging if frustrating start. Of its eight pilots airborne, two fired on LZ97 albeit at extreme range, and four others sighted her in the distance. When she was reported near Chelmsford at about 22.30 hr, Higgins, the squadron commander, decided to launch four B.E.2cs immediately and follow up with a similar patrol an hour later. As it became apparent that any early threat to London was from a single airship this plan was modified, and only two aircraft were held for the later patrol.

A significant feature of the night's operations was the issue of the still experimental Brock explosive bullets to at least one pilot. He was Arthur Travers Harris, OC B Flight at Suttons Farm then nick-named 'Ginger'. During his rise in the inter-war RAF he was known as 'Bert', and to the Bomber Command crews of the Second World War, perhaps harshly but with due realization of his unswerving dedication to the task, he was 'Butch(er)'. To the postwar world he became simply 'Bomber' Harris.

Harris, the first pilot away, climbed east of the aerodrome to 5,000 ft, and at 22.45 hr spotted LZ97 held by searchlights at an estimated 9,500 ft while bombing near Chipping Ongar. He urged his B.E. into its best rate of climb, but when he reached 12,000 ft the Zeppelin had attacked Barkingside and turned east for home—and was still some 2,000 ft above him. As it flew directly overhead he opened fire, only to suffer a jam after six rounds. Harris cleared the stoppage and gained another 500 ft, then made a second attack from the rear. Again his Lewis jammed after only a few rounds. While clearing this jam he inadvertently sideslipped and lost the Zeppelin, which moved out of searchlight range. He climbed to 13,000 ft and had one more fleeting glimpse of LZ97 before she finally disappeared.

Capt A. T. Harris, No.39 Squadron, was the first RFC pilot on record as having used Brock bullets on an anti-Zeppelin sortie—on 25/26 April, 1916. This photograph was used on his Royal Aero Club pilot's certificate; and (*right*) Capt J. W. Woodhouse, No.50 Squadron, who attacked Zeppelin L32 on 24/25 August, 1916. This photograph was taken in 1915 when he was in No.4 Squadron.

In his report Harris wrote that an aircraft with better climbing ability would have offered a reasonable chance of success—'but I had the utmost difficulty in getting my machine up to 13,000 ft, the last 4,500 ft taking a great time'. He was also critical of the Hainault Farm flare layout, which 'had to be studied for some time before it was certain that they (the flares) delineated a landing ground at all'.

Although airborne later, William Leefe Robinson was able to attack LZ97 before his flight commander, thanks to a better climbing B.E. He had reached 7,000 ft and saw the Zeppelin at about the same time as Harris, then climbed to a position some 2,000 ft below as it approached Barkingside. His initial burst had no effect and was abruptly terminated by a stoppage. Robinson cleared this but suffered four more jams in quick succession and managed to fire only about 20 rounds before losing his target.

Birley and Holme from Hounslow both saw LZ97 coned by searchlights but were some miles to the west and well beyond range. Birley's engine then gave trouble—once stopping completely and failing to pick up until he was down to 500 ft—so he landed at Joyce Green. Holme's engine also stopped when he was unable to transfer petrol after the front tank ran out and he was fortunate to make a successful dead-stick landing at Chingford.

Both Hainault pilots saw LZ97 but their sluggish B.Es were not equal to the task. Brandon wrote: 'I seemed to make no headway', and Black, 'My aircraft was not climbing at all well above 8,000 ft'.

Official statements that two No.39 Squadron aircraft crashed are clearly exaggerated references to the two emergency landings, for No.18 Wing reported all aircraft down safely. Harris' machine bore a bullet hole in the tailplane. All pilots—except those based there—found the Hainault flarepath highly confusing, and Stewart abandoned an attempt to land and went to Suttons Farm instead.

The two Dover B.Es which patrolled after receiving reports of the LZ87 and LZ88 activities to the north saw nothing. Both carried mixed loads of Ranken darts, HE and incendiary bombs, but no guns.

B.E.2c 7324 was flown by Lieut R. C. L. Holme, No.39 Squadron, from Hounslow on 25/26 April, 1916. This photograph taken at a later date shows the white fuselage ring carried for a time on black-doped home-defence aircraft. (*RAF Museum*)

26/27 April, 1916 (Night)

Target: London.
Enemy force: Army Zeppelin LZ93 (Hptmn W. Schramm).
Results: No casualties or damage.
Defence sorties: Eight.

RNAS
Westgate: B.E.2c 8497 (Flt Cdr C. H. Butler) 22.40–23.55 hr (Manston).

RFC
No.39 Squadron, Hounslow: Two B.E.2c sorties. Details not known.
No.39 Squadron, Suttons Farm: Two B.E.2c sorties. Details not known.
No.39 Squadron, Hainault: Three B.E.2c sorties. Details not known.

LZ93's intended raid on London was abandoned when she developed engine trouble on reaching the coast off Kingsdown at 23.30 hr. She dropped three bombs off Deal and crossed Thanet to depart over Westgate at 22.50 hr.

Searchlights held the Zeppelin for a few seconds only, and Butler could find nothing. In his report he pointed out that unless searchlights could hold the target they were a great hindrance, making it difficult for a pilot to see anything else. Instead of waving in all directions he urged that they should indicate the general track of the enemy.

No details have been traced of the seven sorties totalling nearly six hours flown by No.39 Squadron.

2/3 May, 1916 (Night)

Targets: Rosyth, Forth Bridge (navy); Manchester (army).
Enemy forces: Navy Zeppelins L11 (Kvtkpt V. Schütze), L13 (Kptlt E. Prölss), L14 (Kptlt A. Böcker), L16 (Oblt-z-S W. Peterson), L17 (Kptlt H. Ehrlich), L20 (Kptlt Franz Stabbert), L21 (Kptlt Max Dietrich), L23 (Kptlt O. von Schubert); Army Zeppelin LZ 98 (Oblt E. Lehmann).

Results: Nine killed, 30 injured, £12,030 damage.
Defence sorties: 14 plus.

RNAS

Felixstowe: Short 184 8351 took off 18.50 hr; Sopwith Baby 8200 took off 19.00 hr. Crews not recorded.

Redcar: B.E.2c 1145 (Flt Lieut B. P. H. de Roeper) 23.00–00.01 hr, damaged landing.

Scarborough: Avro 504C 8600 (Flt Sub-Lieut J. C. Croft) 20 min; B.E.2c 1144 (Flt Sub-Lieut J. F. Roche) 25 min.

Whitley Bay: B.E.2cs 1114 (Flt Sub-Lieut Sanders) 50 min; 1119 (Flt Sub-Lieut A. A. Wallis) 40 min.

RFC

No.15 R.A. Squadron, Doncaster: Unspecified B.E.2c (Capt J. H. Herring) 23.00–00.15 hr (Bramham Moor) and 03.10–04.50 hr (Doncaster).

No.33 Squadron, Bramham Moor: Unspecified B.E.2cs (Maj P. B. Joubert) 22.40–23.45 hr and 00.10–00.40 hr; (Capt T. W. P. L. Chaloner) 22.45–00.05 hr.

No.36 Squadron, Cramlington: Sortie(s) flown but not recorded.

No.47 Squadron, Beverley: B.E.2cs 2720 (Lieut N. H. Bottomley) 03.05–03.50 hr; 2721 (Lieut D. C. Rutter) 03.00–03.45 hr.

This was another instance of a substantial raid being severely hampered by bad weather—which also caused the loss of one airship.

Adverse winds encountered well off the Scottish coast influenced all the naval Zeppelins except L14 and L20 to make for the Midlands rather than the Forth. Heavy cloud aggravated the navigational problems for the entire force.

L11 came in over Holy Island at 22.20 hr, flew down the coast and departed an hour later over Amble having dropped only two bombs.

L23 crossed Robin Hood's Bay at 21.15 hr and shortly afterwards dropped an incendiary 15 miles inland on Danby High Moor, possibly to check drift. She then turned north and released eleven bombs on the long-suffering Skinningrove Iron Works, a few more on Easington and departed at 22.25 hr. L16 came in at 21.40 hr a few miles south of L23 and followed a roughly parallel course. By this time an extensive heath fire had developed from von Schubert's incendiary on Danby High Moor, and Peterson dropped a large proportion of his load on the blazing 'buildings and railway tracks'. He released a few more bombs also in open country and flew out over Saltburn at 23.25 hr.

The Danby conflagration was soon acting like a magnet, and L17, which had entered over Saltburn at 22.50 hr and dropped a dozen bombs a mile east of Skinningrove, released her remaining cargo on the blazing heather. She departed north of Whitby shortly after midnight. L13 came in south of Whitby at 22.30 hr, wandered south to Market Weighton and went out near Scarborough at 00.50 hr. The 'Hartlepool' claimed as the aiming point was probably Danby Moor, since only two other random bombs were plotted along L13's track. L21 made landfall north of Scarborough at 21.40 hr, began a 10-min attack on York an hour later and flew out near Bridlington at about midnight.

The two airships which pressed on for Scotland became more drastically lost. L14 reached the coast south of St Abbs Head at 20.25 hr, overshot the Forth and bombed open fields near Arbroath at 22.50 hr. Thoroughly confused after mistaking the Tay for the Forth, Böcker was last reported departing off Fife Ness around 01.00 hr.

L20 crossed five miles south of Montrose at 21.55 hr, failed to obtain radio bearings from base and finally pin-pointed herself over Loch Ness at midnight. Stabbert steered south above the clouds unaware of his slow progress against the strong winds, and left over Peterhead at 02.40 hr, having dropped a few bombs en route. When he eventually achieved radio contact he realized that he could not regain base and made for the Norwegian coast, crash-landing near Stavanger. The crew survived and Stabbert later escaped from captivity and returned to flying.

The army's LZ98 approached Spurn Head at about 19.00 hr and spent an hour cruising off shore before her commander decided to abandon the Manchester mission because of the weather.

Little is recorded about the night's RNAS effort. The Scarborough and Whitley Bay patrols were presumably mounted against the four incursions into their operational areas, and the Felixstowe sorties were made in an unsuccessful attempt to locate LZ98.

De Roeper from Redcar made a valiant attempt to reach L17, briefly lit by searchlights near Skinningrove, but the task was beyond the capabilities of his old Renault-engined B.E.2c and the airship was gradually lost in the mist. He continued patrolling from Hartlepool to Whitby and was unlucky to miss L16 on her departure. On landing he hit a small aerodrome searchlight, just extinguished, and his aircraft was damaged.

B.E.2c 1145 after Flt Lieut B. P. H. de Roeper's landing mishap at Redcar following his unavailing attempt to reach the L17 over Skinningrove. (*RAF Museum*)

The bad weather which presented such difficulties for L14 and L20 evidently prevented operations from RNAS bases in Scotland.

Farther south, Philip Joubert, CO of No.33 Squadron RFC, had trouble in starting his B.E. and did not get away until ten minutes after the Leeds air defence commander had warned of a Zeppelin in the York–Ripon area. Chaloner followed, and both pilots patrolled at 9,000 ft north of Leeds—the most likely target—and thus missed L21 retiring 25 miles to the east after her attack on York. Soon after midnight Joubert flew a second sortie, cut short by falling visibility, but any targets must have been well out of range.

The York bomb explosions, heard 30 miles south at Doncaster, stimulated a stout effort from No.15 RAS. Although the unit was not given take-off orders, Herring flew a voluntary patrol over Leeds, Pontefract and York, unfortunately too late to see anything of the enemy. He landed at Bramham Moor, where the weather was closing in, and after it cleared he returned to Doncaster by an easterly route in the hope of finding stragglers, since the alert was still in force.

At Beverley, where No.47 Squadron's B.E.2cs were on standby each loaded with four 16 lb HE bombs, six incendiaries and a box of Ranken darts, driving rain and heavy cloud persisted for most of the night, though pilots were prepared to take off had a firm threat to Hull developed. When two aircraft were eventually airborne to patrol the Humber and nearby coast for stragglers, heavy cloud still caused navigation difficulties.

One of the French-built REP (Robert Esnault-Pelterie) Parasol monoplanes (8458) which operated from RNAS Eastchurch. (*RAF Museum*)

3 May, 1916 (Daylight)

Target: Deal.
Enemy force: One Hansa-Brandenburg NW.
Results: Four injured, £720 damage.
Defence sorties: 12.

RNAS

Dover: Nieuport 10 3968 15.50–16.17 hr; FBA flying-boat 3207 (Flt Lieut J. C. Brooke, AM Fanshawe) 16.10–17.20 hr.

Eastchurch: B.E.2cs 8295 (Flt Lt H. G. Henley) 15 min; 8609 (Flt Sub-Lieut E. T. Bradley, AM Casting) 25 min; R. E. P. Parasol 8458 (Flt Sub-Lieut Wood) 68 min.

Grain: Sopwith Babies 8151 (Flt Cdr H. M. Cave-Browne-Cave) 15.45–17.15 hr; 8168 took off 15.41 hr.

Westgate: Bristol Scout Cs 3054 (Flt Sub-Lieut J. A. Carr) 15.52–16.29 hr; 3055 (Flt Sub-Lieut J. S. Browne) 15.52-16.10 hr; B.E.2c 8413 (Flt Lieut H. A. Buss, LM Tinsley) 15.52–16.11 hr; Sopwith Schneiders 3766 (Flt Sub-Lieut A. J. Nightingale) 15.52–16.06 hr; 3767 (Flt Sub-Lieut B. A. Millard) 15.52–16.10 hr.

First spotted off Ramsgate, this Brandenburg floatplane of SFA 1 dropped three bombs near a Sandwich gun battery then flew on to drop another seven on Deal, at 15.59 hr.

Damage was mainly to a public house, not the railway station as stated in an official report. This error raised a protest from the local chamber of trade, doubtless worried about any effect on holiday visitors.

Although the raider was over the coast for some ten minutes, mist and low cloud prevented any of the defenders from making contact. RNAS Dunkirk was alerted, and Flt Lieut H. R. Simms in a Nieuport chased what may have been the culprit for 20 min as it made for Zeebrugge. He could not get closer than 800 yards, and the 1½ drums from his Lewis had no effect. The German crew did not report any combat.

Sopwith Baby 8151 flew several unsuccessful interception sorties from RNAS Grain in April–May 1916. Flt Cdr H. M. Cave-Browne-Cave flew it on 19/20 May when seven assorted German floatplanes bombed Kent coast towns.

19/20 May, 1916 (Night)

Target: Kent coast.
Enemy forces: Three Friedrichshafen FF 33, three Hansa-Brandenburg NW, one Gotha Ursinus W.D.
Results: One killed, two injured, £960 damage.
Defence sorties: Eight.

RNAS

Dover: Bristol Scout C 3045 (Flt Sub-Lieut S. J. Goble) 40 min.

Eastchurch: Bristol Scout C 3059 (Flt Lieut H. G. Henley) 02.20–03.10 hr.

Grain: Sopwith 1½ Strutter 9380 (Flt Lieut P. Legh, LM Osborne) 02.43–03.30 hr; Short 827 3106 (Flt Sub-Lieut F. U. Y. Weldon, AM Daly) 02.25–05.10 hr; Sopwith Babies 8151 (Flt Cdr H. M. Cave-Browne-Cave) 03.20–04.50 hr, 8168 (Flt Sub-Lieut H. G. R. Malet) 04.00–05.20 hr.

Westgate: B.E.2cs 8497 (Flt Cdr C. H. Butler) 02.12–03.42 hr; 1158 (Flt Sub-Lieut J. S. Browne, AM H. Phipps).

The precise object of the most ambitious night aeroplane raid to date is not clear—unless it was retaliation for recent heavy RNAS night attacks against German aerodromes in Belgium.

In bright moonlight between 02.08 and 02.17 hr a mixed force of seven floatplanes from SFA 1 attacked Dover, Broadstairs, Deal and Walmer. The

British plotted 59 bombs, each of 22 lb (10 kg), while the Germans claim to have dropped 90 – 45 on Walmer/Deal, 25 on Dover and 20 on Ramsgate. Thirty came from the Gotha Ursinus. For the size of the attack, casualties and damage were light.

There was no advance warning, and at first a Zeppelin was thought to be responsible. The raiders approached from a considerable height, barely heard with their engines well throttled back, and were on their way home before defence aircraft were airborne in any strength. There were no sightings.

RNAS Dunkirk claimed to have shot down two of the returning raiders, though one encounter, by Flt Lieut R. S. Dallas, flying a Nieuport, took place off Blankenberghe at 07.00 hr, well after the aircraft should have landed. The crew of Brandenburg No.521 reported an attack near Calais which could relate to the other RNAS claim, but in fact all the German machines returned safely.

9 July, 1916 (Daylight)

Target: Manston.
Enemy force: One aeroplane, type not known.
Results: No casualties or damage.
Defence sorties: 19.

RNAS

Dover: Bristol Scout C 3039 (Flt Sub-Lieut E. W. Norton) 30 min; Nieuport 10 3966 (Flt Sub-Lieut Young) 30 min; FBA flying-boats 3655 (Flt Sub-Lieut E. J. Cuckney, PO Wood) 10.57–13.15 hr; 9601 (Flt Sub-Lieut M. R. Buckland, LM Robinson) 11.00–14.00 hr.

Eastchurch: Two sorties—details not known.

Felixstowe: Sopwith Baby 8187 (Flt Sub-Lieut Helbert).

Grain: Bristol Scout C 3051 (Flt Sub-Lieut E. M. Morgan) took off 11.07 hr, landed Eastchurch; Sopwith Baby 8160 (Flt Cdr H. M. Cave-Browne-Cave) 11.02–12.05 hr.

Bristol Scout C 3051, piloted by Flt Sub-Lieut E. M. Morgan, RNAS Grain, was among the nineteen aircraft which attempted to intercept an unidentified machine reconnoitring Manston on 9 July, 1916.

Sopwith 1½ Strutter 9667 at RNAS Manston. (*J. M. Bruce/G. S. Leslie collection*)

Manston: Bristol Scout C 3055 (Flt Sub-Lieut C. W. Greig) 10.40–11.35 hr; Bristol Scout Ds 8957 (Flt Sub-Lieut F. S. Mills) 10.45–11.50 hr; 8960 (Flt Cdr C. H. Butler) 10.55–11.40 hr; B.E.2c 8413 (Flt Lieut H. A. Buss) 10.48–11.41 hr; Sopwith 1½ Strutter 9667 (Flt Cdr R. L. G. Marix).

Westgate: Sopwith Schneiders 3767 (Flt Sub-Lieut C. F. M. Chambers) 10.50–11.15 hr; 3766 details not known; Sopwith Baby 8146 (Flt Lieut N. S. Douglas) 11.00–11.30 hr.

RFC

No.39 Squadron, Suttons Farm: One sortie. Details not known.

No.39 Squadron, Hounslow: One sortie. Details not known.

Despite the two-month interval since the last daylight intrusion, this reconnaissance over Manston—probably by Marine Landflieger Abteilung 1—produced rapid and substantial reaction from the defences, with one pilot engaging the enemy.

The North Foreland lookout heard the machine at 10.38 hr and moments later saw it at about 12,000 ft between the clouds. It flew inland, circled Manston aerodrome, then went out over Birchington, and after rounding the North Foreland, disappeared south of Ramsgate at 11.05 hr.

Three Bristol Scouts and a B.E.2c were airborne before the enemy arrived overhead but all except one of the pilots lost it in cloud. Flying his first operational sortie, Mills kept it in view for 25 min until he was 40 miles out to sea, at 12,000 ft in brilliant sunshine with the enemy only 200 yards ahead. He climbed another 200 ft and made a diving attack from the rear, firing a complete drum from his Lewis gun. Re-loading during a wide S-turn, he repeated the attack without any apparent effect, and himself came under fire from the enemy gunner—seated in front of the pilot. Mills was not hit, but nearing Ostende and out of ammunition he had no option but to return.

This spirited performance by a novice earned the formal approbation of the Admiralty, and Mills' station commander put down his lack of success to bad luck. This was always a factor, though inexperienced pilots often failed to appreciate the vital importance of the most careful aiming from very close quarters.

The only other sighting was by Chambers from Westgate, who lost contact when the enemy flew into cloud.

9/10 July, 1916 (Night)

Target: Dover.
Enemy force: One Friedrichshafen FF 33h.
Results: No casualties, £48 damage.
Defence sorties: None.

This night nuisance raider crossed the Kent coast between Folkestone and Dover at 23.50 hr, quietly with engine throttled back, and after displaying some indecision as to a suitable target dropped seven 22 lb bombs on Dover, causing minimal damage. It then departed low down at high speed and no pursuit was attempted.

A Friedrichshafen FF 33h of the type used for the night hit-and-run attack on Dover on 9/10 July, 1916.

Three other aircraft of SFA 1 had embarked on this attack, but one came down off Ostende with engine trouble and another alighted to assist. The third turned back after an instrument-lighting failure.

According to German records Gotha Ursinus No.120 dropped 36 bombs on Harwich at 23.00 hr but there are no British reports of any activity in that area.

28/29 July, 1916 (Night)

Target: Eastern England.
Enemy forces: Navy Zeppelins L11 (Lt-z-S Otto Mieth), L13 (Kptlt E. Prölss), L16 (Kptlt Erich Sommerfeldt), L17 (Kptlt H. Ehrlich), L24 (Kptlt Robert Koch), L31 (Kptlt H. Mathy).
Results: No casualties, £257 damage.
Defence sorties: One.

RFC
No.33 Squadron, Bramham Moor: Unspecified B.E.2c (Capt R. C. L. Holme) 02.00–02.15 hr.

The first airship raid after a lull, dictated by the short nights, of nearly three months was something of an anti-climax. Four of the ten raiders setting out

Kptlt Heinrich Mathy's L31, second of the R-class 'super Zeppelins'.

returned early for various reasons, then widespread fog hampered the attack by the remaining six and grounded defence aircraft. Mathy's L31 was one of the new R-type Zeppelins making its first raid against England.

The airships came in at various points between Spurn Head and Yarmouth from midnight until 02.35 hr, and except for L13, which reached Newark, they penetrated only short distances inland. Nearly 70 bombs were scattered mostly on open ground.

Fog blanketed aerodromes on the eastern side of the country. There was a fleeting clearance at Bramham Moor shortly after L24 was reported in the Hull area, and Holme climbed over the aerodrome until he began to lose sight of the flares at 3,500 ft, so wisely decided to land. At Castle Bromwich, where the weather was better, No.38 Squadron had aircraft on standby, but no action was taken because of what official reports call 'faulty information'.

30/31 July, 1916 (Night)

Target: Not known.
Enemy forces: Not known.
Defence sorties: 16

RNAS

Felixstowe: Sopwith Baby 8167 (Flt Sub-Lieut Helbert) 21.05–21.30 hr; Short 827 8632—details not known.

Killingholme: Sopwith Baby 8206—details not known.

Yarmouth: B.E.2cs 8420 (Flt Lieut B. D. Kilner) 20.20–21.25 hr; 8492 (Flt Lieut E. Cadbury) 20.26–21.35 hr; 8618 (Flt Sub-Lieut E. B. Thompson) 03.53–04.35 hr and 05.45–06.50 hr; 8492 (Flt Sub-Lieut A. V. Robinson) 04.40–05.35 hr; 8492 (Flt Lieut C. H. C. Smith) 05.47–06.30 hr; Bristol Scout C 1253 (Flt Lieut C. H. C. Smith) 20.30–20.50 hr; Short 184 8062 (Flt Lieut B. D. Kilner, CPO Heywood) 04.20–09.45 hr.

Bacton: B.E.2c 8418 (Flt Sub-Lieut E. L. Pulling), 20.05–21.34 hr and 04.10–05.45 hr.

Covehithe: B.E.2c 8612 (Flt Sub-Lieut J. C. Northrop) 03.30–05.30 hr.

Holt: B.E.2c 8613 (Flt Sub-Lieut G. W. R. Fane) 19.56–21.14 hr and 04.45–06.30 hr.

But for a plausibly described encounter with an airship engaged on some activity not covered in available German records, this night's operations would have been attributed to false alarms.

Reports of Zeppelins off the Norfolk coast came during the evening, and six sorties were flown from Felixstowe, Yarmouth and its satellites between approximately 20.00 and 21.00 hr, but there were no sightings. Further information received in the small hours then stimulated the air defences into renewed activity.

At about 05.00 hr an airship was seen some 30 miles off the coast by Northrop, from Covehithe, flying a B.E.2c laden with four 16 lb bombs, two boxes of Ranken darts and a Lewis gun fixed to fire vertically upwards. The raider was about 1,500 ft above him and he followed it northeastwards, gradually shortening the distance, and when about 1,000 ft underneath he fired two drums of Brock and tracer ammunition, which appeared to score some hits. He loaded a third drum, but after four shots this flew off the gun and struck him a considerable blow on the forehead. He was dazed for some seconds but when he recovered, the airship had vanished in cloud. No other pilots made sightings, and no airships were reported as crossing the coast.

31 July/1 August, 1916 (Night)

Targets: London, Eastern England.
Enemy forces: Navy Zeppelins L11 (Kvtkpt V. Schütze), L13 (Kptlt E. Prölss), L14 (Hptmn Kuno Manger), L16 (Kptlt E. Sommerfeldt), L17 (Kptlt H. Ehrlich), L22 (Kptlt Martin Dietrich), L23 (Kptlt O. von Schubert), L31 (Kptlt H. Mathy).
Results: No casualties, £139 damage.
Defence sorties: 12.

RNAS
Eastchurch: B.E.2c 8610 (Flt Sub-Lieut E. P. Hicks, AM Greenwood) 60 min.
Felixstowe: B.E.2c 8301 21.15–21.45 hr, returned early due to fog.
Killingholme: Sopwith Babies 8148 22.00–22.33 hr; 8161 22.10–22.46 hr; Short 184 8391, details not known.

B.E.2c 8298 flown by Flt Cdr C. H. Butler at RNAS Manston.

Yarmouth: B.E.2c 8492 (Flt Sub-Lieut E. B. Thompson) 03.15–06.30 hr (Wymondham).

Bacton: B.E.2c 8418 (Flt Sub-Lieut E. L. Pulling) 20.25–20.29 hr, returned early due to fog; unspecified B.E.2c (Flt Sub-Lieut E. Cadbury) 20.30–22.30 hr.

Holt: Unspecified B.E.2c, six-minute sortie, returned due to fog.

Manston: B.E.2cs 8298 (Flt Cdr C. H. Butler) 23.30–00.25 hr; 8413 (Flt Sub-Lieut J. S. Browne) took off 23.58 hr.

RFC

No.51 Squadron, Mattishall: One sortie, 00.52–01.06 hr, crashed.

This was another ineffectual raid, with the Zeppelins becoming widely scattered by unpredicted winds after crossing the North Sea mainly above cloud.

Seven airships made landfall at various points from Covehithe to Skegness between 22.40 and 02.00 hrs, while Mathy in L31, apparently thinking he was near London, was briefly over Thanet at 23.30 hr. Of the other Zeppelins, L16 reached Newark, L14 the March area, while L22 flew inland as far as Haverhill. Bombs fell mainly in open country.

Most of the comings and goings were over the territory covered by Yarmouth and its satellites, all badly affected by fog. The first sorties were flown rather prematurely, following reports from a ship spotting several raiders still more than an hour's flying time from the coast. Thompson, who took off just after the last Zeppelin had departed, became well and truly lost in the poor visibility, but it was engine trouble which forced him down at Wymondham, with substantial damage to the aircraft.

Mathy's brief flight over Thanet brought a quick response from Eastchurch and Manston, but the pilots saw nothing of the enemy.

The RFC sortie by No.51 Squadron ended in a crash, with the pilot variously reported as slightly or seriously injured. The aircraft, type unrecorded, took off immediately after L17 had dropped a bomb several hundred yards from Mattishall. Airborne for only 14 min, it was still low down when it stalled and crashed, probably after the pilot lost control in a patch of mist.

2/3 August, 1916 (Night)

Target: Eastern England:

Enemy forces: Navy Zeppelins L11 (Kvtkpt V. Schütze), L13 (Kptlt R. Prölss), L16 (Kptlt E. Sommerfeldt), L17 (Kptlt H. Ehrlich), L21 (Hptmn A. Stelling), L31 (Kptlt H. Mathy).

Results: One injured, £796 damage.

Defence sorties: 32.

RNAS

Cranwell: B.E.2c 8302 (Flt Cdr the Master of Sempill) 03.50–06.00 hr; Bristol Scout C 3016 (Flt Sub-Lieut A. H. Gilligan) 04.50–06.00 hr.

Dover: FBA flying-boats 3656 (Flt Sub-Lieut J. C. Watson, AM Pearson) 04.30–06.00 hr; 9601 (Flt Lieut G. G. Hodge, PO Hanna) 04.30–05.45 hr.

Felixstowe: Sopwith Baby 8187 took off 20.45 hr; Short 184 9068 took off 20.45 hr; Short 184 modified 9085, details not known.

Killingholme: Sopwith Babies 8131 (Flt Sub-Lieut G. H. Simpson) 20.13–21.18 hr; 8148 (Flt Sub-Lieut K. N. Smith) 20.20–21.40 hr; unspecified Baby (Flt Sub-Lieut F. M. Fox) 04.15–06.54 hr (Lowestoft).

Manston: B.E.2cs 8298 (Flt Cdr C. H. Butler) 01.05–02.30 hr; 8497 (Sqn Cdr R. L. G. Marix) 01.00–02.30 hr; Sopwith 1½ Strutter 9414 took off 02.38 hr.

Yarmouth: B.E.2cs 8420 (Flt Lieut B. D. Kilner) 20.20–21.25 hr; 8417 (Flt Cdr V. Nicholl) 21.45–22.45 hr; 8418 (Flt Sub-Lieut E. L. Pulling) 23.30–01.15 hr (Burgh Castle); 8419 (Flt Lieut C. H. C. Smith) 04.45–05.15 hr; Sopwith Baby 8132 (Flt Lieut C. E. Wood) 19.27–20.50 hr; Sopwith Schneider 3776 (Flt Lieut C. J. Galpin) 20.15–21.45 hr (off Cromer).

Bacton: B.E.2cs 8618 (Flt Lieut E. Cadbury) 20.15–22.06 hr and 23.47–02.10 hr; 1155 (Flt Sub-Lieut A. V. Robinson) 03.45–04.10 hr.

Covehithe: B.E.2c 8612 (Flt Sub-Lieut S. Kemball) 01.25–01.45 hr.

Holt: B.E.2c 8613 (Flt Sub-Lieut G. W. R. Fane) 05.35–07.35 hr.

HMS *Vindex*: Bristol Scout D 8953 (Flt Lieut C. T. Freeman) took off 19.50 hr.

HMS *Brocklesby*: Sopwith Baby 8149 (Flt Sub-Lieut G. H. Bittles) 19.40–20.40 hr, (Yarmouth); Sopwith Schneider 3736 (Flt Sub-Lieut H. B. Smith) 19.45–21.10 hr, (Yarmouth).

RFC

No.33 Squadron, Beverley: Unspecified B.E.2c (Capt R. C. L. Holme) 02.25–03.35 hr.

No.50 Squadron, Dover: B.E.2cs 2711 (2nd Lieut W. A. McClaughry) 01.30–02.15 hr; 2699 (Maj M. G. Christie) 01.45–02.25 hr.

No.51 Squadron, Thetford: Aircraft and crew not known, 00.35–00.50 hr, returned early with engine trouble and took off again 01.35 hr.

This eventful night witnessed the first use of an aircraft carrier in the air-defence role, several contacts with the enemy and some competent sea rescues. Still lacking was that elusive objective—the destruction of a Zeppelin.

All the airships except Mathy's L31 came in over the East Anglian coast between Wells and Orfordness, at irregular intervals from 23.45 until 01.00 hr. None journeyed far inland—L21 reached Thetford, L13 flew as far as Wymondham and L17 was over Eye. The only apparent attempt to hit a specific target was L11's bombing of Harwich, the other vessels scattering their bombs mostly in open country.

Mathy, now regarded as one of the ablest Zeppelin commanders, suffered another uncharacteristic lapse and repeated his performance of 48 hr earlier by briefly appearing over the Kent coast and dropping his bombs in the sea off Dover. Again he thought he had attacked London, and in his anxiety to reach the target with minimal assistance from wireless fixes, he perhaps misjudged wind strength at the greater cruising altitudes obtainable by his new airship.

Action started several hours before the Zeppelins reached the coast. Following early warning of a raid, the Admiralty ordered to sea various vessels including the small carrier *Vindex* from Harwich and the seaplane tender *Brocklesby* from Lowestoft. *Vindex* was about 50 miles out when a Zeppelin was sighted in the distance, and at 19.50 hr Charles Freeman successfully flew off the carrier's 64-ft flight deck. His Bristol Scout climbed only slowly due to fuel pressure trouble, but on reaching 5,000 ft he saw two airships, one at 8,500 ft about ten miles away and the second another ten miles further east. As Freeman continued to climb, apparently unnoticed by the enemy, the Bristol's air-bags to provide buoyancy after ditching (the *Vindex* deck was too small for landing) began to expand and foul the tail controls, making the rudder very stiff to operate, and at 7,000 ft causing further handling difficulties. Eventually he managed to get 500 ft above the nearest Zeppelin (the L17) and released his first box of Ranken darts, which missed. He banked round for a second attack, dropping a half-container, but the airship was skilfully turned to avoid the missiles. On a final attempt with his remaining darts he saw a puff of smoke from the envelope suggesting a hit, after which the Zeppelin dived to 5,000 ft. Although under fire from the forward upper machine-gun, Freeman followed and tried to cut her off, but she headed east, apparently undamaged.

As he turned back towards *Vindex* his engine failed—possibly damaged by enemy bullets—and he made a perfect ditching near the North Hinder lightship. His Very pistol was flung into the sea but he managed to light several spare cartridges with matches. Gradually the Bristol's nose sank and Freeman climbed on to the tail, where he crouched in the gathering darkness for 90 minutes. Suddenly he saw the dim outline of a steamer and attracted her attention by firing his revolver and lighting some letters which he had in his pockets. She was the Belgian vessel *Anvers*, which landed him at 05.00 hr next morning at the Hook of Holland—to be released a few days later as a shipwrecked mariner.

Bristol Scout D 8953, flown by Flt Lieut C. T. Freeman from HMS *Vindex* and ditched after his unsuccessful attack on L17 on 2/3 August, 1916—a photograph taken at Filton before the aircraft was delivered to the RNAS. (*R. C. B. Ashworth*)

In his report Freeman described the view from the Bristol Scout as hopeless for attacking from above, and suggested that dropping all darts together would increase the chances of disabling an airship. He added: 'I am fully confident that with a gun of some description I could not have failed to hit every time by nose diving.'

Shortly before Freeman took off, the *Brocklesby*, on station some 40 miles to the northwest, also spotted a Zeppelin and smartly lowered two seaplanes, airborne within five minutes of each other. Smith, flying a rather elderly Sopwith Schneider, had minor engine trouble shortly after take-off but this cleared and he climbed close enough below the airship to read (as he thought) L33 on her bow. In fact L33 had not then been launched, so it might have been L13.

Smith got in a very brief attack before the Zeppelin rapidly ascended beyond his reach, and after circling a few times flew to Yarmouth. Bittles in the Baby managed to follow for a little longer and fired a few bursts at long range, then he too lost the airship after it entered cloud, and departed for Yarmouth.

Wireless reports from British warships of the raiders' unexplained proximity to the coast so long before their landfall times stimulated early reaction from the coastal aerodromes. The only sighting was by Galpin, from Yarmouth, in a Schneider seaplane, who observed a Zeppelin far to his north after breaking cloud at 6,000 ft—probably that seen by Smith and Bittles. Galpin chased for 20 min, making little headway while climbing to 8,000 ft, and gave up when it disappeared into cloud.

It was almost dark when he reached the coast, so he alighted near a steamer anchored four miles north of Cromer. To his alarm he found that strong tides were rapidly sweeping him away from the vessel—the *Albertville* on passage from the Congo to Belgium via Hull—and he was already several miles distant when her co-operative master, Capt Joseph Bernaerts, lowered two boats which towed him alongside. The Schneider was finally hoisted aboard at 04.15 hr and later disembarked at Killingholme.

Of the pilots patrolling over East Anglia, only Pulling in a Yarmouth B.E.2c made a sighting—and an attack. He took off when L16 and L17 were approaching the coast at about 8,000 ft a few miles to the north. The station commander decided to light up Burgh Castle landing ground as 'bait', and shortly afterwards L17 obligingly headed in that direction. She was spotted by Pulling 1,000 ft beneath, who opened fire with his Lewis, only for it to jam after a few shots. He then attempted to get above the Zeppelin to drop darts, but she drew ahead as he climbed, so with some difficulty he cleared his gun for another attack from below. This time the drum flew off, and after replacing it he fired several long bursts and saw some bullets hit the hull. While fitting a third drum he lost his quarry, and after a fruitless search put down at Burgh Castle. He landed down wind in error, hit a fence and badly damaged the aircraft, though was himself unhurt.

From RFC Thetford an unspecified No.51 Squadron aircraft took off after L21 had aimed some bombs at the aerodrome flares, but returned 15 min later with engine trouble. By the time it was airborne again the enemy was departing over the coast. No.33 Squadron (and various RNAS units) flew belated patrols while the alert was still in force, though in fact the raiders had departed.

In the south, Manston despatched two B.E.2cs as Mathy flew over Deal at 01.00 hr, but there was some delay in warning Dover and No.50 Squadron's aircraft did not take off until 20 min after L31 had turned out to sea. None of these crews saw anything.

8/9 August, 1916 (Night)

Target: Northeast England.
Enemy forces: Navy Zeppelins L11 (Kvtkpt V. Schütze), L13 (Kptlt E. Prölss), L14 (Hptmn K. Manger), L16 (Kptlt E. Sommerfeldt), L21 (Hptmn A. Stelling), L22 (Kptlt Martin Dietrich), L24 (Kptlt R. Koch), L30 (Kptlt H. von Buttlar), L31 (Kptlt H. Mathy).
Results: Ten killed, 16 injured, £13,196 damage.
Defence sorties: Two.

RNAS
Redcar: B.E.2c 1109 (Flt Lieut B. P. H. de Roeper) 00.10–02.45 hr.
Whitley Bay: One sortie, took off 02.30 hr, details not known.

With the exception of L14, which flew in over Berwick upon Tweed at 00.25 hr and departed over Alnwick at 02.00 hr, and L16 briefly over the Hunstanton area

RNAS Redcar's obsolescent Renault B.E.2c, 1109, which Flt Lieut B. P. H. de Roeper found so inadequate against the Zeppelins raiding northeastern England on 8/9 August, 1916. It was still in use that November. (*RAF Museum*)

at 00.30–01.00 hr, this force made landfall between Tynemouth and Flamborough Head at various times from 00.15 until 02.00 hr, without penetrating more than about 20 miles inland. L24 bombed Hull, which suffered most of the casualties and damage.

The fog which hampered the enemy's navigation also prevented operations at all aerodromes except Redcar—though Whitley Bay cleared to permit one sortie towards the end of the raid period.

Redcar had become a purely training station with no aircraft allocated for home defence and the only machine available was a solitary 80 hp Renault-engined B.E.2c. Bruno de Roeper took off in this venerable hack, carrying four 16 lb bombs and twelve Ranken darts to combat a Zeppelin reported near Hartlepool. From 6,000 ft he saw bombs bursting to the south, and as he continued climbing, he spotted an airship some 2,000 ft higher briefly held by a searchlight near Saltburn. He laboured up to 9,300 ft, trailing the enemy as it followed the coast down to Hornsea and reached about 12,000 ft. He took station below the Zeppelin's starboard quarter, and realizing that his ancient B.E. had reached its ceiling, jettisoned his bombs and managed to stagger up to just over 11,000 ft. The airship was still out of range above him and about ¾-mile ahead, but he doggedly followed 20 miles out to sea off Flamborough Head until it gradually faded into the mist.

Deeply frustrated by the outcome of this one-sided contest, de Roeper wrote in his report:

> ' . . . if an effective machine had been available, say a 1½-Strutter or a RAF-engined B.E., with a quick climb to 15,000 ft and about 20 knots faster than mine, bombs could have effectively been dropped on the Zeppelin.'

It is difficult to say which Zeppelin (or Zeppelins) de Roeper chased, because the night's tracks were closely interwoven and some locations and timings in the official plot do not correspond with Redcar's own report—which is probably more accurate in local detail. For example, Redcar logged six bombs cratering the aerodrome at 00.35 hr, whereas the official plot puts this bombing—by L22—at 01.00 hr.

De Roeper's first sighting could have been either L21 or L22—both in the Saltburn area at the time—then, as he flew southwards he could have picked up L22 which departed south of Whitby at 01.50 hr. The situation is further confused by a much later report from a German prisoner, formerly in L11's crew, that she was 'attacked' by two aircraft at 02.15 hr that night. The British plotted L11 near Tynemouth, and de Roeper was unable to 'attack'—but he was the only defender airborne at the time.

De Roeper's determined effort earned the personal approbation of Balfour, First Lord of the Admiralty, and started the predictable probe into the absence of more warlike aircraft in the northeast. The Director of Air Services explained that Redcar could not have 100 hp RAF-engined B.E.2cs without weakening resources of more important stations 'owing to the failure of the War Office to supply engines for these machines as promised'.

This comment was typical of the gratuitous inter-Service sniping which increasingly garnished the minute sheets of Whitehall files. An example from the army side was this comment by a GHQ Home Forces intelligence officer on an RNAS suggestion about illuminated decoy aerodromes—'. . . the trouble is that the RNAS are "suspect" in the Admiralty for want of accuracy and a thirst for DSOs'.

12 August, 1916 (Daylight)

Target: Dover.
Enemy force: One aeroplane, type not known.
Results: None killed, seven injured, no damage.
Defence sorties: Ten.

RNAS

Dover: Nieuport 10s 3966 (Flt Sub-Lieut F. C. C. Calder) 12.30–13.45 hr; 3967 (Flt Sub-Lieut A. D. Carey) 12.30–13.02 hr; FBA flying-boat 3656 (Flt Lieut G. G. Hodge, LM White) took off 12.32 hr, alighted Dunkirk.

Manston: Bristol Scout C 3055 (Flt Sub-Lieut E. M. Morgan) 12.38–13.03 hr; Bristol Scout Ds 8951 (Flt Lieut J. A. Carr) 12.34–13.04 hr; 8956 (Flt Sub-Lieut C. W. Greig) 12.38–13.13 hr; B.E.2c 8413 (Flt Lieut H. A. Buss).

Westgate: Sopwith Schneider 3766, 12.34–13.20 hr.

RFC

No.50 Squadron, Dover: B.E.12s 6146 (2nd Lieut C. A. Hore) 12.30–14.00 hr; 6510 (2nd Lieut W. A. McClaughry) 12.32–14.00 hr.

This was another skilfully executed sortie by Walther Ilges of Marine Landflieger Abteilung 1. The aircraft—type not recorded—approached Dover unseen, flying very high, and at 12.27 hr dropped four bombs, at least one falling on the RNAS Guston Road aerodrome.

Despite the lack of warning, defenders were airborne with commendable promptness, but it was a day of poor visibility and only one pilot spotted the enemy. This was Hore, who followed for 30 min, climbing steadily and gradually gaining until he lost his quarry in a thick bank of cloud.

The four-month gap since the last daylight nuisance attack on Dover is the

B.E.12 No.6510, piloted by 2nd Lieut (later Air Vice-Marshal) W. A. McClaughry, was one of two No.50 Squadron aircraft which operated from Dover on 12 August, 1916. This fairly common attitude for the period (responsible pilot not known) shows to advantage the Le Prieur rocket rails and flare brackets. (*J. M. Bruce/G. S. Leslie collection*)

likely reason for the disproportionate concern over the lack of warning for this minor example.

From the Air Board the 68-year-old Lord Sydenham querulously demanded 'can we not ask why this incident was possible?' Christie, CO of No.50 Squadron, had already complained to Holt at Home Defence Wing that their first intimation had been the sound of bombs bursting at Guston Road, and that more alert observations from the Anti-Aircraft Command Post might have enabled the bomber to be cut off. Holt suggested to the Dover Garrison Commander, Brig-Gen C. Bickford, that even the most general preliminary warning in such terms as 'unknown aeroplane approaching Dover at great height' would have enabled fighters to take off five minutes earlier. Bickford regarded the criticism as unreasonable and doubted whether the extra few minutes would have made any practical difference. Unidentified aircraft movements were already reported, he said, and the usually alert and competent observers should not be too harshly blamed for missing one intruder flying very high over broken cloud. However, he agreed to establish an observer post near the South Foreland lighthouse. The War Office tended to side with Bickford, and regarded the whole affair as a storm in a teacup.

23/24 August, 1916 (Night)

Target: East Anglia.
Enemy force: Army Zeppelin LZ97.
Results: No casualties or damage.
Defence sorties: None.

Intelligence rarely received advance warning of German army airship raids and LZ97 came in unheralded over Bawdsey at 23.55 hr, flew a few miles inland and dropped bombs in open country. She departed over Orfordness about 20 min later. The airship was not picked up by searchlights and no defence sorties were flown.

24/25 August, 1916 (Night)

Target: London.
Enemy forces: Navy Zeppelins L16 (Kptlt E. Sommerfeldt), L21 (Oblt-z-S Kurt Frankenburg), L31 (Kptlt H. Mathy), L32 (Oblt-z-S W. Peterson).
Results: Nine killed, 40 injured, £130,203 damage.
Defence sorties: 16.

RNAS

Eastchurch: B.E.2cs 8426 (Flt Cdr A. K. Robertson) 23.46–00.56 hr; 8295 (Flt Sub-Lieut E. T. Bradley) 01.41–03.15 hr.

Felixstowe: Short 827s 3324 (Flt Sub-Lieut Helbert, PO R. W. A. Ivermee) 05.25–07.50 hr; 8631 (Flt Sub-Lieut C. E. Fox, AM Shorter) 05.35–07.45 hr.

Grain: B.E.2cs 8500 (Flt Lieut E. de C. Hallifax) 01.47–02.15 hr; 8296 took off 01.37 hr.

Manston: B.E.2c 8298 (Flt Cdr C. H. Butler) 02.21–03.45 hr; Sopwith 1½ Strutters 9400 (Flt Cdr C. Draper, PO Walker) 02.15–03.30 hr; 9414 (Sqn Cdr R. L. G. Marix) 02.25–03.35 hr.

RFC

No.39 Squadron, North Weald: B.E.2cs 2042 (2nd Lieut C. S. Ross) 01.34–05.05 hr (Joyce Green); 2023 (2nd Lieut J. I. Mackay) 01.48–03.00 hr (Burnham).

No.39 Squadron, Suttons Farm: B.E.2cs 2693 (Lieut W. L. Robinson) 01.17–02.25 hr; 2092 (2nd Lieut F. Sowrey) 01.49–02.25 hr.

No.39 Squadron, Hainault: B.E.2c 4193 (Lieut A. D. Broughton) 01.45–01.50 hr, crashed.

No.50 Squadron, Dover: B.E.2cs 4142 (Capt J. W. Woodhouse) 02.15–04.30 hr; 2699 (Maj M. G. Christie) 02.20–03.05 hr.

The four airships which crossed the coast—two over Suffolk and Essex and the 'super Zeppelins' over Kent—were the survivors of an initial raiding force twelve strong, eight commanders having abandoned the mission for various reasons.

L16 was over the country for little more than an hour, and her bombs fell harmlessly northeast of Ipswich at 00.15 hr. L21 crossed over Frinton at 01.43 hr, flying very high, and made for Harwich, but her bombs, dropped at 02.00 hr, undershot by several miles and caused only minor damage.

Mathy in L31 made landfall off Margate at 23.30 hr and flew direct to London, where his attack two hours later—the first on the capital since October 1915—caused all the night's casualties and most of the property damage. L32 came in east of Folkestone at 02.10 hr and followed the coast to Deal, dropping her bombs in the sea.

The two northerly raiders encountered no opposition from the air. Only days earlier the Admiralty had transferred Felixstowe's four B.E.2cs to Yarmouth since most airships came in over that station's area. When by chance L16 and L21 flew well south of the usual track all that Felixstowe could provide was a couple of first-light sorties, more to look for an airship believed damaged by naval gunfire at sea than to find stragglers.

Official files contain no explanation why Manston did not react to L31's inbound passage off the north Kent coast. From Eastchurch, where visibility was indifferent, Robertson patrolled over Sheppey at 9,000 ft, seeing nothing except searchlights sweeping ineffectually to the west.

Cockpit of B.E.2c 2693, flown by Lieut W. Leefe Robinson on 24/25 August, 1916. (*J. M. Bruce/G. S. Leslie collection*)

There was evidently some delay in reporting L31's progress to the RFC since only Leefe Robinson from Suttons Farm was airborne before Mathy began his bombing run. He saw nothing, and No.39 Squadron's only sighting was by Mackay, from North Weald, who caught a fleeting glimpse of the Zeppelin and followed for some miles before losing it. He then lost himself and put down at Burnham, wiping off his undercarriage. Broughton flew into a patch of mist just after take-off at Hainault, spun and crashed on the aerodrome.

Bradley from RNAS Eastchurch and Draper from Manston saw the departing L31 in the Southend searchlights, but lost her as she flew out to sea. Both pilots, and Marix, also spotted L32 at 9–10,000 ft in the searchlights along the Kent coast, and Draper was gaining ground when she disappeared in cloud.

Closest to success that night was John Woodhouse, No.50 Squadron, recently returned from the Western Front with a high reputation as a special duties pilot, flying 'cloak and dagger' missions to land agents behind the enemy lines.

Woodhouse saw L32 in the Dover searchlights shortly after taking off, and pursued her up Channel until he entered cloud at 4,000 ft. Fortunately she was still visible when he broke clear, and he positioned underneath at 7,000 ft, about 200 ft below the Zeppelin. He fired a drum and a half of Pomeroy ammunition, which fell short, and while reloading lost sight of his target. He continued climbing to 11,000 ft and eventually abandoned the hunt. By this time he was uncertain of his own position, and it was with much relief that he saw the distant Dover aerodrome searchlights. Christie, who had landed earlier, ordered them to be lit as a navigation aid. He also saw L32, but lost her on emerging from the cloud layer.

Chapter X

Defeat of the Zeppelins—and the Great Wireless Mystery

Suddenly the whole picture changed. Less than 36 hr after the break-up of the depressing Air Board meeting which had offered so little indication of progress towards defeating the night-bombing campaign, an airship was brought down in flames—the first to suffer that fate since Warneford had destroyed LZ37 more than a year before.

The victim on the night of 2/3 September was the army's SL11, one of the wooden-framed Schütte-Lanz ships of approximately the same size and performance as the Q-type Zeppelins.

The great significance of this notable victory was its achievement by an aeroplane using the new explosive and incendiary ammunition. The fall was seen by six of the other raiders over England that night, and some of their commanders correctly appreciated that a fighter was responsible. The spectacle understandably dented the morale of the airship services and brought a corresponding rise in that of Home Defence Wing—and of the British public. To the present generation, which has only passing acquaintanceship with small postwar airships, it is difficult to convey the brooding menace projected by the night monsters of 1915–18, three times as big, or the awe-inspiring yet exhilarating spectacle of SL11's crash to earth at Cuffley in a mass of lurid flame from a million cubic feet of hydrogen. Despite the 'unsocial' hour of 02.25, it was seen by hundreds of thousands of cheering people over a radius of some 40 miles.

Like other pilots in No.39 Squadron, William Leefe Robinson, who destroyed the airship, had become convinced that the new ammunition promised the best chance of success, and with the tacit agreement of the squadron commander had discarded the officially specified darts and rockets. This lightened the B.E.2c and enhanced its performance, allowing the Lewis gun to be used to better advantage. By chance he also discovered the correct—and with hindsight, the most logical—technique for machine-gun attack. Having sprayed two drums of Brock and Pomeroy bullets along virtually the entire length of the airship with no visible result, he concentrated the third in one place, seeing the glow of fire inside the hull immediately after the drum was exhausted.

On receiving the news, Holt advised GHQ Home Forces by immediate signal:

> 'It is very important that the successful method of attack remains secret, and instructions have therefore been issued that the public are to be told that the attack was made with incendiary bombs from above.'

This was the story given to the Press—and also recorded by the zealous compiler of Secret Air Raid Circular No.112 of 3 September, which blandly stated that the airship was destroyed 'by an aeroplane which dropped a number of incendiary bombs into her hull'. However, the facts soon became common knowledge and it is doubtful whether the Germans were for a moment deceived.

A strong claim by HQ London District that SL11 had been shot down by AA fire from the Temple House battery, Waltham Abbey sub-command, was rejected after a thorough investigation of all facts and reliable eye-witness reports. The London AA Commander, Col M. St L. Simon, remained unconvinced, and wrote in a postwar report.

> 'There can be no doubt that the Temple guns crippled the enemy airship simultaneously with the arrival of Lt Robinson on the scene. The gunfire was twice corroborated by distant observations. Corroborative evidence from searchlights illuminating the target pointed to a sudden drop in the height of the airship before she caught fire.'

Later examination did in fact show evidence of shell damage to an engine, which could have slowed SL11 during her last moments.

Any few lingering doubts within Home Defence Wing were dispelled by further successes which followed quickly. In five raids during the remaining weeks of the year, 29 airships came over the country and five were shot down—four by machine-gun fire from B.E.2c pilots and one by anti-aircraft guns.

The disposition of the fighter victories—three by No.39 Squadron defending London, one by No.36 in the northeast and one by RNAS Yarmouth—provided

This photograph, known to be of No.39 Squadron B.E.2c No.2693 at RNAS Eastchurch in June 1916, suggests that the RFC sought the advice of naval armament specialists in devising an effective Lewis gun installation for anti-Zeppelin work. The guard wire intended to prevent bullet damage to the wing centre-section is visible at the top of the picture. The RFC flight sergeant has not been identified. B.E.2c 2693 was flown by Lieut W. Leefe Robinson on 24/25 August, 1916, and possibly on 2/3 September. (*J. M. Bruce/G. S. Leslie collection*)

satisfying confirmation that air defence deployments were generally well placed to meet the threat.

One apparent gap remaining was exposed after a flight by L31 over Portsmouth on 25/26 September, countered only by two hopelessly inadequate seaplanes from Calshot. Although the onus for attacking raiders approaching the country rested on the RNAS, GHQ Home Forces nevertheless asked the War Office for a squadron to cover this area, recommending the temporary redeployment south of No.37 Squadron, forming at Chelmsford to deal with day raiders approaching London over the Essex coast. Intelligence did not expect any such attacks for at least another three months.

In the event No.37 Squadron did not move, because No.78 was due to form on 1 November with headquarters at Hove and aerodromes at Telscombe Cliffs (Newhaven) and Chiddingstone Causeway (Tonbridge). Telscombe was ready by the end of September, and was used as necessary by No.50 Squadron aircraft to meet any likely Portsmouth threat. However, neither base proved of long-term value to the defence chain, and in 1917 No.78 Squadron moved northeast of London. No.37 Squadron, with Nos.75, 76 and 77 deferred earlier in the year because of Western Front priorities, were formed between 15 September and 1 October.

The run of RFC successes eventually destroyed the Admiralty's stubborn faith in anti-Zeppelin bombs, and on 19 October the Director of Air Services advised the Commodore, Lowestoft (who was responsible for RNAS Yarmouth), that the best armament for B.E.2cs was a machine-gun firing over the top wing, loaded with alternate Brock, Pomeroy and Buckingham or Sparklet bullets. Pilots were advised to concentrate fire at one spot on the airship's envelope. Le Prieur rockets might be used from a position slightly above the target, but much practice was required to obtain satisfactory results.

The defences' greatest night was 27/28 November, when two Zeppelins were shot down, fittingly one each by the RNAS and RFC. In the resulting euphoria a significant happening on the morning of the 28th caused remarkably little stir among the public at large or in Whitehall. A single naval L.V.G. biplane flew to central London and dropped half-a-dozen bombs in broad daylight, meeting no opposition in either direction. A few newspapers appreciated this portent, and *The Times* warned of the dangerous possibility that it could be a prelude to further visits on an extended scale. The next issue of *The Aeroplane* weekly carried this comment from its outspoken editor, Charles Grey:

> 'When the aeroplane raids start, and prove more damaging than the airship raids, the authorities cannot say that they have not had a fair warning of what to expect.'

In August the specialist nature of night operations was recognized by the transfer to Home Defence Wing of No.11 Reserve Squadron, Northolt, the principal night-flying training unit. In the early days a pilot was considered night qualified after successfully completing five flights in darkness and demonstrating his knowledge of the current anti-airship armament. Later the syllabus was widened to include firing Le Prieur rockets at a 'Zeppelin' target on the ground, and air firing from a Lewis gun at small hydrogen balloons. In the absence of anything resembling operational training units, the more advanced exercises were conducted in the squadrons. In September, for example, No.39 Squadron pilots practised dropping Ranken darts on a target towed by a launch in the lower reaches of the Thames.

There were no significant developments in home-defence aircraft during the rest of the year. A few F.E.2bs entered service, and in August the War Office decided that Nos.37, 39 and 50 Squadrons defending London should be re-armed with the type. This was not effected because of a likely requirement for the F.Es in the bomber role, and in any case, the B.E.2c was demonstrably proving itself in the anti-airship function. For dealing with the contemporary airships there was little to choose between the two machines and in some situations the F.E's pusher layout, giving an unrestricted view for the observer/gunner, offered an advantage. Another type issued was the B.E.2e, an ungainly development of the 2c, with wings of unequal span and offering no significant advance in performance. Holt considered it inferior to the B.E.2c for home defence, and asked the War Office to continue allotting the older aircraft where possible. Then came the B.E.12a, the result of mating B.E.2e wings to the B.E.12 fuselage.

A typical B.E.2e, possibly of No.76 Squadron. Despite Home Defence Wing's initial lack of enthusiasm, B.E.2es were widely employed from late 1916, though they were demonstrably incapable of effective combat with the later Zeppelins or aeroplane bombers. (*R. C. Bowyer*)

Experiments with landing lights continued, and reports refer briefly to a 'Lucas headlamp' being found very useful at RNAS Burgh Castle, and a 'French landing searchlight' fitted to a B.E.2c. The Orfordness experimental station tested an unspecified type of RNAS landing light, and also ordered some special electric bulbs with the upper half silvered for fitting under the wings of aircraft. Although no detailed reports covering this area of research have been traced, the general conclusion was that such installations were complicated and cumbersome, producing results not significantly better than the simple Holt flares.

There were also trials with airborne searchlights to assist in finding airships, and an F.E.2b was fitted with a narrow-beam light coupled to paired Lewis guns. Such devices were found to be of little practical value and had the disadvantage of disclosing the fighter's position to the enemy.

In the wider problem of directing fighters towards the approximate track of the enemy, highly encouraging results were being achieved in the RFC wireless trials.

On 18 February, two days after taking over the air-defence responsibility, the War Office had called a meeting to discuss a scheme for signalling orders by wireless telegraphy to home-defence aircraft during raids. Signals experts

An RNAS Whitley Bay B.E.2c fitted with a CAV car headlamp adapted as a landing light. (*J. M. Bruce/G. S. Leslie collection*)

A French Sautter-Harlé searchlight powered by a wind-driven generator and coupled to twin Lewis guns, fitted to F.E.2b A781 at the Royal Aircraft Factory, Farnborough. The demonstrator is Lieut W. S. Farren, who was again at Farnborough, as Director of the RAE, in 1941–6. He was later knighted and held various leading posts in aviation. (*RAE*)

reported that a prototype lightweight aircraft receiver, very simple to operate, had been constructed for use with a half-kilowatt transmitter nearing completion. Such ground transmitters of 30-mile range could be located on appropriate aerodromes in raid-threatened areas. There was some risk of interference with the navy's intelligence direction-finding stations, though the less important functions of those units once enemy airships had crossed the coast should be weighed against the great advantage of being able to issue orders to home-defence aircraft in flight.

Transmissions would be only on GHQ Home Forces orders, to single aircraft, or small groups, giving the latest position reports on any raiders within striking distance. Not all transmitters would operate at once, and everything possible would be done to minimize risk of interference.

The War Office report on the meeting, circulated two days later, was C-in-C Home Forces' first news of this major project, and his Chief of Staff, Maj-Gen F. C. Shaw, protested to Henderson that they should have been represented. It then emerged that the War Office's telephoned invitation had been declined by an officer failing to appreciate its importance.

Shaw felt that the advantage of communicating with the fighters might well outweigh the risk of losing some information from the DF stations and, given all relevant reports, GHQ was competent to decide when it was safe to dispense with the DF data. Operations staffs, however, remained nervous about the risk of surprise attacks on vulnerable places and postulated a situation where, say, a group of Zeppelins crossed the Wash and flew south for 30 min, when fighters were signalled W/T orders to cut them off. If those W/T signals jammed the Peterborough DF station, that might fail to pick up a second Zeppelin force farther north, and thus expose an important target to attack without warning.

Preliminary experiments on Salisbury Plain were promising, and on 1 April the War Office requested Admiralty agreement to practical working trials at Newcastle. Since the Admiralty was accepted as exercising almost divine rights over all wireless matters, the approach was made formally by the Army Council, and there was much relief when Their Lordships' blessing was received within a week.

No.36 Squadron at Cramlington, commanded by Maj C. S. Burnett, started the trials on 30 May, using a Marconi transmitter operating on 525 metres wavelength, with callsign WXO. The aircraft receiver was tuned in advance, and the pilot merely had to unreel a 150-ft aerial from its drum and switch on. Initial tests showed that signals were easily heard up to ten miles' range, but at longer distances they weakened, demanding careful concentration and a good operator—which would have defeated one object of the exercise since the equipment was intended to be pilot-operated. At 20–24 miles results were unreliable, and use of a sound-proofed helmet was recommended.

Experiments continued through the summer, with improved equipment and different wavelengths, and Holt was hopeful that a working scheme could be operating by January 1917.

During November, after flying trials had moved to the newly-opened aerodrome at Ashington, 16 miles north of Newcastle, significantly better results were obtained. The Brooklands-type receiver installed in the observer's seat weighed 32 lb and had no effect on the B.E.2c's performance. In a test flight to establish this point a wireless-fitted aircraft actually reached 8,500 ft in several minutes' less time than a standard machine—probably because its engine happened to be in better tune.

The set was fitted and adjusted by a specialist, then locked to prevent inexpert tampering. The pilot's control was a simple sliding wire resistance for tuning in to the ground signal. A single telephone earpiece was worn in the left ear underneath a well-fitting flying helmet. The ground transmitter, which remained at Cramlington, was a half-kilowatt musical spark Marconi pack set, with a 70-ft mast and an 8-wire umbrella aerial.

On 21 November, 2nd Lieut Douglas Hood picked up loud and clear signals at 24 miles' range with perfect ease. Next day 2nd Lieut M. H. Butler, having no advanced knowledge of the apparatus, was sent off without a map and simply told to move the sliding contact up and down a resistance wire until he obtained the clearest signal, then follow Morse code orders directing him to points on a special clock-face chart with concentric circles lettered from A to D.

Butler lowered his aerial on reaching 2,000 ft, switched on and immediately began receiving. Tuning was a matter of seconds, and he was ordered to climb northwards to 8,000 ft, then after covering 24 miles, directed to two other points on the chart and finally back to Ashington. Asked on return what signals he had received and where he had been, his answers showed that he had correctly followed all transmitted instructions. He reported that signals were clearly audible throughout the flight, and found no difficulty in interpreting the clock code.

Capt C. Gordon Burge, commanding C Flight, who was in charge of the flying trials, considered the 20-mile plus range of the transmitter fully adequate for operational use. A pilot could now be far better informed about hostile aircraft movements and thus have a greater chance of successfully intercepting. He could be briefed when airborne, eliminating the need to wait on the ground for information which often arrived too late—as in a recent case when the first intimation of an approaching Zeppelin was its bombs falling five miles away. Burge pointed out that W/T would dispense with the need for recall and other ground signals, and reduce the risk of a pilot becoming lost.

The prospect of some contact, however nebulous, through darkness, cloud and rain, with the security of the home flarepath, was clearly attractive to pilots.

Technical aspects were supervised by 2nd Lieut J. M. Furnival, a Marconi engineer, who reported that with further experience it should be possible for an aircraft with a 150-ft aerial to pick up signals from a half-kilowatt transmitter at 30–40 miles. There was no falling off with height, and reception was better at night. He estimated that to man the system on a three-flight squadron required only one wireless officer, three operators and one electrician. If need arose to carry an observer, the receiver could be repositioned and modified for operation by either or both crew members.

On the strength of these results and while Furnival's full technical report was being drafted, Holt notified the War Office Director of Air Organization on 23 November of his proposals for incorporating W/T in the general air defence scheme.

At this point the story as unfolded in the traceable files becomes obscure and much detail is missing. On 8 November the War Office had directed—without giving reasons—that the project should be taken over by the Signals Experimental Establishment, Woolwich, and on the 13th Capt Trew of that unit arrived at Cramlington. On 22 November, the very day of the squadron's breakthrough, eight months after the project was launched, the Director of Air Organization bluntly notified Home Defence Wing that 'as a result of certain technical difficulties arising out of the requirements of the Admiralty for the use of a restricted wavelength at Cramlington, it has been decided to discontinue the wireless experiments now being conducted at that place'.

Between the lines of this masterly piece of official obfuscation one message emerged clearly—the Admiralty was no longer prepared to countenance the army messing about with the navy's wireless waves. Furnival was moved to an SEE out-station at Joyce Green, and all equipment was placed at the immediate disposal of the SEE Chief Experimental Officer.

What happened next is not recorded. Holt's letter of 23 November presumably crossed with the War Office bombshell of the 22nd, but with the War Office and Home Defence Wing barely a mile apart there must have been some personal discussions. At all events, Holt wrote to DAO on 25 December detailing his proposals and called a conference for 1 January, 1917.

Holt maintained that the entirely satisfactory outcome of the experiments now justified the incorporation of tactical control by wireless telegraphy into the overall home-defence system. He recommended installation of transmitters near Kelso, Newcastle, Ripon, Gainsborough, Stamford, Hingham (Norfolk), Braintree, Harrietsham (Kent) and Brighton, each with a radius of 30 miles and where possible situated at squadron or flight headquarters. Suggested wavelengths were between 500 and 700 metres—subject to discussions with the Admiralty—and adjacent transmitters would operate on substantially different wavelengths to avoid confusion. They would be visually identified to pilots by a system of aerial lighthouses.

The conference duly took place at 11.00 hr at Adastral House, but no report on the deliberations can be traced—beyond the basic fact that Admiralty objections were sufficiently strong to veto flatly any continuation of the work.

What went wrong? The sparsity of preserved facts or references in official histories invites speculation. At the very least there appears to have been a lamentable lack of liaison and consultation at appropriate levels. A possible clue lies in a remark in Furnival's report—that since the authorities had specified wavelengths not exceeding 300 metres, and the half-kilowatt transmitter normally gave ranges of 525, 625 and 725 metres, some redesign was necessary.

However, trials on these longer wavelengths were approved—only one request, for 19 October, being rejected—and the area Senior Naval Officer reported that there had been no interference with naval W/T activity. Perhaps these trials were sanctioned by someone unaware of any wider implications, for it seems hardly credible that responsible Admiralty authorities should have allowed work to proceed so far knowing that it could never attain operational maturity because the longer wavelengths would indeed interfere with more vital traffic.

Another possibility is that the RFC home-defence enthusiasts dismissed any tentative Admiralty objections which may have been voiced early on as nothing more than expressions of disappointment that the RNAS had not evolved something similar, and believed that these would ultimately be waived in the wider air-defence interest. A factor which cannot be ruled out is a possibility of friction between some of Marconi's highly-qualified 'boffins' commissioned for technical duties and the more conservative bastions of military protocol.

Clearly the scheme had considerable potential, though full exploitation depended on the rapid passage of accurate information from various ground sources to the transmitters. Despite inevitable teething troubles there is little doubt that it would have enabled the air defences to react more efficiently to the increased enemy offensives of 1917. Holt, an enthusiastic supporter throughout, had no time to brood over any frustrations and a few weeks later left to command a wing on the Western Front. As AOC Fighting Area, Air Vice-Marshal Holt was killed in April 1931 when the Gipsy Moth in which he was flying collided with a Siskin of No.43 Squadron over Sussex.

In the purely ground operational sphere, the warning organization became so complex as to require the introduction of an airship code. After the 2/3 September raid, when fourteen airships not immediately identifiable by their official numbers were over the country, it was decided to reduce confusion by labelling intruders with personal names when passing messages between GHQ Home Forces and subordinate formations. These were first picked at random—girls' names for naval airships and boys' names for the army raiders. During the next raid, Mary, Rose, Kate, Lily, Jane, Sally, Hilda and Nora were prowling the skies.

This had the effect of transforming the raiders into personalities, which added to the interest, relaxed tensions and thus increased efficiency. There was a certain poignancy about some messages. One of the last recorded on the night of 27/28 November—'Mary is now going home'—was passed not long before L21, fatally delayed over England by engine trouble, was shot down off Lowestoft.

Later the scheme was modified to label raiders in alphabetical order as they made landfall—Ada, Betty, Chloe, Dinah and so on. The boys' names were never used, as the Army Airship Service made no more raids over Britain, confining itself to reconnaissance work. It was gradually run down, some crews transferring to the navy, and was disbanded in August 1917.

Chapter XI

Operations—September to November 1916

2/3 September, 1916 (Night)

Target: London.
Enemy forces: Navy Zeppelins L11 (Kvtkpt V. Schütze), L13 (Kptlt E. Prölss), L14 (Hptmn K. Manger), L16 (Kptlt E. Sommerfeldt), L17 (Kptlt Hermann Kraushaar), L21 (Oblt-z-S K. Frankenburg), L22 (Kptlt Martin Dietrich), L23 (Kptlt Wilhelm Ganzel), L24 (Kptlt R. Koch), L30 (Kptlt H. von Buttlar), L32 (Oblt-z-S W. Peterson); Navy Schütte-Lanz SL8 (Kptlt Guido Wolff). Army Zeppelins LZ90, LZ97 (returned early), LZ98 (Oblt-z-S E. Lehmann); Army Schütte-Lanz SL11 (Hptmn W. Schramm).
Results: Four killed, 12 injured, £21,072 damage.
Defence sorties: 16.

RNAS

Grain: Farman F.56 9167 (Flt Cdr A. R. Arnold) 01.30–02.55 hr (crashed Chelmsford).

Yarmouth: B.E.2c 8626 (Flt Lieut E. Cadbury) 22.15–00.40 hr.

Bacton: B.E.2c 8625 (Flt Sub-Lieut E. L. Pulling) 00.01–00.43 hr, 00.58–02.10 hr and 02.57–04.14 hr.

Covehithe: B.E.2c 8420 (Flt Sub-Lieut S. Kemball) 22.45–00.14 hr.

RFC

No.33 Squadron, Beverley: B.E.2c 2661 (Capt R. C. L. Holme) crashed on take-off at 00.55 hr.

No.39 Squadron, A Flight, North Weald: B.E.12 6484 (Lieut C. S. Ross) 23.11–01.00 hr, crashed landing; B.E.2c 2574 (2nd Lieut J. I. Mackay) 01.08–04.10 hr.

No.39 Squadron, B Flight, Suttons Farm: B.E.2c 2092 or 2693 (Lieut W. L. Robinson) 23.08–02.45 hr; unspecified B.E.2c (2nd Lieut F. Sowrey) 01.07–01.20 hr, returned with engine trouble.

No.39 Squadron, C Flight, Hainault: B.E.2cs 2090 (2nd Lieut A. de B. Brandon) 23.12–01.38 hr; 2727 (2nd Lieut B. H. Hunt) 01.22–03.44 hr.

No.50 Squadron, Dover: B.E.2cs 4588 (Capt J. W. Woodhouse) 23.30–01.35 hr (Manston); 2711 (Capt J. Sowrey) 23.30–23.35 hr, returned early with engine trouble; unspecified B.E.2c (2nd Lieut H. H. M. Fraser) 23.30–01.25 hr.

With the German navy and army combining for the first—and only—time to attack London, this was the biggest airship raid of the war.

It was, however, an utter failure, for adverse winds combined with belts of heavy rain and icing at high altitudes en route widely dispersed the raiding force. Only one airship penetrated to within seven miles of Charing Cross, and the 16–17 tons of bombs scattered from the Humber to Gravesend caused minimal casualties and relatively light damage.

The night's memorable feature was the destruction of the army's Schütte-Lanz SL11 by a B.E.2c using the new explosive and incendiary ammunition—the first enemy airship shot down on British soil.

Naval intelligence learned of the impending raid in the early evening, and the first Zeppelin, L14, made landfall near Wells-next-the-Sea at 21.50 hr. The others followed at irregular intervals during the next two hours, most of them crossing over the East Anglian coast. Because of weather, navigational or technical problems, six naval airships (L11, 13, 22, 23, 24 and SL8) abandoned the attempt to reach London and sought alternative targets. The L13 severely damaged the East Retford gasworks.

Satisfaction over the destruction of SL11 appears to have diverted official attention from the pitifully small response by the defences to so substantial a raid—only sixteen sorties, three of them by one pilot. Available records offer no obvious explanation, such as prohibitive weather, though poor visibility on some aerodromes may have interrupted flying, and it is also possible that the warning organization was saturated to the point of confusion. No.51 Squadron's lack of response from its Norfolk bases suggests that despite having managed single sorties against two recent raids, the unit was not yet fully operational. Yarmouth and its satellites may have been temporarily short of adequate aircraft, for only days before the station commander had reported that four of his eleven B.E.2cs lacked the performance for anti-airship work. RNAS Holt, situated in the centre of the enemy comings and goings, failed to produce a single sortie.

First sighting of the night was by Cadbury and Kemball. They spotted an airship held by searchlights near Lowestoft at about 23.00 hr, but it vanished in cloud before they could gain combat distance. Both L11 and L30 were in the vicinity at the time, and von Buttlar (L30), in an imaginative description of his assault on London (his bombs fell on Bungay, 90 miles away) reported that he was chased by two aircraft. A crew member of L11, taken prisoner later in the war, said that they were 'attacked' by an aircraft off the coast.

On landing at Bacton after a fruitless sortie, Pulling learned that an airship was still around and promptly took off again. About 50 minutes later he saw bombs exploding a few miles southwest of the aerodrome. These were from L24, which claimed to have bombed Yarmouth. Pulling was unable to find her, nor any others departing eastwards when he later flew his third sortie of the night.

No.33 Squadron's attempt to intercept L22, which passed about ten miles south of Beverley after dropping a few bombs on Humberston, ended when Holme crashed his B.E.2c on take-off. He was unhurt. L22 reported an attack by aircraft shortly after departing south of Hornsea, but no fighters were near that area.

While the naval airships were still moving southwestwards, London was alerted by the unheralded approach of the army's SL11 off Foulness at about 22.40 hr, followed by LZ90 off Frinton at 23.05 hr. However, LZ90 turned east, bombed Haverhill and then departed, while SL11 embarked on a roundabout course to approach London from the northwest, presumably to avoid the main air defences. Thus there were no immediate targets for the first three B.Es despatched by No.39 Squadron shortly after 23.00 hr to patrol an 18-mile line from North Weald to Joyce Green. Clifford Ross took the most northerly North Weald–Hainault stretch, Arthur Brandon from Hainault to Suttons Farm, and William Leefe Robinson from Suttons Farm across the Thames to Joyce Green.

With the introduction of the new ammunition, No.39 squadron pilots had been allowed to tacitly 'forget' about rockets and darts—still regarded as official anti-airship armament—in the hope that the reduced weight would allow the B.E.2c to reach combat heights more rapidly. Even so, it was still taking the average B.E. more than 50 min to attain 10,000 ft.

Brandon and Ross saw nothing, since most of the approaching raiders were well northwest of their patrol line. Ross had some unspecified trouble—probably with his engine—cut short his patrol and crashed while attempting an emergency landing at North Weald. He was unhurt.

Robinson was nearing the end of his patrol when he spotted a Zeppelin held in searchlights to the southeast. This was LZ98, which had flown in over New Romney just after midnight and bombed Gravesend at 01.15 hr. Robinson was at 12,900 ft—about 800 ft above the airship—and was gradually gaining when she disappeared in cloud. He searched for 15 min with no result.

He had now exceeded his allotted patrol time, but when about to descend, at 01.50 hr, he decided to investigate a red glow several miles to the north. Fifteen minutes later he came upon the SL11, which had skirted the capital and, lit by searchlights, was ineffectually bombing some of the northern suburbs.

Robinson was several hundred feet higher, and diving to gain an attacking position underneath, soon caught up with the airship. He made a head-on attack from 800 ft below, spraying a drum of mixed Brock and Pomeroy bullets along the belly of the vessel. This had no effect, so he reloaded and fired along her side. This likewise produced no result. With a now or never determination Robinson began a third attempt, climbing until he was 500 ft or less below the enormous hull blotting out the stars above. This time he attacked from the rear, concentrating the entire drum on one spot underneath, and at first it seemed like another failure. Then, a split second after the hammering of his Lewis stopped, a red glow blossomed inside the hull and in moments the entire rear of the airship was ablaze.

After some rapid manoeuvring to avoid the blazing hulk as it fell to the ground at Cuffley, Robinson fired off Very lights and dropped a parachute flare from sheer exuberance, then returned to base. Mechanics found that he had somehow shot away the guard wire that prevented the Lewis gun fire from hitting the aeroplane's structure, damaging the centre section and rear spar of the top wing.

Lieut W. L. Robinson seated in the B.E.2c flown during his successful engagement with the SL11 on 2/3 September, 1916. It is not definitely known whether this aircraft was 2092 or 2693. The airmen are holding the wing centre-section damaged by Robinson's fire. (*Air Marshal Sir Frederick Sowrey*)

The Schütte-Lanz SL11, shot down by Lieut W. L. Robinson on 2/3 September, 1916, was for a short period after the event misidentified by some British authorities as Zeppelin L21. It is seen here in its construction shed at Leipzig.
(*Marine-Luftschiffer-Kameradschaft and Douglas H. Robinson*)

There is some uncertainty about the number of the B.E.2c flown by Robinson, which is not quoted in his report or the No.39 Squadron records. An article by former squadron member, T. A. Lloyd, in the August 1929 issue of the magazine *Air* included a retouched photograph of Robinson's aircraft with '2092' on the fin. Since the article, written not long after the event, contained so much authentic detail there was no reason to question that identification. However there have been more recent assertions that Robinson was flying No.2693—the B.E.2c he used on 24/25 August. The fact that 2092 is not recorded, and 2693 only once, in the No.39 Squadron operational returns is not significant because these frequently omitted aircraft numbers—and pilots—during the spring and summer of 1916. Whether Lloyd got his facts wrong or whether the alternative number has resulted from confusion over dates is a question which still awaits a positive answer.

It was fortunate that Robinson had been poaching in the preserves of the squadron's second patrols, which took off soon after 01.00 hr, for only one aircraft (Mackay) was allotted to cover the entire North Weald–Joyce Green line and two (Sowrey and Hunt) to patrol south of the Thames. In the event Sowrey returned early with engine trouble, so, when the real threat to London developed with the approach of the naval airships from the north, a mere three B.Es were airborne.

Mackay was over Joyce Green at 10,000 ft on the second run down his beat when he saw SL11 in searchlights about 12 miles to the northwest. He flew to the scene and 25 min later, when only half a mile away, witnessed her fall in flames.

He returned to his patrol line and shortly afterwards spotted another airship to the northeast, which he lost after a 15-min chase. This was evidently L32 homeward bound after bombing at Ware.

Hunt had a similarly frustrating experience. Unaware that Robinson was in the area, he had approached to within 200 yards of SL11 and was about to attack when she fell. In the blaze of her destruction he clearly saw L16, only half a mile away and slightly below—which had just bombed a village near Hatfield. Unable to wrest his gaze from the awesome spectacle, he temporarily destroyed his night vision and was unable to find the second airship again. Half an hour later he also sighted—and lost—the homeward-bound L32.

Schramm and the fifteen crew of SL11 were killed, and the usual pathetic personal items were found in the wreckage—leave passes, a Stuttgart bookshop receipt and three Cologne tram tickets. The control gondola clock had stopped at 03.23 hr German Summer Time (02.23 hr British Summer Time). Robinson was awarded an immediate Victoria Cross for his achievement.

LZ98's arrival off the Kent coast brought vigorous reaction. No.50 Squadron had two aircraft airborne, with Woodhouse patrolling between Dover and the North Foreland and Fraser making wide circuits of the Dover area, but neither saw the enemy. From RNAS Grain, Arnold took off shortly after the Zeppelin had bombed Gravesend, and in his 150 hp Renault-engined Farman F.56 reached 11,000 ft in only 30 min. He saw nothing of his intended quarry, but spotted SL11 in the searchlights far away to the northwest. He set off in that direction, climbing to 13,000 ft, and as he approached saw her fall in flames. Uncertain of his position, he then made for a landing ground visible to the north—Broomfield Court near Chelmsford—but at 200 ft he lost the flares in the mist, touched down in an adjacent ploughed field and turned over. He escaped from the badly damaged Farman with a sprained ankle and a few cuts.

Although the horrifying spectacle of SL11's fiery end may understandably have weakened the resolve of one or two airship commanders to press on to London it did not cause the wholesale scuttle implied in some published accounts. As

Farman F.56 No.9167 in which Flt Cdr A. R. Arnold, of RNAS Grain, came to grief after his abortive airship chase on 2/3 September, 1916. (*J. M. Bruce*)

mentioned earlier, six of the airships sought alternative targets at an early stage and another four had already bombed and were returning home before the SL11 went down.

22 September, 1916 (Daylight)

Target: Dover.
Enemy force: One aeroplane, type not known.
Results: No casualties, £5 damage.
Defence sorties: 11.

RNAS

Dover: Bristol Scout C 3039 (Flt Lieut J. P. Coleman) 15.16–15.25 hr; Bristol Scout D 8971 (Flt Sub-Lieut F. C. C. Calder) 15.16–16.10 hr, damaged landing; Short 830 1341 (Flt Sub-Lieut M. R. Buckland, PO Hanna) 15.10–15.45 hr; FBA flying-boat 3655 (Flt Sub-Lieut A. H. Sandwell) 15.10–15.55 hr.

Grain: Sopwith Baby 8160 (Flt Sub-Lieut F. E. Sandford) 15.28–15.52 hr, returned with fuel leak.

Manston: Bristol Scout Ds 8960 (Flt Cdr C. H. Butler) 15.12–15.58 hr; 8951 Flt Lieut J. A. Carr) 15.13–16.02 hr.

Westgate: Sopwith Schneider 3761 (Flt Sub-Lieut C. F. M. Chambers) 15.20–15.50 hr; Sopwith Baby 8146 (Flt Lieut E. J. Burling) 15.22–16.22 hr.

RFC

No.50 Squadron, Dover: B.E.12 6493 (Capt Williams) 15.10–15.45 hr; Vickers F.B.19 A2992 (Maj M. G. Christie) 15.10–15.45 hr.

This conventional hit-and-run attack was made by a single raider which appeared at 15.00 hr four miles off Deal at 10,000 ft, then turned west to drop seven small bombs on Dover five minutes later. It was described vaguely as an 'Albatros', and was probably from Marine Landflieger Abteilung 1.

Christie and Williams, No.50 Squadron, kept the intruder in sight for about 20 min until it flew into cloud at 11,000 ft. Sandwell, in the FBA from RNAS Dover, chased an aircraft eventually identified as British—the most likely explanation being unfamiliarity with the tubby little Vickers F.B.19 prototype, flown by Christie. Calder badly damaged his Bristol Scout in a landing accident but was unhurt.

No.50 Squadron again had no warning until bombs were falling near their aerodrome. Christie felt that the observer posts should have spotted the enemy, flying below cloud, and again pleaded with the AA Command Post to be warned of any unknown aircraft approaching at high altitude, so that immediate patrols could be mounted. Home Defence Wing considered that with ten minutes' warning they could guarantee to catch a raider, and suggested that Dover observation posts be given suitable telescopes.

23/24 September, 1916 (Night)

Targets: London, the Midlands.
Enemy forces: Navy Zeppelins L13 (Kptlt Franz G. Eichler), L14 (Hptmn K. Manger), L16 (Kptlt E. Sommerfeldt), L17 (Kptlt H. Kraushaar), L21 (Oblt-z-S K. Frankenburg), L22 (Kptlt Martin Dietrich), L23 (Kptlt W. Ganzel), L24 (Kptlt R. Koch), L30 (Kptlt H. von Buttlar), L31 (Kptlt H. Mathy), L32 (Oblt-z-S W. Peterson), L33 (Kptlt A. Böcker).

This immaculate single-seat B.E.2c, 8294, of RNAS Eastchurch was flown by Flt Sub-Lieut A. F. Buck on 23/24 September, 1916. (*J. M. Bruce/G. S. Leslie collection*)

Results: 40 killed, 130 injured, £135,068 damage.
Defence sorties: 26.

RNAS

Cranwell: B.E.2c 2737 23.55–00.20 hr.

Eastchurch: B.E.2cs 8610 (pilot not listed) 21.36–21.56 hr, returned with engine trouble; 8295 (Flt Lieut H. G. Henley) took off 22.20 hr (forced landed Sandwich); 8294 (Flt Sub-Lieut A. F. Buck) 22.40–23.45 hr, returned with engine trouble.

Manston: B.E.2cs 8298 (Flt Cdr C. H. Butler) 21.50–22.15 hr and 23.00–23.10 hr, returned with engine trouble; 8413 (Flt Lieut H. A. Buss) 23.45–00.45 hr.

Yarmouth: Short 184 8074 (Flt Lieut B. D. Kilner, CPO Rose) took off 17.30 hr, forced alighted; B.E.2cs 8625 (Flt Lieut E. Cadbury) 22.00–00.35 hr; 8499 (Flt Lieut C. H. C. Smith) 22.10–23.50 hr (Burgh Castle); Sopwith Babies 8149 (Flt Lieut C. J. Galpin) 18.25–19.55 hr; 8196 (Flt Lieut E. Cadbury) crashed in sea, time not known.

Bacton: B.E.2c 8626 (Flt Sub-Lieut E. L. Pulling) 21.05–00.01 hr.

Covehithe: B.E.2c 8493 (Flt Sub-Lieut S. Kemball) 23.50–00.20 hr.

RFC

No.33 Squadron, Beverley: Unspecified B.E.2c (Capt G. F. Richardson) 22.45–00.01 hr.

No.39 Squadron, A Flight, North Weald: B.E.2c 2581 (2nd Lieut J. I. Mackay) 00.20–02.20 hr; sortie also flown by Lieut C. S. Ross who returned with engine trouble, details not known.

No.39 Squadron, B Flight, Suttons Farm: B.E.2c 4112 (2nd Lieut F. Sowrey) 23.30–01.40 hr.

No.39 Squadron, C Flight, Hainault: Unspecified B.E.2cs (2nd Lieut A. de B. Brandon). 23.33–02.28 hr; and 2nd Lieut B. H. Hunt. Times not known.

No.50 Squadron, Dover: B.E.2cs 2699 (Lieut W. Glenny) 21.28–23.45 hr; 4588 (2nd Lieut W. A. McClaughry) 22.55–01.10 hr.

No.50 Squadron, Bekesbourne: B.E.2cs 4142 (2nd Lieut C. A. Hore) 23.00–01.00 hr; unspecified (2nd Lieut H. H. M. Fraser) 23.30–00.30 hr.

No.51 Squadron, Thetford: Aircraft type and other details not recorded; (Lieut O. J. F. Scholte) 22.50–01.50 hr (Frettenham). 2nd Lieut M. H. Thunder killed in take-off crash.

Any disposition by the German navy to dismiss the fate of SL11 as an isolated army misfortune was brutally shattered by their own more severe losses on this night. Two of their new 'super Zeppelins' were destroyed, one shot down by a B.E.2c to confirm in spectacular fashion the lethality of the new ammunition, and the other—on her maiden United Kingdom raid—forced down after crippling anti-aircraft shell damage and a prolonged attack by a B.E.2c.

Because of adverse winds the older airships made for targets in the Midlands while the four new vessels retained London as the objective, flying via Belgium and intending to approach the capital from the south.

Some Zeppelin movements before the Midlands attack are obscure and it is not certain which airship or airships were seen by the two Yarmouth seaplanes airborne in the early evening. Kilner and Rose in their lumbering Short 184 delivered a brief attack at about 19.00 hr when 45 miles east of Yarmouth and were then forced down by engine trouble. Fifteen minutes later, from 7,000 ft, Galpin attacked a Zeppelin which he estimated as some 30 miles east of Lowestoft, but while reloading he lost it. This may have been L21, which eventually came in over Aldeburgh at 21.40 hr, but no airships reported attacks during the inbound flight.

The first close approach was not until 20.55 hr, when an airship off Cromer—plotted as L30—slowly followed the coast and was vainly sought by Pulling from RNAS Bacton. Since L30 was in reality many miles to the south (and her commander later produced an imaginative report of bombing London at a time far removed from any attack actually delivered) it was probably one of the older airships. These belatedly crossed the Lincolnshire coast between 22.00 and 23.00 hr.

Little was achieved by this group and, apart from substantial damage and a few casualties in Nottingham caused by L17, the bombs fell mostly in open country. Nor were the few defence sorties any more effective. The official history states that an RNAS Cranwell pilot unsuccessfully engaged L13 near Sleaford, but unit reports say that he saw nothing. From the RFC, Richardson of No.33 Squadron patrolled from Beverley to south of the Humber until forced by low cloud and fog to return, thus missing any of the returning airships.

Scholte, No.51 Squadron, was airborne shortly after L21 had bombed near Stowmarket, and becoming lost towards the end of his three-hour patrol, came down on the first flarepath sighted—at Frettenham, Norwich. Had he been able to remain airborne a little longer he might have encountered L31 returning from London. No details have been traced of the take-off crash in which Thunder was killed.

What was intended as a short, sharp attack against London from the south by the four R-class airships ended in disaster. They all crossed the Belgian coast uneventfully, after which L30's movements remain a mystery. Böcker in L33 switched to a conventional approach from the east, and passed over Foulness at 22.40 hr.

Shortly afterwards L33 was seen in a searchlight north of Shoeburyness by Henley from Eastchurch, flying much lower down, and after a rather optimisitic chase he lost her to view. With mist patches obscuring the ground he then lost himself, and after flying east for a time he decided to land on an unfamiliar flarepath seen near the coast. He misjudged his height, hit a fence and badly damaged the aircraft, though was himself unhurt. He had come down on a new night-landing ground at Downs Farm, Sandwich.

Meanwhile L33 made good progress and Böcker launched his main attack on east London shortly after midnight. At 12 minutes past the hour, over Bow, a shell from the Beckton or Wanstead battery scored a direct hit, exploding in the gas cell just aft of the control gondola and causing massive hydrogen losses.

No.39 Squadron's fighters were not ordered off until L33 was a mere ten miles away and thus had no prospect of intercepting on the inbound journey. The patrols were as before, with North Weald, Hainault and Suttons Farm aircraft covering areas to their south, and all carrying Brock, Pomeroy and Sparklet ammunition. Sowrey and Brandon both saw the airship very shortly after she had been hit, and both promptly lost her as she flew out of the searchlights. She was in fact already losing height, and before long Böcker ordered all disposable items to be jettisoned in the hope of at least reaching the Belgian coast.

Lieut A. de B. Brandon, No.39 Squadron, who attacked L15 and L33 with no decisive results during the 1916 raids. In 1917–18 he commanded No.50 Squadron; and (*right*) Lieut F. D. Holder, from Orfordness, who attacked L48 on 16/17 June, 1917, and also flew six daylight sorties against the Gothas. (*G. Kinsey*)

Brandon found her again near Kelvedon Hatch but, while preparing to attack, was beset by problems of his own. His automatic petrol pump failed, which called for hand pumping, and this hampered him when cocking his gun. Then the gun came adrift from its mounting, and by the time order was restored in the cockpit Brandon had overshot the airship. He turned round to make another approach from the rear port side, then fired a complete drum, seeing the Brock bullets bursting along the underside with no result. He reloaded and began a second attack, but this time his gun jammed after nine rounds. Though not stated in official reports it seems likely that Brandon was carrying Le Prieur rockets and/or Ranken darts, because he next attempted to climb above L33, but lost sight of her against the ground.

Brandon must rate as the unluckiest home-defence pilot of the war, and this action closely paralleled his attack on the crippled L15 six months earlier. L33 was virtually defenceless because all but the upper hull machine-guns had been jettisoned, and it was later established that Brandon's bullets had holed some of her petrol tanks.

Böcker's valiant struggle to keep L33 airborne ended at 01.20 hr when she grounded at Little Wigborough, north of the Blackwater estuary. The crew fired the vessel before being arrested by a local reserve policeman and marched off to captivity.

L31 and L32 adhered to the original raid plan and flew down Channel to cross Dungeness at about 22.45 hr. Peterson in L32 was then delayed for an hour, apparently by engine trouble. Mathy in L31 flew a textbook course, first to London where he began his bombing run at 00.30 hr, then out again along a direct line northeast to Yarmouth, where he departed at 02.15 hr. He met little opposition from AA guns and was not seen by any of the defending aircraft—probably because of the diversion created by L33 a few miles to the east.

Cadbury was airborne from Yarmouth in the early hours of the morning, and while adjusting his goggles, he lost control of his Sopwith Baby and crashed into the sea. He received only minor injuries.

No.50 Squadron had one aircraft on early patrol but the other three were not airborne until the two Zeppelins had flown well beyond Dover and then covered an area many miles east of the enemy's actual route. This was the first time that a patrol was flown from the squadron's new aerodrome at Bekesbourne, near Canterbury.

Peterson's L32 eventually got under way again and was picked up by searchlights well southeast of London. She was under heavy AA fire as she flew northwards over the Thames just after 01.00 hr, and dropped most of her bombs around South Ockenden.

The defences were now fully alert and L32 was spotted by all three of the No.39 Squadron pilots airborne. First to see her, at 00.45 hr some ten miles south of the river, was Sowrey, flying the most southerly patrol. After a 25-min chase at 13,000 ft he was ready to attack. The airship was still lit by searchlights but the gunfire had stopped, and Sowrey was so close underneath that he could easily see the great 17-ft diameter propellers churning round. He throttled down to keep pace at about 60 mph and distributed his first drum along the underside—which had no effect apart from making the airship 'wriggle' considerably and alter course. With cavalier disregard for the effects of one more missile among the night's shower of AA shell fragments, Sowrey hurled the empty drum overboard and reloaded.

During his second attack, equally ineffective, Sowrey was under vigorous fire from the airship's gondola guns. He then fired a third drum, and immediately this was exhausted he saw flames burst from several points in the hull, and within moments the whole ship was ablaze, falling to the ground at 01.20 hr near Billericay.

An account Sowrey wrote in April 1919 differs in some respects from his combat report made at the time. In the latter he wrote 'all firing was traversing fire along the envelope', whereas his later version stated that he concentrated the last drum 'on one spot, about the middle'. He also gave his height as 14,000 ft in the later account. However, these small discrepancies are immaterial to the undisputed fact that the L32 fell to his B.E.2c.

Brandon spotted L32 about five minutes before Sowrey began his attack. His

2nd Lieut Frederick Sowrey seated in his B.E.2c, and two unidentified No.39 Squadron ground crew, after the destruction of L32 on 23/24 September, 1916. This aircraft is preserved in the Canadian War Museum.

Another view of 2nd Lieut F. Sowrey's B.E.2c, No.4112. The Le Prieur rocket rails have been removed but their strut fittings remain.

engine had cut shortly after he lost the L33 and he came down to 9,000 ft before it picked up. He then saw L32 being 'hosed with a stream of fire', after which it caught alight internally in several places. Mackay was close enough to fire a few rounds at extreme range, but Sowrey had delivered the coup de grâce before he could reach effective attacking distance.

Apart from scattered patches of ground mist it was an exceptionally clear night and L32's fall was seen from great distances. It was noted by L17 and L23 from the Lincoln area some 125 miles away, and Scholte of No.51 Squadron saw it from 80 miles away, near Norwich.

25/26 September, 1916 (Night)

Targets: London, the Midlands.
Enemy forces: Navy Zeppelins L14 (Hptmn K. Manger), L16 (Kptlt E. Sommerfeldt), L21 (Oblt-z-S K. Frankenburg), L22 (Kptlt Martin Dietrich), L30 (Kptlt H. von Buttlar), L31 (Kptlt H. Mathy). L23 (Kptlt W. Ganzel) returned early.
Results: 43 killed, 31 injured, £39,698 damage.
Defence sorties: 15.

RNAS

Calshot: Short 827 8554 (Flt Lieut E. J. Cooper) 23.30–00.40 hr; White & Thompson No.3 3807 (Flt Cdr A. W. Bigsworth) 23.25–00.01 hr, returned early with engine trouble.

Cranwell: B.E.2c 2731 (pilot not known) 21.45–23.40 hr.

Manston: B.E.2c 8413 (Flt Lieut H. A. Buss) 21.40–22.50 hr.

Yarmouth: B.E.2c 8420 (Flt Lieut C. H. C. Smith) 20.30–21.32 hr (Burgh Castle).

Bacton: B.E.2c 8626 (Flt Sub-Lieut E. L. Pulling) 20.23–23.20 hr.

Holt: B.E.2c 8608 (Flt Sub-Lieut F. W. Walker) 21.05–22.12 hr (Norwich).

RFC

No.33 Squadron, Coal Aston: Unspecified B.E.2c (Capt E. N. Clifton) 22.55–23.15 hr, forced landed due to fog.

No.33 Squadron, Bramham Moor: Unspecified B.E.2c (Capt W. C. K. Birch) 22.50–01.10 hr.

No.50 Squadron, Dover: Unspecified B.E.2cs (Lieut W. H. Dolphin) 21.35–23.45 hr and 02.40–04.10 hr; (Maj M. G. Christie) 21.35–22.45 hr and 02.45–03.50 hr; (2nd Lieut W. A. McClaughry) 22.00–00.20 hr.

No.50 Squadron, Bekesbourne: Unspecified B.E.2c (Lieut H. H. M. Fraser) 22.10–23.50 hr.

For this raid the older airships were intended to attack Midlands industrial targets while L30 and L31 went for London. Strasser's concern over the recent losses was reflected by his instruction that due caution must be exercised in the event of clear weather.

L14 and L16 both came in near Hornsea at 20.05 hr and the latter flew only about 25 miles inland to scatter a few ineffective bombs. L14 bombed York at 23.00 hr, then steered towards Leeds, but turned homewards after bombing near Wetherby. L21 made landfall at Sutton-on-Sea at 21.45 hr, passed north of Sheffield shortly after 23.00 hr, flew on to attack Bolton at 00.45 hr and departed over Whitby at 03.05 hr. L22 followed a parallel, slightly northerly course 50 min later and made a sharp attack on Sheffield.

L30 and L31 were again routed over Belgium, and for the second successive raid von Buttlar claimed a heavy attack where no bombs fell—in this instance Margate and Ramsgate.

Mathy in L31 made landfall off Dungeness at 21.35 hr, but because of the good visibility decided to go for a target well clear of the main fighter patrol areas. He kept out to sea, turned north over the Isle of Wight and approached Portsmouth at 23.50 hr. Although dazzled by searchlights, Mathy thought that his bombs fell in the town and dockyards. In fact not one did so, nor did British observers report any explosions at sea, which suggests that the bombs had not been fused. The ship returned, flying inland parallel to the coast, crossing near St Leonards at 01.15 hr and departing off Dover at 02.30 hr.

After their outstanding successes 48 hr earlier, the defenders had a disappointing night. Yarmouth and its satellites despatched aircraft to seek airships out at sea which did not penetrate in the immediate area. One was L23, which spent some time off the coast before turning back with engine trouble. Another flying offshore between Trimingham and Yarmouth at about 20.00 hr was wrongly plotted as the L30, and its true identity is not certain. The Cranwell aircraft vainly sought L21 as she flew some miles to the north en route for Sheffield and Bolton.

It was foggy in the Sheffield area, and Clifton, No.33 Squadron, who took off from Coal Aston also to look for L21, abandoned the attempt, then lost himself and forced landed on high ground in the vicinity. His aircraft was badly damaged but he was unhurt.

Birch from Bramham Moor was airborne when L14 appeared to be making for Leeds. After investigating searchlight activity near Goole, with no result, he turned north and at 00.28 hr saw more searchlights at Collingham, near Wetherby, but L14 had vanished before he could reach the area.

Mathy's flight up-Channel and return over the South Downs generated the biggest response from the air defences. No.50 Squadron flew four fruitless patrols at 10,000 ft while L31 was making for Portsmouth and two more at the time of her departure, while RNAS Manston mounted one patrol.

The White and Thompson No.3 from RNAS Calshot, flown by Flt Cdr A. W. Bigsworth in an unsuccessful attempt to reach L31 on 25/26 September, 1916.

The only pilots to see L31 were Bigsworth and Cooper from RNAS Calshot. Bigsworth, in a White & Thompson flying-boat, returned with engine trouble shortly after spotting the Zeppelin in the searchlights and slightly damaged his machine on alighting. Cooper, in a Short, saw it still illuminated and moving inland north of Portsmouth. Both aircraft lacked the performance to enable any effective chase.

1/2 October, 1916 (Night)

Targets: London, the Midlands.
Enemy forces: Navy Zeppelins L14 (Hptmn K. Manger), L16 (Kptlt E. Sommerfeldt), L17 (Kptlt H. Kraushaar), L21 (Oblt-z-S K. Frankenburg), L24 (Kptlt R. Koch), L31 (Kptlt H. Mathy), L34 (Kptlt Max Dietrich). L13 (Kptlt F. G. Eichler), L22 (Kptlt Martin Dietrich), L23 (Kptlt W. Ganzel), L30 (Kptlt H. von Buttlar) returned early.
Results: One killed, one injured, £17,687 damage.
Defence sorties: 15.

RNAS

Yarmouth: B.E.2c 8498 (Flt Sub-Lieut J. C. Northrop) 20.30–21.11 hr (Burgh Castle).

RFC

No.33 Squadron, Coal Aston: Unspecified B.E.2c (Capt E. N. Clifton) 30 min, returned due to weather.

No.38 Squadron, Leadenham: B.E.12 6159 (Capt C. T. Black) 20.25–21.05 hr, forced landed.

No.39 Squadron, A Flight, North Weald: B.E.2cs 2581 (2nd Lieut J. I. Mackay) 21.50–00.45 hr; 4577 (2nd Lieut W. J. Tempest) 22.00–00.10 hr, crashed landing; unspecified B.E.2c (2nd Lieut P. McGuiness) 23.25–01.55 hr; B.E.12 6645 (Capt C. S. Ross) 01.05–02.50 hr.

No.39 Squadron, C Flight, Hainault: B.E.2cs 2736 (Lieut L. G. S. Payne) 21.56–00.30 hr; 4544 (2nd Lieut A. de B. Brandon) 01.37–03.40 hr.

No.50 Squadron, Telscombe Cliffs: B.E.2c 4108 (Capt W. H. Dolphin) 22.00–00.05 hr, crashed landing.

No.51 Squadron, A Flight, Mattishall: B.E.2d 6256 (Capt D. Gilley) 20.55–21.45 hr, returned early due to weather; B.E.12 6161 (Lieut Hill) took off 20.55 hr, crashed landing.

No.51 Squadron, B Flight, Harling Road: F.E.2bs 7004 (Capt W. E. Collison) 20.55–22.00 hr; 7005 (Lieut Holmes) 90 min sortie, forced landed.

No.51 Squadron, HQ Flight, Thetford: B.E.2c 4575 (Lieut O. J. F. Scholte) 23.15–23.57 hr, returned early due to weather.

This raid was another calamity for the Zeppelins, with unfavourable weather over the North Sea presenting navigation difficulties from the outset. Then heavy cloud and mist blanketed large areas of central England, and some vessels encountered severe icing. The culminating disaster was the loss of L31, shot down by a B.E.2c. Bombing from the seven airships which crossed the coast was widely scattered.

The highly experienced Mathy in L31 was the first to make landfall—at 20.00 hr off Lowestoft—and thereafter flew a perfect course southwestwards to London. The others came in at intervals from 21.20 to 01.45 hr between Cromer and

Kptlt Heinrich Mathy, commander of Zeppelin L31, shot down over Potters Bar on 1/2 October, 1916, by 2nd Lieut W. J. Tempest; and (*right*) 2nd Lieut Ian Vernon Pyott, No.36 Squadron, who shot down L36 off the Tees on 27/28 November, 1916.

Theddlethorpe. L34, latest of the R-class, penetrated to Corby, but her bombs fell in open country. L21 got as far as Oakham, L24 reached Hitchin, L14 was plotted near Digby, L16 near Horncastle and L17 about 15 miles east of Norwich.

L31 had progressed some ten miles beyond Chelmsford in reasonable weather when she was illuminated by the very efficient Kelvedon Hatch searchlight at 21.45 hr. Presumably with the intention of attacking from a less obvious direction Mathy then steered north, and by 22.30 hr he was near Buntingford. Surprisingly No.39 Squadron was not ordered up until L31 was less than ten miles away, and had Mathy maintained his original course he could have been bombing London well before any fighters reached his altitude. In the event, although none of the three flying the first patrol saw anything for 90 min, they had been able to gain operational height during the diversion north.

At 23.40 hr, the L31 was approaching Cheshunt, having finally set course for the capital after extensive meanderings over Hertfordshire. At this moment, coned by searchlights, she was spotted by Wulstan Tempest, the third pilot airborne, who was in fact covering the southernmost sector to Joyce Green. He was at 14,500 ft some 15 miles away to the south and immediately made for the airship flat out, passing through what he later described as a 'very inferno' of AA fire. When about five miles away his petrol pressure pump failed and he was obliged to resort to hand pumping.

About this time L31 was also seen by Mackay, McGuiness and Payne—all from greater distances—with Payne flying a very sluggish aircraft which took 20 min to progress from 8,000 to 9,000 ft. The airship's crew saw one or more of the B.Es, promptly jettisoned the bombs, and began climbing to the west.

Tempest continued to gain and was slightly above L31 when he reached firing range. After a final frenzied assault on his fuel pump he dived and delivered two short bursts. He then positioned underneath, so close that he was apparently inside the limits of the field covered by the gondola guns, and fired off the rest of the drum. Before this was exhausted he saw the hull 'begin to go red inside like an enormous Chinese lantern', as he later described it, then the fire rapidly engulfed the entire ship. It was six minutes before midnight when she crashed to earth at Potters Bar, with no survivors.

In an account written in 1920, Tempest described how he put his aircraft into a spin to avoid the flaming airship as it fell. A pilot would not normally seek to place his aircraft temporarily out of control in such circumstances, and it is more likely that Tempest spun involuntarily, perhaps having briefly lost consciousness without realizing the fact. After the combat he complained of feeling sick, giddy and exhausted—symptoms which could well result from the combined effects of reduced oxygen after two hours above 10,000 ft, the severe cold, and the physical effort of working the petrol pump. As he came down he encountered poor visibility on the landing approach and crashed his aircraft.

After this quickest Zeppelin destruction to date, Tempest fittingly wrote the briefest of combat reports:

> 'Sir, I have the honour to report that on 1st October at 10 pm I left the ground on B.E.2c 4577 to patrol between Joyce Green and Hainault. Approximately at 11.40 I first sighted a Zeppelin. I immediately made for her and fired one drum which took effect at once and set her on fire at about 12,700 ft. I then proceeded to North Weald to land and wrecked the machine on the aerodrome, without hurting myself, at 12.10 am.'

RNAS Yarmouth activity was restricted by misty weather to one patrol—flown shortly after L31 had passed inland. Weather also affected No.33 Squadron's aerodromes, and the sole sortie flown, to investigate conditions before any airships reached the area, was cut short by low cloud and heavy rain. Black, No.38 Squadron, was also on a weather reconnaissance when he forced landed after a short trip, meeting thick cloud at 2,500 ft. Reports describe his B.E.12 as 'wrecked', but he suffered only minor injuries.

The three No.39 Squadron pilots who destroyed German airships in 1916: left to right; Lieut William Leefe Robinson, 2nd Lieut Wulstan Joseph Tempest and 2nd Lieut Frederick Sowrey.

No.51 Squadron had an unproductive and expensive night while attempting to find L17, 24 and 34, all in their area of activity either inbound or outbound. Scholte took off to look for L24, reported about ten miles to the north, but abandoned the sortie when he found himself still in solid cloud at 8,500 ft.

Holmes from Harling Road broke clear at 9,000 ft, and an hour later his engine stopped dead. After a seemingly interminable glide he emerged from the clouds at 2,000 ft, and seeing no aerodrome lights attempted a landing by his wingtip flares. This ended in a wood with the F.E. a write-off, but with no significant damage to pilot or observer. The report on Hill's sortie says merely that his B.E.12 got out of control, whereupon he returned to base, smashing his undercarriage on landing.

To calm Admiralty fears of attacks on Portsmouth, Dolphin of No.50 Squadron flew a two-hour patrol between Newhaven and Eastbourne, though the nearest Zeppelin was some 70 miles to the north. He crashed on landing.

22 October, 1916 (Daylight)

Targets: Sheerness, North Foreland.
Enemy forces: Two aeroplanes, types not known.
Results: No casualties, £20 damage.
Defence sorties: Eight.

RNAS

Dover: Bristol Scout Cs 3045 (Flt Sub-Lieut Bailey) 14.15–14.18 hr, returned with engine trouble; 3039 (Flt Sub-Lieut Bailey) 14.53–16.04 hr; Short 830s 1340 (Flt Sub-Lieut C. Laurence, AM Norris) 13.50–15.15 hr; 1342 (crew not known) 14.40–15.15 hr; 1343 (Flt Sub-Lieut W. Perham, Obs Sub-Lieut E. J. Travers) 14.25–15.15 hr; FBA flying-boat 3655 (crew not known) took off 14.35 hr.

Manston: Bristol Scout C 3049 (Flt Sub-Lieut E. S. Boynton) 14.03–15.19 hr; Bristol Scout D 8951 (Flt Lieut J. A. Carr) 13.48–15.10 hr.

This was another enterprising sortie by Walther Ilges, with Sheerness as the unaccustomed target for a high-flying hit-and-run attack. It took place at 13.37 hr, and only one of the four bombs fell on land. The aircraft was probably an L.V.G.

There is no recorded explanation for the lack of reaction by Grain and Eastchurch to this incursion. Dover and Manston despatched aircraft in reasonable time, but nothing was seen of the enemy.

About an hour later another enemy off the North Foreland turned back after being fired on by two naval vessels. This may have been that shot down by Flt Lieut D. M. B. Galbraith, RNAS Dunkirk, at 15.30 hr off Blankenberghe. Flying a Nieuport, Galbraith dived on an enemy seaplane he observed approaching from the west at about 8,000 ft. He fired two drums and it crashed into the sea.

23 October, 1916 (Daylight)

Target: Margate.
Enemy force: One aeroplane, type not known.
Results: Two injured, £229 damage.
Defence sorties: 12.

Flt Lieut J. A. Carr, RNAS Manston, flying Bristol Scout D No.8951, was the only one of twelve pilots who saw—but could not catch—the high-flying enemy which attacked Cliftonville on 23 October, 1916. Carr also flew this aircraft against three daylight raiders earlier in the year.

RNAS

Dover: Nieuport 10s 3966 (Flt Lieut S. B. Joyce) 10.12–11.08 hr; 3967 (Flt Sub-Lieut F. C. C. Calder) 10.12–11.18 hr; Bristol Scout C 1254, details not known; Sopwith Baby 8167 (Flt Sub-Lieut H. G. R. Malet) 10.15–11.15 hr (Dunkirk).

Eastchurch: Bristol Scout D 8977 (Flt Cdr E. H. Dunning) 10.55–11.20 hr.

Manston: Bristol Scout C 3049 (Flt Sub-Lieut E. S. Boynton) 10.15–11.15 hr; Bristol Scout Ds 8951 (Flt Lieut J. A. Carr) 10.05–10.50 hr (Dunkirk); 8956 (Flt Sub-Lieut J. M. Ingham) 10.20–11.12 hr; 8957 (Flt Sub-Lieut M. W. H. Evans) 10.10–11.05 hr; B.E.2c 8413 (Flt Lieut H. A. Buss) 10.20–10.47 hr.

Westgate: Sopwith Schneider 3766 (Flt Sub-Lieut Wood) 10.30–11.20 hr; Sopwith Baby 8146 (Flt Cdr N. S. Douglas) 10.22–11.32 hr.

This typical hit-and-run attack was probably made by Marine Landflieger Abteilung 1. A solitary enemy aircraft approached virtually without warning at about 12,000 ft, dropping three bombs on Cliftonville at 10.05 hr. Fighters were airborne promptly, but only the first away—Carr in a Scout D from Manston—appears to have seen the enemy, and he soon realized that he had no hope of overtaking.

27/28 November, 1916 (Night)

Targets: The Midlands, Tyneside.

Enemy forces: Navy Zeppelins L13 (Kptlt F. G. Eichler), L14 (Hptmn K. Manger), L16 (Kptlt Hans-Karl Gayer), L21 (Kptlt K. Frankenburg), L22 (Kptlt Heinrich Hollender), L24 (Oblt-z-S K. Friemel), L34 (Kptlt Max

Dietrich), L35 (Kptlt H. Ehrlich), L36 (Kvtkpt V. Schütze). L30 (Kptlt H. von Buttlar) returned early.
Results: Four killed, 37 injured, £12,482 damage.
Defence sorties: 40.

RNAS

Cranwell: B.E.2cs 2735 (Sqn Cdr R. E. C. Peirse) 03.10–04.40 hr; 2737 (Flt Lieut F. Maynard) 03.10–04.40 hr.

Redcar: B.E.2c 1109 (Flt Lieut B. P. H. de Roeper) 23.50–00.15 hr.

Scarborough: B.E.2c 1144 (Flt Sub-Lieut J. F. Roche) 00.40–01.30 hr, crashed landing.

Yarmouth: B.E.2cs 8411 (Flt Cdr V. Nicholl) 06.45–08.15 hr; 8625 (Flt Lieut E. Cadbury), times not known, landed Burgh Castle.

Bacton: B.E.2c 8626 (Flt Sub-Lieut E. L. Pulling) 04.45–07.15 hr.

Burgh Castle: B.E.2cs 8420 (Flt Sub-Lieut G. W. R. Fane) 23.00–00.30 hr and took off again at 04.35 hr; 8625 (Flt Lieut E. Cadbury) 06.18–07.05 hr (Yarmouth).

Holt: B.E.2c 8499 (Flt Sub-Lieut A. V. Robinson) 04.45–06.06 hr.

RFC

No.33 Squadron, A Flight, Brattleby: Lieut F. Egerton crashed on take-off, no details recorded.

No.33 Squadron, B Flight, Kirton-in-Lindsey: B.E.12 6661 (Lieut J. B. Brophy) 21.10–00.03 hr; aircraft not known (Lieut L. H. Jull) crashed on take-off, details not known.

No.33 Squadron, C Flight, Elsham: B.E.2c 2665 (Capt G. Richardson) aborted take-off at 21.50 hr because of engine failure, airborne 22.08–01.05 hr; B.E.12 6660 (Lieut G. Talbot-Willcox) 21.45–01.45 hr; aircraft not known (Capt C. H. R. Johnston) crashed on take-off, details not known.

Note: Two additional No.33 Squadron aircraft took off at 01.45 hr, details not known.

No.36 Squadron, A Flight, Seaton Carew: B.E.2c 2738 (2nd Lieut I. V. Pyott) 21.50–22.10 hr; and 22.22–00.01 hr.

No.36 Squadron, details not recorded: B.E.2c 7344 (2nd Lieut F. McD. C. Turner) 22.11–01.00 hr; 7342 (Capt J. P. Inglefield) 23.45–02.55 hr; aircraft not known (Lieut A. T. Williams); plus three sorties, one aircraft of C Flight, Ashington, crashing on landing at 02.40 hr.

No.38 Squadron, A Flight, Leadenham: Unspecified B.E.2es (Capt C. T. Black) 22.40–00.55 hr; (Lieut Bennett) 23.25–00.40 hr; B.E.2e 6290 (2nd Lieut D. S. Allan) 02.22–03.55 hr.

No.38 Squadron, B Flight, Buckminster: Unspecified B.E.2e (Capt G. H. Birley) 01.55–04.15 hr.

No.38 Squadron, C Flight, Stamford: B.E.2e 6297 (Lieut H. D. Harman) 02.00–04.00 hr.

No.51 Squadron, A Flight, Mattishall: Two sorties, at 03.32 and 04.20 hr, details not known.

No.51 Squadron, B Flight, Harling Road: F.E.2bs 7682 (Lieut L. C. Angstrom) 04.30–05.50 hr; 7004 (Capt W. E. Collison) 06.42–06.57 hr, returned with engine trouble; unspecified F.E.2b took off at 03.32 hr.

No.51 Squadron, C Flight, Marham: F.E.2b 7680 (Lieut W. R. Gayner) took off 04.30 hr, crash-landed Tibbenham; unspecified F.E.2b took off at 03.32 hr.

Apart from being another disastrous night for the naval Zeppelin service, this last raid of 1916 brought especial satisfaction to the defence organization by demonstrating that it offered protection for more than just the London area. RNAS B.E.2cs shot down the L21 off Lowestoft, and an RFC B.E.2c pilot destroyed L34 off Hartlepool.

Although there are gaps in the night's records, it is clear that forty sorties were attempted—the highest figure to date—with the RFC Home Defence Wing alone logging 58 flying hours. There were five take-off or landing crashes which resulted in aircraft being listed as 'wrecked', but no pilot received worse than a severe shaking.

After an uneventful North Sea crossing the Zeppelins split into two groups, L24, 34, 35 and 36 making for Tyneside and the remainder for the Midlands. Reports of the first group's approach were received at 22.15 hr, though 90 min passed before just two crossed the coast, L34 coming in to bomb West Hartlepool, followed by L35.

First of the second group was L14, which made landfall 15 miles north of Spurn Head at 21.10 hr, with the remaining four coming in between Spurn and Filey during the next hour. Most of the bombing was aimless, and the one attack of some determination—by L21 on the Potteries—caused little damage and no casualties. The four fatalities were in Hartlepool.

Despite a long spell of idleness, No.36 Squadron was fully alert, and two B.E.2cs were briefly airborne from Seaton Carew at 21.50 hr following a spurious report that five Zeppelins were over Seaham Harbour. For one of the pilots, Pyott, this recall was the second frustration of the day: during the morning he was stuck at Howden for two hours after forced landing a B.E.2e which developed engine trouble on its delivery flight.

This time, however, he was soon airborne again on a genuine alert, and at 23.30 hr, flying at 9,800 ft, saw L34 lower down and held by the Castle Eden searchlight a few miles north of Hartlepool. He dived, firing as he passed underneath at right angles, then climbed round to fly parallel with the Zeppelin as it approached the town at about 70 mph. He aimed several long bursts at one spot on its port quarter and saw his tracers entering the hull. Suddenly a small patch of flame, which he first mistook for a machine-gun returning his fire, spread rapidly until the entire airship was ablaze. Close enough for his face to be scorched, Pyott watched it fall into the sea a mile off the mouth of the Tees. There were no survivors.

B.E.2c 2738 flown by 2nd Lieut I. V. Pyott. (*L. B. Latham*)

Ian Pyott, son of an expatriate Scot living at Port Elizabeth, Cape Province, was born in South Africa and educated at George Watson's College, Edinburgh. He was clearly meticulous beyond his 20 years, reporting that he fired 71 rounds in his main attack. He could hardly have counted so precisely at the time, so presumably based the figure on the number remaining unspent. However, the notable point is that he had emulated Tempest by destroying a Zeppelin with one drum from a Lewis gun. The old 47-round drum had been superseded in early 1916 by the so-called 'double drum' holding 97.

Turner, another No.36 Squadron pilot who was about to attack L34 when she took fire, saw Pyott's aircraft in the glare. De Roeper was also in the close vicinity.

L35, only ten miles north of the encounter, promptly abandoned the raid. The blazing airship was also seen by crews in the southern group, and Oberleutnant-zur-See Richard Frey, in L22 some 70 miles away, later described the 'gruesome picture of destruction' which unfolded.

> 'First she burned right along the top, then fell stern first' he wrote. 'The heat of the burning gas made the entire framework red hot, and this outlined the form of the ship sharply against the dark sky. The fall seemed to last several minutes, and we saw her break into two pieces on the sea.'

Despite the considerable Zeppelin traffic in their area, it was a frustrating night for No.33 Squadron—apart from three take-off crashes. Several pilots saw airships but none managed to reach attacking range. After being lured towards bomb bursts near York without finding the ship responsible (L13 or L22), Richardson, from Elsham, later spotted a Zeppelin in the Hornsea searchlights—but it gradually vanished out to sea. This was L22, which was severely holed by AA fire. Talbot-Willcox also briefly glimpsed the same airship before losing himself and putting down at the nearest visible landing ground to establish his position. He was at Roxby, where he was given a course to Elsham.

Brophy, from Kirton-in-Lindsey, reported a sighting near Beverley at 21.55 hr, which did not fit tidily into the British plot of the overall enemy movements. He was at 8,500 ft when he saw a Zeppelin 3,000 ft higher up, and followed it northwards for about 50 min, gradually reaching 13,000 ft. He was unable to close the distance and abandoned the chase near Flamborough Head. He probably chased two Zeppelins—first L14 which was near Beverley during a 75-minute journey inland before departing to the south, and then L21 which made landfall near Hornsea and followed the coast towards Flamborough Head before turning inland at the start of a nine-hour journey to disaster. Brophy returned to his patrol line south of the Humber and saw bombs bursting near York, though the raider was not illuminated. Shortly afterwards his engine revolutions dropped drastically and his entire energies were devoted to nursing a severely vibrating B.E.12 safely back to base.

After some delay in setting course, L21 proceeded southwestwards, passing between Leeds and Sheffield, and bombed mainly around the Potteries towns. Frankenburg, her commander, was clearly uncertain of his position, and at some point the ship developed engine trouble, but for whatever reason, his curving southerly return course covered nearly twice the distance of the direct route to the Wash. More significantly it led him through one of the biggest concentrations of defence aerodromes. After flying south of Nottingham, L21—labelled 'Mary' by the raid plotters—led a charmed life, passing almost directly over Buckminster, then within 5–15 miles of Leadenham, Cranwell, Stamford, Marham, Harling Road and Mattishall.

At 02.50 hr, the precise moment that the message 'Mary is now going home' was being transmitted over the ground reporting network, she was seen by Birley from No.38 Squadron, Buckminster, held by the aerodrome searchlight. Birley was at 9,500 ft and the airship about 2,000 ft lower, and as he dived she was lost to view. Shortly afterwards he spotted her again, now higher up and apparently still climbing, and began a 25-min chase at 11,000 ft, gaining height very slowly and making little headway. The Zeppelin continually changed course, but Birley eventually positioned 2,000 ft below and fired a drum in two long bursts. While struggling to change drums with hands numbed by cold he again lost his quarry.

At 03.00 hr Allan, from Leadenham, also saw L21. He was at 12,000 ft and estimated the Zeppelin as at 13–14,000 ft. He saw nothing of Birley—though Birley saw him. It is likely that one or both B.Es were spotted, for Allan made particular comment on the airship's continual evasive action which prevented him from lining up to attack. After 15 min he lost sight of her completely. Although L21 was handled with great skill during these encounters the outcome might have been different had the pilots been flying anything but such mediocre performers as B.E.2es.

Flt Sub-Lieut Edward Laston Pulling (*left*) and Flt Lieut Egbert Cadbury, whose combined efforts destroyed L21 off Yarmouth on 27/28 November, 1916.

All aerodromes to the east were now fully alert and an hour later L21 had an even narrower escape. Gayner, No.51 Squadron, saw her near East Dereham shortly after taking off from Marham in an F.E.2b, and was almost in range when his engine revolutions dropped and she drew away. He continued the chase, but his badly vibrating engine finally gave out, and he just stretched his glide to Tibbenham, where he crash-landed.

Against all odds, by 06.05 hr the L21 reached the coast at Yarmouth without further harrassment from the air, and was then seen in the pale dawn light at 8,500 ft nine miles east-southeast of Lowestoft by Egbert Cadbury, 15 min after he had taken off. Pulling and Fane were on the scene shortly afterwards, having been attracted by the Yarmouth gunfire.

Cadbury began his attack from about 700 ft below and fired four drums, gradually closing the distance and attracting considerable return fire. Then 18-year-old Gerard Fane took up a position 100 ft off L21's starboard side, but his Lewis jammed due to frozen oil and he climbed to attempt a bombing attack.

L21 was moving slowly—Cadbury estimated that she increased speed from 35 to only about 55 mph during his attack—and when Edward Pulling closed in she had assumed an angle of 45 deg. He opened fire from 50 ft below, but his gun stopped after the second shot—according to his report, though some accounts say about ten shots—and he turned right to clear the jam. He heard machine-gun fire from the airship, and glancing over his shoulder saw her start to burn from the stern. He dived to avoid the flaming hulk as it began to fall stern first, and noticed that the gunners were still valiantly firing away. The wreckage hit the water at 06.42 hr and all on board were killed.

Fane, who looped in youthful exuberance as L21 fell to the sea, was at one point so close that his face and helmet were scorched and parts of his aircraft blistered.

Despite the overwhelming probability that Cadbury's four drums of explosive, incendiary and tracer ammunition were the prime cause of L21's destruction, the navy gave chief credit to Pulling. He was made a DSO while Cadbury and Fane received DSCs. Commodore A. A. Ellison, in command of Lowestoft and Yarmouth, bracketed Cadbury and Pulling together in his report as both having shown the utmost keenness and devotion to duty in night operations, often flying long hours in dangerous weather. However, Pulling, the last to attack, was perhaps given the senior award in recognition of his thirteen anti-Zeppelin sorties—the highest number flown by any RNAS or RFC pilot at the time.

The occupant of B.E.2c 8626's cockpit is believed to be Flt Sub-Lieut E. L. Pulling, who flew this aircraft in combat with L21. It broke up in the air when looping on 2 March, 1917, and Pulling and his passenger, Flt Sub-Lieut J. C. Northrop, were killed. (*FAA Museum*)

28 November, 1916 (Daylight)

Target: London.
Enemy force: One L.V.G. C IV.
Results: Ten injured, £1,585 damage.
Defence sorties: 21.

RNAS

Dover: Bristol Scout C 3045 (Flt Sub-Lieut N. D. M. Hewitt) 11.45–13.46 hr; Short 184 9065 (Flt Sub-Lieut J. E. Potvin, Obs Sub-Lieut E. J. Travers) 12.00–14.15 hr.

Eastchurch: Bristol Scout D 8977 13.35–15.40 hr.

Grain: Bristol Scout D 8958 (Flt Cdr A. R. Arnold) 13.25–13.52 hr; Short 827 3102 (Flt Sub-Lieut C. V. Bessette, CPO Hartley) 13.00–15.45 hr; Sopwith Baby 8168 (Flt Lieut E. de C. Hallifax) 14.40–14.50 hr.

Manston: Bristol Scout C 3049 (Flt Sub-Lieut H. A. Pailthorpe) 61 min; Bristol Scout D 8960 (Flt Cdr C. H. Butler) 13.05–14.50 hr; B.E.2c 8413 (Flt Lieut J. A. Carr) 50 min—forced landed at Sandwich with engine trouble.

Westgate: Sopwith Schneider 3767, details not known; Sopwith Baby 8146 (Flt Sub-Lieut C. G. Bronson) 13.00–13.55 hr; Short 184 8092 (Flt Sub-Lieut R. Y. Bush, Flt Sub-Lieut L. G. Maxton) 13.13–15.13 hr; Short 827 3072 (Flt Sub-Lieut R. E. Spear, AM Lewis) 13.08–15.08 hr.

RFC

No.37 Squadron, Rochford: Type not recorded (Capt K. N. Pearson) 13.45–15.25 hr.

No.39 Squadron, A Flight, North Weald: B.E.12s 6609 (Capt S. R. Stammers) 13.01–13.30 hr, returned early with engine trouble; 6491 (Lieut L. G. S. Payne) 13.18–15.00 hr (Hounslow).

No.39 Squadron, B Flight, Suttons Farm: B.E.12 6607 (Lieut F. Sowrey) 13.01–16.01 hr.

No.39 Squadron, C Flight, Hainault: B.E.2c 4544 (Lieut C. V. Kerpen) 13.05–14.10 hr.

No.50 Squadron, Dover: B.E.12 6509 (2nd Lieut A. J. Hamer) 13.00–15.00 hr.

No.50 Squadron, Bekesbourne: B.E.12s 6146 (Capt J. Sowrey) 13.05–13.35 hr, returned early with engine trouble; 6593 (2nd Lieut C. A. Hore) 13.08–14.08 hr.

This culminating sortie in the career of Leutnant Walther Ilges must rate as among the most audacious of the war.

In broad daylight and virtually clear skies, his L.V.G. C IV (No.272/16), piloted by Deck Offizier Paul Brandt,* penetrated to central London. At 11.50 hr it dropped six 22 lb bombs between the Brompton Road and Victoria Station, and returned without being intercepted, taking photographs en route for good measure.

Ilges' target was the Admiralty, and for such small bombs dropped from about 13,000 ft he was commendably close. What prompted this bold venture has never

* In German two-seat aircraft the commander was not normally the pilot, the latter usually being of lower rank.

An L.V.G. C IV similar to that flown by Ilges and Brandt.

been explained, but having noted the weakness of the Thames estuary defences during previous sorties, Ilges perhaps decided to demonstrate a safe route to a prestige target in central London, retaining the option of breaking off if intercepted on the way in.

Taking off from Markiakerke near Ostende, the L.V.G. passed seven miles north of the North Foreland at 10.35 hr, skirted the Isle of Grain, then steered south at All Hallows to keep well away from No.39 Squadron's patrol lines, and approached London over Croydon and Mitcham. The few people who saw the aircraft assumed it to be British. It returned well to the west of any home defence bases and crossed the coast near Hastings. Luck deserted the crew on the home stretch; engine failure brought them down at 14.15 hr near Boulogne, where they were captured.

Nothing in the available files explains how this raider so easily slipped through the net, nor is there evidence of any 'inquest' into the inept showing of the defences. This would have disclosed the incredibly slow reactions in Whitehall after the bombs had fallen—though few people in the bombed area realized immediately that the puny explosions were from an air raid.

The Admiralty Air Department received no firm notification until 12.34 hr, while Home Defence Wing did not order any RFC patrols until 12.45 hr. Aircraft were then instructed to cover an arc running roughly from Clacton to Dungeness, but another 15 min elapsed before the first was airborne. By that time the L.V.G. must have been somewhere near the Sussex coast and quite safe from interception. None of the defenders saw anything, and the two aircraft which Ilges noticed leaving an unspecified aerodrome during his return flight were clearly engaged in some routine activity.

Chapter XII

Premature Optimism—and Defence Cuts

Britain's home-defence organization faced the opening of 1917 in a mood of cautious optimism.

There were now eleven full-time home-defence squadrons disposed between Edinburgh and Sussex, mostly with three flights each operating from fully-equipped aerodromes, and squadron headquarters normally located at some convenient central site. The more recently formed squadrons were, however, well below established strength in both aircraft and pilots.

More than 140 additional night-landing grounds were available, graded according to condition: 1st class having no obstructions and a good surface enabling flarepaths to be laid out in any direction; 2nd class with approach obstacles or ground irregularities limiting landings from certain directions; 3rd class permitting landings along one line only (from either direction) but the sole possible emergency-landing area in the neighbourhood.

Each squadron had control of a searchlight company. There were about 200 anti-aircraft guns, 65 deployed for the defence of London. The RNAS had no specific number of aircraft established for their home defence duties, but at least 30 were probably so committed.

Since the start of the war there had been 42 airship raids—with 160 airships crossing the coast—and the 162 tons of bombs dropped had caused 500 deaths and 1,224 injuries. The 2½ tons dropped by 39 aeroplanes in 25 minor attacks had killed 20 people and injured 67. Total property damage was calculated at nearly £1½ million. Although this was not an impressive direct return for the immense German effort, the raids had imposed a substantial burden on British resources. Apart from the large commitment of aircraft, guns and searchlights, more than 17,000 officers and men were tied up in the home-defence organization—and the raids and alarms greatly interfered with war production.

While arrangements to deal with the Zeppelins were reasonably satisfactory, serious shortcomings had been exposed by the audacious daylight aeroplane raid on London on 28 November, 1916. On 13 January Holt conferred with his southern squadron commanders and the following patrol pattern was devised:

No. 37 Squadron Rochford–Farningham–Biggin Hill–Esher.
All Hallows–Rochford–Goldhanger–Easthorpe.
No. 39 Squadron North Weald–Farningham.
No. 50 Squadron Rye–Pluckley–Herne Bay.
Dover–Margate.
Rochford–Herne Bay–Throwley.
No.78 Squadron Telscombe Cliffs–Rye.

If 'concentration' was ordered by Home Defence Wing, squadrons were to launch 'vic' formation patrols of three, with flight commanders' aircraft flying 4-ft identification streamers from their rudders—No.78 Squadron black, No.50

yellow, No.37 red and No.39 blue. 'Grand concentration' over a nominated place required flights of three aircraft to assemble, with the first flight commander reaching the rendezvous point to act as wing leader. It was emphasized that when engaging large numbers of enemy aircraft, flights should avoid becoming broken up, and that where events upset prearranged plans, commanders must use their initiative.

Discussions about RNAS assistance between Home Defence Wing and the Divisional Commander of Air Stations, Nore, predictably escalated to GHQ Home Forces/Admiralty level, and the eventual outcome was that the RFC, with twenty-four B.E.12/12as available for daylight patrols, was considered able to deal with day raiders over southeast England except in the immediate Dover area. It was agreed that the RFC should maintain responsibility for the defence of Sheerness and Chatham, taking over the RNAS aerodrome at Detling from 3 April. RNAS Manston was nominated to patrol between Herne Bay and Deal, while Grain covered the Sheerness–Foulness line. Westgate and Felixstowe seaplanes would patrol between the two stations. The RNAS had discretion to mount ad hoc night defence sorties.

B.E.12a No.A597 with night-flying equipment and externally mounted RL tube.

GHQ's confidence in the ability of B.E.12s to combat daylight raids, expressed to the Admiralty on 24 February, was not shared by Home Defence Wing, and four days later Charles Higgins—who had taken over from Holt—informed the War Office Directorate of Air Organization that these aircraft were quite unsuitable for the purpose. Lack of manoeuvrability and generally mediocre performance had already terminated their brief spell of fighter service in France, but there was nothing in the immediate domestic situation to warrant the issue of newer front-line fighters. One encouraging move—the allotment of three Bristol M.1 monoplanes—was regrettably short-lived, and a few weeks later these excellent aircraft were allocated for the Middle East. It is not clear whether any actually reached a home-defence squadron, but one (A5140) was certainly on the paper strength of Home Defence Wing during March.

It was normal practice for odd prototypes and specimens of aircraft not selected for full squadron use to find their way into home-defence units. In June, for example, Higgins complained to the War Office that two 160 hp Vickers F.B.14

two-seaters (A726 and 727) allotted to him were of no greater value than two useless 120 hp models (A678 and 686) already held by No.51 Squadron. On the other hand the fast Vickers E.S.1 single-seater used by No.50 Squadron was a popular machine, with a better chance of intercepting enemy day bombers than the standard squadron aircraft. Thanks to the unsophisticated state of contemporary aircraft construction and equipment, there were no real difficulties in operating virtually 'one-off' types—which should not be confused with the occasional prototypes specifically attached to squadrons for evaluation.

The RNAS continued to use Bristol Scouts, and various seaplanes which had small prospect of intercepting determined day raiders. From February Manston had a single Sopwith Triplane, though there were few opportunities to exploit its ability to reach 10,000 ft in about 10½ min, and top speed of 114 mph at that height. In May Yarmouth received its first Sopwith Pup, which had a performance almost as good and was renowned for its excellent handling qualities. However, Flt Lieut Egbert Cadbury, a very experienced pilot, was not enamoured of its potential as a night fighter, writing to a friend 'it was pretty rotten flying an unstable fast machine in the dark'.

With the principal enemy—the Zeppelin—apparently mastered, the home-defence organization inevitably became more vulnerable to pressing demands from other areas. In January the planned expansion of the anti-aircraft gun network was halted so that nearly 200 weapons could be diverted to arm merchant ships against U-boats.

On 6 February Henderson recommended to the Chief of the Imperial General Staff, General Sir William ('Wullie') Robertson, that the 'diminished risk from Zeppelin attack' permitted some urgent needs of the RFC in France to be temporarily met from home-defence resources. The immediate requirement was for thirty-six night-trained pilots to man two new F.E.2b night bomber squadrons, followed by nine replacement pilots a month. Neither the Cabinet, nor French,

Single Lewis gun installation on a Bristol Scout at RNAS Dover.

A twin Lewis gun installation on a Bristol Scout at RNAS Dover.

raised objections to this reduction of home-defence pilots below the minimum strength earlier agreed by the CIGS.

The War Office at first considered disbanding Nos.75 and 77 Squadrons, but in the event only one squadron, No.100, was urgently embodied for duty in France. Pilots were withdrawn from various home-defence units, and the new BEF squadron was formed on the aerodromes of No.51 Squadron, which also surrendered four of its F.E.2bs. In mid-March some home-defence B.E.2es and pilots were transferred to the BEF.

The somewhat disturbing strength situation as at 7 March—before the cuts had been fully implemented—is shown in the table:

Sqn	Aerodromes	Aircraft Estab	Aircraft Strength	Aircraft Available	Pilots Estab	Pilots Strength	Pilots Available
33	Brattleby Kirton Lindsey Elsham	18	13	13	18	12	10
36	Seaton Carew Hylton Ashington	18	15	13	18	13	9
37	Rochford Goldhanger	24	15	14	18	11	10
38	Stamford Buckminster Leadenham	18	16	15	18	8	6
39	North Weald Suttons Farm Hainault Farm	24	25	21	18	16	8
50	Dover Bekesbourne Throwley	24	16	13	18	16	10
51	Harling Road Mattishall Marham	18	20	16	18	8	8
75	Yelling Old Weston Therfield	18	7	6	18	4	4
76	Copmanthorpe Helperby Catterick	18	7	5	18	9	6
77	Turnhouse Whiteburn New Haggerston	18	5	4	18	8	7
78	Telscombe Cliffs Chiddingstone Causeway Gosport	24	8	5	18	8	4
		222	147	125	198	113	82

Note: No.98 Depot Squadron, Rochford, had 10 aircraft available and 14 pilots attached for training.

On 7 March after further discussions about reducing home-defence personnel strength, French issued an extraordinary instruction prohibiting all anti-aircraft guns—except those for specific coastal defence in the Dover, Newhaven, Shoeburyness, Harwich, Thames and Medway areas—from firing by day or night on enemy aeroplanes or seaplanes even when identified as such. This enabled a reduction in manning levels and released men for service in France.

An explanatory letter circulated on the same date by Shaw, Chief of Staff, Home Forces, was notably lacking in conviction. Enemy aeroplanes usually attacked from such heights as to make recognition practically impossible, he wrote, and in any case the gunners' lack of aircraft-recognition experience exposed our own aircraft to greater risk than the enemy. Operations in France had shown that a very large number of rounds was necessary to account for one target, and the chance of inexperienced home-based gunners inflicting damage was remote. The probable results obtained against the enemy would not justify the damage and casualties in populous areas from unexploded shells and fragments.

Col Simon, the forceful and energetic London AA Defence Commander, already grappling with problems caused by the cut in weapons establishments, was a great believer in the deterrent effect of guns and searchlights even if chances of success were small, and also appreciated their boost to civilian morale. He was dumbfounded by the new edict—which in a post-war memorandum he called one of the most remarkable in the history of air defence—and without official backing, prudently went ahead with preparing a gun defence scheme for rapid implementation should French's order be rescinded.

Any defence planners who really believed that the Zeppelin menace was over were soon disillusioned. Strasser was not of the mould to accept defeat easily, and the German navy's airship experts in collaboration with the Zeppelin works urgently sought means to regain the initiative. Higher speeds or greater altitudes could clearly reduce interception risks, and after detailed studies the more practical second alternative was adopted.

By relatively easily achieved weight savings the Zeppelins were enabled to reach heights which gave virtual immunity from guns and the contemporary British home-defence fighters. Bomb loads and defensive armament were reduced, fuel loads cut and the structure weight lessened in various ways. A lighter and more streamlined control car was designed, and the bulky rear gondola housing three engines, each driving its own propeller, was replaced by a neater type containing two engines geared to a single propeller.

L44, one of the black-doped 'height climbers'. She was shot down by AA fire over France after the 'silent raid' of 19/20 October, 1917.

Improvements were introduced by stages, and in January and February L35, 36, 39, 40 and 41 each had a rear engine removed as an initial step, enabling them to reach heights of 16–17,000 ft. In February L42 was delivered with some of the alterations embodied and attained nearly 20,000 ft, and in May came L47 with the new rear gondola. Earlier airships were modified to this standard. Apart from the reduced bomb load there were other penalties affecting crew comfort and efficiency, such as exposure to severe cold and lack of oxygen. Navigation problems were increased by the strong and unpredicted winds at high altitudes.

The improved 'height climbers' as they were termed first ventured over Britain on 16/17 March. Bad weather which prevented effective bombing also hampered the defences, and it is doubtful whether anyone realized that the Zeppelins had moved to a height band some 5,000 ft above most of the patrolling fighters.

However, French now altered course and blamed the defence cuts for the escape of the raiders. On 20 March he addressed the first of a long series of letters to the Army Council on the need for maintaining adequate home defences. He pointed out that the average strength of pilots and aircraft to patrol the allotted areas from Edinburgh to Worthing was now reduced from 130 to 71, and that many experienced anti-Zeppelin pilots had been posted overseas. While recognizing the all-important overseas requirements, he declared that Home Defence Wing was now:

> '. . . reduced to a dangerously low point, and one which does not enable the general scheme of defence on which the present disposition of squadrons is based to be carried out effectively'.

French asked for an undertaking that the minimum strength of trained night pilots should not fall below 100.

In their reply of 5 April the War Office declined to commit themselves to any minimum strength figure and maintained that Home Defence Wing deficiencies were not disproportionate to those overseas. However, some notice was, perhaps, taken of French's plea, for when the Zeppelins next attacked, on 23/24 May, the RFC achieved 39 sorties and the RNAS 37, compared with only 13 and three respectively against the March raid. Although the circumstances of the two raids were different, the figures do suggest some improvement in the overall strength.

The RNAS faced a new challenge from April, when German torpedo bombers made a determined, though unsuccessful, attack on coastal shipping. It was accordingly decided to increase fighter strength on the Kent coast as soon as possible, while warships were granted virtual blanket authority to shoot first and challenge later—a long-lasting policy of which some Second World War RAF crews retain rueful memories.

The night of 6/7 May witnessed an event comparable in audacity and portent with the naval L.V.G's London daylight raid of November 1916. A single Albatros from a German army reconnaissance squadron in Belgium dropped five small bombs on north London. Surprisingly, its unopposed flight over 150 miles of heavily defended territory caused little apparent stir in defence circles.

The early months of 1917 brought a series of useful technical and administrative developments rather than any dramatic major progress. With reliance now centred on the machine-gun, installations were improved and the Strange-Hutton mounting for B.E.2cs was superseded by the Admiralty Top Plane type. F.E.2bs were fitted with the Anderson mount for their Lewis guns. Sergeant A. E. Hutton, an enterprising armourer in No.39 Squadron, moved on from gun

Sgt A. E. Hutton checking the Lewis gun of an S.E.5a.

mounts to produce the first effective night sight. The Hutton 'V and bead' sight had illuminated pinholes, with three green spots in the 'V' and one red in the bead. The light was provided by two small bulbs and a torch battery, and the technique was to centralize the bead's red point in the greens marking the base and extremities of the 'V'.

After further trials Le Prieur rockets were discarded because of the aircraft performance penalty imposed by their installation and their erratic course when fired. The RFC also stopped using the Brock bullet, preferring the Buckingham and the Pomeroy PSA—though the RNAS persevered with the Brock for anti-Zeppelin work. Ranken darts appear to have been withdrawn at about this time.

There were various changes in ground organization. In March, Home Defence Wing became a Group, with Northern and Southern Wings. The increased demand for pilots enforced a temporary return to training in the squadrons when it was found that No.98 Depot Squadron—formed at Rochford in February from the old No.11 RAS transferred from Northolt—could not meet requirements.

Anti-aircraft operations rooms introduced an additional code using flower names—Buttercup, Camellia, Carnation, Crocus, Daffodil, Dahlia, Dandelion, Geranium, Hawthorn and Lilac. Thanks to the zeal of security conscious staffs no explanatory key appears to have been filed, so the significance of all the words, relating to airship and aeroplane movements, is not known. However, operational messages indicate that Carnation meant 'aircraft heard' and Dahlia 'aircraft seen', while Dandelion denoted 'hostile'.

The RNAS suffered a sad loss on 2 March, when Flt Sub-Lieut Edward Laston Pulling, who helped to shoot down L21 in November 1916, was killed flying the B.E.2c he had used on that occasion. Pulling, a competent aerobatic pilot, was returning from Burgh Castle to Yarmouth in the afternoon with Flt Sub-Lieut J. C. Northrop as passenger. Officers present at take-off told the subsequent inquiry that Northrop, who had never looped the loop, asked Pulling to demonstrate the manoeuvre. There was no suggestion that the aircraft was overloaded, for Pulling had transferred his gun and bombs to another machine. At about 2,000 ft the B.E. was completing the loop when horrified observers saw the outer bay of the lower starboard wing start to crumple. The aircraft dived, then pulled up to about 45 deg above the horizontal, when the wing collapsed completely. The B.E. plunged to the ground and both occupants were killed.

Chapter XIII

Operations—February to May 1917

14 February, 1917 (Daylight)

Target: Coastal shipping.
Enemy force: One Sablatnig SF 5.
Results: No casualties or damage.
Defence sorties: None.

Shortly after 08.00 hr, Deal AA guns fired 18 rounds at an enemy aircraft emerging from cloud at about 10,000 ft.

It flew off to the east and was almost certainly the Sablatnig floatplane of See Flieger Abteilung 1, crewed by Leutnant Frantz and Flugmeister Elsasser, which soon afterwards dropped 15 bombs among shipping in the Downs.

No hits were scored and the decision not to attempt pursuit, made after the initial sighting, was not questioned.

A Sablatnig SF 5 similar to that which made unsuccessful shipping attacks on 14 and 16 February, 1917. (*H. J. Nowarra*)

16 February, 1917 (Daylight)

Target: Coastal shipping.
Enemy force: One Sablatnig SF 5.
Results: No casualties or damage.
Defence sorties: Six.

RNAS

Manston: Sopwith Triplane N5424 (Sqn Cdr C. H. Butler) 07.53–09.05 hr; Bristol Scout Ds 8956 (Flt Sub-Lieut C. B. Wincott) 07.15–08.05 hr; 8956 (Flt Sub-Lieut E. S. Arnold) 08.30–09.07 hr; 8951 (Flt Sub-Lieut R. R. Thornely) 08.05–08.15 hr, returned early with engine trouble.

Westgate: Short 827 3111 (Flt Sub-Lieut W. N. Tees) 07.30–08.40 hr; Sopwith Baby 8146 (Flt Sub-Lieut C. G. Bronson) 08.10–09.00 hr.

This unsuccessful attack on shipping in the Downs by the same aircraft and crew which flew the 14 February sortie was lucky to escape interference from a Manston Bristol Scout and a Westgate Short, already airborne on routine coastal patrols, before it was sighted from the land.

Wincott, flying the Scout, saw the raider at 07.50 hr about four miles east of Ramsgate at 11,000 ft, but he could make no significant headway and being short of petrol had to return. The newly introduced Sablatnigs were faster than SFA 1's earlier floatplanes, with a top speed of more than 90 mph.

Manston was alerted at 07.50 hr by gunfire which followed sightings from Ramsgate and Foreness, and Butler was airborne in three minutes, flying the first home-defence sortie in one of the sprightly Sopwith Triplanes. He rapidly closed on an aircraft heading west—which turned out to be Wincott's Bristol returning to base. Nothing was seen by the other pilots.

Wing Commander R. Peel Ross, Westgate's station commander (who was also responsible for Manston) reported that despite the absence of warning, the Triplane would probably have intercepted had the enemy ventured a little nearer to the coast, but that Bristol Scouts clearly lacked the performance for successful operations from bases so close to the coast.

16/17 February, 1917 (Night)

Target: Calais.
Enemy force: Army Zeppelin LZ107.
Results: No casualties or damage.
Defence sorties: Six.

RNAS

Manston: B.E.2c 8298 (Sqn Cdr C. H. Butler) 01.49–02.53 hr.

RFC

No.50 Squadron, HQ Flight, Dover: B.E.2cs 1767 (Capt Storey) took off 02.05 hr; 4588 (2nd Lieut C. C. White) took off 02.05 hr.

No.50 Squadron, A Flight, Bekesbourne: B.E.2c 2711 (Lieut Rawson) 02.36–02.54 hr, returned early with engine trouble; B.E.12 6597 (Capt R. G. H. Murray) 02.36–03.22 hr.

No.50 Squadron, B Flight, Throwley: B.E.12 6493 (Lieut Butler) 03.15–03.22 hr, returned early due to weather.

An airship reported off Walmer at 01.45 hr and subsequently seen or heard from other places in east Kent was later established as LZ107 returning from a raid on Calais. No bombs were dropped on British soil. Defence pilots encountered misty weather and made no sightings.

1 March, 1917 (Daylight)

Target: Broadstairs.
Enemy force: One floatplane, type not known.
Results: Six injured, £700 damage.
Defence sorties: 24.

An unlikely-looking fighter—this Short 830 was despatched on patrol from RNAS Dover after a hit-and-run attack on Broadstairs on 1 March, 1917. (*Mrs P. Fane*)

RNAS

Dover: Short 830s 1342 (Flt Sub-Lieut L. C. Pincott, LM G. R. Hodgson) 10.02–10.57 hr; 1342 (Flt Sub-Lieut H. H. Gonyou, LM Hodgson) 10.58–12.34 hr; 1346 (Flt Sub-Lieut A. W. Farquhar, AM Lawson) 10.46–12.00 hr; Short 184 8102 (Flt Lieut R. Graham, CPO Hanna) 10.30–11.50 hr.

Grain: Bristol Scout D N5391, 10.45–11.10 hr; Sopwith Baby 8160, 10.45–11.20 hr. Pilots not known.

Manston: Bristol Scout Ds 8951 (Flt Sub-Lieut C. B. Wincott) 10.04–10.20 hr; 8957 (Flt Sub-Lieut J. E. Scott) 10.10–10.45 hr.

Westgate: Sopwith Babies 8186 (Flt Sub-Lieut W. N. Tees) 10.10–11.05 hr; 8146, details not known.

RFC

No.37 Squadron, Rochford: Two sorties, details not known.

No.37 Squadron, Goldhanger: Two sorties, details not known.

No.39 Squadron, A Flight, North Weald: B.E.12 6645 (Lieut Norris) took off 10.37 hr; one sortie, details not known.

No.39 Squadron, B Flight, Suttons Farm: Two sorties, details not known.

No.39 Squadron, C Flight, Hainault: B.E.12 6517 (Capt W. T. F. Holland) took off 10.30 hr; B.E.12a A6325 (Lieut V. T. Norminton) took off 10.31 hr.

No.50 Squadron, HQ Flight, Dover: Two sorties, details not known.

No.50 Squadron, A Flight, Bekesbourne: Two sorties, details not known.

A single floatplane from Zeebrugge—the type is not specified in Seeflugstation Flanders 1 records—attacked Broadstairs at 09.45 hr, four bombs falling in the sea and six on land.

There was evidently some failure in the warning system, since the first RNAS aircraft was not airborne for more than 15 minutes and RFC readiness was not ordered until 10.12 hr. There was then a lavish response, but too late for any defending aircraft to claim even distant sightings.

16 March, 1917 (Daylight)

Targets: Westgate, coastal shipping.
Enemy force: One floatplane, type not known.
Results: No casualties, £45 damage.
Defence sorties: Seven.

RNAS

Dover: Short 830 1342 (Flt Sub-Lieut A. W. Farquhar, AM Morris) 06.35–07.15 hr.

Manston: Sopwith Triplane N5424 (Sqn Cdr C. H. Butler) 05.35–06.00 hr; Bristol Scout D 8951 (Flt Sub-Lieut E. S. Arnold) 05.37–06.40 hr.

Westgate: Sopwith Baby 8146 (Flt Sub-Lieut C. G. Bronson) took off 05.45 hr.

RFC

No.37 Squadron, Rochford: One sortie, details not known.
No.50 Squadron, HQ Flight, Dover: One sortie, details not known.
No.50 Squadron, A Flight, Bekesbourne: One sortie, details not known.

At 05.20 hr an aircraft emerged from low cloud near Westgate and dropped twenty bombs. Most of them fell in open country causing only minor damage and broken windows in nearby buildings. One dropped 150 yards from the RNAS station.

Several eye-witnesses asserted that the machine was a Handley Page, and a keen-eyed special constable claimed to have seen red white and blue rudder stripes in the faint morning light. People in the area were familiar with the recently introduced Handley Page O/100s at Manston, and some perhaps knew that one had landed, undamaged, inside the enemy lines on 1 January. Despite one report clearly describing the raider as a seaplane, intelligence appeared confident that it was the captured British bomber, flown by a German crew.

German records show that in fact the aircraft was from SFA 1, Zeebrugge, attempting a routine attack on shipping in the Downs. However, when the crew broke through the thick cloud layer at 1,300 ft they found themselves off Westgate, so turned to make a surprise attack on what was claimed as the railway station and sheds at Margate.

The type of aircraft is not given in the German report, and there are no indications that SFA 1 was currently flying twin-engined machines. However, the bombs were only of 5 kg weight, and the total was well within the capacity of a single-engined floatplane.

The British fighter pilots encountered the same thick cloud which had diverted the raider from its intended shipping target, and soon abandoned the search.

16/17 March, 1917 (Night)

Target: London.
Enemy forces: Navy Zeppelins L35 (Kptlt H. Ehrlich), L39 (Kptlt R. Koch), L40 (Kptlt E. Sommerfeldt), L41 (Hptmn K. Manger). L42 (Kptlt Martin Dietrich) returned early.
Results: No casualties, £163 damage.
Defence sorties: 17.

RNAS

Eastchurch: Sopwith 1½ Strutter 3686 (Flt Cdr L. P. Openshaw, Lieut A. N. Hansford) 22.50–00.25 hr; B.E.2c 8294, crew not known, took off 00.12 hr.

Manston: B.E.2c 8298 (Sqn Cdr C. H. Butler) 22.14–00.36 hr.

RFC

No.37 Squadron, A Flight, Goldhanger: B.E.12a A4032 (Capt W. Sowrey) 22.30–00.05 hr and 00.30–02.22 hr; B.E.2e A2767 (Lieut L. P. Watkins) 00.11–02.41 hr.

No.37 Squadron, B Flight, Rochford: B.E.2es 6820 (Capt K. N. Pearson) 22.41–00.01 hr; 5877 (Lieut Carpenter) 00.25–01.40 hr; 6820 (Lieut Ransome) 01.10–02.25 hr.

No.39 Squadron, A Flight, North Weald: B.E.2c 2089 (Capt S. R. Stammers) 00.14–01.15 hr.

No.39 Squadron, B Flight, Suttons Farm: B.E.12 6480 (Capt J. I. Mackay) 23.25–01.44 hr.

No.39 Squadron, C Flight, Hainault: B.E.12 6495 (Capt W. T. F. Holland) 23.24–00.05 hr, returned early with engine trouble.

No.50 Squadron, HQ Flight, Frinsted: B.E.12a A6313 (Capt R. G. H. Murray) 23.57–00.15 (Throwley).

No.50 Squadron, A Flight, Bekesbourne: B.E.2e 6817 (Lieut J. B. Hine) 22.10–23.20 hr.

No.50 Squadron, B Flight, Throwley: B.E.2c 2699 (2nd Lieut A. J. Arkell) 22.15–23.45 hr (Marden); B.E.12a A6313 (Capt R. G. H. Murray) 02.05–03.05 hr (Bekesbourne).

No.78 Squadron, Telscombe Cliffs: B.E.2e 7181 (2nd Lieut D. D. Fowler) 00.01–00.10 hr, crashed, pilot killed.

This first sortie by four R-class Zeppelins modified as 'height climbers' and the new S-class L42 constructed from the outset to achieve increased altitudes was badly affected by weather. The few scattered bombs caused no casualties.

L39 and L35 came in over Thanet at 22.20 hr and 22.40 hr respectively and followed a broadly similar course to Ashford, where L35 turned south to fly out near Dover at 00.25 hr, while L39 continued southwestwards and departed near Pevensey at 23.50 hr. L39 was later shot down by French gunfire near Compiègne. L40 made landfall over Herne Bay at 01.00 hr and flew across Kent to depart near New Romney at 02.15, and L41 was over the Winchelsea–Dungeness area between 01.40 and 02.05 hr. Strasser, recently elevated to a new post, Leader of Airships, was flying in L42, which turned back with mechanical troubles.

The great operating altitudes of 17–19,000 ft attained on this raid exposed the airships to a northwesterly airstream of 45 mph, while cloud obscured much of the ground below. British jamming of the Zeppelins' wireless frequencies prevented them from obtaining fixes, and they all drifted far south of their intended routes, later becoming exposed to a long and hazardous return journey over France.

Defence reaction was prompt, with three B.Es—flown by Butler, Hine and Arkell—airborne before the first Zeppelin had crossed the coast. Fighters continued to take off as the raiders moved over Kent, but they faced a hopeless task. Even if the searchlights had been able to penetrate the cloud, which generally extended from 3,000 to 9,000 ft, they would have experienced great difficulty in tracking airships at such heights.

Only Mackay, from Suttons Farm, who reached 16,100 ft, approached the Zeppelins' altitudes, but none were near his patrol area. Arkell, from Throwley, cruised at 9,000 ft above cloud for 30 min, seeing nothing, and passed through three heavy rainstorms during his descent. With his engine running badly he put down on the 2nd class landing ground at Marden. Murray reached 11,000 ft on his second sortie, from Throwley, and found the weather much improved. Hine broke his undercarriage on landing.

No.78 Squadron began its operational career on a sad note, and the cause of Fowler's fatal accident is not known. His B.E.2e crashed about one-and-a-half miles from the aerodrome at Telscombe Cliffs and was burned out. It came down nine minutes after take-off, and Fowler was probably attempting to return for some reason.

17 March, 1917 (Daylight)

Target: Dover.
Enemy force: One aeroplane, type not known.
Results: No casualties or damage.
Defence sorties: Two.

RNAS

Dover: Short 184 8102 (Flt Lieut M. R. Buckland, LM G. R. Hodgson) 15.45–16.10 hr, returned early with engine trouble.

Manston: Bristol Scout D 8957 (Flt Sub-Lieut J. E. Scott) 15.52–16.42 hr.

This ineffective attack was probably made by Marine Landflieger Abteilung 1. A single-engined biplane approached from the sea, without warning and dropped four bombs near the Dover submarine pens.

The two aircraft despatched in pursuit were too late to locate the raider. Scott crashed on landing, damaging the undercarriage and engine cowling of his Bristol Scout.

25 March, 1917 (Daylight)

Target: Coastal shipping.
Enemy forces: Three aeroplanes, type not known.
Results: No casualties or damage.
Defence sorties: Two.

RNAS

Dover: Short 184 8102 (Flt Lieut M. R. Buckland, CPO Hanna) 13.40–14.43 hr; Short 830 1342 (Flt Sub-Lieut A. W. Farquhar, LM G. R. Hodgson) 13.43–15.23 hr.

Little is on record about this incident. Buckland sighted three enemy aircraft off Dungeness at about 14.25 hr, but was unable to catch up with them.

The machines may have been from a Marine Landflieger Abteilung attempting a shipping strike. SFA 1, Zeebrugge, which recorded no operational sorties, was that day testing its newly-acquired torpedo-carrying aircraft, but those are unlikely to have ventured near the English coast.

5/6 April, 1917 (Night)

Targets: Ramsgate, coastal shipping.
Enemy forces: Two aeroplanes, type not known.
Results: No casualties, £4 damage.
Defence sorties: None.

A single floatplane of SFA 1, type not recorded, was over the Ramsgate area between 22.03 and 22.30 hrs, dropping eight bombs which caused no significant damage. Another aircraft attacked shipping in the Downs. No defence sorties were ordered.

19 April, 1917 (Daylight)

Target: Coastal shipping.
Enemy forces: Six floatplanes.
Results: No casualties or damage.
Defence sorties: None.

This first attack by torpedo-carrying floatplanes of SFA 1 was an exciting performance despite the lack of success. The strike force comprised four unspecified torpedo-carriers—probably Gotha WD 11s—one fighter and one W/T communications aircraft.

Fog and low cloud hampered the attack and also prevented fighters from taking off. Torpedoes aimed at the armed drifter *Carolbank* off the Goodwins at 07.38 hr, and at the ss *Nyanza* a few minutes later, both dived and sank after release, and a third, discharged at a large dredger off Ramsgate, embedded itself in the mud of the harbour. The fourth aircraft lost its bearings in the fog while trying to position for an attack on the monitor, *Marshal Ney*, and returned with its torpedo.

Not mentioned in German reports is an apparent lucky escape for one of the aircraft. According to an onlooker, it alighted off Ramsgate. A crew member then climbed on to a float and apparently re-started an engine, whereupon the aircraft took off successfully.

6/7 May, 1917 (Night)

Target: London.
Enemy force: One Albatros C VII.
Results: One killed, two injured, £510 damage.
Defence sorties: Four.

RNAS
Manston: Two sorties, details not known.

RFC

No.50 Squadron, A Flight, Bekesbourne: Two sorties, details not known.

This audacious night sortie by a single-engined Albatros of the army's Feldflieger Abteilung 19, based at Handzame, near Ostende, was very much a personal effort by an enthusiastic crew—Offizierstellvertreter Rudolf Klimke (pilot) and Oberleutnant Walther Leon (observer). They had the tacit approval of their squadron commander—though not of higher authority, which later delivered a formal reprimand.

Aided by a full moon and favourable winds, the Albatros skirted the North Foreland at 5,800 ft and crossed the coast near Canvey Island, climbing to nearly 14,000 ft. It approached London from the north at 01.00 hr and dropped five 22 lb bombs along a line from Holloway to Hackney. It followed a more southerly track home, flying out near Deal.

As with several other events of special significance, essential details of the defence activity are strangely missing from the generally well preserved file sequences. A possible explanation is that immediate reports demanded by the highest authority before completion of the routine records were subsequently misfiled, or destroyed.

The German crew reported seeing a British aircraft at close quarters during their return flight, which may have been one of the defenders.

23/24 May, 1917 (Night)

Target: London.

Enemy forces: Navy Zeppelins L40 (Kptlt E. Sommerfeldt), L42 (Kptlt Martin Dietrich), L43 (Kptlt H. Kraushaar), L44 (Kptlt F. Stabbert), L45 (Kptlt Waldemar Kolle), L47 (Kptlt Richard Wolff).

Results: One killed, none injured, £599 damage.

Defence sorties: 76.

RNAS

Felixstowe: Curtiss H-12s 8658 (Flt Cdr P. L. Holmes) 04.40–06.55 hr; 8662 (Flt Lieut B. D. Hobbs) 03.52–08.25 hr; Short 184 9068 (Flt Sub-Lieut H. A. Wilson) 04.12–05.22 hr.

Killingholme: Sopwith Babies N1068, 05.11–07.35 hr; N1111, 05.11–07.00 hr; N1113, 05.11–07.00 hr; 8130, 05.13–07.45 hr; Short 184s 8039, took off 05.13 hr; 8055, 05.13–06.15 hr. Pilots' names not recorded.

Manston: B.E.2cs 8298, 23.00–00.33 hr and 02.30–04.12 hr; 8408, 02.55–04.39 hr. Pilots' names not recorded.

Westgate: Sopwith Babies 8186 (Flt Sub-Lieut H. M. Morris) 03.40–06.45 hr; N1065 (Flt Sub-Lieut L. G. Maxton) 03.40–05.15 hr, forced alighting, towed to Grain; Short 827s 3072 (Flt Sub-Lieut H. M. Morris, AM G. O. Wright) took off 08.10 hr, forced alighted; 3111 and 3331 also operated, returning at 06.45 and 06.46 hr respectively, no details.

Yarmouth: B.E.2cs 8411 (Flt Lieut E. Cadbury) 00.50–01.59 hr (Burgh Castle); 8625 (Flt Lieut G. H. Simpson) 02.35–03.00 hr (Burgh Castle); Sopwith Pup 9904 (Flt Lieut E. Cadbury) 04.00–05.00 hr; Bristol Scout D 8959 (Flt Sub-Lieut G. W. R. Fane) 04.10–04.40 hr; Sopwith Babies 8149 (Flt Sub-Lieut H. B. Smith) 04.10–05.35 hr; 8150 (Flt Sub-Lieut H. B. Brenton) 04.15–06.20 hr; N1064 (Flt Sub-Lieut G. H. Bittles) 04.20–06.20 hr; Short 184 8066 (Flt Lieut G. E. Livock, AM Gibbs) 04.30–08.00 hr; Curtiss H-12 8666 (Flt Lieut C. J.

B.E.2c night fighter, 8408, at RNAS Manston in May 1917. The pilot is unidentified. (*RAF Museum*)

Galpin, Flt Sub-Lieut R. Leckie, CPO V. F. Watling, AM J. R. Laycock) 04.15–09.40 hr (Cromer).

Bacton: B.E.2c 8608 (Flt Sub-Lieut T. G. C. Wood) 23.45–00.58 hr, 02.45–03.20 hr and 03.30–05.00 hr.

Burgh Castle: B.E.2cs 8629 (Flt Lieut F. W. Walker) 01.05–02.00 hr and 03.23–05.10 hr; 8411 (Flt Lieut E. Cadbury) 02.40–03.30 hr; 8625 (Flt Lieut G. H. Simpson) 03.15–04.45 hr; 8492 (Flt Sub-Lieut G. R. Halliday) 03.15–05.15 hr.

Covehithe: B.E.2c 8619 (Flt Sub-Lieut C. S. Iron) 23.58–01.02 hr and 03.15–04.57 hr.

Holt: B.E.2c 8498 (Flt Sub-Lieut H. D. Smith) took off 01.43 hr, missing.

RFC

No.37 Squadron, A Flight, Goldhanger: B.E.2d 5778 (Capt C. B. Cooke) 02.28–05.10 hr (Rochford); B.E.2es A2767 (Lieut L. F. Hutcheon) 02.15–04.40 hr; 7237 (Capt F. Sowrey) 03.02–03.35 hr, returned early with engine trouble; B.E.12 6610 (Lieut L. P. Watkins) 23.14–00.24 hr, returned due to weather, and 02.25–04.27 hr; B.E.12as A4032 (Capt W. Sowrey) 23.14–00.22 hr, damaged landing; A6317 (Capt W. Sowrey) 03.05–04.10 hr, forced landed Easthorpe with engine trouble; A590 (Capt F. Sowrey) 04.02–04.13 hr, returned due to weather, and 04.32–05.55 hr.

No.37 Squadron, B Flight, Stow Maries: B.E.12as A6318 (Capt C. A. Ridley) 02.55–06.30 hr; A6345 (Lieut G. D. F. Keddie) 03.00–04.45 hr (Covehithe).

No.37 Squadron, C Flight, Rochford: B.E.2d 5778 (Capt C. B. Cooke) 23.18–00.30 hr (Goldhanger, due to weather); B.E.12a A6312 (Lieut W. R. S. Humphreys) 03.04–03.37 hr, returned due to weather, and 04.40–05.00 hr (Goldhanger).

No.39 Squadron, A Flight, North Weald: B.E.12 6488 (Capt T. Gran) 02.14–05.30 hr, forced landed near Ware; B.E.12a A6326 (Capt S. R. Stammers) 02.55–03.50 hr.

No.39 Squadron, B Flight, Suttons Farm: B.E.12s 6480 (Capt J. I. Mackay) 02.13–05.20 hr; 6138 (Lieut E. S. Moulton-Barrett) 02.48–04.45 hr.

No.39 Squadron, C Flight, Hainault: B.E.2e 7151 (Capt W. T. F. Holland) 02.08–04.13 hr.

No.50 Squadron, A Flight, Bekesbourne: B.E.2e 6817 (2nd Lieut J. G. Goodyear) 23.22–00.15 hr, recalled due to weather, and 02.45–04.25 hr (Burnham); B.E.12a A6313 (2nd Lieut F. A. D. Grace) 02.40–04.10 hr.

No.50 Squadron, B Flight, Throwley: B.E.2c 2699 (2nd Lieut A. J. Arkell) 23.30–23.58 hr, recalled due to weather; B.E.12s 6185 (Capt T. R. Irons) 02.49–03.20 hr; 6493 (Lieut H. T. O. Windsor) 02.38–04.25 hr.

No.50 Squadron, C Flight, Detling: B.E.12 6183 (2nd Lieut C. C. White) 02.32–02.50 hr, returned due to weather.

No.51 Squadron, A Flight, Mattishall: F.E.2bs 4876 (2nd Lieut E. A. W. Kent, AM Brooker) 00.50–01.15 hr; A787 (Lieut W. R. Gayner, Sgt Wigglesworth) 00.45–01.43 hr; 7689 (Lieut O. E. Ridewood, Cpl Dye) 03.48–05.10 hr; 7679 (Capt L. C. Angstrom) 03.40–06.00 hr; 4885 (Lieut V. E. Schweitzer, Cpl Cruselle) 03.25–05.20 hr; A5519 (Lieut Parnell, AM Held) 03.40–05.35 hr.

No.51 Squadron, B Flight, Harling Road: F.E.2bs 4885 (Lieut V. E. Schweitzer, Cpl Cruselle) 00.40–01.40 hr (Mattishall); A5519 (Lieut Parnell, AM Held) took off 00.40 hr, landed Mattishall; 7004 (Capt P. le G. Gribble, Flt Sgt Johnson) 03.10–06.20 hr; 6970 (Capt I. A. J. Duff) 03.15–05.25 hr.

No.51 Squadron, C Flight, Marham: F.E.2bs A5520 (2nd Lieut Duncan, AM Bishop) 00.50–03.00 hr (Harling Road); 4890 (2nd Lieut C. O. Bean, Sgt Bastable) 00.55–04.15 hr; 7676 (Capt Barnes) 03.35–05.15 hr.

The German Naval Airship Service again demonstrated its unfortunate flair for picking bad operating nights. A combination of adverse winds and thick cloud prevented any of the six 'height climbers' from reaching London—the nearest was 40 miles away—and only 60 widely scattered bombs were traced on land.

Yarmouth received reports of Zeppelins 25 miles off the coast at 21.45 hr, but the first penetration was not until 00.18 hr, when L40 came in south of Lowestoft. L42 made landfall over the Naze a few minutes later, and L45 and L43 south of

Surviving photographs of the Harling Road (formerly Roudham), Norfolk, aerodrome, are of poor quality, and this shows a No.51 Squadron F.E.2b there in early 1917. (*RAF Museum*)

Orfordness at 01.00 and 02.15 hr. L44 suffered severe technical troubles off the coast between Harwich and Lowestoft from about 01.45 until 03.15 hr, for a time losing power from all engines. L47 was not plotted inland despite her commander's firm belief that he had spent two hours over the country.

With the airships flying for the most part above 16,000 ft and over cloud, their movements could not be followed with accuracy as they wandered over East Anglia, eventually departing across the Norfolk coast between 01.00 and 04.00 hr. L43, flying at 20,000 ft, mistook Harwich for Sheerness and claimed to have hit London, but her bombs actually fell around Suffolk villages. Some of the airships encountered severe thunderstorms and nearly all crews suffered from anoxia—and the severe cold which also affected mechanical performance in various ways.

After the disappointing lack of contact during the March raid, the defences were on their mettle to repeat the triumphs of 1916 and a tremendous effort was mounted—nearly double the number of sorties flown on any previous occasion.

In the event weather handicapped the fighters as much as the raiders, causing a high proportion of early returns or emergency landings away from base. Pilots displayed great determination—some flying three sorties—labouring up through layers of thick cloud and heavy rain in vain attempts to find the enemy. Conditions largely disguised the fact that the airships were mostly above the fighters' ceiling, and only one was sighted. One RNAS aircraft and pilot did not return.

With Zeppelins over East Anglia for some four hours, RNAS Yarmouth and its satellites and No.51 Squadron, RFC, were the busiest units, together flying more than 30 sorties. Even though the raiders were only rarely anywhere near the fighters' altitudes, they were unlucky not to make any sightings.

Cadbury, whose B.E.2c's navigation lights failed, narrowly escaped collision with Walker when both were approaching Burgh Castle to land at about 02.00 hr. Unperturbed, Cadbury flew a second sortie, then a third on a Sopwith Pup—the first home-defence use of this highly effective little fighter.

The missing pilot was Flt Sub-Lieut H. D. Smith, from Holt, who is believed to have chased L40 far out to sea and run out of petrol while battling his way back against strong headwinds.

One enterprising move by Yarmouth very nearly succeeded. A Curtiss H-12 'Large America' flying-boat, piloted by Galpin and Leckie, took off for the Dutch coast shortly after the last of the raiders had cleared England, hoping to cut them off as they neared their bases. At 06.38 hr, just north of Terschelling, the L40 obligingly appeared through the cloud at 2,000 ft about a mile away. She promptly turned and began to climb, reaching the protection of the clouds as the flying-boat approached to 300 yards. The gunner fired half a drum of Brock, Pomeroy and tracer but the range was too great. Galpin then took his unwieldy machine through a gap up to 10,000 ft, and finding nothing, returned home. He came down at 09.40 hr, short of fuel, off Cromer Knoll and was towed in by a trawler.

The sole sighting was by Douglas Keddie, No.37 Squadron, Stow Maries. Shortly after starting his patrol along the Blackwater–Harwich line he spotted a Zeppelin off Harwich at about 7,000 ft, flying northeast. He gave chase but found difficulty in following its erratic course in and out of cloud. After 20 min trying in vain to urge his B.E.12a into attacking range he lost the raider completely, then while still searching, his engine began to give trouble so he landed at Covehithe. There is little doubt that Keddie saw L44 while she was drifting like a free balloon, with Stabbert's crew frantically trying to rectify the engines. After a nightmare

Curtiss H-12 No.8666 from RNAS Yarmouth which unsuccessfully engaged L40 early on 24 May, 1917. Ten days before, 8666 had shot down L22 while on a North Sea reconnaissance, and had four subsequent encounters with Zeppelins performing this work.

journey the Zeppelin eventually reached her base at 19.00 hr.

No.37 Squadron's attempts to intercept L42 were frustrated largely by weather. Two aircraft from Goldhanger and one from Rochford, airborne after early reports of Zeppelins off the Suffolk coast, were forced back by the conditions, and William Sowrey, youngest of three pilot brothers in the RFC, broke his propeller and bottom port wing while landing in the poor visibility. His second sortie on another aircraft was cut short when sooted plugs forced him down at Easthorpe. Meanwhile, Frederick Sowrey*—who had destroyed L32 the previous September—was enjoying little better fortune. The B.E.2e flown on the first of his three sorties proved incapable of climbing above 9,500 ft, so he took a B.E.12, but gave up the attempt to penetrate a seemingly endless density of cloud. He saw nothing on his third trip.

No.50 Squadron's early patrols were also curtailed by weather, and Arkell and Goodyear, both inexperienced pilots, were complimented for their competent landings in driving rain. On a second sortie patrolling the Dover–Margate line, Goodyear was blown badly off course by the strong wind and put down at Burnham-on-Crouch.

Despite the short-lived threat to London, lifted when L42 turned north near Braintree at about 01.45 hr, GHQ Home Forces had illuminated the searchlights as a deterrent and continued to maintain extensive patrol activity in the south. The RNAS was busy off the coast and altogether fourteen pilots were airborne in very poor weather.

* John Sowrey, the oldest brother, was in No.50 Squadron in 1916. All three later held regular RAF commissions, William retiring as an air commodore and Frederick and John as group captains.

B.E.12 No.6488 of No.39 Squadron, North Weald, flown by Capt Tryggve Gran during the operations of 23/24 May, 1917.

Short 827 No.3331 which flew from RNAS Westgate on 23/24 May, 1917.
(J. M. Bruce/G. S. Leslie collection)

Captain Tryggve Gran, the Norwegian polar explorer and prewar pilot, attached to No.39 Squadron, ran short of petrol and forced landed at Hamels Park, near Ware. Perhaps because of Norway's neutrality, Gran was invariably disguised in No.39 Squadron records as 'Grant'. Stammers put down at Little Laver, five miles northeast of his base because of some unspecified indisposition—possibly suffering from the effects of cold.

The RNAS lost a seaplane from Westgate as an indirect result of the night's activities. Flt Sub-Lieut Morris, with Air Mechanic Wright, left in a Short 827 to search for Maxton's Sopwith Baby, thought to be overdue but in fact under tow en route for Grain. After 35 min the Short came down with engine failure in very choppy seas, and following six hours of pounding by the rising waves, capsized to leave only the floats above water. On the afternoon of the 29th, long after hopes of finding them alive had been abandoned, a Felixstowe H-12 on a routine anti-submarine patrol spotted Morris and Wright clinging to the one remaining float. They were taken on board, then the flying-boat itself became a casualty, being badly damaged trying to take off in the heavy sea. It was eventually towed into Felixstowe by a naval vessel.

Chapter XIV

Rise and Fall of the Day Offensive

The absence of the large-scale aeroplane raids predicted by Intelligence towards the end of 1916 appeared to have justified the Government's calculated risk in running down the defences. During the spring of 1917 a state of inertia seemed to infect GHQ Home Forces—apart from French's near obsession over the Zeppelin threat—and when the new and formidable phase of the air offensive against Britain was actually launched, Germany achieved complete surprise.

At about 17.00 hr on 25 May, 1917—the Friday of Whitsun weekend—twenty-one twin-engined Gotha bombers crossed the Essex coast and headed for London. Thwarted by cloud cover, they turned south to drop most of their bombs on Folkestone, which received no warning. Casualties were 95 killed and 195 injured. During the 90-min flight over England not one bomber was intercepted. The only contacts were made by two ferry pilots as the Gothas returned over the Channel, and by RNAS fighters from Dunkirk. One bomber was shot down.

This unprecedented raid clearly caused chaos and confusion at GHQ Home Forces, but it is difficult to justify the extraordinary decision to delay any news communiqué until after lunch on the following day. This infuriated the Press, already shackled by D Notices, and a formal complaint was later made by the Newspaper Proprietors' Association.

Meanwhile, on 28 May, a *Times* editorial asserted that the home-defence pilots had taken off too late because of obvious shortcomings in the intelligence, observer and warning organizations. *The Times* also criticized the 'childish and dangerous' method of releasing the news. All Fleet Street knew the facts the same evening and the country was full of the wildest rumours, declared *The Times*, yet the Saturday morning newspapers were not allowed to print a line of information. Although there was no mystery about it in Germany, British papers were still ridiculously banned from naming the town suffering most of the casualties—was ever anything better calculated to breed panic and discredit all official publicity?

The introduction of this new major dimension in air warfare required long and careful planning, and it says much for German security that British Intelligence apparently gleaned nothing to warrant any urgent tightening of the defences. The German bomber unit involved, Kampfgeschwader der Obersten Heeresleitung 3—Battle Squadron No.3 of the Army High Command (later titled Bombengeschwader 3, or the Englandgeschwader)—titles normally shortened to Kagohl and Boghol—had its ancestry in the original Ostende Carrier Pigeon Squadron. Its commanding officer was Hauptmann Ernst Brandenburg, succeeded by Hauptmann Rudolf Kleine when Brandenburg was injured in a flying accident on 19 June.

The decision to mount the campaign was made by the GOC of the reorganized German Army Air Service in the autumn of 1916 after concluding that successful airship attacks on London were no longer possible. The squadron role was to

Hptmn Ernst Brandenburg, first commander of the Gotha unit Kagohl 3 (*left*); and Hptmn Rudolf Kleine, who took command of Kagohl 3 after Brandenburg had been injured in a flying accident on 19 June, 1917.

strike at British morale by raids on the capital, to disrupt war industry and communications, attack coastal ports and hamper cross-Channel transport. Preparations went ahead—under the code name Turkenkreuz—on the forecast that thirty new Gotha G IV bombers would be delivered by 1 February, 1917. The first actually arrived in March, and an intensive training programme started at Ghistelles until new bases were completed at St-Denis Westrem and Gontrode, near Ghent.

The second Gotha in this Kagohl 3 line-up may be the red-tailed aircraft captained by Brandenburg. It also displays a hunting-horn device. Serial numbers have been removed by the German censor. (*A. E. Ferko*)

The Gotha G IV was a development of the G III introduced in the autumn of 1916, and apart from minor structural changes the main difference was provision of a 'tunnel' in the rear fuselage to give the aft gunner a much improved downward field of fire, covering what was normally a blind spot exploited by attacking fighters. Powered by two 260 hp Mercedes engines, the G IV with its 78 ft span wings was an ungainly creation to modern eyes, but it had an excellent climb, a ceiling of nearly 17,000 ft and could cruise at about 80 mph—performance figures presenting a formidable challenge to the contemporary British home-defence aircraft. It provided a steady gun platform and its only real shortcoming was a proneness to landing accidents, caused by control difficulties which attended the shift in centre of gravity after bombs had been released and most of the petrol consumed. Landing crashes wrote off more aircraft than all other causes combined.

Gotha G IVs of Kagohl 3 at Ghistelles during an inspection by Generalleutnant Ernst von Hoeppner, Commanding General of the Air Force. (*H. J. Nowarra*)

Two G IIIs had been shot down in France, in February and April, so the existence of the basic Gotha was known. The build-up of G IVs in Belgium can hardly have escaped the notice of friendly agents, but British Intelligence may have assumed that, like the G IIIs, they were for tactical bombing at the Front rather than attacks on England. There is nothing in the files to suggest that their existence worried Home Defence Group.

Even allowing for the Gothas' average operating height of 16,000 ft on 25 May, eye-witness reports demonstrated the prevailing abysmal ignorance of aircraft recognition. The sheer noise generated by the formation probably influenced those who reported 'a Zeppelin escorted by Taubes'. Others described the aircraft as Aviatiks, Rumplers, Albatros, Halberstadts, and D.F.Ws.

Thanks to the ill-conceived restriction on anti-aircraft gunfire, many people assumed the aircraft to be friendly. Apart from the Burnham mobile battery—which discharged one round before somebody remembered the rules—only the Dover guns were in action, firing 384 rounds, after the bombers had finished their work. Police reports included such lyrical descriptions as 'like seagulls', 'white and golden', 'swan-shaped', 'like snowflakes', confirming that the aircraft were viewed with no great apprehension.

A GHQ Home Forces inquiry disclosed that one of the factors responsible for failure to intercept was the 12-min transmission time, through four wireless links, of the first sighting report at 16.45 hr by the Tongue lightship. Appropriate squadrons were on readiness by 17.05 hr and the patrol order followed three minutes later. The navy did rather better and RNAS units were alerted by 16.50 hr. The passing of subsequent information was hampered by irresponsible messages like this example from a Gravesend naval unit to the local AA commander—'a fleet of Zeppelins making a great noise, overhead a stink of paraffin, Zeppelins flying very high towards Snodland'.

Owing to heat haze and an overcast sky many pilots could not read the Ingram ground signals, and had the RFC been allowed to develop its W/T reporting system, more fighters would undoubtedly have been guided in the general direction of the enemy instead of joining an almost aimless shambles. But regardless of the warning and control shortcomings and the lack of co-ordination, the truth is that of the 77 sorties flown—40 RNAS and 37 RFC—only a third were by aircraft having any chance of reaching the bombers let alone joining combat. MPs were told later that the weather was the main reason for lack of success.

With the needs of the Western Front still paramount, no immediate remedies were possible, but at least the Air Board did something. On 28 May a dozen Armstrong Whitworth F.K.8s and eight Sopwith $1\frac{1}{2}$ Strutters were urgently allotted to Home Defence Group—though in no sense were these effective fighters. The F.K.8 was a fairly new artillery spotter and the Sopwith an obsolescent two-seat fighter-bomber. Neither type was noted for manoeuvrability, but Home Defence Group claimed that the Sopwith took only 20 min to reach 10,000 ft, where it had a speed of 90 mph, and the F.K.8 required 30 min and could attain 85 mph. Both aircraft took considerably longer to reach Gotha operating heights, but they did represent an improvement over the B.E.12/12as, which could seldom be persuaded to exceed 70 mph at those altitudes. Next day No.50 Squadron received four F.K.8s and No.39 two, while No.37 took delivery of five $1\frac{1}{2}$ Strutters.

Armstrong Whitworth F.K.8 B215 was one of the Martlesham Heath aircraft called upon for home-defence work. (*Mrs P. Fane*)

At the same time the Air Board ordered southern-based training (formerly reserve) squadrons and other appropriate units to make aircraft available for home defence, and a count produced the following numbers: No.35(T), Northolt, six Bristol Fighters; No.40(T), Croydon, twelve Sopwith Pups; No.56(T), London Colney, six Spads; No.62(T), Dover, six Pups; No.63(T), Joyce Green, six Pups; No.65 (working up for the Western Front), Wye, six D.H.5s. It was accepted that not more than half the nominated quantities were likely to be available on any particular day. Training squadron aircraft not in combat-fit state were to be made so. No.2 Aircraft Acceptance Park, Hendon, would be asked to provide D.H.4s and D.H.5s, and No.8 AAP, Lympne, which handled various combat types en route to France, would also assist.

On 31 May a Home Defence Group guidance letter to units declared that the use of Ingram signals in conjunction with pre-arranged patrol areas should permit consolidation of a large force to attack or pursue enemy bombers. The home-defence pilot's duty was to attack vigorously with a view to breaking up the enemy formation and divert it from its target.

> 'Any delay a home defence pilot can cause by compelling an enemy to defend himself, or compel him to decrease his height by forcing combat upon him will be of the greatest value to the defence organisation as a whole' added the instruction.

This well-meant document pointed out that 'several' Gothas had already been shot down in France—cheering news to pilots flying obsolete B.E.12s—and offered this piece of lethal advice:

> 'It is proved that the best way to attack them is from below and behind, that is, under their tails. An attacker in this position is safe, and he is completely outside the enemy's field of fire.'

This was not strictly true even of the earlier Gotha G III, which had a hatch offering a very limited field of fire below. It was to improve on this that the G IV's tunnel was devised.

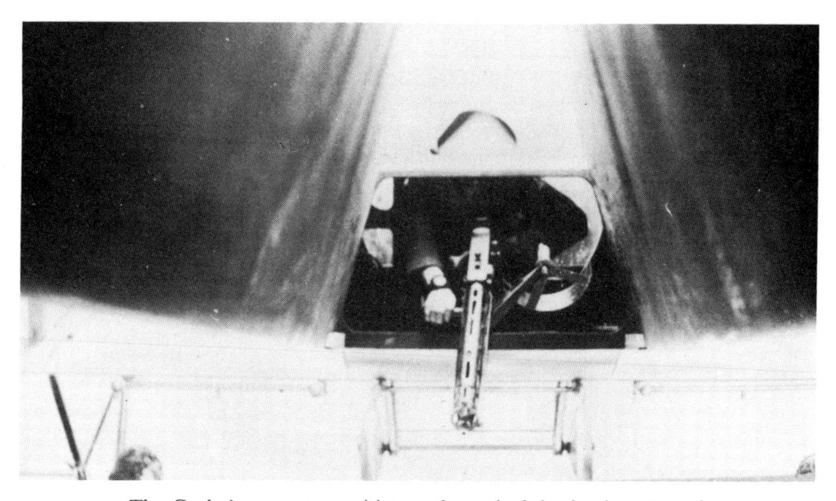

The Gotha's rear gun position at the end of the fuselage tunnel.

Also on 31 May the CIGS chaired a conference to discuss all aspects of air defence which stressed the need for a general speeding up of operational procedures. Home Defence Group claimed that fifty-one aircraft were now available to defend southeast England compared with only twenty-two on 25 May. It was hoped to allot eight Pups each to Nos.37 and 50 Squadrons to improve the prospects of meeting enemy bombers before they reached the outskirts of London, but nothing more could be done without detriment to overseas requirements. Additionally the Martlesham Heath and Orfordness experimental stations were being instructed to provide reinforcements.

The transfer of twenty-four trained anti-aircraft observers from France for duty on lightships was agreed as more practical than flying kite balloons from the North Foreland, Sheppey and Shoeburyness, manned by observers in direct telephone contact with Nos.37 and 50 Squadrons.

There was a suggestion of complacency in the conference's overall conclusion:

> 'It was considered that no measures which could be taken would prevent bombs being dropped on towns, but that under the arrangements proposed there was no likelihood that the enemy aeroplanes would be able to avoid an engagement with our fighting machines.'

Henderson raised the question of wireless communication with the defence aircraft, since ground signals had proved ineffective. Despite Admiralty representatives' attempts to reject this out of hand it was agreed to give the subject further separate consideration. Rear-Admiral George P. W. Hope, Director of Operations, and Commodore Godfrey Paine, Fifth Sea Lord, both thought that any RFC W/T operations would still be strongly resisted because of the risk of jamming Fleet communications, quite apart from reception problems in single-seat aircraft and the training of pilots—for example it took a year to train a seaplane wireless operator. Unimpressed by this transparent attempt to steer the RFC away from arcane naval matters, Henderson firmly maintained his view that there were no insuperable difficulties.

Higgins, who attended the conference, felt that it placed too much emphasis on day operations. Next day he wrote to GHQ Home Forces and the Air Board pointing out that since February, 77 trained night pilots had been withdrawn from Home Defence Group, leaving only 107 against the agreed establishment of 198. There were also deficiencies in servicing trades. He urged that the planned formation of Nos.101 and 102 bomber squadrons for France, which threatened further calls on his resources, should be deferred.

On 5 June French passed Higgins' letter to the War Office with his own comments. The impracticability of securing adequate protection by relying on such aircraft and pilots as happened to be availble in training squadrons had been recognized by the formation of Home Defence Wing more than a year ago, he wrote. Home-defence squadrons could only supply trained personnel for overseas if they were allotted more aircraft than were established for actual defence operations. There were now only 75 machines available for night flying compared with 83 on 20 March. French ended:

> 'I cannot too strongly impress on the Army Council my opinion that the means placed at my disposal for aeroplane defence are now inadequate and that a continuance of the present policy may have disastrous results.'

This letter had barely left the field marshal's out tray when twenty-one Gothas attacked Sheerness and Shoeburyness. One bomber was brought down.

From this date until the end of the daylight raids there were substantial discrepancies between the British—principally RNAS—claims of Gothas shot down and the German figures. In this account it is proposed to follow the line adopted after the Second World War by the Air Ministry over the Battle of Britain, namely that the Germans were unlikely to falsify their own official records. However, this does not exclude the possibility that some aircraft the Germans listed as having crashed in Belgium, or on landing, were actually shot down off the enemy coast by British fighters, or crash-landed as the direct result of damage or casualties sustained in combat.

On 5 June the Germans admitted the loss of one aircraft—but the RNAS claimed two more. During a confused air battle it was difficult to make accurate observations, and the naval authorities tended to be more lenient than the RFC over accepting pilots' claims. This led to several behind-the-scenes wrangles over the accreditation of victories.

Although the public doubtless accepted imaginative newspaper stories suggesting that the defences had turned the bombers away from London, this raid was in fact a large-scale hit-and-run coastal foray, providing no real opportunity to test the efficacy of the makeshift improvements. The bombers were well on their way home before any of the twenty reasonably high-performance aircraft from training and other units could reach them.

Against the likelihood that London would soon be raided, the anti-aircraft gunfire ban was lifted on 7 June, units being notified by telephone ahead of the formal paper promulgation.

The expected attack took place on 13 June, with fourteen Gothas penetrating to the East End and the City and four which developed engine troubles bombing coastal targets. The bombs killed 160 people and injured 414*—the highest casualties from any raid during the war. No fewer than 92 defence sorties were flown, but only five of the eleven pilots who fired their guns claimed to have done so from effective range. The bomber force suffered no loss, and one British observer/gunner was killed.

At urgent Cabinet meetings which followed it was agreed that the overall strength of the flying service should be doubled. Consulted about the feasibility of standing fighter patrols, Maj-Gen H. M. Trenchard, GOC the RFC in France, said that these would be very costly in aircraft and pilots. Also discussed were reprisal raids on Germany and the possibility of augmenting the defences with squadrons from France. Trenchard insisted that any units loaned from the Western Front must be back by 5 July. Field Marshal Sir Douglas Haig, GOC-in-C British Expeditionary Force, was warned by CIGS on 15 June that one or two of his squadrons would be required, and the decision was confirmed at the Cabinet War Policy Committee meeting on 20 June attended by Haig and Trenchard. The signal ordering the moves was sent from London by Trenchard later that day.

No.56 Squadron flew its S.E.5s to England on the 21st, A Flight going to Rochford and B and C Flights to Bekesbourne, while No.66 Squadron with Sopwith Pups moved from Liettres to Calais. Because of unreliable Continental telephone links it was agreed that, failing orders from Home Defence Group, No.66 should act on information from Dunkirk. On notification that Gothas were leaving Belgium for England, its Pups were to patrol in formation from the Long

* The figures showing 162 killed and 432 injured as a result of the daylight raid on 13 June, page 243, include those killed and injured by debris from AA fire.

S.E.5 A8913 of B Flight No.56 Squadron at Bekesbourne. Standing by the aircraft is Sgt Vousden, a technical NCO.

Sand lightship to a point ten miles south of the Kentish Knock. If no enemy were sighted, they would land at Manston when down to 30 minutes' fuel.

Towards the end of June, Home Defence Group was allotted four S.E.5 fighters and a few more Pups, and on 3 July the Air Board instructed that six D.H.4s were to be retained at Hendon ready for action, while the two best fighting aircraft of the day's throughput at Lympne should be held until as late as possible each evening. B.E. pilots transferring to Pups or $1\frac{1}{2}$ Strutters were given short courses on Avro 504 trainers at No.98—later 198—Depot Squadron, Rochford, to learn rotary-engine handling techniques.

Meanwhile the Admiralty had been meditating over the Sheerness raid. Wing Cdr H. P. Smyth-Osbourne, in charge of the Nore air stations, warned Admiral Sir George Callaghan, C-in-C Nore, that the Manston aircraft could not hope to intercept bombers before they reached objectives to the west. Callaghan suggested that the RNAS should defend naval installations with aircraft based at Detling, but Hope at the Admiralty advised that this would not be acceptable and on 19 June wrote to GHQ Home Forces stresssing the need for high-performance aircraft to defend the Chatham area. Shaw answered informally, explaining the extra protection afforded by the reinforcements from France, but French tartly reminded the War Office that the Admiralty had attended all air defence conferences and should be fully aware that protection could not be provided for specific points.

By 23 June the RNAS had modified their patrol arrangements, with Operation 'O' providing for three Short seaplanes—two from Westgate and one from Felixstowe—and a B.E.2c from Manston to patrol out to sea on days when the weather favoured raids. These aircraft were not to engage the enemy, but remain in visual contact and report their movements to base by W/T. Operation 'X' required Manston to maintain at readiness five Sopwith Triplanes, three Camels and a Pup, and Eastchurch similarly to provide three Camels. These aircraft were to patrol in formations of three, the leaders' machines coloured dark brown and flying 4-ft blue streamers for ease of identification. This was the first formal allocation of Sopwith Camels for home defence, though one had flown from Dover in pursuit of the 25 May raiders.

French seems to have been unaware of Trenchard's rigid limit on the stay of No.56 Squadron and the No.66 Calais detachment until Haig reminded the CIGS on 1 July that they should be returned 'as already agreed' on 5 and 6 July respectively. The files indicate that GHQ Home Forces were not sent a copy of Haig's signal until the 3rd, but French learned of its contents and wrote to the War Office on 2 July:

> 'Although the numbers of machines and pilots available for day defence have been to some extent increased during the past few weeks, the withdrawal of these squadrons will leave the means at my disposal to repel enemy aeroplane attacks dangerously weak, and it cannot be supposed that the danger of attack can be any the less after the 5th instant than it is now or has been in the past. In fact it is probably much greater; for so far as is known this new type of enemy machine is now being produced in considerable numbers. Further there is a reasonable probability that the enemy may send fast machines to create alarm on the coast and induce us to put our machines into the air, following these with a strong attack of large Gotha aeroplanes.'

As if to underline French's warning, the Gothas raided again on 4 July, selecting Harwich and Felixstowe as targets since weather was unsuitable for a deeper penetration. There were no early sightings from ships and the raiders were engaged only by a D.H.4 on test from Martlesham Heath. The general patrol order was not given until a minute or two after the Gothas had bombed, and none of the 101 aircraft which took off—not even the high-performance S.E.5s of No.56 Squadron—made contact. For reasons coyly missing from the files, No.66 Squadron at Calais received no patrol orders until 45 min after the raiders had departed. RNAS fighters from Dunkirk claimed two bombers shot down but the Germans admitted no losses.

Although it is unlikely that this coastal raid deluded Robertson or Henderson into thinking that the danger to London was over, they believed—like Haig and Trenchard—that Western Front needs were of greater military importance than home defence. French's communication of 2 July was not shown to the War Minister, but retained by Henderson—according to the official historian so that he could deal with some minor aspect raised. What this could have been is not easily deduced from the text. Neither was the letter apparently seen by Robertson, who nevertheless later accepted full responsibility for returning the BEF squadrons. Had French's warning reached the Cabinet, the moves might well have been deferred.

Cynics might also detect a sinister motive behind some strangely slipshod staff work which could have delayed the actual return order from reaching French, whose HQ received it in roundabout fashion via Home Defence Group. When Shaw protested to the War Office that such orders should be conveyed through GHQ, Brancker, now Deputy Director-General of Military Aeronautics, explained that the staff had too literally followed his instruction to 'let Higgins know'.

The two squadrons returned to their regular bases on the 5th and 6th as arranged, though there is a puzzling note in the records of the 4 July raid stating that No.56 wrote no reports because it 'returned immediately to France'. A possible explanation is that the administrative element had already packed for their return by sea, ahead of the aircraft.

On 6 July French wrote to Robertson pointing out that apart from slower machines with neither the climbing power nor speed for effective use against Gothas, he now had only twenty-one effective fighters—twelve Pups, six D.H.4s and three S.E.5s. The two aircraft on daily standby at Lympne were too far away for defending London.

> 'I desire to place on record my most emphatic opinion that even with the addition of 12 Sopwith Scouts which it is hoped will be available by the 15th instant, the aeroplanes which I can dispose of are not sufficient for effective action against raids in force', he continued. 'Such raids may certainly be expected, and if London is again subjected to attack the results may be disastrous.'

French ended his gloomy story—which underestimated his 'effective' fighter strength by some 30 per cent—on a note suggesting that he had forgotten that Robertson was no longer his Chief of Staff, as in 1915 . . . 'if you care to discuss the question personally, I shall be glad to see you here'.

The City of London photographed by one of the 7 July, 1917, raiders from 14,100 ft. St Paul's Cathedral is prominent on the left of the picture.

With uncanny sense of timing, the Germans launched their second London raid the next morning. Twenty-one Gothas attacked, causing fewer casualties than before, largely because more people took shelter. Also the defences gave a rather better showing, with more than thirty aircraft making contact, though few reached close quarters. If not the disaster predicted by French, it was another humiliation, and only one Gotha was shot down—causing much contention between the Admiralty and Home Forces as to which deserved the credit. The Germans admitted one loss, but not three others claimed by the RNAS. However, combat damage or crew injuries may have contributed to the four landing crashes recorded by the Germans. Two RFC aircraft were lost and their crews killed, while a third returned with the pilot wounded.

Public indignation reached new heights. In spite of four weeks in which to improve the defences, the enemy could still penetrate to the heart of London with impunity in broad daylight. A special Cabinet meeting was held in the afternoon and another on the 9th, when members learned for the first time of French's recent warnings and angrily protested at their suppression. Robertson weathered the storm, but it was decided that the Western Front must again detach two good fighter squadrons for home defence.

Haig immediately signalled a protest that this would seriously prejudice imminent and important operations, and it was agreed that only one unit need be provided. No.46 Squadron, with Pups, duly flew to Suttons Farm on 10 July. What Haig did not then know was that twenty-four new Sopwith Camels were being held back for home defence, which delayed the re-equipment of two squadrons in France still flying obsolescent $1\frac{1}{2}$ Strutters. This news reached Trenchard on 13 July in an Equipment Directorate letter dated five days earlier. Trenchard immediately passed this to Haig, who complained bitterly to the CIGS about the decision and the manner in which it had been conveyed. Robertson, desperately trying to please everybody, was in an unenviable position.

The Camels were for one of the three additional home-defence squadrons which the Cabinet had sanctioned at the 9 July meeting to satisfy French's minimum requirement of sixty-six day fighters—three squadrons and two flights. Counting No.66, he already had half that number, and it was hoped to supply twenty-four by the end of the month.

While the Cabinet spent the Saturday afternoon bickering over major policy questions, operations staffs were assessing reports from the squadrons. Although the first sighting from the Kentish Knock lightship had not been notified to GHQ Home Forces until 09.23 hr—seven minutes after the RNAS—it allowed ample time for the fighters to gain the necessary height since the bombers took nearly an hour to reach London.

The pilot's cockpit of a Gotha G IV.

Home Defence Group blamed the failure on lack of cohesion resulting from the multiplicity of units flying aircraft of differing performance, the pilots' unfamiliarity with new aircraft, and the increased speed and manoeuvrability displayed by the enemy formation. It was estimated that the bombers flew at about 90 mph at 14–15,000 ft, compared with 75 mph at 12,000 ft on the earlier raids (but there is no evidence from German records that this was so). Accepting pilots' reports of the Gothas' apparent invulnerability to considerable machine-gun fire from close quarters, and recovery after falling out of control, the group's experts wrongly claimed this as conclusive indication that every Gotha crew member was a pilot, so that if the first was disabled he could be replaced. A surprising omission was any reference to gunnery troubles, when combat reports mentioned seventeen cases of machine-gun failure.

A letter to French from Sir Reginald Brade, Secretary of the War Office, on 9 July, though perhaps nothing more than convention demanded, suggested a degree of exasperation that the elderly field marshal was so unequivocably able to say 'I told you so':

> 'I am commanded by the Army Council to request that you will be good enough to report, in connection with the air raid on London on the 7th instant, whether you are satisfied with your pilots, and with the manner in which the Officer Commanding Home Defence Group, RFC, performed his duties.'

Brade went on to request suggestions for improving co-operation between Home Forces and BEF squadrons, and any observations on the gun defences.

Higgins told French that pilots flying the better aircraft recently issued to

Field Marshal Lord French, Commander-in-Chief, Home Forces, from December 1915 to May 1918 (*left*); and Major-General E. B. Ashmore, commander of the London Air Defence Area. (*Imperial War Museum, left-hand photograph*)

squadrons had done well considering that they were not used to their handling and gun gear, or to formation flying. Those in machines of indifferent performance could not be blamed for the lack of results. Generally, pilot quality in the southern squadrons was good, though a few who lacked special aptitude for dog-fighting, though otherwise capable, were being transferred to night-fighter squadrons. It took time to train pilots in team work, but no effort was being spared to improve efficiency and in future the squadrons would give a good account of themselves.

Replying to the War Office on 12 July, French put forward Higgins' points and added 'I am satisfied that in these difficult circumstances pilots of the Home Defence Group did all that was possible on the 7th instant'. He expressed complete satisfaction with Higgins—'a capable and energetic officer'.

Of greater significance than these skirmishes was the Cabinet decision of 11 July to form a committee, nominally under chairmanship of the Premier, Lloyd George, but effectively under Lieut-Gen J. C. Smuts, to examine air defence and the overall air organization. Smuts produced his air-defence report on the 19th, recommending that a senior officer with air experience, under C-in-C Home Forces, be placed in command of the London Air Defence Area (LADA)—which included all regions in Gotha range.

Smuts had sought guidance from all those best qualified to advise, and he adopted the main points of a memorandum received from Henderson on the 16th. This was based on Henderson's minute to the CIGS two days earlier, suggesting that air defence should be organized without reference to GHQ Home Forces' wider functions of repelling enemy invasion, and that RFC squadrons, AA guns and the observation posts be placed under the command of one man, with the sole duty of organizing the defences and controlling them during raids. He must come from the RFC because handling the aeroplanes was the major factor to which the disposition of other defence elements must conform.

Another Smuts committee recommendation was that completion of the three additional day-fighter squadrons agreed by the Cabinet on 9 July be pressed ahead rapidly. In fact this was already well in hand, and No.44 Squadron began to form at Hainault Farm on 24 July with 1½ Strutters as interim equipment, receiving fifteen Camels during the first two weeks in August. No.61 started forming at Rochford on 2 August and No.112 at Throwley on 30 July, both with Pups.

Disappointed by the failure to recommend the immediate formation of any more squadrons than already agreed by the Government, Higgins produced, on the day the committee's report was issued, a memorandum suggesting that five additional day squadrons were needed, since existing units were too involved in extraneous duties connected with possible invasion to devote their undivided attention to air combat. As events developed, such duties concerned a declining proportion of the force, and no new squadrons were approved until December.

As to anti-aircraft guns, the committee supported a recommendation made by Col Simon on 14 July that guns be deployed to present barrage fire aimed at breaking up formations before they reached London—though in view of the continued Zeppelin risk, guns in central and northwest London should not be moved. Little was actually done, however, despite a plea from French on 23 July that it was much easier for fighters to deal with individual bombers. 'Isolated attacks by aeroplanes on these unbroken formations are, it is clear, a useless sacrifice' he wrote. French asked for 110 guns to cover London's eastern approaches, but the Cabinet decided that the merchant service still merited priority and he had to make do by redeploying 34 guns from other areas.

The committee defined the principal function of the RNAS fighters as combating raiders on their return journey—a clear sign that the Admiralty had abandoned hope of intercepting them inbound. It was recommended that the aircraft should continue to operate under their separate naval commands, but in close co-operation with the new defence organization.

The committee underlined one fear haunting Home Defence Group—that the enemy might launch small feint raids to draw off fighters so that they would be on the ground refuelling when the main assault was directed elsewhere—and recommended that the defences must be strong enough to meet that situation.

A general tidying-up process had continued while the committee was deliberating, and on 13 July Home Defence Group issued updated orders for meeting daylight raids. 'Readiness' was signified by short Klaxon bursts, whereupon pilots and mechanics doubled to their aircraft. All machines were wheeled from the sheds, likewise at the double, and pilots ran up engines and awaited further instructions. On the 'patrol' order, aircraft were to climb in formation to their allotted areas unless ordered for some special patrol, and thereafter act according to the ground signals. On sighting enemy aircraft, formation leaders must always bear in mind the possibility of feint sorties. These instructions applied to Nos.37, 39, 46, 50, 65 and 78 Squadrons, Nos.49 and 62 (Training) Squadrons and aircraft at Hendon, Lympne, Martlesham and Orfordness. Nos.35, 40, 56 and 63 (Training) Squadrons and aircraft from No.7 AAP, Kenley, were to be held in reserve to await special orders.

Patrol arrangements were also laid down for RFC and RNAS units suitably located in France to engage Gotha formations off the Belgian coast, though Trenchard insisted that instructions to the RFC squadrons must be issued through his HQ.

For the next raid, on Sunday, 22 July, Germany reverted to the hit-and-run technique, with a sharp attack on Harwich by twenty-one Gothas. Patrol orders were not given until a minute or two before the raid began, and only one aircraft, already airborne from Orfordness, made contact. With the enemy over the coast so briefly, and lacking reliable information on bomber movements, Home Defence Group did not order any pursuit in case this proved to be a feint attack. Anti-aircraft batteries between Harwich and the Thames blithely assumed that any formations must be enemy, and engaged British fighters with great abandon.

Aerodrome 'state boards' varied in layout. This is No.37 Squadron's at Stow Maries. (*Mrs M. F. Sadler*)

The social life enjoyed by home-defence units contrasted vividly with the stark existence on the Western Front. This photograph taken at No.50 Squadron's Bekesbourne garden party shows, left to right: 2nd Lieuts N. E. Chandler, J. G. Goodyear and F. V. Bryant, Capt A. J. Capel, Mrs F. A. D. Grace and Miss Bidlake.

The Germans admitted the loss of one bomber in a landing crash—a rather questionable way of describing the Gotha forced down just off Ostende by a Bristol Fighter of No.48 Squadron.

Maj-Gen Edward Bailey Ashmore, 45, commander of the new London Air Defence Area, took up his post at 12 noon on Wednesday, 8 August. 'Splash' Ashmore—the origins of the nickname are obscure—was an Old Etonian who had entered the Royal Artillery in 1891 and learned to fly in 1912. Thereafter he had alternated between RFC and RA postings. His proved efficiency plus considerable personal charm and the ability to get on well with people made him an excellent choice for the new job. His command included fixed and mobile AA guns and searchlights between Harwich and Dover, Nos.37, 39, 50, 51, 75 and 78 Home Defence Squadrons—plus Nos.44, 61 and 112 in process of formation—and aircraft observation posts east of a Portsmouth–Grantham line. Higgins and Simon were retained in their existing posts.

On 28 August the War Office approved the up-grading of Home Defence Group to a brigade, with three wings: Southern (Nos.37, 39, 50, 51 and 75 Squadrons for night fighting and daylight 'wireless tracking', plus No.198 Depot Squadron), Eastern (Nos.44, 61, 78 and 112 day-fighter squadrons) and Northern (Nos.33, 36, 38, 76 and 77 night-fighter squadrons).

Clearly the new organization required time to settle down and some confusion still prevailed when the Gothas attacked Southend on 12 August. However, this was partly because the raiders made landfall some 40 miles north of their planned target, Chatham, due to unexpectedly strong winds. Convinced that they were making for London, Ashmore deployed his forces accordingly. If the enemy had-flown farther inland they would have encountered, among other fighters, fifteen Camels of No.44 Squadron patrolling the Romford–North Weald line. One Gotha was shot down at sea by a Pup from RNAS Walmer.

The next raid, on 22 August, was a disaster for the Germans. Five Gothas turned back with engine trouble leaving only ten to mount an intended

These officers were all engaged in home-defence flying operations during the summer of 1917. They are shown when in No.50 Squadron, but some later transferred to newly-formed units. Left to right: 2nd Lieuts N. E. Chandler and R. W. le Gallais, Capt A. J. Capel, 2nd Lieuts J. G. Goodyear, F. A. D. Grace and T. A. Lloyd (observer). Le Gallais was killed on 15 September flying Sopwith Pup A638 of No.112 Squadron, which broke up in the air.

two-pronged attack, with half the force bombing Sheerness, Chatham or Southend at the discretion of the leader, and the remainder attacking Dover. The plan misfired badly, three Gothas being shot down over the coast by RNAS aircraft and AA guns. Ashmore's vastly improved fighter chain covering inland areas had no opportunity for combat. Of the 120 RFC aircraft operating between the Blackwater and Dover, more than half were from the four day-fighter squadrons—fifteen Camels of No.44, eighteen Pups of No.61 and eleven Pups of No.112, plus the eighteen Pups of No.46 still on loan from France.

Arguments between Home Forces and the Admiralty over responsibility for the destroyed Gothas brought recent inter-Service bickering to a head. On 8 August French had suggested to the Admiralty that the close co-operation between RNAS coastal fighters and the RFC advocated by the Smuts committee could best be achieved if the controlling senior naval officers maintained direct contact with Ashmore's headquarters. Even allowing for the Admiralty's established position as the Senior Service this seemed a reasonable enough suggestion—but it took until 23 August for them to reply, that they would prefer to withdraw their flights used for the defence of English towns and leave the whole commitment to the RFC.

During the month (the date is not recorded) GHQ Home Forces sent the Admiralty a proof copy of their July intelligence summary containing a tolerably objective account of the 7 July raid, crediting the destruction of the single Gotha the Germans admitted having lost to 2nd Lieuts, F. A. D. Grace and G. Murray of No.50 Squadron. But the Admiralty had already credited victories to Sqn Cdr C. H. Butler and Flt Lieut J. E. Scott from Manston, and both pilots were decorated on 20 July.* The doubtless unintentionally patronizing tone of the

* Grace and Murray eventually received MCs in December.

summary's concluding paragraph could not have been better worded to arouse the Admiralty's wrath—'. . . it appears more probable, judging from the reports received, that it [the Gotha] was actually brought down by Lieutenants Grace and Murray, though no doubt the RNAS pilots contributed to its destruction.'

All reports were promptly re-checked at the Admiralty, and almost inevitably no neat and tidy picture emerged. Admiral Hope concluded that the aircraft destroyed by Butler and Scott had no connection with that claimed by the RFC, and on 20 August an icy letter was addressed to French:

> 'I am commanded by my Lords Commissioners of the Admiralty to acquaint you that they are unable to agree to the conclusions arrived at on pages 15 and 26 of this report: and I am to request that the information concerning action by naval aircraft may be confined to an accurate reproduction of the reports forwarded by the Admiralty.'

Home Forces conceded defeat, and the finalized report appeared in September with the offending passages removed and the RNAS pilots' statements printed as originally submitted.

Thus the situation was ripe for further squabbles over the claims of 22 August. The Gotha which fell in flames off Dover was the indisputable victim of an RNAS Manston Camel, but contention arose over two destroyed in the Thanet area, both being claimed by naval fighters and army AA guns. With the laudable intention of clarifying the picture, Lieut Rees Jenkins of Home Defence Group intelligence innocently visited the Manston/Westgate station commander, Wing Cdr R. Peel Ross, on 24 August. To his astonishment Peel Ross refused him any information about ground observations made from his stations and denied access to the pilots who had claimed victories. After some smoothing out at higher level, Peel Ross 'very reluctantly' saw Jenkins next day, and expressed the modified view that one bomber was certainly brought down by an RNAS pilot. Close analysis of all reports indicates that fighters and guns destroyed one each, but Ashmore believed that the guns were responsible for both.

It is difficult to avoid linking this growing ill-feeling with the Admiralty's suggestion of 23 August that they should remove their Kent coastal-defence fighters—about twenty-four aircraft. The withdrawal was considered in the light of No.46 Squadron's imminent return to France (this took place on 30 August) and intelligence appreciations that raiding strength was unlikely to exceed 25–30 Gothas in the immediate future. Ashmore felt that if his three day-fighter squadrons were brought up to a strength of twenty-four aircraft each, No.78 Squadron redeployed to Suttons Farm as a day-fighter unit and some patrol lines reorganized, his force would be adequate—though some bombers would still get through to London and nothing could stop a raid directly from the sea on Harwich. On 4 September the War Office formally agreed the RNAS withdrawal, as soon as RFC squadrons were up to strength. By 12 September they were only one Camel and two Pups deficient.

By that time, however, the matter had become academic with the production of Smuts' second report, on the overall air oganization. This far-reaching document recommending the creation of a unified air Service had been placed before the War Cabinet on 17 August and was accepted in principle on the 24th.

The return of No.46 Squadron produced another of those staff work muddles seemingly endemic to the home-defence organization. It was generally known at all appropriate levels that the unit would leave around the end of August, but executive instructions for actual departure went direct from a War Office movements section to the squadron, causing Ashmore to complain that such actions 'might well cause all sorts of confusion and trouble' and Shaw to protest that it was 'quite impossible to maintain any sort of control if orders were given direct to subordinate officers'.

But this did not affect the normal courtesies, and Shaw told Haig about the squadron's good work. 'They are well advanced in formation flying, and the instruction and example which they have given in their work have been a great help to the new home defence squadrons' he wrote. 'The squadron has kept up a fine record in having available all its machines serviceable, day after day.'

No.46 Squadron, under Maj Philip Babington, created a great impression around Suttons Farm with its lightning take offs and immaculate formation flying. Babington gave much thought to combat techniques, and produced a report arguing that although two or three skilled pilots working in co-operation could distract a single Gotha's gunners and attack the blind spots, it was almost useless for a few fighters to confront an unbroken formation possessing extensive covering fire.

> 'It is therefore imperative for the whole 18 aircraft of a fighter squadron to make a simultaneous attack' he wrote. 'This will have great moral effect and the defending gunners will be disconcerted. Once the formation breaks, small groups of scouts can deal with stragglers, and then re-group and make another squadron attack on the remaining formation.'

Babington evolved a system of air drill, with orders given by hand signals and Very cartridges from a flank position, which unfortunately was denied the opportunity of a practical test.

An important development during the summer was the breaking of the navy's stranglehold on wireless activities, though insufficient progress was made to improve the air defences significantly for many months. The study promised at the 31 May conference evidently favoured the RFC, for on 5 July the War Office informed the Admiralty that an experimental continuous-wave transmitting station was opening at Biggin Hill, where trials had been in progress for some time without complaints of interference. The Admiralty gave qualified approval on 19 July, and by the summer of 1918 air-defence fighters were using reasonably efficient radio-telephony equipment.

In early August 1917 a wireless-telegraphy tracking system was introduced which reversed the procedures tested in 1916 in that aircraft reported the movements of enemy bombers to ground stations. Two B.E.12s of No.37 Squadron equipped with pilot-operated continuous-wave W/T transmitters patrolled north of the Thames and two from No.50 south of the river. Their morse signals reporting enemy movements were received by ground stations at Wormwood Scrubs and the Hotel Cecil in the Strand, and passed on to GHQ Home Forces. Initially only the leader of a tracker pair transmitted, the No.2 machine joining in if a formation diverted.

Each of the four aircraft had its own wavelength—1250 and 1300 metres for No.37 Squadron transmitting from north of the Thames to Wormwood Scrubs, and 1100 and 1150 metres for No.50 Squadron working to the Hotel Cecil. Messages were sent at two-minute intervals in a simple code, giving the location as designated by the appropriate zone squares on a special map, number of hostile aircraft, direction of flight and time—in minutes after the last hour. Surprisingly, no height figure was included. Signal 'QQC 24 W 45' meant 'hostile formation of 24 aircraft over Hazeleigh flying west at (10)45'. The words 'turning', 'dividing' or ‘breaking’ were transmitted in full as necessary. No.78 Squadron was involved in the scheme for a time.

Since the B.E.12 ‘trackers’ did not fly standing patrols and were of generally inferior performance to the Gothas, they could provide little information of value to the defenders during the raids which followed the scheme’s introduction, though some benefit might have accrued had the enemy attempted deeper penetrations.

Also briefly considered was a system involving a number of stations to register continuous bearings on enemy aircraft and transmit these to GHQ Home Forces, providing a continuous plot. This was rejected as being prohibitively costly in money and materials.

The vigorous reception which greeted the Gothas off the Kent coast on 22 August and the threat from the clearly visible patrols inland convinced the Germans that daylight raiding had become too expensive. During eight raids spread over a 13-week campaign, 142 Gothas reached English shores, six being destroyed by fighters and two by anti-aircraft gunfire. Despite the Gotha’s notorious propensity to landing accidents, at least three—and probably more—of the ten recorded by the Germans as having crashed on or near their bases after returning from raids did so because of combat damage. Gotha strength was further depleted by the loss of eight or nine during an abortive raid on 18 August which ran into severe headwinds.

The modest 5½ per cent British success rate should be judged against the fact that the only three raids which ventured inland to any extent took place while the defences were still ill-equipped and poorly organized. Then circumstances conspired to deny Nos.56 and 46 Squadrons any opportunity of meeting the Gothas, while on the few occasions when the better Home Defence Group fighters were able to engage, they experienced excessive gun troubles.

Clearly the British authorities first underestimated, then exaggerated, the Gotha’s performance. Even after its main characteristics must have become known, little apparent effort was given to devising effective methods of attack. The B.E.12/12a pilots, vainly struggling to get to terms during the early raids, rather naively thought that proper fighters would solve all their problems—but when they were given Pups many difficulties still remained.

Capt J. B. McCudden with Sopwith Pup A7311 which he flew against the 13 June and 7 July raiders. This aircraft was his personal ‘hack’ while filling an instructional post and is shown before its Lewis gun was fitted.

Perhaps the greatest weakness was lack of experience, and reports suggest that many pilots, not fully appreciating the Gotha's size, attacked from too far away and failed to concentrate on vulnerable areas. Against this new and formidable target even Western Front expertise provided no guarantee of success, as shown by the experience of James McCudden, then serving as an instructor between operational tours. McCudden, later to become a leading fighter 'ace', had gained five combat victories in France, yet determined attacks on Gothas in two raids brought him no success.

The Admiralty evidently became rather sceptical about the exuberant RNAS claims—four times the true success rate—for on 21 August Capt A. V. Vyvyan, Assistant Director of Air Services, held a meeting attended by Capt Arthur Stopford, head of the armaments section, and other RNAS and RFC experts to consider the Gothas' apparent immunity suggested by consistent pilots' reports that numerous close-range hits brought no results.

It was decided to seek authority to use Brock and Pomeroy anti-airship ammunition against the Gothas, to develop a combined incendiary/explosive bullet and to conduct trials with ·45-in calibre. Although both targets were bombers, the extended use of anti-Zeppelin bullets required Cabinet approval, since, on humanitarian grounds, types of ammunition were governed by international agreement. The introduction of tracer had brought rumours that Germany regarded it as infringing the rules, and there had been similar anxieties about Brock and Buckingham. In October 1916, Trenchard even suggested that the fighter 'ace' Albert Ball should not engage in anti-Zeppelin work during his rest period lest this prejudice his future employment as a fighter pilot at the Front.

British reports about types of German ammunition used over this period are confusing. In October 1916 it was stated that explosive bullets were found on one of the Zeppelins brought down, and an RFC pilot attacking a Gotha on 22 August, 1917, said that it was firing 'the usual type of explosive bullet' leaving a great cloud of smoke. Both these references may in fact have been to the German tracer ammunition. In June two naval pilots claimed that one Gotha was firing explosive shells larger than ·303 calibre, though RFC assessments of later raids reported no supporting evidence.

The destruction of two Gothas by naval fighters on 22 August ended the Gotha invulnerability myth, but Vyvyan nevertheless asked the Air Board on the 25th to raise the matter with the Cabinet. Their approval to use Brock and Pomeroy against the Gothas was given on 28 September—when the next phase of the bomber offensive had caused more than 450 casualties.

Home Defence Group might be criticized for spreading its small initial allocation of Pups and S.E.5s among existing squadrons on several bases rather than operating them as one homogeneous unit. However, with only primitive ground signals to direct squadrons to the threatened area, the dispersal policy improved the chances of some of the better fighters finding the enemy. It also created a bigger pool of pilots with some fighter experience to man the three new squadrons. The need for adequate conversion training—for pilots and maintenance crews—was not universally appreciated, and some Whitehall pundits expected to see immaculate fighting formations from B.E. pilots the day after they had received Pups.

During August, life was frustrating for the RFC fighter squadrons, restricted to rigid inland patrol lines while their RNAS counterparts rampaged among the enemy formations off the coast. It would be unfair to criticize Ashmore for lack of flexibility, since his prime task was to defend London and dispositions were made

A No.37 Squadron Sopwith Camel running-up at Stow Maries, 1918. (*Mrs M. F. Sadler*)

Sopwith Pup A6230 of No.63 (Training) Squadron, photographed at Joyce Green by Capt J. B. McCudden. This aircraft was shot down by one of the Gothas attacking London on 7 July, 1917, and the pilot, 2nd Lieut W. G. Salmon, was killed.

accordingly. He sounded a wistful note in a letter to Trenchard on 24 August: 'I am hoping that the Huns will try to come to London—we have everything ready for them'.

The squadrons were manned by a mixture of recently-qualified pilots—some of them 'naturals' showing great promise—others with considerable previous home-defence experience, of questionable value against Gotha formations, plus a few seasoned veterans from the Fronts. Given greater opportunities and a little more experience they would assuredly have employed their excellent aircraft to good effect.

The Sopwith Camel is rated by some historians as the most effective fighter of the First World War, and it would be near the top of anyone's list. The 130 hp Clerget-engined Camel, used by the RFC and to a lesser extent by the RNAS, had a maximum speed of 104½ mph at 10,000 ft, reaching that height in 11¾ min. The exclusively RNAS 150 hp Bentley-engined model was about six mph faster and took just under ten minutes to reach the same height. Other fighters may have been speedier but few could match the Camel's superb manoeuvrability. It was sensitive on the controls and unforgiving of mistakes, so training accidents were regrettably frequent, but having mastered the beast pilots grew to love it as the dog-fighter par excellence. It was armed with two Vickers machine-guns synchronized to fire through the propeller arc.

Most of the Sopwith Pups in Home Defence Group had the 100 hp Monosoupape engine instead of the 80 hp Le Rhône fitted to earlier models, and were almost as fast as Clerget Camels at 10,000 ft but took about a minute longer to get there. Though lacking the Camel's lightning manoeuvrability, the Pup, too, was an excellent dog-fighter, with highly-praised flying qualities. Pilots' reports indicate that in addition to the standard synchronized Vickers gun, most of the early home-defence Pups carried a Lewis firing over the top wing, but no squadron photographs showing this installation have been found. At least one pilot considered that the modification significantly reduced performance and, since enhanced fire-power meant nothing if the fighters could not reach their targets, it may have been quickly abandoned.

Just over 20 tons of bombs were dropped during the Gotha daylight raids, causing 401 deaths, injuries to 983 people, and property damage estimated at some £391,000. Two British fighters were shot down, their two pilots and one gunner being killed. Three other observer/gunners were killed and one pilot wounded in combats after which the fighters landed safely. Several aircraft received varying amounts of combat damage.

More important from the military viewpoint were the bonus results gained by the enemy over and above the main object of hitting London and southern ports. Apart from the diversion of three trained fighter squadrons, Western Front strength was further depleted by holding back new Camels and D.H.4s for home defence. In a postwar Staff College lecture, Squadron Leader Harry Orlebar,* who went to No.44 Squadron after a duty tour in France, recalled his astonishment on seeing its Camel line-up at a time when units at the Front were desperately needing new equipment. Some squadrons in France were diverted from their normal tasks to fly patrols aimed at intercepting the returning Gothas. Another indirect loss to the Front resulted from the substantial extra manpower and effort poured into home defence.

* Orlebar captained the RAF teams which won the 1929 and 1931 Schneider Trophy races. He died in 1943 when an air commodore.

In the long term, however, the greatest bonus perhaps went to Britain, in that the raids produced the climate which ended many months of indecision regarding overall British air policy, and led to the Smuts report's recommendation for an Air Ministry and a single Air Service.

Previous proposals to this end had failed for various reasons. Smuts cited the daylight attacks on London as clear evidence that air power could be used as an independent means of war operations, and declared '. . . aerial operations with their devastation of enemy lands and destruction of industrial and populous centres on a vast scale may become the principal operations of war.'

An Air Staff was required to conduct the independent strategic operations which would be possible following the increased aircraft-production programme, he argued, and went on 'The enemy is no doubt making vast plans to deal with us in London if we do not succeed in beating him in the air and carrying the war into the heart of his country.'

Zeppelin attacks in June and August were somewhat overshadowed by the furore surrounding the Gotha raids, despite the destruction of Germany's newest 'height climber'.

Before the loss of L48 on 16/17 June, a query from the Kaiser about the continued viability of airship raids on London was vigorously rebutted by the German naval staff and, as though to demonstrate his own confidence, Strasser broke his previous rules by ordering an attack on one of the shortest summer nights. He seemed convinced that the 'height climbers' were immune from fighter attack—and if they remained at 18–20,000 ft he was right. However, circumstances could always force them down to lower altitudes. The army's decision to abandon airship raids possibly strengthened Strasser's determination to show that the navy was made of sterner stuff.

L48 was shot down in combat with three fighters from a height variously estimated between 13,000 and 16,000 ft—probably nearer to the lower figure. The same night L42 flying home at 16,000 ft across the North Sea comfortably outpaced two Sopwith Pups.

Far from becoming complacent after the destruction of L48, and despite preoccupations with the Gotha raids, French resumed his campaign for improved night fighters. He wrote to the War Office on 2 July asserting that his existing B.E.2cs, B.E.2es, B.E.12s and F.E.2bs were incapable of dealing with Zeppelins which could reach 15,000 ft and fly at 60–65 mph, and asked for better aircraft as soon as possible.

Brancker noted on the file that although properly maintained and handled B.E.12s, F.K.8s and the recently-issued 160 hp F.E.2bs flown as single-seaters ought to cope adequately, the new N.E.1 night fighter should nevertheless be produced as quickly as possible. The War Office reply to French on 13 July took this line, pointing out that Home Defence Group now had fifty B.E.12s, eight F.K.8s and twenty-one of the 160 hp F.E.2bs. Additionally, imminent improvements to the RAF 4A engine should substantially enhance B.E.12 performance.

This was followed three days later by an Air Board letter containing this highly questionable statement '. . . information at the disposal of the Air Board does not bear out the view that any existing type of Zeppelin in fighting trim can climb to the height above named (15,000 ft).'

The Board endorsed the Army Council view that some existing home-defence aircraft could deal with the latest known Zeppelins and demanded detailed information to support French's assertion. They hoped that the improved RAF 4A engine would be fitted to the one hundred B.E.12s due for delivery in September–October, and expected the first of six N.E.1s ready for trials within two months.

French retaliated on 30 July with chapter and verse from recent operational reports—including documents found in the L48 wreckage revealing that she had reached 19,357 ft on trials—and North Sea sightings at 15–20,000 ft. He asked whether 'in fighting trim' meant when carrying full bomb load, and pointed out that Zeppelins usually dropped their bombs when illuminated by searchlights.

Reporting to the Cabinet on 18 August, the Air Board maintained its view that no existing Zeppelin could reach 15,000 ft with full bomb load, but conceded that after bombing the L48 could exceed that height. The Board was considering requisite steps, and made optimistic references to the N.E.1. On 21 August they wrote to the War Office about the latest points raised by French, adding some characteristic chairborne advice:

> 'The expression "in fighting trim" . . . was intended to mean fully equipped with bombs and defensive armament, the condition in which Zeppelins may be expected to reach this country, and in which, if their mission is to be frustrated, they should be attacked. Under these circumstances the night flying machines, F.E.2b and B.E.12, should be capable of dealing with the latest types.'

Nevertheless the Board admitted the need for night fighters able to attack Zeppelins in any circumstances—though two months elapsed before they grudgingly conceded that Home Forces might be right about Zeppelin capabilities.

The B.E.2e was the most widely used night-fighter in September 1917; fifty-four were on Home Defence Group strength and this example, A2794, belonged to No.76 Squadron. (*L. B. Latham*)

On 3 September GHQ Home Forces listed current night-fighter strength as 191—made up of thirty-four B.E.12s, twelve B.E.2cs, eleven B.E.2ds, fifty-four B.E.2es, thirty-five F.E.2bs (160 hp Beardmore engine), twenty-one F.E.2bs (120 hp Beardmore), twelve F.E.2ds, seven R.E.7s and five F.K.8s. The 250 hp Rolls-Royce engined F.E.2ds were regarded as the most efficient, but of the remainder only the B.E.12s, the 160 hp F.E.2bs and the F.K.8s were considered just powerful enough to deal with the latest Zeppelins. This gave an average of eight aircraft to each of the eleven night-flying squadrons—less than three per flight.

The War Office ended this phase of the paper war with a letter to Home Forces on 6 October containing a mixture of bad and good news—B.E.12 output was delayed, but thirty-one of the 160 hp F.E.2bs should be delivered during the month. There was no more reference to the improved RAF engine for the B.E.12, but instead there was the surprising information that sixteen for allotment in October would have the 200 hp Hispano Suiza. At that time there was a serious shortage of these engines, and in fact the Hispano-powered B.E.12b did not materialize until December. It was, perhaps, an indication of the importance still placed on inherent stability as a major night-flying requisite that this clumsy expedient was adopted before any evaluation trials to discover how existing fighters could perform in the role. It may also have offered a means of using otherwise valueless B.E.12 airframes already completed.

Towards the end of this exchange, a raid on 21/22 August had provided further evidence of the altitudes being achieved, one pilot estimating the height of a Zeppelin as about 20,000 ft.

While the arguments about anti-Zeppelin aircraft echoed around Whitehall, the controversy in Germany over the continuing viability of the airship as a bomber ended to the navy's disadvantage. On 27 July, four days before the formal dissolution of the German Army Airship Service, General Erich von Ludendorff, holding the key position of First Quartermaster General to von Hindenburg, suggested to Admiral von Holtzendorff, Chief of the Naval Staff, that naval airship building be stopped and materials diverted to aeroplane construction. The navy pointed out that this would curtail raids on targets beyond aeroplane range, but the Kaiser settled for a compromise. He decided on 17 August that the navy should be limited to twenty-five airships, primarily for reconnaissance, and replacement building cut from the previous average of two new Zeppelins a month to one every two months.

Chapter XV

Operations—25 May to 22 August, 1917

25 May, 1917 (Daylight)

Target: Folkestone.
Enemy forces: 23 Gothas despatched, 21 Gothas attacked.
Results: 95 killed, 195 injured, £19,405 damage.
Defence sorties: 77.

RNAS

Dover: Sopwith Pups 3691 (Flt Sub-Lieut R. F. S. Leslie) 18.20–19.30 hr; N5197, 18.15–19.26 hr; N5194, 18.20–18.43 hr, returned with engine trouble; Sopwith Camel N6348, took off 18.40 hr, landed Dunkirk; Short 830 1337 (Flt Sub-Lieut L. C. Pincott, CPO Hanna) 17.25–18.05 hr; 1337 (Flt Sub-Lieut Pincott, AM W. A. Coppins) 18.15–19.50 hr.

Eastchurch: Bristol Scout D 8978, 17.45–18.10 hr.

Felixstowe: Curtiss H-12s 8658, 17.00–20.00 hr; 8662, 17.30–20.55 hr; Sopwith Babies 8137, 17.45–18.30 hr; N1102, 17.40–17.55 hr; N1037, 17.45–1900 hr; Short 184 9068, landed 19.55 hr.

Grain: Sopwith Pups 9912 (Flt Lieut C. T. Freeman) 17.28–19.30 hr; 9922 (Sqn Cdr H. R. Busteed) 18.05–18.52 hr, returned with engine trouble; Sopwith Babies 8168 (Flt Sub-Lieut W. F. Dickson) 17.35–19.30 hr; 8118 (Flt Sub-Lieut F. I. Jacks) 17.55–19.35 hr.

Manston: Bristol Scout Ds 8969 (Flt Sub-Lieut H. R. de Wilde) 16.45–18.25 hr and 18.35–19.55 hr; N5398 (Flt Sub-Lieut A. C. Burt) 16.55–17.50 hr; 8990 (Flt Sub-Lieut R. H. Daly) 16.55–17.25 hr; 8989 (Flt Sub-Lieut Daly) 17.26–18.33 hr; N5390 (Flt Sub-Lieut Daly) 18.39–19.56 hr; 8965 took off at 18.34 hr; Sopwith Pup 9907 (Flt Sub-Lieut J. E. Scott) 16.55–18.22 hr and 18.25–19.40 hr; Sopwith Triplanes N5424 (Sqn Cdr C. H. Butler) 16.55–17.25 hr and 18.05–20.30 hr (with intermediate landing at Dunkirk); N509 (Flt Sub-Lieut Burt) 18.10–19.55 hr.

Westgate: Sopwith Schneider 3766 (Flt Sub-Lieut E. B. Drake) 16.55–19.20 hr; Sopwith Babies 8186 (Flt Sub-Lieut L. G. Maxton) 16.56–17.26 hr; 8186 (Flt Sub-Lieut W. J. de Salis) 18.09–18.30 hr and 19.37–20.30 hr; 8146 (Flt Sub-Lieut F. C. Lander) 17.02–17.45 hr; 8146 (Flt Sub-Lieut L. G. Maxton) 18.45–20.05 hr; N1025 (Flt Sub-Lieut H. C. Lemon) took off 16.55 hr, forced alighted with engine trouble, towed to Burnham.

Walmer: Bristol Scout D 8957 (Flt Sub-Lieut W. H. Chisam) 18.30–18.44 hr; Sopwith Pups 9947 (Flt Sub-Lieut Chisam) 17.30–18.20 hr; 9947 (Flt Lieut S. Kemball) 18.30–19.20 hr; N5182 (Flt Sub-Lieut Chisam) 18.53–19.38 hr.

Sopwith Baby N1025, RNAS Westgate, was forced down by engine failure during its search for the 25 May, 1917, raiders. It also operated on 5 and 13 June.

RFC

No.37 Squadron, A Flight, Goldhanger: B.E.12s 6610 (Lieut C. D. Kershaw) 19.00–20.00 hr; A4032 (Lieut W. R. S. Humphreys) 18.25–19.50 hr, forced landed near Bexhill; B.E.12as A6317 (Lieut L. P. Watkins) 17.13–19.30 hr; A590 (Lieut L. F. Hutcheon) 17.14–20.00 hr.

No.37 Squadron, B Flight, Stow Maries: B.E.12a A6318 (Capt C. A. Ridley) 17.12–21.16 hr.

No.37 Squadron, C Flight, Rochford: B.E.2d 5778 (Capt C. B. Cooke) 18.55–21.00 hr; B.E.12as A6312 (Lieut W. R. S. Humphreys) 17.10–17.25 hr, at Goldhanger with engine trouble; A6306 (Lieut Orr-Ewing) 17.15–20.03 hr; A599 (Capt C. B. Cooke) 17.22–18.15, returned with engine fire.

No.39 Squadron, A Flight, North Weald: B.E.2c 2089 (Lieut E. M. Gilbert) 17.53–18.40 hr, forced landed Hill Hall with engine trouble: B.E.2e 7233 (2nd Lieut A. A. Wilcock) 18.27–19.00 hr; B.E.12 6488 (Capt L. F. Hursthouse) 17.25–19.53 hr; B.E.12a A6326 (Capt S. R. Stammers) 17.14–17.19 hr, returned with engine trouble; A593 (Capt Stammers) 17.30–19.05 hr; A6326 (Capt R. G. H. Murray) 18.25–20.00 hr.

No.39 Squadron, B Flight, Suttons Farm: B.E.2c 2023 (Lieut E. S. Moulton-Barrett) 17.50–19.50 hr; B.E.12 6138 (Capt J. I. Mackay) 17.18–19.50 hr.

No.39 Squadron, C Flight, Hainault: B.E.2e 7151 (Capt W. T. F. Holland) 17.51–19.40 hr; B.E.12as A6325 (Capt W. H. Haynes) 17.16–19.43 hr; A6349 (Lieut G. T. Wix) 17.21–20.15 hr.

No.50 Squadron, A Flight, Detling: B.E.2c 2711 (2nd Lieut C. C. White) 17.38–19.17 hr; B.E.12 6183 (2nd Lieut W. R. Oulton) 17.16–19.59 hr; B.E.12as A577 (2nd Lieut A. J. Arkell) 17.10–19.50 hr (Throwley); A6308 (Lieut Carmichael) 17.30–20.02 hr; A6305 (Lieut R. W. le Gallais) 17.18–19.50 hr (Bekesbourne); A582 (2nd Lieut L. Lucas) 17.18–19.55 hr; A6313 (2nd Lieut N. E. Chandler) 17.19–18.38 hr (Bekesbourne).

No.50 Squadron, B Flight, Throwley: B.E.12s 6493 (Lieut H. T. O. Windsor) 17.34–18.38 hr; 6185 (Lieut Windsor) 18.58–19.59 hr; R.E.8 A3836 (Capt T. R. Irons) 17.53–19.58 hr.

No.50 Squadron, C Flight, Bekesbourne: B.E.2e 6187 (2nd Lieut F. A. D. Grace) 18.13–19.40 hr; Vickers E.S.1 7759 (Capt A. J. Capel) 17.35–18.40 hr and 18.45–20.12 hr.

No.78 Squadron, Telscombe Cliffs: B.E.12as A601 (Lieut J. S. Castle) 17.57–18.40 hr, returned with engine trouble; A595 (Lieut Castle) 18.43–19.45 hr, forced landed, Arlington, with engine trouble; A6320 (Capt E. R. Pretyman) 18.00–19.45 hr.

No.8 Aircraft Acceptance Park, Lympne: D.H.5 B347 (Lieut G. W. Gathergood) 18.40–19.50 hr.

B.E.12a A601 of No.78 Squadron flew from Telscombe Cliffs during the 25 May, 1917, raid. It later operated from Chiddingstone Causeway, renamed Penshurst, where this photograph was taken. (*F. L. Luxmoore*)

Brandenburg's plan to open the daylight bombing campaign with a major attack on London was frustrated by weather.

The twenty-three Gothas of Kagohl 3 set off over the North Sea in a loose gaggle and two soon turned back with mechanical troubles. On approaching England they tightened up into two defensive formations, and one, comprising ten aircraft flying at about 15,000 ft, was sighted from the Tongue lightship at 16.45 hr. They crossed the coast between the Blackwater and Crouch estuaries at 17.00 hr and set course for London. Patchy cloud developed, and as they neared Tilbury half an hour later the ground to the west was completely obscured, so Brandenburg reluctantly turned south to seek an alternative target.

For the next 45 min the formation flew a curving course over Kent, dropping a few bombs at random—including several on Lympne aerodrome. The main attack was made on Folkestone and the nearby Shorncliffe army camp between 18.15 and 18.25 hr. No warning had been given, and most of the casualties were from this area.

Although GHQ Home Forces was not notified of the Tongue sighting until 16.57 hr—seven minutes after the RNAS—there was still ample time to intercept had the squadrons possessed reasonably effective fighters. One enemy formation passed almost directly over No.37 Squadron's aerodromes at Stow Maries and Rochford as though contemptuously aware that there was nothing to fear from the mediocre B.E.12s and 12as.

Capt Cooke, C Flight commander, spotted the Gothas through a break as he took off from Rochford in a B.E.12a, but by the time he had laboured up through the cloud layer starting at 5,000 ft they were out of sight. He pressed on southwestwards and had reached 13,000 ft when his engine burst into flames—which he successfully extinguished by executing a sudden tail-slide. He then noticed that the B.E's centre-section and wings were swaying in an alarming fashion, 'evidently owing to the inability of the machine to withstand rough usage such as it would undergo in an air fight', as he wrote in his report, and gingerly flew back to Rochford.

The flight commanders had obviously been briefed by their CO, Maj W. B. Hargrave, to mince no words about their aircraft's shortcomings, and Cooke went on:

> 'If I had been on a fast climbing scout I would have been able to keep in touch with the hostile aircraft. The B.E.12a will not climb above 14,000 ft and at that height it is impossible to do a sharp turn without losing about 500 ft, owing to the fact that the machine has no [power] reserve, and it is only just able to keep that height.'

Claude Ridley, commanding B Flight at Stow Maries, likewise unable to catch the formation after he eventually penetrated the clouds, wrote:

> 'It seems a great pity that scouts cannot be supplied to flights for this purpose, as the B.E.12a climbs so very poorly and is so very slow at a height in comparison with a good machine. It takes a long time to reach 14,000 ft and at this height there is no reserve of power, which seems absolutely useless when it comes to attacking first-class German machines. If I had been flying a fast scout I am almost certain that I should not have had the slightest difficulty of coming in contact with the hostile formation.
>
> 'If the Germans make a practice of coming over as they did today it seems hardly fair to expect pilots on B.E.12as to gain satisfactory results.'

At 19.05 hr, Humphreys of No.37 Squadron, a Canadian from Ontario, sighted a straggler over the Channel and managed to get his B.E.12 up to 15,000 ft, but the Gotha easily outpaced him. He had started from Rochford, put into Stow Maries to rectify a malfunctioning throttle, then forced landed at Goldhanger with a broken oil pipe. He saw the Gotha after being airborne for 40 min in another aircraft, and became lost over the coast after abandoning the chase. Near Bexhill, Humphreys found a field that looked suitable for a forced landing, but he noticed too late that it sloped steeply and ended at a ditch, and his aircraft was considerably damaged.

Of the thirty other B.E.12/12as and B.E.2 variants floundering about over southeast England that evening, only three—flown by Watkins, Hutcheon and Orr-Ewing, all of No.37 Squadron—came within sight of the enemy but were too distant to attempt a chase. There was no lack of enthusiasm, and several pilots forced to return with engine troubles either took off again when these were rectified or used any other aircraft available. Capel flew two sorties in No.50 Squadron's speedy little Vickers E.S.1 but saw nothing. The communications network was clearly unable to cope with the situation, particularly south of the Thames, and any useful messages displayed by the Ingram signals were difficult to read in the summer evening haze.

The RNAS coastal patrol fighters fared no better, and only an elderly and slow Short 820 seaplane from Dover made a sighting. Flown by Leslie Pincott, it

The Vickers E.S.1 prototype, 7759, with a top speed of over 112 mph, was one of the faster fighters airborne on 25 May, 1917. It was on the strength of No.50 Squadron. (*AVM A. J. Capel*)

landed from a 40-min sortie mounted in response to the initial warning just as the Folkestone attack started, and was immediately sent off again. Pincott saw the enemy formation, but his machine was even less capable than the B.Es of effective intervention.

The Pups, Triplanes and Bristol Scouts from Manston and the Westgate seaplanes, also airborne shortly after the first warning, failed to make contact because they patrolled too far to the east. They were equally unsuccessful on second sorties flown in the hope of engaging the bombers returning from Folkestone. One of the Sopwith Triplanes, N509, used against this and later raids was the experimental version with the 150 hp Hispano Suiza engine—a larger and more powerful aircraft than the production model.

Dover also suffered from the general communications breakdown, and after a standby warning at 17.00 hr, received nothing more until 18.16 hr, when bombs were dropping at Folkestone.

The prototype Hispano-powered Sopwith Triplane, N509, flew from RNAS Manston on 25 May, 1917, and during some of the later raids.

Bristol Scout D No.8990 (*left*) and Sopwith Pup 9947 (*centre*) were both airborne on 25 May, 1917, and during the next three months flew a total of ten operational sorties. Scout D (*right*) with modified fin and rudder did not make any recorded home-defence patrols. Scout D 8990 was initially at RNAS Manston, but this photograph was taken after it had been transferred to the Walmer defence flight.

The Sopwith Pup prototype, 3691, with which Flt Sub-Lieut R. F. S. Leslie, RNAS Dover, engaged a Gotha over the Channel on 25 May, 1917.

However, after the total failure of the regular defences—for which the cloudy weather was partly responsible—it was an RNAS Dover ferry pilot who provided the evening's redeeming feature. Reginald Leslie, who had logged 22 cross-Channel delivery flights by November 1916 and probably doubled that number by May 1917, had briefly engaged one of the single-engined hit-and-run raiders in March 1916.

On this particular evening he was awaiting release from the 'readiness' state so that he could leave for France in a new D.H.4. When the alarm came he grabbed the first available fighter—the Sopwith Pup prototype, which had first flown a year before and was still maintained in full fighting condition by the Dover defence flight.

Ten minutes after take-off Leslie saw the rear machines of the German formation travelling down Channel about midway between Dover and Gravelines and gradually overtook a straggler flying at 11,000 ft. He positioned 150 yards behind and above, then dived to attack. His first shots passed ahead of the Gotha, so he increased his dive, closing to 50 yards and firing 150 rounds. The enemy gunner returned the fire. As Leslie broke off, the Gotha went into a steep dive, with smoke and steam pouring back over the centre-section, but he was diverted from following its progress by a sudden attack from above by two others. Being unfamiliar with the Pup, he banked too steeply and fell into a spin, losing several thousand feet. On recovery he judged that the bombers were now too far away to catch, so after an unsuccessful search for traces of the one he believed he had shot down, he returned to Dover.

RFC ferry pilot Gerald Gathergood took up a D.H.5 awaiting delivery from Lympne to France, only to be thwarted by gun failure. Following the Dover AA shell bursts he climbed rapidly over the Channel and came up with the Gothas at 14,500 ft. He approached to point-blank range under the tail of the rearmost—possibly the aircraft attacked by Leslie—which was trailing the main formation and emitting periodic puffs of black smoke, but his gun refused to fire. He broke away, flying a highly erratic course with his feet while using both hands to rectify his Vickers, and received a few bursts from the Gotha. By the time his gun was eventually working the enemy had drawn well ahead, and Gathergood could fire only a few ineffective bursts at extreme range. The D.H.5 had not been fully checked since arriving from Hendon earlier in the day and its compass was unserviceable, so being out of sight of land, Gathergood decided that further pursuit would be unwise.

A third incident also involved a ferry aircraft. Blissfully unaware of the raid, a Lieut Baker was flying Bristol Fighter A7130 from the makers to France, via Lympne, when he was attacked by a Gotha over Ashford. His gun was not loaded, so he made a hasty dive for Lympne.

As the Gothas approached the Belgian coast at 18,000 ft they were intercepted by nine Pups of Nos.4 and 9 (RNAS) Squadrons from Dunkirk. Reports of the encounter were conflicting, but the consensus was that one Gotha was shot down into the sea while another fell apparently out of control. RNAS Dunkirk said that various pilots had attacked and it was not possible to credit success to any individuals.

The Germans admitted one loss, for which the Dunkirk pilots rather than Leslie were probably responsible—though Leslie received the DSC for his stout effort. Another Gotha crashed near Bruges, killing its crew, the cause rather strangely being attributed to a heart attack suffered by the pilot; it would seem equally likely that it resulted from combat damage, or injury to the pilot, not readily traceable after the event. German crews claimed to have shot down three British fighters—perhaps due to misinterpreting Leslie's spin, Gathergood's erratic 'no hands' spell and Cooke's engine fire.

5 June, 1917 (Daylight)

Target: Sheerness.
Enemy forces: 22 Gothas despatched and attacked.
Results: 13 killed, 34 injured, £5,003 damage.
Defence sorties: 62.

RNAS

Dover: Sopwith Pups 9929, 18.20–19.15 hr; 9900, 18.20–19.30 hr; N5182, 18.20–19.45 hr; Sopwith Camel N6363, took off 18.20 hr, returned with engine trouble; Short 184 8102 (Flt Sub-Lieut S. E. Ball, CPO Martin) 18.45–19.45 hr.

Eastchurch: B.E.2c 8405 (Flt Sub-Lieut R. J. M. St Leger, APmr G. S. Trewin) took off 18.32 hr, forced landed Orfordness (W/T aircraft); Sopwith 1½ Strutter 3686 (Flt Lieut G. A. Cox, Obs Lieut F. J. Dean) 18.45–20.15 hr; Bristol Scout D 8978 (Flt Cdr J. C. P. Wood) 18.30–19.06 hr; Farman F.40 N3216 (Flt Lieut E. M.

Pizey, Flt Lieut A. H. S. Lawson) 18.40–19–50 hr.

Grain: Sopwith Pup 9940 (Flt Cdr R. D. Sibley) 18.25–19.20 hr.

Manston: Bristol Scout Ds 8965 (Flt Sub-Lieut R. H. Daly) 18.05–19.25 hr; N5390 (Flt Sub-Lieut A. C. Burt) 18.05–19.18 hr; 8989 (Flt Sub-Lieut H. R. de Wilde) took off 18.10 hr, returned with broken gun sight; N5392 (Flt Sub-Lieut de Wilde) 18.28–19.45 hr; Sopwith Pup 9907 (Flt Sub-Lieut J. E. Scott) 18.05–19.05 hr; Sopwith Triplane N5424 (Sqn Cdr C. H. Butler) 18.40–20.15 hr (Dunkirk).

Westgate: Sopwith Babies 8186 (Flt Sub-Lieut L. G. Maxton) 18.15–18.50 hr, damaged alighting in rough sea; N1025 (Flt Sub-Lieut W. J. de Salis) damaged taking off at 18.15 hr in rough sea.

Walmer: Sopwith Pups N6438, 18.15–19.25 hr; N6442, 18.25–19.35 hr; 9947 18.25–19.55 hr.

RFC

No.37 Squadron, A Flight, Goldhanger: B.E.2e 6820 (Capt K. N. Pearson) 18.40–20.13 hr; B.E.12 6610 (Capt W. Sowrey) 18.35–19.47 hr; B.E.12a A599 (Lieut L. F. Hutcheon) 18.37–20.30 hr; Sopwith 1½ Strutters A8251 (Lieut L. P. Watkins) 18.17–19.47 hr; A8271 (Lieut R. F. Oakes) 18.18–19.50 hr; R.E.7 2232 (2nd Lieut H. A. Blain) 18.50–20.15 hr.

No.37 Squadron, B Flight, Stow Maries: Sopwith 1½ Strutter A8274 (Capt C. A. Ridley) 18.19–20.20 hr.

No.37 Squadron, C Flight, Rochford: B.E.2d 5778 (2nd Lieut J. E. R. Young) 18.25–19.57 hr; B.E.12a A6312 (2nd Lieut J. V. A. Gleed) 18.15–20.09 hr; Sopwith 1½ Strutter A8249 (Capt C. B. Cooke) 18.18–20.00 hr.

No.39 Squadron, A Flight, North Weald: B.E.12as A593 (Capt L. F. Hursthouse) 18.20–20.03 hr; A6326 (Capt T. Gran) 18.21–19.42 hr; Armstrong Whitworth F.K.8 B213 (Capt S. R. Stammers, Lieut Fraser) 18.25–19.19 hr, returned with engine trouble.

No.39 Squadron, B Flight, Suttons Farm: B.E.12 6138 (2nd Lieut C. L. Brock) 18.25–20.05 hr; Armstrong Whitworth F.K.8 B237 (Capt J. I. Mackay, Lieut E. S. Moulton-Barrett) 19.09–19.47 hr.

No.39 Squadron, C Flight, Hainault: B.E.12as A6325 (Capt W. H. Haynes) 18.18–19.40 hr; A6349 (Capt O. V. Thomas) 18.47–20.06 hr.

No.50 Squadron, A Flight, Detling: B.E.12 6183 (2nd Lieut W. R. Oulton) 18.18–19.58 hr; B.E.12a A6313 (2nd Lieut C. C. White) 18.14–19.55 hr.

No.50 Squadron, B Flight, Throwley: Armstrong Whitworth F.K.8 B229 (Capt C. R. Rowden) 18.18–20.09 hr; R.E.8 A3840 (2nd Lieut A. J. Arkell) 18.17–19.10 hr, returned with engine trouble.

No.50 Squadron, C Flight, Bekesbourne: Armstrong Whitworth F.K.8s B225 (Lieut R. W. le Gallais) 18.20–20.00 hr; B224 (2nd Lieut J. G. Goodyear) 18.21–20.00 hr; B238 (2nd Lieut N. E. Chandler) 18.21–20.11 hr; Vickers E.S.1 7759 (Capt A. J. Capel) 18.21–19.53 hr.

No.78 Squadron, Telscombe Cliffs: B.E.12as A6320 (Capt E. R. Pretyman) 18.19–19.55 hr; A601 (Lieut J. S. Castle) 18.20–19.58 hr; A6305 (2nd Lieut W. H. Howell) 18.20–20.01 hr.

No.65 Squadron, Wye: D.H.5s A9379 (Capt L. E. Whitehead) 18.20–20.00 hr; A9184 (2nd Lieut E. Churcher) 18.35–19.55 hr.

No.35(T) Squadron, Northolt: Bristol Fighters A7135 (Capt C. W. E. Cole-Hamilton) 18.55–20.35 hr; A7122 (Lieut Child) 19.00–20.35 hr; A7136 (Lieut Walmsley) 18.55–21.15 hr, forced landed near Barnet with engine trouble.

No.2 Aircraft Acceptance Park, Hendon: D.H.4 A7471 (Lieut D. W. Clappen) 18.45–20.45 hr; D.H.5 A9174 (2nd Lieut A. G. Alderson) 18.45–18.55 hr, returned with engine trouble; Armstrong Whitworth F.K.8 B251 (Lieut F. L. Hambly) 19.00–20.15 hr.

No.8 Aircraft Acceptance Park, Lympne: Sopwith Pup B1731 (Lieut D. Armstrong); R.E.8s A3699 (2nd Lieut S. Crosfield); A3700 (2nd Lieut E. Carpenter); A4711 (2nd Lieut C. A. Rogers); A4713 (2nd Lieut H. D. Crompton); all aircraft airborne by 18.40 hr, details not recorded.

Under mounting pressure from his superiors to bomb London, Brandenburg was in some quandary. He required ideal weather to attack the British capital, which lay at the extreme range of his aircraft, but was nevertheless anxious to keep his crews occupied. On 5 June conditions were good apart from a strong easterly wind, exposing the bombers to a slow flight home through the alerted defences, so he chose the coastal objectives of Sheerness and Shoeburyness.

British notification procedures had been only marginally improved since the Folkestone raid, and GHQ Home Forces' receipt of the first sighting reports, at 18.10 hr, was still five minutes behind the RNAS and ten minutes after the Gothas had been seen by the Kentish Knock lightship and the *Clacton Belle* steaming near Black Deep. Earlier that afternoon there had been a false alarm from the Admiralty, fortunately established as such before more than a few aircraft, including three from No.78 Squadron and one from Hendon, were airborne.

The real raiders were first spotted flying westwards off the Belgian coast by a routine patrol of three No.4 (RNAS) Squadron Pups under Flt Cdr J. D. Newberry. With no means of transmitting a warning, they could only chase—which they did until nearing the Thames estuary when petrol shortage forced them to land at Manston. The only pilot close enough to engage suffered a gun stoppage.

Bristol Scout D N5392 was among the RNAS Manston fighters airborne during the 5 June and 7 July Gotha raids. The streamlined ammunition drum container can be seen on the side of the fuselage. (*RAF Museum*)

Armstrong Whitworth F.K.8 B224 flew the first of its ten recorded day and night home-defence sorties on 5 June, 1917. The first eight were with No.50 Squadron and the remaining two with No.143.

The first United Kingdom based naval fighters took off at 18.05 hr in the rather forlorn hope of intercepting over the sea, and RFC squadrons went on readiness at 18.04–08 hr followed by the 'patrol' order at 18.12–17 hr. Meanwhile the Gotha formation had crossed the coast near Foulness Point at 18.05 hr, turned south and began bombing at 18.25 hr. With some bombs failing to explode and others falling in the sea, casualties were relatively light.

First away from Manston was a formation of three—Scott in a Pup leading Daly and Burt in Bristol Scouts—de Wilde took off five minutes later but turned back with a broken gun sight. Over Southend Scott saw the Gothas at 15,000 ft, and realizing that the Bristols were nearing their ceiling, he climbed on his own to 17,000 ft. By this time he was well beyond the North Foreland, but despite his height advantage was unable to get within effective combat range of the departing bombers. Daly eventually reached 16,000 ft and attacked one with no result, then came under fire from four others. Both Scott and Daly reported seeing a Gotha firing explosive shells larger than standard machine-gun calibre, but they were probably mistaken since experiments with 20 mm cannon did not start until several months later.

The indefatigable Charles Butler, despite a bout of water on the knee and difficulty in starting his Triplane, eventually got away though his engine was still running badly. However, he caught the departing formation east of the Kentish Knock and attacked one aircraft which dived into the haze. He flew to within ten miles of Ostende and fired 150 rounds into a second, which also put its nose down and was lost to view.

The only other British-based RNAS machine to make contact was a Bristol Scout from Eastchurch, flown by Wood, who engaged a Gotha at 11,000 ft over the Thames estuary with no visible result. The Eastchurch B.E.2c, equipped to transmit W/T reports on enemy movements, came down near Orfordness, well away from the activity, having apparently lost its bearings.

The major RNAS reaction came from the Dunkirk squadrons as the Gothas neared home and were under fighter protection. Three Pups from No.4 Squadron, and seven Pups and Triplanes from No.9, were involved in a substantial battle, during which two bombers were claimed destroyed and four other aircraft sent down out of control.

Improvements to RFC capability since the first Gotha assault were inconsequential, and the few Sopwith 1½ Strutters and Armstrong Whitworths issued to squadrons represented only a slight advance on the mediocre B.Es. Of the thirteen aircraft produced by training and other supporting units just over half were capable of meeting the Gothas on reasonable terms.

With no knowledge of the raiders' intentions, patrols were mounted on the assumption that London was the target, which eliminated any possibility of interception before they reached Sheerness. In the event only Arkell, Capel, Goodyear and Ridley, flying at 14–15,000 ft, sighted the enemy force several thousand feet higher up and moving eastwards from the Girdler lightship, but their efforts to get within combat range were unavailing.

What role was expected of the R.E.8s from Lympne, with their 11,000 ft ceiling, is difficult to surmise, though the Gotha's excellent performance was not then perhaps generally appreciated, and the unit was doubtless anxious to appear willing. These aircraft were urgently required in France, and by arrangement they proceeded directly across the Channel on sighting the all-clear signal.

One Gotha fell in the sea at 18.31 hr while being shelled by the Sheerness and Shoeburyness guns, which fired 329 rounds. It sank nearly two miles off Barton's Point, and the pilot, Vizefeldwebel Erich Kluck was drowned. The badly injured observer, Leut Hans Francke, died soon after being picked up, but the gunner, Unteroffizier Georg Schumacher, escaped with a broken leg. The aircraft, number G IV/660/16, was salvaged, and technical examination showed that the starboard engine stopped after the magneto drive teeth had stripped. This does not invalidate the claim of the Barton's Point battery to have brought the aircraft down, as the magneto damage could have resulted from engine over-speeding after the propeller had been shot away. RNAS pilots asserted that AA shells were mostly bursting some 3,000 ft beneath the bombers, but the machine which came down was reported as flying below the main formation, at 9,000 ft.

Although only this one loss was admitted by the Germans, the Press gave prominence to the RNAS claims and presented the action as a great British victory. 'So efficient were the defences that they [the bombers] only succeeded in penetrating the coastal districts for a few miles, and after dropping bombs made off at high speed' wrote *The Daily Telegraph*. The *Express* claimed that only half

B.E.12a A593, No.39 Squadron, North Weald, flew against the Gothas attacking Sheerness on 5 June, 1917, and during two of the following raids.

Gotha G IV/660/16, shot down on 5 June, 1917, being salvaged two days later. (*J. M. Bruce/G. S. Leslie collection*)

the bomber force escaped, and hoped that the attacks would be repeated so that more might be destroyed.

13 June, 1917 (Daylight)

Target: London.
Enemy forces: 20 Gothas despatched, 18 Gothas attacked.
Results: 162 killed, 432 injured, £129,498 damage.
Defence sorties: 94.

RNAS

Dover: Sopwith Pups 9929, 11.09–12.15 hr; N6189, 12.14–13.35 hr; N6202, 12.14–13.35 hr; Sopwith Baby 8157, 11.15–12.10 hr.

Eastchurch: Bristol Scout Ds 8972 (Sqn Cdr A. F. Bettington) 11.10–13.30 hr; 8978, 11.15–11.45 hr; Sopwith 1½ Strutter 3686, 11.10–12.45 hr.

Felixstowe: Sopwith Schneiders 3794 (Flt Sub-Lieut H. A. Wilson) 11.20–12.30 hr; 3794 (Flt Sub-Lieut C. C. Purdy) 13.25–15.00 hr; Sopwith Babies 8187 (Flt Sub-Lieut Purdy) 11.23–12.23 hr; 8187 (Flt Sub-Lieut A. G. Simms) 12.45–13.50 hr; N1105, 12.35–14.05 hr; N1102, 12.40–14.25 hr; N1037 (Flt Sub-Lieut H. A. Wilson) 13.30–14.00 hr.

Grain: Sopwith Pups 9940 (Flt Lieut F. M. Fox) 11.05–12.34 hr (Manston); 9497 (Flt Lieut C. T. Freeman) 11.50–13.00 hr; Sopwith Babies 8168 (Flt Sub-Lieut W. F. Dickson) 11.05–13.00 hr; 8160 (Flt Sub-Lieut J. M. McCleary) 11.13–12.30 hr, forced down near Nore lightship with engine trouble.

Manston: Bristol Scout Ds 8969 (Flt Sub-Lieut H. R. de Wilde) 10.45–11.30 hr and 12.20–13.37 hr; N5391 (Flt Sub-Lieut A. C. Burt) 10.45–11.30 hr; N5391 (Flt Cdr G. L. Thompson) 12.30–13.37 hr; 8990 (Flt Cdr Thompson) 11.45–12.22 hr; Sopwith Pup 9907 (Flt Sub-Lieut R. H. Daly) 10.45–12.20 hr (Aldeburgh); Sopwith Triplanes N5424 (Sqn Cdr C. H. Butler) 10.45–11.35 hr and 12.20–13.37 hr; N509 (Flt Sub-Lieut A. C. Burt) 12.20–13.37 hr.

Westgate: Sopwith Babies 8146 (Flt Sub-Lieut H. C. Lemon) 11.30–12.15 hr; 8146 (Flt Sub-Lieut E. B. Drake) 12.35–14.40 hr; N1025 (Flt Sub-Lieut L. G. Maxton) 10.48–12.25 hr; N1025 (Flt Sub-Lieut F. C. Lander) 12.45–13.30 hr.

Walmer: Sopwith Pups 9947 (Flt Lieut S. Kemball) 11.20–13.14 hr; N6439 (Flt Sub-Lieut W. H. Chisam) 11.10–13.10 hr; N6441 (Flt Sub-Lieut W. M. Lusby) 11.50–12.45 hr; N6442 (Flt Sub-Lieut J. A. Shaw) 12.35–13.41 hr.

RFC

No.37 Squadron, A Flight, Goldhanger: B.E.2e A2767 (Lieut L. F. Hutcheon) 11.04–13.30 hr; B.E.12 6610 (Lieut L. P. Watkins) 11.03–13.10 hr; R.E.7 2232 (Capt W. Sowrey) 11.04–12.45 hr; Sopwith 1½ Strutter A8271 (Lieut R. F. Oakes) 11.04–13.15 hr.

Sopwith Pup 9497 (with the prefix N wrongly added during maintenance work) was flown by Flt Lieut C. T. Freeman, RNAS Grain, on 13 June, 1917. It is seen here during land-based deck-landing experiments. (*J. M. Bruce/G. S. Leslie collection*)

No.37 Squadron, B Flight, Stow Maries: B.E.12a A6318 (2nd Lieut H. A. Blain) 11.08–12.31 hr and 12.58–13.56 hr; Sopwith 1½ Strutter A8274 (Capt C. A. Ridley) 11.00–13.45 hr.

No.37 Squadron, C Flight, Rochford: Sopwith 1½ Strutters A8249 (Capt C. B. Cooke, Lieut A. A. C. Garnons-Williams) 11.03–12.28 hr; A8250 (2nd Lieut J. E. R. Young, Lieut Bennett) 11.05–13.15 hr; A8275 (Lieut G. D. F. Keddie, Cpl W. Rowley) 11.01–13.45 hr.

No.39 Squadron, A Flight, North Weald: B.E.2e A8626 (2nd Lieut A. A. Wilcock) 11.15–12.17 hr; B.E.12 6488 (Capt T. Gran) 10.32–13.00 hr (Rochford); B.E.12as A6326 (Capt S. R. Stammers) 10.30–13.00 hr; A593 (Lieut E. M. Gilbert) 10.45–13.25 hr.

No.39 Squadron, B Flight, Suttons Farm: B.E.2c 2023 (Lieut C. B. van Leonhof) 11.44–12.09 hr; B.E.12s 6491 (Capt O. V. Thomas) 11.04–13.14 hr; 6480 (Lieut E. S. Moulton-Barrett) 11.05–13.10 hr; B.E.12a A6349 (Lieut G. T. Wix) 11.03–12.49 hr; Armstrong Whitworth F.K.8 B237 (Capt J. I. Mackay, Lieut G. T. Stoneham) 11.04–11.55 hr, returned with engine trouble.

No.39 Squadron, C Flight, Hainault: B.E.2e 7151 (Capt J. O. C. Orton) 11.23–13.14 hr.

No.50 Squadron, A Flight, Detling: B.E.2c 2711 (2nd Lieut W. R. Oulton) took off 11.07 hr, forced landed Kingsnorth; B.E.12as A6313 (2nd Lieut C. C. White) 11.03–13.05 hr; A6309 (2nd Lieut L. Lucas) 11.05–13.23 hr.

No.50 Squadron, B Flight, Throwley: B.E.12 6185 (2nd Lieut F. V. Bryant) 11.08–13.10 hr; R.E.8s A3836 (2nd Lieut A. J. Arkell) 11.00–13.12 hr; A3840 (2nd Lieut N. F. Perris) 11.11–13.20 hr; Armstrong Whitworth F.K.8 B229 (Capt C. R. Rowden) 11.07–13.30 hr.

No.50 Squadron, C Flight, Bekesbourne: Vickers E.S.1 7759 (Capt A. J. Capel)11.00–11.29 hr and 11.35–13.15 hr; Armstrong Whitworth F.K.8s B225 (Lieut R. W. le Gallais) 11.02–13.02 hr; B224 (2nd Lieut J. G. Goodyear) 11.03–12.55 hr; B247 (2nd Lieut F. A. D. Grace) 11.04–13.11 hr; B238 (2nd Lieut N. E. Chandler) 11.08–13.10 hr.

No.78 Squadron, Telscombe Cliffs: B.E.12a A6320 (Capt E. R. Pretyman) 12.12–13.55 hr, landed at Arlington due to sea mist.

No.65 Squadron, Wye: D.H.5s A9184 (2nd Lieut E. S. Weiss) 11.00–13.15 hr; A9379 (Capt L. E. Whitehead) 11.07–13.15 hr.

No.98 Depot Squadron, Rochford: B.E.2d 5778 (Capt I. T. Lloyd) 11.10–12.19 hr; B.E.2e 6820 (Maj B. F. Moore) 11.15–12.35 hr; B.E.12a A6312 (Capt K. N. Pearson) 11.12–12.43 hr.

No.35(T) Squadron, Northolt: Bristol Fighters A7135 (Capt C. W. E. Cole–Hamilton, Capt C. H. Keevil) 11.19–13.00 hr; A7136 (2nd Lieut J. Chapman, 2nd Lieut F. G. C. Weare) 11.18–12.45 hr.

No.40(T) Squadron, Croydon: Sopwith Pups A7341, 11.22–13.20 hr; B1738, 11.45–13.50 hr.

No.62(T) Squadron, Dover: Sopwith Pup, unrecorded, (Lieut F. W. Kilgour) 11.40–12.30 hr and 12.40–13.25 hr.

No.63(T) Squadron, Joyce Green: Sopwith Pup A7311 (Capt J. T. B. McCudden) 11.25–13.20 hr.

No.2 Aircraft Acceptance Park, Hendon: D.H.4s A7486 (Lieut F. L. Hambly) 11.50–13.25 hr; A7477 (Lieut D. W. Clappen) 12.15–13.30 hr; D.H.5 B354 (Lieut E. M. Roberts) 11.40–13.15 hr.

No.8 Aircraft Acceptance Park, Lympne: D.H.4 A7481 (2nd Lieut H. J. McKenzie) 11.30–13.05 hr; D.H.5 B348 (Lieut L. G. Wood) 11.10–12.40 hr;

F.E.8 A4929 (Lieut G. H. Hackwill) 11.05–12.40 hr; Sopwith 1½ Strutter A1095 (Lieut F. Garrett) 11.13–12.45 hr; Bristol Fighter A3345 (Lieut R. S. Carroll) 11.10–13.25 hr; R.E.8 A3705 (Lieut G. S. Frost) 11.25–13.15 hr.

Experimental Station, Orfordness: Sopwith Triplane N5430 (Lieut N. Howarth) 11.17–12.40 hr; N5430 (Lieut Clarke) 13.10–13.25 hr; D.H.4 A2129 (Lieut F. D. Holder, Capt B. M. Jones) 11.30–12.50 hr; A2129 (Lieut Howarth, Lieut F. W. Musson) 13.10–13.40 hr.

Orfordness D.H.4 A2129, crewed by Lieut F. D. Holder and Capt B. Melvill Jones on 13 June, 1917.

Despite having lost the element of surprise, the success achieved when conditions eventually permitted the London raid exceeded Brandenburg's best expectations. Not one British fighter managed to intercept the Gothas on their way to the target, and only a handful gained effective combat range during their departure. All the bombers returned safely, but one RFC observer-gunner was killed in combat.

Of the twenty Gothas which took off, two turned back with engine trouble. Probably by accident rather than design the remainder escaped detection by the off-shore light vessels and the first indications of a heavy raid came when an Essex coast army unit reported engine sounds out to sea, half an hour before the formation crossed at Foulness. Meanwhile a third Gotha had signalled engine trouble and made for Margate, being sighted off the town at 10.43 hr, and three more fell behind with various problems. Two of these unloaded their bombs in the Shoeburyness area and the third followed an erratic course south of the Thames, eventually crossing to bomb the Royal Victoria docks. The remaining fourteen aircraft tightened up into a diamond-shaped formation, flying at about 16,500 ft, and approached London north of their principal aiming areas—Liverpool Street station and East End docks and warehouses.

Over Regent's Park, Brandenburg—whose aircraft was distinguished by its red tail—fired a white signal cartridge and the whole formation swung round to begin bombing at 11.35 hr, each crew selecting a target almost at leisure. Including those which fell in coastal areas, 128 bombs totalling four tons' weight were dropped, one hitting a school in Poplar, killing sixteen young children. After the attack the bombers had some difficulty in resuming a compact, defensive formation, and British pilots met groups of seven, four and two aircraft over Essex. These closed up beyond the coast.

None of the RNAS Manston aircraft, airborne within two minutes of the first sighting, found the Margate raider—which at the time was thought to be trying to decoy fighters from the main formation. However, Daly in a Pup did encounter a single machine off Southend, lost it in cloud and then lost himself, landing at Aldeburgh.

RFC home-defence squadrons were given the 'patrol' order at 10.53 hr, and although more than two-thirds of the aircraft were airborne within six minutes, their chances of intercepting en route were negligible. The bombers were actually seen by No.37 Squadron crews at Rochford before take-off orders were given. The better-performance machines—Pups, D.H.4s and Bristol Fighters from training and other units to the west—were not ordered off for another 15–20 min, which in turn minimized their chances of intercepting before the Gothas bombed.

Home Defence Group reports show that only three pilots got anywhere near the formation before bombing started. Sidney Stammers, already airborne on a routine flight from North Weald, spotted the 'patrol' signal on the ground, and when over Joyce Green at 11.20 hr, he saw the Gothas under AA fire some distance to the northwest. He put down the nose of his B.E.12a with the idea of gaining enough speed to cut them off, but realized as he approached that they had turned and were several thousand feet above his own 10,500 ft. Relieved of their bomb loads, the Gothas climbed even higher and when Stammers eventually caught up, over Romford, they were still a long way above. Nevertheless he pulled up the B.E's nose and blasted off with his Vickers into the centre of the formation, and when this achieved nothing, fired three drums from his elevated Lewis. But he was well beyond effective range, and falling engine revolutions caused him to abandon the hopeless task.

No.35 (Training) Squadron at Northolt received the 'patrol' order at 11.17 hr, only four minutes before London was given the raid warning, and two Bristol Fighters were airborne within two minutes. Cole-Hamilton headed south of the Thames while Chapman kept to the north, and both had reached about 10,000 ft when they saw the enemy flying west over Hackney. However, even the excellent Bristol Fighter could not perform miracles, and the bombers had released their

Capt C. W. E. Cole-Hamilton, No.35 (Training) Squadron, Northolt, running-up Bristol Fighter A7135. He was flying this aircraft on 13 June, 1917, when his observer, Capt C. H. Keevil, was killed in combat with a Gotha. (*Peter W. Brooks*)

loads and were beyond Ilford on the return journey before the altitude gap had narrowed enough for combat.

At this point Cole-Hamilton was closing on three Gothas behind a larger group and gradually got within 600 ft below the tail of the rearmost and fired 98 rounds from his Vickers. He turned away allowing Keevil, his observer, to attack with the Lewis. Soon afterwards, when approaching Southend and concentrating on the same aircraft, they came under fire from one of the flanking machines which had dropped back. Keevil responded—altogether he fired 157 rounds—but was killed by a bullet through the neck. Cole-Hamilton then found that his own gun had jammed, and he returned to Northolt.

Chapman attempted to attack the same Gotha flight but could not gain enough height to use his front gun effectively, though his observer fired a few optimistic bursts from below at extreme range. With his Bristol climbing badly, he abandoned the chase on reaching the coast.

Gran, No.39 Squadron, also airborne when patrol was ordered, briefly saw—and lost—the single Gotha approaching Greenwich south of the main force, and he later encountered a group of four flying out to sea off Foulness. He fired from 100 yards behind and 500 ft below the last machine, which retaliated, and in trying to attain the enemy's altitude fell further behind, and then gave up. Near Shoeburyness a close AA burst damaged his B.E.12's port exhaust stack, which began to vibrate alarmingly, so he landed at Rochford.

The Gotha seen by Gran over the Thames was briefly attacked by Lloyd in a B.E.2d from the depot squadron at Rochford, who picked it up northwest of Maidstone. As it followed the river, Lloyd tried to cut it off, and there were several long-range exchanges of fire before he lost it in cloud. Shortly afterwards he saw four Gothas flying east near Rayleigh at a speed far beyond the capabilities of his B.E.

Incensed by their ground-level view of the Gothas serenely heading for London, No.37 Squadron 1½-Strutter crews at Rochford made valiant attempts to get them on their way back. No system of co-ordinated attack had been devised, and each crew tackled the departing bombers independently. Keddie saw them near Stow Maries at about 16,000 ft and although the Sopwith was 2,000 ft below, Rowley, his gunner, fired three drums of Lewis to no visible effect. Keddie then concentrated on a straggler, allowing Rowley to fire four more drums forward and over the top wing, but again the range was too great, and after nearly an hour's chase the Gothas were mere specks in the distance.

Sopwith 1½ Strutter A8250 of No.37 Squadron, Rochford, engaged Gothas from long range on 13 June and 7 July, 1917, but gun failures and performance shortcomings prevented effective combat. (*Mrs C. Alexander*)

Although not positively identified, this R.E.7 is probably one of No.37 Squadron's flown during the summer of 1917. At that time a role of this obsolescent type was target-towing.

Cooke attacked a group of six over North Benfleet, firing about 200 rounds from his Vickers, and his gunner using five drums of Lewis, all from reasonably close range. One bomber was thought to receive many hits, and Cooke considered it to be nearly out of control—possibly an illusion created by some vigorous evasive action. Cooke was then obliged to terminate the engagement, having accidentally released his petrol tank pressure.

Young's attempt to attack a group of six was frustrated by Vickers gun failure. However, his observer fired a drum of Lewis, seeing hits on the fuselage of one machine—whose aft gunner slumped as though wounded—before the bombers gradually pulled away and were lost in cloud.

Two Sopwith Pups operating independently were perhaps closest to achieving success. Frederick Fox from RNAS Grain was at 17,000 ft above the Thames estuary when he saw the Gothas over Southend and dived on one of the rear aircraft, firing a drum of Lewis at close quarters and seeing tracers entering the fuselage. He then came under fire from three others, so spun down 500 ft to change drums. This took about five minutes, as he had difficulty in releasing the muzzle anchoring clips and then found that the gun would not swing down far enough to reach comfortably. When he eventually reloaded, the Gothas had moved well ahead and he climbed after the rearmost, which greeted him with bursts of fire through the fuselage tunnel. Fox fired off another dozen rounds before his gun jammed, and he broke off 25 miles east of Foulness. He landed at Manston, wrecking his undercarriage and damaging the wings.

The other Pup was flown by James McCudden, later to become one of the greatest fighter 'aces', whose sortie from Joyce Green was a freelance effort not included in Home Defence Group records. He had reached 15,000 ft when he saw the enemy near Shoeburyness, and it took him some 15 min to position 500 ft below and behind the rearmost aircraft. Aware that he was barely within range, he nevertheless fired off three drums, since the Pup was incapable of getting any closer. It is likely that both Pups attacked the same Gotha, for as McCudden broke off to change his first drum, he noticed another approach to close quarters and then turn off as though with gun troubles.

Of the nineteen different aircraft types or variants airborne that morning, the most improbable to be masquerading as a day fighter was one of No.37 Squadron's R.E.7s—an unwieldy day bomber with a 57-ft wing span, designed in 1915. William Sowrey coaxed it up to 12,000 ft to patrol between Rochford and Stow Maries and lurked beneath a group of seven Gothas overtaking several thousand feet above. He opened fire with his elevated Lewis at one aircraft a little lower than the rest, only for the drum to fly off when it was nearly exhausted. He discharged a replacement drum into the formation—which he estimated was flying five to ten mph faster than his own maximum speed of 70.

Apart from Fox's spirited attack it was clearly not the navy's day, and none of the Manston pilots despatched to cut off the returning bombers made contact. There were German and British observations of a triplane making a long-range attack on one Gotha, but no Sopwith Triplane pilot reported such an attempt. RNAS patrols from Dunkirk were unable to intercept a group of seven Gothas seen in the distance.

Brandenburg's estimate of about thirty British fighters airborne was reasonable, since he would know nothing of the large number on patrol far removed in time or distance from his formation. German crews reported seventeen combats, again a reasonable figure, since gunners from several different Gothas sometimes fired at the same fighter. Their claim that two fighters were shot down could be explained by the sight of Cole-Hamilton's Bristol turning away after Keevil was killed, and Fox spinning down to change ammunition drums.

An account by a Gotha captain, Leut von Seydlitz-Kurzbach, published shortly after the raid, broadly correlated with the actual sequence of events, allowing for some journalistic licence and propaganda considerations. He described seeing three British aircraft before reaching central London—presumably Cole-Hamilton, Chapman and Stammers—and a later series of combats with aircraft which could have been No.37 Squadron's Sopwiths. He then reported shooting down a third—'the first enemy to be defeated over England's isle'. The writer described this aircraft as 'falling end over end into the depths', which although not the manner in which Cole-Hamilton departed after his gun stoppage—if his Bristol was the aircraft referred to—sounded better to the lay public. Finally, after crossing the coast, he mentioned a persistent attack 'showing the practised hand of a Somme pilot'—which could have been McCudden or Fox—or both since they were flying Pups with only minor differences in appearance.

16/17 June, 1917 (Night)

Target: London.
Enemy forces: Navy Zeppelins L42 (Kptlt Martin Dietrich), L48 (Kptlt F. G. Eichler); L44 and L45 returned early.
Results: Three killed, 16 injured, £28,159 damage.
Defence sorties: 32 plus.

RNAS

Felixstowe: Curtiss H-12s 8677, 03.00–09.21 hr; 8662, 04.20–09.00 hr; Sopwith Baby 8137, 02.55–04.20 hr.

Manston: B.E.2cs 8298, 00.40–03.35 hr; 8413, 01.10–03.45 hr (Throwley, due to weather); 8628, 01.15–01.45 hr returned due to weather, 02.00–03.00 hr.

Yarmouth: B.E.2cs 8619 (Flt Sub-Lieut C. S. Iron) took off 23.15 hr, landed Aldeburgh, took off 03.00 hr for Yarmouth; 8608 (Flt Sub-Lieut T. G. C. Wood) 03.17–05.17 hr; Sopwith Pups 9904 (Flt Lieut E. Cadbury) took off 03.20 hr; 9905 (Flt Lieut G. W. R. Fane) 03.20–04.05 hr; Sopwith Babies N1108 (Flt Sub-Lieut H. B. Brenton) 03.25–05.45 hr; N1064 (Flt Sub-Lieut G. H. Bittles) 03.25–05.05 hr; Curtiss H-12 8666 (Flt Cdr V. Nicholl, Flt Sub-Lieut R. Leckie) 04.05–08.50 hr.

Bacton: One B.E.2c sortie—details not known.

Burgh Castle: B.E.2c 8629 (Flt Sub-Lieut C. V. Halford Thompson) took off

23.15 hr; 8629 (Flt Sub-Lieut F. W. Walker) landed 04.30 hr; 8301 (Flt Sub-Lieut Halford Thompson) 01.15–03.35 hr.

Covehithe: B.E.2c 8625 (Flt Lieut G. H. Simpson) took off 23.15 hr and 03.00–04.20 hr.

RFC

No.37 Squadron, A Flight, Goldhanger: B.E.2e 7237 (Lieut G. D. F. Keddie) 03.07–04.04 hr; B.E.12 6610 (Lieut L. P. Watkins) 02.06–04.03 hr; R.E.7s 2232 (Capt W. Sowrey) 01.54–02.30 hr, returned with engine trouble; 2231 (Capt C. A. Ridley) 02.43–04.12 hr.

No.37 Squadron, C Flight, Rochford: B.E.2d 5778 (Capt C. B. Cooke) 03.21–05.00 hr; B.E.2e 6820 (2nd Lieut H. A. Edwardes) 03.22–05.20 hr.

No.50 Squadron: Details not recorded. All aerodromes affected by fog. 2nd Lieut A. J. Arkell forced landed near Faversham without damage. An unspecified aircraft damaged its undercarriage landing at a No.50 Squadron aerodrome—presumably Manston B.E.2c 8413 at Throwley.

Experimental Station, Orfordness: B.E.2c A8896 (Lieut E. W. Clarke) 01.50–04.45 hr (Covehithe); F.E.2b B401 (Lieut F. D. Holder, Sgt S. Ashby) 01.55–04.05 hr; D.H.2 A5058 (Capt R. H. M. S. Saundby) 02.55–03.50 hr.

Strasser's imprudent decision to mount a Zeppelin raid on London during a short mid-summer night was a major factor contributing to the destruction of one of the two airships which reached England.

Of six vessels detailed for the raid, two could not leave their sheds because of strong winds and two turned back with engine failure. Only L42 and L48 participated, the latter being the first of the new five-engined U-Class Zeppelins designed from the outset to operate at 20,000 ft. On board was Korvettenkapitän Viktor Schütze, who had taken command of the Naval Airship Service after Strasser's elevation to Leader of Airships.

After sighting the Suffolk coast at 21.30 hr, Dietrich in L42 flew south intending to make landfall at Dungeness, but strong winds affected navigation and at 02.00 hr he bombed Ramsgate, having abandoned any idea of reaching London. None of the naval aircraft from Manston made sightings, though one machine was spotted from the airship. This could have been an RNAS aircraft, or one from No.50 Squadron, which attempted to operate from its fog-affected aerodromes. One of L42's 660 lb bombs hit a naval ammunition store, causing considerable damage.

L48 was reported about 40 miles off Harwich at 23.34 hr and at some point thereafter—accounts are conflicting—experienced trouble with two engines and was further hampered by a compass failure. It is unlikely that the faults had been rectified when she crossed the coast near Orfordness around 01.45 hr at 17–18,000 ft, and the crew's efficiency in tackling the problems was doubtless impaired by the effects of anoxia, while Schütze's continuous hectoring must have done nothing to improve matters. At 02.50 hr, bombs aimed at Harwich fell harmlessly in fields five miles to the north. L48 then called base for a wireless bearing, and the reply included news that tailwinds for the homeward flight could be expected at lower altitudes. With her speed now reduced to about 33 mph by engine troubles, the airship came down to 13–14,000 ft and headed northeast.

By chance, L48 had made landfall just north of the Orfordness armament experimental station, which had been given a home-defence commitment after the onset of daylight raiding and on this night received a preliminary warning at

F.E.2b B401, crewed by Lieut F. D. Holder and Sgt S. Ashby, from Orfordness, attacked L48 on 16/17 June, 1917. The aircraft is shown as modified for experiments in cutting barrage-balloon cables.

21.58 hr. The airship arrived overhead at about 01.50 hr, her engines barely audible, and remained in view for some 20 min.

Clarke and Holder were both airborne within five minutes of the sighting and both followed L48 towards Harwich, though Clarke could not get his B.E. above 11,000 ft and fired four drums at long range without expecting—or achieving—any result.

Holder was at 14,200 ft—still well below L48—after she had bombed, and he had some difficulty in climbing and at the same time following her erratic course, but both he and Ashby, his gunner, opened fire regardless. Holder's front gun then jammed and would not clear. At about 03.10 hr, just inland from Aldeburgh, the Zeppelin started descending and Holder followed, enabling Ashby to fire four more drums. Five miles beyond Leiston, after firing 30 rounds

Capt R. H. M. S (later Air Marshal Sir Robert) Saundby, who flew the Orfordness D.H.2 which contributed to the destruction of L48 on 16/17 June, 1917; and (*right*) Capt Loudon Pierce Watkins—a portrait taken after his successful attack on L48.

from the fifth drum at 300 yards' range, Ashby's Lewis jammed, and as Holder turned away for him to clear it, the Zeppelin began to fall in flames.

While L48 had been limping towards the coast she was again spotted from Orfordness aerodrome and the CO, Maj P. C. Cooper, had authorized Robert Saundby to take off in a D.H.2 in case she eluded the two slower machines already airborne. Saundby was an experienced D.H.2 pilot, though he had done no previous night flying, nor was this particular machine equipped for it. However, dawn was approaching and if necessary the landing could be delayed until daylight. He saw the airship at 03.10 hr and climbed under its tail, firing three drums at rapidly shortening range. Halfway through the third, fire started at one point and rapidly spread along the hull.

Shortly after L48 was first seen, Cooper had conscientiously notified No.37 Squadron headquarters at Woodham Mortimer and the CO ordered patrols from Goldhanger and Rochford. The squadron's 1½ Strutters were regarded essentially as day fighters, and the only reasonable performer among the six aircraft despatched was the B.E.12 flown by Pierce Watkins, from Toronto. He was detailed to search specifically in the Harwich area.

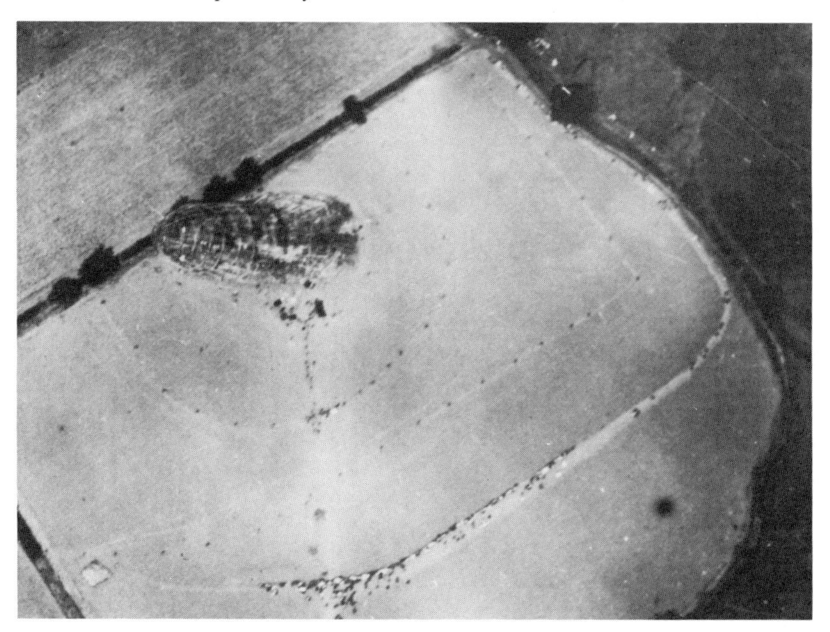

The remains of L48 photographed at 12 noon on 17 June, 1917.

Watkins came upon L48 when she was making for the coast at about 13–14,000 ft. He was 2,000 ft below and fired two drums while halving this distance. He then decided that he must get closer to achieve results and climbed to 500 ft under the Zeppelin before firing a third drum. He began with three short bursts, then delivered a long one, starting a fire at the tail which quickly spread. L48 came down at 03.30 hr, at Holly Tree Farm, Theberton, and three crew members survived the impact and fire—though one died from his injuries 17 months later.

A navy salvage party removing the nose section from the wreckage of L48. (*J. S. Waddell*)

With two single-seater pilots and the crew of a two-seater all convinced that they alone were responsible for L48's destruction it was clearly difficult to allocate specific credit. Holder and Ashby did not claim to have actually seen the fire start from the impact of their bullets, as did Watkins and Saundby, but their final attack is as likely to have caused the lethal damage. Cooper was convinced that the Orfordness D.H.2 and F.E.2b were responsible, and his report to Home Defence Group stated that those aircraft could see each other—but no additional machine—the whole time while manoeuvring around the Zeppelin. However, in their own reports the pilots were less specific, Saundby seeing 'another machine higher than myself . . . firing bursts of tracer', while Holder described 'tracer from a machine below the Zeppelin'. Watkins noticed one aircraft firing tracer fairly early in the engagement, then lost sight of it until just before he fired his last drum.

All the evidence pointed to a shared victory by Watkins, Saundby and Holder/Ashby, but the War Office arbitrarily awarded prime credit to Watkins. The pundits who made this equivocal decision may have been a little sceptical at the over-confident tone of Cooper's report, and felt that in the wider interests of morale, credit should go to a full-time home-defence squadron rather than to the part-timers from Orfordness.

While the L48 drama was nearing its final act, Dietrich in L42, having bombed what he claimed to be Dover and Deal, was passing perilously close to the East Anglian coast on his way home. L42 was seen by five aircraft from Yarmouth, but only one managed a brief attack. Bittles spotted her at 11,000 ft about 30 miles east of Lowestoft and fired a drum from 100 ft below, whereupon she shot up to an altitude far beyond the reach of his Sopwith Baby. Brenton then saw the Zeppelin and chased it for 70 mins without being able to get within range.

Cadbury and Fane, airborne in Pups at first light, just in time to see L48 go down, soon located L42 at 16,000 ft but could not get high enough to attack. Cadbury gave up when a petrol pipe broke—he returned plugging the leak with a finger—and Fane persevered for another ten minutes before deciding that pursuit was useless. Nicholl and Leckie found the Zeppelin 45 miles east of Yarmouth and tailed her for 95 mins until ten miles off the Friesian Islands without being able to persuade their ponderous H-12 flying-boat high enough to even consider an attack.

There were puzzling indications of a third airship over the country and Yarmouth was alerted after alleged sightings near Norwich, and from Lowestoft at 03.00 hr. Brenton reported seeing another Zeppelin at 10,000 ft out to sea after he had abandoned pursuit of L42.

The destruction of Germany's newest Zeppelin provided a tonic for morale at a time when the air services were still groping for an answer to the Gotha menace. The night's operations also confirmed that provided the 'height climbers' maintained their planned operating altitudes they were virtually immune—but they were easily located in the short, light summer night, and descent to the modest fighter heights invited attack.

Flt Lieut G. W. R. Fane running-up Sopwith Pup 9905 at RNAS Yarmouth. This was the aircraft in which he vainly chased L42 out to sea after seeing L48 shot down on 16/17 June, 1917. (*Gp Capt G. E. Livock*)

4 July, 1917 (Daylight)

Targets: Harwich, Felixstowe.
Enemy forces: 25 Gothas despatched, 18 Gothas attacked.
Results: 17 killed, 30 injured, £2,065 damage.
Defence sorties: 103.

RNAS

Dover: Sopwith Pups 3691, 07.38–08.25 hr; N6202, 07.40–08.45 hr; Sopwith Baby 8145, 08.25–09.10 hr.

Manston: Sopwith Triplanes N5382, 07.50–09.00 hr; N5383, 07.50–09.00 hr; N5424, 07.50–09.00 hr; Sopwith Camel B3774, 07.40–09.10 hr; Sopwith Pup 9907, 07.40–09.10 hr; Bristol Scout D 8989, 07.40–09.10 hr.

Walmer: Sopwith Pups N6438 (Flt Sub-Lieut W. H. Chisam) 08.10–09.15 hr; N6439 (Flt Sub-Lieut W. M. Lusby) 07.50–08.25 hr.

Yarmouth: Sopwith Babies 8149, 07.50–08.05 hr and 08.25–10.10 hr; N1107, 08.05–09.25 hr; N1109, 08.25–10.10 hr; N1110, 08.25–10.10 hr.

Burgh Castle: Farman F.40 9160, 07.55–09.00 hr.

Covehithe: Bristol Scout C 1257, 07.30–08.15 hr.

RFC

No.37 Squadron, A Flight, Goldhanger: B.E.12 6610 (Lieut L. F. Hutcheon) 07.42–08.41 hr; B.E.12as A6318 (Lieut R. F. Oakes) 07.42–08.28 hr: A4032 (Capt W. Sowrey) 07.41–08.41 hr; A6312 (2nd Lieut H. A. Blain) 07.50–08.41 hr.

No.37 Squadron, B Flight, Stow Maries: Sopwith Pups A651 (Capt C. A. Ridley) 07.29–09.20 hr; B1771 (Capt E. B. Mason) 07.29–09.21 hr; B1765 (Capt E. S. Cotterill) 07.29–09.21 hr; B1764 (Lieut J. Potter) 07.30–07.56 hr, returned with gun jam.

No.37 Squadron, C Flight, Rochford: Sopwith 1½ Strutters A8251 (Capt C. B. Cooke) 07.33–09.08 hr; A8250 (2nd Lieut H. A. Edwardes) 07.33–08.57 hr; A8271 (2nd Lieut J. E. R. Young) 07.36–09.10 hr; A8275 (Capt C. E. Holman) 08.19–09.05 hr.

No.39 Squadron, A Flight, North Weald: B.E.12s 6488 (2nd Lieut C. L. Brock) 07.39–08.40 hr; A6326 (Capt S. R. Stammers) 07.40–08.46 hr; B.E.12a A593 (Lieut E. M. Gilbert) 07.38–09.30 hr.

No.39 Squadron, B Flight, Suttons Farm: B.E.12 6480 (Lieut E. S. Moulton-Barrett) 07.39–08.35 hr S.E.5s A8941 (Capt J. I. Mackay) 07.38–08.50 hr; A8924 (Capt Hope) 07.39–08.36 hr.

One of the S.E.5s, A8941, urgently allotted to No.39 Squadron, Suttons Farm, to help counter the Gotha raids. It was flown by Capt J. I. Mackay on 4 July, 1917.

No.39 Squadron, C Flight, Hainault: B.E.12a A6349 (Capt O. V. Thomas) 07.33–08.35 hr; Armstrong Whitworth F.K.8 B212 (Capt W. H. Haynes, AM Gellan) 07.38–08.37 hr.

No.50 Squadron, B Flight, Throwley: Sopwith Pups B1711 (2nd Lieut N. E. Chandler) 07.40–08.50 hr; A638 (Lieut R. W. le Gallais) 07.42–08.43 hr; B1769 (2nd Lieut S. Cockerell) 07.43–08.22 hr; A6153 (2nd Lieut N. F. Perris) 08.05–08.20 hr, returned with engine trouble; Armstrong Whitworth F.K.8s B224 (2nd Lieut W. R. Oulton) 07.45–09.21 hr; B238 (2nd Lieut F. V. Bryant) 07.48–09.05 hr; B247 (2nd Lieut F. A. D. Grace) 07.58–09.15 hr; Vickers E.S.1 7759 (2nd Lieut I. M. Davies) 07.48–08.36 hr.

No.65 Squadron, Wye: Sopwith Camel B3977 (Capt L. E. Whitehead) 07.40–09.00 hr.

No.56 Squadron, A Flight, Rochford: S.E.5s—six sorties, 07.33–09.30 hr.

No.56 Squadron, B and C Flights, Bekesbourne: S.E.5s—13 sorties, 07.31–09.30 hr.

No.35(T) Squadron, Northolt: Bristol Fighter A7136 (Capt A. C. Wright, Capt Bagnall) 08.02–08.46 hr.

No.40(T) Squadron, Croydon: Sopwith Pups A6228 (Sgt Parry) 07.33–08.30 hr; A7319 (Lieut Cummings) took off 07.33 hr, landed at Goldhanger.

No.56(T) Squadron, London Colney: Spads A8803 (Lieut A. Wearne) 08.00–10.00 hr; A8804 (Lieut J. W. Potts) took off 07.45 hr, landed at Stow Maries.

No.2 Aircraft Acceptance Park, Hendon: D.H.4s A7483 (Lieut A. G. Alderson) 07.45–08.15 hr, returned with engine trouble; A7452 (Lieut D. W. Clappen) 07.45–08.50 hr; A7500 (Lieut F. L. Hambly) 07.50–08.45 hr; A7508 (Lieut J. B. Jaques) took off 07.55 hr, landed at Goldhanger with engine trouble.

No.8 Aircraft Acceptance Park, Lympne: R.E.8s A4637 (Lieut J. L. S. Gill) 07.45–09.55 hr; A3855 (Sgt H. G. Thompson) took off 09.50 hr; D.H.4s A7509 (Lieut R. S. Carroll) took off 09.46 hr; A7525 (Sgt A. Reffell) took off 09.55 hr.

Experimental Station, Orfordness: Bristol Fighter A3303 (Lieut F. D. Holder, Lieut H. L. Billinton) 07.30–08.45 hr; F.E.2d A6513 (Capt L. J. Wackett, Lieut F. W. Musson) 07.30–08.20 hr.

Testing Squadron, Martlesham Heath: Sopwith Camels, (Maj H. L. Cooper) 07.35–08.30 hr; (Lieut K. S. Henderson) 07.45–08.30 hr; D.H.4 A7436 (Capt J. Palethorpe, AM J. O. Jessop) 06.50–07.20 hr; A7436 (Capt Palethorpe, Lieut Hoffert) 07.40–08.45 hr.

No.66 Squadron, Calais: Sopwith Pups A6191 (2nd Lieut J. W. Boumphrey) 08.20–09.30 hr; A6197 (2nd Lieut F. A. Smith) 08.20–09.30 hr; A6198 (2nd Lieut J. B. Hine) 08.20–10.50 hr; A6201 (2nd Lieut S. J. Oliver) 08.20–10.35 hr; A6205 (Lieut G. E. C. Round) took off 08.20 hr, landed at Bekesbourne; A6215 (2nd Lieut C. C. Morley) took off 08.20 hr, landed at Lympne; B1703 (Capt J. O. Andrews) 08.20–09.30 hr; B1710 (Lieut C. C. S. Montgomery) 08.20–10.40 hr; B1724 (2nd Lieut T. C. Luke) 08.20–09.30 hr; B1725 (2nd Lieut W. R. Keast) took off 08.20 hr, landed at Dover; B1731 (2nd Lieut E. H. Lascelles) 08.20–10.45 hr; B1744 (2nd Lieut R. A. Stedman) 08.20–10.00 hr; B1746 (Capt C. C. Sharpe) 08.20–10.40 hr; B1747 (2nd Lieut E. L. Ardley) 08.20–10.45 hr; B1756 (2nd Lieut D. F. Cox) took off 08.20 hr, landed at Lympne; B1757 (2nd Lieut J. M. Warnock), 08.20–10.40 hr; B1758 (Capt G. W. Robarts) took off 08.20 hr, landed at Lympne; B1762 (Lieut T. V. Hunter) 08.20–10.40 hr.

Rudolf Kleine, who took command of the Gotha squadron after Brandenburg's injury in a flying accident, possessed the 'press-on' spirit to an almost obsessive degree and was eager to emulate his predecessor's success. However, he appreciated that a London raid required ideal conditions, and while awaiting these was content to start his leadership with what a later bomber generation would call a 'piece of cake'.

Harwich, with its naval installations, and the RNAS station at Felixstowe lay on opposite sides of the Orwell estuary, and out at sea there were fewer lightships to give early warning than lay along the route to more southerly targets. Raiders could therefore expect to bomb and be well on their way home before defending aircraft could hope to reach them.

On this occasion defence reaction was slower than the enemy's most optimistic expectations. Heavy engine sounds out to sea were reported from Orfordness at

06.55 hr, and five minutes later the Gothas approached the coast near Bawdsey. The attack took place at 07.20–25 hr, and many of the Harwich bombs fell in the water. Two 26-pounders dropped at Felixstowe destroyed one H-12 flying-boat and damaged another. The AA gunners, hampered by low coastal cloud, fired 135 rounds without success.

Home Defence Group did not give the 'patrol' order until 07.26 hr, possibly because they first assumed that the Gothas would make for London. Less explicable is the failure of No.66 Squadron—moved to Calais for the specific purpose of covering the bombers' arrival and departure routes—to get airborne in time to play any part. Records show that No.66 was not given 'patrol' order until 08.10 hr, because of what Home Forces intelligence called 'some error in liaison'—which could mean simply that a harassed duty officer forgot about the squadron across the Channel. The stop-gap system to meet this eventuality by acting on information from Dunkirk also failed. Had the unit got away 30 min earlier, eighteen Pups might have been straddling the Gothas' return route near the Belgian coast.

The sole RFC encounter happened quite by chance. John Palethorpe, from the Testing Squadron at Martlesham, had been airborne for 15 min faced with several tedious hours' endurance testing a RAF-engined D.H.4. He was accompanied by Air Mechanic James Jessop. At 07.05 hr he saw the eighteen Gothas at 14,000 ft in straggling formation spread over about five miles, moving southwest across the coast. Rather rashly he went for the centre machine, but his front gun refused to work and the D.H.4 came under fire from several Gothas at about 300 yards' range. Jessop fired one drum as they closed to about 100 yards and was then hit in the heart and killed by an enemy bullet.

Palethorpe turned away, with no option but to land, and saw the whole formation swing to the east. Twenty minutes later he was airborne again with another gunner. He was awarded the MC for his determination and aggression.

Capt John Palethorpe, awarded the MC for his determined attack on the Gothas which bombed Harwich and Felixstowe on 4 July, 1917; and (*right*) Lieut (later Gp Capt) E. S. Moulton-Barrett, No.39 Squadron, the only S.E.5 pilot to engage the Gothas during the 1917 daylight raids. During the Second World War he administered the first Hurricane 'catafighters' on merchant ships. (*Mrs E. Moulton-Barrett*)

Some of the No.56 Squadron pilots at Bekesbourne in June 1917: left to right, Lieut C. A. Lewis, Capt G. H. Bowman, Capt I. H. D. Henderson, Lieut V. P. Cronyn and Lieut A. P. F. Rhys Davids—with Thais Marson, daughter of the squadron Recording Officer.

When No.66 Squadron's Pups were eventually airborne at 08.20 hr, half were ordered to patrol between Dunkirk and the North Hinder lightship—a sound idea but for the fact that the returning enemy aircraft were already about to cross the Belgian coast. The remainder was allotted a more westerly area. Unaware of the futility of their task, pilots diligently searched for two hours, with cloud increasing until they lost sight of sea or land, and some became detached from their formations to lose themselves. Five came down on English aerodromes—and records include an intriguing note that Round, who put down at Bekesbourne, did not return for two days and was listed as missing.

Nor did the other squadrons—including No.56 transferred to England from the Western Front—stand any better chance of finding the enemy, since they also took off too late and patrolled areas well south of the bombers' homeward track. The S.E.5s could conceivably have still caught them had there been any rapid decision, or means to convey it, to engage in pursuit.

An encouraging feature of the day's operations was the appearance of some Sopwith Pups in Home Defence Group, though these were dispersed among flights in Nos.37 and 50 Squadrons rather than grouped into a single unit.

Again it was the RNAS at Dunkirk which came closest to success. Some twenty aircraft took off to seek the returning Gothas, and five Camels of No.4 Squadron found them about 30 miles northwest of Ostende. Flt Cdr A. M. Shook and Flt Sub-Lieut S. E. Ellis both reported attacking aircraft which went down emitting quantities of black smoke, while Shook saw another descending with an engine stopped. These were not formally claimed as destroyed, and the Germans admitted no losses. They reported six inconclusive combats.

7 July, 1917 (Daylight)

Target: London.
Enemy forces: 24 Gothas despatched, 22 Gothas attacked.
Results: 57 killed, 193 injured, £205,622 damage.
Defence sorties: 108. Note: Records for this date have much detail missing.

RNAS

Dover: Sopwith Pup N6177 took off 10.30 hr and returned with engine trouble; Sopwith Babies 8145 (Flt Sub-Lieut H. H. Gonyou) 09.40–10.25 hr, returned with engine trouble; N1011 (Flt Sub-Lieut A. C. Reid) 11.15–11.40 hr.

Eastchurch: Sopwith Camels B3795 (Flt Cdr C. Draper) 09.37–11.37 hr; B3798 (Flt Lieut S. R. Watkins) 09.41–11.30 hr.

Grain: Sopwith Pup 9912 (Flt Cdr C. T. Freeman) landed 10.15 hr, and 10.25–11.19 hr.

Manston: Sopwith Pup 9907 (Flt Sub-Lieut C. H. Fitzherbert) 09.27–11.15 hr and 11.22–13.25 hr; Sopwith Camels B3774 (Flt Lieut J. E. Scott) took off 09.27 hr and 11.00–12.17 hr; B3761 (Flt Sub-Lieut A. H. Lofft) 09.27–10.05 hr, returned with engine trouble; B3773 (Flt Sub-Lieut Lofft), took off 11.05 hr, forced landed near Manningtree; Sopwith Triplanes N5424 (Sqn Cdr C. H. Butler) took off 09.35 hr and 11.00–13.00 hr; N5382 (Flt Sub-Lieut R. H. Daly) took off 09.35 hr and 10.55 hr; N5383 (Flt Sub-Lieut A. C. Burt) took off 09.35 hr and 11.05–13.46 hr, crashed landing; N509 (Flt Sub-Lieut M. A. Harker) took off 11.00 hr; Bristol Scout Ds N5391 (Flt Sub-Lieut Lord Ossulton) 11.20–13.00 hr; N5392 (Flt Sub-Lieut S. Quayle) took off 11.00 hr; N5398 (Flt Sub-Lieut H. C. Lemon) 11.50–12.45 hr.

Walmer: Sopwith Pups 9947 (Flt Lieut S. Kemball) 09.30–11.35 hr; N6439 (Flt Sub-Lieut W. M. Lusby) 09.30–10.25 hr; N6439 (Flt Sub-Lieut W. H. Chisam) 10.50–12.10 hr; N6441 (Flt Cdr T. C. Vernon) took off 09.30 hr, landed at Furnes; N6442 (Flt Sub-Lieut J. A. Shaw) 09.30–11.35 hr.

RFC

No.37 Squadron, A Flight, Goldhanger: B.E.12 6610 (Lieut L. P. Watkins) 09.38–11.30 hr; B.E.12as A4032 (Capt W. Sowrey) 09.35–11.45 hr; A6318 (Lieut R. F. Oakes) 09.38–11.52 hr; plus two B.E.12/12a sorties, one B.E.2e sortie and one R.E.7 sortie—details not recorded.

No.37 Squadron, B Flight, Stow Maries: Sopwith Pups B1771 (Capt E. B. Mason) 09.28–10.36 hr; B1764 (2nd Lieut G. A. Thompson) 09.29–11.05 hr; A653 (Capt C. A. Ridley) 09.30–11.44 hr; B1765 (Capt E. S. Cotterill) 09.46–11.47 hr; plus two sorties—details not recorded.

No.37 Squadron, C Flight, Rochford: Sopwith 1½ Strutters A8251 (Capt C. B. Cooke, Lieut A. A. C. Garnons-Williams) 09.28–11.50 hr; A8275 (Capt C. E. Holman, AM Burtenshaw) 09.28–11.36 hr; A8271 (2nd Lieut J. E. R. Young, AM C. C. Taylor) took off 09.31 hr—shot down, crew killed; A8250 (2nd Lieut H. A. Edwardes, Lieut Brooks) 09.32–11.45 hr; A8233 (Lieut L. F. Hutcheon, Sgt MacDonald) 09.34–11.25 hr; plus one sortie—details not recorded.

No.39 Squadron, A Flight, North Weald: B.E.12a A6326 (Lieut E. M. Gilbert) 09.35–11.15 hr; plus one B.E.12a sortie, 10.31–11.30 hr.

No.39 Squadron, B Flight, Suttons Farm: B.E.12 6480 (Lieut R. S. Bozman) 09.35–11.43 hr; unspecified B.E.12 took off 09.34 hr, returned with engine trouble; S.E.5 A8939 (Lieut E. S. Moulton-Barrett) 09.35–11.28 hr; unspecified S.E.5 took off 09.34 hr, returned with engine trouble.

No.39 Squadron, C Flight, Hainault: B.E.12/12a, two sorties 09.32–11.55 hr, details not recorded; Armstrong Whitworth F.K.8 B212 (Capt W. H. Haynes, Lieut G. T. Stoneham) 09.35–11.55 hr.

No.50 Squadron, A Flight, Detling: B.E.12a A6313 (2nd Lieut L. Lucas) 09.30–12.10 hr; unspecified B.E.12a, 09.28–12.10 hr.

No.50 Squadron, B Flight, Throwley: Sopwith Pup B1711 (2nd Lieut N. E. Chandler) 09.29–11.27 hr; Armstrong Whitworth F.K.8 B247 (2nd Lieut F. A. D. Grace, 2nd Lieut G. Murray) 09.32–13.00 hr (Orfordness); plus three sorties—details not recorded.

No.50 Squadron, C Flight, Bekesbourne: Vickers E.S.1, one sortie; Sopwith Pups, five sorties—details not recorded.

No.78 Squadron, Chiddingstone Causeway: B.E.12a A601 (Capt S. P. Gamon) 09.46–12.04 hr; unspecified B.E.12a (Lieut H. Hamer) took off 09.39 hr.

No.78 Squadron, Telscombe Cliffs: B.E.12as A595 (Lieut R. F. W. Moore) 09.31–11.54 hr; A6308 (Capt F. Billinge) 09.31–11.54 hr; A592 (Capt G. M. Boumphrey) 09.31–11.54 hr.

No.35(T) Squadron, Northolt: Bristol Fighter A7135 (Capt G. D. Hill, Capt R. Stuart-Wortley) 09.40–11.25 hr; unspecified Bristol Fighter, 09.30–11.15 hr.

No.40(T) Squadron, Croydon: Sopwith Pup A6228 (2nd Lieut R. Martin) 09.25–11.55 hr; plus two sorties, 09.39–12.10 hr—details not recorded.

No.56(T) Squadron, London Colney: Spad, one sortie 09.52–10.05 hr, returned with gun jam.

No.62(T) Squadron, Dover: Sopwith Pup (2nd Lieut J. C. Hopkins) 09.40–11.55 hr.

No.63(T) Squadron, Joyce Green: Sopwith Pups A7311 (Capt J. T. B. McCudden) 10.00–11.45 hr (took off from Dover); A6230 (2nd Lieut W. G. Salmon) take-off time not recorded, shot down, pilot killed.

No.198 Depot Squadron, Rochford: Vickers F.B.12C A7351 (Maj B. F. Moore) 09.28–11.03 hr.

No.2 Aircraft Acceptance Park, Hendon: D.H.4s A7508 (Lieut F. L. Hambly, 2nd Lieut M. A. E. Cremetti) 09.35–12.03 hr; A7483 (Lieut D. W. Clappen, AM Wills) 09.29–11.00 hr; plus three D.H.4 sorties, details not recorded; D.H.5 A9408 (2nd Lieut L. N. Mitchell) 09.37–11.30 hr.

No.7 Aircraft Acceptance Park, Kenley: F.E.8 one sortie, took off 10.30 hr.

No.8 Aircraft Acceptance Park, Lympne: Bristol Fighter—three sorties; F.E.2d—one sortie; F.E.8—two sorties; D.H.5—one sortie; Armstrong Whitworth F.K.8—one sortie—details not recorded.

Experimental Station, Orfordness: Bristol Fighter A3303 (Lieut F. D. Holder, Lieut F. W. Musson) 09.50–12.05 hr; Sopwith Triplane N5430 (Capt V. Brown) 10.15–11.35 hr; D.H.2 A5058, 09.50–12.05 hr; F.E.2b, Sopwith 1½ Strutter, Armstrong Whitworth F.K.8, R.E.8, one sortie each—details not recorded.

Testing Squadron, Martlesham Heath: Sopwith Camel B3751 (Capt H. T. Tizard) 10.00–11.45 hr; unspecified Sopwith Camel, 09.45–12.00 hr; D.H.4 A7436 (Capt J. Palethorpe, AM F. James) 09.45–11.10 hr (Rochford).

The second daylight raid on London aroused intense indignation at all levels. The man in the street wanted to know why, six weeks after the Folkestone attack, large enemy formations could still fly with impunity over the country. Cabinet ministers asked why Service chiefs had permitted the return of the two Western Front fighter squadrons without Government blessing—but were doubtless much relieved that the public was unaware of those moves. The Service chiefs were embarrassed because by electing to raid London only 24 hr after those redeployments were completed, the Germans had made them look a little foolish.

But the story was not one of unmitigated gloom. A new high total of 108 defence sorties was flown and a few pilots managed to attack the raiders before they reached central London. Another twenty or so engaged the returning bombers, shooting one down—though two RFC aircraft were lost. Casualties were lower than in the first London raid.

The initial sighting report from the Kentish Knock lightship at 09.14 hr, giving an accurate count of twenty-two Gothas, was received by the RNAS commander at Chatham two minutes later. There was the usual slight time-lag in passing the message on to the army network, and Home Defence Group began issuing the 'patrol' order at 09.24 hr. Meanwhile the Gotha force crossed the mouth of the Crouch at about 09.45 hr—less one machine suffering from engine trouble which had broken away to bomb Margate. Kleine flew at the head of two flanking formations, each of eight, with four aircraft bringing up the rear apparently having some difficulty in keeping station. The force continued almost due west to Hendon, where the leader turned southeast, causing the following aircraft to spread out considerably. The bombs fell between 10.20 and 10.25 hr in a rough triangle bounded by Kentish Town, Hackney and Tower Hill.

There was an uncharacteristic and unexplained delay of some ten minutes before any RNAS machines were airborne from Manston, which meant that Scott and Fitzherbert covering the Burnham area arrived too late, while Butler, Daly and Burt, detailed to patrol over the aerodrome in Sopwith Triplanes, were still on the ground when the single Gotha bombed Margate at about 09.30 hr. After it became apparent that the real threat was to London, the fighters were recalled to refuel in readiness for the returning raiders.

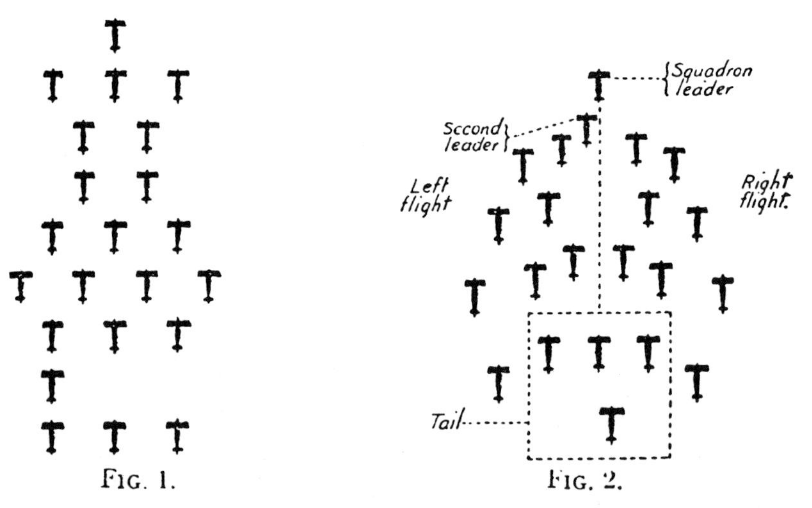

These diagrams from an Air Ministry publication of October 1918 represent an official portrayal of the Gotha formation of 7 July, 1917. The bombers were said to have crossed the coast grouped as in Fig. 1, and changed to the Fig. 2 pattern on approaching London, maintaining unbroken formation throughout the return flight. This is contradicted by the gaggle shown in the apparently genuine photograph opposite.

This unique photograph shows the entire Gotha formation of twenty-one returning from London on 7 July, 1917. Newspapers generally printed crude montage pictures with aircraft scraping the rooftops, but this untidy formation is unlikely to have been faked. Any one of the trailing aircraft in the original picture could have been the straggler mentioned by several British pilots. (*Public Record Office*)

Sopwith Pup A653 flown by Capt C. A. Ridley, No.37 Squadron, on 7 July, 1917, shown with the normal armament of one Vickers gun. This aircraft was later transferred to No.61 Squadron, and written off after it had collided with an Avro trainer just after take-off at Rochford on 6 October. The pilot, Lieut J. D. Belgrave, escaped with slight concussion. (*J. M. Bruce/G. S. Leslie collection*)

From the RFC, No.37 Squadron was well situated to cover the northeastern approaches to the capital, though only its few Pups, most of them up-dated with the 100 hp Monosoupape engine and an upper wing-mounted Lewis to supplement the synchronized Vickers gun, were capable of overtaking the bombers before they reached the target.

Mason caught them over Billericay and had difficulty in keeping up when his engine started misfiring. However, after shooting indiscriminately into the formation from below, he concentrated on the right-hand rearmost aircraft and fired eight bursts while closing from 200 to 100 yards. These had no visible effect, and his engine then began missing badly enough for him to break off and return home. After landing he found four enemy bullet holes in his Pup's interplane struts, top main wing spar and wing fabric.

Cotterill was not far behind but after firing ten short bursts at two of the bombers his Vickers jammed. He then used his Lewis to attack a Gotha from the supposedly blind area underneath, and immediately saw bullet holes appear in his own wings as the German gunner fired through the fuselage tunnel. His Lewis then jammed, so he landed at Hainault to have both guns rectified, and although on the ground for only eight minutes, was unable to catch the bombers on their return flight.

Thompson found his engine revolutions much reduced by an oiled-up plug and had only reached 8,000 ft when he sighted the enemy. He got within range over London and saw tracers from his Lewis pass through the wings of his first selected target. He then put up his nose and aimed at another Gotha, only for his Vickers to jam after one round, and when he cleared the gun his engine was running so badly that he was outpaced. On inspecting his Pup after landing he was shaken to find a neat group of four bullet holes around the seat.

William Sowrey caught the bombers over Romford, but his B.E.12a was incapable of getting within 1,000 ft of their height, and two drums of Lewis at the tailmost machine had no effect. He maintained contact with the formation until it bombed, after which the Gothas climbed away and left him standing.

Ernest Gilbert, No.39 Squadron, patrolling in a B.E.12a between Hainault and Joyce Green, engaged the inbound Gothas over the Ongar area with both guns, causing two of the pilots to start weaving. Then his Vickers jammed, and while he tried without success to clear the stoppage the bombers drew a long way ahead. He attacked again as they returned over the City, using all his remaining Lewis drums. Gilbert's report included the remarkable statement that the enemy formation was 'escorted by two or three small, dark-coloured scouts'. Having flown on the Western Front, Gilbert cannot have been completely ignorant of aircraft recognition, and his comment might have been an ironic suggestion that British fighters were not showing enough aggression—not realizing that some apparently 'escorting' were experiencing gun troubles, or out of ammunition.

Moulton-Barrett in one of the three S.E.5s recently allotted to No.39 Squadron, spotted the enemy at 10.15 hr over north London and had no difficulty in overtaking. He fired at three Gothas in quick succession, then concentrated on one flying a little apart from the rest, giving it his last two drums of Lewis and seeing tracer enter the fuselage below the nose cockpit. Out of ammunition, he flew on the north side of the formation as far as the coast, hoping to edge it within range of the Shoeburyness guns.

The No.39 Squadron F.K.8 crewed by Haynes and Stoneham trailed the Gothas from Epping to central London and back to the coast without ever being able to close sufficiently for an effective attack, and a parting gesture of 37 rounds fired at the rearmost group of three produced no result.

The only other interceptions of the inbound raiders were by training squadrons and supporting units flying good-performance aircraft conveniently based to gain the necessary altitude for attack. Croydon-based aircraft patrolled from Biggin Hill to Joyce Green, while Northolt machines reinforced the Joyce Green–Chingford line. Hendon pilots, although allocated to the Woolwich area, in the event engaged the enemy well to the east.

Ferry pilot Donald Clappen, flying a Hendon D.H.4, found the formation crossing the coast and positioned behind, but suffered an immediate Vickers stoppage which he could not rectify. He manoeuvred to give Wills, his gunner, a target from below, and during several attacks on one Gotha the D.H.4 came under fire from two flanking aircraft. Clappen continued this harassment all the way to London, and while returning over Hornchurch he moved in very close for a final attack, Wills seeing tracers from his last drum entering the Gotha's fuselage. On turning away the D.H.4's engine seized, but there was ample height to glide back to Hendon and a safe landing. The aircraft had been hit in the tail and centre-section area.

Frank Hambly—from the USA—and Max Cremetti in another D.H.4 also fought the Gothas to London and back. After his Vickers had jammed at the outset, Hambly dived through the formation several times hoping to break it up. In a long-drawn-out engagement Cremetti then fired one-and-a-half drums of Lewis into one bomber, which eventually banked steeply and was lost to view. His gun jammed four times, and in desperation he dismantled and reassembled it, only for a burst from another Gotha to put it completely out of action—and shoot away his windscreen. With neither gun working and the engine 'conking'—to use Hambly's word—the sortie was abandoned.

Mitchell in the Hendon D.H.5 saw both D.H.4s in action after his own gun had jammed when he engaged a Gotha, which he described as having one engine stopped.

Hill flying a Bristol Fighter from Northolt was also thwarted by a jamming

Although not in a front-line unit, Sopwith Pup A6228 of No.40 (Training) Squadron, Croydon, flew more operational sorties than some aircraft of the regular home-defence squadrons. It was airborne during four of the daylight raids, and its pilot on 7 July, 1917, 2nd Lieut Robert Martin, engaged a Gotha which bombed London. (*RAF Museum*)

Vickers as he attacked two Gothas straggling slightly on the approach to London. After his observer had fired a few bursts he endeavoured to clear his own gun, but eventually he gave up and decided to carry on with just his observer to do battle. However, the enemy had made too much ground to be overtaken.

Robert Martin, in a Pup from No.40 (Training) Squadron, Croydon, made a pass at one Gotha over London, firing a 50-round burst from 50 yards, which, he said, sent it down in a spinning nose-dive. His report then described how he shook off two others which dived on him. Having lost much height he was unable to catch the formation again as it sped to the coast. Martin's account, with its rather improbable picture of bombers behaving more like fighters, suggests the inexperience of a newly-qualified pilot.

If the fighters achieved no success against the inbound bombers, their attacks at least helped to break up the formation, and it was more of a gaggle which returned eastwards a few miles south of the inbound track, to cross the coast soon after 11.00 hr. Several aircraft were straggling, and the hundreds of bullets aimed at what different pilots described as 'the' tail-ender were probably distributed among various machines.

No.37 Squadron's 1½ Strutter pilots later complained bitterly that, despite official assurances to the contrary, their aircraft could neither overtake nor effectively keep up with the Gothas in level flight. One put the Gothas' speed advantage as high as 20 mph.

Hutcheon saw them west of Burnham at 10.55 hr and got to about 300 ft below the last three in the formation, but fired only 40 rounds from his Vickers before it jammed. His observer fired three drums from his Lewis with no visible result as the bombers gradually pulled away to the coast. Edwardes' Vickers discharged only five rounds before jamming, and he then found it impossible to keep up sufficiently for his gunner to fire even at extreme range. Holman attacked the four rear machines from the flank at 400 yards, but after turning to follow was unable to catch them again. Cooke dived on the rearmost Gotha as the formation crossed the coast, firing a full belt from his Vickers. He continued 30 miles out to sea, but the Sopwith could not keep up and the nine drums fired by his gunner were from too great a range to have more than moral effect.

Watkins and Ridley of No.37 Squadron also made brief attacks. Watkins, in a B.E.12, trailed the bombers to London and back, never really getting within range. Ridley found his Pup unusually slow—for which he blamed the drag created by the top-wing Lewis gun installation—and when he did reach an attacking position, east of the Girdler lightship, his Vickers jammed after one round. His report commented: 'I doubt if attacking underneath is the best position as they [Gothas] can shoot vertically downwards, as is proved by holes in our planes.' This was before he discovered that a main wing spar had been shot through.

Among the more notable encounters by aircraft from support units was that by Palethorpe from Martlesham, flying the D.H.4 he had used on 4 July. Attacking the leading starboard aircraft as the formation flew east over Essex, he found that he had very little speed advantage. His Vickers jammed, so he made a series of passes moving in to 35 yards, enabling James, his gunner, to fire in all seven drums. The Gotha retaliated, and on the final approach Palethorpe was hit in the bottom, and with blood trickling into his boots, landed the badly-shot-about aircraft at Rochford.

Henry Tizard, flying a Martlesham Camel, noticed Moulton-Barrett turn away from his 'escort' task, then himself went for a Gotha crossing the coast. He dived from 17,000 ft, but both Vickers' jammed soon after he opened fire from 100 yards, and although he cleared the starboard gun it failed again during a second attack. With the precision expected from a Farnborough scientist—who later became a leading figure in aviation research—Tizard noted that the port gun jammed with a cross feed after 30 rounds, and the starboard with a defective round after 45.

The prototype Bristol Fighter, A3303, based at Orfordness, flew five sorties against the daylight Gotha raiders. The pilot was Lieut F. D. Holder, and his gunner on 7 July, 1917—the only occasion on which an enemy was engaged—was Lieut F. W. Musson. This photograph was taken when the aircraft visited Rochford.

McCudden was keen to add a Gotha to his 'bag' and was at Dover collecting his Pup after overhaul when readiness was ordered. With the idea of making it less visible when flying above the enemy, the Pup's under surfaces had been painted a pale powder blue. McCudden found the raiders near Southend and made three carefully planned attacks, one from the rear and two on the flank of the hindmost Gotha, closing to 50 yards, without causing visible damage. Reproaching himself for carrying only three Lewis drums, he 'escorted' the bomber for 25 min with the intention of drawing its fire so that other nearby fighters might attack, and his Pup received several bullet holes—one passing through the windscreen. From the unsympathetic tone of his report he was unaware of the gunnery problems being experienced by other pilots—'either our machines did not appreciate my attention, or they did not want to' he wrote, 'but they had a splendid opportunity if they had availed themselves of it'.

Sopwith Triplane N5430, here being flown by Capt Vernon Brown, made five sorties from Orfordness during the Gotha daylight campaign.

Two Orfordness aircraft made contact. Holder in the prototype Bristol Fighter began chasing the formation east of Southend but, after 30 miles and running low on fuel, was not perceptibly gaining, so settled for a 30 round burst at long range. Musson, his observer, fired one drum from his Lewis. Vernon Brown found his Sopwith Triplane had the necessary performance, but was frustrated by a series of gun stoppages and a final irremediable jam.

Moore's sortie in the Vickers F.B.12c, known at Rochford as the 'spider', demonstrated why, despite early promise, this fighter was not chosen for front-line service. After trying to cut off the formation, Moore could make no headway, so fired a drum from 500 yards' range. Then despite every effort he was unable to change the drum, thanks to the gun's inaccessible position.

When the bombers began their return flight, Home Defence Group had ordered the display of ground signals diverting patrols to the Girdler lightship, though the prospects of successful intervention by many aircraft seemed remote. In the event it paid off handsomely.

The leggy and angular lines of the Vickers F.B.12C indicate why it was known as the 'spider'. It flew two sorties while in No.198 Depot Squadron, Rochford.

Frederick Grace, a sugar planter, and George Murray, an architect, who had both travelled from Argentina to enlist, quickly spotted the signal from their No.50 Squadron F.K.8 and were north of the Girdler at 16,000 ft in time to see the enemy approaching from the coast, under attack from a Triplane—probably Brown's. Grace dived on a group of three Gothas, opening fire from 1,000 yards, and Murray attacked with his Lewis. This produced some retaliatory fire, one bullet piercing the F.K.8's port wings and others passing close to its nose.

Grace then turned to another bomber in the rear, flying much lower than the 14,000 ft of the main group. He dived on this machine, firing his Vickers as they closed from 800 to 400 yards, jinking to distract the gunners, then pulled up above its starboard side. Murray took over with his Lewis, and within moments black smoke poured from around the Gotha's centre-section and it dived into the sea, the starboard wing becoming submerged. Shortly afterwards two of the crew were seen on the sinking bomber's port wing, but being short of fuel Grace could do no more than fire Very lights in the hope of attracting ships to the scene. He landed at Orfordness, and some reporting delay caused his aircraft to be listed as missing for a time.

Three aircraft of No.50 Squadron at Bekesbourne, which in aggregate flew at least twenty-seven sorties against enemy day- and night-bombers; Armstrong Whitworth F.K.8 B247 (eleven), Vickers E.S.1 7759 (seven) and B.E.12 6509 (nine). B247 was crewed by 2nd Lieuts F. A. D. Grace and G. Murray when they shot down a Gotha on 7 July, 1917. B.E.12 6509, which operated between November 1916 and February 1918, was mostly flown by Capt J. S. Shaw, who had several unproductive night and day contacts. The Vickers was flown by various pilots, including Capt A. J. Capel, who took the photograph.

Reverting to RNAS activities, reports are not clear whether the Camels flown by Draper and Watkins of the Eastchurch War Flight engaged the enemy on their way to London or during the return—though the latter is more likely. In any case, both had to abandon combat with their guns jammed after firing 100–150 rounds. They both thought they had scored hits.

The Manston pilots who had landed after failing to intercept the inbound raiders, refuelled and took off to try again as they returned. Butler led a patrol north of the Tongue lightship, and after sighting the enemy near the Kentish Knock, the mixed formation of Camels and Triplanes became dispersed during the subsequent chase.

After a 30-min pursuit, Butler fired 100 rounds from his Triplane into one Gotha from close quarters, then administered similar treatment to a second. Breaking off, he saw what he thought was his first target hit the sea and sink at a point about 20 miles west of Ostende. Rowan Daly, also in a Triplane, reported shooting down in flames an aircraft of unspecified type from 17,000 ft, some 15 miles off the coast between Ostende and Zeebrugge. He then followed another machine up the Scheldt estuary, but his gun jammed when he tried to engage. These were probably fighters sent to escort the returning Gothas.

Scott, in a Camel, came up with a Gotha at 8,000 ft about 35 miles east-northeast of the North Foreland and made a prolonged attack, firing 475 rounds, after which it spun into the sea. The tail and part of a wing remained visible on the surface and Scott saw one of the crew swimming.

Lofft had a long chase after three Gothas and was in sight of Walcheren when his Camel closed sufficiently for him to aim a burst of 150–200 rounds into the fuselage of one. It put its nose down as though intending to land, but Lofft did not follow because his engine was running badly and both guns were jammed. By the time he had cleared one the enemy was no longer visible so he headed for home. His engine failed completely soon after crossing the coast 40 miles north of Manston, and he crash-landed near Manningtree, without injuring himself.

So the morning ended with Butler, Scott and Daly each credited by the RNAS with an enemy aircraft definitely destroyed—for which Butler received a Bar to his DSO and Scott and Daly DSCs.

The enemy admitted the loss of only one Gotha, captained by Leut Max Elsner, and the bickering between the Admiralty and GHQ Home Forces over the accreditation of responsibility has already been described. Whereas pilots were often mistaken about the ultimate fate of aircraft apparently falling out of control, it is most improbable that three could wrongly claim to have seen a Gotha hit the sea. Despite small differences in their descriptions of the impact and sinking, the logical conclusion is that they all saw the same aircraft. There are enough significant similarities in the Scott and Grace/Murray reports—the low altitude of the combat, the general appearance of the wreck and the sighting of crew members—to confirm this beyond any reasonable doubt.

It is surprising that none of the pilots reported seeing other aircraft actually attacking, though such situations were not uncommon. Murray mentioned a Triplane flying off after the Gotha hit the water—probaby Butler, who made no claim beyond expressing the opinion that it was the first of the two he had attacked shortly before. Butler reported an unspecified RFC machine in the area, but did not see it engage the enemy, while Scott saw no other aircraft.

The official history's placing of the Grace/Murray engagement as 'near the North Foreland' creates an apparent discrepancy, since the RNAS attacks were made much closer to the Belgian coast. But in fact Grace was already some 20 miles north of the North Foreland when he first sighted the Gotha formation at 11.30 hr, and although his report quoted no further timings, he clearly flew a long way east during the remainder of his patrol. Had this been a combat involving one squadron of either Service, each pilot would have been credited with one-third of a victory.

A force of twenty-two aircraft from Nos.3 and 4 (RNAS) Squadrons, Dunkirk, failed to find the Gothas but became involved with German fighters sent to cover their return, and claimed four destroyed.

Despite the high incidence of gun failures, the home-based fighters expended in all some 3,500–4,000 rounds, and although much firing was admittedly at extreme ranges, some bullets found targets. One Gotha captain, Leut S. R. Schulte, captured later in the year, disclosed that his aircraft, on the right of the formation, was forced to land on the beach at Ostende because of damage from incessant attacks. It was found to have 88 bullet holes. Three other Gothas were written off in approach and landing crashes in which combat damage may have been a factor.

No British crew reported seeing the combat in which Wilfred Salmon, No.63(T) Squadron, was shot down. He fired 55 rounds before receiving a fatal head wound, and some ground witnesses thought that his Pup was still under control until moments before it crashed near Joyce Green aerodrome.

Deeper mystery surrounds the circumstances of the morning's second fighter loss, off the Essex coast. Young and Taylor were crewing one of No.37 Squadron's 1½ Strutters airborne from Rochford between 09.28 and 09.34 hr, and the official history states that they were shot down in combat with the incoming bombers. But since the Gothas were at 14,000 ft or higher, the Sopwiths could not have reached them until at least 10–15 min after they had crossed the coast—which is confirmed by the other crews' accounts of engagements with the returning bombers. Strangely not one No.37 Squadron crew mentioned seeing a squadron colleague go down, and the only significant reports were from pilots of

2nd Lieut J. E. R. Young, No.37 Squadron, who, with his gunner, AM C. C. Taylor, was killed when his Sopwith 1½ Strutter A8271 was shot down during the raid of 7 July, 1917; and (*right*) Capt Vernon Brown, from Orfordness, who attacked Gotha bombers on two of the four home-defence sorties he flew during the summer of 1917, but to no visible effect.

other units attempting to pursue the raiders out to sea. Martin, No.40(T) Squadron, saw an aircraft of unspecified type spinning down near the Maplin Sands, and Moore, No.198 Depot Squadron, noticed a 1½ Strutter diving steeply and lost to sight at 12,000 ft.

Young's aircraft fell near the Maplin light vessel, and a launch quickly picked up the badly-injured Taylor. He was transferred to HMS *Wolfe* but died soon afterwards from a compound skull fracture and other injuries. It was impossible to recover the pilot's body before the wreckage sank, leaving one tyre floating nearby.

Observers on the lightship thought the aircraft was hit by an AA shell burst, and a signal of obscure origin among the day's official reports also mentioned a defending aircraft believed to have been shot down by the guns. One No.37 Squadron pilot complained that they were considerably hindered by AA fire. The Germans claimed only one fighter shot down—presumably Salmon—which strengthens the suspicion that the 1½ Strutter was one of the two fighters shown in postwar statistics as falling casualties to the AA guns during the German day offensive. The possibility of such a tragic and unavoidable accident is supported by Henderson's remark in his 14 July minute to the CIGS on air defence reorganization, that the RFC 'cannot go on taking its present risks of being brought down by the fire of our own guns whilst attacking the enemy'.

For obvious reasons the authorities would not wish to admit such a mistake, and a letter from Hargrave, CO of No.37 Squadron, to Young's father was published in the next issue of *The Aeroplane*, describing in almost macabre detail how the pilot had unhesitatingly flown into the combined fire from twenty-two Gothas. Hargrave's claim that he witnessed the whole affair invites question, since he was not airborne but presumably at his Woodham Mortimer headquarters, 18 miles from the scene and a long way for accurate observation from the ground.

22 July, 1917 (Daylight)

Targets: Harwich, Felixstowe.
Enemy forces: 23 Gothas despatched, 21 Gothas attacked.
Results: 13 killed, 26 injured, £2,780 damage.
Defence sorties: 122. Note: records for this date have much detail missing.

RNAS

Dover: Sopwith Pups N6191, 08.30–10.20 hr; N6200, 09.05–10.00 hr.

Eastchurch: Sopwith Camels B3795, 08.45–10.20 hr; B6333, 08.50–10.20 hr; B3798, 09.00–10.55 hr.

Manston: Sopwith Triplanes N509, 08.20–10.03 hr; N5382, 08.20–10.07 hr; N5424 (Flt Sub-Lieut G. K. Cooper) 08.55–09.08 hr, returned with gun jam, took off 09.25 hr, forced landed Fort Darland; Sopwith Camels B3844, 08.20–10.06 hr; B3843, 08.24–10.04 hr; B3761, 08.55–10.10 hr; B3842, 08.55–10.08 hr; B3774, 08.55–10.03 hr; B3834, 08.25–10.05 hr; Sopwith Pup 9907, 08.55–10.03 hr.

Westgate: Sopwith Schneider 3760, 08.55–10.10 hr; Sopwith Baby 8160, 08.55–09.50 hr.

Walmer: Sopwith Pups N6441 (Flt Cdr T. C. Vernon) 08.30–09.50 hr; N6439 (Flt Lieut S. Kemball) 08.35–10.25 hr; N6442 (Flt Sub-Lieut J. A. Shaw) 08.35–10.50 hr; N6438 (Flt Lieut H. S. Kerby) 08.40–10.35 hr; 9947 (Flt Sub-Lieut W. M. Lusby) 08.40–09.00 hr.

This immaculate Sopwith Pup, N6442 of RNAS Walmer, was flown by Flt Sub-Lieut J. A. Shaw against the 22 July, 1917, and earlier raids.

Yarmouth: Sopwith Babies 8133 (Flt Sub-Lieut A. M. FitzRandolph) 09.00–11.00 hr; N1109 (Flt Lieut L. E. R. Murray) 09.00–11.00 hr; N1110 (Flt Sub-Lieut F. W. Dolman) 09.50–11.30 hr.

RFC

No.37 Squadron, A Flight, Goldhanger: B.E.12as A4032 (Capt W. Sowrey) 08.23–09.53 hr; A6312 (Lieut C. V. Clayton) 08.32–10.07 hr; unspecified B.E.12/12as 08.23–09.01 hr, returned with engine trouble; 08.26–10.01 hr.

No.37 Squadron, B Flight, Stow Maries: Sopwith Pups B1723 (Capt C. A. Ridley) 08.23–09.42 hr; A6246 (Capt C. E. Holman) 08.25–09.30 hr; A6248 (2nd Lieut H. A. Edwardes) 08.26–10.11 hr; plus eight sorties, details not recorded.

No.39 Squadron, A Flight, North Weald: B.E.12/12a, three sorties, 08.25–09.40 hr; Armstrong Whitworth F.K.8, 08.44–09.17 hr; details not recorded.

No.39 Squadron, C Flight, Hainault: Sopwith Camels, ten sorties, 08.24–09.20 hr, details not recorded.

No.50 Squadron, A Flight, Detling: Sopwith Pups, five sorties, 08.22–10.30 hr, details not recorded.

No.50 Squadron, B Flight, Throwley: Armstrong Whitworth F.K.8, five sorties, 08.25–10.30 hr, details not recorded.

No.50 Squadron, C Flight, Bekesbourne: B.E.12/12a; five sorties, 08.25–10.10 hr, details not recorded.

No.78 Squadron, Penshurst: B.E.12a, three sorties, 08.24–10.25 hr; S.E.5, two sorties, 08.28–10.20 hr, details not recorded.

No.78 Squadron, Telscombe Cliffs: B.E.12as A592, A595, A6305, A6308 airborne 08.21–10.35 hr, details not recorded.

No.46 Squadron, Suttons Farm: Sopwith Pups, eighteen sorties 08.13–09.30 hr, details not recorded.

No.62(T) Squadron, Dover: Sopwith Pup, 09.20–12.40 hr, with intermediate landing at Croydon; D.H.4, 09.15–10.15 hr; details not recorded.

No.2 Aircraft Acceptance Park, Hendon: D.H.4s, five sorties; D.H.5s, two sorties, 08.40–10.20 hr, details not recorded.

No.8 Aircraft Acceptance Park, Lympne: Sopwith Camels, two sorties; D.H.4s, two sorties; D.H.5, one sortie; Martinsyde, one sortie; F.E.2b, one sortie; R.E.8, one sortie; details not recorded.

Experimental Station, Orfordness: Vickers F.B.14D C4547 (Capt V. Brown, Capt B. M. Jones) 08.05–09.15 hr (Manston); Sopwith 1½ Strutter A8255 (2nd Lieut H. A. Francis, Lieut B. H. M. Jones) 08.30–10.15 hr; Armstrong Whitworth F.K.8 B215 (Lieut G. Barrett, Flt Sgt T. Bosworth) 08.20–09.45 hr (Rochford); Bristol Fighter A3303 (Lieut F. D. Holder, Sgt S. Ashby) 08.20–10.15 hr; unspecified aircraft, 08.20–10.15 hr.

Testing Squadron, Martlesham Heath: Sopwith Camel, 08.20–09.45 hr; Martinsyde, 08.24–10.17 hr; Vickers F.B.16D, 08.58–10.30 hr, details not recorded.

First warning of this Sunday morning hit-and-run attack on Harwich and Felixstowe came at 08.00 hr from the Sunk lightship, nine miles off The Naze, only about five minutes before the twenty-one Gothas crossed Hollesley Bay, thus ruling out any chance of effective interception. The Gothas bombed at 08.10–08.17 hr, damaging port and RNAS installations, and were last reported disappearing southeast of the Sunk at 08.34 hr. One was later shot down by a French-based RFC aircraft.

From the 122 home-based defence sorties there was only one contact—by an Orfordness aircraft already airborne on a quite unconnected mission. Denied success on this occasion, its crew achieved distinction in later life. Vernon Brown, the pilot, reached air commodore rank in the RAF, then spent 15 years as the Air Ministry and later Ministry of Civil Aviation, Chief Inspector of Accidents, being knighted in 1952. Bennett Melvill Jones, the observer, was a Cambridge science graduate, employed at Farnborough before his attachment to Orfordness, where he did valuable work on gun sights. He was Mond Professor of Aeronautical Engineering at Cambridge in 1919–52, and Chairman of the Aeronautical Research Council in 1943–47. He was knighted in 1942. (His brother, also at

Vickers F.B.14D C4547, crewed by Capts Vernon Brown and B. Melvill Jones, from Orfordness, was the only home-based aircraft to make contact when Gothas raided Harwich and Felixstowe on 22 July, 1917. (*J. M. Bruce/G. S. Leslie collection*)

Orfordness and airborne in a 1½ Strutter that morning, was killed in a flying accident in April 1918.)

Brown and Jones were flying in a Vickers F.B.14D, intending to test one of Melvill Jones' new sights against a towed target. It was hardly the aeroplane Brown would have chosen for combat, since he was an adept performer in the Sopwith Triplane, and had recently posed that nimble fighter for a unique series of aerobatic photographs. The F.B.14 had started life in 1916 as an undistinguished reconnaissance two-seater with a 120 hp Beardmore engine, entering limited production but not seeing squadron service. The 14D version, which had flown in March 1917, embodied a different wing layout and although performance was improved by a 250 hp Rolls-Royce engine, it failed to gain a production order.

They saw the Gothas flying east soon after they had bombed, and welcomed the opportunity to test the new gun sight against a live target. However, the F.B.14D lacked fighter performance and they chased for about 50 miles before getting within range. The bombers proved difficult to see against the sun, and the 100 rounds which Jones fired from below produced no result. Returning well south of their base and short of petrol, they landed at Manston to refuel.

No detailed Home Defence Group reports for the morning's activities have survived and the sketchy available information reflects the state of upheaval prevailing while the defences were being strengthened and reorganized. Two S.E.5s—presumably aircraft formerly used by No.39 Squadron—operated in No.78 Squadron at Penshurst, the name promulgated two days earlier for the aerodrome at Chiddingstone Causeway. The ten Camels officially attributed to C Flight of No.39 Squadron at Hainault were clearly aircraft destined for No.44 Squadron, then in the formation stage, and probably flown by pilots posted to that unit. But No.44 was not due to form until 24 July, and bureaucratic niceties perhaps barred any pre-empting of that date. Preparations for the imminent creation of No.61 Squadron at Rochford could explain the absence of sorties from that aerodrome.

With the patrol order not issued until after the Gothas had bombed, not even the experienced No.46 Squadron—hastily transferred from France after the second London raid—could hope to catch the enemy. Soon after the fighters were airborne a confused situation arose when a British formation was wrongly reported as a breakaway Gotha section heading for Southend. This decided Home Defence Group not to divert aircraft away from their prescribed patrols to chase bombers over the North Sea.

From about 08.45 hr the anti-aircraft guns deployed between the Blackwater and Thames estuaries had a field day, firing at anything and everything, single machines and formations, in the blind belief that they were enemy. It is a sorry reflection on contemporary aircraft-recognition standards that in justification the gunners could plead 'the difficulty of distinguishing the markings of the aeroplanes owing to their height and the glare of the sun'.

The indestructible Claude Ridley had his engine cowling shot away when leading a formation of six No.37 Squadron Pups at 14,000 ft over Shoeburyness. An official report said that it was thanks only to his skill and experience that the aircraft landed safely. The gunners proudly claimed a hit, and Ridley was doubly incensed because only the day before he had led a Pup formation over the area with the specific object of familiarizing the AA sites with its appearance. Eight pilots from other units complained of being shelled, and Barrett from Orfordness landed his F.K.8 at Rochford with two gashes in the wing fabric.

'Gunners do not seem to have realised that the aircraft might not be German' reported GHQ Home Forces intelligence. 'Such a mistake points to a want of familiarity with aeroplane tactics on the part of personnel of the anti-aircraft batteries and observer companies'

The only event of note among the RNAS activities was of domestic rather than operational concern. Flt Sub-Lieut G. K. Cooper at Manston had the temerity to use Sqn Cdr Charles Butler's favourite Sopwith Triplane while its 'owner' was on leave. After returning to rectify his gun, which jammed during the normal test burst, he took off again but failed to find the rest of his formation. To complete his embarrassment he then shot off his propeller because of a gun synchronization fault and forced landed at Fort Darland, Chatham.

Of the aircraft despatched from French bases, the Camels of Nos.3 and 4 (RNAS) Squadrons missed the returning bombers, and the D.H.4s of No.55 Squadron RFC sighted them too far away to chase. No.48 Squadron at Bray Dunes scored a notable success. At 10.40 hr Capt Brian E. Baker, with 2nd Lieut G. R. Spencer as his observer/gunner in Bristol Fighter A7146 patrolling at 16,000 ft spotted five Gothas low down about eight miles northwest of Ostende, Baker dived towards them and engaged one from the flank at 3,000 ft, continuing the attack down to 2,000 ft and seeing his tracers hitting the bomber in the nose. Meanwhile, Lieut R. D. Coath and 2nd Lieut A. D. Merchant in Bristol A7164 were attacking from the rear. Both crews saw the Gotha crash just off Ostende and remain with the top wing awash and the tail showing above the surface. No.48 Squadron's CO, Maj A. V. Bettington, reported the wreck as still visible four hours later.

This aircraft had clearly ditched close enough to the shore to be resting on the bottom, and could thus be strictly described as having crashed on landing—the only casualty admitted by the Germans. In similar circumstances the British authorities would doubtless have employed such terms to avoid admitting an enemy victory.

12 August, 1917 (Daylight)

Target: Southend.
Enemy forces: 13 Gothas despatched, 11 Gothas attacked.
Results: 33 killed, 46 injured, £9,600 damage.
Defence sorties: 139.

RNAS

Dover: Sopwith Pup N6191 (Flt Cdr G. E. Hervey) took off 17.25 hr, returned with gun jam, 17.40–19.00 hr; Sopwith Babies N1024 (Flt Sub-Lieut A. W. Farquhar) 17.50–19.00 hr; N1118 (Flt Sub-Lieut A. C. Reid) 17.45–19.45 hr.

Eastchurch: Sopwith Camels B3798 (Flt Cdr A. F. Bettington) 17.30–19.45 hr; N6333 (Flt Lieut A. A. Wallis) 17.32–19.06 hr; B3795 (Flt Lieut E. M. Pizey) 17.43–18.45 hr; Nieuport 24 N5863, 17.34–19.10 hr.

Grain: Sopwith Pup 9912 (Flt Cdr C. T. Freeman) 17.50–19.20 hr.

Manston: Bristol Scout Ds N5390 (Flt Sub-Lieut H. J. Nelson) 17.18–17.55 hr, returned with engine trouble; N5391 (Flt Sub-Lieut S. Quayle) 17.18–18.38 hr; N5398 (Flt Sub-Lieut C. F. D. Ash) 17.18–19.30 hr; Sopwith Triplanes N5382 (Flt Sub-Lieut H. C. Lemon) 17.23–19.18 hr; N535 (Sqn Cdr G. L. Thompson) 17.45–18.50 hr; Sopwith Camels B3844 (Flt Sub-Lieut A. C. Burt) 17.23–18.23 hr, forced landed; B3925 (Flt Sub-Lieut H. R. de Wilde) 17.23–18.27 hr;

B3834 (Flt Sub-Lieut R. H. Daly) 17.23–19.25 hr; B3761 (Sqn Cdr C. H. Butler) 17.30–19.25 hr; B3843 (Flt Sub-Lieut M. A. Harker) 17.30–19.18 hr (Eastchurch); B3923 (Flt Sub-Lieut E. B. Drake) 17.30–18.50 hr; B3774 (Flt Sub-Lieut C. H. Fitzherbert) 17.30–18.50 hr; B3924 (Flt Sub-Lieut A. H. Lofft) 17.40–18.25 hr.

Walmer: Sopwith Pups N6440 (Flt Lieut H. S. Kerby) 17.30–20.20 hr; N6439 (Flt Sub-Lieut M. R. Kingsford) 17.30–19.33 hr; N6441 (Flt Cdr T. C. Vernon) 17.30–18.50 hr; 9947 (Flt Lieut R. A. Little) 18.20–20.40 hr.

RFC

No.37 Squadron, A Flight, Goldhanger: B.E.12 6610 (Lieut P. R. Cawdell) W/T tracker, 17.21–19.18 hr; B.E.12as A4032 (Capt W. Sowrey) 17.20–19.13 hr; A6312 (2nd Lieut S. Armstrong) W/T tracker, 17.21–18.10 hr, returned with W/T unserviceable, and 18.14–19.07 hr; A6318 (2nd Lieut C. L. Milburn) 17.22–18.50 hr.

No.39 Squadron, North Weald: B.E.12s 6480 (Lieut P. W. L. Jarvis) 17.20–19.20 hr; 6488 (Capt G. D. F. Keddie) 17.24–19.14 hr; B753 (2nd Lieut C. L. Brock) 17.24–17.35 hr, returned with broken drift wire.

No.44 Squadron, Hainault: Sopwith Camels, A Flight, B3852 (Capt C. J. Q. Brand) 17.32–18.45 hr; B3826 (Lieut D. V. Armstrong) 17.33–18.47 hr; B3930 (Lieut C. A. Lewis) 17.33–18.45 hr; B3765 (Lieut C. Patteson) 17.40–18.50 hr. B Flight, B3827 (Capt J. I. Mackay) 17.30–19.00 hr; B3815 (Capt T. Gran) 17.32–18.12 hr, returned with engine trouble; B3776 (Lieut E. S. Moulton-Barrett) 17.32–19.40 hr, forced landed, out of petrol; B3883 (Capt G. A. H. Pidcock) 17.37–18.55 hr; B3886 (Lieut G. R. Craig) 17.41–18.55 hr. C Flight, B3859 (Capt G. W. M. Green) 17.29–18.31 hr; B3763 (Capt W. H. Haynes) 17.30–18.32 hr; B3788 (Lieut R. G. H. Adams) 17.30–18.32 hr; B3816 (Lieut G. H. Hackwill) 17.31–18.34 hr; B3767 (Lieut L. F. Lomas) 17.32–18.33 hr; B3828 (Sgt S. W. Smith) 17.32–18.34 hr.

No.50 Squadron, B Flight, Detling: Armstrong Whitworth F.K.8s B229 (2nd Lieut N. F. Perris) 17.25–19.29 hr; B225 (2nd Lieut F. V. Bryant) 17.27–19.30 hr; B223 (Capt C. J. Truran) 17.28–19.24 hr; B224 (2nd Lieut W. R. Oulton) 17.38–19.37 hr; B247 (2nd Lieut F. A. D. Grace) 17.33–18.05 hr, returned with loose cowling, and 18.35–19.16 hr.

No.50 Squadron, C Flight, Bekesbourne: B.E.12s 6157 (2nd Lieut L. Lucas) 17.20–19.17 hr; 6509 (2nd Lieut W. G. Latham) 17.22–19.17 hr; 6185 (2nd Lieut C. C. White) 17.26–19.11 hr; B.E.12as A6309 (Lieut J. Metcalfe) 17.20–19.12 hr; A6313 (2nd Lieut T. V. Villiers) 17.22–18.11 hr, returned with engine trouble.

No.61 Squadron, Rochford: Sopwith Pups B1771 (Lieut L. F. Hutcheon) 17.18–19.00 hr; A6243 (Lieut J. D. Belgrave) 17.19–19.20 hr; B1811 (2nd Lieut P. Thompson) 17.19–19.10 hr; B2157 (Lieut J. T. Collier) 17.19–19.20 hr; B2159 (Capt C. B. Cooke) 17.20–18.40 hr; not recorded (Capt S. H. Starey) 17.20–19.25 hr; A6246 (Capt C. E. Holman) 17.23–18.55 hr; A6249 (Capt E. B. Mason) 17.23–19.17 hr; B735 (2nd Lieut A. H. Bird) 17.23–19.20 hr; B1723 (Capt C. A. Ridley) 17.23–18.55 hr; B1764 (Sgt W. A. E. Taylor) 17.23–18.50 hr; B1765 (2nd Lieut H. A. Blain) 17.23–18.21 hr; B1774 (2nd Lieut E. E. Turner) 17.23–19.50 hr; B1806 (2nd Lieut J. S. Wood) 17.23–19.17 hr; B1809 (Capt H. C. Stroud) 17.23–19.11 hr; A653 (2nd Lieut G. Howe) 17.25–18.59 hr.

No.78 Squadron, Penshurst: B.E.12a A6320 (2nd Lieut F. L. Luxmoore) 17.21–19.21 hr; Sopwith 1½ Strutter A8275 (Lieut C. J. Marchant) 17.21–19.07 hr.

No.78 Squadron, Telscombe Cliffs: B.E.12as A6305 (2nd Lieut R. F. W. Moore) 17.19–19.07 hr; A6308 (2nd Lieut A. Barker) 17.19–19.30 hr.

No.112 Squadron, Throwley: Sopwith Pups A638 (Lieut R. W. le Gallais) 17.24–19.00 hr; B1711 (2nd Lieut N.E. Chandler) 17.24–18.58 hr; B1763 (2nd Lieut I. M. Davies) 17.24–19.09 hr; B2158 (2nd Lieut A. J. Arkell) 17.25–17.46 hr, returned with engine trouble; A6153 (Capt C. Sutton) 17.25–18.20 hr and 18.23–19.08 hr; B1769 (2nd Lieut S. Cockerell) 17.25–18.59 hr; B1773 (Capt S. H. Pratt) 17.25–17.30 hr, returned with gun trouble, and 17.35–19.17 hr; B1807 (2nd Lieut J. G. Goodyear) 17.40–19.07 hr; B1810 (2nd Lieut J. W. R. Thompson) 17.25–18.15 hr, returned with gun trouble, and 18.30–19.17 hr.

No.46 Squadron, Suttons Farm: Sopwith Pups A6155 (Lieut E. F. Hughes) 17.14–18.35 hr; A6200 (2nd Lieut R. S. Asher) 17.14–18.47 hr; A7335 (Lieut C. A. Brewster-Joske) 17.14–18.47 hr; A7337 (Lieut A. W. Wilcox) 17.14–18.50 hr; B1701 (Lieut A. F. Bird) 17.14–18.50 hr; B1716 (2nd Lieut F. B. Barager) 17.14–18.50 hr; B1719 (2nd Lieut R. L. Ferrie) 17.14–18.50 hr; B1727 (2nd Lieut N. H. Dimmock) 17.14–18.50 hr; B1766 (2nd Lieut L. M. Shadwell) 17.14–18.50 hr; B1777 (Lieut A. S. G. Lee) 17.14–18.40 hr; B1795 (Maj P. Babington) 17.14–19.25 hr; B1802 (Lieut C. Courtneidge) 17.14–18.40 hr; B1837 (2nd Lieut E. Armitage) 17.14–18.35 hr; B1841 (2nd Lieut G. Thompson) 17.14–18.50 hr; B1842 (2nd Lieut C. W. Odell) 17.14–18.50 hr; B1843 (Capt M. D. G. Scott) 17.14–18.35 hr; not recorded (Capt S. H. Long) 17.14–18.50 hr; not recorded (Lieut MacDonald) 17.14–18.43 hr.

No.65 Squadron, Wye: Sopwith Camels B3850 (Capt T. E. Withington) 17.23–18.50 hr; B3861 (Lieut V. Wigg) 17.40–19.35 hr.

No.40(T) Squadron, Croydon: Sopwith Pups A6228 (Lieut A. G. Taylor) 17.18–19.15 hr; A650 (2nd Lieut J. F. Bremner) 17.19–19.20 hr; A7341 (Lieut N. Clarke) 17.20–19.10 hr; A7318 (2nd Lieut A. C. Hurst) 17.21–19.25 hr; B1738 (Lieut R. M. Collingwood) 17.22–19.15 hr.

No.56(T) Squadron, London Colney: Spads A8816 (2nd Lieut R. H. Stocken) 17.30–19.00 hr; A8818 (Lieut J. M. Stubbs) 17.30–18.45 hr, crashed on landing due to engine failure.

No.62(T) Squadron, Dover: Sopwith Pup B1740 (Lieut D. M. Faure) 17.37–18.55 hr.

The 30 mm Coventry Ordnance Works gun, fitted here to D.H.4 No.A2168 at Orfordness, was considered as an anti-Zeppelin weapon. This aircraft flew an anti-Gotha sortie on 12 August, 1917—but it is thought not with the COW gun.

No.63(T) Squadron, Joyce Green: D.H.5, two sorties 17.45–19.15 hr, details not recorded.

No.198 Depot Squadron, Rochford: Vickers F.B.12C A7351 (Maj B. F. Moore) 17.25–19.12 hr.

No.8 Aircraft Acceptance Park, Lympne: D.H.4 A7556 (2nd Lieut O. Matson) 17.40–19.20 hr; D.H.5s B372 (2nd Lieut H. Kirton) 17.35–18.25 hr; not recorded (2nd Lieut E. S. T. Cole) 17.20–18.42 hr; Bristol Fighters A7117 (Lieut R. S. Carroll) took off 17.30 hr; A7106 (Lieut H. Slingsby) 17.20–19.09 hr; F.E.2b A5505 (Lieut P. T. Chamberlayne) 17.20–19.15 hr; F.E.2d B1894 (Lieut M. Campbell) 18.10–19.10 hr; R.E.8 A4424 (2nd Lieut F. Litchfield) 17.38–19.02 hr; Martinsyde G.100 A6280 (Capt C. W. Carleton) 17.49–19.22 hr.

Experimental Station, Orfordness: Sopwith Pup B1717 (Lieut N. Howarth) 17.35–18.35 hr; Sopwith Triplane N5430 (Capt V. Brown) 17.35–18.20 hr; Bristol Fighter A3303 (Lieut F. D. Holder, Lieut Wallace) 17.45–18.45 hr; D.H.4 A2168 (Capt L. J. Wackett, Lieut F. W. Musson) 17.40–18.40 hr.

Testing Squadron, Martlesham Heath: Vickers F.B.16D (Capt O. M. Sutton) 17.30–18.45 hr; Sopwith Camels B3751 (Lieut G. W. Gathergood) 17.23–18.52 hr; unrecorded (Flt Lieut H. L. Wood) 17.36–19.00 hr; Martinsyde G.100 A3997 (2nd Lieut G. E. Cushing) 17.35–19.15 hr.

The primary target for this raid was Chatham naval base, with Southend and Margate as alternatives. Its ordering at short notice on a Sunday produced only thirteen available aircraft with crews, and two of these turned back with engine trouble.

First sightings were made from the Sunk light vessel at 17.00 hr, and the RFC readiness order at 17.09 hr was followed by 'patrol' at 17.14 hr. Strong winds had driven the formation considerably farther north than intended, and skirting the coast southwards it made less than 50 mph ground speed, passing Clacton at 17.20 hr, Bradwell at 17.35 hr, and approached Rochford at 17.50 hr. One aircraft broke off to bomb Margate at about 17.40 hr. Nearing Canvey Island, the formation leader, Oberleutnant Richard Walter, realized that another 20 min over heavily defended territory at this crawling pace could expose the squadron to unacceptable risk from the numerous alerted and visible fighters, so he fired a double green signal cartridge, turned east and bombed Southend. Many of the bombs dropped in the sea, and a few fell on the aerodrome at Rochford.

Among the first fighters to arouse Walter's anxieties were five Camels of No.3 (RNAS) Squadron, which sighted the formation at 16.30 hr having been airborne for 105 minutes on a routine fleet-protection patrol from Furnes. One Camel turned back with engine trouble and the remaining four found that their low fuel state prevented them from making effective attacks when they caught up with the bombers near the English coast. Flt Sub-Lieut G. S. Harrower, who got closest, fired all his ammunition at the rearmost Gotha with no visible result, and the others made brief attacks from extreme range. Flt Lieut H. P. Beamish scraped into Rochford troubled with the flow from his gravity tank, and Flt Sub-Lieut E. T. Hayne landed at Manston with a damaged propeller resulting from faulty gun synchronization. Flt Sub-Lieut R. P. F. Abbott also landed at Manston, and Harrower at Eastchurch.

According to most accounts, the Gotha which diverted to Margate did so after a straightforward mechanical failure, but one German report asserts that an engine was put out of action in an air combat—in which case one of the No.3 Squadron Camels must have been responsible. Certainly it was not, as some believed,

Sqn Cdr C. H. Butler (*right*), RNAS Manston, flew more home-defence sorties—at least 29—than any other pilot. With him is Sqn Cdr G. L. Thompson, a Handley Page pilot, who flew fighter patrols when the opportunity arose. (*C. Ross*)

consciously acting as a decoy—though it admirably fulfilled that function, drawing perhaps nine of the United Kingdom based RNAS fighters from the main formation and miraculously surviving their numerous assaults.

Surprisingly, since he was flying a Bristol Scout of modest performance, Quayle was the first to attack, at about 12,000 ft, shortly after the Gotha had bombed, and despite four gun stoppages he managed to fire 40 rounds. Ash in another Scout fired one 97 round drum, then a succession of faster fighters took up the chase—the Camels flown by Butler, Burt, de Wilde and Daly, a Sopwith Triplane (Lemon), and two Pups flown by Kerby and Vernon from Walmer.

Burt's engagement was brief, with both guns jamming after 30 rounds, then after a centre-section wire snapped—possibly hit by an enemy bullet—he forced landed a mile northeast of Manston. Butler picked up the Gotha 20 miles east of the North Foreland and fired 420 rounds in a series of attacks until spent

Sopwith Pup B1727 *Normie*—flown by 2nd Lieut Norman H. Dimmock—of No.46 Squadron, which flew from Suttons Farm against the later Gotha daylight raids.

ammunition forced him to break away near the Belgian coast, and de Wilde fired 180 rounds before both his guns jammed. Daly also attacked and left the bomber at about 1,000 ft nearing Zeebrugge. Lemon discharged 350 rounds in five attacks, only to see the Gotha gently diving off the Scheldt estuary, still under control. Vernon and Kerby both chased until it was lost to view 10–15 miles off Zeebrugge.

The Gotha staggered over the coast at about 600 ft to crash-land near Ostende, having against all odds escaped any lethal damage from more than 1,100 rounds fired by the fighters. Steadily losing height on its one good engine, the aircraft could not indulge in any vigorous evasive action, and only Quayle mentioned seeing any return fire—though Butler later found that his Camel had received four hits. Four pilots were confident that they hit the Gotha, but the concensus was that it was under control as it neared the coast. There is no simple explanation of their failure and they were evidently suffering one of those occasional off days, which a high incidence of gun failures did nothing to improve. The German crew claimed one fighter shot down, which they doubtless felt they had earned.

A substantially improved RFC fighter force was waiting to do battle with the main bomber formation. The Pup flights had been removed from Nos.37 and 50 Squadrons, while No.39 had ended its brief flirtation with SE.5s and Camels, and these units had reverted to the pedestrian B.E.12s and Armstrong Whitworth F.K.8s having no serious pretensions as day fighters. The Pups were grouped into two new day fighter squadrons, No.61 at Rochford and No.112 at Throwley, while the Camels went to another new squadron, No.44 at Hainault. Some pilots transferred from the previous units.

However, the only experienced combat team was No.46 Squadron, still on loan from France, which demonstrated by its take-off technique the high degree of professionalism achieved by Philip Babington, its energetic CO. All engines were running 2½ min after the 'readiness' call, and aircraft taxied to pre-arranged positions on the aerodrome for a squadron take-off. On the firing of the white Very cartridge denoting 'patrol', the eighteen Pups were airborne within 45 seconds.

Ashmore, the new air-defence commander, had no doubts that his principal task was to protect the capital, preferably by destroying bombers before they got there, but also by inflicting such mayhem on the formations after bombing as to render London raids too costly to continue. His main patrols were deployed accordingly—Nos.44 and 39 Squadrons operating between Romford and North Weald; No.46, Joyce Green–Romford; No.112, All Hallows–Dover; No.50, Bekesbourne–Throwley–Dover; and No.78, Penshurst–Biggin Hill–Joyce Green. Supporting units either backed up the home-defence squadrons or patrolled their immediate coastal areas.

Once it became evident that this was not another Harwich raid, Ashmore reasonably—but wrongly—deduced that London would be the target, and some curious confusion surrounds the subsequent movements of No.61 Squadron.

An official report says Ashmore intended to hold it in reserve to harry the bombers on their homeward journey, but other accounts relate how Maj E. R. Pretyman, the CO, ordered the Pups airborne on his own authority when the Gothas were seen approaching Rochford. There is, however, evidence which casts doubt upon this story. No.61 Squadron's operational return shows take-off times between 17.18 and 17.25 hr, apparently in response to the general Home Defence Group 'patrol' order passed to other squadrons between 17.14 and 17.20 hr, before the Gothas would have been visible from Rochford. Strangely,

Maj E. R. Pretyman, CO of No.61 Squadron, Rochford, whose Sopwith Pups harried the Gothas returning from the Southend raid of 12 August, 1917; and (*right*) Capt Cecil Lewis, who flew at least nine day and night sorties in Nos.44 and 61 Squadrons. Author of the First World War classic, *Sagittarius Rising*, he was associated with broadcasting from its earliest days.

these take-off times have been amended, each meticulously initialled by Pretyman, to read 20 min later—from 17.38 to 17.45 hr. It is unlikely that a mistake of 20 min was made in the initial logging, and in any case several pilots sighted the bombers—admittedly some thousands of feet higher up—about ten miles northeast of Rochford. If Pretyman did indeed order his squadron airborne against the intentions of Home Defence Group—perhaps thinking that it had been left out by mistake—he might conceivably have altered the figures to match the official patrol order for his unit when it was ultimately received.

Whatever the truth of the matter, Pretyman did the right thing, and No.61 was virtually the only home-defence squadron to engage the enemy. Ten pilots sighted the bombers and strove to reach them as they sped homewards, lightened of their loads and climbing to 14–15,000 ft, and some broke off only when they were 40–50 miles out to sea. However, six suffered gun stoppages, two were affected by engine troubles and nothing was achieved.

Cooke and Wood saw the Gothas over Burnham and were still climbing after them as they left Southend, some of them dropping bombs when six miles out to sea. Cooke gave up after an incurable gun jam, and Wood continued for another 40 miles, firing all his ammunition without seeing any hits. Ridley, Belgrave, Hutcheon and Thompson were all in combat 40–50 miles out, firing from 20 to 270 rounds before their guns jammed. Hutcheon's aircraft was hit in the engine cowling and lower port wing by a Gotha gunner shooting down the fuselage tunnel. A badly missing engine caused Holman to return after he had aimed 100 rounds at one bomber about 45 miles out, and Stroud abandoned the chase 30 miles at sea for the same reason. Bird, the only pilot other than Wood to enjoy a trouble-free sortie, fired all his ammunition into the rearmost Gotha to no apparent effect.

Moore, flying No.198 Depot Squadron's Vickers F.B.12C, was still 9,000 ft below the Gothas when he saw them turn to bomb Southend, and attributed the move to their sighting of No.61 Squadron's Pups. His aircraft was too slow to reach close quarters, and the two drums he fired from 1,000 yards were little more than a gesture.

No.112 Squadron's only pilot to engage was Stuart Pratt. Being ten minutes behind the rest after returning to cure a gun fault, he felt justified in taking independent action and diverted from the patrol line to investigate AA activity over Southend. He was probably the first to attack, for when he engaged the tail-end Gotha near the Shingles no other fighters were in the vicinity. His gun jammed after 50 rounds, and while vainly trying to clear it several other fighters appeared, but still some 2–3,000 ft below the bombers' height.

A spirited attack by Gerald Gathergood, flying a Camel from Martlesham, must have missed success by the narrowest margin. From 17,500 ft he saw probably the same aircraft tackled by Pratt, and dived to open fire from 500 yards, only for both guns to jam after 20 rounds each. Having rectified the stoppage he made altogether nine attacks from behind and below, on four occasions closing in until the Gotha overlapped his Aldis sight. For part of the time a Pup attacking from above attracted most of the bomber's return fire. Gathergood was obliged to abandon combat when a sticking valve caused severe back-firing. It took him 42 min to fly back to Martlesham.

Gathergood's effort was seen by fellow Martlesham pilot Oliver Sutton, flying the prototype Vickers F.B.16D, which although the fastest fighter of its day, with a top speed of 135 mph, was rejected for service largely because its good streamlining created excessive maintenance problems. He went for another Gotha, firing two 97-round double drums from his Lewis and closing to 300 yards, but was hampered by engine trouble. Sutton had established his place in history by inventing the Sutton Harness, the system of shoulder and thigh straps secured by a quick-release lock, which proved such a boon to the fighter pilot hitherto held in his cockpit by a simple seat belt.

Sopwith Pup B1806, with 100 hp Monosoupape engine, from which 2nd Lieut J. S. Wood, No.61 Squadron, fired all his ammunition to no effect against a departing Gotha on 12 August, 1917. This photograph was taken after the aircraft had been transferred to No.112 Squadron, Throwley.

No.61 Squadron reports indicate that there had not been time for its pilots to work up as a disciplined team, though ironically it was strict discipline which kept the one fully-trained squadron—No.46—away from the enemy. Babington saw anti-aircraft activity 20 miles east of his patrol line and was sorely tempted to investigate, but accepted that a successful defence scheme demanded adherence to orders and could not degenerate into a general free-for-all.

The only Manston aircraft to engage the main formation was the Sopwith Triplane—one of the few two-gun versions—flown by Thompson, a Handley Page bomber pilot who seized any opportunity to study the German counterpart. He fired 250 rounds into one Gotha from below, after which both guns jammed. He got one functioning again for a short time, and although he seemed to be scoring hits there was no result. Gun troubles also afflicted the Eastchurch Camels flown by Pizey and Wallis after brief attacks, and Wallis later found that several enemy bullets had struck his engine. Bettington, also hit in the engine, thought he had damaged one Gotha and wounded its gunner.

Freeman, flying a Pup from Grain, fortuitously encountered the Gothas when very well situated, only to be denied success by the gun troubles which plagued so many pilots that evening. He was at 10,000 ft on a carburettor height test when AA fire over Southend drew his attention to the Gothas a few miles out to sea. He overhauled other pursuing fighters and aimed at one of two Gothas bringing up the rear, but his gun jammed after ten rounds. He cleared this stoppage, then suffered two more and could only fire two or three shots.

Returning with Vernon, his flight commander, from pursuing the Margate raider, Harold Kerby spotted in the distance eight Gothas of the main force being harried by the Eastchurch Camels and decided to join the fray. Vernon did not see them and continued for base. Kerby climbed above the bombers and made a diving attack, then noticed a single aircraft 4,000 ft below and trailing behind. He made a diving frontal attack on this Gotha, which flew straight on down into the sea and turned over. Circling the wreck, Kerby saw one man clinging to the tail

Flt Sub-Lieut H. S. Kerby, RNAS Walmer, who shot down a Gotha on 12 August, 1917. Kerby had already scored combat victories on the Western Front.

Sopwith Camel B3850 was flown by Capt T. E. Withington, No.65 Squadron, during the 12 August, 1917, raid. No.65 Squadron, working up at Wye before moving to the Western Front, mounted eight sorties during the Gotha daylight offensive. This was a Basutoland presentation aircraft.

and threw him his life-jacket, then, as he returned to Walmer, he fired red Very cartridges hoping to divert four nearby destroyers to the spot, but they failed to understand and continued on their course. Kerby's 170-min sortie was the longest of the day, and he was awarded the DSC for his victory.

One final crack at the enemy as they approached the Belgian coast was attempted by four Camels of No.3 (RNAS) Squadron, Dunkirk, but every one suffered gun troubles.

A feature of the day's operations was the first employment by RFC Home Defence Wing of 'wireless tracker' aircraft, described in the previous chapter. In the event neither of No.37 Squadron's W/T-equipped B.E.12s was ever close enough to the enemy to signal any useful observations.

The Germans announced the loss of the Gotha shot down by Kerby—No. G IV 656/16, crewed by Leutnant Kurt Rolin (navigator and captain) and Unteroffiziers Rudi Stolle (pilot) and Otto Rosinsky (gunner). In addition to the aircraft achieving the remarkable single-engined return sea crossing, three others—perhaps with combat damage—crashed on landing. One which landed safely bore sixteen bullet holes.

Gotha crews claimed three British fighters destroyed, and one pilot, Unteroffizier Kurt Delang, graphically described in an article 20 years after the event how his gunners shot down one in flames. The British combat report which might have provided substance for Delang's account was Gathergood's, despite discrepancies and the fundamental fact that he was not shot down and survived the war to become a successful London dentist. Delang described repeated attacks at close quarters, very similar to Gathergood's, and bursts of smoke from the Camel's back-firing engine might have given the impression that it caught fire on breaking away.

Apart from the high incidence of gun failures, there were few troubles during the 139 fighter sorties involving more than 190 flying hours. Several pilots landed and took off again after rectifying minor faults and a few returned with ailing engines. Stubbs crashed his Spad attempting a dead-stick landing at London Colney after engine over-heating, but Burt from Manston put his damaged Camel down a mile northeast of the aerodrome without further harm. The circumstances which caused Moulton-Barrett to run out of petrol and crash 40 min after the rest of No.44 Squadron had landed are not recorded.

After the raid an unattributable release from the Press Bureau stated that:

> 'reports of pilots show conclusively that the enemy . . . was making for London. On sighting the large numbers of our aeroplanes which were sent up against them they turned abruptly and made the best of their way out to sea again, dropping some bombs in Southend and unloading the rest when out to sea.'

Although the only written statement to that effect was made by Moore, of No.198 Depot Squadron, this was a reasonable snap assessment. However, a perceptive minute from Brancker to Intelligence four days later argued that since Harwich was clearly not the intended target—otherwise it would have been attacked—the bombers evidently reached the coast well north of their planned landfall. They would not then have had enough fuel to reach London, and their subsequent course skirting the coast suggested that the leader had decided to bomb the first suitable target, which happened to be Southend. Brancker was warning against complacency rather than questioning the value of the fighters, and could not know that their presence had saved Chatham.

21/22 August, 1917 (Night)

Target: Northern England.
Enemy forces: Navy Zeppelins L41 (Hptmn K. Manger), L42 (Kptlt Martin Dietrich), L44 (Kptlt F. Stabbert), L45 (Kptlt Waldemar Kolle), L46 (Kptlt Heinrich Hollender), L47 (Kptlt Michael von Freudenreich); L35 (Kptlt H. Ehrlich) and L51 (Kptlt Walter Dose) returned early.
Results: One injured, £2,272 damage.
Defence sorties: 21.

RNAS
Holt: B.E.2c 8301 (Flt Sub-Lieut C. V. Halford Thompson) 23.18–00.50 hr.
Killingholme: Curtiss H-12 8669, 04.59–11.50 hr.

RFC
No.33 Squadron, A Flight, Scampton: B.E.2e A8707 (Lieut Keene) 22.45–22.55 hr, returned early, pilot sick; B.E.12a A6317 (2nd Lieut H. P. Solomon) 23.25–02.20 hr (Elsham); F.E.2bs A5536 (Lieut E. G. Roberts, 2nd Lieut A. R. Kingsford) 22.50–01.45 hr; A5660 (Capt S. W. Price, 2nd Lieut D. R. Brook) 00.05–03.05 hr; F.E.2d B1883 (Lieut N. L. Garstin, 2nd Lieut J. D. Watson) 23.15–01.45 hr.

No.33 Squadron, B Flight, Kirton-Lindsey: B.E.2e 7226 (2nd Lieut J. R. Cudemore, 2nd Lieut H. P. Solomon) 22.20–23.20 hr (Scampton); F.E.2d B1882 (Capt D. H. Dabbs) 23.05–00.01 hr, returned early, pilot sick.

No.33 Squadron, C Flight, Elsham: B.E.2e 7184 (Lieut W. Mc L. Walbank) 22.50–00.40 hr, returned early with engine trouble, and 00.55–03.00 hr; F.E.2bs A869 (Capt G. Mackrell) 22.45–23.45 hr; A5656 (Maj A. A. B. Thomson, 2nd Lieut J. R. Smith) 03.20–04.00 hr (Scampton).

No.33 Squadron, HQ Flight, Gainsborough: F.E.2bs A5656 (Maj A. A. B. Thomson, 2nd Lieut J. R. Smith) 01.20–03.00 hr (Elsham); A838 (2nd Lieut G. C. Peters) 01.30–04.45 hr; F.E.2d A6434 (2nd Lieut F. H. Barton) 01.25–05.15 hr.

No.76 Squadron, A Flight, Copmanthorpe: B.E.2es A8704 (2nd Lieut H. B. Evans) 00.06–02.30 hr; 7205 (2nd Lieut J. A. Dales) 00.58–03.05 hr, crashed landing.

No.76 Squadron, B Flight, Helperby: B.E.2es A8628 (2nd Lieut E. D. Hall) 01.20–01.35 hr, crashed; A1331 (Lieut K. R. Fletcher) 01.40–03.10 hr; B.E.12 6660 (Capt J. O. C. Orton) 00.45–01.15 hr, returned with engine trouble.

The records of this raid present a confusing picture. Two of the airships—L35 and L51—turned back near the British coast and did not bomb, while L42 and L45 were claimed to have attacked shipping near Spurn Head. All faced operating problems at their heights of about 20,000 ft, with various permutations of strong headwinds, frozen compasses and impaired human performance caused by the inadequacies of primitive oxygen equipment.

Of the four which reported having flown over England, only L41 was tracked. She came in north of Withernsea just after midnight, scattered her bombs east of Hull and left about 30 min later. L44 claimed to have bombed Lincoln, L46 Louth and L47 Grimsby, and although these places were not attacked, unsubstantiated reports of airship sightings or distant bomb explosions came from Rochdale, York, Doncaster and Lincoln. Of the 24,000 lb of bombs the Germans recorded as dropped, less than a tenth was traced—those in the Hull area. It is improbable that such a high proportion fell in the sea, and with contemporary resources unable to track such high-flying raiders accurately, some bombs may have been scattered in remote moorland and any craters found long afterwards never reported.

Zeppelins L41 and L44, which both operated on 21/22 August, 1917. L41 was an R-class vessel much modified to enhance performance, while L44 was of the T-class, built with an improved and streamlined rear gondola.

The fighters' experiences showed that the 15,000 ft, which the C-in-C Home Forces was trying to convince a sceptical War Office represented the latest Zeppelins' operating height, was a conservative figure, and that northern-based home-defence aircraft were quite inadequate for their task.

Herbert Solomon, No.33 Squadron, patrolling at around 15,000 ft, saw a Zeppelin under shell fire near Beverley at 00.25 hr. The bursts were some 2,000 ft below the airship, which he estimated as at 20,000 ft. He found that his B.E.12a would climb no higher while he approached the raider, but nevertheless he fired three Vickers bursts on the remote chance of scoring a hit. After chasing for 20 miles out to sea without gaining ground, and getting low in fuel, he turned back to land at Elsham.

Walbank, a Canadian, had reached 8,000 ft on his second sortie—the first was cut short by engine trouble—when he observed searchlights near Lincoln, but found nothing on closer approach. He then climbed eastwards to 11,000 ft and saw three searchlights coning a Zeppelin near Hessle. It was at about 15,000 ft, and the lights lost it as he approached. Altogether he spent nearly four hours on patrol. Despite the different heights quoted by Solomon and Walbank, it is likely that both saw L41 during her brief journey inland.

Thomson, the dynamic CO of No.33 Squadron, also flew two sorties. Taking off from Gainsborough, he patrolled for 100 minutes, investigating searchlight concentrations over the Humber and Spurn Head without seeing any airships, and landed at Elsham. His second sortie was equally unproductive. Several other pilots reported searchlights directed at friendly aircraft.

Two landing accidents to No.76 Squadron aircraft both originated from the same cause—failure of cockpit instrument lighting. Dales hit the ground short of the flarepath at Copmanthorpe, wrecking his B.E.2e and receiving head injuries, while Hall was unhurt when he crashed on landing at Helperby after being airborne for only 15 minutes.

Douglas Dabbs, No.33 Squadron B Flight commander, who had gained two victories over Fokkers on the Western Front in 1916, was still suffering minor effects from the bullet wound which had invalided him home. The impact of the cold at high altitude on the old injury caused severe cramp, affecting his control of his F.E.2d, so he returned after less than an hour.

22 August, 1917 (Daylight)

Targets: Margate, Ramsgate, Dover.
Enemy forces: 15 Gothas despatched, 10 Gothas attacked.
Results: 12 killed, 27 injured, £17,145 damage.
Defence sorties: 138.

RNAS

Dover: Sopwith Pups N6191 (Flt Cdr G. E. Hervey) took off 10.20 hr; N6438 (Flt Cdr C. T. MacLaren) 10.15–12.00 hr; N6189, 10.20–10.45 hr, returned with engine trouble; Sopwith Baby N1024 (Flt Sub-Lieut A. C. Reid) 10.50–12.30 hr (Westgate); Short 184 9046, 11.05–11.40 hr.

Eastchurch: Sopwith Camels B3798 (Flt Cdr A. F. Bettington) 10.20–12.06 hr; B3795 (Flt Lieut E. M. Pizey) 10.20–12.06 hr; N6333 (Flt Lieut A. A. Wallis) 10.20–12.06 hr.

Manston: Sopwith Camels B3761 (Sqn Cdr C. H. Butler) took off 10.15 hr; B3843 (Flt Sub-Lieut C. H. Fitzherbert) took off 10.15 hr; B3844 (Flt Sub-Lieut E. B. Drake) took off 10.15 hr; B3926 (Flt Sub-Lieut M. A. Harker) took off

10.15 hr; B3834 (Flt Lieut A. F. Brandon) 09.30–10.55 hr; B3923 (Flt Lieut A. F. Brandon) took off 11.00 hr.

Walmer: Sopwith Pups N6440 (Flt Lieut H. S. Kerby) 10.24–11.20 hr; N6439 (Flt Sub-Lieut M. R. Kingsford) 10.20–12.00 hr; 9947 (Flt Lieut R. A. Little) took off 10.35 hr, landed Dunkirk.

RFC

No.37 Squadron, A Flight, Goldhanger: B.E.12 6610 (Lieut P. R. Cawdell) 10.21–11.27 hr; B.E.12as A6312 (2nd Lieut C. L. Milburn) 10.20–11.29 hr; A4032 (Capt W. Sowrey) 10.22–11.20 hr.

No.39 Squadron, North Weald: B.E.12s 6488 (Lieut C. J. Chabot) 10.33–11.40 hr; B753 (2nd Lieut C. L. Brock) 10.36–11.30 hr; 6480 (2nd Lieut W. B. Thomson) 10.36–12.05 hr; 6138 (2nd Lieut G. S. Bozman) 10.36–11.35 hr; B.E.12a A6325 (2nd Lieut A. M. Bennett) 10.35–12.00 hr.

Camels of B Flight, No.44 Squadron, lined up for a formal inspection at Hainault in the late summer of 1917. All these aircraft patrolled during the last two Gotha daylight raids.

No.44 Squadron, Hainault: Sopwith Camels B3852 (Capt C. J. Q. Brand) 10.17–11.20 hr; B3930 (2nd Lieut Smith) 10.19–10.34 hr, returned with engine trouble, and 10.53–11.25 hr; B3765 (Lieut C. Patteson) 10.19–11.15 hr; B3826 (Lieut D. V. Armstrong) 10.19–11.25 hr; B3837 (Lieut C. A. Lewis) 10.20–11.22 hr; B3859 (Capt G. W. M. Green) 10.21–11.13 hr; B3816 (Lieut G. H. Hackwill) 10.22–11.27 hr; B3828 (Sgt S. W. Smith) 10.23–11.13 hr; B3827 (Capt J. I. Mackay) 10.23–11.10 hr; B3815 (Lieut E. M. Gilbert) 10.23–11.10 hr; B3763 (Capt W. H. Haynes) 10.24–11.19 hr; B3752 (Lieut A. H. Orlebar) 10.24–11.10 hr; B3886 (2nd Lieut C. C. Banks) 10.24–11.24 hr; B3767 (Lieut L. F. Lomas) 10.25–11.12 hr; B3899 (Maj T.O'B. Hubbard) 10.25–11.10 hr.

No.50 Squadron, B Flight, Detling: Armstrong Whitworth F.K.8s B225 (2nd Lieut F. V. Bryant, 2nd Lieut T. A. Lloyd) 10.25–12.20 hr; B247 (2nd Lieut F. A. D. Grace, 2nd Lieut G. Murray) 10.32–12.15 hr; B229 (Capt C. J. Truran, Lieut R. Robertson) 10.33–12.15 hr; B223 (2nd Lieut H. T. W. Oswell, Capt Kirkby) 10.54–12.14 hr.

No.50 Squadron, C Flight, Bekesbourne: B.E.12s 6509 (Capt J. S. Shaw) 10.23–11.59 hr; 6493 (2nd Lieut W. G. Latham) 10.24–12.10 hr; 6185 (2nd Lieut C. C. White) 10.25–12.11 hr; 6157 (2nd Lieut L. Lucas), W/T tracker, 10.45–11.48 hr; B.E.12as A6309 (Lieut J. Metcalfe) 10.22–12.02 hr; A6313 (2nd Lieut T. V. Villiers) 10.23–12.00 hr.

No.61 Squadron, Rochford: Sopwith Pups A6249 (Capt E. B. Mason) 10.22–11.35 hr; B1811 (2nd Lieut P. Thompson) 10.23–11.40 hr; B1808 (Capt H. C. Stroud) 10.22–11.30 hr; B1806 (Capt S. E. Starey) 10.22–11.25 hr; B1809 (2nd Lieut J. S. Wood) 10.23–11.40 hr; B1764 (Sgt W. A. E. Taylor)

10.22–11.30 hr; B2159 (Capt C. B. Cooke) 10.23–11.32 hr; A6248 (Lieut H. A. Edwardes) 10.24–11.25 hr; A6243 (Lieut J. D. Belgrave) 10.24–11.28 hr; B1771 (Lieut L. F. Hutcheon) 10.25–11.30 hr; B1774 (2nd Lieut E. E. Turner) 10.26–11.33 hr; A6246 (Lieut L. B. Blaxland) 10.25–11.25 hr; B1723 (Capt C. A. Ridley) 10.24–11.30 hr; B2159 (Lieut J. T. Collier) 10.24–11.24 hr; B1765 (2nd Lieut H. A. Blain) 10.24–11.24 hr; A6245 (2nd Lieut E. H. Chater) 10.25–11.29 hr; A653 (2nd Lieut G. Howe) 10.24–11.29 hr; B735 (2nd Lieut A. H. Bird) 10.30–11.30 hr.

No.78 Squadron, Penshurst: Sopwith 1½ Strutters A8275 (Lieut C. J. Marchant) 10.21–12.05 hr; B2554 (2nd Lieut F. L. Luxmoore) 10.22–12.05 hr; B.E.12as A595 (2nd Lieut N. H. Auret), W/T tracker, 10.20–11.55 hr; A592 (2nd Lieut A. T. Kemp), W/T tracker, 10.20–12.00 hr; A6320 (2nd Lieut J. F. Ellor), W/T tracker, 10.35–11.50 hr.

No.78 Squadron, Telscombe Cliffs: B.E.12as A6308 (2nd Lieut R. F. W. Moore) 10.16–12.48 hr; A6305 (2nd Lieut W. H. Howell) 10.17–11.49 hr.

B.E.12a A6308, No.78 Squadron, flew four anti-Gotha sorties from Telscombe Cliffs, the last on 22 August, 1917. This photograph, with its unidentified 'owner' and friends or relations, was taken later at Penshurst.

No.112 Squadron, Throwley: Sopwith Pups B2158 (2nd Lieut A. J. Arkell) 10.17–12.05 hr; B1763 (2nd Lieut I. M. Davies) 10.17–12.02 hr; A6153 (Capt C. Sutton) 10.20–11.52 hr; A638 (Lieut R. W. le Gallais) 10.20–12.16 hr; B1711 (2nd Lieut Cox) 10.20–12.00 hr; B1772 (Capt Thomas) 10.20–11.45 hr; B2195 (Lieut C. R. W. Knight) 10.20–11.45 hr; B1803 (2nd Lieut J. W. R. Thompson) 10.20–11.05 hr, returned with engine trouble; B1807 (2nd Lieut N. E. Chandler) 10.20–12.06 hr; B2194 (Lieut J. S. Poole) 10.21–12.05 hr; B1769 (2nd Lieut S. Cockerell) 10.21–11.35 hr, returned with petrol feed trouble.

No.46 Squadron, Suttons Farm: Sopwith Pups—Eighteen sorties, 10.10–11.20 hr, details not recorded.

No.65 Squadron, Wye: Sopwith Camel—one sortie, 10.50–12.15 hr.

No.35(T) Squadron, Northolt: Bristol Fighter A7173 (2nd Lieut F. G. C. Weare) 10.32–12.00 hr.

No.40(T) Squadron, Croydon: Sopwith Pups B1738 (Lieut T. W. L.

Stallibrass) 10.30–11.35 hr; A650 (Lieut N. O. Vinter) 11.00–11.45 hr; A6228 (Lieut A. G. Taylor) 10.20–11.45 hr; D.H.5 A9163 (Maj C. C. Miles) 10.35–11.45 hr.

No.56(T) Squadron, London Colney: Spads A8817 (Capt C. E. Foggin) 10.20–11.40 hr; A8815 (Capt W. H. L. Copeland) 10.21–11.20 hr; A8816 (2nd Lieut R. H. Stocken) 10.22–10.27 hr, returned with burst radiator; A8802 (Lieut J. M. Stubbs) 10.23–11.35 hr.

No.62(T) Squadron, Dover: D.H.5s A9250 (Lieut J. G. Aaronson) 10.28–11.30 hr; A9254 (Capt H. M. Sison) 10.48–11.30 hr.

No.63(T) Squadron, Joyce Green: D.H.5s A9252 (Lieut P. O. Ibbett) 10.25–11.40 hr; A9442 (Lieut R. Erskine) 10.25–11.25 hr; A9215 (2nd Lieut L. Hale) 10.20–11.20 hr.

No.7 Aircraft Acceptance Park, Kenley: R.E.8s A3889 (Lieut R. Goudie) 10.30–12.00 hr; A3890 (2nd Lieut Sutton) 10.35–11.10 hr.

No.8 Aircraft Acceptance Park, Lympne: F.E.2ds B1881 (Lieut H. Slingsby) 10.20–12.40 hr; B1894 (Lieut P. R. T. Chamberlayne) 10.25–12.10 hr; B1896 (2nd Lieut A. N. Dupont) 10.25–11.55 hr; B1898 (2nd Lieut O. Matson) 10.35–11.45 hr; Bristol Fighters A7106 (2nd Lieut J. G. Dainty) 11.00–12.30 hr; A7116 (2nd Lieut S. J. Riley) 11.20–12.00 hr; Sopwith Camel A2322 (Lieut L. G. Wood) 11.20–12.10 hr; D.H.4 B2127 (2nd Lieut G. H. Drew) 11.10–12.10 hr.

Experimental Station, Orfordness: Martinsyde F.1 A3933 (Capt L. J. Wackett, Capt F. W. Musson) 10.25–11.40 hr; Sopwith Triplane N5430 (Capt V. Brown) 10.28–11.45 hr; Sopwith Pup B1717 (Lieut A. J. Francis) 10.30–12.00 hr; Bristol Fighter A3303 (Lieut F. D. Holder, Capt B. M. Jones) 10.30–12.00 hr; Armstrong Whitworth F.K.8 B224 (2nd Lieut W. R. Oulton, 2nd Lieut Lamb) 10.50–12.15 hr; D.H.5 A9186 (Maj C. H. Norman) 10.35–11.50 hr.

Testing Squadron, Martlesham Heath: Sopwith Camel (Lieut G. W. Gathergood) 10.30–11.40 hr; Vickers F.B.16D (Lieut K. S. Henderson) 10.35–12.15 hr.

Rudolf Kleine could muster only a much-depleted force for this raid after severe losses on 18 August, when eight or nine of the twenty-eight Gothas which took off to attack London came to grief without ever reaching the English coast. They had left in defiance of an adverse weather forecast, and after abandoning the raid because of violent winds, drifted across neutral Holland where two were shot down, while others crashed in Belgium.

Despite having only fifteen aircraft available on the 22nd, Kleine rashly planned a two-pronged attack—which ended in disaster. On reaching the coast one group was to bomb Sheerness, Southend, or Chatham, according to the situation encountered, and the other was to attack Dover. This idea became even less tenable after four aircraft turned back with mechanical problems; then, nearing the English coast, Kleine himself had engine trouble, leaving his deputy, Richard Walter, to execute the plan.

The ten remaining aircraft were reported by the Kentish Knock lightship at 10.06 hr and as they proceeded southwestwards came under a considerable barrage from various ships, with the destroyer HMS *Kestrel* and the armed trawler *Plym* over-optimistically claiming hits. The formation's progress over the 20 miles to the coast was unaccountably slow, taking another 30 min to reach Margate and thus allowing ample time for fighters to gain their height, estimated variously as between 14,000 and 16,000 ft. Gun batteries around the North Foreland were also fully alerted.

Believed to be Flt Lieut A. F. Brandon, posing at RNAS Manston with Camel B3923, the second aircraft he flew on 22 August, 1917, after his Gotha combat. (*R. Shelley*)

Within moments two of the Gothas went down—one in the sea and one on the Hengrove golf course at Margate—and the formation was reduced to some disarray, though the precise sequence of events is not clear. Realizing the strength of the opposition, Walter fired white signal cartridges, meaning to indicate that the entire formation should make for Dover, and turned southeast. However, this was not fully understood, and some aircraft bombed Margate and others Ramsgate, but they all followed Walter out to sea, then down the coast to Deal and across the land to Dover, where the remaining bombs were dropped at about 11.15 hr. Another Gotha was shot down off Dover.

Since only five of the Manston War Flight pilots were available, Smyth-Osbourne, commanding the Nore aerodromes, ordered them to patrol over the aerodrome to await events. Already airborne on his first Camel flight, Arthur Brandon felt sufficiently at home after 40 min in the responsive little fighter to engage the enemy about a mile out to sea, having been alerted by the 'readiness' signal visible on the aerodrome 13,000 ft below. He selected a Gotha on the left of

Camels and a Pup of the RNAS Manston war flight. The nearest Camel, B3843, was flown on 22 August by Flt Sub-Lieut C. H. Fitzherbert, who made a prolonged but inconclusive attack on a Gotha off Margate.

the formation, opening fire at 200 yards and closing to 20, made a second attack closing to 15, and then a third, after which the bomber started to spin. Brandon had now exhausted his ammunition, and before returning to base he followed his victim down to 1,000 ft. At the same time he noticed another Gotha falling in flames.

When Brandon was starting his attack, Butler in a Bentley-engined Camel leading Fitzherbert, Drake and Harker in Clerget-powered models, was at 15,000 ft a few miles west of Margate and also saw the formation. As he approached to engage, an enemy bullet cut the cable activating his joy-stick gun button, and while pondering this problem he saw a Camel—which he took to be Brandon's—attack a Gotha and set its starboard engine on fire. He found that he could still fire his guns with their levers and chased the formation to Dover, engaging one bomber at close quarters until one gun was exhausted and the other jammed. On landing he discovered a bullet embedded in an engine cylinder and that an aileron cable was holding by a single thin strand.

Camel B3926, flown by Flt Sub-Lieut Mark Harker, RNAS Manston, inconclusively engaged a Gotha on 22 August, 1917. The name *Happy Hawkins*, forward of the roundel, has no apparent relevance to Manston, and is likely to have been applied, with the elaborate colour scheme, when the aircraft was later on the Redcar training station—where the photograph was taken.

Drake delivered two attacks between Ramsgate and Deal before his port gun jammed. He managed to clear this and off Dover singled out another Gotha which burst into flames after a prolonged attack. He resisted the temptation to follow it down, preferring to continue pursuit of the formation, and thus did not see it hit the water. A final attack on the departing enemy was frustrated when his port gun again jammed, and he returned to base having fired 632 rounds.

Fitzherbert and Harker both made several determined attacks between Margate and Dover without causing any major damage. Fitzherbert, who thought that he had incapacitated one rear gunner, fired 600 rounds despite several stoppages, while Harker broke away with engine trouble after firing 300 rounds.

Meanwhile Brandon had spent only five minutes on the ground before getting airborne in another Camel, the first having shown signs of engine trouble as well as suffering some combat damage. He saw the departing Gothas off Ramsgate, caught them about 30 miles out and made repeated attacks without success until his ammunition ran out when nearing the Scheldt estuary. In the course of his two sorties Brandon fired 1,020 rounds. When 50 miles out to sea he saw one Gotha drop seven bombs, which had presumably failed to be released over England.

The Manston pilots possessed no exclusive rights over Gothas in the Thanet area and among those attracted to the scene was Gerald Hervey in a Pup from RNAS Dover. While still about three miles off Margate he engaged a Gotha on the right of the formation, opening fire at 100 yards from dead astern and delivering 100 rounds before his gun jammed. The bomber began a slow spin, and Hervey, after rectifying his gun, fired only another 25 shots before it jammed again. While trying to clear this, he stalled his Pup and got into a rapid engine-on spin. On recovering he saw what he thought was the same Gotha hit the sea about half a mile off Margate. After brief attacks on several more machines he gave undivided attention to one, firing 200 rounds while closing to 20 yards and silencing the rear gunner.

While Hervey was making his first attack from the rear, Harold Kerby from Walmer tackled the same aircraft from slightly below and to the side. He saw his tracers entering the fuselage and almost immediately the Gotha went into a spin. He followed it down, firing an occasional burst, and saw it hit the sea off Margate. Then to his considerable embarrassment his engine oiled up and he was obliged to land on the beach. Kingsford from Walmer saw the Gotha spinning after Kerby's attack. So, the best co-ordinated action of the morning was achieved—probably by accident—by pilots from two different stations.

MacLaren, the Walmer CO, who took off just before Hervey, had collected a newly-repaired aircraft from Dover. He landed at Walmer to rectify a gun fault which occurred on his test burst and, although airborne with minimal delay, was unable to overtake the Gothas, which he chased to Dover and out to sea.

The bulk of the considerable RFC force—which included eighteen Camels and fifty-one Pups—was again deployed along set patrol lines well inland to protect the capital and thus denied any contact with the enemy.

However, the prompt issue of the patrol order at 10.15 hr and the slow progress of the bombers allowed the less effective aircraft based south of the Thames to reach operational height, and No.50 Squadron made contact. John Shaw, C Flight commander, with Latham, Metcalfe and Villiers flying B.E.12s and 12as, had reached 11,000 ft when he saw eight Gothas under AA fire near the North Foreland. He climbed his formation east of the enemy, intending to attack from out of the sun, but found himself still 1,000 ft below, so flew directly underneath and fired 90 rounds from his Lewis to no perceptible effect.

This was the point when the Gothas turned south for Deal, and unaware that he had encountered them during a short breathing space between vigorous onslaughts by the vastly more effective naval fighters, Shaw believed that the presence of his puny force had deterred them from penetrating inland. The B.Es followed the Gothas out to sea after they bombed Dover but could make no headway and abandoned the chase after 20 min. Of the other pilots only Metcalfe engaged, firing 70 rounds from extreme range as he flew underneath with Shaw after the initial sighting.

On seeing the AA fire towards Dover, Cyril Truran in an F.K.8 felt justified in diverting south of his prescribed patrol line and pursued the departing Gothas, though he was still two miles behind as they passed off the North Foreland. He fired a few bursts at extreme range, then began a long and fruitless chase over the sea, eventually reaching the bombers' height of 15,000 ft when in sight of the Belgian coast but still too far away for effective attack. Bryant kept company with Truran, and his observer fired one long burst from 1,000 yards.

No.50 Squadron made a small contribution to British military aviation history

RNAS Manston Camel B3834, with the outlandish name *Wonga Bonga*, was twice in action against Gothas—flown by Flt Sub-Lieut R. H. Daly on 12 August, 1917, and by Flt Lieut A. F. Brandon on the 22nd, when he contributed towards the destruction of Gotha G IV/663/16 off Margate. (*M. Burrows*)

Capt J. S. Shaw (*seated centre*), No.50 Squadron C Flight commander, with his pilots. Apart from 2nd Lieut L. Lucas (*seated right*), they are unidentified.

when Leonard Lucas, flying a B.E.12 'tracker' transmitted the first air-to-ground W/T message for home-defence use. He saw the Gothas near Dover and signalled '9H WW B55 NE15'. No key to the locations grid has been found, but the first and last groups meant '9 hostile aircraft . . . flying northeast at 11.15'. He evidently miscounted the Gothas, for numbers had then been reduced to eight.

Of the five pilots from supporting units who chased the bombers, only Sison in a D.H.5 from the Dover training squadron got within range, and his efforts came to naught because of mechanical troubles. He attempted to engage when they were about six miles off Dover on the way home, but his gun jammed during the initial burst, then he suffered a series of engine stoppages due to a petrol-feed fault. Aaronson in a similar aircraft, and Slingsby, Matson and Dupont in F.E.2ds from Lympne all chased for varying periods but found their machines incapable of getting close enough for attack.

D.H.5 A9163, flown on 22 August, 1917, by Maj C. C. Miles, CO of No.40 (Training) Squadron, Croydon.

A substantial effort was mounted by RNAS and RFC units from the Dunkirk area with the object of inflicting further damage as raiders neared base. Ten Camels of No.4 (RNAS) Squadron were diverted by twenty-five German fighters sent out to protect the Gothas, but two Camels of No.3 (RNAS) Squadron and three Pups of the Dunkirk Defence Flight engaged without success.

The RFC put up six Pups from No.66 Squadron and six Bristol Fighters from No.48. The Pups, patrolling between Nieuport and Blankenberghe missed the enemy, and one flown by Lieut Garland ditched off Ostende after engine failure.

The No.48 Squadron formation, led by Capt J. H. T. Letts, with 2nd Lieut H. R. Power as observer/gunner in Bristol Fighter A7219, met the Gothas—one fairly concentrated group, with two stragglers—at 11.45 hr about 30 miles off Nieuport. The Bristols were at 14,500 ft and the Gothas 1,000 ft higher. Letts closed on the rearmost, opening fire at 200 yards, with Power taking over with his Lewis and firing above the top wing as the range shortened. Letts made several more attacks, firing 300–400 rounds and Power discharged three drums while the remainder of the patrol, lagging behind for some reason, gradually caught up.

Throughout the engagement the Gotha's rear gunner retaliated with spirit, and as the Bristol closed to 60 yards for its final attack Power was shot through the heart and killed. Letts was momentarily unaware of what had happened, being struck on the head by the observer's gun as it fell forward. Recovering from his dizziness, he fired a green Very cartridge meaning to indicate that he was returning. This was misinterpreted by the other pilots as a general recall in view of the long homeward flight against the wind, and they followed to Bray Dunes, landing at 12.45 hr. Letts had the impression that after his last attack the Gotha's port propeller was turning erratically.

Sole survivor from Gotha G IV 663/16 which hit the sea about ¾-mile off Margate was the gunner, Unteroffizier Bruno Schneider, aged 19, picked up by HMS *Kestrel*. The pilot and observer, Leutnants Werner Joschkowetz and Walter Latowski, were drowned. When salvaged a few days later the aircraft—which bore a large '2' on the fuselage—was found to have a number of new bullet holes as well as patched ones dated 12.8.17.

Salvaging Gotha G IV/663/16, shot down off Margate on 22 August, 1917. (*C. Ross*)

The aircraft—number not known—which came down in flames on the Hengrove golf course, with one engine falling some distance from the main wreckage, was crewed by Unteroffizier Heinrich Schildt (pilot), Oberleutnant Echart Fulda (observer) and Vizefeldwebel Eichelkamp (gunner), all being killed. No bodies or wreckage were recovered from the aircraft shot down off Dover.

Although RFC pilots claimed no successes, ample scope remained for inter-Service dispute as to whether the navy's aeroplanes or the army's AA guns had brought down the three Gothas. At Dover the matter was resolved amicably, and the fair-minded AA defence commander, Lieut-Col W. M. Thompson—whose guns fired 1,455 rounds—regretfully conceded that there was insufficient evidence to substantiate the claims of his Citadel and Frith Farm batteries, both of which believed they had brought down the bomber. There was thus no reason to dispute Drake's positive claim.

Circumstances were different for the two shot down over Thanet, where pilots' stories conflicted regardless of claims by the gunners. Of the three whose attacks

Smouldering wreckage of the Gotha which came down on the Hengrove golf course on 22 August, 1917. Fragments from this aircraft were sold in aid of war charities. (*C. Ross*)

appeared successful, only Kerby followed the spinning Gotha all the way down and actually saw it crash into the sea. Hervey was temporarily unsighted while his own aircraft was spinning, and did not categorically identify the aircraft he saw hit the water with the one that spun after his attack. Both Kerby and Hervey attacked the right-hand Gotha of the formation, and their stories are sufficiently similar to credit them with a shared victory. Brandon's report that he engaged the Gotha on 'the left' did not indicate the direction of attack—which, if from the front, could have been against the same machine. He made no reference to any engine fire as it spun down, nor did he see it strike the surface, since his attention was diverted by the sight of another Gotha going down in flames.

Butler from the air, and Peel Ross, the Manston/Westgate station commander from the ground, both saw what they believed was Brandon's attack, after which the victim's starboard engine caught fire and the aircraft went down on land. To complicate the issue further, Kerby reported seeing two Camels attack a Gotha, which burst into flames. However, the odd fact remains that no pilot made a positive claim.

From the gunnery side, the Hengrove and St Peters batteries reported hits, the latter unit, which fired 169 rounds in 13 min, claiming the Gotha which fell in the sea. Both batteries insisted that no aircraft were attacking at the time of their hits. The CO of the Cliffsend site, whose signature is unfortunately illegible, reported with admirable objectivity—'It is impossible to give an accurate record in prolonged action of this nature.' It was equally impossible, he added, to judge whether Cliffsend could claim any credit for the Gotha down at Hengrove.

The recently-promoted Divisional Commander of Air Stations, Nore, Wing Captain H. P. Smyth-Osbourne, quoted pilots' opinions that the Thanet guns were generally ranging 2–3,000 ft below the enemy formation, with only the occasional shell reaching higher altitudes.

According to witnesses questioned by the GHQ Home Forces intelligence officer given the unenviable task of sorting things out, the aircraft which fell at Hengrove appeared to be lifted bodily by a shell explosion, then swung round to the west, burst into flames and dived to the ground. The Margate observer post agreed that this aircraft was hit by AA fire, but considered the one in the sea as definitely brought down by fighters.

Matters were further confused by survivor Schneider's statement under interrogation that a shell burst stopped their starboard engine, sending the aircraft into a spin from which the pilot could not recover. However, this admission would have been made before salvage revealed fresh bullet holes in the aircraft, undoubtedly made that morning since those from previous raids were neatly patched and labelled as battle souvenirs.

The stolid Schneider, a farmer's son, disclosed some accurate information about his unit and is unlikely to have deliberately misled his interrogators about the combat. He possibly missed seeing the first fighter—which could have killed the pilot or caused major damage with its initial burst—and genuinely believed that they fell victim to the AA barrage. Arthur Brandon reported that his first attack apparently took the Gotha by surprise, which could have happened if its crew were concentrating on the threat from the other Manston fighters airborne long after Brandon.

The question cannot be resolved with certainty, and Intelligence admitted the impossibility of piecing together such confused fighting into a consecutive narrative, but the balance of evidence indicates that the Gotha in the sea should be credited jointly to Brandon, Hervey and Kerby, and that falling at Hengrove to the anti-aircraft guns. This accords with the German assessment that one bomber was lost to gunfire and two to fighters.

During the bickering over the apportionment of credit both sides predictably took a partial view, with the navy exasperated that Senior Service opinions should even be questioned. The slightly defensive tone of a memorandum from Peel

Spad S.7s of No.56 (Training) Squadron mounted nine sorties against the Gotha raids of July and August, 1917. A8817 was flown by Capt C. E. Foggin on 22 August, but the allotted patrol line was too far north of the bombers' route for any prospect of interception. (*RAF Museum*)

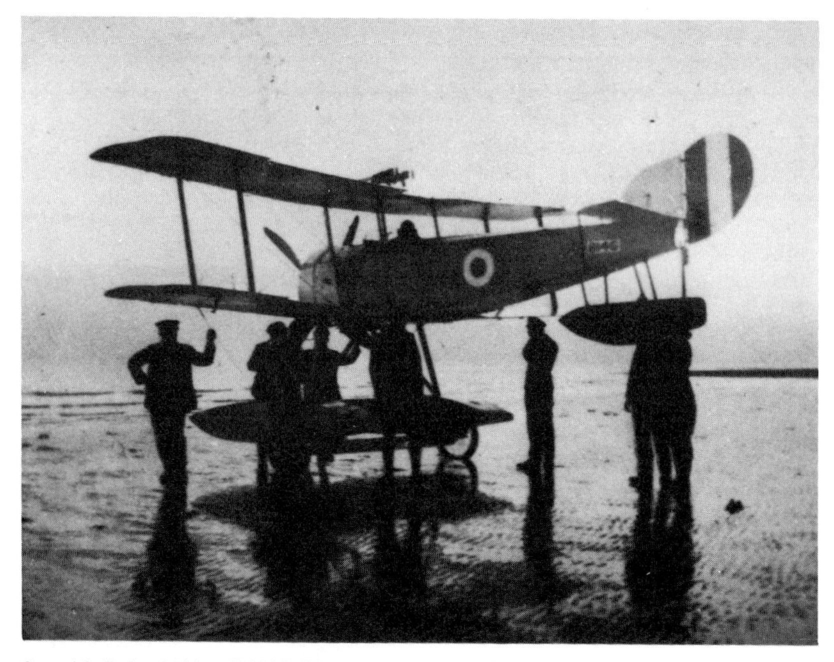

Sopwith Baby 8146 at RNAS Westgate. This aircraft flew several home-defence sorties during the summer and was damaged when Flt Sub-Lieut L. G. Maxton alighted near the Gotha shot down off Margate on 22 August, 1917. (*C. Ross*)

Ross, dated 23 August, suggests that he may have been mildly chided by his superior, Smyth-Osbourne, for allowing him so confidently to claim both the Thanet Gothas for RNAS fighters.

'Pilots immediately on landing after a long patrol and engaging hostile aircraft are not in a sufficiently stable frame of mind to give an accurate report of their proceedings' wrote Peel Ross. He added that during operations he was too busy to correct reports personally, and recommended that pilots on landing should mention only matters of immediate importance: a full account of the whole operation, including pilots' reports, could be prepared by the CO at the earliest convenience.

Brandon and Hervey were awarded DSCs for their morning's work, while Butler, Drake, Fitzherbert and Harker received 'Mentions'. Kerby, just decorated for his victory of the 12th, was omitted.

For such an intensive spell of flying activity there were again remarkably few accidents. Rex Stocken landed safely when his Spad's radiator burst just after take-off, and Flt Sub-Lieut Maxton, in a Sopwith Baby from Westgate, not on a defence patrol, crashed when trying to alight beside the ditched Gotha, but he was picked up unhurt.

Chapter XVI

Gothas by Night

Having created an apparently adequate day-fighter organization—though being denied the opportunity of proving its efficiency by the competent performance of the coastal guns and RNAS fighters on 22 August—the RFC faced the dispiriting task of starting once again from the beginning in order to oppose night bombers.

The Germans had anticipated that steadily improving British defences might inflict prohibitive casualties on their daylight formations, but Kleine did not at first regard a switch to night raiding as a permanent new role for his squadron. However, the Gotha G V did not offer sufficiently improved performance for long-range day operations, and more advanced bombers failed to progress beyond the prototype stage. For the Germans the new problems posed by night flying were partly eased by allowing crews reasonable freedom to attack unspecified targets of military importance instead of demanding pin-point accuracy against key points. For the British pilots, many now reasonably experienced in night flying, it brought a reversion to the frustrating old needle-in-the-haystack problem—but with the quarry shrunk from a sizeable bodkin, the vast unwieldy Zeppelin, to the smallest sewing needle.

The new phase of the offensive began undramatically with two single-engined aircraft from Kagohl 4 bombing Dover in bright moonlight on the night of 2/3 September, 1917. Kagohl 3's first attack was led by Kleine the following night. The target was Chatham and although the four Gothas caused little material

The Gotha G V was introduced during the autumn of 1917. (*H. J. Nowarra*)

damage 130 naval recruits were killed and 88 injured in the worst bomb incident of the war.

Meeting no difficulties in this operation, Kleine confidently despatched eleven Gothas against London on 4/5 September and five reached the target. One was shot down by the guns.

The Cabinet's predictable first reaction to these raids—which caused in all 152 deaths and 177 injuries—was to seek the view of that air policy oracle, Jan Smuts, who produced an instant memorandum on 6 September. He cannot have had time to consult the same range of authorities as in his earlier inquiries, and his report included this sweeping generalization:—

> 'Our aeroplanes afford no means of defence at night as they find it impossible to see the enemy machines even at a distance of a couple of hundred yards. In the recent night raids they have been sent into the air but to no purpose, and they might just as well have remained on the ground. They are at night useful only against very large and conspicuous objectives, like Zeppelins, once these have been picked up by them.'

This may have reflected the views of Trenchard, who was known to favour guns as the better means of defence, though Smuts himself was not very sanguine over their prospects. The Smuts report also advocated more powerful searchlights—to hamper navigation by dazzling bomber crews rather than to indicate targets for guns and fighters—and proposed some form of balloon barrage. It also dispelled comfortable beliefs that raids might be expected only during bright moonlight periods, pointing out that they were equally feasible on any dark, clear night.

Although only two enemy aircraft sightings resulted from the thirty-six fighter sorties flown during the first three night raids, there had been one highly significant development which was soon to disprove Smuts' pessimistic pronouncement on the night-fighter's role. At the end of August home-defence squadrons had been categorized as day- or night-fighter units, the latter equipped with sedate and stable aircraft which it was fondly hoped could cope with Zeppelins—though they were demonstrably incapable of coming to terms with Gothas even in daylight. There was no suggestion that day-fighter squadrons, least of all No.44 flying the unstable Sopwith Camel, with its reputation as a 'hot' aeroplane, should operate at night.

On the night of 3/4 September, when Kleine's Gothas were making their first night raid on England, official policy was calmly overturned and the stability myth buried for ever by what Ashmore later described as 'perhaps the most important event in the history of air defence'. The spontaneous decision by No.44 Squadron's Commanding Officer that Camels could be flown at night, is the more remarkable since 22-year-old Capt Gilbert Ware Murlis Green, C Flight commander, had been acting squadron commander for less than a week—and inexplicably remained thus for another four months before receiving his majority.

Murlis Green had achieved notable success during the winter of 1916–17 flying B.E.12s in No.17 Squadron on the Macedonian Front. He shot down three two-seaters and shared in the destruction of a fourth, and also destroyed one twin-engined bomber and damaged a second. A skilled pilot and excellent shot, he was an ebullient personality, unawed by higher authority to a degree remarkable in one of such modest years.

With enemy bombers reported over the North Foreland, the idea of sitting idly on the ground at Hainault Farm was anathema to Murlis Green, so he telephoned

This No.44 Squadron group, taken in December 1917, includes the three pilots who made the first home-based night Camel sorties on 3/4 September. Left to right: standing: 2nd Lieuts J. L. Wingate, W. A. Pritt and L. S. V. Gedge, Lieut C. S. T. Lavers, 2nd Lieut T. M. O'Neill, Lieut J. T. Collier, 2nd Lieut L. F. Lomas,—Roberts and Lieut J. H. Summers; seated: Lieuts A. E. Godfrey and R. N. Hall,—Herbert (equipment officer), Capt C. J. Q. Brand, Maj G. W. M. Green,—Ripley (recording officer), Capt C. J. Marchant, 2nd Lieuts R. M. Foster and C. C. Banks.

Home Defence Brigade and extracted permission to take off. Whether he mentioned that neither he nor the other two pilots prepared to go with him had previously flown a Camel at night is doubtful. However, Capt C. J. Q. 'Flossie' Brand, the South African commander of A Flight, was another highly experienced pilot, and 2nd Lieut Charles 'Sandy' Banks, though relatively recently qualified, was a natural flier whose mastery of the Camel soon earned him a reputation as an outstanding aerobatic pilot.

The three took off from an improvised flarepath without difficulty and patrolled the Thames estuary for more than an hour, then returned to encounter none of those gloomily prognosticated perils on landing. Despite having seen nothing—perhaps not surprising in the circumstances—they came back in a state bordering on euphoria. Their first experience of that special magic surrounding night flying was sharpened by the satisfaction of having demonstrated that the redoubtable Camel was not a creature to be handled with kid gloves in daylight only, but could be flown with complete safety by night. Records show that in the course of more than 200 subsequent operational night patrols by home-defence Camels there was not one fatal accident.

By remarkable coincidence, that same night saw a similar demonstration by a Camel squadron in France, though more of a planned operation than the spontaneous performance by the pilots of No.44. The aim was to intercept German aircraft which regularly bombed St-Omer, and by arrangement with Advanced RFC HQ, the anti-aircraft guns ceased firing two minutes after the fighters took off from Estrée-Blanche. Two Camels of No.70 Squadron, flown by Capt C. F. Collett and 2nd Lieut F. H. Bickerton, were airborne but neither made contact with the enemy. The second of this pair landed 35 min before the first of No.44's took off, and No.70 Squadron thus marginally pre-empted Murlis

Green's bold venture. However, this in no way detracts from its significance, for although news of No.70's experiment was ordered to be widely promulgated, the reaction of GHQ Home Forces would probably have been to initiate protracted official trials. As it was, the night conversion of other No.44 Squadron pilots began immediately, and news of this major development spread rapidly through the home-defence organization.

Mention of squadron personalities recalls a hilarious episode in the annals of No.44, first related by Cecil Lewis, a squadron pilot, in his classic *Sagittarius Rising*, with the hero—or villain—identified only as 'Sandy'. It happened on 15 September, 1917, when, stimulated by the effects of some superior ale recently acquired by the Officers' Mess, the pilots embarked on a low-level follow-my-leader over the Essex countryside. For the ground observer such a tail-chase presents an exhilarating spectacle, rarely performed by jet-age display teams.

While this was in progress Ashmore arrived with his ADC to discuss certain weighty matters with Murlis Green, and when all pilots had apparently landed the three strolled on to the aerodrome to check some point. However, Charles Banks was still airborne, and seeing what he took to be three ignorant air mechanics foolishly obstructing the landing area, he decided to educate them with an alarming 'beat-up', which culminated in the lowest of low passes causing the general to lie flat on the muddy grass to escape the Camel's undercarriage hurtling inches above his head. Lewis' report that 'Sandy' was 'deprived of his Sam Browne and put in irons for three days' may be literary licence, but certainly Banks left Murlis Green's office somewhat chastened. He noted in his log book—'Zoomed at General Ashmore by mistake. Trouble!'

B Flight of No.112 Squadron, waiting at Throwley in late 1917 for the daylight raids which never came.

By the end of September at least ten pilots of No.44 Squadron were qualified for night flying. But for some reason which surviving documents fail to explain, and although a few uneventful ad hoc night sorties on Pups had been flown by individual RNAS and RFC pilots, the two Pup squadrons—Nos.61 and 112—never converted to night-flying operations. A report by Higgins several months later on general re-equipment matters baldly dismissed the Pup as 'impossible to fly at night'. This remarkable statement confounds most popular assessments of the relative characteristics of the two famous Sopwith fighters—that while the Pup was docile and tractable, the Camel could turn round and bite the unwary pilot.

Oliver Stewart in *The Clouds Remember* wrote of the Pup: 'Its handling qualities were so good and its wing loading so light that it could be put down "anywhere" by a pilot who knew it well.' The Camel he summed up as a great aeroplane, 'at once difficult and yet responsive; wilful yet with those who knew

Inexplicably barred from night operations, Sopwith Pups of No.61 Squadron seen here lined up at Rochford in the autumn of 1917.

how to handle it, enthusiastically obedient'—but he also recalled that several early, unexplained, accidents endowed it with all kinds of vices. However, it had one especially valuable quality described by Group Capt Gilbert Insall VC, formerly of No.50 Squadron, in a personal recollection—'the Camel could be landed in 50 yards without undue difficulty . . . this had an important bearing on night fighting morale.' In correspondence with the authors shortly before his death in 1979, Capt Gerard Fane, who flew both types in the RNAS, commented: 'the Pup was much nicer and easier to fly at night than the Camel, but its chief drawback was that it had a high and rather flimsy undercarriage and small tyres, and being very lightly loaded, would tip over on a wing unless landed dead into the eye of the wind'.

The answer would appear to lie with the relative wing loadings of the two aircraft—6·4 lb/sq ft for the Camel and 5·1 lb/sq ft for the Pup. This may seem academic in comparison with figures more than ten times greater for modern fighters, but it represented a significant difference for the period. The result was that the Camel could be flown firmly down to the flarepath where it stayed put, while the Pup tended to 'float' for some distance and bounce on touching down.

It is unlikely that the Pup squadrons would remain content with their inactive day role while Camel pilots were happily converting to night flying, and perhaps an unacceptably high incidence of landing accidents during early night training caused the authorities to restrict the Pups to daylight operations. But this is pure speculation, unsupported by any facts which have come to light. Whatever the

This Lewis-armed Sopwith Pup was habitually flown by Flt Lieut Gerard Fane at RNAS Yarmouth. It is not known whether he was responsible for its sorry state shown here—which was clearly a humorous shot for personal albums.

reason, the home-defence organization was deprived of some forty good fighters and pilots, which would have greatly increased the interception prospects.

The balloon barrage proposal in Smuts' report had in fact been put forward by Ashmore the day before. It was not, as sometimes suggested, his own invention but an idea which had been around since prewar days. Suggestions had come from Service men and civilians, one keen protagonist being Halifax engineer Edgar Booth, who early in 1916 deluged MPs and others with his 27-page pamphlet on the subject. The suspended wires of Booth's barrage were intended to carry electrically-detonated charges, and there was provision for a built-in W/T warning system. In turning it down the Ministry of Munitions claimed that the balloons would be seen by enemy aircraft—to which the exasperated Booth retorted that it was essentially for protection at night. His prophetic parting shot on retiring from

A section of the London balloon barrage.

the fray was that the value of such 'aerial nets' would eventually be recognized.

Germany and Italy had introduced balloon barrages in early 1917, and during the Gotha daylight campaign an RFC specialist had inspected the installation at Venice. The system chosen for London was a series of 'aprons' comprising three Caquot-type balloons 500 yards apart, linked with cables from which 1,000-ft steel wires hung vertically at 25-yard intervals. The initial 7,000 ft operating height was later increased to 9,500. There was provision for flying single balloons in vital areas where an apron could not be deployed.

The first trial, in Richmond Park on 21 September, 1917, was marred by a fatal accident. A violent gust of wind struck the balloons, and in a valiant but forlorn attempt to control them, Air Mechanics H. E. James and W. J. Pegge clung to their handling lines and were carried aloft. James plummeted to his death in the park from 1,000 ft and Pegge, who had struggled up into the balloon rigging, fell from a greater height over Croydon.

The first of twenty balloon aprons authorized became operational in the northern and eastern outskirts of London during early October, but in the event no more than ten were completed, the last in June 1918.

The night raids also brought some reorganization of the anti-aircraft guns, with the outer defences covering a rough semi-circle of some 25 miles radius east of Charing Cross. Fighters were briefed to avoid a 'silent area' immediately east of this gun line as well as central London. If bombers were not picked up by the searchlights they were plotted by sound, and barrage fire was ordered in the appropriate position shown on a map with numbered squares. The various barrages each had their own code names.

On Monday, 24 September, the sinister, undulating hum of Gotha engines off the North Foreland barely 15 min after sunset signalled the start of the most intensive night bombing phase which England experienced during the entire war. Zeppelins also bombed that night, confining their activities to northern England. During the next seven nights of the harvest-moon period there were five more aeroplane raids, with 60 of the 97 bombers despatched attacking London and southeastern England. Despite relatively few casualties—95 killed and 260 injured—these raids, sometimes dragging on for several hours with a succession of unseen raiders interminably within earshot, caused long-lasting feelings of anger and revulsion in the population comparable with those produced by the 1940–41 'blitz'.

This is reflected in some of the early writings about the air war, heavily tainted by propaganda, such as this extract from Wilson and Hammerton's *The Great War*, published in 1919:

> 'For their aeroplane raids the Germans were unable to spare the best pilots or the best machines. The service was unpopular among the pick of the German airmen, as there were some men who were revolted by the cruel and unnecessary murder of civilians and who realised that sooner or later it would bring stern retribution. A couple of hours before the Gothas started their crews were summoned from the brothels in which they spent most of their time, and one after another the machines were made ready and rose.'

While the anti-aircraft guns did well, destroying four Gothas, the performance of the night fighters was disappointing, with only nine sightings in the course of 157 sorties. However, there is strong circumstantial evidence that a Sopwith 1½ Strutter of No.78 Squadron accounted for a Gotha missing on 25/26 September which Germany attributed to anti-aircraft fire. It was more probably ditched after its fuel had drained from tanks punctured by the Sopwith's fire.

Of major significance during this phase was the introduction, on 28/29 September, of vast multi-engined bombers designated by the letter R—Riesenflugzeug (giant aeroplanes)—as distinct from the Grossflugzeug (large aeroplanes) which included the G category Gothas.

Evolution of the Giants owed much to the prophetic drive of Count von Zeppelin. The success of Igor Sikorsky's pioneering four-engined aeroplanes in Russia during 1913–14 had awakened thoughts of trans-Atlantic flight, and when the war indefinitely postponed projects to win the *Daily Mail*'s £10,000 prize for the first crossing, von Zeppelin—perhaps already visualizing the airship's long-term limitations—partly financed formation of the Versuchsbau GmbH Gotha-Ost (Experimental Works Gotha-East) and commissioned a skilled design team to produce a large long-range aeroplane bomber. The V.G.O. concern was quite unconnected with the Gothaer Waggonfabrik which built the G class machines.

The three-engined prototype V.G.O.I, which flew in April 1915, was followed by the V.G.O.II and the six-engined V.G.O.III, both operating with Riesenflugzeug (Giant Aeroplane Section) No.500—Rfa 500—on the Eastern Front. In 1916 the V.G.O. factory moved to Staaken, near Berlin, and the R prefix was used for its subsequent aircraft.

During the summer of 1917, Rfa 501, commanded by Hauptmann Richard von Bentivegni, was recalled to Germany from the Eastern Front—where it had flown Siemens-Schuckert Giants—to re-arm with new Zeppelin-Staaken aircraft and work up for operations in the west, including raids on England.

The Giants allotted to Rfa 501 were the R.IV, with six engines driving one tractor and two pusher propellers; the R.V, with five engines driving three tractor propellers; and the R.VI, with four engines driving two tractor and two pusher propellers. Individual aircraft were also identified by an R prefix, which can cause confusion. For example, aircraft R.12 was of the R.IV type, R.13 was an R.V, while R.25–39 were R.VIs.

The R.IV and R.V were prototypes, and the R.VI with its simpler installation of four 245 hp Maybach or 260 hp Mercedes engines in tandem pairs was the main production version. The aircraft were heavily defended, with gun positions in sundry precarious-looking locations—though some crews were critical of the machines' capacity to deal with fighters. Like the earlier V.G.Os, they spanned 138½ ft (compared with the 102 ft of the Second World War Lancaster) and were approximately double the size of the Gothas. Loaded weight of the R.VI—more than 26,000 lb—approached that of the Wellington and Whitley, Britain's largest bombers in 1939, though it had only half their power. All versions had a maximum speed of about 80 mph and carried 2,200 lb of bombs.

Although sometimes belittled as white elephants, the Giants were technically far ahead of their time and would have earned lavish praise had they been British products. The R.VI had an enclosed cabin with extensive instrumentation, had W/T for contact with base, and a primitive system of intercommunication for the crew, who were provided with parachutes. For their time they were reasonably 'clean' aircraft, though marred by the clumsy undercarriage, using up to sixteen mainwheels in some versions and imposing a drag penalty of perhaps ten miles an hour. Despite problems arising from their complex engine installations and sheer size, they operated with remarkable efficiency and proved capable of remaining airborne after suffering extensive damage or mechanical failures. In the course of

Zeppelin Staaken Giant R.12—the R.IV prototype.

Zeppelin Staaken Giant R.13—the R.V. prototype.

A Zeppelin Staaken Giant R.VI of the main production batch.

twenty-eight sorties against England not one Giant fell to the defenders.

The introduction of the Giants produced a strangely unco-ordinated and unhelpful performance by the Home Forces intelligence staff. As early as 27 July a British W/T monitoring station in France intercepted Cologne calling aircraft FR-O, and during the next four weeks logged FR-B, H and Z. Then FR-L was heard while flying from Hanover to the Ghent area on 6 September—the same date that a four-engined aircraft was independently reported as having landed at St-Denis Westrem.

Other scraps of information came from various sources, and on 19 September Home Forces intelligence reported that new Riesenflugzeuge or Giant aircraft, perhaps as many as six, had recently gone to Belgium. Their limited circulation report went on:

> 'From such information as we have at present, it is impossible to foretell the uses to which these machines will be put, but it is reasonable to assume that if they prove successful they will in time take part in the bombing attacks on England.'

A reconnaissance photograph of St-Denis Westrem taken on 25 September showed an aircraft considerably larger than a Gotha.

None of this important information appears to have been passed either down to the gunners and flying squadrons or upwards to the Cabinet. There is little doubt that the 'five aeroplanes' allegedly held by a London searchlight unit on 29/30 September were a single Giant picked up on its first visit to the capital, and subsequent raids provided further clues.

A fuller GHQ Home Forces intelligence memorandum of 10 October disclosed that among seven Giants seen at St-Denis Westrem four days earlier was a six-engined machine. On 14 December it was further reported that of twenty-one W/T transmissions recently monitored, at least three were possibly connected with raids on England.

At last, on 19 December, after the eighth Giant sortie, the authorities let the directly involved soldiers and airmen into the secret, and Colonel Simon sent this note to his London anti-aircraft sub-commanders:

> 'The last attack last night was made by a very large machine, probably of a span of nearly 120 ft between wing tips. It was flying comparatively slowly, about 60 mph. The engines were very loud and, as is usual, were worked intermittently. The height was probably not very great, somewhere about 10,000 ft. Future raids will probably be made by this machine and it is particularly desirable to destroy it. When information is received of its approach it will be notified to you by the name *Bertie*'

Although not to be found on the files, it is probable that a similar notification was passed to the flying squadrons.

The reference to the 'intermittent' working of the engines is explained by the widely-held belief that Gotha pilots habitually switched off and made gliding approaches to targets. Observers had not then become accustomed to the almost arbitrary fading of engine sounds caused by atmospheric conditions.

The unfortunate delay in widening the circle of knowledge about the Giant threat probably began with the laudable desire to obtain firm evidence of their employment and was then governed by over-zealous application of the 'need to know' principle and a belief that any leakage to the public would create alarm and despondency. There is no indication that the early clues provided by strange searchlight sightings were followed up, or that the improbability of Gothas flying in close formation at night was ever questioned.

What is certain is that withholding such a fundamental fact as the existence of a second and vastly larger possible aeroplane target greatly added to the difficulties of gunners and fighter pilots, with consequent delay in creating an efficient night-defence organization—quite apart from the confusion caused when the Penshurst wireless monitoring station picked up Giant transmissions which it understandably assumed were coming from Zeppelins.

Apart from the Giant threat, the harvest-moon offensive added impetus to the home-defence research programme. Having abandoned the idea of airborne searchlights, the Orfordness experimental station turned to other ways of

The Eeman triple Lewis gun installation in Martinsyde G.102 Elephant A6299. (*H. J. T. Saint*)

locating, and destroying, the bombers. Capt Bennett Melvill Jones conducted trials using F.E.2bs as bombers and B.E.2es as fighters to prove what had long been suspected—that targets were much more easily spotted from below than from above. Extrapolating the results, he calculated that on a moonless night a Gotha should be seen from a distance of 600–1,400 ft underneath, while in moonlight this was increased to 4,000 ft. The target aircraft was difficult to pick up from the side or from above, and the fighter should therefore attempt to attack from below at fairly long range before it could be seen by the bomber.

Concurrently, ballistic experts had been studying the behaviour of bullets discharged from Lewis guns and established that when fired at an angle of 45 deg from an aircraft flying at 100 mph, the force of gravity and the air resistance counter-balanced one another and the bullets followed a straight course for 600–800 yards. For a time the theorists were rather carried away by the possible applications, particularly when mock combats at the Central Flying School involving a two-seater and various fighters produced the most accurate shooting from an S.E.5 with its Lewis angled at 45 deg.

Martinsyde F.1 A3933 fitted with two upward-firing guns, in this picture aligned to fire vertically through the wing centre-section. The noticeably high-gloss finish seems inappropriate for night operations but was doubtless applied for some trial at Orfordness.

The next step was to fit a Martinsyde G.102 Elephant single-seater with a triple mounting, designed by Capt L. E. Eeman at Orfordness, with the guns housed in the fuselage and angled upwards at about 47 deg to fire through a cut-out in the top wing centre-section. By the time this was ready for trials in early August, however, the revelation of the Gotha's tunnel gun had much reduced the prospects of success against the day raiders. Sound enough in theory, the upward-firing technique was clearly not practical for daylight interception—and suicidal for dog-fighting which demanded well-tried methods involving rapid manoeuvre. But it had obvious merit at night, when the fighter could make a stealthy approach from below. Eeman flew the modified G.102 on one anti-Zeppelin patrol but found nothing, and the installation was never tested 'in anger'.

Following the widely-held belief that two pairs of eyes were better than one for night operations, Orfordness adapted the prototype Martinsyde F.1 two-seater for special trials. Though classed as a fighter, this aircraft probably originated as a reconnaissance design, for the observer was positioned ahead of the pilot, an arrangement which had proved highly unsatisfactory in early B.E.2c operations. This is perhaps why the F.1, despite excellent stability, and a good performance bestowed by the 250 hp Rolls-Royce engine, received no production order.

The F.1 was fitted with an upward sight developed by Melvill Jones for the pilot and two Lewis guns angled at about 45 deg to fire above the propeller for the observer, who lay on his back in the front cockpit. The idea was for the pilot to fly the aircraft into the correct attacking position, then signal to the observer when to fire. Piloted by Capt L. J. (later Sir Lawrence) Wackett, with Lieut H. H. Hussey as observer, the Martinsyde patrolled from Rochford during two successive raids. However, the searchlights could do no more than indicate the general direction of targets and the crew saw nothing, probably because the Gothas were flying below their daylight operating heights and the Martinsyde was above them instead of underneath.

Despite this lack of success, further trials confirmed that the method was sound, and during one Orfordness test in early 1918 Murlis Green, flying a Camel, scored 83 hits with 84 rounds fired from 200–250 yards at an 18 by 10 ft flag target towed by a Bristol Fighter, and 162 hits out of 194 rounds during a second attack from over 250 yards. A Bristol Fighter crewed by Lieuts C. P. Donnison and Fox of No.39 Squadron scored 99 hits out of 194 rounds from 400–450 yards. From about this time the 45 deg sight became a standard fitting for the night fighters, proving its value on several occasions.

The night attacks also stimulated research on sound locators, and simple double-trumpet devices were aiding the searchlights and guns at the end of 1917. A later, more sophisticated, pattern employing four 24-in trumpets connected to stethoscopes enabled the operator to assess direction of a target in elevation and azimuth up to an effective range of 10,000 yards in favourable conditions.

Parallel work was undertaken with vastly larger sound mirrors and other fixed installations, the first being located at Fan Bay east of Dover. It is not known

A quadruple-trumpet sound locator which indicated the direction of a target in elevation and azimuth. (*Imperial War Museum*)

The site of the Fan Bay (Dover) sound mirror—a 1975 photograph. (*D. G. Collyer*)

whether this derived from Mather's early experiments or was an original project of the Munitions Inventions Department acoustical section. It was of the fixed spherical type, a 15-ft diameter reflector cut into the chalk cliff and its surface rendered with concrete, focussed on a point midway between Dunkirk and Calais. The sound reflected off the sides was received in a 3-ft trumpet universally pivoted at the centre of the sphere, connected to stethoscopes and graduated to give the bearing and direction of the target. Experiments were later made using two trumpets, then with resonators instead of trumpets.

This device was first used during the raid of 1/2 October, 1917, picking up the sounds of enemy aircraft flying down Channel some 12–15 miles out to sea and inaudible to the gun crews.

A 4 ft diameter paraboloid concrete sound mirror, mounted on a cast iron stand permitting movement in elevation and azimuth was also tested in the Dover area. These sites were probably chosen to assist the interception of the persistent tip-and-run attacks—which in fact dwindled away in 1917–18—and were too far west to be of much value during the night offensive.

Research was later moved to Joss Gap, near Broadstairs, where a spherical 12½-ft concrete sound mirror on a movable mounting was working by May 1918. A more sophisticated 20-ft diameter plywood double-disc locator, which received the sound via microphones, was installed below the cliffs, but was not completed until after the bombing campaign had ended. During trials in September 1918 it picked up a B.E.2e flying at 3,000 ft 15 miles away, which was not heard by the unaided ear until it had approached to about one mile.

Research into better illumination of enemy night bombers had been in train before the main offensive opened. The versatile F. W. Lanchester, whose 1916 theories about night-fighter design had received such a lukewarm welcome from practical pilots, evolved a scheme for projecting beams of light horizontally so that fighters flying above the bombers would see them silhouetted against the ground. A trial at Upavon on 16 July, 1917, showed that with as little as 500 ft height separation the upper aircraft could only faintly see the lower machines, and further tests indicated that the scheme was unlikely to offer practical benefits. Another project, investigated by the Munitions Inventions Department anti-aircraft experimental section at Rochford, was to deploy a group of searchlights in a fan formation to produce a belt of light at 10,000 ft which would take an aircraft 3–5 seconds to cross. The idea was to illuminate all the bombers as they approached, each one then being taken over by the conventional searchlights.

Numerous other proposals were submitted, many from well-meaning members of the public, and the Government sought the advice of Dr Horace Parshall, a leading electrical engineer. No copy of his report has been traced, but there is little doubt that all the schemes were prohibitively costly in money, materials and labour, of questionable efficiency in good weather, and useless on cloudy nights.

The MID Rochford detachment investigated the more orthodox and promising possibilities of using the searchlights in conjunction with sound locators—known as 'ears'. Employing two sets of 'ears' positioned three miles apart to direct a pair of 60 cm searchlights, it was found possible to lead a fighter into visual range of a bomber—simulated by an R.E.9 and an F.E.2b respectively. Observations during actual raids showed that distinguishing and following a Gotha was possible while only a few defending aircraft were within hearing, but a saturation point was rapidly reached.

One of the most promising methods of interfering with the enemy night bombers was tried on 29/30 September, when a heavily-armed RNAS Handley Page from Coudekerque patrolled off the Belgian coast in the hope of making interceptions. Two enemy aircraft were engaged, with indecisive results. There

The 20 ft double-disc sound locator at Joss Gap, near Broadstairs, which was tested in 1918. (*Royal Radar Establishment*)

were no further such patrols, which the Admiralty probably regarded as a misuse of the heavy bombers.

The defences consistently over-estimated the size of the night raiding forces, sometimes by as much as 100 per cent. Inquiries among British night-bomber units should have dispelled any beliefs that the Gothas flew in formation and produced an answer close to the truth—that they operated individually, taking off at about five-minute intervals. But the daylight formations had left an indelible impression, and with the occasional Giant adding to the confused sound pattern created by single aircraft scattered over a vast area of sky, mistakes were understandable.

These over-estimates were perpetuated by Lieut-Col Sir Alfred Rawlinson, the West London Anti-Aircraft Sub-Commander, in a book published in 1923 which nevertheless relied extensively on old official wartime internal communiqués for its sources. Rawlinson described thirteen Gothas on 18/19 December as 'five separate divisions, each consisting of numerous groups of aeroplanes advancing in succession on a broad front on both sides of the Thames'. Breaking up Gotha 'formations' by gunfire on 5/6 December was 'a necessary prelude to enable our glorious fighting pilots to mop them up, and no doubt need be entertained that full advantage was, as usual, taken by them of their opportunity'.

Pilots are a modest, rather cynical breed and a more accurate version would hardly have offended the thirty-three airborne that night. Not one made contact with any of the eighteen individual bombers wandering over southeast England.

Home Defence Brigade optimistically maintained its wireless tracking scheme, though with hindsight any useful results were clearly unlikely. The first recorded night sighting by a 'tracker' came on 30 September from a No.50 Squadron pilot over Faversham, who lost the suspected enemy after a few seconds. W/T 'trackers' also transmitted weather information at the start of patrols, then at 30-min intervals or on meeting any significant change.

Individual aircraft identification numbers were allotted—3, 4 and 5 to No.39 Squadron, 6 and 7 to No.37, and 8 and 9 to No.50. Messages were passed in simple code, and this example—'8 LLB CT 8 F3 CJ'—meant 'aircraft No.8 reporting from map zone LLB. Cloud thick at 800 ft, wind east, ground features difficult to observe above 300 ft, thick mist, unfit for flying'. Reception generally was good, equipment reliable and the few problems were usually mechanical, such as recalcitrant aerial reels. Pilots found the transmitter useful for passing general messages—warning of an early return with engine trouble, or reporting friendly shell-fire in fighter zones. 'Trackers' were expected to concentrate on keeping an enemy in sight rather than combat.

Cabinet meetings on 1 and 2 October discussed various matters arising from the intensified German raids—wear and tear on AA guns, falls in war production by night shifts, alleged signs of panic among sections of the population and the possibility of reprisal raids—but nothing emerged of consequence to the aircraft defences. A lengthy daylight alert caused by three R.E.8s bringing Trenchard and party from France for the 2 October meeting was an indication of the prevailing state of jitters. The Press was castigated for sensationalism and the Prime Minister asked editors for more restrained air raid reporting. He produced figures showing that whereas 2,102 people had been killed and 60,402 injured by traffic accidents in the Metropolitan Police area from January 1915 to the end of August 1917, air raid casualties were only 328 killed and 1,178 injured.

With the populace becoming conditioned to Gotha raids during moon periods, there was some dismay when London received several bombs from a Zeppelin on the moonless night of 19/20 October—the first airship attack on the capital for more than a year. Ironically a 660-lb bomb which fell in Piccadilly Circus, traditional 'hub of the Empire', was launched more by accident than design, for the eleven Zeppelins seeking targets in the Midlands encountered gales which swept them helplessly southwards—five to eventual destruction over France or beyond. They flew mostly above the reach of fighters, which reported only two engagements. The faint sound of Zeppelin engines at the great operating heights was minimized by atmospheric conditions and with only a few guns firing because targets were invisible above cloud, this biggest naval airship disaster became known as the 'silent raid'.

The fortuitous impact of Zeppelin bombs on London inevitably raised another outcry from the Press and politicians. There was no disguising the fact that German losses were due to weather, and that Zeppelins had been over England for several hours with the defences apparently as powerless to intervene as two years earlier.

French, who sometimes gave the impression of being more concerned with Zeppelins than with the greater threat from Gothas and Giants, registered his predictable protest about inadequate equipment even before all the hapless raiders had come to earth. In a letter to the War Office on 20 October he complained that of the 229 aircraft on the night's order of battle, 110 were inefficient B.E.2cs, B.E.2es, R.E.7s or 120 hp F.E.2bs. Of his efficient machines 72 were serviceable, giving an average of less than three per flight on the night-fighter squadrons—a most dangerous state of affairs demanding special remedial effort. French quoted the experience of a B.E.2e pilot a few hours earlier who had found his aircraft utterly inadequate to reach a Zeppelin at 16,000 ft.

A remarkable omission from French's diatribe was any reference to his most effective fighters, No.44 Squadron's Sopwith Camels, which had already flown 38 sorties against night-bombing aeroplanes. There are no obvious operational reasons for their exclusion from the anti-Zeppelin resources, which suggests some purely administrative inertia.

Maj-Gen John Salmond, who, at the age of 36, had become Director General of Military Aeronautics, freeing Henderson to concentrate on the approaching formation of the Royal Air Force, reminded the CIGS that new aircraft for home defence could be provided only at the expense of overseas units, which were already under strength.

French's communication was considered by the Cabinet on 27 October, with a memorandum from the Air Board still expressing doubts whether loaded Zeppelins could reach the extreme heights credited to them, though conceding that many of the home-defence aircraft did lack a sufficiently high ceiling.

The Board bemoaned the difficulty of producing a fighter combining good climb with a landing speed slow enough to minimize night flying accidents, and predicted that the new N.E.1 under trial was likely to prove satisfactory in these respects. This hope proved sadly over-optimistic. The N.E.1 (Night Flying Experimental 1) was a pusher design from the Royal Aircraft Factory, powered by a 200 hp Hispano Suiza engine and incorporating various features intended to facilitate night operations, including an exceptionally sturdy wide-track undercarriage. Unfortunately, while it was very stable and easy to fly, poor climb and ceiling condemned it as a non-starter.

The War Office reply to French on 31 October disarmingly admitted that better fighters were required to counter the latest Zeppelins, but blamed the delay in

The Royal Aircraft Factory designed N.E.1—with Crayford rocket gun mounted forward—which lacked the performance to become an effective night-fighter. Maximum speed at 10,000 ft was 89 mph, and ceiling 17,500 ft.

giving Home Defence Brigade any existing high-performance aircraft on the need for a more thorough examination of their night-flying suitability rather than priority demands from the Front. This cautious attitude was evidently a delaying tactic, for there had been no recorded night-flying accidents to the sole high-performance type introduced—the Camel—since its unpremeditated introduction to night operations by No.44 Squadron, whereas during the same period seven of the well-tried and supposedly safer machines—four F.E.2b/ds and three B.E.2es—had suffered night accidents causing death or serious injury.

The War Office offered some consolation with the news that an initial batch of ten B.E.12s was being fitted with the 200 hp Hispano Suiza engine to produce 'a highly efficient machine' while some S.E.5s, Bristol Fighters and D.H.4s would be issued to Home Defence Brigade to assess their suitability for night operations.

B.E.12bs of No.77 Squadron, Penston, in 1918.

An early Sopwith 1½ Strutter single-seat 'Comic' conversion (A6906) of No.78 Squadron, Suttons Farm. Clearly the pilot was too distant from the Vickers gun to take remedial action after a failure.

Sopwith 1½ Strutter single-seat 'Comic' B762 at Martlesham Heath, with a twin Lewis gun installation. (*Mrs P. Fane*)

Squadrons would then be given such allotments of the recommended types as might be possible. A few Bristols, S.E.5as and Hispano-engined B.E.12bs joined the squadrons in December, but the limited pilot's view caused second thoughts about the D.H.4.

The B.E.12b which looked like the illegitimate offspring of a union between a B.E.2c and an S.E.5, was hardly the paragon implied by the War Office. The extra 50 hp of the Hispano Suiza gave it a ceiling of 19–20,000 ft, and Home Defence Brigade considered that at 15,000 ft it was fast enough to attack current enemy bombers, though it was likely to be obsolescent by the summer of 1918. No official performance figures for this B.E. variant appear to have survived.

December also saw the introduction of a 'do-it-yourself' home-defence fighter. Disenchanted with the performance of the early 1916 vintage Sopwith 1½ Strutter, Capt F. W. Honnett of No.78 Squadron evolved a single-seat version, with the front cockpit faired over and the pilot transferred to the observer's position. The pilot thus had a better view, while the cleaning-up and reduced weight improved performance. Armament was one or two Lewis guns mounted to fire above the top wing, since the forward Vickers was no longer accessible for clearing stoppages. Pilots initially regarded this conversion with some misgivings because Billy Honnett, aged 24 (a farmer in South Africa before the war), though a skilled pilot who had flown D.H.2s at the Front, possessed no qualifications as an aircraft engineer. In fact the modification involved no significant structural changes, and the machine was fully cleared by the Martlesham Heath testing squadron. At least twelve were used by No.78 Squadron, where they were dubbed Sopwith 'Comics'—a name also applied to a later Camel modification.

Similar efforts had been made to improve the performance of the 160 hp F.E.2bs and the Rolls-powered F.E.2ds in home-defence units. A single-seat version with the cavernous, drag-creating forward gunner's cockpit faired over, had been tested at Martlesham in August, and conversions were subsequently made in squadron workshops. These had variously shaped plywood and/or fabric nose fairings as well as different armament installations with one or two fixed or movable Lewis guns. In some cases the pilot's seat was moved forward.

These 'Chinese scouts', as they were called by the pilots, obviously had better speed, rate of climb and ceiling, but no actual figures have been traced. In a letter to DGMA on 13 December, Higgins (a brigadier-general since the end of October when Home Defence Brigade had been reorganized as No.6 Brigade) said that a 160 hp F.E.2b so modified could still only reach a maximum ceiling of 17,000 ft after a considerable time—though the average was probably nearer 16,000—and was thus of little use against Zeppelins which might reach 20,000 ft.

Repetition of heavy and sustained Gotha raids during the remaining moonlight phases of 1917 was largely frustrated by the advancing winter. Inevitably the German meteorological forecasts of conditions to the west were not always accurate, and in December Bogohl 3 introduced weather reconnaissances by single-engined Rumplers, which flew to the English coast before the bombers took off and reported by W/T whether conditions appeared favourable for

An F.E.2b single-seat conversion with one horizontal and one elevated Lewis gun. Note the cartridge-case collectors and the Hutton battery-powered gun sights. (*R. C. Bowyer*)

A more extensively modified F.E.2b single-seater—possibly A5724 of No.51 Squadron—with two enclosed Lewis guns.

operations. They also acted in a primitive pathfinder role, flying ahead of the bomber stream to drop parachute flares off some prominent feature such as the North Foreland.

Two major attacks on 31 October and 5 December were notable for the high proportion of incendiaries dropped. However, the new type 10 lb incendiary bombs employed proved to have poor performance, causing far less damage than the Germans had anticipated.

With only a handful of sightings resulting from the 84 fighter sorties flown, it began to seem that anti-aircraft guns were the answer, particularly after they shot down two Gothas during the December raid, and may have been responsible for a third machine reported missing.

On the night of 18/19 December the picture changed. Murlis Green, flying a Camel with upward-firing Lewis guns attacked a Gotha over east London and damaged one of its engines, causing it to ditch off Folkestone. It was fitting that the pilot who had demonstrated that the Camel was safe to fly in the dark should provide the proof that it could also fight in those conditions.

When it became clear that by design or because of navigation difficulties the Gothas were employing a more flexible attack pattern than hitherto seen by day or night, some redisposition of the fighter forces was necessary. During September, D Flight of No.39 Squadron was formed at Biggin Hill to cope with bombers approaching London from a more southerly direction, and in December this detachment was transferred to the parentage of No.78 Squadron. Towards the end of the year the Government sanctioned the formation of two additional fighter squadrons, one to be based at Biggin Hill.

In mid-November the basic LADA (London Air Defence Area) patrol pattern to meet night attacks by aeroplanes provided for No.37 Squadron to cover the northern approaches from Goldhanger to Leigh-on-Sea, No.50 to patrol south of the Thames between the Nore lightship and Swingfield, while Nos.39, 44 and 78 Squadrons shared an arc stretching from Enfield to Grove Park. The anti-Zeppelin pattern brought in Nos.51 and 75 Squadrons, and extended the line into Suffolk and Norfolk. The daylight patrol scheme dispensed with No.39 Squadron, but included the two Pup squadrons—Nos.61 and 112.

The night aeroplane patrol areas were lettered as follows: B Chingford–Enfield, C Chingford–Woodford, D Woodford–Goodmayes, E Goodmayes–Dagenham, F Dagenham–Eltham Park and G Eltham Park–Grove Park.

Chapter XVII

Operations—September to December 1917

2/3 September, 1917 (Night)

Target: Dover.
Enemy forces: Two aeroplanes, type not known.
Results: One killed, ten injured, £3,486 damage.
Defence sorties: Two.

RFC
No.62(T) Squadron, Dover: Sopwith Pup B1740, 23.05–00.05 hr; D.H.5 A9250, 23.25–00.15 hr.

Chronologically this raid must be regarded as opening the German aeroplane night-bombing offensive against England, despite indications that it was an ad hoc hit-and-run affair. Some details remain obscure.

British reports state that two aircraft arrived, without warning, over Dover at 23.03 hr, dropped fourteen bombs totalling 804 lb from about 2,500 ft and departed before searchlights or guns could be brought to action. Two of the bombs were adaptations of the 9·84-in mortar shells known in trench jargon as Crashing Christophers.

German records suggest that the attack was made by a single aircraft of Kagohl 4, which was primarily occupied that night with its usual programme of bombing mainland targets behind the Allied lines. This unit operated various aircraft types, and while the bomb load quoted—650 kg (1,430 lb)—far exceeds that of its single-engined L.V.Gs and Rumplers, it could have been within the capacity of the twin-engined A.E.G loaded for short missions.

Two instructors from No.62(T) Squadron patrolled east and west of Dover at 10,000 ft but saw nothing.

The motive for the attack is not apparent, and a Continental raider can hardly have got lost in the bright moonlight. It is just conceivable that a Kagohl 4 crew knowing of Kleine's intentions for Kagohl 3 decided to pre-empt his first night.

3/4 September, 1917 (Night)

Target: Chatham.
Enemy forces: Five Gothas despatched, four Gothas attacked.
Results: 132 killed, 96 injured, £3,993 damage.
Defence sorties: 16.

RFC
No.37 Squadron, Goldhanger: B.E.2d 5778 (Capt W. Sowrey) 21.12–22.52 hr; B.E.2es B4456 (2nd Lieut C. L. Milburn) 21.12–22.56 hr; B4456 (2nd Lieut S.

Armstrong) 23.05–23.46 hr; B752 (Lieut P. R. Cawdell) 21.12–22.52 hr.

No.37 Squadron, Stow Maries: B.E.2es A8659 (Capt G. D. F. Keddie) 21.12–22.30 hr; A8709 (2nd Lieut L. T. Onslow) 22.30–23.45 hr; 5768 (Capt J. L. Horridge) 22.35–00.01 hr.

No.39 Squadron, North Weald: B.E.2es B4484 (Lieut C. J. Chabot) 23.29–01.00 hr; B4483 (Capt W. St J. Boultbee) 23.59–01.10 hr.

No.44 Squadron, Hainault: Sopwith Camels B3852 (Capt C. J. Q. Brand) 23.40–00.30 hr; B3886 (2nd Lieut C. C. Banks) 23.43–00.45 hr; B3899 (Capt G. W. M. Green) 23.47–01.15 hr.

No.50 Squadron, Bekesbourne: B.E.2c 2711 (2nd Lieut L. Lucas) 21.35–22.33 hr; B.E.12s 6185 (2nd Lieut C. C. White) 21.40–22.30 hr; 6493 (2nd Lieut W. G. Latham) 22.57–00.50 hr; 6157 (Lieut W. L. Phillips) 23.00–00.40 hr.

Five Gothas flown by volunteer crews and led by Kleine took off for Kagohl 3's first night raid on England, one turning back with engine trouble.

Despite perfect weather, an easy target and minimal AA opposition, only about half the 46 bombs plotted fell on or near the primary objective, Chatham naval base, the others being scattered around Sheerness and Margate.

Due to some communications failure Chatham received no warning, and by tragic ill chance two bombs hit a drill hall used as a temporary dormitory for naval recruits, killing 130 and injuring 88. The German figure of 2,898 lb bombs dropped was 500 lb more than British estimates and probably included those which fell into the sea.

The first Gotha came in over Westgate at 22.35 hr, others arrived during the next half hour and the main Chatham attack began at 23.10 hr. The observer organization was thoroughly confused and grossly over-estimated numbers, reporting most fighters as 'hostile'—in one instance listing two as eight bombers. The final official estimate of ten bombers was still a 100 per cent exaggeration.

Home Defence Brigade was holding an exercise following concern raised by the previous night's unwarned raid on Dover, and this clearly increased confusion when a real emergency developed. Six of the aircraft officially listed in the total of sixteen anti-Gotha sorties were in fact airborne on this exercise an hour or more before the first bomber crossed the coast, and three had actually landed. The two fighters taking off at 22.30 and 22.35 hr were also probably flying exercise sorties, and surviving documents do not record when the 'patrol' order was given.

Although pilots on some of these training flights obviously acted on ground signals displaying patrol orders, it appears that only five B.Es from the regular night-fighter squadrons actually took off after the alarm was raised. They gave thin cover along patrol lines from Goldhanger to Dover but saw nothing of the enemy. The searchlights were largely ineffective in the bright moonlight, holding only one bomber for fleeting seconds.

The night's outstanding feature, discussed in the previous chapter, was the bold decision by the CO of No.44 Squadron, Capt Gilbert Murlis Green, to fly some of his Sopwith Camels. Authority duly obtained, three were airborne in seven minutes, Brand patrolling the Woolwich–Tilbury area and Banks covering a northeasterly line to Rochford. Murlis Green stayed airborne for nearly an hour-and-a-half, patrolling between Hainault and Joyce Green. Their lack of any sightings was insignificant against the demonstration that one of Britain's latest day fighters could safely be flown at night.

Recalling the occasion several years later Brand wrote: 'We were convinced of the delightful qualities of our machines, and the exhilaration of our new adventure created the most intense excitement among the other pilots.' Banks' log book comment was typically terse: 'Air raid (planes). Patrolling London to Southend. First night flying on Camels'.

No RNAS aircraft were airborne in accordance with the Admiralty's current policy not to attack enemy aeroplanes at night.

4/5 September, 1917 (Night)

Target: London.
Enemy forces: Eleven Gothas despatched, nine Gothas attacked.
Results: 19 killed, 71 injured, £46,047 damage.
Defence sorties: 18.

RFC

No.37 Squadron, Goldhanger: B.E.2d 5778 (2nd Lieut C. L. Milburn) 22.41–01.10 hr; B.E.2e B4456 (2nd Lieut S. Armstrong) 22.41–01.26 hr; B.E.12a A4032 (Capt W. Sowrey) 01.01–01.56 hr.

No.37 Squadron, Stow Maries: B.E.2es B4457 2nd Lieut J. H. Hayward) 01.01–02.00 hr; 5768 (Capt J. L. Horridge) 01.01–01.56 hr.

No.39 Squadron, North Weald: B.E.2es B4483 (Capt W. St J. Boultbee) 21.30–01.45 hr; B4484 (Lieut C. J. Chabot) 23.15–00.30 hr; B4462 (2nd Lieut L. Taylor) 23.16–01.30 hr; B.E.12s 6480 (2nd Lieut P. W. L. Jarvis) 23.13–01.13 hr; 6488 (2nd Lieut A. M. Bennett) 23.24–01.55 hr; B753 (2nd Lieut W. B. Thomson) 23.20–01.05 hr.

No.44 Squadron, Hainault: Sopwith Camels B3899 (Capt G. W. M. Green) 23.20–00.30 hr; B3852 (Capt C. J. Q. Brand) 23.27–01.10 hr; B3885 (Capt J. I. Mackay) 23.29–01.12 hr; B3886 (2nd Lieut C. C. Banks) 23.30–00.55 hr.

No.50 Squadron, Bekesbourne: B.E.12s 6185 (2nd Lieut C. C. White) 22.44–00.30 hr; 6493 (2nd Lieut W. G. Latham) 22.55–00.33 hr.

No.50 Squadron, Detling: Armstrong Whitworth F.K.8 B247 (2nd Lieut F. A. D. Grace, 2nd Lieut G. Murray) 22.55–00.15 hr.

Sopwith Camel B3885 *Thaba Bosiu* of No.44 Squadron, flown by Capt J. I. Mackay on 4/5 September, 1917.

Encouraged by the minimal opposition over the English coast, Kleine grasped the opportunity to raid London while the good weather held.

The first Gotha was airborne at 20.30 hr and ten more followed at five-minute intervals. Two returned with engine trouble and the others became widely scattered, making landfall at various points from Orfordness to Dover between 22.20 and 00.10 hr. This dispersal increased the confusion of the inexperienced observer organization, and the official assessment was that twenty-six bombers crossed the coast in seven groups. There were several wild reports from AA posts, one of which 'clearly saw' five aircraft flying up the Thames. The last of the bombers departed over Deal at about 02.15 hr.

Only five Gothas reached London, attacking at irregular intervals between 23.20 and 00.50 hr. The others bombed Dover, Margate and various places in Essex and Suffolk. Bombs dropped near Aldeburgh came from an aircraft immediately after it had crossed the coast, more likely because of incipient engine trouble than a fainthearted crew performance since again all taking part were volunteers. British authorities estimated the total weight of the 90 bombs plotted as about 6,000 lb—some 750 lb short of the German figure.

Fighter pilots patrolling between Maldon and Dover were generally confused by the difficulty of distinguishing between bomb bursts and AA guns firing, and several reported bomb explosions in places which were not hit.

Two fighter attacks were made, one by Grace and Murray flying the same F.K.8 from which they had shot down one of the 7 July day raiders. Patrolling at 6,500 ft, they were attracted by ground flashes near Faversham, then spotted twin exhaust flames below and ahead on their port side. Grace flashed the 'AAA' recognition challenge with his navigation lights and fired a Very signal, and on receiving no response Murray opened fire from the rear cockpit. After a few bursts the aircraft was lost to view.

Armstrong, No.37 Squadron, reported seeing two enemy aircraft at about his own height of 6,000 ft, flying west over the Thames estuary. He followed for five minutes, firing one drum from his Lewis to no visible effect, until they gradually drew away from his slow B.E.2e. His report suggests that he may have seen the twin exhausts of a single Gotha.

The four Camel pilots saw nothing more than the occasional parachute flares and friendly navigation lights.

A Gotha admitted by the Germans as missing was probably the victim of the Borstal AA gun, commanded by 2nd Lieut Charles Kendrew. His searchlight operator, Corporal J. Letley, held an aircraft for about seven minutes from 23.30 hr, and after what appeared to be a direct hit, it went into a steep dive. It was not seen to crash and subsequent dredging in the Medway produced no wreckage. However, 15 miles to the east a Sheppey gun section reported an aircraft with heavily labouring engines and showing a white light slowly descending out to sea off Eastchurch.

One Camel pilot was fired on by AA guns over Ilford, though in the adjacent Epping area the mobile AA brigade reported that fighters had been most co-operative with their ready use of recognition signals.

24/25 September, 1917 (Night)

Target: London.
Enemy forces: 16 Gothas despatched, 13 Gothas attacked.
Results: 21 killed, 70 injured, £30,818 damage.
Defence sorties: 30.

RFC

No.37 Squadron, Goldhanger: B.E.2es 6318 (2nd Lieut C. L. Milburn) 19.51–21.02 hr; B752 (Lieut P. R. Cawdell) 21.10–22.25 hr; B.E.12 A4032 (Capt W. Sowrey) 20.05–22.00 hr.

No.37 Squadron, Stow Maries: B.E.2es 5768 (Capt J. L. Horridge) 19.50–22.02 hr; B4505 (2nd Lieut A. C. Goldsmith) 21.50–22.29 hr; B.E.12 A6312 (Capt G. D. F. Keddie) 20.02–22.48 hr.

No.39 Squadron, North Weald: B.E.2es B4454 (Capt J. M. Clarke) 19.57–22.08 hr; B4482 (2nd Lieut A. A. Wilcock) 19.59–21.12 hr; B4462 (2nd Lieut L. Taylor), W/T tracker, 20.01–22.05 hr; B4483 (Lieut C. J. Chabot) 20.03–20.23 hr, returned with engine trouble; B.E.12 6488 (2nd Lieut P. W. L. Jarvis) 20.15–22.07 hr.

No.39 Squadron, Biggin Hill: B.E.12a A595 (2nd Lieut N. H. Auret) 20.20–22.10 hr.

No.44 Squadron, Hainault: Sopwith Camels B3852 (Capt C. J. Q. Brand) 19.50–22.05 hr; B3899 (Capt G. W. M. Green) 19.55–21.45 hr; B3763 (Capt W. H. Haynes) 20.00–22.10 hr.

No.50 Squadron, Bekesbourne: B.E.12s 6157 (2nd Lieut L. Lucas) 19.40–21.40 hr; A6313 (Lieut W. L. Phillips), W/T tracker, 19.56–21.35 hr; 6185 (2nd Lieut W. G. Latham), W/T tracker, 20.05–22.17 hr; 6509 (Capt J. S. Shaw), W/T tracker, 20.10–22.13 hr; 6493 (2nd Lieut H. T. W. Oswell) 21.50–22.31 hr.

No.50 Squadron, Detling: B.E.2e B4507 (2nd Lieut C. C. White) 20.03–22.06 hr; Armstrong Whitworth F.K.8s B224 (2nd Lieut W. R. Oulton, Capt Kirkby) 20.06–22.13 hr; B223 (2nd Lieut F. V. Bryant, Lieut R. Robertson) 21.45–22.58 hr, crashed on landing.

No.78 Squadron, Suttons Farm: F.E.2ds B1883 (2nd Lieut N. L. Garstin, Lieut H. I. Fordred) 19.39–21.40 hr; B1882 (2nd Lieut F. H. Barton, 1st AM W. Merchant) 19.41–21.35 hr; Sopwith 1½ Strutters A1040 (Capt D. J. Bell, 2nd Lieut G. G. Williams) 19.42–21.47 hr; B745 (Capt F. Billinge, 1st AM E. Cooper) 21.35–22.00 hr.

Experimental Station, Orfordness: Three sorties—details not recorded.

F.E.2ds B1882 and 1883 (nearest) flown by No.78 Squadron, Suttons Farm, in the autumn of 1917 while it was building up to its full complement of Sopwith 1½ Strutters. These aircraft were later transferred to No.33 Squadron. (*J. M. Bruce/G. S. Leslie collection*)

This was intended as the first phase of a major two-pronged attack, with a force of Gothas bombing London followed by Zeppelins raiding the Midlands and northeast.

Navigation inadequacies were manifest and, with both forces widely dispersed, damage and casualties were relatively small. The defences also had a bad night, and there were five crashes—one fatal. Another aircraft and crew were missing and there were numerous early returns for weather and mechanical reasons.

Of the sixteen Gothas airborne for London at the opening of what became known as the harvest-moon offensive, three turned back with various troubles. The remainder failed to achieve a neat stream to the target and crossed the coast at various points between Orfordness and Dover, the first at 19.03 hr and the last 70 min later. Only three reached London, bombing between 20.05 and 20.50 hr and scoring several telling hits, while six attacked Dover between 19.15 and 19.45 hr and at 21.30 hr. The remaining four scattered their bombs around Southend, Tilbury, Chatham, Sheppey and West Malling. It was estimated at the time that twenty-one bombers were involved.

The absence of a single sighting was due to the haphazard courses of the bombers as much as any lack of vigilance by the fighter pilots, several of whom clearly recognized 'friendlies'. A few fighters were held by the searchlights and it was apparent that recognition signals flashed by their downward identification lights were seldom seen from the ground.

Four B.Es were equipped as 'wireless trackers' to signal sightings and weather reports. Taylor, No.39 Squadron, used his W/T to report engine trouble and was comforted to receive a loud and clear OK to land from the ground. His engine cut completely at 500 ft over North Weald, but he touched down safely.

Wilcock, also of No.39, had been airborne for about an hour when increasing sloppiness of control made him decide to return. On landing he found that a strip of fabric had torn from his B.E.2e's under-fuselage following acid spillage from the lighting battery.

An event of historic interest—despite any productive outcome—was the mounting of the first fighter sortie from Biggin Hill, flown by 2nd Lieut Norman Hugh Auret of D Flight, No.39 Squadron, in a B.E.12a. Auret, aged 20, had been studying at the South African School of Mines and Technology before joining the RFC.

One of No.50 Squadron's F.K.8s crashed on landing without injury to the crew. Orfordness aircraft on unscheduled sorties caused some confusion in the Harwich area, where one was slightly damaged by AA fire.

24/25 September, 1917 (Night)

Target: Midlands and northeast.

Enemy forces: Navy Zeppelins L35 (Kptlt H. Ehrlich), L41 (Hptmn K. Manger), L42 (Kptlt Martin Dietrich), L44 (Kptlt F. Stabbert), L46 (Kptlt H. Hollender), L47 (Kptlt M. von Freudenreich), L50 (Kptlt Roderich Schwonder), L51 (Kptlt W. Dose), L53 (Kptlt E. Prölss), L55 (Kptlt Hans Kurt Flemming); L52 (Oblt-z-S Kurt Friemel), returned early.

Results: Three injured, £2.210 damage.

Defence sorties: 36.

RNAS

Cranwell: B.E.2e A1286, 02.10–04.50 hr.

Bacton: B.E.2c 8608, 01.45–03.56 hr.

Burgh Castle: B.E.2c 8629, 01.45–04.00 hr.
Holt: B.E.2c 8483 (also recorded as 8485), 01.50–04.00 hr.

RFC

No.33 Squadron, A Flight, Scampton: F.E.2bs A5659 (2nd Lieut D. R. Brook) 23.20–02.10 hr; A5536 (2nd Lieut E. G. Roberts) 00.03–00.30 hr, returned with engine trouble; F.E.2d B1884 (Capt S. W. Price) 03.28–04.30 hr.

No.33 Squadron, C Flight, Elsham: B.E.2e 7216 (Lieut Fall) 23.40–01.40 hr and 03.30–04.20 hr; F.E.2d A12 (2nd Lieut C. Pinnock, Lieut J. A. Menzies) 23.40–01.40 hr, crashed, observer killed; B1896 (Lieut E. E. H. Hamilton-Jackson) 00.45–02.25 hr (Beverley); A6356 (Lieut Carruthers) 00.10–01.05 hr, returned with engine trouble.

No.33 Squadron, HQ Flight, Gainsborough: F.E.2d B1885 (Maj A. A. B. Thomson) 03.15–05.50 hr.

No.36 Squadron, Seaton Carew: F.E.2b A5542 (2nd Lieut R. J. Paull, 2nd Lieut G. H. Box) 01.55–03.40 hr; F.E.2d A6461 (2nd Lieut H. J. Thornton, 2nd Lieut C. A. Moore) took off 01.50 hr, missing.

No.38 Squadron, A Flight, Leadenham: B.E.2e 6290 (Capt M. D. Barber) 00.50–04.10 hr (Elsham).

No.38 Squadron, B Flight, Buckminster: B.E.2e 6291 (Capt L. P. Watkins) 01.10–04.00 hr; F.E.2b A5566 (Lieut G. H. Harrison, 2nd Lieut C. C. Abrahams) 00.35–01.10 hr, returned with engine trouble.

No.38 Squadron, C Flight, Stamford: B.E.12 6182 (2nd Lieut C. R. Gaffney) 00.47–01.10 hr, crashed.

No.51 Squadron, A Flight, Mattishall: F.E.2bs A5525 (2nd Lieut A. W. Simon) 00.35–00.50 hr, returned with engine trouble; B417 (2nd Lieut Simon) 01.21–05.20 hr; A5543 (Capt L. C. Angstrom) 02.40–05.10 hr; A5525 (Lieut Lynn) 02.40–05.10 hr.

F.E.2d A6356 *Ceylon No.4 Flying Fox* flown by Lieut Carruthers, No.33 Squadron, on 24/25 September, 1917. (*J. M. Bruce/G. S. Leslie collection*)

A B.E.12 of No.76 Squadron at Copmanthorpe, as operated on 24/25 September, 1917. This is a 'straight' shot by No.46 Wing photographer, Cpl A. L. Hitchin, who used ground-to-air pictures of aircraft to produce montages of operational situations. (*L. B. Latham*)

No.51 Squadron, B Flight, Tydd St Mary: F.E.2bs A5551 (Lieut O. E. Ridewood) 00.41–02.15 hr; 7004 (Capt Savery) 02.50–05.03 hr (Marham).

No.51 Squadron, C Flight, Marham: F.E.2bs 7021 (Lieut T. H. Gladstone) 00.38–01.10 hr, returned with engine trouble; A5548 (Lieut D. H. Montgomery) 01.12–03.29 hr.

No.75 Squadron, Elmswell: B.E.12 A6344 (Capt C. W. Mackey) 02.30–04.30 hr.

No.75 Squadron, Harling Road: One sortie, 00.27–04.30, details not recorded.

No.76 Squadron, A Flight, Copmanthorpe: B.E.2es 7226 (2nd Lieut N. H. Hampton) 00.45–01.00 hr, returned due to weather; A1331 (2nd Lieut H. B. Evans) 02.30–06.20 hr, crashed landing; B.E.12s 6156 (Lieut J. L. N. Bennett-Baggs) 02.15–02.48 hr, returned due to weather; 6156 (Capt J. C. Griffiths) 03.03–03.35 hr, crashed, Shipton.

No.76 Squadron, B Flight, Helperby: B.E.2e A8663 (2nd Lieut W. W. Cook) 01.00–06.15 hr (Flamborough).

No.76 Squadron, C Flight, Catterick: B.E.2e 6301 (2nd Lieut D. Darby) 01.45–03.00 hr (Seaton Carew); B.E.12 A590 (Capt T. R. Irons) 02.01–03.10 hr (Seaton Carew) with engine trouble.

The first Zeppelins of the northbound force, led by Strasser flying in L46, arrived about two-and-a-half hours after the last of the Gothas had departed in the south.

Despite German claims that eight airships attacked land targets, only five were tracked by the defences. These were L35, 41, 46, 53 and 55, which came in between Bridlington and King's Lynn from around midnight until 01.25 hr, finding their efforts to reach major targets greatly hampered by strong winds at 16–18,000 ft and patchy cloud lower down. Bombs from L35, 41 and 55 fell reasonably close to industrial installations near Rotherham, in Hull and at Skinningrove, but those from L46 and 53, possibly intended for aerodromes, fell in Lincolnshire countryside.

The defenders' experiences were no more satisfactory. Only three pilots made sightings, and their aircraft were unable to close with the high-flying airships.

Nearest to success was 2nd Lieut William Wallace Cook, No.76 Squadron, who, remarkably, encountered three different Zeppelins. A New Zealander from Palmerston North, Cook penetrated the cloud and climbed northeastwards towards searchlights coning L55 south of Middlesbrough. He reached the area at 01.45 hr to find the Zeppelin some 4,000 ft higher than the 12,000 ft of his B.E.2e, and well above the AA bursts. While he strove for more height the lights lost the airship, which shortly afterwards dropped parachute flares and aimed for the Skinningrove iron works. The bombs landed several miles off target.

Despite a 60 mph tailwind Cook realized that he had little prospect of finding or overtaking the Zeppelin, so he turned back to his patrol line. He had reached 14,000 ft near Beverley when he saw L41 held in searchlights at about 16,000 ft. Again the lights lost their quarry as he approached, so he decided to patrol out to sea in the hope of catching one of the returning raiders.

F.E.2b A5548, flown by Lieut D. H. Montgomery. No.51 Squadron, on 24/25 September, 1917. (*J. M. Bruce/G. S. Leslie collection*)

Later, when ten miles off Bridlington, Cook saw a Zeppelin against the first glimmer of dawn in the sky. His B.E. was now at its 14,500 ft ceiling and the airship a good 1,500 ft higher, but he managed to close the range to 800 yards and fired four drums upwards at its rear end. He saw tracers hitting the hull and had high hopes of some result, but the Zeppelin arrogantly climbed away. It was probably the L42, which had attacked shipping off the Humber and on return found two bullet holes in a gas cell.

As the airship disappeared from view Cook realized with some concern that he had been airborne for four hours and was faced with a 60-mile flight to the coast against strong winds. After 75 interminable minutes he sighted land, with just enough petrol to safely reach a field at Flamborough about 400 yards from the shore. He was awarded the MC for what was described as an intelligent and determined sortie which failed only through bad luck.

Barber of No.38 Squadron noticed bombs falling at several points in Lincolnshire, evidently from L53, and at about 03.00 hr briefly saw a Zeppelin caught by searchlights many miles to the north—presumably the L41. After a forlorn chase he became lost and eventually landed at Elsham.

Mackey, No.75 Squadron, saw a Zeppelin northeast of Elmswell at 03.20 hr and kept it in view for some 15 min until losing it near Bungay. Although not listed among the raiders officially plotted that night, when great operating heights and the weather made accurate reporting very difficult, a later Intelligence assessment suggested that this was the L44.

No trace was found of the No.36 Squadron F.E.2d crewed by Thornton and Moore, believed to have run out of petrol while trying to regain the coast after chasing a Zeppelin far out to sea. Pinnock, No.33 Squadron, in a similar aircraft, hit some trees when letting down near Elsham, and his Canadian observer, Lieut James Arthur Menzies, was killed. Gaffney, No.38 Squadron, apparently lost consciousness because of the cold or lack of oxygen and could recall nothing of the accident in which he was injured. After labouring up to 9,500 ft he throttled back to avoid some cloud, and the next thing he remembered was struggling out of his wrecked B.E.12 in a field near Stamford.

Griffiths, No.76 Squadron, experienced severe engine vibration soon after take-off and decided to put down on the Shipton emergency landing ground, but

Capt S. W. Price, who was No.33 Squadron A Flight commander in the autumn of 1917 and later became CO of No.36; and (*right*) Capt F. W. 'Billy' Honnett, No.78 Squadron A Flight commander, who devised the single-seat 'Comic' version of the Sopwith 1½ Strutter.

he hit a ridge short of the flares, damaging his propeller, undercarriage and lower wings. Evans from the same unit crashed on landing at Copmanthorpe, and a taxi-ing accident at Scampton caused an abortive sortie.

To complete the tale of misfortune, there were five early returns for mechanical reasons and two because of weather—which also caused four aircraft to land away from their bases. One aircraft diverted with engine trouble.

25/26 September, 1917 (Night)

Target: London.
Enemy forces: 15 Gothas despatched, 14 Gothas attacked.
Results: Nine killed, 23 injured, £16,394 damage.
Defence sorties: 20.

RNAS

Manston: B.E.2cs 8298 (Sqn Cdr C. H. Butler) 18.40–20.25 hr; 8628 (Flt Lieut A. F. Brandon) 18.50–21.00 hr.

RFC

No.37 Squadron, Goldhanger: B.E.2d 5778 (Capt A. Dennis) 19.09–22.26 hr; B.E.2e B752 (Lieut P. R. Cawdell) 19.13–21.00 hr.

No.37 Squadron, Stow Maries: B.E.2e B4457 (2nd Lieut A. O. Beckett) 19.13–21.00 hr; B.E.12 6610 (Lieut J. H. Hayward) 19.13–21.03 hr, crashed landing.

No.39 Squadron, North Weald: B.E.2es B4483 (Lieut C. J. Chabot) 19.27–20.33 hr; A8711 (2nd Lieut A. A. Wilcock) 19.30–20.30 hr; B4454 (Capt J. M. Clarke) 19.27–20.43 hr; B4462 (2nd Lieut L. Taylor), W/T tracker, 19.30–20.40 hr.

No.39 Squadron, Biggin Hill: B.E.2c 4575 (2nd Lieut A. T. Kemp) 19.35–19.45 hr, returned due to weather; B.E.12a A6305 (2nd Lieut V. C. Chapman) 19.35–19.45 hr, returned due to weather.

No.44 Squadron, Hainault: Sopwith Camels B3852 (Capt C. J. Q. Brand) 19.33–20.50 hr (Shenfield); B3763 (Capt W. H. Haynes) 19.40–21.00 hr (North Weald); B3886 (2nd Lieut C. C. Banks) 19.45–20.45 hr (North Weald).

No.50 Squadron, Detling: B.E.2e B4507 (2nd Lieut C. C. White) 19.19–19.34 hr, returned due to weather.

No.78 Squadron, Suttons Farm: F.E.2d B1882 (2nd Lieut F. H. Barton, 1st AM H. L. Daws) 19.32–20.37 hr; Sopwith 1½ Strutters A1040 (Capt D. J. Bell, 2nd Lieut G. G. Williams) 19.35–20.40 hr; B2593 (Capt S. P. Gamon, Lieut G. T. Stoneham) 19.40–20.03 hr; A1051 (2nd Lieut R. F. W. Moore, 1st AM A. T. C. Stagg) 20.20–20.55 hr, crashed landing.

The bombers achieved notably better concentration during this raid, coming in on a line from Foulness to Dover between 19.00 and 19.45 hr. However, they showed no greater determination to reach London—always clearly visible despite patches of low cloud and mist which temporarily obscured some districts.

Only three Gothas bombed the capital, between 19.55 and 20.10 hr, and most of the others attacked near Kent coastal towns from Margate to Folkestone. The big discrepancy between the British estimate of 3,922 lb of bombs dropped (which works out at only some 280 lb per aircraft) and the German figure of 8,816 lb suggests that a large percentage fell in the sea.

Home Defence Brigade issued the readiness instruction at 19.02 hr, and the first patrols were ordered off ten minutes later.

The only RFC sighting was by a No.78 Squadron 'Colonial' crew—Douglas Bell from Johannesburg and George Williams, an Australian. They also apparently scored the fighters' first night victory—though since the evidence was circumstantial, no particular significance was accorded to this historic event. At 20.15 hr, south of Brentwood at about 9,400 ft, their 1½ Strutter was the target for some tracers from an aircraft flying due east. This failed to respond to repeated challenges, so Bell followed it for 10–15 min firing frequent bursts from his Vickers gun until it disappeared. The encounter, clearly with a Gotha returning from London, was seen by Taylor of No.39 Squadron.

Sopwith 1½ Strutters of C Flight No.78 Squadron at Suttons Farm. The third aircraft from the left is possibly A1040 from which Capt D. J. Bell attacked a returning Gotha on 25/26 September, 1917.

Next day local English newspapers reported that substantial quantities of petrol had fallen near an Essex town—unspecified because of censorship. The authorities were generally disinclined to accept Press stories as serious evidence, and there appears to have been no attempt to correlate this phenomenon with Bell's combat report. No German crew reported any aerial engagement, which supports the strong presumption that the Gotha listed as missing was lost at sea, ditching after its fuel had drained from tanks punctured by the Sopwith's fire. It was understandable that Germany should have attributed the loss to AA gunfire, which was the only form of opposition mentioned by returning crews.

During the evening, weather deteriorated and most airfields were affected by fluctuating ground mist. No.50 Squadron, and No.39 Squadron D Flight at Biggin Hill, were unable to mount any productive sorties, and the weather was the likely factor in landing accidents at Suttons Farm and Stow Maries. There were several weather diversions, and Dennis of No.37 Squadron put down at Stutton, Suffolk, then at Stow Maries before finally returning to his base at Goldhanger.

All three Camels diverted without difficulty when Hainault was temporarily fog-bound. Home Defence Brigade eventually decided to recall the fighters for weather reasons, but not before the last bombers were clearing the country at about 20.45 hr.

A sighting was also reported by Brandon from Manston, the Admiralty having abandoned its rigid non-patrol policy for night aeroplane raids. He encountered a Gotha at 12,000 ft, flying east four miles north of Westgate and fired one Lewis drum at long range before losing it.

28/29 September, 1917 (Night)

Target: London.

Enemy forces: 25 Gothas despatched, three Gothas attacked. Two Giants despatched and attacked.

Results: No casualties, £129 damage.
Defence sorties: 23.

RFC

No.37 Squadron, Goldhanger: B.E.2es A8659 (2nd Lieut C. L. Milburn) 19.53–21.06 hr; B752 (Lieut P. R. Cawdell) 21.10–22.45 hr; 7237 (2nd Lieut S. Armstrong) 19.54–22.12 hr.

No.37 Squadron, Stow Maries: B.E.2es 6820 (2nd Lieut N. H. Colson), W/T tracker, 19.54–20.10 hr, returned with W/T trouble; A2767 (2nd Lieut Colson), W/T tracker, 20.21–22.10 hr; B.E.12 A6318 (2nd Lieut L. T. Onslow) 19.53–20.24 hr and 20.51–22.45 hr.

No.39 Squadron, North Weald: B.E.2es B4481 (2nd Lieut W. B. Thomson) 19.54–21.34 hr; B4453 (2nd Lieut C. B. van Leonhof) 19.56–20.13 hr, returned with engine trouble; B4483 (Lieut C. J. Chabot) 20.03–21.25 hr; B.E.12s 6480 (2nd Lieut P. W. L. Jarvis) 19.53–22.00 hr; 6488 (2nd Lieut A. M. Bennett) 20.27–21.20 hr.

No.39 Squadron, Biggin Hill: B.E.2c 4575 (2nd Lieut A. T. Kemp) 20.24–21.20 hr; B.E.12as A6308 (2nd Lieut E. J. Stockman), W/T tracker, 19.59–20.21 hr, returned with engine trouble; A6305 (2nd Lieut V. C. Chapman) took off 20.01 hr, forced landed at Staplehurst; A595 (2nd Lieut N. H. Auret) took off 20.47 hr, forced landed at West Malling.

No.44 Squadron, Hainault: Sopwith Camels B3852 (Capt C. J. Q. Brand) 20.15–21.15 hr (Suttons Farm); B3886 (2nd Lieut C. C. Banks) 20.17–20.58 hr, B3763 (Capt W. H. Haynes) 20.20–20.40 hr—Banks and Haynes recalled due to weather.

No.78 Squadron, Suttons Farm: F.E.2d B1883 (2nd Lieut N. L. Garstin, Lieut H. I. Fordred) 20.24–21.59 hr; Sopwith 1½ Strutters B2592 (2nd Lieut W. Hubbard, 1st AM W. Eatock) 20.20–21.25 hr; B745 (Capt F. Billinge, Lieut W. N. Fraser) 20.21–20.29 hr, returned due to weather.

Planned as the heaviest aeroplane attack yet mounted on London, by twenty-five Gothas and—for the first time—two of the multi-engined Giants, this raid was rendered utterly ineffective by the weather.

Because of last-minute reservations about the forecast, Kaghol 3 crews were advised to turn back without hesitation if conditions deteriorated. One Gotha did so early because of engine trouble, and, as cloud thickened to an unbroken carpet over the North Sea, fifteen more abandoned the mission. Whether any of these aircraft actually reached the coast is not clear, and the number of bombers over England remains largely guesswork. British observers thought there were eighteen, but only a modest 2,680 lb of bombs was traced—less than half the weight to be expected from the three Gothas and two Giants which claimed to have bombed.

Home Forces intelligence had not seen fit to disclose the Giants' existence to the air squadrons or ground defences, and with Gotha strength already subject to consistent multiplication it was not surprising that single Giants were assessed as formations.

It was probably a Giant which scattered bombs in the Ipswich–Harwich area at about 21.00 hr. One Gotha crew claimed to have attacked central London on dead reckoning, but no bombs were plotted closer than Billericay north of the Thames and Meopham to the south. Others dropped at scattered points in Kent and Essex, while those claimed to have hit Thanet towns clearly fell some distance out to sea.

Cloud over southeast England extended in places from 2,000 to 7,000 ft, and thick ground haze presented the fighters with an impossible task. There were no sightings. All aerodromes except No.37 Squadron's were affected to some degree, and those of No.50 were unfit throughout. Two Biggin Hill aircraft landed elsewhere—one safely at Staplehurst and the other being badly damaged when trying to land at West Malling, though without injury to the pilot. Two Camels saw Hainault's recall signal and came in before the weather clamped, but Brand, who had landed at Orsett to check his whereabouts, was too late and went to Suttons Farm. The almost casual fashion in which Camels were now flying by night in conditions likely to require landings away from base is a tribute to the superb job performed by No.44 Squadron's more skilled pilots in rehabilitating the rather sinister early reputation of this great fighter.

On realizing that the cloud layer was impenetrable by searchlights, Chabot of No.39 Squadron landed to suggest to the authorities that the AA guns firing on sound would greatly help any bombers to find London. Home Defence Brigade praised this intelligent thinking, but whether they in fact ordered any cease fire is not recorded. Chabot took off again, but gave up after three unsuccessful attempts to break cloud. His first essay at take-off that night was frustrated when his B.E.2e sank in a muddy patch and broke its propeller: he was away in a replacement five minutes later.

Two of No.37 Squadron's 'tracker' pilots suffered mechanical problems with their equipment. Colson's aerial drum jammed and he returned to change aircraft, while Onslow came back twice with aerial difficulties. On his first attempt the aerial fouled a projection under the fuselage and would not release. Airborne again he experienced greater embarrassment when a considerable length of the wire unwound itself inside the cockpit, but all went well on his third attempt.

Anti-aircraft guns on Sheppey, at Deal, and on the monitor HMS *Marshal Ney* off Ramsgate, claimed to have brought down bombers, and although no wreckage was found it was assumed that these were the three Gothas admitted by the Germans as missing. But the weather should not be ruled out, for one Gotha pilot recovered almost at sea level from a spin which followed his loss of orientation in the dense cloud. Others may have been less fortunate in similar circumstances. Six Gothas crashed during let-downs or landings.

29/30 September, 1917 (Night)

Target: London.
Enemy forces: Seven Gothas despatched, four Gothas attacked.
Three Giants despatched and attacked.
Results: 40 killed, 87 injured, £23,154 damage.
Defence sorties: 33.

RNAS

Manston: B.E.2cs 8298 (Sqn Cdr C. H. Butler) 19.39–19.50 hr, returned with engine trouble; 8628 (Flt Lieut A. F. Brandon) 20.05–22.15 hr; 8413 (Sqn Cdr Butler) 21.00–22.40 hr.

RFC

No.39 Squadron, North Weald: B.E.2es A8711 (2nd Lieut A. A. Wilcock) 20.32–22.30 hr; B4453 (2nd Lieut C. B. van Leonhof) 20.31–22.40 hr; B4454 (Capt J. M. Clarke) 20.30–22.59 hr; B4462 (2nd Lieut L. Taylor) 20.33–22.13 hr; B4481 (2nd Lieut W. B. Thomson) 22.12–00.28 hr; B4483 (Lieut C. J. Chabot)

22.24–00.17 hr; B.E.12s 6534 (2nd Lieut P. W. L. Jarvis), W/T tracker, 22.22–00.27 hr; 6488 (2nd Lieut A. M. Bennett), W/T tracker, 22.20–00.42 hr.

No.39 Squadron, Biggin Hill: B.E.2c 4575 (Capt J. A. Dennistoun) 20.44–21.10 hr, returned with engine trouble; 4575 (2nd Lieut A. T. Kemp) 21.15–22.45 hr; B.E.12a A6308 (2nd Lieut E. J. Stockman) 20.46–22.45 hr.

No.44 Squadron, Hainault: Sopwith Camels B3852 (Capt C. J. Q. Brand) 20.59–23.01 hr; B3886 (2nd Lieut C. C. Banks) 21.00–22.34 hr; B3763 (Capt W. H. Haynes) 21.02–22.55 hr; B3899 (Capt G. W. M. Green) 21.02–22.26 hr.

No.50 Squadron, Bekesbourne: B.E.12s (Lieut J. Metcalfe) 20.20–22.10 hr; (Lieut W. L. Phillips) 20.26–20.40 hr, returned with engine trouble; (2nd Lieut L. Lucas) 21.02–23.06 hr; (2nd Lieut W. G. Latham) 23.57–01.10 hr; B.E.2e (Lieut W. L. Phillips) 20.45–22.46 hr. Aircraft numbers not recorded.

No.50 Squadron, Detling: Armstrong Whitworth F.K.8 B247 (2nd Lieut F. A. D. Grace, 2nd Lieut G. Murray) 20.36–20.43 hr, returned due to weather; B.E.2e B5404 (Capt C. J. Truran, Lieut R. Robertson) 20.50–21.08 hr, returned due to weather, and 21.52–21.59 hr, returned due to weather; unspecified B.E.2e (2nd Lieut N. F. Perris) 23.53–01.02 hr.

No.78 Squadron, Suttons Farm: F.E.2d B1882 (2nd Lieut F. H. Barton, 1st AM W. T. Merchant) 20.59–23.09 hr; Sopwith 1½ Strutters B2593 (Capt S. P. Gamon, Lieut G. T. Stoneham) 20.58–23.06 hr; B2555 (Capt F. W. Honnett, Lieut N. C. Crombie) 21.06–22.00 hr (Orsett); B745 (Capt F. Billinge, Lieut W. N. Fraser) 21.19–21.25 hr, returned with engine trouble, and 21.38–22.03 hr, returned with airframe trouble.

Experimental Station, Orfordness: Martinsyde F.1 A3933 (Capt L. J. Wackett, 2nd Lieut H. H. Hussey) 19.45–21.05 hr—operated from Rochford.

Despite the previous night's losses, Kleine maintained the pressure on London, and his seven serviceable Gothas were joined by Giants R.25, 26 and 39, all of the R.IV class capable of carrying about three times the Gotha's bomb load.

German reports claim that four Gothas and the three Giants actually bombed, though the British estimate of 4,540 lb dropped is only about half the capacity of that modest force—a large discrepancy even allowing for assessment errors.

The weather was again cloudy, with heavy ground mist affecting some fighter airfields, but the bombers' navigation to the coast was the best to date and all made landfall between Foulness and Deal. They came in from 19.55 until 22.40 hr, and the Giants thoroughly confused the ground reporting organization, each being labelled as a group of four or five aircraft, while some posts identified them as Zeppelins.

No-one at HQ queried such improbable reports as that from the Meath Gardens (Bethnal Green) twin searchlight battery which claimed to have held five aeroplanes in the beam at one time, and another unit's observation of three. The total bomber force was estimated at 18–20 aircraft, and despite persistent reports of '14 machines over London in a group', the final British assessment was that the bombs hitting the capital between 21.10 and 21.45 hr came from four machines. According to the Germans, two Gothas and one Giant (R.39) were involved. Bombs were also dropped at Sheerness and other places in Kent. The last aircraft over the country was a Giant which came in near Margate at 22.40 hr, meandered up and down the Thames estuary before eventually dumping its bombs on Sheppey, and departed south of Margate soon after midnight. Oil splashes found on tents at Tankerton Camp, Whitstable, after its passage overhead suggest that it was suffering some engine trouble.

Home Defence Brigade ordered 'readiness' at 20.03 hr after the first bomber was reported off the North Foreland, but an RNAS B.E.2c from Manston and an experimentally-armed Martinsyde detached from Orfordness to Rochford were airborne earlier. Some aerodromes were badly affected by fog—Detling, for example, being unable to fly an effective patrol until nearly midnight. Of the night's 33 sorties listed, eight were of less than 30 min duration because of weather or mechanical reasons. Three pilots briefly sighted and identified aircraft.

Frank Billinge, No.78 Squadron, had a trying night, returning with engine trouble after six minutes, then abandoning his second attempt when a large area of fabric stripped off his 1½-Strutter's fuselage. Taylor of No.39 Squadron made an immaculate dead-stick landing at North Weald after his engine failed at 8,000 ft, five miles south of base.

The planned first operational trial of the upward-firing attack technique, described in the previous chapter, unfortunately came to nothing because the fighter failed to locate a target. The Martinsyde F.1 employed had a maximum speed of 104 mph at 10,000 ft, and reached that height in less than 14 min. If Hussey, the observer, had any qualms about having to lie on his back to fire the upward-angled twin Lewis guns, he was reassured by the knowledge that Lawrence Wackett was an exceptionally skilled night pilot. There was a

Capt L. J. Wackett (*right*) and 2nd Lieut H. H. Hussey in front of the experimentally-armed Martinsyde F.1 which they flew from Rochford on 29/30 September, 1917.

pre-arranged plan—of which details are not recorded—for nominated searchlight units to indicate, but not directly illuminate, bombers for the Martinsyde. This evidently worked because the ground observers clearly heard a Gotha and the Martinsyde near the end of the beam, but the fighter failed to see the target.

Although Wackett's report omitted his patrol height, it did emphasize his firm belief that the Gothas flew at not less than 14,000 ft, so it may be assumed that he was not below 12,000 ft and searching upwards. According to postwar German accounts, the early Gotha night raids were flown at 6,500–8,200 ft and the later ones at 4,000–5,600 ft. These figures probably related to inbound journeys, and

The Martinsyde F.1 at Rochford, with its 44½ ft wing span, dwarfs a line of No.61 Squadron's daylight-only Sopwith Pups at Rochford.

the lightened bombers would tend to gain height on the return flight. Of the nine British sightings reported in September–October, five were estimated at between 6,000 and 10,000 ft, and four at 12,000 ft. Wackett's faith in a higher figure suggests a lack of communication, and he probably searched above for a Gotha which was actually below his own level, perhaps at 10,000 ft, the estimated height of the AA shell bursts.

There was an enterprising move by No.7/7A Squadron, RNAS, based at Coudekerque, near Dunkirk, which detailed a twin-engined Handley Page to combine a raid on enemy airfields with an anti-Gotha patrol off the Belgian coast. The aircraft was specially armed with five Lewis guns at unspecified points and carried four gunners. During a four-hour patrol at 10,000 ft ten miles out to sea north of Ostende, three enemy aircraft were seen and two engaged.

The first of these was lost to view after the initial attack. The second, encountered between Nieuport and Ostende, was identified as a Gotha and attacked from 50–100 yards' range. Three drums were fired from one rear and two port guns, causing the enemy to enter a steep spiral and disappear below. The Handley Page crew thought that it might have crashed in the sea, but this was probably Gotha G IV/602/16 which Reuter's Amsterdam correspondent reported as landing at Sas Van Gent, a mile or two over the Dutch border, with one of its crew severely wounded.

Despite this encouraging start, no further such patrols were flown. The episode has the stamp of a piece of intelligent private enterprise at squadron or wing level, doomed to provoke Admiralty reminders that the Handley Page was a bomber, not a fighter.

There was a faintly complacent note in the Home Defence Brigade anti-aircraft reports, which spoke of the gunfire breaking up groups of raiders and preventing the penetration of others. However, the Dover guns may have scored a success and the breakwater searchlight crew saw an aircraft spin into the sea about two miles out at 21.40 hr. One Gotha loss was admitted by Germany.

30 September/1 October, 1917 (Night)

Targets: London, Dover.
Enemy forces: Eleven Gothas despatched, ten Gothas attacked.
One single-engined aeroplane despatched and attacked.
Results: 14 killed, 38 injured, £21,482 damage.
Defence sorties: 37.

RNAS
Manston: B.E.2cs 8298 (Sqn Cdr C. H. Butler) 19.55–21.40 hr; 8628 (Flt Lieut A. F. Brandon) 20.05–22.10 hr.

RFC
No.37 Squadron, Goldhanger: B.E.2e B752 (2nd Lieut C. L. Milburn) 19.29–21.05 hr.
No.37 Squadron, Stowe Maries: B.E.2es 6318 (2nd Lieut J. H. Hayward) 18.56–19.35 hr, returned with engine trouble; A2767 (2nd Lieut Hayward) 19.41–21.25 hr; 6820 (Capt G. D. F. Keddie), W/T tracker, 18.59–19.12 hr, returned with faulty W/T, and 19.58–20.19 hr, returned with engine trouble.
No.39 Squadron, North Weald: B.E.2es B4454 (Capt J. M. Clarke) 18.59–21.23 hr; A8711 (2nd Lieut P. F. O. Frith), W/T tracker, 19.00–21.26 hr; B4484 (Lieut C. J. Chabot) 19.02–21.06 hr; B4462 (2nd Lieut L. Taylor), W/T tracker, 20.43–22.15 hr; B.E.12s 6488 (2nd Lieut A. M. Bennett) 20.45–21.43 hr; 6534 (2nd Lieut P. W. L. Jarvis) 21.45–22.10 hr.
No.39 Squadron, Biggin Hill: B.E.12a A6308 (2nd Lieut E. J. Stockman) 19.15–22.10 hr.
No.44 Squadron, Hainault: Sopwith Camels: B3826 (Lieut D. V. Armstrong) 19.09–20.49 hr; B3859 (Lieut C. A. Lewis) 19.11–20.19 hr; B3752 (Lieut A. H. Orlebar) 19.14–19.36 hr, returned with engine trouble; B2402 (Lieut G. H. Hackwill) 19.18–21.31 hr; B3899 (Capt G. W. M. Green) 19.15–20.11 hr, returned with engine trouble; B3852 (Capt C. J. Q. Brand) 19.46–20.56 hr and 21.11–21.52 hr; B3763 (Capt W. H. Haynes) 19.50–20.23 hr and 21.09–21.48 hr; B3886 (2nd Lieut C. C. Banks) 21.05–21.58 hr.
No.50 Squadron, Bekesbourne: B.E.2e (2nd Lieut H. T. W. Oswell) 19.00–21.06 hr; B.E.12 6509 (Capt J. S. Shaw), W/T tracker, 19.00–20.54 hr; unspecified B.E.12 (2nd Lieut W. G. Latham) 19.21–19.26 hr, returned with engine trouble.
No.50 Squadron, Detling: Armstrong Whitworth F.K.8s (2nd Lieut W. R. Oulton, 2nd Lieut Lamb) 19.10–21.35 hr; B247 (2nd Lieut F. A. D. Grace, 2nd Lieut G. Murray) 19.04–20.52 hr.
No.78 Squadron, Suttons Farm: F.E.2d B1882 (2nd Lieut F. H. Barton, Lieut H. I. Fordred) 21.00–22.15 hr; Sopwith 1½ Strutters A1040 (Capt D. J. Bell, 2nd Lieut G. G. Williams) 19.05–21.07 hr; B2592 (Capt G. M. Boumphrey, 2nd Lieut J. W. D. Smith) 19.08–21.14 hr; B745 (Capt F. Billinge, 1st AM E. Cooper) 19.09–20.28 hr, returned with engine trouble, and 20.54–21.42 hr; B2555 (Lieut F. L. Luxmoore, 1st AM A. Coombs) 20.59–22.20 hr; B2593 (Lieut J. S. Castle, 1st AM H. Daws) took off 21.03 hr, forced landed at North Benfleet.
Experimental Station, Orfordness: Martinsyde F.1 A3933 (Capt L. J. Wackett, 2nd Lieut H. H. Hussey) 19.30–21.45 hr—operated from Rochford.

On this third successive night attack against London the bombers reverted to a more widely spaced approach, crossing the coast at points between Clacton and

Sopwith $1\frac{1}{2}$ Strutter B745, piloted by Capt F. Billinge, No.78 Squadron, was one of the three British aircraft which engaged bombers on 30 September/1 October, 1917.

Dover. The first came in at 18.45 hr, just after sunset, and the last about 90 min later, and all had departed by 21.45 hr.

Although no Giants took part, the defences assessed the raid strength as about twenty-five aircraft, attacking in two main groups. One of the more imaginative AA sub-commanders thought there were three attacks, each by three squadrons whose formations were scattered by the barrage fire.

One Gotha returned early with engine trouble and six penetrated to London, bombing between 19.40 and 20.45 hr. They were little hampered by the patchy cloud, which suggests that others were deterred by the intense anti-aircraft fire on the approaches. These attacked Chatham, Margate and Dover, while a few bombs fell in Essex. Dover also received four 55 lb bombs from the single-engined aircraft used by Kagohl 3 as a hack, and flown that night by the unit adjutant.

Fighters were on readiness at 18.40 hr and the first patrols ordered 15 min later. Five sorties were non-effective because of mechanical troubles, and a Sopwith $1\frac{1}{2}$ Strutter forced landed for reasons not recorded. There was a small and encouraging increase in sighting reports, and three pilots fired at fleeting targets. Camel sorties more than doubled any previous figure.

The most positive report came from Camel pilot Bill Haynes, who engaged a London-bound Gotha over Lambourne at 6,000 ft. He fired 300 rounds at 100 yards' range before losing sight of his target. Billinge, flying a No.78 Squadron $1\frac{1}{2}$ Strutter, fired 20 rounds at an aircraft over the Gravesend area at 10,500 ft which made off after ignoring his challenge, and his observer later saw another, unfortunately lost to view before they could position for attack. Grace and Murray, No.50 Squadron, saw machine-gun fire over Throwley which they assumed to be from a Gotha testing its guns and Murray retaliated with a few bursts in its direction, but no aircraft was actually seen.

Shaw of No.50 Squadron signalled the first recorded night sighting from a W/T 'tracker' aircraft. Having duly reported the position of an unidentified machine over Faversham at 7,500 ft which failed to respond to his challenge, he turned to follow but could not find it again.

Wackett's sortie in the Orfordness Martinsyde, flown at 12,000 ft, was again

Capt William Harold Haynes, No.44 Squadron, with his Camel B3763 from which he engaged a Gotha over Lambourne on 30 September/1 October, 1917. Haynes, who was awarded the DSO in December, was killed by a freak accident on 26 September, 1918, in No.151 Squadron. His Camel overturned while taxi-ing at night, and while he and others were inspecting the damage one of the guns was triggered and he was shot.

unproductive. The suspicion that he was too high is supported by other crews' sightings at lower levels.

In apparent contradiction of Orfordness trial results which established that aircraft were more visible from below than above, Taylor, No.39 Squadron, reported clearly seeing beneath him at 6,000 ft three Camels in a loose line abreast. However, this was probably the exception proving the rule, the fighters being outlined by moonlight above the cloud.

Pilots still complained of attacks from AA guns, and not all sites were as polite about it as Dover. Consecutive signals in a home-defence file read: '20.07 Dover guns in action' . . . '20.10 much regret have fired on one of our planes'. A claim by one Dover gun to have shot down a bomber in the sea later that night gained some substance from the sighting of aircraft wreckage near the Varne lightship. However, the Germans reported no losses and the debris may have been from an earlier victim.

1/2 October, 1917 (Night)

Target: London.
Enemy forces: 18 Gothas despatched, 12 Gothas attacked.
Results: 11 killed, 42 injured, £45,570 damage.
Defence sorties: 19.

RFC

No.37 Squadron, Stow Maries: B.E.2e A2767 (2nd Lieut E. H. Chater), 19.19–20.55 hr; B.E.12 A6318 (Capt J. L. Horridge), 19.15–21.05 hr.

No.39 Squadron, North Weald: B.E.2es A8711 (2nd Lieut A. A. Wilcock), 19.20–21.18 hr; B4481 (2nd Lieut W. B. Thomson), 19.17–21.20 hr.

No.39 Squadron, Biggin Hill: B.E.12as A592 (2nd Lieut A. T. Kemp), 19.25–21.25 hr; A6308 (2nd Lieut E. J. Stockman), 19.30–21.50 hr.

No.44 Squadron, Hainault: Sopwith Camels B3852 (Capt C. J. Q. Brand), 19.25–21.49 hr; B3763 (Capt W. H. Haynes), 19.27–21.10 hr; B3899 (Capt G. W. M. Green), 19.30–21.00 hr; B3859 (Capt C. A. Lewis), 19.32–21.02 hr; B3886 (2nd Lieut C. C. Banks), 19.33–21.07 hr; B2402 (Lieut G. H. Hackwill), 19.46–20.58 hr; B3826 (Lieut D. V. Armstrong), 20.34–21.04 hr.

No.78 Squadron, Suttons Farm: F.E.2d B1882 (2nd Lieut F. H. Barton, 1st AM W. T. Merchant), 19.16–19.45 hr, returned with engine trouble, and 20.50–21.35 hr; Sopwith 1½ Strutters B2565 (Lieut C. J. Marchant, 1st AM E. Gudgeon), 19.11–20.40 hr; B2555 (Lieut H. Hamer, 1st AM J. Morgan), engine failed on take-off at 19.14 hr; A1051 (2nd Lieut R. F. W. Moore, 1st AM A. T. C. Stagg), 19.30–21.30 hr, damaged undercarriage; B2592 (2nd Lieut A. F. Barker, 1st AM L. Card), 20.02–22.14 hr.

On this last of the harvest-moon attacks the Gothas achieved good geographical concentration, with landfalls between the Blackwater and Ramsgate—apart from one brief incursion near Harwich. However, the attack extended over a long period, with aircraft coming in between 18.50 and 20.50 hr and the last departing at 22.40 hr, probably because of navigation problems rather than any deliberate prolongation of the nuisance factor.

German records for the night are incomplete, but available information suggests that twelve aircraft actually bombed England, six reaching London and attacking between 20.00 and 21.00 hr. Thickening mist made navigation difficult and one or two Gothas appear to have missed the capital from quite short range.

Bombs also fell in Kent, Essex and Suffolk, but casualties were light. At least one Giant took off but turned back after the crew realized that their W/T transmissions had been intercepted by a British listening station.

GHQ Home Forces Secret Air Raid Circular No.147 reported that some bombers climbed to 12–14,000 ft near the outer defences then glided into the centre of London with their engines switched off. This is highly improbable, and aural indications of such behaviour would have been caused by atmospheric conditions—also doubtless responsible for a report from North Foreland that one aircraft in full and loud flight suddenly shut off its engines, which were not re-started.

Fighters were ordered to readiness at 18.57 hr. Conditions were marginal at most aerodromes and No.50 Squadron's Kent bases remained unfit throughout. Patrols were flown between 8,000 and 14,000 ft, with 1,000 ft spacing. Only Haynes, No.44 Squadron, saw anything—a fleeting glimpse of a Gotha, at 12,000 ft southeast of Epping, which quickly disappeared. The night's mishaps were confined to No.78 Squadron, where Hamer successfully coped with an engine failure on take-off and Moore damaged his undercarriage while landing.

A historic event was the first operational use of the experimental15-ft diameter spherical sound locator at Fan Bay, between Dover and St Margaret's. This picked up enemy aircraft flying down Channel 12–15 miles out to sea and inaudible to the unaided ear. It was assumed that these were bombers making for London via Folkestone and Ashford, and they were reported accordingly. However, subsequent study of the night's operations indicated that they attacked a French coastal target, and the sound of heavy gunfire from the Boulogne area was said to be 'almost unbearable' for operators in the Fan Bay listening post. Lieut-Col W. M. Thompson, the Dover AA Defence Commander, was enthusiastic over the results, and predicted that the device would prove invaluable for obtaining early raid information.

19/20 October, 1917 (Night)

Target: Northern England.
Enemy forces: Navy Zeppelins L41 (Hptmn K. Manger), L44 (Kptlt F. Stabbert), L45 (Kptlt W. Kölle), L46 (Kptlt H. Hollender), L47 (Kptlt M. von Freudenreich), L49 (Kptlt H. K. Gayer), L50 (Kptlt R. Schwonder), L52 (Oblt-z-S K. Friemel), L53 (Kptlt R. Prölss), L54 (Kptlt H. von Buttlar), L55 (Kptlt H. K. Flemming).
Results: 36 killed, 55 injured, £54,346 damage.
Defence sorties: 78.

RNAS

Cranwell: B.E.2e A8697 (Flt Cdr G. G. Simpson) 21.55–22.25 hr (Waddington).

Frieston: B.E.2c 9951, 19.45–20.07 hr.

Manston: B.E.2cs 8628 (Flt Lieut A. F. Brandon) 20.45–22.25 hr; 8298 (Sqn Cdr C. H. Butler) 23.20–23.35 hr, returned due to weather; 8626 (Flt Lieut Brandon), times not recorded.

Yarmouth: B.E.2c 8411 (Flt Cdr E. Cadbury) 23.20–00.45 hr (Burgh Castle).

Bacton: B.E.2c 8607 (Flt Sub-Lieut C. V. Halford Thompson) 21.07–22.30 hr (Holt), crashed landing.

Burgh Castle: B.E.2cs 8629 (Flt Lieut F. W. Walker) 21.15–22.04 hr (Bacton);

8492 (Flt Lieut C. S. Nunn) 22.56–00.04 hr, crashed landing; unspecified B.E.2c, 23.05–00.06 hr.

Covehithe: B.E.2c 8619 (Flt Lieut C. S. Iron) times not recorded, crashed.

RFC

No.33 Squadron, A Flight, Scampton: F.E.2bs A5659 (2nd Lieut A. R. Kingsford, Lieut C. W. Reid) 20.10–22.35 hr (Kelstern, with engine-trouble); A5536 (2nd Lieut D. R. Brook, Lieut G. E. Lucas) 22.45–01.15 hr; F.E.2ds B1884 (2nd Lieut E. G. Roberts, Lieut Tatham) 19.55–22.20 hr (Kirton-Lindsey); A6353 (2nd Lieut T. E. Carley, Cpl Smith) 20.55–22.55 hr; B1885 (Maj A. A. B. Thomson) 01.00–01.45 hr (Kirton-Lindsey).

No.33 Squadron, B Flight, Kirton-Lindsey: F.E.2bs B409 (2nd Lieut G. E. P. Elder, 1st AM Bayley) 19.10–20.25 hr, returned with engine trouble; A5655 (2nd Lieut J. D. Watson) 19.30–19.40 hr, returned with engine trouble; 19.50–22.40 hr; A5635 (2nd Lieut A. S. Harris) 00.03–01.55 hr; F.E.2ds A6375 (Lieut J. A. Harman, 1st AM Booth) 20.00–20.40 hr, returned with engine trouble; A6375 (2nd Lieut N. J. Whittingham, 2nd Lieut Dixon) 21.30–23.55 hr (Elsham, due to fuel shortage); B1884 (Lieut Harman, Lieut Stevenson) 01.00–01.50 hr.

No.33 Squadron, C Flight, Elsham: F.E.2ds B1896 (Lieut R. Affleck, 2nd Lieut D. Fraser) 19.10–22.10 hr; B1885 (Maj A. A. B. Thomson) 22.30–00.01 hr (Scampton).

No.33 Squadron, HQ Flight, Gainsborough: F.E.2d B1885 (Maj A. A. B. Thomson) 19.45–21.45 hr (Elsham); F.E.2b A5656 (2nd Lieut H. P. Solomon, 2nd Lieut H. Preston) 19.55–19.56 hr, crashed, pilot killed.

No.37 Squadron, Goldhanger: B.E.2d 5778 (2nd Lieut S. Hay) 23.00–00.55 hr (Stow Maries due to weather); B.E.2es B752 (Lieut P. R. Cawdell) 22.04–00.19 hr; 7237 (2nd Lieut S. Armstrong) 20.12–21.32 hr, forced landed Blackheath due to engine trouble; B.E.12 A4032 (2nd Lieut C. L. Milburn) 22.32–00.40 hr.

No.37 Squadron, Stow Maries: B.E.2es 5768 (Capt J. L. Horridge) 20.18–22.23 hr; B4457 (2nd Lieut A. O. Beckett) 22.05–23.59 hr, crashed landing; B4537 (2nd Lieut J. H. Hayward) 22.35–00.35 hr; A8709 (2nd Lieut L. T. Onslow) 22.37–23.20 hr.

No.38 Squadron, A Flight, Leadenham: F.E.2bs A5584 (Capt M. D. Barber) 23.07–23.55 hr, returned due to engine trouble; B419 (Lieut H. C. Calvey, Lieut R. A. Varley) 00.40–03.50 hr, forced landed at Great Gonerby.

No.38 Squadron, B Flight, Buckminster: F.E.2bs A5566 (2nd Lieut A. E. Ikin, Lieut Blyth) 21.20–00.35 hr (Stamford due to fuel shortage); A5568 (Capt L. P. Watkins, Sgt Edwards) 23.55–02.10 hr.

No.38 Squadron, C Flight, Stamford: F.E.2bs B419 (2nd Lieut E. Vredenburg) 20.05–23.40 hr (Leadenham); A5578 (Sgt C. R. L. Falcy, 2nd Lieut J. O. Holliday) 20.25–22.55 hr; B422 (Lieut G. H. Harrison) 21.25–22.45 hr; A5578 (2nd Lieut S. N. Pike, 1st AM G. W. Moorhouse) 23.45–01.45 hr.

No.39 Squadron, North Weald: B.E.2es B4462 (2nd Lieut L. Taylor) 20.23–22.25 hr; B4454 (Capt J. M. Clarke) 20.20–22.43 hr; B4481 (2nd Lieut W. B. Thomson) 22.25–00.15 hr; 7151 (2nd Lieut A. M. Bennett) 20.32–22.53 hr; B4484 (Lieut C. J. Chabot) 20.30–23.16 hr; B4534 (2nd Lieut T. B. Pritchard) 22.30–01.20 hr, forced landed, Hooe; B4532 (2nd Lieut W. Hunt) 23.50–02.16 hr (Joyce Green due to weather). Attached: Martinsyde G.102 A6299 (Capt L. E. Eeman) 21.30–23.35 hr (Stow Maries, crashed landing).

No.39 Squadron, Biggin Hill: B.E.2c 4575 (2nd Lieut V. C. Chapman)

20.50–21.55 hr; B.E.12 6534 (2nd Lieut A. E. Simmons) 23.45–02.10 hr; B.E.12a A592 (Lieut E. J. Stockman) 21.05–21.07 hr, crashed.

No.50 Squadron, Bekesbourne: B.E.2e B4511 (2nd Lieut H. T. W. Oswell) 21.58–00.15 hr; B.E.12s A6309 (Lieut J. Metcalfe) 21.42–23.52 hr; A6313 (2nd Lieut W. G. Latham) 23.10–01.19 hr; 6157 (2nd Lieut L. Lucas) 23.17–23.57 hr, returned with engine trouble.

No.51 Squadron, A Flight, Mattishall: F.E.2bs A5543 (2nd Lieut A. W. Simon) 19.45–23.30 hr (intermediate landing at Harling Road due to engine trouble); B417 (Lieut H. C. Burdett) 19.47–21.40 hr (Tibbenham due to weather).

No.51 Squadron, B Flight, Tydd St Mary: F.E.2bs A5551 (Lieut O. E. Ridewood) 19.40–23.05 hr; 7004 (2nd Lieut A. Critchley) 19.40–21.10 hr.

No.51 Squadron, C Flight, Marham: F.E.2bs A5723 (Lieut A. R. Nock) 19.42–00.15 hr; A5724 (2nd Lieut T. H. Gladstone) 20.07–23.55 hr.

No.75 Squadron, A Flight, Hadleigh: B.E.2es B4456 (Lieut C. F. Wolley-Dod) 21.20–23.05 hr; B4518 (Lieut E. A. Lloyd) 21.20–23.00 hr; A8701 (Capt C. B. Cooke) 20.15–23.30 hr; B.E.12 A6349 (Lieut L. Neville-Smith) 20.15–23.25 hr.

No.75 Squadron, B Flight, Harling Road: B.E.2es B723 (2nd Lieut C. F. Cowper) 20.30–21.50 hr; 7253 (2nd Lieut J. E. G. Hassall) 19.30–22.20 hr; B.E.12 A6325 (2nd Lieut C. F. Cowper) 19.30–20.20 hr, returned with burst petrol pipe.

No.75 Squadron, C Flight, Elmswell: B.E.2e B4514 (Lieut W. A. Forsyth) 19.45–22.25 hr.

No.76 Squadron, A Flight, Copmanthorpe: B.E.2es A1273 (Lieut J. L. N. Bennett-Baggs) 19.58–22.16 hr; 7232 (2nd Lieut G. W. Wall) 20.15–23.15 hr; A1273 (2nd Lieut H. B. Evans) 22.50–01.35 hr (Pocklington, due to weather); B.E.12 A590 (Capt T. R. Irons) 23.59–01.09.

No.76 Squadron, B Flight, Helperby: B.E.2e A8663 (2nd Lieut R. A. Vosper) 19.37–22.18 hr; B.E.12 6485 (2nd Lieut R. Wilson) 22.13–00.15 hr.

Instead of its intended devastating blow against northern industrial targets, this raid was reduced to a fiasco because of the weather, which then inflicted the biggest-ever disaster on the German Naval Airship Service—the loss of five Zeppelins.

The limited resources available to the German meteorologists promised good conditions, and while two airships could not leave their sheds because of a cross-wind, the remaining eleven set off between 11.15 and 12.54 hr. The North Sea crossing was uneventful and none turned back.

The plan was to rendezvous off Flamborough Head, but as the airships climbed they encountered increasingly strong northwesterly winds, reaching 45–50 mph at their operating height of 16–20,000 ft. They crossed at various points from the Humber to Happisburgh between 18.45 and 20.15 hr—except for L46, flying near the upper extremity of the height band, which met the full force of the gale and did not reach the coast until 22.20 hr.

With a few exceptions the Zeppelins' navigation difficulties began even before they were over land, and as they battled on in the teeth of the wind they became hopelessly lost. The deepest penetration was by L41, which attacked the western outskirts of Birmingham—reported as Manchester—and bombs from other vessels fell near Northampton, Bedford, Leighton Buzzard, and many in open country, some 250 in all. Apart from the wind strength, which cut ground speed to 10–15 mph, navigation problems were aggravated by lowered crew performance brought about by anoxia and temperatures of minus 30 deg F. Engine handling and W/T procedures were also impaired.

Among the Zeppelins driven southeastwards while still seeking a worthwhile target was L45, whose crew first appreciated the great strength of the wind when they unexpectedly found themselves over London instead of many miles farther north. Bombs from L45, including three 660-pounders—one falling at 23.30 hr in Piccadilly Circus—caused 33 deaths and 50 injuries.

In L54, von Buttlar, a most experienced if ultra-cautious commander, with a reputation for exaggerating his achievements, alone recognized the dangers of the situation and reduced altitude after a brief sortie inland near Ipswich. He flew a normal return course across the North Sea, reaching base at 08.40 hr. Five more got home between 12.00 and 14.05 hr, some desperately short of fuel.

Four Zeppelins were swept across France to their destruction. L44 was shot down by AA fire, L45 hit the earth near Sisteron and L49 at Bourbonne-les-Bains. L50 grounded at Dommartin, leaving behind her forward control car and most of the crew. Four men were trapped in the main wreck, which rose again and was last seen from Fréjus, at 17.30 hr, drifting out to sea at a great height. L55 crash-landed at Tiefenort, in Germany, but some 200 miles southeast of her Ahlhorn base, and was scrapped.

Had Strasser been commanding the attack from one of the airships, as was his normal practice, he might well have appreciated the hazards and ordered a general return. But despite early indications of trouble from the W/T bearings plotted, no guidance was signalled from headquarters at Ahlhorn. One embittered prisoner from L45's crew uncharitably remarked that now Strasser had received the Pour le Mérite he no longer needed to risk his life.

This attack was known as the 'silent raid' for two reasons. Atmospheric conditions dispersed any noise from the high-flying Zeppelins—for example, some authorities wrongly asserted that L45's engines were shut down as she careered, unheard, across London. Also, when it became apparent that searchlights in the outer suburbs, guided only by the faintest engine sounds, could not serve any useful purpose, they were covered and the AA gun barrage withheld to avoid attracting raiders to the capital.

A preliminary raid warning was issued by the Admiralty at 16.00 hr, but the time of Home Defence Brigade's readiness order is not recorded. The difficulty of tracking the raiders produced some surprises—one, for example to the No.33

L49, which scattered bombs across the Norfolk countryside on 19/20 October, 1917, suffered prolonged engine troubles and finally crashed at Bourbonne-les-Bains in France.

U-class Zeppelin L48 was a sistership of the L49, L52 and L54 used on the 19/20 October raid.

Squadron crews standing by their aircraft at Scampton awaiting patrol orders, when two bombs exploded a few hundred yards from the flarepath. They were dropped at 19.40 hr by L41, whose approach had been inaudible.

The response in all threatened areas was good, but it soon became clear that the enemy was operating well above the fighters' reach. Of the six pilots who saw Zeppelins, only two were able to make the briefest of long-range attacks before being outpaced. There was one fatal accident and seven landing crashes—three aircraft being listed as 'wrecked'. Four fighters returned early with engine troubles. In a dozen successful forced landings or precautionary landings away from base because of mechanical or weather problems the pilots generally displayed excellent airmanship.

B.E.2e B4518 of No.75 Squadron, flown by Lieut E. A. Lloyd on 19/20 October, 1917.

Harrison, flying one of No.38 Squadron's few F.E.2b single-seaters, was at 13,500 ft near Leicester when, at 22.00 hr, he saw a Zeppelin some 2,000 ft higher up. He narrowed the gap to 1,000 ft, and three bursts aimed directly under the airship's tail seemed to be hitting before his gun jammed. He spent some minutes trying unsuccessfully to clear the stoppage and broke away at 22.25 hr. His impression that he received some return fire was confirmed by the later discovery of several holes in his F.E's wing fabric. The official history suggests that Harrison attacked L45, but survivors from her crew said that she was flying some 4,000 ft higher and did not mention a fighter. However, the circumstances of the night were such as to make accurate plotting difficult.

Further south, Chabot, No.39 Squadron, left his North Weald–Hainault patrol line at 22.15 hr to investigate bomb bursts near Waltham Abbey. From his height of 12,000 ft he saw two Zeppelins—later identified as L52 and the L44 or 53—flying due east and 3–4,000 ft higher up. His B.E.2e gained height painfully slowly, and though his chances of overtaking were nil he tried to keep them in sight, switching off his cockpit lighting to avoid any distraction. This led to his undoing, for he stalled the aircraft and by the time he had recovered the airships were lost to sight.

> 'I have no doubt whatever that had I been on a machine with a superior climb and better turn of speed I could have got into close touch with the airships'

wrote Chabot in his report.

An hour later Thomas Pritchard, also from No.39 Squadron and patrolling between North Weald and Ware, saw the L45 about 15 miles to the south making her bombing run across London. He estimated her height at about 15,000 ft and immediately headed southeast, intercepting near Chatham at 00.10 hr, having meanwhile coaxed his B.E.2e from 11,500 to 13,000 ft. The Zeppelin was still 2,000 ft higher, and although Pritchard's burst of fire from some 150 yards behind caused no visible damage, it did force her commander to increase altitude rapidly. L45 thus encountered the full force of the gale and was driven far south of her intended course, which would probably have allowed a safe return to Germany.

Pritchard had no difficulty in keeping L45 in sight as he followed her across Kent, though cloud gradually obscured the ground. His B.E. eventually attained its ceiling, with never a hope of reaching the airship, and at about 01.00 hr as it faded into the distance he realized that his fuel was alarmingly low and put his nose down for the coast. When his altimeter read 600 ft he dropped a parachute flare and saw that he was still over the sea. After another five minutes he released his remaining flare, but this failed to ignite. There was no response to his repeated W/T and identification light signals which he hoped might galvanise some friendly emergency landing ground into action.

Cautiously letting down to 50 ft he lit a wingtip flare, which showed that the ground below was impossible for landing. After being temporarily blinded by a well-meaning searchlight he fired his second wing flare and tried to turn into a field mercifully revealed in its light. Unfortunately the flare burned out before he could complete his approach and he stalled, escaping from the badly damaged aircraft with concussion and a cut near his left eye. He had crashed close to the emergency landing ground at Hooe, near Bexhill.

Pritchard, from Kimberley, South Africa, was commended by French for his courage, resource and determination in difficult and dangerous circumstances, and awarded the MC. Sadly he died on 5 December from injuries sustained in a flying accident on 21 November.

The failure of the Hooe landing ground personnel to assist Pritchard's approach resembles the odd behaviour at North Weald, reported by Taylor of No.39 Squadron. Shortly before he began his let-down the aerodrome searchlight was extinguished, then his own recognition signals went unacknowledged and he narrowly avoided a taxi-ing aircraft as he landed. He heard later that orders had been given to ignore signal lights from the air—which suggests some confusion arising from the decision not to expose the London searchlights.

The night's unluckiest pilot was Clarence Nunn from RNAS Burgh Castle, who, at 23.30 hr ten miles north of Yarmouth and against all probabilities, spotted von Buttlar's L54 flying home at 5,000 ft, well below the influence of the gales. Nunn was at 8,800 ft and dived after the Zeppelin, but found to his chagrin that his B.E.2c was not fast enough to gain an attacking position. He abandoned the attempt after realizing that all was not well with his engine—which cut completely at 3,500 ft over the coast, resulting in a crash on landing.

2nd Lieut T. B. Pritchard, No.39 Squadron, awarded the MC for his determined pursuit of L45 on 19/20 October, 1917. This photograph was taken shortly before his death, when the squadron was re-arming with Bristol Fighters.

Roberts, No.33 Squadron, and Calvey of No.38 saw Zeppelins in the far distance south of the Humber and near Grantham respectively, but lost them long before they could attain combat range. Later Calvey put in to the Swinstead emergency landing ground for some unrecorded reason, and shortly after leaving for Leadenham ran out of fuel and successfully landed by wingtip flares in a turnip field at Great Gonerby, three miles north of Grantham.

2nd Lieut A. R. Kingsford, No.33 Squadron, is just visible in F.E.2b A5659. On 19/20 October, 1917, Kingsford diverted to Kelstern because of engine trouble.

The reason for No.33 Squadron's F.E.2b crash at Gainsborough, causing the death of the New Zealand pilot, Herbert Solomon, was not established. The aircraft took off normally and at about 200 ft dived steeply to the right, hit the ground with engine running, turned over and caught fire. Solomon was killed by the impact, but Preston, the observer, was thrown clear and escaped with a severe shaking. Thomson, the squadron commander, thought that the crash might have been caused by Solomon's clumsy, thigh-length 'fug boots' fouling the controls.

Thomson again showed himself to be one of the most energetic home-defence squadron COs, flying three sorties in a single-seat F.E.2d armed with two Lewis guns on a movable mounting, and visiting all his flights. His example undoubtedly stimulated keenness among the No.33 Squadron crews. Watson suffered engine failure at 1,000 ft soon after taking off from Kirton-Lindsey and executed a faultless landing in an adjacent field using his wingtip flares. Far from regarding this as sufficient work for one night, he took off again after mechanics had rectified the trouble. However, his enthusiasm was ill rewarded and after about two hours the engine was vibrating badly and his F.E. would climb no higher than 11,000 ft, so he returned.

Less fortunate was Edgar Stockman of No.39 Squadron, an ex-farmer from Victoria, Australia, who had an engine failure shortly after taking off from Biggin Hill. He crashed on the airfield, and his B.E.12a was described as wrecked. Another aircraft similarly listed was Halford Thompson's B.E.2c after its landing crash at RNAS Holt.

There was disappointment for Leon Eeman, flying the Martinsyde Elephant fitted with his experimental upward-angled triple Lewis gun installation. He spent nearly two hours patrolling at 15,000 ft between Chingford and Ware, and although Zeppelins were in the neighbourhood he saw nothing—for which the Martinsyde's limited field of view may have been partly to blame. He lost his bearings descending through cloud and landed at Stow Maries. He touched down successfully, but nearing the end of his landing run the starboard wheel collapsed and the undercarriage broke. Although the aircraft appears to have escaped major damage, no further operational trials of this promising night-fighting armament development were made.

29/30 October, 1917 (Night)

Target: Southeast coastal towns.
Enemy forces: Three Gothas despatched, one Gotha attacked.
Results: No casualties or damage.
Defence sorties: Seven.

RFC

No.37 Squadron, Goldhanger: B.E.2e B752 (Lieut P. R. Cawdell) 22.20–23.07 hr; B.E.12 A4032 (Capt W. Sowrey) 22.19–23.01 hr.

No.37 Squadron, Stow Maries: B.E.2es B8835 (2nd Lieut E. H. Chater) 22.20–22.55 hr, crashed landing; B4505 (2nd Lieut A. C. Goldsmith) 22.21–23.09 hr.

No.39 Squadron, North Weald: B.E.2es B4454 (Capt J. M. Clarke) 22.27–23.00 hr; B4483 (Capt W. St J. Boultbee) 22.30–22.53 hr.

No.198(NT) Squadron, Rochford: One sortie—details not recorded.

Having planned a series of major London raids for the next full-moon period, Kleine postponed the first—due to take place on this night—because of an unfavourable weather forecast. Instead, three of the more experienced crews were sent to bomb southeast coastal towns.

In the event, two chose the alternative target of Calais, and the third scattered eight bombs between Burnham and Southend, claiming to have attacked Sheerness.

The weather was equally bad for the defences, with strong winds and thick cloud generally around 2–6,000 ft, but lower in places which closed all aerodromes south of the Thames and grounded No.44 Squadron's Camels. Readiness was ordered at 21.51 hr, and the six fighters airborne from 22.19 hr saw nothing and were recalled after half an hour. The aircraft operating from Rochford may have been Wackett's experimental upward-firing Martinsyde.

The solitary raider was reported as several detachments, possibly totalling ten aircraft, and the Press communiqué proudly claimed that 'enemy machines were unable to penetrate far inland owing to the activity of our own aircraft, which went up to meet them in spite of the rising gale'.

30/31 October, 1917 (Night)

Target: Dover.
Enemy forces: Not known.
Results: No casualties, £2 damage.
Defence sorties: None.

Kagohl 3 did not make this attack, about which little is recorded. It was typical of the earlier hit-and-run coastal incursions which had proved almost impossible to counter. One or two aircraft crossed the coast east of Dover at 04.30 hr, dropped seven bombs near the RFC Swingate Down aerodrome and another four in the harbour. The raiders were briefly engaged by AA fire, but no fighter sorties were ordered.

31 October/1 November, 1917 (Night)

Target: London.
Enemy forces: 22 Gothas despatched and attacked.
Results: Ten killed, 22 injured, £22,822 damage.
Defence sorties: 50.

RNAS

Eastchurch: Sopwith 1½ Strutters N5613, 23.25–01.20 hr (Dunkirk); N5617, 23.25–00.48 hr.

Manston: Sopwith 1½ Strutters N5528, 23.40–00.15 hr; N5174, 00.34–00.55 hr; D.H.4 N6416, 23.50–02.10 hr.

RFC

No.37 Squadron, Goldhanger: B.E.2es 7237 (2nd Lieut S. Armstrong) 23.19–01.05 hr; B4535 (2nd Lieut C. L. Milburn) 23.20–01.30 hr; B4545 (2nd Lieut S. Hay) 01.10–02.56 hr.

No.37 Squadron, Stow Maries: B.E.2es B4505 (Capt J. L. Horridge) 23.20–01.30 hr; B4457 (2nd Lieut A. O. Beckett), W/T tracker, 01.38–02.43 hr; 5768 (2nd Lieut E. H. Chater) 02.03–02.54 hr.

No.39 Squadron, North Weald: B.E.2es B4481 (2nd Lieut A. M. Bennett) 23.25–01.48 hr; B4485 (2nd Lieut A. E. Simmons) 01.03–02.14 hr; B4484 (2nd Lieut L. Taylor) 01.35–02.58 hr; B.E.12 6138 (2nd Lieut P. W. L. Jarvis), W/T tracker, 22.23–01.20 hr.

No.39 Squadron, Biggin Hill: B.E.2es B4543 (Maj J. A. Dennistoun) 23.24–01.26 hr; B4536 (2nd Lieut W. Hunt) 23.27–00.10 hr, returned with engine trouble; B.E.12s A6308 (2nd Lieut V. C. Chapman) 00.25–02.30 hr; B753 (Lieut

A B.E.12 of D Flight, No.39 Squadron, at Biggin Hill—one of the units airborne on 31 October/1 November, 1917.

E. J. Stockman) 01.36–01.50 hr, returned with airframe trouble.

No.44 Squadron, Hainault: Sopwith Camels B3852 (Capt C. J. Q. Brand) 23.28–02.15 hr; B3763 (Capt W. H. Haynes) 23.31–01.43 hr; B3826 (Lieut D. V. Armstrong) 23.32–01.12 hr; B2378 (Lieut A. H. Orlebar) 23.37–00.14 hr, returned with engine trouble; B3827 (Lieut R. G. H. Adams) 00.45–02.35 hr; B3752 (Lieut Orlebar) 01.00–02.50 hr; B3765 (2nd Lieut C. H. Clifford) 01.25–02.40 hr; B4601 (2nd Lieut R. M. Foster) 01.25–02.25 hr; B3860 (2nd Lieut C. C. Banks) 01.26–02.45 hr; B3899 (2nd Lieut R. N. Hall) 01.28–03.00 hr; B2378 (Lieut E. Gribbon) 01.30–02.50 hr; B3767 (Lieut T. M. O'Neill) 01.30–02.50 hr; B3816 (2nd Lieut A. E. Godfrey) 01.34–03.40 hr.

No.50 Squadron, Bekesbourne: B.E.12s A6313 (Lieut W. L. Phillips) 22.55–00.55 hr; 6493 (2nd Lieut H. T. W. Oswell), W/T tracker, 22.50–01.25 hr; 6157 (Lieut L. Lucas), W/T tracker, 23.20–01.20 hr; B.E.12a A6309 (Lieut J. Metcalfe) 00.40–01.45 hr.

No.50 Squadron, Detling: Armstrong Whitworth F.K.8s B229 (Capt C. J. Truran, Lieut R. Robertson) 23.23–01.30 hr; B247 (2nd Lieut F. A. D. Grace, 2nd Lieut G. Murray) 23.24–01.37 hr; B224 (2nd Lieut W. R. Oulton) 00.57–01.18 hr; B226 (2nd Lieut F. V. Bryant) 01.27–02.30 hr; B.E.2e A3134 (2nd Lieut C. C. White) 02.10–03.07 hr.

No.78 Squadron, Suttons Farm: Sopwith 1½ Strutter SSs* A5259 (Capt D. J. Bell) 23.24–23.40 hr, returned with engine trouble; A6906 (Lieut N. H. Dimmock) 23.27–02.20 hr; A5238 (Capt F. Billinge) 01.15–03.00 hr (Orsett, forced landed); Sopwith 1½ Strutters A1050 (Lieut W. H. Howell, 1st AM I. Elder) 23.25–01.10 hr, crashed landing; B862 (Capt S. P. Gamon, 1st AM A. Coombs) 23.26–01.35 hr; A8778 (Capt D. J. Bell, 2nd Lieut G. G. Williams) 23.47–02.05 hr; A8777 (2nd Lieut W. Hubbard, 1st AM W. Eatock) 01.18–02.51 hr; A1040 (2nd Lieut J. R. Cote, 1st AM E. Gudgeon) 01.20–02.30 hr; (Hainault) broke undercarriage; B2567 (Capt G. M. Boumphrey, 2nd Lieut J. W. D. Smith) 01.21–02.25 hr.

Germany's high hopes for this maximum effort on London, with nearly half the 12,800 lb bomb load comprising new and much-vaunted incendiaries, seemed likely of fulfilment when the entire force of twenty-two Gothas reached England without the usual crop of early returns.

The plan for the bombers to approach over Kent, and thus avoid the main fighter concentrations north of the Thames, somewhat miscarried when later crews failed to appreciate that freshening winds were driving them well north of the intended route. They were also bothered by patchy cloud. The first aircraft made landfall at 22.37 hr over Deal as intended, but as the night wore on some were crossing in the Foulness area. The last was plotted in over Canvey Island at 01.15 hr, and all had cleared the country by 02.40 hr.

German reports show that only ten of the raiders reached London, where casualties were very light. Some crews made no attempt to penetrate inland, and Dover, Ramsgate, Margate and Herne Bay received sharp attacks, while bombs also fell in other parts of Kent. The British count showed that 183 of the 274 bombs plotted were in that county, compared with only 85 in London.

The almost derisory results from a raid of such size were due to the small proportion of high explosive dropped. Furthermore, whatever the trials results

* SS = Single-seat conversions.

B.E.2e B4545, flown by 2nd Lieut S. Hay of No.37 Squadron on 31 October/1 November, 1917, is shown here after its transfer to No.187 Night Training Squadron. (*P. H. Liddle*)

with the new incendiary bomb, in practice it was a dismal failure, and the expected conflagrations did not develop.

No.6 Brigade's assessment that about thirty bombers took part was slightly more accurate than hitherto, but it was still believed that the raiding force flew in defined groups each of three or four aircraft.

Fighters were put on readiness at 22.38 hr and the last came down from patrol nearly five hours later. Four RFC pilots briefly saw bombers, which quickly vanished. The crew of a naval $1\frac{1}{2}$ Strutter from Eastchurch reported two combats. All sightings were made without the aid of searchlights. Two of the RFC pilots, Oswell and Lucas, were flying B.E.12 'trackers' of No.50 Squadron and both dutifully signalled their sightings back to base. Oswell followed a Gotha flying at 11,500 ft northwest from Dover for about 30 seconds before it disappeared in cloud, and Lucas saw two at 11,000 ft over the Thames estuary heading towards London. Dimmock, No.78 Squadron, was at 8,500 ft over Joyce Green when he saw a bomber 500 ft below, but as he dived to follow it turned into cloud. Haynes, No.44 Squadron, saw one at 12,000 ft.

The unidentified crew of $1\frac{1}{2}$ Strutter N5617 from Eastchurch picked up Gotha exhaust flames at 23.50 hr between Southend and Sheerness. They closed in and the observer fired a drum from his Lewis, whereupon a white light showing from

This RNAS Eastchurch Sopwith $1\frac{1}{2}$ Strutter, fully night-equipped and with a modified gunner's cockpit, may be N5617 which engaged a Gotha on 31 October/1 November, 1917.

the bomber was extinguished. Shortly afterwards they lost sight of the machine. Later they claimed to have seen 'five enemy machines in formation off Whitstable, all with white lights forward', and fired one-and-a-half drums at the nearmost—which retaliated. There is no obvious explanation of this strange sighting, and no Gothas reported fighter attacks.

No.78 Squadron had two landing accidents, both after problems had arisen in the air. Howell's engine cut over Joyce Green, and he was congratulating himself on stretching his glide to Suttons Farm when he stalled on the aerodrome. Cote became lost and went in to Hainault, destroying his undercarriage. To add to No.78's excessive share of the incidents, Bell returned early with engine trouble and Billinge forced landed at Orsett. Both were flying Sopwith 1½ Strutter single-seat 'Comic' conversions, which made their début that night.

Stockman of No.39 Squadron, unscathed in a major crash during the 'silent raid', decided to take no chances when he found his B.E.12 alarmingly sloppy in handling. He returned after fourteen minutes, and faulty rigging was diagnosed. Orlebar, No.44 Squadron, came in early with engine trouble but was off in another Camel soon afterwards.

Some drama over Kent suggests that the Ightham section of the 2nd Mobile AA Brigade was close to achieving a victory. At 00.25 hr the engines of a Gotha under heavy fire suddenly stopped and the aircraft came down to about 200 ft near Borough Green railway station before they picked up. It then flew off eastwards. The incident was reported by five independent witnesses from different points, and after daylight fragments of machinery and copper tubing were found. Home Forces intelligence later identified them as parts of a fuel system, and suggested that the aircraft had switched over to an emergency or reserve supply after identifying the damage.

Five Gothas crashed on landing or in the final stages of their return flights, but it is not known whether the Ightham incident made any contribution.

5/6 December, 1917 (Night)

Target: London.
Enemy forces: 19 Gothas despatched, 16 Gothas attacked.
Two Giants despatched and attacked.
Results: Eight killed, 28 injured, £103,408 damage.
Defence sorties: 34.

RFC

No.37 Squadron, Goldhanger: B.E.2d 5778 (Capt A. Dennis) 02.28–03.45 hr and 04.14–06.15 hr; B.E.2es B4535 (2nd Lieut S. Armstrong) 02.31–05.35 hr; B752 (2nd Lieut F. R. Kitton) 04.59–06.25 hr; unspecified B.E.2e, 06.20–06.35 hr; B.E.12 A4032 (2nd Lieut S. Hay) 02.28–05.00 hr.

No.37 Squadron, Stow Maries: B.E.2es B4457 (2nd Lieut A. O. Beckett) 02.30–04.50 hr; B4505 (2nd Lieut A. C. Goldsmith) 02.30–04.10 hr; unspecified B.E.2e (2nd Lieut E. H. Chater) 05.10–06.40 hr.

No.39 Squadron, North Weald: B.E.2es B4454 (Capt J. M. Clarke) 02.54–04.55 hr; B4462 (2nd Lieut L. Taylor) 02.56–05.13 hr; Bristol Fighters C4823 (Lieut C. J. Chabot, Lieut V. A. Lanos) 05.05–07.01 hr; A7249 (2nd Lieut C. P. Donnison, Lieut W. N. Fraser) 04.59–07.35 hr.

No.39 Squadron, Biggin Hill: B.E.12s 6181 (2nd Lieut A. M. Bennett) 02.55–04.20 hr and 04.50–06.43 hr; A6305 (2nd Lieut A. J. Winstanley) 03.05–05.05 hr; A6308 (Capt A. B. Fanstone) 04.48–06.20 hr.

No.44 Squadron, Hainault: Sopwith Camels B3860 (2nd Lieut C. C. Banks) 02.53–05.07 hr; B3852 (Capt C. J. Q. Brand) 02.59–05.22 hr; B2402 (Capt G. H. Hackwill) 05.06–07.18 hr; B3826 (Lieut D. V. Armstrong) 04.58–06.29 hr; B3859 (Lieut J. T. Collier) 05.08–06.05 hr; B2517 (Capt G. W. M. Green) 05.09–06.11 hr.

No.50 Squadron, Bekesbourne: B.E.12s 6509 (Capt J. S. Shaw) 02.38–04.45 hr; A6313 (Lieut W. L. Phillips) 02.53–04.54 hr; 6157 (Lieut L. Lucas) 04.38–06.40 hr—all W/T trackers.

No.50 Squadron, Detling: Armstrong Whitworth F.K.8s B247 (2nd Lieut F. A. D. Grace, 2nd Lieut G. Murray) 02.55–05.17 hr; B224 (2nd Lieut W. R. Oulton) 02.50–03.50 hr (Throwley, with engine trouble); B229 (2nd Lieut N. F. Perris) 04.29–06.30 hr; B3316 (Capt C. J. Truran) 04.25–06.50 hr.

No.78 Squadron, Suttons Farm: Sopwith 1½ Strutter SSs A6907 (Lieut A. F. Barker) 02.55–05.10 hr; A5259 (Lieut C. J. Marchant) 02.56–03.25 hr; A6906 (Lieut J. S. Castle) 04.40–06.40 hr; A8781 (Capt J. Potter) 04.40–06.45 hr, crashed landing.

After a spell of bad weather had prevented operations for five weeks, conditions eventually improved enough for the Germans to attempt another major fire-raising raid on London. In the interim, Kagohl 3 had been restyled as a Bombengeschwader OHL, henceforward abbreviated as Bogohl 3.

Three Gothas turned back with engine trouble, but the remaining sixteen, and two Giants, came in at intervals between 02.00 and 04.30 hr most of them over the Kent coast from the North Foreland to Walmer. A few crossed north of the Thames. Only six penetrated to London, where the main attack was delivered between 04.30 and 05.40 hr. The majority of bombs fell in Kent, notably at Sheerness, Margate, Ramsgate, Dover and Whitstable. The two Giants distributed their 4,450 lb load mostly on Sheerness and Dover. The last of the bombers departed at 06.15 hr over Folkestone.

More than three-quarters of the bomb load was made up of incendiaries difficult to plot, which is probably why the British estimate of an overall total of 7,170 lb, with 3,863 lb falling in London, was less than half the German figure of 17,125 lb. Casualties were light but the material damage was substantial, the London estimate of nearly £92,500 being the biggest since the daylight raids of the summer. However, results were far below the enemy's expectations of conflagrations causing widespread panic and disorder, and it was 'back to the drawing board' for the bomb designers.

From the defence viewpoint an encouraging feature of a night devoid of any firm sightings was the introduction of the superlative Bristol Fighter, albeit with some caution on sorties offering the option of remaining airborne until daylight. This resulted from French's agitations after the 'silent raid'. Readiness was ordered at 02.00 hr and patrols totalling more than 60 hr flying were maintained until after the last raider had departed.

Barker of No.78 Squadron received no response when he challenged an aircraft showing a green light, above him at 14,000 ft, but he lost it while climbing to investigate. This may have been a friendly machine.

William Oulton, No.50 Squadron, displayed first-class airmanship when the 160 hp Beardmore engine of his F.K.8 shed a cylinder, its connecting rod cutting through the crankcase, sump and an engine bearer. He glided down to a successful landing at Throwley. Potter, No.78 Squadron, damaged the wings of his Sopwith 'Comic' after the engine seized on the landing approach.

The night provided further clues to the presence of Giants, whose existence was still a jealously guarded Intelligence secret. At 01.39 hr RNAS Grain intercepted W/T signals suspected of coming from an aeroplane, while the AA Eastern sub-command reported that some raiders seemed lower than usual, their black-cross wing markings being clearly visible.

Notable successes were achieved by the guns. Gotha G V/906/16, whose young pilot, Gemeiner J. Rzechtalski, was heavily outranked by the gunner, Vizefeldwebel O. E. A. Jakobs and Leutnant R. W. O. Wessells (navigator and aircraft commander), made landfall off the North Foreland at 03.40 hr and proceeded steadily up the Thames estuary. At 04.20 hr over Canvey Island the port propeller was shattered by a shell burst. Bombs were jettisoned but the Gotha could not maintain height, so the pilot made for Rochford aerodrome, clearly visible a few miles northeast. Firing the British recognition colours of the night by pure chance, he made an unharrassed approach, only to strike a tree—all too familiar to the resident British pilots—and crash on the nearby golf course. The time was 04.45 hr. The Gotha crew was uninjured but the wreckage was destroyed shortly afterwards in a fire caused by the accidental discharge of a signal cartridge.

Another Gotha, captained by Leutnant S. R. Schulte and piloted by Vizefeldwebel B. Senf—both on their 13th United Kingdom raid—with Leutnant P. W. Bernard as gunner, was hit at about 05.00 hr over London while bombing. The port radiator was wrecked, causing the engine gradually to become red hot. When it caught fire the crew accepted the inevitable, and at 05.50 hr put down in a small field at Sturry, near Canterbury. During the descent they smashed the instruments and jettisoned one machine-gun, later found by police in a gravel pit. They set fire to the aircraft and altogether behaved in textbook fashion before surrendering to a local clergyman in his capacity as a special constable. A Herne Bay AA unit and No.50 Squadron's triple-Lewis aerodrome defence battery near Bekesbourne both claimed this Gotha, and although the latter may have scored some hits, its fate had been decided over London.

The Germans reported another Gotha missing—presumably down in the sea—one crashed on landing and two came down in Belgium before reaching their aerodromes.

18/19 December, 1917 (Night)

Target: London.
Enemy forces: 15 Gothas despatched, 13 Gothas attacked.
One Giant despatched and attacked.
Results: 14 killed, 83 injured, £238,861 damage.
Defence sorties: 47.

RFC

No.37 Squadron, Goldhanger: B.E.2e B752 (2nd Lieut F. R. Kitton) 20.20–22.40 hr, crashed landing; B.E.12 A4032 (2nd Lieut S. Hay) 18.35–20.40 hr, crashed landing; B.E.12bs C3091 (Capt W. Sowrey) 18.50–19.48 hr, returned with radiator leak; C3082 (2nd Lieut S. Armstrong) 20.10–22.20 hr.

No.37 Squadron, Stow Maries: B.E.2es B4505 (2nd Lieut E. H. Chater) 18.50–21.05 hr; B4457 (2nd Lieut A. O. Beckett) 18.38–20.50 hr.

No.39 Squadron, North Weald: B.E.2es B4532 (2nd Lieut L. Taylor) 18.48–20.56 hr; B4484 (2nd Lieut A. T. Kemp) 20.30–22.23 hr; Bristol Fighters

B1184 (2nd Lieut P. W. L. Jarvis, Lieut Robbins) 18.54–20.49 hr; C4815 (Capt O. V. Thomas, Cpl Gee) 18.57–21.05 hr; B1186 (Lieut C. R. W. Knight, Lieut L. Speller) 20.31–22.23 hr; A7265 (Lieut A. E. Simmons, Lieut A. L. Harrow-Bunn) 20.35–22.17 hr.

No.44 Squadron, Hainault: Sopwith Camels B3859 (Lieut J. T. Collier) 18.36–19.39 hr; B5192 (Capt G. W. M. Green) 18.43–19.35 hr and 19.54–21.30 hr; B2402 (Capt G. H. Hackwill) 18.43–20.31 hr; B3826 (Lieut D. V. Armstrong) 18.48–20.46 hr; B3860 (2nd Lieut C. C. Banks) 18.52–20.39 hr; B2517 (Lieut G. W. Gathergood) 18.55–19.45 hr; B4601 (2nd Lieut R. M. Foster) 20.19–20.53 hr; B3899 (2nd Lieut R. N. Hall) 20.20–21.30 hr.

No.50 Squadron, Bekesbourne: B.E.12s 6509 (2nd Lieut W. G. Latham) 19.05–21.18 hr; A6309 (Lieut J. Metcalfe) 21.19–22.08 hr; 6493 (Lieut Stocks) 21.20–22.10 hr.

No.50 Squadron, Detling: Armstrong Whitworth F.K.8s B3316 (Capt C. J. Truran) 18.30–19.55 hr; B225 (2nd Lieut F. V. Bryant) 18.36–20.55 hr; B247 (2nd Lieut F. A. D. Grace, 2nd Lieut G. Murray) 18.55–21.10 hr; B229 (2nd Lieut N. F. Perris) 18.55–21.15 hr; B4017 (2nd Lieut C. C. White) 20.40–22.00 hr; B3316 (2nd Lieut W. R. Oulton, Lieut H. Harris) 20.22–22.10 hr.

No.61 Squadron, Rochford: S.E.5as B655 (Capt E. B. Mason) 19.10–21.10 hr; B679 (Lieut P. Thompson) 19.15–20.15 hr; C1051 (Capt H. C. Stroud) 19.16–20.55 hr; C9486 (Capt C. A. Lewis) 20.25–21.00 hr.

No.78 Squadron, Suttons Farm: Sopwith 1½ Strutter SSs A1100 (Capt D. J. Bell) 18.35–21.04 hr; A6907 (Capt J. Potter) 18.50–19.54 hr; B715 (Capt G. M. Boumphrey) 18.53–21.08 hr; A5259 (Lieut W. H. Howell) 19.00–20.15 hr, crashed landing; B4016 (Lieut J. S. Castle) 19.02–21.19 hr; A5280 (Capt F. Billinge) 20.00–21.06 hr; A6907 (Lieut A. F. Barker) 20.30–20.55 hr, returned with engine trouble; A6906 (Maj C. R. Rowden) 21.10–21.58 hr; B812 (Lieut A. F. Barker) 21.30–22.00 hr; Sopwith 1½ Strutter A8777 (2nd Lieut W. Hubbard, 1st AM W. Eatock) 18.40–21.03 hr.

No.78 Squadron, Biggin Hill: B.E.2e A3146 (2nd Lieut W. Hunt), W/T tracker, 18.50–21.15 hr; B.E.12s A6305 (2nd Lieut A. M. Bennett) 18.55–21.45 hr; A595 (2nd Lieut A. J. Winstanley) 21.00–22.09 hr.

The outstanding feature of this night's operations was the first positive success against a bomber by a night fighter over England, achieved by Murlis Green.

Since its last England raid, Bogohl 3 had lost Kleine, shot down and killed during a daylight attack on troop concentrations near Ypres on 12 December. His place was taken by the senior flight commander, Oberleutnant Richard Walter. Though less imbued with the 'press on regardless' spirit, Walter was probably a more knowledgeable aviator, and this attack diverted from previous practice by being launched on a darker night, only five days after a new moon.

Nevertheless good concentration was achieved and most of the Gothas came in at 18.00–19.15 hr between the Blackwater and Ramsgate. Six reached London, bombing between 19.10 and 20.30 hr. Others raided Margate, the Canterbury area, and various random points, while one claimed to have attacked Harwich—though no aircraft was plotted within 20 miles. The single Giant, No. R.12—the six-engined R.IV prototype—made landfall north of the Crouch at 20.20 hr, dropped two 660-pounders and some incendiaries in London at 21.10 hr and departed about 50 min later close to its entry point. Altogether 11,300 lb of bombs were dropped, causing the greatest property damage since the Zeppelin raid of 8/9 September, 1915.

Capt G. W. Murlis Green, CO of No.44 Squadron, who achieved the first positive success against the 1917–18 night offensive when the Gotha he attacked on 18/19 December, 1917, ditched off Folkestone; and (*right*) Lieut F. L. Luxmoore, No.78 Squadron, whose attack on Giant R.39 was terminated by an ammunition mishap on 29/30 January, 1918.

Murlis Green's victim, piloted by Leut Friedrich Ketelsen, with Oblt G. von Stachelsky as navigator and Gefreiter A. Weissmann as gunner, made landfall over the Blackwater at 18.35 hr and headed straight for London. Murlis Green was flying a Camel with two upward-angled Lewis guns mounted above the top wing instead of the usual pair of synchronized Vickers.

At 19.15 hr, at 10,000 ft over Goodmayes, he turned to investigate nearby searchlight activity and picked up the Gotha's exhaust flames. Closing to 30 yards under the bomber—with both aircraft now held in a searchlight beam—he opened fire to find that the starboard Lewis had frozen solid and the flash from the other temporarily destroyed his night vision. At this point he noticed bombs dropping from the Gotha and banked away to avoid being hit. They fell in Bermondsey at 19.25 hr. He kept his quarry in sight for the next five minutes, then moved in to make two more attacks from slightly longer range, again being blinded by gun flash and also distracted by a persistent searchlight. This left him alone for his fourth attack, during which he fired some 60 rounds to finish the drum. The Gotha then began to dive, causing the Camel to spin as it hit the slipstream, and after regaining control Murlis Green was unable to find it again. Throughout the encounter the Gotha's return fire was wild, and the Camel received no hits.

The German crew's relief on finding themselves apparently unscathed was short-lived, for soon after crossing the Thames the bullet-damaged starboard engine began running badly and finally expired in a sheet of flame when they were about halfway to the coast. At first they lost height gradually and there seemed some prospect of scraping across the Channel to Belgium on the remaining engine, but when the Gotha was down to 3,000 ft and only ten miles out to sea, Ketelsen realized that it was hopeless and turned back. They ditched off Folkestone at about 21.00 hr, and shortly afterwards the armed trawler *Highlander* was on the scene. She took two of the fliers on board but, by ill

Sopwith 1½ Strutter 'Comics' lined up at Suttons Farm. No.78 Squadron had at least twelve of these conversions, and eight of them flew on 18/19 December, 1917, without making any sightings.

fortune, after Ketelsen's display of excellent piloting, he fell from his refuge on the upper wing moments before rescue and was drowned.

When *Highlander* optimistically tried to take the wrecked Gotha in tow it began to break up and there was an explosion, according to some accounts caused by a destruction device. The German crew's denial of this is supported by the special efforts made by crews of other crashed Gothas to destroy their aircraft, and a hung-up bomb is the more likely cause.

Murlis Green's report, written before he knew the outcome of the combat, ended on a diffident note:

> 'This is my first attempt at attacking a hostile machine at night, consequently I found distance very difficult to judge, so that although tracers appeared to enter the hostile machine, the bullets may have been falling behind.'

However, after analysis of AA reports and interrogation of the German survivors there was no hesitation in crediting Murlis Green with the victory, for which he was awarded a second Bar to his Military Cross.

Two other Camel pilots encountered Gothas and were similarly tossed into sudden spins by their slipstreams. Collier was in combat at about the same time and place as Murlis Green, and it is surprising that neither apparently saw the other's tracer. He climbed up close behind a Gotha, firing about 120 rounds, and met the slipstream as he pulled away. On recovery from the spin he could not re-locate the bomber, and since his port gun had jammed and instrument lights failed, he returned to base.

Hackwill, who spotted a Gotha over Woodford at 20.05 hr at 10,300 ft, was upset by its slipstream as he moved in close behind for his initial attack. He recovered after spinning for a few turns, picked up the bomber again but lost it after firing a short burst.

Oulton, No.50 Squadron, followed a bomber indicated by AA bursts on its homeward journey across east Kent, but his F.K.8 had only a marginal speed advantage and he abandoned the chase over Dover.

No.61 Squadron, which had not operated since August because of the ban on Sopwith Pup night patrols, staged a rather inauspicious first night with its new

S.E.5as, issued on a trial basis. None of the four pilots saw anything, and Lewis and Thompson flew only short sorties because of engine trouble.

The night also marked the introduction of the Hispano-powered B.E.12b single-seater. No.37 Squadron had two airborne, one returning early with a leaking radiator. No.37 suffered two landing crashes, and one of No.78's 'Comics' wrote off its undercarriage as it touched down.

Contemporary British estimates of the raiding force were again much exaggerated and Rawlinson thought that it was the biggest yet employed. There were the inevitable identification problems, as for example when the Epping guns fired at an aircraft held in searchlights which the CO stoutly maintained was a Bristol Fighter flying some miles off its prescribed patrol line. Later inquiries confirmed that it was indeed a Bristol.

The night's activities finally convinced the authorities that Giants were operating over England. Apart from the distinctive sound of the six-engined monster flying on its own between the Gotha streams, the Wanstead AA battery was emphatic that an aircraft engaged at 20.50 hr was much larger than a Gotha. The Penshurst W/T station reported extensive air-to-ground traffic which at times jammed British signals. No public announcement was made, but during the morning all units were instructed to exert their best efforts against the new bomber, code-named 'Bertie'.

Several incidents supported the night's intelligence assessment that two Gothas were destroyed. At about 18.55 hr, North Foreland and Ramsgate independently reported a large descending flame out to sea—though this could have been a signal flare from a weather-reconnaissance Rumpler. The labouring progress and final ditching of Ketelsen's Gotha might explain two claims. Folkestone guns believed that they shot down a bomber at about 21.00 hr, and the Wrotham guns claimed a near miss at 20.21 hr, which caused one to swerve. Later a large splinter of polished wood, believed to be from an aircraft, was found. Ketelsen's aircraft could have been in this area when its starboard engine finally blew up, perhaps breaking the propeller.

The Germans admitted only one loss, though two aircraft were destroyed by fire after landing crashes and five damaged in other accidents or forced landings and combat damage cannot be ruled out as a possible contributory cause.

B.E.12bs from No.37 Squadron, Goldhanger, were first flown operationally on 18/19 December, 1917. These two, flanking a pair of B.E.12s, were photographed at Stow Maries in 1918. (*Mrs M. F. Sadler*)

A group of No.37 Squadron pilots at Goldhanger in the winter of 1917–18 including, left to right: 2nd Lieut S. Hay, Capt A. Dennis and Capt W. Sowrey. The others are not identified, but among them may be pilots who were active during the period, such as S. Armstrong, Cawdell and Milburn. (*Miss H. Sowrey*)

22/23 December, 1917 (Night)

Target: Southeast coastal towns.
Enemy forces: Gothas—number despatched not recorded.
Two Giants despatched.
Results: No casualties or damage.
Defence sorties: 18.

RFC

No.37 Squadron, Goldhanger: B.E.2e B4512 (Capt W. Sowrey) 21.42–22.55 hr; B.E.12b C3091 (Capt A. Dennis) 21.45–22.58 hr.

No.37 Squadron, Stow Maries: B.E.2e B4457 (2nd Lieut A. C. de Fleury) 21.45–23.33 hr; B.E.12 B1500 (2nd Lieut A. C. Goldsmith) 21.49–23.24 hr.

No.39 Squadron, North Weald: B.E.2e B4484 (Lieut A. A. Wilcock), W/T tracker, 21.39–23.10 hr; Bristol Fighters A7249 (Lieut C. P. Donnison, Lieut W. N. Fraser) 21.38–22.49 hr; B1184 (Lieut P. W. Deane, Lieut A. L. Harrow-Bunn) 21.44–23.35 hr.

No.44 Squadron, Hainault: Sopwith Camels B3842 (Capt C. J. Q. Brand) 21.43–23.06 hr; B3859 (Lieut J. T. Collier) 21.45–22.41 hr; B3826 (Lieut D. V. Armstrong) 21.47–23.02 hr; B2402 (Capt G. H. Hackwill) 21.49–23.00 hr; B5603 (Capt W. H. Haynes) 21.49–23.04 hr; B3860 (2nd Lieut C. C. Banks) 22.10–22.41 hr; B5192 (Capt G. W. M. Green) 21.54–22.27 hr.

No.78 Squadron, Suttons Farm: Sopwith 1½ Strutter SSs B2555 (Lieut C. J. Marchant) 21.38–22.59 hr; A1100 (Lieut F. L. Luxmoore) 21.38–22.57 hr; B812 (Lieut R. F. W. Moore) 21.39–23.03 hr; B862 (2nd Lieut D. G. Lewis) 21.40–22.06 hr, returned with engine trouble.

German records are reticent about Bogohl 3's intentions for this last attack of 1917, but several Gothas destined for England apparently turned back because of bad weather over the North Sea.

At 17.45 hr an aircraft approaching at very low level near Westgate was reported as a British flying-boat, so no alert was given—but as it passed over the Hengrove AA site the keen-eyed gun commander immediately recognized it as a Gotha. Unfortunately he was beyond shouting distance of his four-machine-gun battery, which blissfully ignored an easy target.

In the event this bomber—crewed by Unteroffizier G. Hoffman (pilot), Leut W. Döbrick (navigator) and Vizefeldwebel H. Klaus (gunner)—offered no threat. After a stormy passage over the sea its starboard engine stopped and severe vibration set in. On breaking cloud the coast was visible ahead, so the crew jettisoned bombs and decided to land, putting down successfully at 18.00 hr in a field at Hartsdown Farm south of Margate. Döbrick set fire to the aircraft with a signal cartridge.

The initial misidentification was followed by other happenings which heightened the incident's comedy flavour. Police officers arrived on the scene in a taxi, and a few days later there was much wrangling between the War Office and Alderman Pilcher, JP, of Grosvenor Place, Margate, who unsuccessfully pleaded to retain a dumped German machine-gun—which landed in his garden—as a town war trophy.

Of the three Giants which took off for England one diverted to the alternative target of Boulogne because of bad weather. Signals from this aircraft were intercepted at 19.36 hr, and it was probably the machine showing a green light seen from the North Foreland shortly afterwards, and which had also been tracked down the Channel by the Fan Bay listening post until 20.05 hr.

Giants R.12 and R.39 were off the North Foreland at about 21.30–21.40 hr, clearly uncertain of their whereabouts. They claimed to have attacked shipping in the Thames estuary, but their bombs fell harmlessly in the sea between Ramsgate and Sandwich.

Weather prevented flying from fighter aerodromes south of the Thames, and for the pilots who did take off there was nothing to be found within miles of their patrol areas. But Whitehall had no inhibitions about implying, for public consumption, that a raiding force had been severely handled off the English coast.

Chapter XVIII

Evolution of the Night Fighter

The early months of 1918, which saw the start of the major air reorganization recommended by the Smuts report in August 1917, were politically turbulent, with personality clashes and resignations in high places.

The Air Council was formed on 3 January, with Lord Rothermere as Secretary of State and Trenchard as Chief of the Air Staff. The Trenchard appointment was made at Rothermere's insistence, and Henderson, the obvious candidate, was relegated to the lesser position of Additional Member and Vice President of the council. However, major differences soon arose between Rothermere, the newspaper baron turned politician, and Trenchard, the soldier turned airman, who did not then fully accept the need for a unified air service—and on 19 March Trenchard tendered his resignation. With the formation of the Royal Air Force already decided for 1 April, formal acceptance was deferred, and the announcement that Maj-Gen F. H. Sykes would replace Trenchard was not made until 15 April. Henderson, again passed over, felt unable to work with the new CAS, who was very much his junior, and accordingly resigned. Then on 25 April Rothermere himself resigned and was succeeded by Sir William Weir.

Major-General Sir Hugh Trenchard, first Chief of the Air Staff; and (*right*) Fregattenkapitän Peter Strasser, chief of the German Naval Airship Service from 1913 until his death in L70 on 5 August, 1918.

For the air defences, the year opened in more auspicious fashion when a pair of Camels scored a spectacular victory, shooting a Gotha down in flames during the first raid of the year, on 28/29 January. Then followed three months of frustrated effort against four raids by Giants and three small-scale Zeppelin attacks. Airship activity would have been greater but for the loss of five vessels (L46, 47, 51, 58 and SL20) in a disastrous explosion at Ahlhorn on 5 January, judged to have been accidental though some airship men always suspected sabotage.

This blow was additionally galling to the enemy, coming when improved high-altitude performance had greatly reduced any likelihood of another 'silent-raid' fiasco. This was provided by the new 245 hp Maybach MBIVa high-compression engine delivering 142 hp at 19,700 ft, where the Zeppelins could now achieve 60 mph compared with the modest 45 mph of those using the older engines. L58, the first Zeppelin with these new 'altitude' engines, was delivered in November 1917, and some older vessels were later re-engined.

Gotha operations were halted while Bogohl 3 rebuilt up to establishment after heavy aircraft and crew losses, largely in accidents. This rehabilitation period was at the insistence of Brandenburg, who, despite the artificial leg necessitated after his crash the previous summer, had returned to command his old unit. When the unit was again operational, in March, the German High Command decreed that targets more directly associated with the struggle in France must temporarily have priority over raids on England.

By this time Germany retained few illusions that any bombing offensive within her forseeable capabilities would significantly affect British morale or cause major industrial damage. But it was clear that the build-up of the British defences was diverting more and more men and material from the fighting fronts, while air-raid alerts interrupted war production over a wide area.

In the early part of the year the Giants of Rfa 501 operated from St-Denis Westrem and Gontrode, using Ghistelles, near Ostende, in emergencies. On 7 March the squadron moved to Scheldewindeke, south of Ghent, a new base specially built and equipped for Giant operations.

Against the total of fourteen Giants and six Zeppelins raiding between 29/30 January and April the defences mounted nearly 300 fighter sorties, but sightings were depressingly few and far between. Despite the facility to check their positions by W/T the Giants confined their operations mainly to the moonlight nights. There were several determined combats but not one enemy was destroyed. With the proportion of effective, modern fighters increasing during this period, the lack of success was clearly due to a combination of inexperience and various technical factors, while the problem of locating the bombers seemed no nearer to solution. Four RFC pilots were killed in accidents while on operational patrols.

Much thought was devoted to producing a really effective night fighter, and after studying detailed reports on the 'silent raid' and discussions with Salmond, Ashmore had written to No.6 Brigade on 7 November, 1917, seeking their views. Higgins' reply of 22 December reviewed in some detail the various aircraft with night-fighting potential.

Although both the recently Farnborough-designed pushers, the N.E.1 and the F.E.9, had been found by the new Service Testing Squadron at Suttons Farm to fall far below minimum performance requirements, Higgins still believed that the ideal aircraft for attacking Zeppelins and night bombers was a fast two-seat pusher with a ceiling of at least 20,000 ft. He had earlier put in a bid for one hundred and forty-four of a projected 200 hp BHP-engined version of the F.E.2

An RAF reconnaissance photograph of the German bomber aerodrome at Scheldewindeke, about six miles south-southeast of Ghent, taken on 30 May, 1918. Another photograph, taken on 30 September, 1917, showed three R-type aircraft on the same area, then virtually indistinguishable from the surrounding fields. The concrete T has been reported as runways, with estimated lengths of about 400 and 500 m and a width of 50 m. The numerous drainage works give an impression of the state of the aerodrome and emphasize the need for paved surfaces. It is not known whether the bombers could take off from the concrete or whether they used it to improve initial acceleration. A photograph taken on 22 August, 1918, shows a pattern on the ground which may have been a form of visual approach guidance while other marks suggest earthworks to house cables serving a lighting system. It seems likely that Scheldewindeke was the first aerodrome anywhere with paved runways. The concrete area was first used on 7 March, 1918.

to equip six squadrons, but this appeared to be stagnating.

'The only tractor machine which approaches the ideal for night flying is the Sopwith Dolphin' wrote Higgins, 'and in view of the fact that this machine is already in production . . . efforts should be made to allot as many of these to 6 Brigade as the demands from other sources will admit.'

This latest single-seater differed from earlier Sopwith fighters in using a liquid-cooled engine, and had the Rolls-Royce been installed instead of the 200 hp Hispano Suiza its history might have been different. To provide the best possible forward and upward view, the pilot was seated immediately behind the engine, and the wings were given negative stagger. With the pilot's head protruding through the wing centre-section, he was vulnerable to serious injury should the aircraft turn over on the ground—and the geared Hispano's current reputation for unreliability promised fairly frequent forced landings. The unconventional backward stagger was viewed with perhaps unjustified suspicion because the earlier D.H.5 with that layout had been a disappointment.

A Sopwith Dolphin modified for night fighting, with 4 deg wing-dihedral and protective hoops on the upper wings. This aircraft clearly has a balanced rudder, unlike the version described by Babington.

The Dolphin's performance, particularly at altitude, was impressive; a top speed of 119½ mph at 15,000 ft—reached in 20 min—a ceiling of 21,000 ft and excellent manoeuvrability. Large orders were placed, and No.19 Squadron in France was equipped in January 1918. The Dolphin suffered more than the average run of teething troubles, which may be why only four squadrons were equipped, though it eventually emerged as an excellent high-altitude day-fighter.

Higgins listed the modifications being made to a Dolphin in the Sopwith factory to make it more suitable for night flying, with only a small performance penalty. To improve fore and aft and lateral stability, a 4 deg dihedral angle was being added to the wings, and the angle of incidence increased. An adjustable-incidence, lever-operated tailplane was being fitted. Two tubular steel hoops above the wing centre-section safeguarded the pilot should the aircraft turn over, while a new centre-section Lewis gun mounting offered additional protection. Stronger landing wheels were specified.

As for the Camel, Higgins said that with the 130 hp Clerget engine it was not very suitable for dealing with day raiders since it lost height badly in turns above 14,000 ft and its ceiling was only about 16,000 ft. With the 110 hp Le Rhône, however, it was satisfactory and better suited to formation flying. It was also less

Sopwith Dolphin C3778 with the protective centre-section gun mounting.

One of the standard Sopwith Dolphins (C3942) issued to No.141 Squadron, Biggin Hill, in early 1918.

sensitive to throttle adjustments—a considerable advantage for night flying. He added this significant comment:

> 'In the standard machine the pilot's view upwards is very restricted, and when the positions of the main petrol tank and the pilot are reversed, this is greatly improved. Camel allotments should be the Le Rhône Camel, with this reversal.'

This was the first official reference to the specialized Camel night-fighter, discussed later in this chapter.

The Hispano-powered B.E.12b was described as 'valuable for giving pilots night experience on a fairly fast water-cooled tractor' and, despite limited upward view, good enough to attack current German bombers. But it would be of little use against the improved Zeppelins and new bombers to be expected by mid-1918.

Other potential night fighters were briefly assessed: 'Bristol Fighter very satisfactory, though the pilot's view forward and upward is somewhat restricted; S.E.5—easy to fly at night and has a big margin of performance over Zeppelins and bombers; D.H.4—pilot's view so restricted as to put it out of court, undercarriage somewhat weak.'

Higgins listed the favoured aircraft in order of suitability: 1–modified Dolphin; 2—S.E.5; 3—Bristol Fighter; 4—modified Camel. For reasons not then foreseen by the Brigade staff this order proved to be the precise reverse of the machines' ultimate operational value as night fighters.

Plans for the introduction of the Dolphin went ahead quickly. No.141 Squadron was scheduled to start equipping in January, No.143 in February, No.78 in March, and No.112 in May. Since modifying aircraft on the assembly lines would delay production, No.6 Brigade suggested that the necessary components be supplied and the work done on the squadrons. No.141 Squadron at Rochford duly received, and crashed, its first Dolphin in January, and a few more arrived—all unmodified—during the next six weeks while the squadron moved to Biggin Hill. But the only operations flown were by B.E.12s retained as interim equipment. At least one more Dolphin was crashed, though without serious consequences. Apart from engine unreliability, pilots found the aircraft much less stable than they had expected, with a tendency to spin easily from a left-hand turn.

In March the squadron at last received a modified aircraft, which still lacked the new Lewis gun mounting. According to the CO, Maj Philip Babington, this machine had an unbalanced rudder, a feature of the first prototype criticized by Martlesham test pilots. Babington's report, dated 17 March, effectively ended the Dolphin's night-fighting career before it had started.

> 'The machine is still balanced, without being really stable, though it is more stable laterally than fore and aft. The movable tailplane and increased dihedral are improvements over the ordinary Dolphin, making the machine much easier to fly. The rudder is a failure, making flying rather tricky.
>
> 'I do not consider that the machine is sufficiently stable at present to fly on a night when there is no horizon to guide the pilot, but for ordinary moonlight nights, or dark nights when there is a horizon, it will be possible to fly the Dolphin provided the pilot is possessed of fair skill. The view for landing purposes is not so good as from some tractors, but upward and forward view is vastly superior.
>
> 'As a day fighting machine the Dolphin offers excellent view and quick manoeuvre.'

Two days later the CO of No.49 Wing, Lieut-Col Malcolm Christie, informed Brigade that the machine could not be recommended for fighter operations on dark nights, and that even on moonlit nights pilots of considerable skill would be required. Additionally, the engine, with its inaccessible components requiring daily servicing, seemed unlikely to show that reliability to which night pilots were entitled.

So an embarrassed Higgins saw his hopes for the favourite dashed, and wrote to the Chief of the Air Staff on 3 April: 'after protracted trials of a modified machine the conclusion was arrived at that the machine was too delicate on the controls and not stable enough to be flown on dark nights when the stars are obscured'.

How the Camel might have fared in such trials at a comparable stage of development instead of being thrown in at the deep end by Murlis Green is a matter for speculation. This implies no criticism of those who rejected the Dolphin, for aviation was already starting to move out of the era dominated by the decisions of pilots flying 'by the seat of their pants'.

When the Dolphin's shortcomings were becoming evident, No.6 Brigade reassessed various aircraft for climb, ceiling, speed, stability, ease of landing at night, engine reliability, crew outlook and survival prospects in accidents. The Bristol Fighter emerged top of the table and the Camel was highly placed, with its stability described as good for moonlight and fair for dark nights. The S.E.5a was credited with good stability for dark nights, but its 200 hp Hispano Suiza engine was considered unsuitable for night flying.

The Dolphin fiasco enforced changes in the planned re-arming programme, No.141 Squadron receiving Bristol Fighters, Nos.78 and 112 Camels, and No.143 Viper-engined S.E.5as after a short spell with F.K.8s.

With the standard Camel accepted as suitable for night operations, it is not clear who initiated the major modifications which made it unquestionably the best single-seat night fighter of the First World War. The impetus probably came from No.44 Squadron following the relative success of No.78 Squadron's 1½ Strutter

A Sopwith Camel of No.44 Squadron modified for night fighting, with two Lewis guns mounted above the top wing instead of the usual Vickers installation.

conversion. Also unknown is the date the first example was completed—though its existence was implied by Higgins' letter of 22 December, and the Lewis-armed Camel B5192 flown in combat by Murlis Green four days earlier may have been the original conversion.

Higgins sent this glowing report on the modified Camel's performance to the Air Council on 10 January, 1918.

> 'The machine is greatly improved for night flying and climbed to 10,000 ft in 10 minutes, 16,000 in 20 minutes 25 seconds and to 20,000 in 31½ minutes. At 20,000 ft it was very easy to manoeuvre and was climbing on turns. The losing of height and tendency to spin when turning at high altitudes, which is common with the standard Camel, was entirely absent with the converted machine.
>
> 'A great advantage in weight has been gained by reducing the petrol carrrying capacity and by the fitting of the two Lewis guns on the top plane in place of the Vickers guns.
>
> 'Perhaps the most important point in the conversion is the pilot's view, which is infinitely better than in the standard machine—a point of the utmost importance in night flying.'

It was in this letter that Higgins stressed the urgent need to re-equip No.112 Squadron because it was 'impossible to fly the Sopwith Scout [Pup] at night'.

On 5 February Lieut Michael Doyle, on the staff of the Controller, Technical Department, inspected the aircraft at Hainault and listed all the alterations, later summarized and given official recognition in the CTD printed fortnightly reports. These were: removal of both Vickers guns, chutes and magazines, and the upper fuselage covered with three-ply decking from the engine cowling to the cockpit; wing centre-section cut away for a central width of 30¼ in; two Lewis guns, each with 97 round double drums, 16-inches apart on the top centre-section, on S.E.5 mountings, arranged to fire 15 deg upwards from the line of flight when in a fixed position, pivoted to fire at any angle upward when pulled down and fitted to fire simultaneously or singly; pilot's cockpit moved back 18 in; main petrol tanks replaced by an 18-gal B.E.2e tank carried on bearers fitted across the fuselage in the place previously occupied by the cockpit.

Doyle reported that the view now left very little to be desired, being no longer obstructed by the Vickers guns and obviating the need for the pilot to crane his neck over the side to see forward. Upwards there was practically a clear view all round. The reduced tankage made the aircraft unsuitable for long patrols or escort as required overseas, but it seemed ideal for short night home-defence sorties.

> 'Pilots are unanimous that at about 18,000 ft the modified aircraft is very much livelier than the original Camel' wrote Doyle, 'and that . . . it was possible to land more slowly as it seemed to float on to the ground, wheels and skid together, instead of touching wheels first and then dropping the tail as on the standard aircraft. This is due in great extent to the absence of downwash on the tail from the centre-section.'

Like the single-seat $1\frac{1}{2}$ Strutter, the modified Camel was also known as the 'Comic' and, although not formally recognized, the name was used in some official documents. From this point the 'Comic' Camel story becomes confused. On 17 January DGMA agreed to allot the necessary 110 hp Le Rhône engines, conversion sets, and a 20-strong working party to alter the Camels in No.44 Squadron, then move on to other units listed for re-arming. However, a month

This well-known photograph of B2402 best illustrates the features of the Sopwith Camel modified for night fighting. The pilot is believed to be Capt G. H. Hackwill, No.44 Squadron, who regularly flew B2402 before and after modification.

later the Equipment Directorate was still reiterating that since the modifications could not be made in contractors' works, they should be done by the squadrons if and when necessary. In May CTD reported that 91 per cent of the drawings for the conversion were 'to hand', and the following month the CAS was advised of a production requirement for 204 converted night-flying Camels.

Clearly there was some hold-up in the original plans for rapid conversion in the squadrons, and the number actually modified is not known. They were not specially annotated in operational records, and photographic evidence suggests that relatively few saw squadron service.

Despite the promise of the Camel and Bristol Fighter, No.6 Brigade continued its quest for the ideal night fighter, and a memorandum of 26 January to the Air Ministry on eventual B.E./F.E replacements still expressed preference for a two-seat pusher, but of higher performance than originally visualized. The

The first D.H.10 prototype, C8658, at Marham for assessment by No.51 Squadron.

requirement was now for a ceiling of 22,000 ft and armament comprising one Lewis gun for the pilot and two—or a 1 lb shell gun—for the observer. For southern squadrons having day- and night-fighting responsibilities a higher rate of climb was needed—45 min to 20,000 ft compared with 60 min to the same altitude for northern units with the anti-Zeppelin and night-bomber training role.

The pusher was favoured for its wide range of view and two-man crew, allowing the pilot to concentrate on the flying and the observer on finding and fighting the enemy. A specially designed twin-engined night-fighter was not considered, though during May a D.H.10 twin-engined bomber was sent to No.51 Squadron for evaluation in the face of No.6 Brigade's expressed scepticism.

With the F.E.9 and N.E.1 pushers already rejected, there was a forlorn attempt to rejuvenate the F.E.2 which had been around since 1915 and survived as a night bomber until the end of the war. No more Rolls-engined F.E.2ds were available,

The F.E.9 A4818, another candidate for the night-fighter role, lacked the performance for effective combat.

so the basic airframe was fitted with the new 220 hp BHP engine, to become the F.E.2h. Performance was estimated as superior in all respects to earlier versions, as shown:

	F.E.2b 160 hp Beardmore	F.E.2d 250 hp Rolls-Royce	F.E.2h (estimate) 220 hp BHP
Top speed, ground level	90 mph	92 mph	100 mph
,, ,, 10,000 ft	76 mph	88 mph	$97\frac{3}{4}$ mph
Time to 10,000 ft	39–44 min	18 min	18–30 min
Ceiling	16,000 ft	17,500 ft	21,000 ft

Endorsing the general preference for a two-seat pusher, Trenchard commented: '. . . the F.E. is recognised as an inefficient type, but we ought to get a 25% improvement with a better designed machine'—though it is not clear whether he meant a new aircraft or the re-engined F.E.2.

The outcome was another fiasco. Converted by Ransomes, Sims and Jefferies of Ipswich, the F.E.2h (A6545) received a withering report on 22 March from Maj R. Bourdillon of the Aeroplane Testing Squadron, Martlesham Heath, who found it inferior in all respects to the rejected N.E.1. It took seven minutes longer to reach 14,000 ft and its best speed was $81\frac{1}{2}$ mph. The main fault lay with the propeller, and various examples tried brought no improvement. Solution of this problem should have been within the competence of current research facilities, and perhaps some courageous individual decided not to waste further effort on the unnatural marriage between an elderly airframe and an untried engine already acquiring an unsavoury reputation.

No.6 Brigade then adopted the desperate expedient of reviving that venerable 1915 Zeppelin hunter, the Avro 504 which was extensively used as a trainer. The 1918 night-fighter version of the Avro 504K had its front cockpit faired over and carried a single Lewis gun on a Foster mounting to fire over the propeller. Some were fitted with a V undercarriage instead of the more familiar pattern with characteristic 'hockey stick' central skid. The Avro was powered by a 110 hp Le

Avro 504K night fighters of No.77 Squadron. E3273 is about to be started and E3278 is beyond.

Rhône engine, and the only available performance information states that it could reach 18,000 ft—clearly of doubtful value against Zeppelins operating at 20,000 ft. However, actual ceiling may have been greater, and a No.33 Squadron pilot claimed to have attained 22,100 ft. An advantage of the Avro—eventually issued to six northern squadrons—was that pilots accustomed to its rotary engine could quickly convert to Camels.

Although only a single-seater, the Vickers F.B.26 Vampire pusher was assessed as a potential night-fighter. Three 200 hp Hispano-powered prototypes were built, each armed with three Lewis guns on Eeman mountings, and after official Martlesham trials one (B1484) was evaluated by No.141 Squadron at Biggin Hill. There is no formal record of the results, only Babington's comment that it was 'most unpleasant in a spin, rotating at an appalling speed'. In March, No.61 Squadron at Rochford also received an F.B.26—with its guns movable in

Vickers F.B.26 Vampire B1484 evaluated by No.141 Squadron at Biggin Hill in early 1918.

elevation—which may have been B1486, though no number was given in a discouraging test report dated 23 March by an unidentified, experienced S.E.5a pilot. Top speed was quoted as 114 mph at ground level, 90 mph at 10,000 ft and 69 mph at 17,000 ft—reached in 55 min. Stability was good, but the aircraft lost height badly on turns at 15,000 ft. Landing speed was a little higher than the S.E.5a's, and the narrow wheel-track made the aircraft liable to turn over if landed with drift. The engine was inaccessible for servicing and difficult to change.

'The machine would be fairly suitable for use against night bombers, but of little use against day bombers or Zeppelin raids' wrote the anonymous test pilot.

By the end of the Giant offensive, No.6 Brigade could deploy more than fifty Camels, Bristol Fighters, S.E.5as and B.E.12s against London raiders. While the difficulty of locating targets was apparent, the failure of the fighters to destroy any bombers that were found and attacked was more puzzling. The most likely reason was that attacks generally were launched from too great a distance—though the Giants were remarkably lucky, and one returned with more than eighty bullet holes in its vast surfaces without being hit in a vital spot. R.12 also survived an impact with the balloon barrage.

Towards the end of 1917 an illuminated ring-sight, designed by Lieut H. B. Neame of the Technical Directorate, was introduced. It was made in limited numbers by Purdey, the renowned London gunsmith, and cost £1.75. The Neame sight was adjusted so that the Gotha's 77-ft wing span exactly filled the ring at a distance of 100 yards, and was fitted to the No.44 Squadron Camels of Hackwill

A Bristol Fighter of No. 141 Squadron, Biggin Hill, showing the upward-angled Neame sight on wing centre-section.

and Banks, whose beautifully co-ordinated attack had destroyed the Gotha on 28/29 January.

However, the Giant's 138-ft span obviously filled the sight when much farther away, and pilots believing that they were dealing with a Gotha engaged at too great a range. A GHQ Home Forces intelligence assessment of operations on 29/30 January—when four Camels attacked Giant R.25 without success—claimed that the pilots who initially estimated that they were firing from 50 yards later conceded that the true distance might have been 250 yards.

Intelligence condescendingly added that this failure was not the fault of the pilots, who might not yet all realize the Giant's great size. In truth the principal blame could be laid at the Intelligence door, for there is no evidence of any more effort to acquaint pilots with the Giants' main features than was devoted to the Gotha in 1917—though detailed information about vulnerable areas such as the gravity fuel tank in the centre section, and the blind spot below the nose gun's limited forward field of fire, did not emerge until later.

Meanwhile intelligence happily propagated disparaging reports, one originating from a Gotha crew member captured in France during February. This officer, perhaps resentful because the Giants had temporarily assumed the task which the Gothas had pioneered, said of an encounter with four Camels on 29/30 January—'the crew lost their heads and were paralysed with fright; if your man (*sic*) had stuck to them, even without firing, I believe they would have landed'. Although later German reports showed that the Giant crew had the situation well under control, this story has been debased with the passing of time into an official British statement that the Giant was on the point of landing.

Staaken R.VI R.39, one of the frequently disparaged Giants, survived the war, and the list of twenty operations on the nose includes seven against England—three of them on London.

The intelligence assessment continued 'if this is the spirit of all crews, the fighting capacity of the Giant aeroplanes cannot be very good', while another report declared 'the Giant is a heavy, lumbering and clumsy machine, and its occupants are not usually of the first rank among German airmen. Many prisoners speak disparagingly of the crews, declaring them all to be raw recruits with no experience of air fighting.'

This description of the aircraft was reasonable, and R.39's own crew summed up their machine as having 'only a low speed . . . it is impossible to see all parts of the aircraft from the cockpits . . . guns have a restricted range of fire . . . petrol tanks are in locations too exposed to hostile machine-gun fire.' The rest of the British report, with its blatant propaganda tinged with wishful thinking, reveals a degree of gullibility in the intelligence staffs which failed to recognize an extreme form of inter-unit rivalry. In skill and devotion to duty the Giant crews clearly matched those in other branches of the German air services.

There was steady progress in solving various armament problems which contributed to the fighters' early lack of success, though benefits were slow to emerge because many attacks were still made from too great a range. A new bullet, designed by one of Britain's leading chemical engineers who had earlier been concerned with anti-Zeppelin incendiary bombs, Sir Richard Threlfall, of Albright and Wilson, Oldbury, was ordered after successful Orfordness trials in August 1917. Initial production batches were tested in November, and RTS bullets were issued to home-defence squadrons at the end of December. RTS stood for Richard Threlfall and Son, the latter having acted as his father's unpaid mechanic while on sick leave from the Macedonian Front.

The RTS bullet possessed explosive and incendiary properties. On striking aircraft fabric it exploded, distributing a cone of incendiary composition and fine steel fragments over a diameter of about two feet for every yard from the point of impact. Test reports described it as very accurate and many times more incendiary than the Buckingham over a much longer range. It was highly sensitive—perhaps excessively so, since pilots found that an appreciable proportion of rounds exploded prematurely at 70–100 yards, particularly towards the end of long bursts.

A superficial examination to discover whether RTS bullets contributed significantly to the destruction of the Gotha on 28/29 January was inconclusive. Both Camels carried the usual two Vickers guns firing ball and tracer ammunition, but one had an additional Lewis loaded with one in three rounds of RTS. Lieut-Col F. R. Hedges of the No.6 Brigade technical staff claimed that this was not used until both Camels had almost exhausted their Vickers belts, suggesting that the RTS was mainly responsible and certainly caused the fire. However, the brigade's initial operational summary based on pilots' de-briefings stated that the Lewis-armed Camel fired its three guns together. Since altogether nearly 1,000 rounds were discharged—only about 32 being RTS—and unburned parts of wreckage showed many hits, an open verdict seems most reasonable.

Normal loading for the belt-fed Vickers guns, synchronized to fire between the propeller blades, was five rounds of ball ammunition to one of tracer—the improved SPG VIIG, still popularly known as Sparklet. The Buckingham incendiary and PSA Mk II (Pomeroy) were considered hazardous for use in the Vickers because of their high sensitivity, and RTS was similarly restricted to Lewis guns, firing above the propeller. The Mk II RTS, which appeared in March, was described by Air Ministry armament experts as superior to any bullet of similar type. Unlike others it was not affected by the cold at high altitudes, which had led to the development of heated magazines maintaining a constant temperature of 70–80 deg F.

With the emphasis switching from Zeppelins to the more elusive aeroplane targets, the fighter pilots' temporary loss of night vision due to the flash from their machine-guns assumed greater importance. This affected pilots differently, some being blinded after firing a few shots while others seemed unbothered after long bursts. The problem arose when using the fuselage-mounted Vickers and with the Lewis angled to fire upwards, both directly in the pilot's line of vision. Work began on a flash eliminator for the Lewis in February, and progress was made towards solving the problem with the Vickers. Pilots could also be briefly blinded by the not infrequent premature explosion of Sparklet bullets, which were eventually discarded for night use.

The Orfordness experimental station continued to study other aspects of night combat and in January reported on camouflage. Tests showed that a dark-green shade designated NIVO—*N*ight *I*nvisble *V*arnish *O*rfordness—was much more effective than black in concealing an aircraft against a land background. From below, black under-surfaces were less visible in searchlights, but light shades were harder to pick up when not so illuminated. Removal of the white circle from the national roundels was recommended because it could reveal an aircraft before its outline became visible.

Orfordness listed the following prerequisites for successful night combat: the fighter must have superior performance; gun flash to be damped down; non-tracer ammunition used; 45 deg upward-angled guns to be installed; exhaust flames must be reduced.

S.E.5as could advertise their presence by bursts of flame when the engine was throttled back, and flame damper cowlings—including one pattern devised by Lieut G. C. Young, a Canadian pilot in No.61 Squadron—were fitted over the rear part of the exhaust pipes on some aircraft. Similar dampers were also used on B.E.12bs.

S.E.5a D3459 with the exhaust flame damper devised on No.61 Squadron and the suspectedly unofficial camouflage used for a time on the unit. It was photographed after transfer to No.37 Squadron in the summer of 1918, and the pilot is Lieut Mitchell. (*Mrs M. F. Sadler*)

A major German development was the introduction of the 2,204 lb (1,000 kg) high-explosive bomb—the largest used by either side during the war. Only three were dropped on England, the first on 16/17 February causing substantial damage. Some German crews believed that an equivalent weight of medium-sized bombs created more overall destruction, which may be why only one Giant, R.39, appears to have been modified to carry this monster.

Public disquiet after the 18/19 December raid had shown that aeroplane attacks were no longer restricted to the brighter moonlit nights stimulated another Government reappraisal of the threat and necessary countermeasures. There were wild estimates of imminent raids by 500 bombers, and the War Office asked the C-in-C Home Forces for a full report on the London defence situation.

A 60-cm searchlight of 1917–18. (*J. M. Bruce/G. S. Leslie collection*)

French replied on 17 January, quoting the strength of efficient aircraft in the eight fully operational LADA squadrons as 89 day- and 63 night-fighters. Since Camels and some other types were included under both headings the figures can not conveniently be added to give total strength—which was about 100 efficient aircraft, plus another 26 day-fighters from training and other units. The report recapitulated the host of difficulties facing the defences and stressed the need for better AA guns and searchlights. It referred to the wireless tracker scheme as though this was some new and promising development rather than one which had produced minimal benefits over the past six months. It also hailed the special listening-posts capable of detecting approaching aircraft far out to sea—without mentioning that the only working examples were badly sited to yield much benefit.

Meanwhile an Air Council assessment reduced the threat to a more realistic maximum of 80 bombers able to reach Britain at any one time during the early summer. This was still over-generous, even if all available large German bombers were switched to English targets. The threat was regarded seriously enough to stimulate a programme of underground hangar building, a start being made at Manston.

GHQ Home Forces' requirement to meet this scale of attack against London, forwarded to the CIGS on 8 February, was 264 aircraft—twelve squadrons of twenty and four wireless flights of six. At that time LADA had eight squadrons operational, but mostly under strength, and Nos.141 and 143 in process of formation, giving a theoretical total of 200 machines. Also required were 300 of the new 120 cm searchlights and 100 more guns, larger than the existing 3-in type, bringing strength up to 623 searchlights and 349 guns.

Field Marshal Sir Henry Wilson, who succeeded Robertson as CIGS on 16 February, recommended that the Western Front be given priority for aeroplanes—deferring any new home-defence squadrons until October—but that

A three-inch anti-aircraft gun for aerodrome defence at Bekesbourne.

home requirements for AA guns should have precedence over France. This was agreed by the War Cabinet on 27 February. As events developed the wisdom of this decision was not put to the test, but Wilson was no great believer in the fighter's value. In a 1921 assessment of home-defence requirements he claimed that in the first two years of war 87.4 per cent of home-defence pilots never saw the enemy, and that in 1917–18 the figure rose to 91.7 per cent. He did not say how many thousands of AA shells missed their targets, or mention the damage and casualties caused by falling debris—more than 20 killed and 130 injured in seven of the 1917 raids alone.

On 22 January the CAS had reacted cautiously to a suggestion from Shaw, Chief of Staff, Home Forces, that improved searchlight efficiency and better aircraft might justify allowing fighter patrols greater freedom of action over the gun areas.

> 'I do not think we have sufficient information under the improved conditions to determine whether aeroplanes or guns will be most effective against enemy aeroplanes' wrote Trenchard. 'Under certain conditions, such as ground mist, firing to sound will still be important. Giant aeroplanes also have to be allowed for, and probably guns will be more effective than aeroplanes. No alteration in existing principles should take place until further experience has been gained, but I suggest that a modified scheme be worked out with Ashmore, to be put into operation if it is found desirable to give the aeroplanes more freedom of action.'

A new form of barrage fire, named Polygon, was introduced on 28/29 January, which aimed to encircle a bomber with shell bursts rather than confront it with a curtain of fire as in the previous Linear pattern. This brought no dramatic results, and in April the fighter patrol zone was widened by transferring some of the inner guns to the outer barrage line. At the same time more searchlights were placed under the operational control of fighter squadrons.

At the end of February, after a few parting exchanges between the Admiralty and GHQ Home Forces, RNAS aircraft were finally relieved of any responsibility for defence against enemy bombers in the LADA area—a somewhat academic decision since the two air services were within only weeks of amalgamation. Although the RNAS had virtually opted out in September 1917, a few sorties continued to be flown, and during the first two raids of 1918 naval fighters caused some confusion in the Dover area because the AA Defence Commander had not been notified. These were probably free-lance sorties by experienced pilots reluctant to sit idly on the ground when enemy bombers were about.

On 13 February Home Forces reminded the Admiralty of the old principle that naval machines should not take off to deal with enemy aeroplanes over land, but were free to continue pursuits which had started out at sea. However, they welcomed RNAS co-operation provided patrols could be properly integrated. The Admiralty responded to the effect that such patrols were ruled out by lack of suitable aircraft, and on 27 February Home Forces told LADA that no RNAS aircraft would henceforth fly at night during raids.

This rather arid exchange did not reflect the normally cordial relations existing between the army and navy pilots—though on the formation of the Royal Air Force some made no secret of their attachment to their old Services and feelings were strong on certain stations.

In April, in apparent contradiction of the decision to build underground hangars at Manston, the Air Ministry ruled that home-defence flights were not needed there, or at Eastchurch, since AA guns adequately covered the Kent and Essex shores of the Thames estuary.

The need for co-ordinated action was shown by the speed with which false alarms could escalate into extensive patrol activity. A major example on 18/19 February started when German bombers attacking Calais were heard from the Kent coast. Readiness was ordered at 19.50 hr, but through some misunderstanding patrols were launched 40 min later. Events then took over, and as the first fighters reached their patrol areas they were reported as hostiles, so more took off and were still doing so until ten minutes before midnight, when the all-clear was given.

Every LADA squadron except No.112—still limited to daylight operations with its Pups—was involved, and 55 sorties totalling 91 hr were flown. To their credit, no pilots claimed to have seen any hostiles and only two reported aircraft not responding to challenge.

Gunners from the more trigger-happy London sites fired 2,599 rounds at what were described as three attacks between 21.15 and 22.22 coming in from the Thames–Medway area, the intruders sounding 'quite unlike' British aeroplanes. All targets picked up by searchlights were claimed as hostile. However, Col Simon's report did admit that 'targets were lost in every case in the most unexpected manner' while the Central Sub-Commander, Capt L. S. Stansfeld RN, conceded that the distinctive enemy 'double-beat' sound was missing. Lieut-Col C. Buckle, the Epping Sub-Commander, complained that fighters habitually encroaching into the barrage area undermined the basis of the defence system, and it was thanks to the diligence of the operations-room staff that they were not attacked. If gun commanders had rigidly followed the book, said Buckle, several thousands of rounds would have been fired.

The probable offenders were the Camels of No.44 Squadron, whose pilots protested that the guns ignored their recognition signals.

There was more substance to the false alarm of 26/27 April, which generated 26 fighter sorties totalling 24 hr flying time. This was caused by H-12 flying-boat No.8683 from Felixstowe, returning after a five-hour search for a reported enemy destroyer. Fog had grounded fighter squadrons south of the Thames, and the H-12 became lost after approaching the North Foreland, where it was reported as hostile and caused a readiness alert at 22.58 hr. As it moved slowly up the coast AA guns fired on sound until an eagle-eyed gunner at Burnham recognized its silhouette against the moon. It alighted near this battery, established its bearings and returned to Felixstowe.

The AA guns scored a 'success' during a minor scare on 3/4 January which was resolved before any general alert was given. The victim was F.E.2b A5698 of No.38 Squadron on a cross-country training flight from Stamford. The pilot, 2nd Lieut E. F. Wilson, strayed into the outer London defences, forgot the night's recognition colours and was promptly fired on by the Roding guns. The aircraft was hit, then wrecked in a forced landing, but Wilson was unhurt.

Apart from home defence, No.6 Brigade was responsible for certain air operations in the event of enemy invasion, and had growing commitments to train night-flying crews for overseas squadrons. With the increase in fighter and night training (formerly depot) squadrons, some organizational changes became necessary in early 1918.

At the end of 1917 the brigade had four wings—No.46 (Northern) York; No.47 (South Midland) Cambridge; No.49 (Eastern) Upminster and No.50 (Southern) Chelmsford. The formation of Nos.141 and 143 Squadrons meant that Nos.49 and

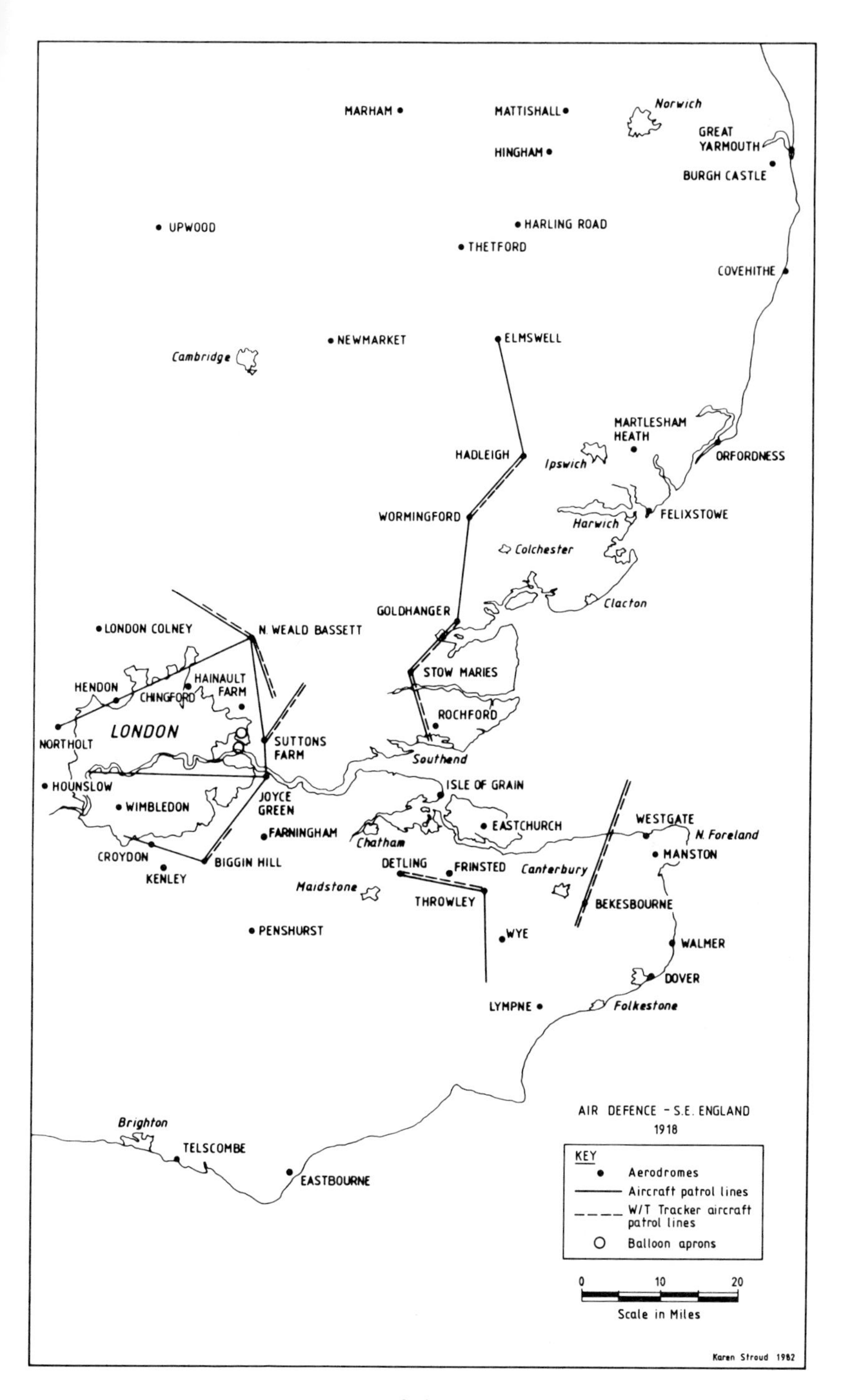
MARHAM
MATTISHALL
Norwich
GREAT YARMOUTH
HINGHAM
BURGH CASTLE
UPWOOD
HARLING ROAD
THETFORD
COVEHITHE
NEWMARKET
ELMSWELL
Cambridge
MARTLESHAM HEATH
HADLEIGH
Ipswich
ORFORDNESS
WORMINGFORD
FELIXSTOWE
Harwich
Colchester
Clacton
GOLDHANGER
LONDON COLNEY
N. WEALD BASSETT
STOW MARIES
HENDON
HAINAULT FARM
CHINGFORD
ROCHFORD
LONDON
NORTHOLT
SUTTONS FARM
Southend
HOUNSLOW
ISLE OF GRAIN
WIMBLEDON
JOYCE GREEN
WESTGATE
EASTCHURCH
N. Foreland
FARNINGHAM
Chatham
MANSTON
CROYDON
BIGGIN HILL
DETLING
FRINSTED
Canterbury
KENLEY
Maidstone
THROWLEY
BEKESBOURNE
PENSHURST
WYE
WALMER
DOVER
LYMPNE
Folkestone
AIR DEFENCE – S.E. ENGLAND
1918
Brighton
TELSCOMBE
EASTBOURNE
KEY
Aerodromes
Aircraft patrol lines
W/T Tracker aircraft patrol lines
Balloon aprons
0
10
20
Scale in Miles
Karen Stroud 1982

50 Wings would be controlling ten LADA squadrons, and, to achieve better administration, a new wing, No.53, was formed at Harrietsham, Kent, on 11 March. The new breakdown became: No.49 Wing—Nos.39, 44, 78 and 141 Squadrons; No.50 Wing—Nos.37, 61, 75 and 198(NT) Squadrons; No.53 Wing—Nos.50, 112 and 143 Squadrons. An additional wing (No.48 at Gainsborough) was formed in February, largely to cope with the increased training requirements.

The confused picture at Biggin Hill, where since September 1917 patrols had been maintained by detached flights—first from No.39 Squadron and then No.78—ended in February when No.141 moved in from Rochford to become the first full resident squadron, eventually flying Bristol Fighters. Several of the original No.39 Squadron pilots stayed on, unbothered by the bureaucratic manoeuvres which had given them three squadron numbers in less than six months.

In January, believing that No.6 Brigade was becoming too large for effective control and supervision, GHQ Home Forces had sought approval for the creation of a new northern group, with HQ at York. This was rejected by the Air Ministry but formed later in the year after the establishment of a Northern Air Defence Area under Brig-Gen Philip Maud, which organized the defences in the LADA manner. Northern squadrons had formerly been controlled by the appropriate Garrison Commanders.

Chapter XIX

Operations—January to April 1918

28/29 January, 1918 (Night)

Target: London.
Enemy forces: 13 Gothas despatched, seven Gothas attacked.
Two Giants despatched, one Giant attacked.
Results: 67 killed, 166 injured, £187,350 damage.
Defence sorties: 103.

RNAS

Dover: Sopwith Camels B7192 (Sqn Cdr R. S. Dallas) 21.55–22.55 hr; also sorties by B6359, B6409 and B6411; Sopwith 1½ Strutter 9414, 21.15–23.05 hr.

Eastchurch: Sopwith Camel B5714, 21.15–22.00 hr.

RFC

No.37 Squadron, Goldhanger: Eight sorties, took off 20.10–00.40 hr, landed 20.27–01.25 hr.

No.37 Squadron, Stow Maries: Seven sorties, took off 20.10–00.43 hr, landed 22.10–01.20 hr.

No.39 Squadron, North Weald: Bristol Fighters C4638 (Lieut J. G. Goodyear, 1st AM W. T. Merchant); B1157 and C4636, plus seven unspecified sorties, took off 20.17–23.23 hr, landed 22.10–01.20 hr.

No.44 Squadron, Hainault: Sopwith Camels: Twenty-five sorties, took off 20.26–00.40 hr, landed 21.37–01.24 hr—including B3827 (2nd Lieut C. C. Banks).

No.50 Squadron, Bekesbourne: Seven sorties, took off 20.14–22.11 hr, landed 21.47–00.14 hr.

No.50 Squadron, Detling: Four sorties, took off 20.15–23.00 hr, landed 22.45–00.30 hr.

No.61 Squadron, Rochford: S.E.5as; Nine sorties, took off 20.15–23.15 hr, landed 21.25–01.00 hr.

No.75 Squadron, Hadleigh: Five sorties, took off 20.42–22.55 hr, landed 21.30–00.30 hr.

No.78 Squadron, Suttons Farm: Sopwith Camels and Sopwith 1½ Strutter SSs; Fifteen sorties, took off 20.20–00.25 hr, landed 20.57–01.22 hr.

No.78 Squadron, Biggin Hill: Seven sorties, took off 20.22–00.35 hr, landed 22.30–01.19 hr.

Normal operational reports covering the first raid of 1918 are unaccountably missing from the regular file sequences preserved in the Public Record Office.

This is particularly unfortunate because the attack stimulated the First World

A B.E.2e of No.75 Squadron after taking off at Hadleigh.

War's biggest reaction from British night fighters, which shot down their first Gotha in flames. The subsequent consolidated intelligence report is equally inadequate, which suggests that all the usual source material was unavailable from the outset. One possible explanation of this strange situation is that the new and autocratic Secretary of State for the Air Force, Lord Rothermere, demanded immediately all information about the raid, and that the papers were either not returned from the all-powerful ministerial office or were misfiled. However, from surviving documents and other sources it is possible to present the essential story.

An intended major effort by Bogohl 3 was baulked from the outset when fog prevented the later take-offs and six of the Gothas which did get airborne returned because of poor visibility. Of the two available Giants, R.35 developed engine trouble, jettisoned its bombs in the sea north of Ostende and went back to base. The Gothas came in between Harwich and the North Foreland, the first at 19.55 hr and the last 30 min later. Three reached London, bombing from 20.30 to 21.45 hr, and the others attacked Ramsgate, Margate, Sheerness, and the

Sopwith Camel B3827 (foreground) flown by 2nd Lieut C. C. Banks on 28/29 January, 1918. Next is B2402 regularly used by Capt G. H. Hackwill and probably when he and Banks shot down Gotha G V/938/16. B2402 was later modified as an aft-seated night-fighter version.

Sandwich neighbourhood. Giant R.12 made landfall over Hollesley Bay at 22.25 hr and followed a tortuous course to reach central London at 00.15 hr. One of its two 660 lb bombs caused the worst London bomb incident of the war when it hit the Odhams Press building in Long Acre, resulting in 38 deaths and 85 injuries. Altogether 8,100 lb of bombs were dropped.

Apart from patchy coastal cloud the night was fine and clear, with brilliant moonlight, and No.6 Brigade reported greatly improved co-operation between aircraft, searchlights and guns.

The armament of two Vickers and one Lewis gun on this Camel suggests that it is the Scarff modification on B3827 flown by Banks on 28/29 January, 1918.

The Gotha which did not return was No.G V/938/16, crewed by Leut Friedrich von Thomsen (navigator and commander), and Unteroffiziers Karl Ziegler (pilot) and Walther Heiden (gunner). It flew in over The Naze at 20.00 hr, skirted Clacton and followed a steady course to London, then, instead of turning south for a major target, unloaded its bombs on Hampstead at 21.45 hr.

Its return across northeast London was indicated by searchlights, which attracted two of No.44 Squadron's Camels, flown by George Hackwill and Charles Banks, who independently sighted it at about 10,000 ft over Romford by its exhaust flames.

Banks' log-book notes that he was flying Camel B3827 'modified to Lt Scarff's instructions'—which could link with a No.6 Brigade technical report stating that one of the two Camels was unconventionally armed with a Lewis gun firing the new RTS ammunition in addition to the two standard Vickers. Lieut F. W. Scarff was the RNAS armaments specialist who had earlier designed machine-gun interrupter gear and observers' gun mountings, and it is therefore reasonable to assume that Banks was flying the three-gun Camel.

Banks attacked first, closing to about 30 yards under the Gotha from the left before opening fire with his three guns. Meanwhile, Hackwill had moved in from the right and also engaged, presenting an almost impossible situation for the enemy gunner firing down the 'tunnel', whose tracer mostly passed between the two Camels. The battle went on for perhaps ten minutes, its progress etched by tracer bullets in full view of the Noak Hill, Shenfield and Billericay AA gunners. Despite the closeness of combat the Gotha at first seemed invulnerable, and Banks had to break off when an electrical fault put two of his cylinders out of action. He turned for another look at the bomber, which had received a few more bursts from Hackwill, and saw it falling, partly on fire, then exploding into a mass of flame on hitting the ground.

The Gotha came down at Frund's Farm, Wickford, at 22.10 hr. The three crew members were killed, the pilot having been shot through the neck. A member of the No.3 Divisional Cycle Company who was among the first on the scene noted the aircraft serial number, and a small metal plate found in the wreckage gave its factory number as 1696.

Hackwill and Banks were awarded MCs for their victory.

The sparse information in surviving documents shows that the five sightings or brief attacks reported by Nos.50, 39, 61 (two) and 78 Squadrons all related to Gothas. Francis Luxmoore, flying one of No.78 Squadron's newly-acquired Camels, was nearing the southernmost limit of his patrol over Joyce Green, hoping to pick up a target silhouetted against the Thames, when his concentration was rudely shattered by an uncomfortably close burst of machine-gun fire from the right-hand side.

'I whipped my head round just in time to see a Gotha's starboard wingtip give my tail a very near miss, and had a clear close-up view of its front gunner' recalled Luxmoore 60 years later.

He was flying slowly, and in turning to keep the Gotha in sight his Camel fell into a spin, but it recovered after half a turn and he climbed eastwards along the Gotha's homing course. He soon picked up its exhaust flames and closed in behind, bumping in the slipstream until its wings overflowed his Neame sight. He

No.78 Squadron Sopwith Camels at Suttons Farm. The unit began operating the type in January 1918.

pulled the trigger—it was an early Camel with a gun trigger similar to a motor-cycle clutch on the triangular joy-stick trip—and nothing happened. While trying to rectify matters the slipstream threw him into another spin, and after further fruitless efforts with the guns he returned to base. It was then found that the trigger levers had been wrongly positioned after a cable replacement. His short test burst on reaching patrol height had stretched the cable just enough to make the gun inoperable.

Staaken R.IV R.12, which shot down the Bristol Fighter B1157 of No.39 Squadron on 28/29 January, 1918. (*P. M. Grosz*)

An RNAS 1½ Strutter from Dover briefly attacked a Gotha off the North Foreland at 21.50 hr—probably one of the aircraft which bombed Sheerness.

From 23.00 hr, when the Giant R.12 was in the Sudbury area and obviously bound for London, another twenty-four fighters took off to join the twenty already airborne and with fuel for at least another hour's patrolling. The last Gotha had cleared the coast by 22.30 hr, and although it was not at the time realized that this substantial force was deployed against a single bomber, that one aircraft's load of 2,645 lb was only 110 lb less than that of the three Gothas which reached the capital.

Available records do not identify the two fighters which, according to the official history, encountered R.12 early during its inward journey. They are not mentioned in the Rfa 501 report nor, surprisingly, is a combat over the Harlow area with a No.39 Squadron Bristol Fighter, crewed by John Goodyear and Walter Thomas Merchant. However, the consolidated German account did claim correctly that one defender was shot down.

The Bristol was patrolling at 10,000 ft between Suttons Farm and Sawbridgeworth when Goodyear sighted a 'four-engined Gotha' at about 23.00 hr. This faulty description of the R.12, with six engines driving three propellers, is of no great significance since the best-known Giants were four-engined and Goodyear clearly realized that he had found something larger than the twin-engined Gotha.

He positioned behind and fired a long burst from his Vickers, but the Bristol was flung to the right by the slipstream churned up by the two great 14-ft pusher propellers as he closed in. The same thing happened on a second attempt, and this time he came under fire from several of the Giant's machine-guns. He turned in again, intending to give Merchant an opportunity with his Lewis, but as he approached to position below, the Bristol was caught by a burst which shattered the main petrol tank and wounded Merchant. Shortly afterwards the engine stopped, presumably from fuel starvation, and with the North Weald flarepath visible to the southeast, Goodyear glided down to a faultless engine-off landing. Merchant was removed to hospital, where his arm wound was found to be relatively slight.

R.12 continued serenely to London, and at about 00.10 hr, according to some British accounts, hit the balloon barrrage at Chingford. This belief was based on the daylight discovery that two streamer wires from the No.5 apron had been torn away. They were never found, and perversely, an AA shell known to have hit one of the balloons during the night was discounted as the cause of the cable damage. Four months afterwards, when a talkative prisoner admitted that a Giant had once hit the barrage, British intelligence linked this with the Chingford incident, though it actually referred to a later occasion. R.12's crew report said nothing about even seeing the barrage, and it is inconceivable that an impact could escape the crew's notice or inflict no damage.

The report described British fighter activity as minimal, and mentioned that one machine had followed for some time without attacking. This was evidently the No.44 Squadron Camel flown by South African Bob Hall, who picked up the Giant east of Woolwich and trailed it to the coast without being able to get his guns functioning. R.12 cleared the coast off Foulness just after 01.00 hr and as it droned out to sea the crew could still see the fire from one of their 660 lb bombs.

The London AA commander estimated the raiding force as twelve aircraft, with eight penetrating to central London. Atmospheric conditions played peculiar tricks with engine sounds, and AA gunners reported that some aircraft shut down engines and glided for a time. Murlis Green diplomatically telephoned Buckle, the local gun commander, to praise the searchlights for initially picking up the Gotha shot down by two of his pilots, and the guns for withholding fire during the aerial combat.

The CO of No.78 Squadron was rather less cordial after one of his Camels had been brought down by gunfire. This was the first time that the new and more widely dispersed Polygon barrage was employed, and the engine of Idris Meredith Davies' Camel was stopped by a close shell burst at 11,000 ft over Woolwich. Davies made a valiant attempt to glide back to Suttons Farm, but he hit telegraph wires near the Hornchurch signal box, was catapulted out and landed unhurt between the railway lines. The Camel caught fire and was a write-off. The crash happened at about 21.30 hr, and 40 min later Davies was sitting in another Camel, ready to take off if necessary.

29/30 January, 1918 (Night)

Target: London.
Enemy forces: Four Giants despatched, three Giants attacked.
Results: Ten killed, ten injured, £8,968 damage.
Defence sorties: 80.

RNAS

Dover: Sopwith Camels B6431 (Sqn Cdr R. S. Dallas) 23.38–00.22 hr; B6411 (Flt Cdr R. P. Minifie) 22.15–23.20 hr; B6429 (Flt Lieut H. V. Rowley) 22.44–00.14 hr; B6420 (Flt Lieut C. B. Ridley) 22.15–00.14 hr; Sopwith 1½ Strutter 9414, 22.12–00.22 hr.

Walmer: Sopwith Camels B3853 (Sqn Cdr B. L. Huskisson) 22.45–23.55 hr; N6364 (Flt Cdr A. M. Shook) 22.12–00.22 hr.

RFC

No.37 Squadron, Goldhanger: B.E.2es B8835 (2nd Lieut F. R. Kitton) 21.40–00.59 hr; B4512 (Lieut P. R. Cawdell) 23.42–01.30 hr; B.E.12bs 6137 (Lieut C. L. Blake) 23.25–01.39 hr; C3091 (Capt A. Dennis) 21.38–23.45 hr.

No.37 Squadron, Stow Maries: B.E.2e B4505 (Lieut H. Lingard) 21.33–23.00 hr; B.E.12s C3183 (2nd Lieut E. H. Chater) 21.35–00.01 hr; A6318 (Capt A. B. Kynoch) 23.33–01.38 hr; B1500 (Capt J. L. Horridge) 23.40–01.42 hr; B.E.12b C3084 (Capt A. B. Fanstone) 22.14–23.40 hr.

No.39 Squadron, North Weald: Bristol Fighters B1157 (Lieut E. S. C. Brooks, 2nd Lieut J. T. Baugh), W/T tracker, 21.59–00.15 hr, crashed landing; C4646 (2nd Lieut A. S. Dickens, Lieut N. C. Crombie) 21.59–23.59 hr; C4639 (Lieut A. E. Simmons, 1st AM Coombs) 22.00–22.45 hr, returned with engine trouble; A7265 (2nd Lieut W. B. Thomson, 2nd Lieut F. J. B. de S. La Terriere) 22.02–00.40 hr (Fyfield); B1186 (Lieut C. R. W. Knight, 2nd Lieut E. J. Ralli) 22.57–23.55 hr; C4815 (Capt O. V. Thomas, Sgt Riches) 23.33–01.33 hr; B1264 (Lieut P. W. Deane, 1st AM W. Eatock) 23.30–01.30 hr; B1260 (2nd Lieut H. P. Lale, Lieut W. N. Fraser) 23.40–01.40 hr; B.E.2e B4485 (Lieut L. Taylor), W/T tracker, 23.35–01.35 hr.

No.44 Squadron, Hainault: Sopwith Camels B3852 (Capt C. J. Q. Brand) 21.59–00.35 hr; B2402 (Capt G. H. Hackwill) 22.03–00.45 hr; C6715 (Capt C. J. Marchant) 22.04–00.12 hr; B5603 (Capt W. H. Haynes) 22.05–00.33 hr; B9245 (2nd Lieut C. C. Banks) 22.09–00.39 hr; B3767 (2nd Lieut A. E. Godfrey) 22.09–00.11 hr; B3815 (Maj G. W. M. Green) 22.15–23.44 hr, returned with gun trouble, and 23.55–01.15 hr; B9177 (2nd Lieut R. N. Hall) 22.17–00.25 hr; B5412 (2nd Lieut T. M. O'Neill) 22.21–00.18 hr; B3827 (2nd Lieut H. A. Edwardes) 22.22–00.12 hr; B5411 (Lieut J. T. Collier) 23.47–01.30 hr; B3899 (2nd Lieut L. S. V. Gedge) 23.50–01.32 hr; B3859 (2nd Lieut W. A. Pritt) 23.57–01.36 hr; C6714 (2nd Lieut R. M. Foster) 00.01–00.55 hr, returned with gun trouble; B5206 (2nd Lieut J. L. Wingate) 00.35–01.52 hr.

No.50 Squadron, Bekesbourne: B.E.12s A6313 (2nd Lieut J. A. C. Kempe-Roberts) 21.36–23.50 hr; C3182 (2nd Lieut W. G. Latham), W/T tracker, 21.37–21.42 hr, returned with engine trouble, and 23.17–01.21 hr; C3206 (Lieut H. T. W. Oswell) 00.21–01.35 hr; B.E.12bs C3095 (Capt J. S. Shaw), W/T tracker, 21.34–22.05 hr, returned due to weather, and 22.41–22.51 hr, returned with engine trouble; C3110 (2nd Lieut A. C. Goldsmith) 21.39–00.34 hr; C3097 (Lieut H. T. W. Oswell) 21.49–21.54 hr, returned due to weather; C3090 (Lieut J. Metcalfe) 23.34–01.30 hr.

No.50 Squadron, Detling: Armstrong Whitworth F.K.8s B3316 (Maj A. A. B. Thomson, Lieut T. E. Garside) 21.36–23.40 hr; B224 (2nd Lieut W. R. Oulton, Lieut H. Harris) 21.34–00.30 hr; B223 (2nd Lieut F. V. Bryant, 2nd Lieut V. H. Newton) 23.20–01.35 hr; B4017 (Lieut C. Ossenton, 2nd Lieut R. C. Cowl) 23.24–01.50 hr; B229 (2nd Lieut N. F. Perris, 2nd AM H. G. Brothers) 23.50–01.55 hr.

No.61 Squadron, Rochford: S.E.5as B658 (Capt C. A. Lewis) 21.40–23.35 hr; B672 (Capt S. H. Starey) 21.43–23.15 hr; C1065 (Lieut J. W. Sheridan) 21.43–23.40 hr; C9486 (Capt E. B. Mason) 23.10–00.45 hr; C5338 (Capt H. C. Stroud) 23.12–00.45 hr; C1756 (Lieut L. B. Blaxland) 23.15–23.31 hr, returned with engine trouble; C1062 (Lieut Blaxland) 23.45–01.20 hr.

No.75 Squadron, A Flight, Hadleigh: B.E.2e A8701 (Lieut C. F. Wolley-Dod) 21.45–23.05 hr; B.E.12 6160 (2nd Lieut L. Neville-Smith) 21.55–23.00 hr, crashed due to engine trouble.

No.75 Squadron, C Flight, Elmswell: B.E.12b C3086 (Capt C. W. Mackey) crashed 21.50–23.50 hr.

No.78 Squadron, Suttons Farm: Sopwith Camels C6713 (Lieut D. V. Armstrong) 21.54–22.45 hr and 23.57–01.24 hr; B9305 (Lieut R. F. W. Moore)

21.54–00.01 hr; B9297 (Capt D. J. Bell) 21.54–00.10 hr; C1555 (Capt F. L. Luxmoore) 21.54–00.20 hr; C1563 (Capt G. M. Boumphrey) 23.52–01.00 hr, returned with engine trouble; B9253 (Capt S. P. Gamon) 23.53–01.42 hr; Sopwith 1½ Strutter SSs A1100 (2nd Lieut V. C. Chapman) 21.54–23.58 hr; B862 (2nd Lieut D. G. Lewis) 23.54–00.41 hr, returned with engine trouble; A1100 (2nd Lieut M. H. G. Liddell) 00.55–01.35 hr.

No.78 Squadron, Biggin Hill: B.E.12s C3195 (2nd Lieut A. M. Bennett) 21.46–23.20 hr; C3210 (Lieut A. F. Barker) 23.02–01.12 hr; A6308 (Lieut E. J. Stockman) 23.12–01.16 hr; B.E.12a A595 (2nd Lieut E. E. Turner) 21.58–00.04 hr; B.E.12b C3152 (Capt F. Billinge) 21.05–23.10 hr.

This first raid conducted solely by the Giants of Rfa 501, while Bogohl 3 with its Gothas was being rebuilt to full strength, produced mediocre bombing results.

The defences reacted creditably, and had the fighters suffered fewer gun troubles the outcome could have been a German disaster. One Giant survived the most remarkable night combat of the war, limping home after an hour of successive attacks by five fighters.

R.12 developed engine trouble over the Channel and bombed fortifications near Gravelines. The remaining three aircraft came in between The Naze and Southend, one venturing no more than 20 miles inland and the other two bombing the outskirts of London. The defences were still confused by the sound of the Giants meandering along at 10,000 ft at 60–70 mph, and it was estimated that a force of fifteen bombers, including some Gothas, was involved.

R.39, which came in over the mouth of the Blackwater at 22.05 hr, was picked up ten minutes later at 12,000 ft southwest of Goldhanger by Arthur Dennis flying

Lieut C. F. Wolley Dod, No.75 Squadron, Hadleigh, who was airborne on 29/30 January, 1918, posing in the wreckage of a B.E.2e which he had crashed a few weeks later. This was typical of many contemporary accidents where low impact speeds enabled pilots to escape without injury. Wolley Dod became an Instone Air Line captain in the early 1920s. (*Mrs M. F. Sadler*)

one of No.37 Squadron's B.E.12bs. He attacked from fairly close range, and despite the Giant's evasive action and return fire from two rear guns, scored some hits on its fuselage. He cleared a stoppage in his Lewis and finished the drum, then on a second approach after re-arming was flung considerably off course by the turbulent slipstream and lost his target. After landing Dennis found 'several' bullet holes in the centre section of his B.E.—which was by no means 'riddled' as some accounts have suggested. The Rfa 501 report confirmed that R.39 was hit, adding that brilliant moonlight assisted accurate shooting.

By accident or design, R.39 skirted the main LADA patrol area and approached London from the northwest at 23.30 hr. However, the crew then mistook Hammersmith Bridge for the Tower Bridge seven miles to the east, and bombs were scattered mainly on residential areas between Acton and Richmond Park, causing the night's only casualties. The crew claimed to have bombed between Charing Cross and the West India Docks.

Shortly before R.39 bombed, she was picked up at 11,000 ft by Bob Hall of No.44 Squadron—who thought he was chasing R.25, of which more later. Despite persistent gun trouble, Hall pursued the Giant until it turned east in a shallow dive over Roehampton, well south of the easily visible balloon barrage, to become lost in the haze. Hall's Camel and the Giant were seen against the moon at 23.41 hr by the Acton AA battery, which reported 'a small machine chasing another with a heart-shaped tail, quite double its size'.

While R.39 thundered home south of the Thames—described first by the Crayford gun battery as a 'V' of five aircraft, then by Dartford as a group of seven—Luxmoore, of No.78 Squadron, patrolling across the river, noticed the searchlight activity and flew over to investigate, hoping for better luck than the previous night. But this was not to be. The Giant passed beneath him at about 10,500 ft and he dived from the rear, firing 50 rounds before he overshot. He turned for a second attack, and when loosing off another 50 rounds one struck the Camel's propeller. This broke off the bullet's brilliant tracer element which flew back and hit the forehead part of Luxmoore's helmet, temporarily blinding him. When his night vision returned he searched again for the bomber without success.

Meanwhile Hackwill, No.44 Squadron, had found R.39, now down to 9,500 ft and still travelling very fast. It shook him off with a steep turn, then he saw it again about 150 yards ahead and followed nearly to Sheppey, firing 600 rounds from long range before dwindling fuel obliged him to return. One more fighter encountered the Giant before it cleared the coast near Hythe. This was the No.50 Squadron F.K.8 crewed by Frank Bryant and V. H. Newton. They saw it near Throwley at 00.15 hr clearly enough to realize that it was not a Gotha, but lost it after turning to chase.

No return fire was mentioned by Hall, Luxmoore or Hackwill, and the R.39 report merely says that three fighters were observed after the initial meeting with Dennis. A surprising aspect of these encounters was that Dennis and Hackwill, both flying aircraft considerably faster than the Giant, were unable to overtake. Dennis (B.E.12b) wrote 'the enemy aircraft's performance was better than my machine . . . he was steadily getting away from me', and Hackwill (Camel) 'I put my engine full on and tried to get close to him but found it impossible.' R.39 was one of the first Giants to have the 245 hp Maybach engines, which although rated at less than the 260 hp Mercedes, delivered substantially more power above 6,500 ft and consumed less petrol. This improved climb and ceiling, but cannot have significantly affected the normal top speed of 84 mph. Hackwill was flying at about 95 mph when he failed to catch the bomber, and the fighter pilots' difficulties were probably caused more by the powerful slipstream than by any performance superiority.

R.25 came in near Foulness at 22.50 hr and five minutes later was spotted by Kitton of No.37 Squadron, flying at about 8,000 ft, against the reflection of the moon on the Crouch. He dived his B.E.2e at 100 mph and fired a complete drum underneath its tail, seeing hits with no apparent effect. While changing drums he lost the raider.

At 23.15 hr Hall, No.44 Squadron, investigating AA and searchlight activity over North Benfleet, picked up R.25 and attacked from behind, but his guns jammed after about five rounds. He cleared them but the same thing happened and recurred several times as he continued chasing the Giant towards London.

At 23.25 hr he was joined by Edwardes, who fired three long bursts from under the bomber's tail from an estimated 40 yards' range. He then suffered stoppages in both guns, a synchronizing gear failure in the starboard weapon causing a bullet to strike his propeller. With the object of attracting other fighters to the scene he switched on his navigation and identification lights and boldly formated above the Giant on its starboard side, and during the next 25 min he saw three other Camels attack.

First of these was probably O'Neill, who despite R.25's evasive action in the form of sharp left- and right-hand turns, delivered one diving attack from above then a second from under the tail, firing 100 rounds before he too had gun trouble—the port Vickers jamming with an immovable stoppage. However, he continued with his remaining gun, firing 200 rounds before that also jammed.

Meanwhile, Murlis Green, flying a Camel armed with two Lewis guns using RTS ammunition, was waiting in the wings for his own opportunity to attack. He had arrived just before Edwardes took up station above R.25, and when another Camel broke away, carefully positioned below, ignoring the vigorous return fire, until he reached close quarters. He was about to open fire when bullets from a Camel in the rear flashed past to one side. This must have been O'Neill who clearly had not noticed his CO's aircraft. The result was that R.25's rear gunner redoubled his attack on Murlis Green, who retaliated with a complete double-drum of RTS and three-quarters of a drum from his second Lewis before it jammed. He watched for a few moments, fully expecting the bomber to take fire, and saw Hall making his final attack, then returned to base to rectify his guns.

Modified Lewis-armed Camels of No.44 Squadron at Hainault. Unit records do not identify modified aircraft, and—as in this photograph—serial numbers are often hidden. But it is likely that some of these aircraft were in combat with Giant R.25 on 29/30 January, 1918.

R.25 was facing a desperate situation. Somewhere over the Brentwood area at about 23.25 hr one of the port engines had seized after bullet damage to the radiator—which could have been caused by Hall or Edwardes—and later another bullet smashed a revolution counter. Surprisingly the Giant crew believed that, apart from Kitton's initial interception, all the attacks—which they estimated as fifteen—were made by the one persistent Camel which found them first, Hall's.

With exemplary devotion to duty they decided to continue for London on three engines, though the Giant could not maintain height with its full bomb load and speed was down to 58 mph. Murlis Green noted that it lost several hundred feet while he followed from Shenfield to Hainault. The next decision was made for them when they saw the Woodford–Southgate balloon apron looming ahead, so they swung round in a wide curve and dropped all bombs around Wanstead, where they fell in open ground. It was at this point that Hall, flying the only Camel still in the chase and struggling to rectify his obstinate guns, lost the aircraft and quite fortuitously found R.39 a few miles farther west.

R.25 bombed at midnight from 5,900 ft and probably lost more height during the homeward journey. Murlis Green re-armed and was airborne again after only 11 min, and more than twenty other fighters were still patrolling before the fortunate Giant departed off Shoeburyness at 00.30 hr. The only sighting was by Oulton and Harris of No.50 Squadron, east of Sheerness.

On landing, R.25 was found to have been hit 88 times. The handling throughout showed the highest standards of competence and discipline, and it is unfortunate that the ill-founded contemporary British intelligence assessment with its allegations of panic has been accepted at face value. The area in which their performance might be faulted was the gunnery. British pilots normally—though not invariably—mentioned any damage to their aircraft, but none did so on this occasion. With the Giant sustaining so many hits it is unlikely that the Camels were untouched, and it may be significant that Murlis Green's B3815 is not recorded as flying on any subsequent home-defence operations.

Had any of the Camels been able to continue the battle for a little longer R.25's remarkable survival could surely not have lasted. In all, 750–850 rounds must have been aimed by five fighters, and their score of 88 hits was no disgrace. Nevertheless Murlis Green's report, written after discussing the action with his pilots, was a typically honest assessment, making no excuses for the failure. He described closing to what he estimated as about 50 yards beneath the Giant, but 'what from other pilots' observations must have been 150 yards'. He expected the Giant to burst into flames after apparently absorbing nearly two drums of ammunition, but accepted other pilots' reports that the RTS was exploding prematurely, his shots apparently passing over the bomber's tail. A Home Forces Intelligence report dated 2 February claimed that the pilots 'now believed that they were at least 250 yards away'.

R.26 evidently mistook the Blackwater for the Thames and made landfall at 22.44 hr over The Naze, not at Southend as reported by the crew. About 40 min later, cruising at 10,000 ft, it developed trouble in two engines and began losing height rapidly, so dumped its bombs around Rayleigh and turned back, maintaining about 5,000 ft on two engines and reaching Ostende at 01.50 hr. The decision to return was not influenced by the formidable Billericay AA barage as claimed in contemporary British records.

Any objective assessment of the night's operations must divide honours evenly. There was some British satisfaction that both Giants making significant penetrations had been intercepted and attacked, while the Germans could take their survival as proof that the big multi-engined bomber was a viable weapon. The Rfa 501 consolidated report, which described the overall defences as strong, with 70 night-flying aerodromes visible in southeast England, sounded one warning note—on such bright moonlit nights, with aircraft easily visible at over 850 yards, raids were not advisable, and should be restricted to occasions with little or no moon.

The fighters experienced a rather higher than average incidence of engine troubles, fortunately without serious consequences. Shaw and Latham of No.50 Squadron both put down safely with failures shortly after take-off, the engine of Shaw's B.E.12b catching fire as the result of a broken exhaust valve. Neville-Smith, No.75 Squadron, crashed four miles short when trying to stretch his glide to reach base at Hadleigh with a dead engine. One of No.39's Bristol Fighters crashed on landing for reasons not recorded.

Maj A. A. B. Thomson, the ever-energetic former CO of No.33 Squadron and nominated to take over No.53 Wing, flew one of No.50 Squadron's F.K.8s to acquire some familiarity with his new parish. He saw no enemy, but experienced one of the chronic problems, being held by searchlights despite lavishly displaying the accepted recognition signals.

RNAS operations were probably a freelance effort, after collusion between Sqn Cdrs R. S. Dallas, No.1 (RNAS) Squadron, and B. L. Huskisson of No.4 (RNAS). Both squadrons, with plenty of experienced pilots, were resting after intensive spells on the Western Front, No.1 at Dover having replaced its Sopwith Triplanes with Camels. No.4 was at Walmer. Their activities raised a protest from Thompson, the Dover AA Commander, that whereas nobody could confuse a single Sopwith with an enemy bomber, several together inevitably caused problems. He complained that at one point the air around Dover seemed crowded with naval Sopwiths not keeping to their patrol lines, and, had enemy bombers appeared, no gunfire could have been brought to bear.

Flt Sub-Lieut Gerard W. R. Fane, who cut short his schooling at Charterhouse to join the RNAS—under the minimum enlistment age. He flew numerous sorties from Yarmouth in 1916–18; and (*right*) Flt Cdr A. M. Shook, No.4 (RNAS) Squadron, who damaged a Gotha on 4 July, 1917. He flew one of the un-notified sorties from Walmer on 29/30 January, 1918, which confused the Dover AA gunners.

16/17 February, 1918 (Night)

Targets: London, Dover.
Enemy forces: Five Giants despatched, four Giants attacked.
Results: 12 killed, six injured, £19,264 damage.
Defence sorties: 60.

RFC

No.37 Squadron, Goldhanger: B.E.2d 5778 (2nd Lieut Foster) 22.10–00.35 hr; B.E.2es B4545 (2nd Lieut F. R. Kitton) 22.05–00.20 hr; B4512 (Lieut P. R. Cawdell) 00.12–00.40 hr; B.E.12 6610 (Lieut S. Hay) 22.15–00.25 hr.

No.37 Squadron, Stow Maries: B.E.2es B4503 (Capt J. L. Horridge) 21.55–00.02 hr; B4535 (2nd Lieut C. L. Milburn) 21.56–23.20 hr, crashed landing; B4457 (2nd Lieut N. H. Colson) 23.20–00.15 hr; B.E.12s B1500 (Capt A. B. Kynoch) 22.05–22.20 hr, forced landed due to engine trouble; C3183 (2nd Lieut E. H. Chater) 22.10–00.25 hr, crashed on landing due to engine trouble; B.E.12a A6312 (2nd Lieut Murray) 22.01–22.53 hr.

No.39 Squadron, North Weald: Bristol Fighters A7265 (2nd Lieut W. B. Thomson, Lieut L. B. Hawkswell) 22.00–00.15 hr; C4636 (2nd Lieut A. J. Arkell, 1st AM E. Gudgeon) 22.01–00.15 hr; C4650 (Capt J. M. Clarke, Lieut L. Speller) 22.04–00.10 hr; C4815 (Capt O. V. Thomas, Sgt Riches) 22.07–00.30 hr; C4635 (Lieut C. P. Donnison, 1st AM A. T. C. Stagg) 23.20–00.30 hr; C4850 (Lieut P. Thompson, Lieut G. T. Stoneham) 23.26–00.27 hr; B1264 (Lieut P. W. Deane, 1st AM W. Eatock) 23.30–00.20 hr.

No.44 Squadron, Hainault: Sopwith Camels B3827 (2nd Lieut J. H. Summers) 21.53–23.55 hr; B5411 (Lieut E. M. Gilbert) 22.05–22.56 hr; C6714 (2nd Lieut R. M. Foster) 22.08–00.09 hr; B3826 (2nd Lieut C. C. Banks) 22.09–00.01 hr; B2517 (Maj G. W. M. Green) 22.17–23.20 hr; B5412 (Lieut T. M. O'Neill) 22.17–00.17 hr; B2404 (Capt G. H. Hackwill) 22.18–00.04 hr; B9251 (Capt W. H. Haynes) 22.18–00.13 hr; B4614 (Lieut R. G. H. Adams) 22.19–00.03 hr; B3816 (Lieut A. E. Godfrey) 22.20–00.20 hr; B9177 (2nd Lieut R. N. Hall) 22.25–00.08 hr; B3859 (Lieut W. E. Nicholson) 22.45–00.01 hr.

No.50 Squadron, Bekesbourne: B.E.12s C3206 (2nd Lieut A. C. Goldsmith) 22.05–00.24 hr; C3182 (Lieut L. Lucas) 22.10–00.10 hr; 6509 (Lieut W. G. Latham), W/T tracker, 22.27–00.40 hr; B.E.12bs C3097 (Lieut C. J. Chabot) 22.19–23.09 hr; C3095 (Capt J. S. Shaw,) W/T tracker, 22.33–00.33 hr; C3110 (Lieut J. Metcalfe) 23.55–00.45 hr.

No.61 Squadron, Rochford: S.E.5as B658 (Capt C. A. Lewis) 22.05–00.05 hr; B655 (Lieut L. B. Blaxland) 22.05–23.50 hr; C1065 (Lieut M. H. Coote) 22.06–22.20 hr, returned with engine trouble; C5302 (Capt J. D. Belgrave) 22.20–23.30 hr; B672 (Capt S. H. Starey) 23.05–00.20 hr; C1072 (Capt E. B. Mason) 23.15–23.50 hr, returned with engine trouble, crashed landing; C5339 (Capt C. E. Holman) 23.15–00.25 hr.

No.78 Squadron, Suttons Farm: Sopwith Camels C6713 (Lieut D. V. Armstrong) 21.53–22.02 hr, returned with engine trouble, 22.21–22.25 hr, returned with gun trouble and 22.38–00.08 hr; C6716 (Lieut I. M. Davies) 21.53–22.03 hr (Orsett, due to weather); C1621 (2nd Lieut W. Algie) 21.53–23.55 hr (Hainault, due to weather); B9311 (2nd Lieut F. D. Hudson) 22.05–23.49 hr; B9297 (2nd Lieut W. Hubbard) 23.39–00.11 hr; B9299 (Capt S Cockerell) 23.40–00.43 hr; C1555 (Capt S. P. Gamon) 23.40–00.01 hr; Sopwith 1½ Strutter SS A1100 (2nd Lieut M. H. G. Liddell) 21.53–00.01 hr.

No.141 Squadron, Biggin Hill: B.E.12s C3195 (Lieut J. S. Castle) 21.55–00.25 hr; A6308 (Lieut E. J. Stockman) 21.57–22.30 hr, returned with engine trouble; C3210 (Lieut E. E. Turner), W/T tracker, 22.32–22.57 hr, returned with W/T trouble, 23.00–23.25 hr, returned with W/T trouble and 23.35–00.15 hr; A6305 (Lieut E. J. Stockman) 23.05–00.30 hr.

No.143 Squadron, Detling: Armstrong Whitworth F.K.8s B3316 (Capt C. J. Truran, Lieut T. E. Garside) 22.10–00.15 hr; B223 (Lieut F. V. Bryant, 2nd Lieut V. H. Newton) 22.15–00.10 hr.

While London was the primary target on this night, the Mercedes-engined Giants were given discretion to attack Dover if the strong winds expected by the weather forecasters made the long flight to the capital appear too hazardous, and R.25, R.33 and R.36 exercised this option.

There were no problems for the six-engined R.12 and Maybach-powered R.39, which had two hours' greater endurance and comfortably made the journey to London. They came in over the Maplin sands six miles apart at about 21.40 hr, then followed roughly parallel courses and converged over Erith, with R.12 a few minutes in front. The closeness of the tracks led the British authorities to credit the London bombing to a single Giant, believed to be the only machine from a six-strong bomber force to penetrate any distance inland.

R.12, commanded by Oberleutnant Hans-Joachim von Seydlitz-Gerstenberg, with Leut Götte as first pilot, crossed the coast at 8,200 ft. It was a poor climber, gaining only another 1,300 ft on the approach to London, and Götte was either unaware that the balloon apron extended to about 10,000 ft or was intending to skirt this obstacle. In the event, when he saw the Woolwich section straight ahead at 22.15 hr it was too late, and the starboard wing hit one of the cables. The aircraft was flung violently to the right, then sideslipped out of control to the left. With great presence of mind Götte shut off all power, then opened up the two port engines, which restored the machine to level flight, albeit after losing nearly 1,000 ft. The mechanic in the starboard engine nacelle made a desperate grab to save himself from being flung out and severely burned his hands on the forward exhaust manifold. The two 660 lb bombs were wrenched from their racks and dropped at Woolwich. One of the port-engine radiator shutter cables was dislodged from its pulley.

Against all probabilities the aircraft's flying ability was unaffected, and later inspection showed only slight damage to the starboard wing leading-edges and propeller and the centre of the fuselage. It went on to bomb the Beckenham area, returning to base at 01.25 hr.

R.39, flying at 10,500 ft and carrying the first 2,204 lb (1,000 kg) bomb delivered to England, claimed to have dropped this awesome weapon east of the City, but it actually fell on a Chelsea Royal Hospital building.

Then unaware of this bomb's existence, the British experts attributed the Chelsea incident to a 660-pounder, and R.12's involuntary Woolwich attack to 112-pounders, which dovetailed neatly into the plotters' assumption that only one Giant was over London. R.39 followed a southerly course home, departing west of Folkestone at 23.40 hr.

R.33 survived a perilous situation thanks to crew enterprise and discipline. At about 20.45 hr, approaching Deal and after symptoms of trouble in both port engines, the forward unit stopped. The bombs were hastily aimed at shipping and the Giant turned back, then shortly afterwards the rear port engine also gave up and the rear starboard dropped to half power. A machine-gun and loose equipment were dumped overboard while the aircraft inexorably descended from 7,200 to 650 ft. Meanwhile the trouble had been identified as interrupted oil circulation caused by the cold. An enterprising mechanic punctured a tank with his pocket knife and transferred oil in his cupped hands to the rear port engine and got it going again. By continuing the process it was kept running to enable R.33 to reach Scheldewindeke.

German reports concerning R.25 and R.36 conflict with the British version, which recorded only one Giant over the coast in the Dover area, dropping eighteen bombs weighing an estimated 1,890 lb near St Margaret's at about 22.40 hr. Since the British consistently underestimated quantities of bombs dropped, this suggests that more than one bomber was involved, in accordance with the German claim that the two Giants dropped a total of 2,750 lb. Although the R.25 report is missing, it may be assumed that this aircraft was primarily responsible, because at 23.40 hr, after some difficulty in seeing the target due to searchlight dazzle, R.36 had bomb-door trouble and dropped only two 550-pounders. However, this does not explain why the British reported only one attack, nor why two crews should miss their target by four or five miles.

An obscure reference in a pilot's report provides a possible clue to the latter mystery. Cyril Truran, of the newly-formed No.143 Squadron, wrote, 'saw Brock flares lit near Dover at 23.00 hr—quite useless'. The next night similar remarks were made by two other pilots from the same squadron, and clearly crews patrolling over east Kent had been asked to comment on these flares. No explanation of their function has been found, but it is a reasonable assumption that they may have been simulated fires to divert bombers away from genuine targets in the neighbourhood. If so, and they did attract bombs on this occasion, it is strange that British records make no reference to the success of the ruse.

With minimal moonlight and some cloud over Essex, conditions were not helpful to the fighters, which had a disappointing night. Returning Giants were seen by three pilots, who could make only fleeting attacks. None of these were mentioned in German reports—suggesting that they were launched well outside effective range.

At 23.15 hr northwest of Sandwich, Lucas of No.50 Squadron saw R.12 flying due east at 10,500 ft after its remarkable recovery from the encounter with the balloon barrage. He positioned 75 yards behind, only to find his Lewis gun jam after the first round. He quickly cleared the stoppage but the Giant pulled away from his B.E.12 as he finished the drum. While changing drums, under considerable AA fire, he lost the enemy. Shortly afterwards, however, it was picked up by Shaw in a B.E.12b, who reported its position by W/T and gave chase. He was below the Giant and climbed after it at 90 mph for 15 min without being able to get closer than 150 yards. He fired half a drum and saw the bomber put its nose down and turn north, disappearing behind his top wing. While searching, Shaw lost his own bearings and eventually crossed the coast near Dover.

At about 22.50 hr James Belgrave, in a No.61 Squadron S.E.5a, was attracted by searchlights south of the Thames and came across R.39 flying southeast, very fast, at 10,500 ft. He fired six long bursts from an estimated 100 yards' range, then lost the bomber while clearing a gun stoppage. He soon found it again, but abandoned the chase southeast of Maidstone after another gun stoppage.

A No.6 Brigade communiqué claiming that a bomber had crashed in the Channel was disputed by Thompson at Dover, who considered that it had recovered at low altitude. This report doubltess originated from sightings of R.33 in difficulties.

Bristol Fighters of No.39 Squadron at North Weald. Capt J. M. Clarke was flying C4650 (*centre*) on 16/17 February, 1918, when he opened fire in error on a squadron colleague.

North of the Thames there were numerous complaints of fighters crossing into gunnery zones and of guns ignoring the fighters' recognition signals—which were manifestly inadequate. In most cases fighters could be identified by their higher speeds, and any rounds fired were normally intended as a challenge. The general confusion led to several fighters chasing each other. Clarke, No.39 Squadron, followed exhaust flames over Epping and opened fire on an aircraft described as resembling a D.H.4. It was in fact a Bristol Fighter from his own unit, piloted by Thomas, whose observer said that an aircraft behind them opened fire immediately after flashing an identification challenge. However, they realized that it was friendly and turned sharply away. Milburn, No.37 Squadron, was also fired on by a friendly aircraft near Rayleigh.

The night's operations produced one forced landing and three landing crashes. The only one reported in any detail was that to Eric Chater's B.E.12 (No.37 Squadron) which received undercarriage and wing damage.

17/18 February, 1918 (Night)

Target: London.
Enemy force: One Giant despatched and attacked.
Results: 21 killed, 32 injured, £38,922 damage.
Defence sorties: 69.

RFC

No.37 Squadron, Goldhanger: B.E.2es B4512 (Lieut P. R. Cawdell) 21.57–00.20 hr; B4545 (Lieut S. Hay) 23.10–00.30 hr; B.E.12 6610 (2nd Lieut S. Armstrong) 23.00–01.10 hr, crashed, pilot killed; B.E.12b 6137 (Lieut C. L. Blake) 22.00–00.24 hr.

No.37 Squadron, Stow Maries: B.E.2es B4505 (Lieut H. Lingard) 21.55–00.06 hr; B4537 (Lieut Lawrence) 21.57–23.15 hr; B4457 (2nd Lieut Spencer) 23.10–00.57 hr; B.E.12s A6312 (2nd Lieut Murray) 23.17–00.25 hr; A6318 (Capt A. B. Kynoch), W/T tracker, 22.02–23.04 hr, returned with W/T trouble, and 23.15–00.35 hr; B.E.12bs C3084 (Capt A. B. Fanstone) 21.53–00.46 hr; C3085 (Capt J. L. Horridge) 22.00–00.20 hr; B718 (2nd Lieut E. H. Chater) 23.16–00.41 hr.

No.39 Squadron, North Weald: Bristol Fighters C4639 (Lieut C. R. W. Knight, 2nd Lieut E. J. Ralli) 21.56–23.55 hr; B1264 (Lieut P. W. Deane, 1st AM L. Card) 22.01–00.05 hr; B1261 (Lieut C. Evans, 2nd AM Parks) 22.02–23.55 hr; C4650 (Capt J. M. Clarke, Lieut L. Speller) 22.03–00.15 hr; C4850 (Lieut P.

Thompson, Lieut G. T. Stoneham) 23.02–00.30 hr; C4635 (Lieut C. P. Donnison, 1st AM A. T. C. Stagg) 23.10–00.25 hr; C4636 (2nd Lieut A. J. Arkell, Sgt Mjr Wyatt) 23.15–00.38 hr.

No.44 Squadron, Hainault: Sopwith Camels B3827 (2nd Lieut J. H. Summers) 21.55–00.15 hr; C1561 (Lieut J. T. Collier) 21.56–00.01 hr; B4614 (Lieut R. G. H. Adams) 21.58–00.02 hr; B3767 (2nd Lieut L. F. Lomas) 21.59–23.45 hr; B5603 (Capt W. H. Haynes) 22.04–23.56 hr; B3826 (2nd Lieut C. C. Banks) 22.07–23.54 hr; B2402 (Capt G. H. Hackwill) 22.16–00.20 hr; B2517 (Maj G. W. M. Green) 22.30–23.35 hr; B3816 (Lieut A. E. Godfrey) 22.50–00.24 hr; C6714 (2nd Lieut R. M. Foster) 22.56–00.12 hr; B5411 (Lieut E. M. Gilbert) 23.12–00.28 hr; B9177 (2nd Lieut R. N. Hall) 23.17–00.35 hr.

No.50 Squadron, Bekesbourne: B.E.2es 6817 (Lieut J. E. King) 21.59–23.59 hr; B4463 (2nd Lieut W. J. McSweeney) 23.17–00.15 hr (Swingfield); B.E.12s 6509 (Capt J. S. Shaw), W/T tracker, 21.52–23.35 hr; C3182 (Lieut W. G. Latham), W/T tracker, 21.54–00.08 hr; unrecorded (Lieut H. T. W. Oswell) 22.00–00.13 hr; C3206 (2nd Lieut A. C. Goldsmith) 23.05–00.35 hr; B.E.12a A6313 (Lieut J. A. C. Kempe-Roberts) 21.54–00.15 hr; B.E.12bs C3110 (Lieut C. J. Chabot) 21.53–00.30 hr; C3090 (Lieut J. Metcalfe) 23.10–00.40 hr.

No.61 Squadron, Rochford: S.E.5as B655 (2nd Lieut W. A. E. Taylor) 22.00–23.50 hr (Goldhanger, with engine trouble); B679 (Capt H. C. Stroud) 22.06–23.45 hr; B672 (Capt S. H. Starey) 22.10–00.15 hr; B658 (Capt C. A. Lewis) 22.15–23..55 hr; C5302 (Capt J. D. Belgrave) 22.21–23.42 hr; C5338 (Lieut J. E. Johnston) 23.10–00.25 hr; C1062 (Lieut G. Howe) 23.10–00.20 hr; D239 (Capt E. B. Mason) 23.20–00.43 hr.

No.78 Squadron, Suttons Farm: Sopwith Camels B9305 (Lieut R. F. W. Moore) 21.51–23.08 hr; B9299 (2nd Lieut N. E. Chandler) 21.51–23.58 hr, crashed landing; C6718 (2nd Lieut G. Clapham) 21.51–00.05 hr; C1555 (Capt S. P. Gamon) 21.51–00.07 hr; C6717 (Capt S. Cockerell) 22.54–00.30 hr; C1580 (Lieut G. O. Shiner) 22.56–00.20 hr (North Weald); B9311 (2nd Lieut F. D. Hudson) 22.59–23.12 hr, returned due to lost windscreen, and 23.18–00.23 hr; C1653 (Capt G. M. Boumphrey) 22.59–00.22 hr, crashed landing; C6716 (Lieut I. M. Davies) 23.12–00.07 hr; Sopwith 1½ Strutter SS A1100 (Lieut-Col M. G. Christie) 23.15–23.55 hr, returned with engine trouble.

No.141 Squadron, Biggin Hill: B.E.12s 6534 (Capt E. Pownall) 22.05–00.05 hr; C3210 (Lieut A. F. Barker) 22.05–00.10 hr; 6181 (Lieut A. M. Bennett) 23.05–00.45 hr; 6138 (Lieut E. E. Turner) 23.08–00.30 hr; B.E.12b C3152 (Capt N. H. Dimmock) 22.05–00.10 hr.

No.143 Squadron, Detling: Armstrong Whitworth F.K.8s B223 (Lieut F. V. Bryant, 2nd Lieut V. H. Newton) 21.54–00.20 hr; B3316 (Capt C. J. Truran, Lieut T. E. Garside) 22.03–00.10 hr; B224 (2nd Lieut W. R. Oulton, Lieut J. Tennant) 23.05–00.50 hr; B220 (2nd Lieut N. F. Perris, 2nd Lieut R. C. Cowl) 23.56–00.30 hr.

R.25, the only Giant serviceable after the previous night's operations, took full advantage of the weather to make one of the most competent raids of the war.

Commanded by Leut Max Borchers, R.25 made landfall off the North Foreland at 21.45 hr, crossed the coast near All Hallows and began bombing with incendiaries from 8,200 ft at Eltham an hour later. During the next ten minutes it dropped eighteen bombs (110-pounders) along a neat northwesterly line, the final stick of eight hitting St Pancras railway station and hotel, causing most of the night's casualties.

Lightened of its load, the Giant climbed to 9,800 ft, flew across Kent and went out to sea over Folkestone at 00.13 hr. It met intermittent heavy gunfire and at some unspecified point on the homeward journey the port rear propeller was damaged. Power from the engine was immediately reduced, and cut off altogether for the sea crossing. Fighters were seen, but no attacks reported.

The night's defence operations provided a sharp reminder that two major problems were still far from resolved—the wildly inaccurate plotting of enemy movements from the ground and misjudgment of the Giant's size by fighter pilots. Paradoxically the very slowness of the great Staaken-Zeppelin bombers could trigger off the initial plotting errors. R.25's 385-mile journey took 6 hr 23 min—at an average speed of 62 mph—and as the machine crawled above the Thames estuary it was heard from places 15 miles apart on a north–south line and reported as two aircraft. Then as fighters inevitably strayed into gun zones miles away from the solitary raider's track they were liable to be listed as hostile, their recognition signals seldom being seen from the ground.

Many fighters were persistently held by searchlights and a good number fired on by the guns. No.39 Squadron was the main offender—or victim—in the Epping area, where a near miss caused Cyril Donnison temporarily to lose control of his Bristol Fighter. The gunners complained that two Bristols sounded like one Gotha, and after the all-clear their Commander conferred with the CO of No.39 and pilots in an attempt to find some solution. To the southeast, Cecil Lewis, No.61 Squadron, had his S.E.5a holed by fire from the Benfleet guns.

From the sixty-nine fighter sorties totalling 114 flying hours, No.6 Brigade claimed five indecisive combats against the estimated raiding force of one Giant and four or five Gothas. In fact only three Camel pilots of No.78 Squadron appear to have seen R.25, and engaged from very long range. Chandler fired 50 rounds at a large aircraft near Joyce Green, but lost it after being dazzled by his gun flash. He gave no time, so this could have been during the Giant's inbound or outbound flight. At 23.30 hr Hudson, flying his second sortie after the ground staff had smartly fixed him a new windscreen in six minutes to replace one blown away, also aimed a burst at a large aircraft and likewise lost it because of gun-flash dazzle. At 23.20 hr Shiner reported a strange sighting of 'four enemy aircraft' below him, flying east at 12,500 ft. He fired 400 rounds before losing 'them'. This can only have been R.25, its four propellers somehow giving the illusion of four aircraft, and its size causing Shiner to think that it was much nearer his own altitude than its

S.E.5a B658 of No.61 Squadron, regularly flown by Capt C. A. Lewis in the early months of 1918, was holed by AA fire on 17/18 February. The experimental colour scheme was applied later in the year.

actual height of about 10,000 ft. If so, he probably attacked from more than 800 yards.

Had any of the night's fighter attacks remotely threatened R.25 they would surely have been reported by its crew, who possessed the normal desire of any fighting team to present their mission in the most active light.

Lewis, No.61 Squadron, was fired on over Benfleet at 22.55 hr by an aircraft flying west. He spun away, assuming it to be friendly—which it clearly was despite the absence of any correlating reports. Conversely, no British pilot mentioned being on the receiving end of a drum fired by the No.39 Squadron Bristol Fighter crewed by Evans and Parks when an aircraft failed to answer their challenge over Passingford Bridge.

B.E.12b C3152 of No.141 Squadron, flown by Capt N. H. Dimmock on 17/18 February, 1918, photographed at Biggin Hill after the squadron had started to re-equip with Bristol Fighters. (*E. F. Haselden*)

One of No.37 Squadron's more experienced pilots, Sydney Armstrong, was killed when his B.E.12 crashed and caught fire at Tolleshunt Major, four miles north of Goldhanger aerodrome. He had been patrolling the Goldhanger–Easthorpe line for two hours and may have come down while trying to reach base with engine trouble. It was initially reported that Armstrong had been killed in combat with an enemy aircraft, but this theory was rejected even before it was known that R.25 had never been within 20 miles of his patrol line, on the dubious basis that medical examination revealed no bullet wounds. No consideration was apparently given to the likely destruction by fire of any evidence showing airframe or engine damage sustained in combat. The No.39 Squadron Bristol Fighter can be exonerated since its brief attack on an unidentified aircraft took place 20 miles to the southwest, and it had landed long before Armstrong crashed.

Malcolm Christie, former CO of No.50 Squadron and now commanding No.49 Wing, flew No.78 Squadron's last Sopwith 1½ Strutter single-seat 'Comic' on its final operational sortie.

The Rfa 501 report boasted with some justification that even a single Giant sortie amply justified maintaining the bombing policy, being enough to alert all defence measures and waste enormous quantities of ammunition—sheer nervousness had caused guns 30 km distant to fire blindly into the sky. It also sounded a warning note, suggesting that the slow-climbing Mercedes-engined R.VIs, with their poor defensive armament, should operate only when conditions hampered the fighters—or if they must attack in bright moonlight, be given targets away from the main defended areas.

7/8 March, 1918 (Night)

Target: London.
Enemy forces: Six Giants despatched, five Giants attacked.
Results: 23 killed, 39 injured, £42,655 damage.
Defence sorties: 42.

RFC

No.37 Squadron, Goldhanger: B.E.12 C3222 (Lieut S. Hay) 23.27–01.08 hr; B.E.12b 6137 (Capt A. Dennis) 23.30–01.10 hr.

No.37 Squadron, Stow Maries: B.E.2es B4535 (2nd Lieut C. Milburn) 23.25–01.10 hr; B4505 (2nd Lieut Burfoot) 23.28–01.25 hr; B.E.12 C3208 (Capt A. B. Kynoch) took off 23.29 hr, collided with S.E.5a B679, pilot killed; B.E.12bs C3084 (Capt A. B. Fanstone) 23.28–01.15 hr; B718 (Lieut A. O. Beckett) 23.30–01.25 hr.

No.39 Squadron, North Weald: Bristol Fighters C4850 (Capt P. Thompson, Lieut G. T. Stoneham) 23.25–01.00 hr, forced landed due to engine trouble; C4636 (Lieut A. J. Arkell, 1st AM E. Gudgeon) 23.30–01.37 hr; C4650 (Capt J. M. Clarke, Lieut L. Speller) 23.35–01.45 hr (Hainault); B1186 (Lieut C. R. W. Knight, 1st AM Easton) 23.49–01.50 hr (Hainault); C4670 (Lieut J. L. N. Bennett-Baggs, Lieut A. J. F. Bawden) 00.24–01.37 hr; A7265 (2nd Lieut W. B. Thomson, 2nd Lieut F. J. B. de S. La Terriere) 00.51–01.50 hr; C4638 (Lieut J. G. Goodyear, Lieut Forrest) 00.52–02.00 hr; B1264 (Lieut P. W. Deane, 1st AM W. Eatock) 00.46–02.00 hr (Hainault).

No.44 Squadron, Hainault: Sopwith Camels B3826 (2nd Lieut J. H. Summers) 00.11–01.25 hr; B2517 (Capt R. N. Hall) 00.13–01.37 hr; C1561 (Lieut G. O. Shiner) 00.35–01.18 hr (Chingford, crashed landing); B3816 (Maj G. W. M. Green) 00.40–01.35 hr.

No.50 Squadron, Bekesbourne: B.E.12s C3220 (2nd Lieut W. G. Latham), W/T tracker, 23.22–01.30 hr; C3182 (Capt J. S. Shaw), W/T tracker, 23.45–01.55 hr; C3206 (2nd Lieut C. Packham) 23.50–01.00 hr, returned with engine trouble; B.E.12bs C3110 (2nd Lieut A. C. Goldsmith) 23.35–02.05 hr; C3097 (Capt C. J. Chabot) 23.40–02.05 hr; C3090 (Lieut J. Metcalfe) 01.15–20.05 hr.

No.61 Squadron, Rochford: S.E.5as B658 (Capt S. H. Starey) 23.30–01.20 hr; B679 (Capt H. C. Stroud) took off 23.30 hr, collided with B.E.12 C3208, pilot killed; D3434 (2nd Lieut Brown) 23.40–01.15 hr, C9578 (2nd Lieut H. A. Blain) 01.00–01.32 hr; D3459 (Capt E. B. Mason) 01.10–01.50 hr; C1051 (2nd Lieut W. A. E. Taylor) 01.20–01.55 hr; last three aircraft recalled due to weather.

No.78 Squadron, Suttons Farm: Sopwith Camels B9253 (Capt A. E. Godfrey) 23.45–01.45 hr; D6401 (Lieut D. V. Armstrong) 23.47–00.56 hr, returned with engine trouble; C6717 (Capt S. Cockerell) 23.48–01.40 hr.

No.112 Squadron, Throwley: Sopwith Camel, sorties by Capt C. J. Q. Brand, 23.32–23.43 hr, and 00.11–00.13 hr, returned due to weather.

No.141 Squadron, Biggin Hill: B.E.12s C3195 (Lieut J. S. Castle) 23.43–02.00 hr; A6308 (2nd Lieut J. Hetherington) took off 23.45 hr, landed

Hounslow; C3210 (Lieut W. Hunt) 00.01–01.45 hr.

No.143 Squadron, Detling: Armstrong Whitworth F.K.8s B4017 (Lieut C. Ossenton) 23.25–00.15 hr; B224 (2nd Lieut W. R. Oulton) 23.33–01.35 hr; B3316 (2nd Lieut F. V. Bryant) 00.23–02.00 hr.

This biggest effort by the Giants of Rfa 501 produced mediocre results. It was also a bad night for the defences, with no fighter sightings and two experienced pilots killed in an inflight collision.

Just as the full British reports on the maximum fighter effort of 28/29 January are missing, so too are detailed German accounts for 7/8 March, leaving some aspects of the raid policy open to speculation.

Apart from the fact that there was no moon—though some light from an aurora display—statements on the weather are conflicting, from the 'fine and clear' of the British official history, to the patchy cloud actually encountered by some of the bombers. London itself enjoyed exceptionally clear skies, and the poor visibility and cloud lay to the east. Heavy mist restricted flying from some fighter

Capt C. J. Q. Brand made No.112 Squadron's initial Camel sortie on 7/8 March, 1918—possibly in this aircraft (D6435) which is said to have been the first delivered to the unit.

aerodromes, and at Throwley, where No.112 Squadron was replacing its 'daylight only' Pups with Camels, only the CO, Capt 'Flossie' Brand, was airborne, having ruled that conditions were unfit for pilots with limited experience of the new aircraft. Three of No.39 Squadron's Bristol Fighters diverted from North Weald because of the visibility, and at Rochford No.61 Squadron's last three S.E.5a sorties were recalled.

One Giant—probably R.27—came in over Deal at 22.56 hr, three over Maplin between 23.00 and 23.20 hr, and a fifth over Broadstairs at 23.35 hr. R.13, 27 and 39 reached London, bombing between 00.10 and 00.35 hr. Most of the damage and casualties were caused by the 2,204 lb bomb from R.39 which demolished Nos.61–67 Warrington Crescent, Maida Vale, and seriously affected another nineteen houses. R.13's front starboard engine failed over London but she returned safely on the remaining four.

One of the bombers which made landfall over Maplin was plotted along a northwesterly course into Bedfordshire, bombing south of Luton at about midnight. A stick of bombs also fell near Ware 40 min later, probably aimed at a nearby night landing ground. If London was the intended target, such a gross navigation error by Rfa 501 standards could be explained by some failure preventing the receipt of W/T fixes. But the R.25 commander's recently-expressed reservations about using the Mercedes-engined R.VIs against heavily defended areas poses the question whether Luton was in fact the objective.

The British estimated that seven or eight bombers were over England, and plotting was as usual somewhat confused. One Giant, possibly in difficulties, penetrated no farther than Billericay, then dropped bombs on Southminster and Herne Bay. The first to depart went out over Dymchurch at 01.10 hr and the others left during the next hour at various points northwards to Felixstowe.

R.27 encountered unexplained problems—possibly navigational—on the return flight and eventually crash-landed just inside the German lines near Courtrai. It was clearly well off course, and a report that all engines had stopped suggests that it was out of fuel. Another Giant was damaged on landing at Ghistelles.

There were no witnesses of the fatal collision over Rayleigh between Alex Kynoch's B.E.12 and Clifford Stroud's S.E.5a, for which no time is recorded. The aircraft took off from Stow Maries and Rochford at 23.29 and 23.30 hr

Capt H. C. Stroud, No.61 Squadron, killed when his S.E.5a collided with a No.37 Squadron B.E.12 on 7/8 March, 1918; and (*right*) Lieut C. C. Banks, who shared in the destruction of the first Gotha to fall on English soil, on 28/29 January, 1918, showed the qualities of a great all-round fighter pilot in his short operational career. He never flew again after the war, and became a preparatory school classics teacher, latterly at Cheltenham College junior school. His son, Arthur, a sergeant pilot in No.112 Squadron, was awarded a posthumous George Cross for heroism with a resistance group after his Mustang was brought down by ground fire near Ravenna, Italy, in August 1944. He was eventually captured, tortured and shot by the Fascist Black Brigade.

In contrast with crashes from which pilots walked away, this one at Stow Maries caused the death of 2nd Lieut Cyril Lawson Milburn, from Alberta. Milburn flew at least eleven sorties in No.37 Squadron from August 1917, until his last on 7/8 March, 1918, and was one of the many unsung pilots who patrolled nightly but never found the opportunity to engage the enemy. He was killed on 23 April, probably flying his regular B.E.2e, B4535.
(*Mrs M. F. Sadler*)

respectively and may have collided while still climbing through cloud. On the other hand, the presence of the B.E. ten miles south of its patrol line suggests that Kynoch had perhaps spotted a Giant and legitimately diverted in pursuit. In both fighters the pilots' forward and upward view was restricted by the top wing, and despite the allocation of well-separated patrol height bands, the collision risk was always present.

The two aircraft fell in neighbouring fields and Kynoch's body was found several hundred yards from the B.E.12 wreckage.

After the 'readiness' alert at 23.01 hr there was an unexplained delay in giving the 'patrol' order, and the fighters did not begin to take off until 23.22 hr, when some bombers were 25–30 miles inland. Thereafter the searchlights probably illuminated more fighters than bombers, and not one pilot claimed even a tentative sighting.

An immediate search for an aircraft reported as falling in flames near Epping at 00.45 hr, after sounds of machine-gun fire, produced nothing, and following other similar stories next morning, soldiers thoroughly combed the forest. It was later established that a British pilot, who had unwittingly lit his Holt flares, put down in a clearing, believing that his aircraft was on fire. This incident was not reported by any unit flying patrols that night, and the aircraft may have been one from No.38 Squadron, Stamford, briefly reported overdue on a training flight.

12/13 March, 1918 (Night)

Target: The Midlands.
Enemy forces: Navy Zeppelins L53 (Kptlt E. Prölss), L54 (Kptlt H. von Buttlar), L61 (Kptlt H. Ehrlich), L62 (Hptmn K. Manger), L63 (Kptlt M. von Freudenreich).
Results: One killed, none injured, £3,474 damage.
Defence sorties: Nine.

RFC

No.33 Squadron, A Flight, Scampton: F.E.2b A5660 (2nd Lieut F. A. Benitz) 20.29–20.40 hr, returned due to weather.

No.33 Squadron, B Flight, Kirton-Lindsey: F.E.2b B430 (Capt W. E. Kemp) 20.30–20.50 hr, returned due to weather.

No.36 Squadron, A Flight, Ashington: F.E.2d B1883 (2nd Lieut N. S. Jones, 2nd Lieut H. Cock) 22.24–00.24 hr.

No.36 Squadron, B Flight, Hylton: F.E.2d A6429 (Sgt R. Mann, Cpl Douglas) 22.11–01.15 hr.

No.36 Squadron, C Flight, Seaton Carew: F.E.2d A6451 (Lieut A. H. Hinton, 2nd Lieut R. D. Linford) 22.00–02.30 hr, with refuelling stop at Hylton.

No.76 Squadron, B Flight, Helperby: B.E.12 A6317 (2nd Lieut J. D. Edge) 00.08–01.10 hr; B.E.12b C3143 (2nd Lieut S. Hill) 23.14–01.25 hr.

No.76 Squadron, C Flight, Catterick: B.E.12s 6659 (Capt S. R. Stammers) 21.12–00.25 hr; 6660 (2nd Lieut F. W. Butt) 22.45–00.53 hr.

This first Zeppelin attack since the disastrous 'silent raid' of October 1917 failed because of the weather.

As the airships neared England at 16–18,000 ft, thick cloud increasingly obscured the surface and navigation errors led crews to believe that they had flown farther west than was the case and two Zeppelins dropped their bombs in the sea. L61, 62 and 63 crossed between Bridlington and Hornsea at 20.30–21.50 hr, penetrating no more than 30 miles inland—not to Leeds as two commanders claimed. Bombs fell in Hull and near Pocklington.

Fighter operations were equally hampered by the weather, and of the nine sorties flown, the two from No.33 Squadron were non-effective. Kemp came back after meeting three cloud layers between 200 and 2,500 ft, and the less experienced Benitz wisely gave up when he found some patches as low as 150 ft. Two brief weather reconnaissances made by A Flight from Copmanthorpe revealed equally impossible conditions.

There were no sightings—hardly surprising in view of the weather—and in any case the patrol lines of the new fighters able to operate were generally too far north. No.76 Squadron B Flight, Helperby, responsible for the Pocklington area, was unable to despatch any aircraft until after L62 had left. No.76 commented favourably on its first B.E.12b—'the machine went well and was still climbing fast at 13,000 ft'.

Shortly before the first Zeppelin approached Yorkshire, aircraft sounds off the Kent coast had triggered off a patrol by five fighters from No.50 Squadron, Bekesbourne. Giants R.13, 33 and 39 had set off for London, but R.33 soon turned back with engine trouble. Then when R.13 also developed mechanical problems and its crew went for Boulogne, R.39's crew did likewise rather than continue alone.

13/14 March, 1918 (Night)

Target: The Midlands.
Enemy forces: Navy Zeppelins L42 (Kptlt Martin Dietrich); L52 and L56 recalled because of weather.
Results: Eight killed, 39 injured, £14,280 damage.
Defence sorties: 15.

RFC

No.36 Squadron, A Flight, Ashington: F.E.2b A5741 (2nd Lieut H. E. Ebrey) 22.00–23.45 hr; F.E.2ds A6642 (2nd Lieut N. S. Jones, 2nd Lieut J. M. le Mee) 20.10–22.10 hr; B1883 (Capt J. A. Boret, 2nd Lieut L. J. Ingram) 21.10–23.56 hr.

No.36 Squadron, B Flight, Hylton: F.E.2b A5470 (Sgt A. J. Joyce) took off 21.15 hr, crashed, pilot killed; F.E.2d A6474 (Lieut E. T. Carpenter, 2nd Lieut T. V. Preedy) 20.20–21.45 hr.

A No.36 Squadron F.E.2b at Hylton. The crew is unidentified. (*L. B. Latham*)

No.36 Squadron, C Flight, Seaton Carew: F.E.2b A5683 (Lieut C. MacLaughlin) 22.00–00.01 hr, crashed landing; F.E.2ds A6451 (Lieut A. H. Hinton, 2nd Lieut H. Hutchinson) 20.15–00.05 hr (Helperby); A6422 (2nd Lieut E. C. Morris, 2nd Lieut R. D. Linford) 20.49–23.15 hr (Hylton).

No.76 Squadron, A Flight, Copmanthorpe: B.E.2e B4506 (Lieut W. E. Watt) 22.08–01.15 hr; B.E.12b C3142 (2nd Lieut G. W. Wall) 22.13–00.22 hr.

No.76 Squadron, B Flight, Helperby: B.E.12 A6317 (2nd Lieut J. D. Edge) 21.50–23.06 hr; B.E.12b C3143 (2nd Lieut S. Hill) 22.08–01.02 hr.

No.76 Squadron, C Flight, Catterick: B.E.2e A3136 (2nd Lieut P. C. Matthews) 20.05–23.40 hr; B.E.12s 6660 (Lieut F. W. Butt) 21.20–23.50 hr; 6659 (Capt S. R. Stammers) 23.35–00.50 hr.

Although 'operations', the preliminary readiness state, was notified by No.6 Brigade at 18.50 hr, subsequent uncertainties about enemy airship movements resulted in the absence of any public warning when this raid actually developed two-and-a-half hours later.

Confusion arose after Strasser had recalled the force on receiving a forecast of strong northeasterly winds. When this message was transmitted at 19.15 hr, Dietrich in L42 was nearing England and decided to turn a deaf ear, standing off the Norfolk coast until the last light faded. Meanwhile L52 and L56, some miles behind, had obeyed the recall, and those operating the British monitoring service doubtless believed that all the raiders had done so.

Dietrich came in at 21.20 hr and, with all street and industrial lights blazing, had no difficulty in identifying the West Hartlepool docks from his height of 16,400 ft. However, casualties and damage from the twenty-one bombs were relatively light.

Indecision over the public warning had not prevented fighters from taking off, though of the six airborne before L42 bombed, only two from Seaton Carew were patrolling the right area. Unhappily the first of these, airborne long enough to reach its ceiling, became lost and eventually landed at Helperby.

Morris and Linford in an F.E.2d had reached only 14,500 ft when they saw the airship flying due south at 21.35 hr after bombing. She was briefly illuminated by the Redcar searchlights and Morris estimated her height as at least 20,000 ft—about 2,000 ft higher than actually recorded in the airship's log. However, the point is academic since Morris was unable to force his machine above 17,500 ft during a 40-mile chase out to sea.

Until the Zeppelin turned east beyond Redcar, the F.E. crew thought that it might be making for Middlesbrough, and although aware that they were out of range, attacked as a deterrent gesture. Linford fired 280 rounds—nearly three double drums—from his Lewis gun and Morris 50 from his fixed gun. They gradually lost L42 in the haze, then on returning found heavy mist over Seaton Carew so diverted north to Hylton.

This episode underlined the utter inability of the F.E. to cope with the newer Zeppelins. There was no opportunity for No.76 Squadron's B.E.12bs to flex their muscles as both were airborne after the raider had departed, and they patrolled to the southwest against the possibility of more incursions. Hill, flying at 17,000 ft, saw Wall briskly engaged by the Howden AA guns at 23.00 hr. The gunners later protested their unfamiliarity with the new sound of the B.E.12b.

Sergeant Joyce, No.36 Squadron, was killed when his F.E.2b crashed on Pontop Pike, ten miles southwest of Gateshead, at about 22.45 hr. It is not clear from reports whether he flew straight into this 1,018-ft hill or crashed while attempting to make a forced landing. Two other pilots from No.36 Squadron were more fortunate. MacLaughlin was unhurt when he crashed on landing at Seaton Carew, and Jones glided down to a perfect touchdown at Ashington after his engine cut at 17,000 ft.

12/13 April, 1918 (Night)

Target: The Midlands.
Enemy forces: Navy Zeppelins L60 (Kptlt H. K. Flemming), L61 (Kptlt H. Ehrlich), L62 (Hptmn K. Manger), L63 (Kptlt M. von Freudenreich), L64 (Kvtkpt Arnold Schütze).
Results: Seven killed, 20 injured, £11,673 damage.
Defence sorties: 27.

F.2A N4283 from RNAS Yarmouth, piloted by Flt Cdrs G. E. Livock and R. Leckie, who sighted Zeppelin L61 on 12/13 April, 1918.

RNAS*

Yarmouth: D.H.4 A7848 (Sqn Cdr V. Nicholl, Obs Sub-Lieut H. G. Owen) 04.45–06.00 hr; D.H.9s D1655 (Flt Cdr E. Cadbury, Obs Sub-Lieut F. L. Wills) 03.55–05.00 hr; D1656 (Flt Cdr G. W. R. Fane, Obs Sub-Lieut S. Plowman) 04.25–04.50 hr; F.2A N4283 (Flt Cdr G. E. Livock, Flt Cdr R. Leckie) took off 04.30 hr.

Bacton: B.E.2c 9973 (Flt Sub-Lieut F. R. Bicknell) 21.20–22.55 hr and 00.20–01.10 hr.

Burgh Castle: B.E.2cs 8417 (Flt Sub-Lieut L. L. King) 00.50–01.40 hr and 03.00–04.05 hr; 9980 (Flt Sub-Lieut R. C. Packe) 03.00–04.30 hr, forced landed near Beccles; 9982 (Flt Lieut C. S. Iron) 03.05–04.40 hr.

Covehithe: B.E.2c 9971 (Flt Sub-Lieut G. R. Halliday) 03.05–05.45 hr (Hadleigh, with engine trouble).

RFC*

No.33 Squadron, A Flight, Scampton: F.E.2b B4005 (Lieut L. Murphy, 2nd AM W. Taylor) 21.48–00.23 hr, damaged landing; F.E.2d A6587 (2nd Lieut J. Heyes, 2nd Lieut E. H. Canning) 21.10–23.15 hr, forced landed due to engine trouble.

No.33 Squadron, C Flight, Elsham: One sortie, 21.11–21.35 hr, returned due to weather, details not recorded.

No.38 Squadron, B Flight, Buckminster: F.E.2b A5707 (Lieut C. H. Noble-Campbell) 23.25–01.30 hr, crashed near Coventry.

No.38 Squadron, C Flight, Stamford: F.E.2b A5578 (Lieut W. A. Brown) 23.18–01.30 hr, crashed near Coventry.

No.51 Squadron, A Flight, Mattishall: F.E.2bs A5754 (Capt A. R. Nock) 22.20–23.25 hr, A5732 (Lieut Coombs) 22.24–01.25 hr; B417 (2nd Lieut Munro) 23.06–23.25 hr, forced landed with engine trouble.

No.51 Squadron, B Flight, Tydd St Mary: F.E.2bs A5753 (Lieut F. St C. Sergeant) 21.50–00.45 hr; A5733 (2nd Lieut C. O. Bird) 23.00–00.05 hr, returned with engine trouble; F.E.2d A6453 (2nd Lieut L. A. Bushe) 21.54–00.34 hr.

No.51 Squadron, C Flight, Marham: F.E.2bs A5724 (2nd Lieut J. R. Smith) 22.00–00.47 hr; A5729 (Lieut T. H. Gladstone) 23.02–01.42 hr; F.E.2d A6465 (2nd Lieut S. W. Smith) 22.07–23.38 hr.

No.75 Squadron, B Flight, Harling Road: B.E.12 C3231 (Lieut P. Plant) 22.13–00.50 hr.

No.75 Squadron, C Flight, Elmswell: B.E.12b C3089 (Capt F. G. B. Reynolds) 22.14–23.25 hr.

This attack by five of the latest Zeppelins with the improved Maybach engines further emphasized that while the great operating altitudes attainable provided immunity from attack, they also created navigation and weather forecasting problems which severely prejudiced the success of operations.

Claiming significant attacks on Leeds, Grimsby, Hull, Sheffield, Coventry, and Birmingham, the Germans were unaware that their 33,340 lb of bombs had fallen mostly in open country with little effect. The British on the other hand retained no illusions about the indifferent equipment of the northern defence squadrons, and

* Although the RAF had been formed on 1 April, sorties were still listed as RNAS and RFC.

Higgins reported:

> 'Taking into consideration the adverse weather conditions, low cloud and mist, it is evident that the pilots who took part put up a very fine performance, showing extraordinary courage and determination.
>
> 'There is no doubt that if machines with a performance equal to, say, the Bristol Fighter, had been available, two Zeppelins would have been brought down.'

The raiding force was well concentrated as to timing, with all Zeppelins making landfall between 21.20 and 22.00 hr. Geographically they were dispersed along a 70-mile line stretching from Cromer to Spurn Head. L60 scattered its bombs south of the Humber during a brief sortie inland, while L63 and L64 bombed various places in Lincolnshire. L61, making for Sheffield, misjudged the wind strength and flew west as far as Runcorn, then turned north to bomb Wigan in the belief that it was indeed Sheffield. L62 came in over Cromer and made steady progress towards her objective—Birmingham—aiming three bombs en route at No.51 Squadron's Tydd St Mary aerodrome. From this point navigation and bomb aiming went astray, and the main load was dropped south of Coventry and southwest of Birmingham. L62 returned over Yarmouth at 03.35 hr.

'Operations' was notified at 19.35 hr and the patrol order issued at 22.05 hr. Bad weather prevented any flying from six aerodromes in the general raid area, and Elsham launched only one tentative sortie to investigate conditions. None of the four F.E.2bs which reported sightings could attain effective combat range.

Murphy, No.33 Squadron, fleetingly glimpsed L64 through a break in the clouds at 23.00 hr near the southern limit of his Grimsby–Dunston patrol line. He climbed at full throttle, but his F.E. could not exceed 9,200 ft—some 5,000 ft below the apparent height of the Zeppelin, which he lost after a few minutes.

Sergeant, No.51 Squadron, was at 14,000 ft over his Tydd St Mary base when L62 dropped her bombs. He spotted the airship 4–5,000 ft higher up and gave chase as it moved off southwest. He kept it in sight for 80 min, unable to get closer than 3–4,000 ft, and with a few optimistic bursts of fire abandoned pursuit near Rugby at 23.45 hr.

At 00.15 hr Noble-Campbell of No.38 Squadron, patrolling at 16,000 ft, reported sighting an airship northeast of Birmingham—presumably L62 after she had bombed. He estimated the height as 17,500 ft, and aware that his F.E. was already wallowing along at its ceiling, fired at 500 yards' range on the off-chance of scoring a lucky hit. After temporarily losing the Zeppelin in cloud, he decided to follow in case it reduced height.

Seven minutes before Noble-Campbell was airborne from Buckminster, the only other No.38 Squadron pilot flying that night, Brown of C Flight, had taken off from Stamford 12 miles to the southeast. At 01.00 hr he also claimed a Zeppelin sighting, and a ten-minute chase showed that he had no better chance of overtaking. He saw nothing of Noble-Campbell, who was still trailing behind.

If this was L62 fighting the strong headwind at 18,700 ft, none of her crew reported seeing either of the F.E.2bs labouring along well below and to the rear. In any case, they shortly ceased to offer any threat, for at about 01.30 hr both crashed in the northern environs of Coventry.

Precisely how this came about is not clear. Both pilots were injured, and their recollections, from different hospitals, were doubtless hazy—Noble-Campbell's recorded by his CO, Maj C. C. Wigram, and Brown's by the CO of No.1 Aircraft Acceptance Park. Noble-Campbell said that at 01.15 hr he was hit in the head, his propeller smashed and his aircraft controls damaged. He immediately began to descend, breaking cloud at about 4,000 ft. As he came lower his Holt flares showed trees and a tall chimney ahead, and moments before hitting the ground he noticed a flarepath being lit just beyond his reach. He crashed at 01.30 hr, a few feet short of the White & Poppé filling factory's boundary wall and managed to scramble clear before the aircraft caught fire.

Brown's briefer account merely said that at about 01.10 hr his engine failed, and that for a time he was held by a searchlight as he came down. He fired Very signals, then saw a lighted aerodrome but unfortunately hit a hedge and crashed about 200 yards short. With commendable speed the flarepath had been activated by the AAP staff at Radford on their recognition of an emergency.

D.H4 A7848 flown by Sqn Cdr Vincent Nicholl on his last home defence sortie. Although rejected by No.6 Brigade as a potential night-fighter, RNAS Yarmouth successfully employed the type in the anti-Zeppelin role.

Without the hind-knowledge that L62 had not opened fire, it was reasonable to assume that Noble-Campbell had been shot down by the Zeppelin, and this was the story put out for public consumption. However, there is evidence that his F.E. was the accidental victim of some defence action—though it is unlikely that the full facts will ever be known. The Warwickshire police reported shortly after the crash that the pilot's scalp wound was believed to have been caused by fire from the other F.E., a theory that can hardly have come from any other source than Noble-Campbell himself. Brown said nothing about having opened fire, but neither did he explain his engine failure. Wigram thought that Noble-Campbell might have been hit by AA fire, but whether subsequent inquiries confirmed this or indicated that the two F.Es had fired at one another, no findings were recorded. The consolidated intelligence report diplomatically stated that Noble-Campbell was wounded 'when in action' with the L62.

Soon after this incident L62 descended to 11,000 ft to escape the headwind, and as she approached the coast there was reaction from Yarmouth and its satellites—some of which had earlier flown unfruitful sorties against the same airship inbound and the L63 outbound.

One potentially hazardous situation ended in high comedy. After letting down through several cloud layers to check his bearings, Robert Packe, from Burgh Castle, finally broke cloud at 200 ft, whereupon his engine refused to pick up. He narrowly missed a tree and, on hitting the ground, wrote off his undercarriage. He was about three miles east of Beccles, and a helpful special constable agreed to stand guard while Packe telephoned base. When he returned soon afterwards the B.E.2c was a charred wreck, the 'Special' having somehow managed to fire the Holt flares.

Fog at Yarmouth delayed take-offs and L62 was well over the North Sea, down to 5,000 ft with a leaking gas cell but in no serious difficulty, before any aircraft were airborne. After flying northeast for 80 min, Livock and Leckie sighted L61, which had departed off Spurn Head an hour before their intended quarry, the L62. The Zeppelin spotted their F.2A flying-boat and rapidly went up to 22,000 ft, hopelessly beyond reach.

At 01.10 hr LADA squadrons were put on readiness after a Giant had been reported off the Kent coast. Nothing developed and units were stood down 45 min later.

Chapter XX

The Final Raids

With the German 1918 spring offensive in France offering little hope of an early end to the war, No.6 Brigade pressed ahead with its planned defence improvements. This was despite a temporary halt in raids against England while the heavy bombers were committed to targets behind the Allied battle lines.

On 19/20 May, after breaks of sixteen and ten weeks respectively, the Gothas of Bogohl 3 and Giants of Rfa 501 resumed their attacks on London, to be confronted by a vastly more effective night-fighter force—seventy-four Camels, S.E.5as and Bristol Fighters, and only six of the mediocre B.E.12s and B.E.12as. It was the largest aeroplane raid of the war—with 33 bombers attacking out of 43 despatched—and also the last. Forty-nine people were killed and 177 injured. On the same night, heavy raids by Bogohl 6 against railway and ordnance installations in northern France, in which some 600 bombs caused 214 deaths and over 700 injuries, underlined the still formidable strength of the German bomber arm.

At this time the LADA patrol areas and Order of Battle were:—

	Patrol	Squadron and CO	Base	Aircraft
B	Ball's Park— North Weald— Crabtree Hill	39 Capt W. T. F. Holland	North Weald	Bristol Fighter
C	Greensted Farm— Suttons Farm	44 Maj G. W. Murlis Green	Hainault	Sopwith Camel
D	South Weald— Tilbury	78 Maj G. Allen	Suttons Farm	Sopwith Camel
E	Joyce Green— South Ash— Biggin Hill	141 Capt B. E. Baker	Biggin Hill	Bristol Fighter
F	Northey Island— Tiptree	37 Maj F. W. Honnett	Goldhanger (C Flt)	B.E.12/12a
J	Hatfield Peverel— Stow Maries	37 —	Stow Maries (A and B Flts)	B.E.12/12a/12b
G	1 mile S of Stow Maries— Leigh on Sea— Yantlet Creek	61 Capt E. Henty	Rochford	S.E.5a
H	Throwley— Judds Hill— Warden Point	112 Maj C. J. Q. Brand	Throwley	Sopwith Camel
K	Wingham— Margate	50 Maj A. de B. Brandon	Bekesbourne	S.E.5a, B.E.12/12b
M	Detling— Marden	143 Maj F. Sowrey	Detling	S.E.5a

Note: The recently-appointed COs of Nos.39, 61 and 141 Squadrons were still awaiting their formal promotions to major.
Locations: Ball's Park = Hertford; Crabtree Hill = $2\frac{1}{2}$ miles NE of Hainault; Greensted Farm = 3 miles SE of North Weald; Judds Hill = Faversham; Yantlet Creek = Grain.

Normal procedure on receipt of the patrol order was for three or four aircraft to take off and cover their area at 10–12,000 ft, with strict 500-ft height separation, so that in theory any aircraft seen on the fighters' level was hostile. Patrols were relieved according to the developing raid pattern.

No.37 Squadron, covering the northernmost patrol zones between Stow Maries and Tiptree, was still struggling on with the obsolete B.E.12s and B.E.12as and makeshift B.E.12bs, and had just received its first S.E.5a. This unit had the lowest re-equipment priority since most bombers came in between Foulness and the South Foreland, and the few making landfall farther north normally entered areas patrolled by the modern fighters as they converged on London.

Brandenburg's basically sound decision to await an unequivocal forecast of good weather for his major blow rebounded badly, for with the moon two days past the first quarter and exceptionally clear visibility, conditions were even better for the fighters, which shot down three Gothas, The guns destroyed two, while a sixth crashed in Essex after an engine failure, adding up to Germany's biggest bomber loss over England.

Rfa 501 had already appreciated that its Giants were very vulnerable in bright moonlight—but they were under the operational control of Bogohl 3, and Brandenburg evidently thought that the Gothas were not at undue risk from this cause. On that brilliant Whit-Sunday night the fighter pilots, now completely at home in their high-performance single-seaters, were able to pick up bombers at 400 yards' range, and with four times more targets than usual on offer, a good success rate was almost guaranteed. Even so, with individual bombers dotted in a vast wedge of sky bordered by The Naze, London and Dungeness, it was still something of a needle-and-haystack situation, as evidenced by the failure of No.61 Squadron, patrolling the busy area north of the Thames estuary, to make a single positive sighting. The searchlights also had an unsatisfactory night, contributing to only one of the eleven interceptions. Success was mainly due to the ideal weather, the preponderance of effective fighters and increased overall squadron efficiency.

Discounting aircraft which crashed on landing or let-down, the percentage of the bomber force destroyed over England or missing from unknown causes—weather the likely suspect—had been exceeded in some of the earlier and smaller raids. Although the saturation factor created by so many bombers over England in the space of three hours might arguably have produced a lower loss rate, Brandenburg was undismayed and planned to fit occasional London raids into the growing pattern of operations against targets behind the battle lines. Two such planned for July were called off by the German High Command, and in August a massive attack using the new 2·2 lb Elektron incendiary bomb was similarly cancelled just before take-off time.

Between April and July there were at least nine enemy reconnaissance flights over southern England and coastal towns by army Flieger Abteilung or the navy's See Frontstaffel. Only three, on 17 June, 18 July, and 20 July, were detected and those too late for fighters to reach the high-flying photographic aircraft—usually Rumpler C VIIs, though the navy made a few sorties with Halberstadt CL IIs.

The Margate guns, which shelled the naval Rumpler passing high overhead at noon on 17 June, had been in action earlier that morning against an unidentified aircraft which flew in over Kingsdown at 03.00 hr and eventually landed near the North Foreland coastguard station, revealing itself as an F.E.2b with strong homing instincts. It was from No.38 Squadron, recently transferred to Dunkirk as a night-bomber unit. The crew, Sgt Falcy and Lieut Reid, got lost returning from a raid on Zeebrugge, and believing themselves in enemy territory, were about to burn their F.E. when they saw British uniforms. (The main body of No.38 went to France on 31 May, but a detachment remained on home defence until replaced in mid-August by the newly-formed No.90 Squadron.)

Boldest of the German photographic-reconnaissance flights was the London sortie by Leut Carl Drechsel (pilot) and Leut Reinhold Foell (observer) of F1 Abt 5Lb, based at Tournai. The 375-mile return trip was far longer than the unit's normal sorties, and since higher authority was unlikely to approve such a foolhardy enterprise, extra tankage to give the Rumper C VII seven hours' endurance was installed surreptitiously. Modifications were conveniently completed in time to make the flight, in perfect weather, on 21 May—24 hr after Germany's biggest bombing raid.

The Rumpler crossed Shoeburyness at 18,700 ft, was over London at about 11.30 hr and back at base by 14.00 hr, having been airborne just over six hours. It was neither heard nor seen from the ground, nor spotted by any British pilot fortuitously at high altitude near its track.

Despite the euphoria which followed the defences' success on 19/20 May—heightened by a congratulatory message from the Lord Mayor of London to Ashmore, the LADA commander—there was nothing in the forward intelligence assessments to permit any relaxation of the home-defence build-up beyond a few minor concessions. During July a prisoner disclosed that a new Gotha with greatly improved ceiling was under development—presumably the G VII—and on the 29th Higgins advised GHQ Home Forces that No.6 Brigade would require fighters capable of meeting enemy formations at 15,800 ft and single hit-and-run raiders operating up to 25,000 ft.

> 'Time is the essence of the contract' he wrote 'and air-cooled engines have the pull every time as regards home defence. At present our machines of 6 Brigade with air-cooled engines should be able to cope with the first, but not with the 20–25,000 types. Water-cooled engines mean a delay of ten minutes after a warning is received in getting machines off the ground in summer, and a longer time in winter.'

Higgins stated that the Le Rhône Camel could normally reach 20,000 ft in 50 min, and the Bristol Fighter with 275 hp Rolls-Royce Falcon III in 75 min. He quoted the 'extreme' ceilings of these aircraft as 22,000 and 21,000 ft respectively.

At the time of this appreciation, measures were in fact already in hand to increase the proportion of Camels, with their air-cooled rotary engines, by issuing them to Nos.50, 61 and 143 Squadrons to replace their S.E.5as with water-cooled engines. This burst of official enthusiasm for air-cooled engines, and for the Camel, came about quite suddenly, for on 29 May the aircraft requirements for No.6 Brigade's single-seater squadrons were listed as ninety-eight S.E.5as and only seventy-two Camels. At that time, too, the new Martinsyde F.4 Buzzard powered by the 300 hp water-cooled Hispano Suiza engine was nominated as a potential home-defence fighter.

In reality there was little difference between the times taken to 'scramble' the two categories of fighters during the 1918 raids. On 19/20 May, intervals between receipt of 'patrol' orders and first take-off were Camels: No.44 Sqn—none, No.78—2 min, No.112—2 min; S.E.5as: No.50 Sqn—4 min, No.61—1 min, No.143—2 min; Bristol Fighters: No.39 Sqn—two patrols, 1 min each, No.141—two patrols, 5 min and 1 min. While the opponents remained 70–80 mph Gothas and Giants flying at only 8,000–12,000 ft, there was normally ample time between

Three Camels of No.112 Squadron about to leave Throwley on 14 June, 1918, for Hainault to join others forming No.151 Squadron for service in France.

the 'readiness' and 'patrol' orders for engines to be warmed up, but with faster, higher-flying bombers reducing this standby period, the water-cooled types might have shown to disadvantage.

Another benefit claimed for rotary-powered fighters was that the positive on-off engine control by the 'blip switch' made for easier landing approaches. This was a reversal of the 1915 Central Flying School thinking that the pilot's job was simplified by a stationary engine which could be throttled back. The enthusiasm for air-cooled types favoured the extensive employment in the northern squadrons of the Avro 504—a questionable move, since apart from a good ceiling it had neither the performance nor armament to make an effective fighter.

The principal reason why the S.E.5a squadrons were re-equipped with Camels, starting in June, was that the S.E. was difficult to land in a small area and thus handicapped for forced landings. Even in daylight on good aerodromes it was easily tipped on to its nose because of the undercarriage positioning close to the centre of gravity. Another factor was that many home-defence S.E.5as were powered by the 200 hp Hispano Suiza, regarded as unreliable for night flying.

The Bristol Fighter, with some tendency to 'float' during the approach, also acquired a reputation for being difficult to land at night, but nevertheless remained on home-defence duties until the end of the war.

A familiar sight on S.E.5a aerodromes—C8711 of No.37 Squadron at Stow Maries. (*Mrs M. F. Sadler*)

During June the Air Council accepted a slight weakening of home fighter strength in order to provide better protection from the persistent enemy raids against back areas in France. Some Camels and experienced pilots were accordingly withdrawn from Nos.44, 78 and 112 Squadrons to form No.151 Squadron which, under Murlis Green, left Hainault on 19 and 20 June for Fontaine-sur-Maye.

Murlis Green's departure from Hainault saw vacation of probably the first ever squadron commander's ex-officio married quarter in the Royal Air Force. This unique dwelling was not provided by a benevolent Air Ministry but grew from a piece of typical Murlis Green private enterprise. Anxious to be on hand for operations, and with his wife nearing the end of a pregnancy, he created a shanty-type bungalow from aircraft packing cases and other oddments to be found on the aerodrome. Though hardly elegant, the completed dwelling boasted a bathroom, running water, electric light, a telephone—and a flock of chickens.

Maj G. W. Murlis Green's elegant dwelling at Hainault.

There had been no significant follow-up of No.70 Squadron's initial 1917 Camel night sorties, probably because fighter squadrons in France were fully extended by daytime operations. A few ad hoc patrols were flown by experienced night pilots, and on 30 May Charles Banks—who had been with No.43 Squadron for two months, shot down a Friedrichshafen in flames. He was the first pilot to destroy an enemy night bomber over England and the Western Front, and also achieved eight victories in day combats.

Documents concerning the formation of No.151 Squadron provide superficial evidence that some numbers of the aft-seated 'Comic' Camel had become available. A minute by Higgins of 5 June referred to the diversion of eighteen 'converted' Camels from No.44 Squadron to the new No.151, though this figure was later reduced to twelve, the balance being made up by 'unconverted' aircraft from Nos.78 and 112 Squadrons. The immediate home deficiency was to be restored by delivery of twenty-four Camels to depots for conversion. The long-term requirement for LADA units, including rearming S.E.5a, B.E.12 and night-training squadrons, was stated as 204 'converted' Camels.

The word 'converted' implied the 'Comic' night-fighter version rather than the standard aircraft merely fitted with navigation lights and flare brackets for night flying. Doubts must remain, however, because no more than five 'Comics' are visible in any single squadron photograph which has so far emerged. Also, since some LADA squadrons did not fit flares, arguing that lighted aerodromes were always within reach for forced landings, to do even that could be described as 'conversion'. The shorter endurance of the 'Comic' would clearly handicap the intruder operations developed by No.151 Squadron in France, and accounts of the unit's work suggest that it flew standard Camels, though some Lewis-armed aircraft were on strength during its early weeks.

A modified (*left*) and an unmodified Camel of No.44 Squadron at Hainault. Four other modified aircraft are in the background.

The threat of new high-altitude bombers did not change an earlier Air Council decision about the balloon barrage. After completion of the tenth apron on 4 June—the halfway stage of the original plan—it was agreed not to extend the barrage further. Ashmore favoured completion in slow time and opposed suggestions that the balloons were not worth their keep. To withdraw them, he told GHQ Home Forces on 28 May, would require the fighters to cover all heights instead of a relatively narrow upper zone, and London would certainly be bombed from low altitudes. Home Forces rejected the latter view, arguing that the bombers would remain high to minimize risks from gunfire and to improve prospects of returning to base in the event of an engine failure. Though the aprons encouraged the bombers in this, their main benefit was moral effect.

The most significant development in the First World War home-defence field reached operational status just too late to make any impact. Early in 1917 the Wireless Experimental Establishment's 'testing park' at Joyce Green and some of the wireless training facilities from Brooklands were moved to Biggin Hill. In charge of the technical side was Lieut J. M. Furnival, whose promising Cramlington W/T trials had been so unceremoniously terminated at the end of 1916. One of Biggin Hill's priority tasks was to develop the earlier wireless telephony work of H. J. Round and C. E. Prince and produce efficient, reliable ground-to-air and air-to-air direct-speech equipment. It was estimated that this would speed up operational communications threefold and be of incalculable value in directing pilots towards enemy bombers.

However, the first practical sets to emerge were for air-to-air speech, and after successful trials in September 1917 by No.11 Squadron flying Bristol Fighters in France, other two-seat fighter squadrons on the Western Front were equipped. A wireless telephony school for the aircrews was formed at Biggin Hill, and later moved to Penshurst.

From this point it is more convenient to use the later terminology—radio telephony (R/T) to avoid confusion with wireless telegraphy (W/T).

The break-through on ground-to-air R/T was achieved early in 1918, and during April the Bristol Fighters of No.141 Squadron took part in trials. A long-range transmitter was installed in the grounds of Aperfield Court, a mile southeast of Biggin Hill aerodrome, primarily for daylight operations. At night

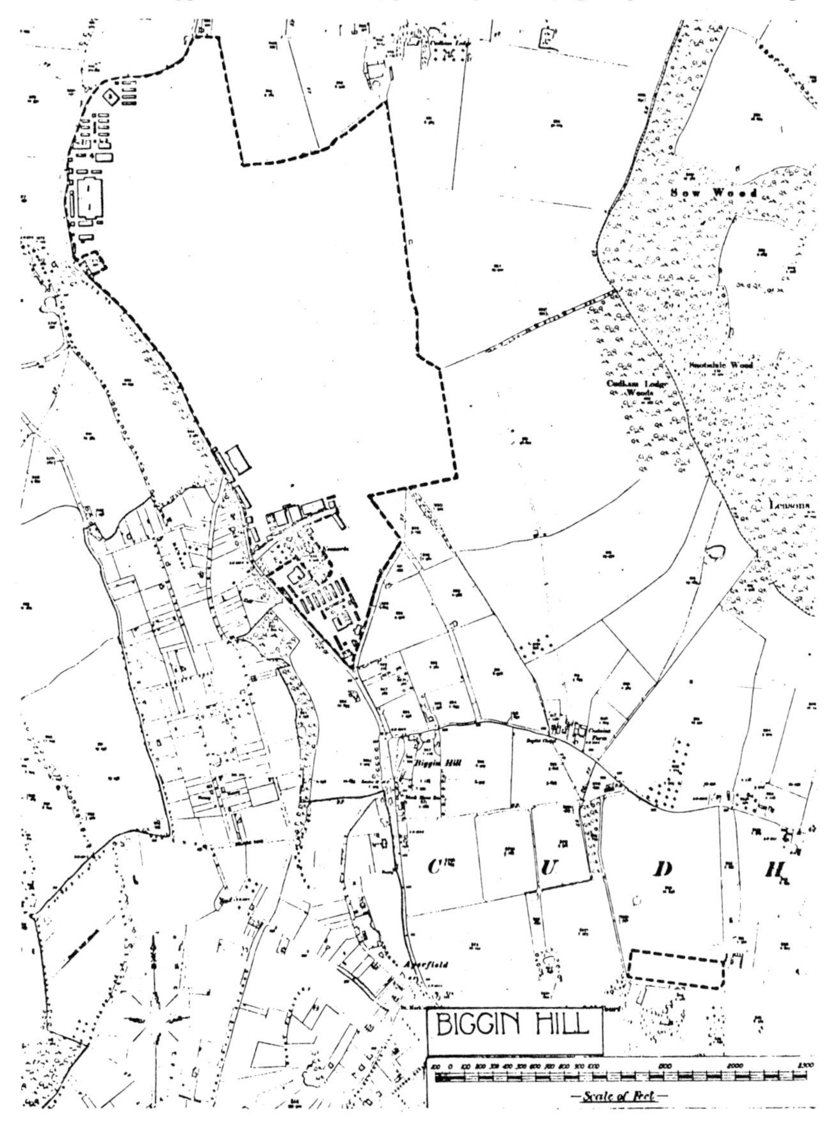

Biggin Hill aerodrome in mid-1918. The Wireless Experimental Establishment buildings are at the southern end. The small detached enclosure to the southeast housed the R/T transmitter.

Biggin Hill aerodrome in 1979. (*L. Pilkington*)

there were inevitable delays in filtering the numerous and often conflicting ground reports of enemy bomber positions and movements, so the LADA aerodromes were equipped with short-range transmitters communicating directly with their own squadron aircraft. In the early stages, while all the aircraft carried receivers, only flight commanders had transmitters.

According to No.53 Wing's immediate operational summary after the 19/20 May raid, messages were transmitted to several of No.143 Squadron's S.E.5as equipped with R/T receivers. However, this report was written before pilots had been debriefed and without any knowledge about reception quality. It is likely that some No.141 Squadron Bristol Fighters were also equipped, though this aspect is not mentioned in the brief squadron reports. Entries in the log-book of Lieut F. S. Mockford, the unit wireless officer, show that two Bristols flying that night certainly had the installation five days later. It is remarkable that various surviving reports on First World War wireless development contain virtually nothing on the important home-defence aspects.

Although the aeroplane bomber menace dominated defence requirements in the summer of 1918, the airship threat was still present. During the predictable suspension of Zeppelin raiding because of the short nights, the German Naval Airship Service had been weakened by several losses. The L62 blew up during a North Sea reconnaissance on 10 May, and L54 and L60 were destroyed in their shed at Tondern by the historic carrier-borne Camel attack on 19 July.

However, the few raids earlier in the year appear to have strengthened Strasser's stubborn belief that his newer craft were immune from attack by British guns or fighters, and on 8 July an even better Zeppelin, the L70, had been commissioned. With seven engines, a top speed of 81 mph and an 8,000 lb bomb load, this 694-ft airship was the first of a new X-class and the largest Zeppelin built—apart from two specially 'stretched' for flights to German East Africa.

On 5/6 August, flying in L70 and leading four of the earlier types, Strasser displayed an uncharacteristic and almost suicidal lack of caution in an attack which resulted in the destruction of the ship with all on board before it had even crossed the coast. This was achieved by one of a dozen modern aircraft which took off to intercept from Yarmouth and nearby aerodromes—something at last resembling the 'swarm of hornets' which five years earlier Churchill had promised would rise to meet the Zeppelins.

This was the last German air raid of the war.

Chapter XXI

Operations—May to August 1918

19/20 May, 1918 (Night)

Target: London.
Enemy forces: 38 Gothas despatched, 28 Gothas attacked.
Three Giants despatched and attacked.
Two Rumpler C VII weather-reconnaissance aeroplanes.
Results: 49 killed, 177 injured, £177,317 damage.
Defence sorties: 88.

RAF

No.37 Squadron, A and B Flights, Stow Maries: B.E.12s C3221 (2nd Lieut Wooding) 23.12–00.34 hr; C3221 (2nd Lieut Foster) 01.30–02.27 hr; C3192 (Lieut G. F. Hollington) 00.22–00.58 hr, returned with engine trouble, and 01.07–01.42 hr, returned with engine trouble; B.E.12a A4032 (Lieut H. Lingard) 23.02–01.04 hr; A4032 (Lieut Stokes) 01.30–02.15 hr; B.E.12bs C3091 (Lieut A. O. Beckett) 23.05–01.20 hr; C3085 (Capt S. Hay) 23.12–00.20 hr, returned with engine trouble; S.E.5a C8710 (Capt S. H. Starey) 23.12–01.15 hr and 01.55–02.11 hr.

No.37 Squadron, C Flight, Goldhanger: B.E.12s C3237 (Capt C. L. Blake) 23.05–01.25 hr; C3232 (Lieut J. J. C. Hamman) 01.05–02.10 hr.

No.39 Squadron, North Weald: Bristol Fighters C4636 (Lieut A. J. Arkell, 1st AM A. T. C. Stagg) 22.56–00.45 hr; B1264 (Lieut P. W. Deane, Lieut Robinson) took off 22.57 hr, crashed after fire; C4711 (Lieut A. F. Barker, 1st AM Hill), W/T tracker, 22.57–01.07 hr; C4671 (Lieut S. H. Love, 1st AM W. T. Merchant) 22.57–01.30 hr, crashed landing; B1263 (Capt W. T. F. Holland, 1st AM Easton) 23.43–01.24 hr; C964 (Capt C. L. Wauchope, 1st AM L. Card) 00.41–02.12 hr; B1331 (Capt O. V. Thomas, Lieut Fox) 00.41–02.20 hr; D8001 (Capt J. M. Clarke, Lieut L. Speller) 00.40–02.13 hr.

No.44 Squadron, Hainault: Sopwith Camels B5412 (Lieut J. H. Summers) 22.55–01.20 hr; B4614 (Lieut W. E. Nicholson) 22.56–23.45 hr (Chingford, with pressure trouble); B3852 (Capt R. N. Hall) 22.57–01.25 hr; B3816 (Capt W. H. Haynes) 22.58–00.19 hr; C6712 (Maj G. W. M. Green) 23.14–01.10 hr; B5206 (Lieut C. R. W. Knight) 00.02–02.07 hr; B2517 (2nd Lieut F. V. Webb) 00.22–02.07 hr; D6660 (2nd Lieut H. A. Sparks) 00.44–01.35 hr; B3827 (Lieut E. M. Gilbert) 00.44–02.10 hr; B3767 (2nd Lieut W. B. Detmold) 00.44–02.08 hr; D9391 (Lieut L. S. V. Gedge) 00.45–02.14 hr.

No.50 Squadron, Bekesbourne: B.E.12 C3220 (Capt J. M. Taylor), W/T tracker, 22.55–01.05 hr; B.E.12b C3106 (2nd Lieut W. G. Latham), W/T tracker, 00.43–02.35 hr; S.E.5as C1073 (Lieut W. Partridge) 22.57–23.20 hr, returned with engine trouble; D5995 (Lieut L. Lucas) 22.59–00.49 hr; D5984 (Capt C. E. Holman) 23.00–23.55 hr; C1087 (Lieut M. L. F. A. Aymard) 23.33–01.25 hr;

Lieut L. Lucas, No.50 Squadron, flying S.E.5a D5995, was among the unlucky fighter pilots who saw nothing of the enemy on 19/20 May, 1918.

C1756 (2nd Lieut A. C. Goldsmith) 00.23–02.40 hr; D6020 (Lieut H. T. W. Oswell) 00.52–02.40 hr; D5984 (Lieut C. W. D. Bell) 01.19–02.48 hr.

No.61 Squadron, Rochford: S.E.5as B656 (Lieut L. B. Blaxland) 23.08–00.56 hr; C1061 (Capt R. G. Holt) 23.08–00.30 hr; C1062 (Lieut G. Howe) 23.09–00.25 hr; B658 (Capt C. A. Lewis) 23.10–00.50 hr; D3434 (2nd Lieut W. A. Taylor) 00.40–01.50 hr; D3459 (Capt E. B. Mason) 00.42–02.05 hr; B672 (Lieut C. F. Briggs) 01.00–01.51 hr, returned with engine trouble; C9582 (Lieut J. W. Sheridan) 00.58–01.10 hr; D239 (Lieut G. C. Young) 01.21–02.20 hr.

No.78 Squadron, Suttons Farm: Sopwith Camels C6713 (Capt D. V. Armstrong) 22.59–00.05 hr; C6716 (Capt S. Cockerell) 22.59–00.30 hr; D6623 (2nd Lieut G. Clapham) 23.00–01.12 hr; D6688 (Lieut H. R. Clarke) 23.00–01.25 hr; C6714 (Lieut L. L. Carter) 23.38–01.26 hr; C1582 (2nd Lieut T. L. Tebbitt) 23.38–00.30 hr (Orsett, with engine trouble); B9249 (2nd Lieut C. G. Salmond) 00.43–01.44 hr; D6698 (Lieut W. Algie) 00.43–02.40 hr (Rochford); D6675 (2nd Lieut C. W. Middleton) 00.43–02.19 hr; D6677 (2nd Lieut C. G. Joyce) 00.46–02.12 hr.

No.112 Squadron, Throwley: Sopwith Camels D6469 (Lieut W. G. Scotcher) 23.00–00.50 hr; D6635 (Lieut F. B. Barager) 23.01–23.10 hr, returned with unserviceable lighting; D6437 (Lieut W. Aitken) 23.01–00.50 hr; D6473 (Capt J. T. Collier) 23.00–00.03 hr; D6465 (Lieut G. N. Blennerhassett) 23.12–00.25 hr; D6423 (Maj C. J. Q. Brand) 23.15–01.15 hr; D6435 (Lieut F. B. Barager) 00.10–02.10 hr; D6429 (Lieut D. F. Lawson) 00.28–02.10 hr; B9301 (Lieut E. P. Mackay) 00.50–02.25 hr; D6473 (Capt T. M. B. Newton) 00.50–02.15 hr; D6415 (Lieut A. C. S. Irwin) 00.52–02.20 hr; D6682 (Lieut F. C. Broome) 00.51–02.20 hr.

No.141 Squadron, Biggin Hill: Bristol Fighters C820 (Lieut E. F. Haselden, Lieut R. C. Cowl) 23.00–01.08 hr; C823 (Lieut Kelsey) 23.07–01.07 hr; C4715 (Lieut F. R. S. Southon) 23.05–01.00 hr; C851 (Lieut E. E. Turner, Lieut H. B. Barwise) 23.02–01.25 hr (Detling); C4778 (Capt B. E. Baker) 00.55–02.15 hr; C863 (2nd Lieut A. K. Bamber, 2nd Lieut G. R. Barker) 00.55–02.15 hr; C875

(Lieut H. Slingsby) 01.00–02.25 hr.

No.143 Squadron, Detling: S.E.5as C1879 (Capt J. Potter) 23.02–00.40 hr; C1803 (Capt C. J. Truran) 23.05–00.05 hr, returned with engine trouble; C1809 (Lieut N. F. Perris) 23.04–01.08 hr; C1805 (Lieut W. R. Oulton) 23.05–01.00 hr; C1804 (Maj F. Sowrey) 23.30–00.55 hr; C1118 (Lieut Northwood) 00.23–02.40 hr; C1802 (Lieut Jones) 00.50–02.45 hr; C1873 (Lieut C. Ossenton) 00.55–02.20 hr, damaged landing; C1808 (Lieut W. C. M. Harbottle) 00.58–02.00 hr; C1810 (Lieut F. V. Bryant) 01.08–02.50 hr.

Despite the continuing commitment to maintain heavy night attacks behind the battle front, Brandenburg was anxious to resume major Gotha raids against England, which was becoming the exclusive province of the Giant squadron.

The need to await a favourable weather forecast for the entire route was underlined by a disaster which struck Rfa 501 on 9 May, when three of four Giants returning from a French coastal raid were destroyed while attempting to land in fog. That same night Brandenburg had only with great reluctance accepted his own squadron meteorologist's advice to keep the Gothas on the ground. When the weather chart did promise trouble-free conditions, the moon was two days after the first quarter and the skies were clear, apart from some patchy cloud over Essex.

Bogohl 3 produced an impressive line-up of thirty-eight Gothas for this maximum effort, but the depleted Giant unit could muster only three—R.13, R.39 (carrying a 2,200 lb bomb) and probably R.12. Two Rumpler C VIIs were detailed for weather reconnaissance.

The first aircraft was reported off the North Foreland at 22.17 hr. It circled and dropped a flare to indicate clear skies ahead, then flew south to bomb Dover. This was the Rumplers' primary target and the alternative for any main-force aircraft unable to reach London. The spearhead of the Gotha contingent came in off Foreness 20 min later, and several raiders were approaching Sheppey at about 23.00 hr. The procession continued at irregular intervals, with aircraft crossing the coast between the Blackwater and Dover until midnight. The first bombs fell

Staaken R.IV R.12 is believed to have been one of the three Giants taking part in the last aeroplane raid on England in the 1914–18 war—on 19/20 May, 1918. (*Peter M. Grosz*)

Types of German bombs dropped on England during the raids of 1917–18, ranging in weight from 25 to 300 kg (55 to 660 lb). Larger bombs also used are not shown. In the background is a Gotha G V. (*H. J. Nowarra*)

on London at 23.30 hr and the attack lasted for an hour, with eighteen Gothas and one Giant penetrating to the capital. Other aircraft bombed at scattered points in Kent and Essex. Two Giants, one being R.39 with its one-ton bomb, claimed to have bombed Chelmsford, though no incidents were plotted within ten miles. The last of the departing bombers had cleared the coast by 01.40 hr.

The British estimated the total weight of bombs dropped as 23,724 lb, though the German figure was 32,000 lb—only 2,400 lb short of that delivered by the biggest Zeppelin raid of 1916. All bombing deaths were in the London area, where 17,850 lb were dropped according to German reports. The British count was 12,128 lb.

Despite problems caused by the size of the raiding force and the presence of 88 fighters, the British estimate that 34 bombers crossed the coast was remarkably accurate, reflecting the growing efficiency of the reporting organization. The actual number was probably 31, comprising twenty-eight Gothas and three Giants, but excluding the two Rumplers. There is some doubt as to how many Gothas turned back for various reasons before reaching the coast.

Fighters were put on readiness shortly after the Rumplers appeared. No.6 Brigade began issuing the patrol order at 22.53 hr, and eight squadrons had received it within five minutes. There was an unexplained delay with No.61 Squadron, which, as one of the more easterly-based units covering a regular bomber route, should logically have been among the first airborne, but it did not receive the order until 23.07 hr. Nevertheless it got four S.E.5as away within three minutes, to join the thirty-one aircraft from other squadrons already airborne—twelve Camels, eight S.E.s, eight Bristol Fighters and three B.E.12s. Apart from No.50 Squadron at Bekesbourne (only 15 miles from the coast), being the first to receive the patrol order, the promulgation appears to have followed no logical pattern. No.141 well to the west at Biggin Hill was in the second batch of units notified at 22.55 hr, while No.37, attempting to cover a sometimes active area with low-performance B.E.12s, was among the last at 22.58 hr.

The night's first fighter success came with astonishing speed. Brand, CO of No.112 Squadron, was airborne from Throwley at 23.15 hr in his Camel, *Makhabane II*, a standard aircraft armed with two Vickers guns. Having gained height over the aerodrome, he was making his first run along his patrol line to Warden Point, Sheppey, at 8,500 ft when he saw a Gotha flying west over Faversham 200 ft higher up, its exhaust flames clearly visible from more than 400 yards. This aircraft, crewed by Oberleutnant Rudolf Bartikowski (observer and captain) and Vizefeldwebels Fritz Bloch (pilot) and Heinrich Heilgers (gunner), had come in south of Ramsgate at about 23.00 hr.

As Brand approached, the Gotha's front gun opened up at 50 yards' range, firing high and to the left, and he retaliated with two 20-round bursts which stopped the bomber's starboard engine. The Gotha banked steeply and dived away to the northeast, making desperate S-turns as Brand followed, gradually closing the distance to 25 yards. There was no fire from the rear gunner perhaps killed or wounded in the initial attack, and Brand aimed three 25-round bursts, causing the bomber to burst into flames and then fall to pieces. Brand's face and moustache, and the nose of his Camel, were scorched by the flames but he followed the main wreckage down to 3,000 ft, watched it hit the ground near the Harty landing ground and then climbed back to continue his patrol.

Brand first saw the Gotha at 23.23 hr and his timing of the crash at 23.26 hr was confirmed by other pilots flying in the vicinity. The victory had been achieved just 11 min after take-off.

To the obvious delight of his pilots, Maj C. J. Q. Brand, CO of No.112 Squadron, poses in Camel D6423 *Makhabane II* from which he shot down a Gotha on 19/20 May, 1918. This aircraft was probably linked with the Basutoland (now Lesotho) presentation scheme, for Makhabane was a famous Basuto warrior, and Brand, of South African birth and upbringing, flew the original *Makhabane* (B3852), which was presented by the Paramount Chief and the Basuto Nation, throughout his service in No.44 Squadron. B3850 *Lepoqo* of No.65 Squadron was another Basuto warrior Camel.

The second success came about an hour later, achieved by one of No.39 Squadron's most experienced crews, and the unit's first victory since the great Zeppelin triumphs of 1916. Pilot of Bristol Fighter C4636, rather flamboyantly named *Devil in the Dusk*, was Tony Arkell, a parson's son, only 19, who had flown in Nos.50 and 112 Squadrons before joining No.39 in February and was flying at least his eleventh home-defence sortie. His gunner, Albert Stagg, had begun his career in $1\frac{1}{2}$ Strutters of No.78 Squadron, and his enthusiasm was unabated by the landing accidents terminating his first two patrols in 1917. After the squadron re-equipped with Camels he transferred to No.39, and this was his fifth operational trip.

Bristol Fighter C4636 of No.39 Squadron was crewed by Lieut A. J. Arkell and 1st AM A. T. C. Stagg, when they shot down the second Gotha destroyed on 19/20 May, 1918.

Arkell was first away from No.39 Squadron and had been flying at 11,000 ft for just over an hour when, at 00.05 hr, north of Hainault and near the southern extremity of his 'B' patrol line, he picked up the twin exhaust flames of a Gotha 1,000 ft lower down. He dived and began closing from 200 yards under its tail, giving Stagg the opportunity to fire half a drum. He then zoomed up to deliver a long burst from his forward Vickers, levelling off to offer Stagg another chance. The Gotha started to dive, making flat turns, with both its gunners firing as opportunity offered, and Arkell delivered several more bursts. He then moved in much closer, sitting under its tail and able to make out all its details, while Stagg fired two more drums. He zoomed up once more for another long burst of Vickers—in all he fired 350 rounds—and noticed that the fight was now down to 3,000 ft, with the Gotha still descending.

At 1,500 ft Arkell once more positioned underneath, and a final burst from Stagg set the Gotha's starboard engine on fire. The bomber spun for about one-and-a-half turns and hit the ground off Roman Road, East Ham, bursting into flames. Arkell noted the time as 00.20 hr. Two of the crew, Vizefeldwebel Hans Thiedke and Paul Sapkowiak (whose rank is not recorded) jumped to their deaths before the crippled bomber hit the ground, and the third, Gefreiter Wilhelm Schulte, perished in the wreckage.

Lieut A. J. Arkell and 1st AM A. T. C. Stagg inspecting the remains of the Gotha they shot down.

Apart from the uniforms, this could be a 1940 Battle of Britain post-combat 'inquest'. No.78 Squadron pilots at Suttons Farm, left to right in the centre group: Lieut W. Algie, 2nd Lieut G. Clapham (*facing camera*) and Capt D. V. Armstrong.

On return to North Weald numerous bullet holes were found in the Bristol, one only inches from Stagg's seat. Arkell was full of praise for his gunner, who 'displayed the greatest coolness, taking no notice of much tracer which was going all round us'.

The official history states that this Gotha was first attacked by D'Urban Victor Armstrong of No.78 Squadron, but times and locations given in the pilots' reports make this unlikely. At 23.55 hr, while northwest of Orsett at 12,000 ft, Armstrong saw a Gotha below, which proved to be carrying a very alert gunner. As he positioned his Camel carefully behind and beneath, he came under immediate fire down the bomber's fuselage tunnel, then as he zoomed up over its tail the gunner smartly switched to the upper position. Armstrong made a complete right-hand circle, the Gotha remaining clearly visible in the moonlight, then closed to 50 yards and fired several bursts until his gun jammed. Clearing the stoppage he fired the rest of his ammunition at point-blank range with no result, except that the return fire became rather wild.

He fought the Gotha down to 9,000 ft, and left it between Hainault and Suttons Farm at 00.15 hr. By that time Arkell had been chasing his opponent for ten minutes, and it is unlikely that the two fighters—one with a second pair of eyes in the rear cockpit—could have attacked the same bomber without noticing one another.

D'Urban Victor Armstrong, like his home city named after Sir Benjamin D'Urban, a former Governor of Cape Colony, was acknowledged as probably the greatest exponent of aerobatics in the Sopwith Camel. On this occasion his marksmanship was rather below par, but he was being buffeted by the Gotha's slipstream and at one point momentarily lost control. His gunnery clearly improved after he went to France with No.151 Squadron, where he destroyed three night bombers. He was killed two days after the Armistice when his Camel failed to recover from a spin.

There was some contention over allocation of the night's third fighter victory. In his provisional report to HQ LADA, Higgins, No.6 Brigade, credited the destruction of a Gotha which crashed near Frinsted landing ground at 00.45 hr to Maj Fred Sowrey, CO of No.143 Squadron, Detling, flying an S.E.5a, but later information showed that Edward Turner and Henry Barwise, crewing a No.141 Squadron Bristol Fighter from Biggin Hill, were ultimately responsible. Strangely, neither pilot saw the Gotha hit the ground in the sort of 'no man's land' bordering the two squadron patrol lines—it did not catch fire—and neither lodged any immediate claim.

Sowrey had earlier seen an inbound bomber northeast of Maidstone at 23.45 hr, only 15 min after he was airborne. He moved up underneath until it filled his Neame sight and fired one drum from his elevated Lewis. There was no result nor retaliation, and during re-arming the empty drum fell into the fuselage. While rummaging for this, Sowrey lost his target.

At 00.25 hr in about the same place he encountered an outbound Gotha and again had no difficulty in positioning directly below, the exhaust flames glowing as he edged in until the aircraft overflowed his gun sight. He fired two double drums from his Lewis, and was sufficiently far forward for the return fire down the enemy's gun tunnel to pass over his tail. Despite some spirited evasive action, Sowrey kept the Gotha in sight and pulled up his S.E's nose to attack with the Vickers, but he stalled and spun a few turns, losing sight of his opponent.

Mindful of his earlier trouble, after exhausting the second Lewis drum, Sowrey resorted to the remedy used during his successful combat with the Zeppelin L32 in

1916 and hurled the drum overboard. However, this one did not embellish some unknown individual's collection of war souvenirs. Next morning it was dutifully returned by Mr Roland White, having crashed through the roof of his house in Holland Road, Maidstone. Fortunately he was in the street watching the action overhead and escaped injury.

While endeavouring to escape from Sowrey, the Gotha had diverted from its homeward track, flying some miles west, and was picked up at 00.30 hr over South Ash, near the present Brands Hatch motor-racing circuit, by Turner and Barwise at the eastern edge of their patrol area.

Lieut Edward Eric Turner, pilot of No.141 Squadron Bristol Fighter C851, which shot down the third Gotha on 19/20 May, 1918. Turner stayed in the RAF and was killed during Indian North-West Frontier operations on 28 December, 1922. His No.27 Squadron D.H.9A was apparently hit by a bomb from a higher aircraft in the formation. (*E. F. Haselden*)

Turner, aged 21, who for some long-forgotten reason acquired the inelegant nickname of 'Bum', had joined No.61 Squadron in time to fly Pup sorties during the last two Gotha daylight raids of 1917. He was posted to Biggin Hill in December, and if this was because he was considered to show better aptitude for night operations, the authorities must have been gratified by their action.

It was Turner's fourth listed night sortie, and he positioned with great care below and behind the Gotha until it filled his 45 deg Neame sight on the upper wing. He signalled for his observer to fire, and Barwise delivered a text-book attack with his Lewis, the first burst of RTS ammunition hitting the port engine. The Gotha put its nose down and went into a flat turn, but Barwise nevertheless managed two more bursts, hitting the fuselage and starboard wings before the gun jammed.

The Gotha continued to lose height, with the rear gunner shooting erratically for some moments, then Turner saw its front gun firing vertically downwards—possibly as a signal of surrender. Whatever the intention, the Bristol was unable to resume the attack because its engine, throttled back during the descent, refused to pick up for some time, and the Gotha was lost to sight without Turner having fired a shot from his Vickers.

Gotha G V/979/16 down near Frinsted after being attacked by a No.143 Squadron S.E.5a and a No.141 Squadron Bristol Fighter on 19/20 May, 1918. This aircraft was modified with additional forward undercarriage wheels to minimize the risk of nosing-over during a bad landing.

Now some 20 miles east of their patrol area, Turner and Barwise lost themselves while trying to re-locate the bomber and at 01.25 hr landed at Detling to refuel. They left for Biggin Hill an hour later.

Gotha G V/979/16 crashed between Frinsted and Harrietsham at about 00.45 hr, and the only survivor, Unteroffizier Hermann Tasche, the fuselage gunner, received a broken arm. The crew members killed were Leutnant Joachim Flathow (captain and observer) and Vizefeldwebel Albrecht Sachtler (pilot). The aircraft had the large white letters FST—the crew's initials—on the fuselage.

No details were known while Turner and Barwise were on the ground at Detling, where they merely told No.143 Squadron officers that they had had 'a bit of a scrap' between South Ash and Throwley before Barwise's gun jammed. It was thus quite logically assumed that the Gotha's crash was the result of the longer engagement by Sowrey. Further facts did not emerge until Tasche had been interrogated some time afterwards. He confirmed that they were attacked by two fighters after bombing the Peckham–Rotherhithe area at 23.50 hr—but the files contain two slightly different versions of the rest of his story. One was that the first fighter (Sowrey's S.E.5a) caused no damage or injury. The other more widely-circulated, and probably correct, version was that it wounded the pilot, and the second attack came when they were looking for a place to land—not easy

The first (C1802) and third (C1808) S.E.5a in this line-up at Detling were among the No.143 Squadron aircraft operating on 19/20 May, 1918. The projections under the rear fuselage appear to be pyrotechnics, though the original location of Holt flares under the lower wingtips remained standard in the RAF during the 1920s.
(*J. M. Bruce/G. S. Leslie collection*)

said Tasche, as German crews knew that most of the illuminated landing grounds were decoys. He confirmed that a burst from the second fighter (Turner's Bristol) stopped the port engine as the Gotha was making for the Frinsted flarepath.

No.143 Squadron was naturally disappointed when credit for the victory was switched to No.141. There were still a few unclear aspects, and on 25 May, from his newly-formed squadron's viewpoint rather than any personal motive, Sowrey queried the decision with No.53 Wing. This produced no change, though a shared victory between the two squadrons might have been a fairer verdict.

The successful aircrews were suitably decorated—Brand with the DSO, Arkell and Stagg with the MC and MM respectively, while Turner and Barwise both received the new Distinguished Flying Cross.

Gotha G V/925/16 *Pommern* which crashed at St Osyth.

A fourth Gotha down on British soil, G V/925/16 named *Pommern*—suggesting that the crew were from Pomerania—came to grief through a combination of bad luck and faulty airmanship. Crewed by Leutnant Wilhelm Rist (captain and observer) and Vizefeldwebels Max Gummelt and Rudolf Huhnsdorf, it encountered cloud on approaching the coast and let down for a position check. It broke clear at 2,000 ft and the Blackwater estuary was mistaken for the Thames. However, this error proved academic, for the pilot choked the starboard engine while opening up to check their descent, and despite the jettisoning of the bombs the aircraft hit the ground at St Osyth at 23.50 hr. It was little damaged, but Rist in the front cockpit was killed.

Several other fighter pilots reported spirited though indecisive combats. Holman, No.50 Squadron, fired 300 rounds at a bomber flying northwest near Canterbury at 23.20 hr. It returned his fire, then turned and dived so steeply as to appear to be out of control. No.6 Brigade suggested that this was the aircraft later destroyed by Brand, but the pilots' timings make that unlikely, for Holman lost his target at 23.26 hr—the time Brand's victim crashed at Harty. Neither pilot reported any other combat in progress.

Clearly there were several bombers in this area, and at 23.23 hr over Whitstable, Collier, No.112 Squadron, briefly attacked one before being dazzled by a would-be helpful searchlight. He picked up another at 23.53 hr north of Frinsted at 10,000 ft which skilfully evaded his fire with steep S-turns. Collier fired some 500 rounds before his guns jammed, and was much bothered by their flash—which he attributed to an excessive proportion of Buckingham in the ammunition belts. He relieved his frustration by firing a Very cartridge at the Gotha before departing.

Haynes, No.44 Squadron, flying a Camel armed with one Lewis gun fixed to fire forward and a second angled upward at 45 deg, had a protracted engagement with one bomber. He picked it up at 8,500 ft over Romford at 23.30 hr and remained in contact while it flew on to bomb east London, then followed to North Benfleet on its homeward journey. A skilled and conscientious pilot, Haynes positioned with great precision behind and 500 ft below, firing two carefully aimed bursts while it was still flying west and another after it had bombed, using a full drum of armour-piercing ammunition from the 45 deg gun. The only response was a few ponderous S-turns. On switching to the horizontal Lewis loaded with RTS, he

Sopwith Camel D6473, No.112 Squadron, was flown by Capt J. Tessimond Collier who unsuccessfully attacked two enemy bombers on 19/20 May, 1918. The occupant of the cockpit in this photograph has not been identified. (*Imperial War Museum*)

climbed and closed in behind the bomber, making several attacks and apparently scoring some hits. Now more easily visible against the moon, his Camel was greeted by short, accurate bursts every time he turned in to attack, and after landing, out of ammunition, he found bullet damage to his propeller and a neat group of holes in the lower starboard wing. He had the impression that his adversary 'floundered' slightly after one attack, and that its flying was 'distinctly unnatural' when he disengaged.

This bomber may have been a Giant. Unlike some pilots who clearly identified Gotha features, Haynes offered no more than the opinion that it was twin-engined—an impression sometimes given by the Giant's tandem engine layout. He gave its speed on the inbound flight as 60–65 mph, against the 80 mph quoted for identified Gothas pursued—though it was flying a little faster after bombing—and there was no retaliatory fire when he attacked from below as might have been expected from a Gotha's fuselage tunnel. The lack of results from the three carefully aimed bursts from below suggests that Haynes was initially well out of range, having been misled by the size of a Giant.

This Camel of No.44 Squadron (occupant unknown) has the armament installation of horizontal and upward-angled Lewis guns fitted to B3816, flown by Capt W. H. Haynes on 19/20 May, 1918.

Nicholson, No.44 Squadron, made two attacks on a bomber over Loughton at 23.33 hr, but a broken pressure valve obliged him to break away and forced land at Chingford.

Cockerell, No.78 Squadron, attracted by searchlights and AA fire concentrating over Orsett at 23.55 hr, saw the Gotha causing the activity and remained in contact for 25 min. It was at 11,000 ft, and after Cockerell made a head-on diving attack, opening fire at 200 yards, it put its nose down and started jinking, though still maintaining course for London. He turned and attacked from below with a short burst, then dropped back to a level position about 20 yards behind. On opening fire both his Vickers guns ran away, and although he managed to hold the Gotha in his sights while they exhausted their ammunition, there was no visible result beyond some aimless fire from the rear gunner.

Two of the night's bombs fell on Detling aerodrome at about 23.30 hr. These caused no damage, but another which cratered an adjacent meadow produced a minor incident. Ossenton, No.143 Squadron, put down in this field with an ailing engine which just failed to carry him to the flarepath, and some uncanny magnetism drew his S.E.5a to the crater, where it nosed over and received fire damage when the Holt flares inadvertently ignited.

Operationally the night was relatively trouble free. No.39 Squadron had two accidents, not recorded in detail but causing no injuries. Of the ten aircraft developing technical snags while airborne, most completed some useful patrol time before returning. The unexplained diversion by Algie, No.78 Squadron, to Rochford was probably because he was uncertain of his whereabouts.

No.37 Squadron, suffering serviceability problems with its variegated B.E.12s, had only six fit for operations and two of those made early returns with engine trouble—Fred Hollington, from Brockville, Ontario, having to go back twice. However, double sorties were flown where possible, enabling more pilots to acquire experience. Stephen Starey flew two sorties in the squadron's first S.E.5a.

Anti-aircraft gunners claimed three bombers shot down in flames—off Dover, Shoeburyness and Foreness Point—but German figures show only two losses to this cause. Next morning the armed trawler *W. H. Podd* recovered Gotha wreckage and a body from the Channel to confirm the Dover claim, while Cecil Lewis, No.61 Squadron, saw from the air what could have been the Shoeburyness victim falling.

A depressing feature of the night was the indifferent performance of the searchlights, which aided only one fighter sighting and aroused considerable criticism from the fighter-squadron commanders: Murlis Green (No.44) '. . . searching too fast . . . concentration not at all confident . . . at no time was it possible to ascertain from searchlight action the course of a Hun, coming or going'; Brandon* (No.50) '. . . too fast . . . no enemy (or friendly!) aircraft seen by searchlights'; Sowrey (No.143) '. . . searchlights throwing beams too low'; Brand (No.112) '. . . of some value in indicating direction of aircraft but lagged behind.'

Brand was also unimpressed by the star shells intended to indicate the positions of bombers, asserting that their brilliant light blinded pilots to everything in the area.

Official raid files contain only a tantalisingly brief report by the Dover AA commander on the performance of the two bowl-shaped sound reflectors at Fan Bay and Joss Gap—that they proved invaluable in picking up enemy aircraft five to ten minutes in advance of first warnings received at the gun stations.

5/6 August, 1918 (Night)

Target: The Midlands.

Enemy forces: Navy Zeppelins L53 (Kptlt E. Prölss), L56 (Kptlt Walter Zaeschmar), L63 (Kptlt M. von Freudenreich), L65 (Kptlt W. Dose), L70 (Kptlt Johann von Lossnitzer).

Results: No casualties or damage.

Defence sorties: 35.

RAF No.4 Group

Yarmouth: D.H.4s A8039 (Lieut R. E. Keys, AM A. T. Harman) 20.55–01.10 hr (Kelstern); A8032 (Maj E. Cadbury, Capt R. Leckie) 21.05–23.05 hr (Sedgeford); D.H.9s D5802 (Capt B. G. Jardine, Lieut E. R. Munday) took off 20.55 hr, missing; D5809 (Capt C. B. Sproatt, Capt J. Hodson) 21.10–22.20 hr; D5793 (Capt C. S. Iron, Lieut H. G. Owen) 21.10–23.15 hr (Sedgeford); D5709 (Lieut W. K. Prendergast, 2nd Lieut E. Gray) 21.10–21.55 hr (Bacton); Sopwith Camels N6622 (Capt G. D. Kirkpatrick) 21.10–

* Brandon did not fly that night.

23.15 hr (Saxthorpe); N6625 (Lieut G. W. Stallard) 21.15–21.50 hr (Bacton); F.2A N4303 (Capt S. J. Fetherston, Capt E. A. Mossop) 21.00–22.30 hr.

Burgh Castle: Sopwith Camels N6620 (Lieut G. F. Hodson) took off 21.05 hr, missing; N6624 (Lieut J. Tomkins) 21.05–21.20 hr, returned with engine trouble; B5706 (Capt G. W. R. Fane) 21.10–21.40 hr (Yarmouth, with gun trouble).

Covehithe: D.H.4 A8044 (Lieut Plaskett, Sgt Keeling) 21.25–22.00 hr; D.H.9 D1079 (Lieut F. R. Bicknell, Sgt Bull) 21.25–23.00 hr (Sedgeford).

RAF No.6 Brigade

No.33 Squadron, A Flight, Scampton: Bristol Fighter C4698 (Lieut F. A. Benitz, Lieut H. Lloyd-Williams) 22.37–22.50 hr, returned with petrol pressure trouble, 23.10–00.55 hr (Atwick, crashed, pilot killed).

No.33 Squadron, B Flight, Kirton-Lindsey: F.E.2b A5660 (Lieut J. T. G. Murison) 22.45–01.30 hr; F.E.2ds A6375 (Lieut R. E. Butler) 22.38–01.30 hr; B1898 (Lieut G. N. Smith, Capt S. T. Goodman) 23.43–00.10 hr, returned due to weather.

No.33 Squadron, C Flight, Elsham: Bristol Fighters B1186 (Capt A. B. Fanstone, AM Ridley) 22.30–00.30 hr; C8003 (Lieut G. Cameron, Cpl Booth) 23.45–01.50 hr (Pocklington).

No.38 Squadron, Leadenham: F.E.2b C9806 (2nd Lieut A. J. Marsden) 21.39–23.45 hr.

No.38 Squadron, Buckminster: F.E.2b C9809 (Capt P. W. Rutherford) 23.36–23.50 hr, returned due to weather.

No.51 Squadron, A Flight, Mattishall: F.E.2bs A5754 (Lieut J. Day) 21.41–23.30 hr, returned with engine trouble; A5732 (2nd Lieut J. L. Drummond) 21.38–00.40 hr, forced landed, Skegness.

No.51 Squadron, B Flight, Tydd St Mary: F.E.2b A5549 (Lieut L. A. Bushe) 21.43–22.53 hr; F.E.2d A6453 (2nd Lieut A. E. Rowell) 21.43–23.04 hr.

No.51 Squadron, C Flight, Marham: F.E.2bs A5724 (Lieut H. W. Steele) 21.41–22.37 hr, returned with engine trouble; A5548 (Capt T. J. C. Martyn) 21.41–00.50 hr (North Coates).

No.75 Squadron, A Flight, Hadleigh: Avro 504K E1722 (Sgt R. Mann) 21.43–22.10 hr (Elmswell).

No.75 Squadron, C Flight, Elmswell: Avro 504K D9355 (Lieut J. Hutcheson) 21.35–22.20 hr (Thetford).

No.76 Squadron, A Flight, Copmanthorpe: B.E.12b C3094 (Lieut W. E. Watt) 22.50–01.45 hr.

No.76 Squadron, B Flight, Helperby: B.E.12bs C3143 (Lieut S. Hill) 22.01–00.58 hr; C3085 (Lieut F. H. Wrenn) 00.28–01.10 hr, returned with faulty oil pressure.

US Naval Air Service

Killingholme: F.2A (Lieut G. F. Lawrence, Ensign A. W. Hawkins) 22.30–05.30 hr (Tynemouth).

Several puzzling features surround the last Zeppelin raid of the war, led by Strasser flying in L70. Paramount among these is Strasser's uncharacteristic disregard of basic operating precautions by bringing his force within sight of the English coast before it was fully dark.

This led to the destruction of Germany's latest Zeppelin, with the deaths of all on board, but the satisfaction generated by that spectacular event diverted attention from defence shortcomings comparable with those of early 1916. Two

L70 at Friedrichshafen in 1918 before entering German navy service.

aircraft were missing and a third crashed, causing the death of its pilot.

A major factor affecting both sides was the weather. The strong westerly wind declined as Strasser's force climbed across the North Sea to operating altitude, and by 18.30 hr three airships—L53, L65 and L70—were within 60 miles of the coast. There had been no early warning of the raid, but as the Zeppelins edged slowly westwards they were sighted at 20.10 hr from the Leman Tail light vessel 30 miles northeast of Happisburgh, which kept them in sight for 75 min. It was still daylight, and the thick bank of cloud accompanying a deep depression moving east across the Midlands, which the German meteorologists probably calculated would have extended well out to sea, had barely progressed beyond the coast.

Strasser had appointed Kapitänleutnant Johann von Lossnitzer, rather than one of the surviving veterans with United Kingdom raiding experience, to command the magnificent new L70, commissioned in July. Von Lossnitzer had flown ten operations, mostly in command of the ex-army LZ120 over the Baltic during 1917, then spent some months as Strasser's adjutant. He had no personal knowledge of operating conditions over England, but he shared his chief's faith in the military future of the airship and doubtless the belief that on this occasion they would be immune from attack high above the clouds.

For unexplained reasons Yarmouth and other nearby No.4 Group stations were not alerted until 20.50 hr, by which time L56 and L63, flying some 30 miles south of the other three airships, were less than ten miles from the aerodrome. There was a wild scramble for aircraft from the astonished aircrews who could see the two Zeppelins in the clear evening sky, east of the rapidly gathering cloud.

The Yarmouth pilots rightly considered that the station's best aircraft for Zeppelin hunting were the two D.H.4s powered by 375 hp Rolls-Royce Eagle VIII engines, and Keys grabbed the first of these. Egbert Cadbury, who had been largely responsible for the destruction of L21 in November 1916, hastily deserted the audience at a nearby charity concert where his wife was singing and took off ten minutes later in the second. Acting as his gunner was Robert Leckie, co-pilot of the H-12 which had shot down L22 over the North Sea in May 1917. Another D.H.4, five D.H.9s, five Camels and an F.2A flying-boat were also airborne from Yarmouth, Burgh Castle and Covehithe.

Meanwhile, L56 and L63 had turned north, eluding most of the pilots, who broke through the increasing cloud formations to see L53, L65 and L70 flying in a

Egbert Cadbury (*left*) and Robert Leckie photographed at Yarmouth after shooting down L70 on 5/6 August, 1918. They then held the respective ranks of major and captain in the RAF. Yarmouth was one of the old RNAS stations with tenacious naval loyalties, which may explain why both officers are still wearing their old flight-commander rank insignia.

broad V pattern. L70 was in the southernmost position, then L65 and L53, with about a mile between each airship.

Because of the thick cloud and varying wind speeds at different heights the RAF pilots had difficulty in estimating their positions, and correlating their reports is further complicated by conflicting times. Some aspects of the action therefore remain obscure.

Cadbury's D.H.4 carried two 100 lb bombs, but action to jettison them shortly after take-off brought no appreciable improvement in the aircraft's climb. Leckie also discovered that the Lewis gun lacked its sight. They broke cloud at about 7,000 ft, and by 22.10 hr, with the altimeter reading 16,400 ft, saw L70 some 1,000 ft above and to the rear.

Cadbury turned and approached head-on, slightly to the left, and the absence of any opposing fire suggests that the D.H.4 was not noticed against the dark cloud background. Leckie aimed for the airship's nose, but his first few rounds missed before he managed to concentrate fire on a point three-quarters of the way along the hull. Cadbury saw the Pomeroy explosive bullets blow 'a great hole' in the fabric, then flames rapidly spread the length of the Zeppelin. The blazing hulk broke into two main pieces before plunging into the cloud below.

Omitted in most accounts is a virtual counter-claim for L70's destruction by Keys in the other D.H.4. Uncharitable thoughts that he was attempting to 'poach' the victory can be discounted, as his report was telephoned from Kelstern, where he forced landed, unaware that Cadbury had already claimed what proved to be the only airship destroyed. Keys reached 17,000 ft and attacked from 75–100 yards with his front gun. This soon jammed, and he turned, allowing Harman, his gunner, to fire about 70 rounds of armour-piercing and tracer bullets, whereupon the airship burst into flames from the stern and fell to the sea.

L70 came down eight miles off Wells-next-the-Sea and much closer to the coast than any of the aircrews estimated. According to the logs of other Zeppelins which saw her destruction, the time was 22.15 hr. Her barograph, later recovered with some of the wreckage, showed that she had just reached 5,500 metres (18,000 ft) when attacked.

Despite discrepancies in Keys' account—which gave the time as 21.55 hr and the position as 40 miles north of Yarmouth, 20 miles out to sea—it is inconceivable that he and his gunner invented the story. Keys was an airship expert, and paradoxically his claim is strengthened by his incorrect identification of the victim as a Schütte-Lanz. L70 was slightly different in proportions from the earlier Zeppelins, and more likely to be mistaken for the better-streamlined Schütte-Lanz types. This was evidently another instance where two crews, hidden from one another by the bulk of their target, both believed that they were the sole agents for the destruction of the same Zeppelin, and intelligence accepted that both crews attacked. However, the arbitrary final verdict favoured Cadbury and Leckie—who received DFCs—and Keys' claim is not mentioned in the official history.

At 22.00 hr, L70 had also been fired on at extreme range by Sproatt, flying one of the lower-powered D.H.9s. He could not exceed 13,000 ft, and his 100 rounds at the airship 4,000 ft above inevitably had no effect.

Cadbury next turned to L65, which had swung north on witnessing the L70 calamity. His engine cut for a few moments—probably because of icing—and he knew that with the D.H.4 now at its ceiling any attempt to raise the nose and use the Vickers gun would produce a stall. He positioned 500 ft below L65 to give Leckie a head-on shot firing above the centre-section, but after a short burst the

Lewis jammed, resisting five minutes of strenuous attempt at rectification. A brief stab of light from the Zeppelin's port midships gondola, which gave the impression of a fire starting, was later learned to have come from an interior lamp when a mechanic incautiously raised a porthole shutter.

Returning to the coast Cadbury became lost after descending through four thick cloud layers. In a letter to his father he described the next 30 min as the most terrible in his flying career, particularly having 'been told that [the D.H.4] could not land at night'. Cadbury's accounts leaned towards the dramatic, and a pilot of his experience must have known that rumours about difficult landing characteristics when Yarmouth got its first D.H.4s in 1917 had long been disproved. Evidence of this reputation is seen in the over-emphasis on landing in Gerard Fane's log-book comments after his first D.H.4 flights—19 August, 1917 ' . . . landed very well'; 22 August ' . . . landed in dark at Bacton OK'; 26 August ' . . . landed OK.'

Eventually Cadbury found an aerodrome—Sedgeford—and apart from narrowly missing another machine in the circuit, put down with no difficulty. It was only after climbing out that he discovered that his two bombs had failed to release.

Keys also went after L65, though he too had been experiencing engine trouble, and his gunner delivered a drum and a quarter of accurate fire from the port quarter. Then the port cylinders cut out completely and Keys abandoned the action. At about 23.45 hr, having descended below the clouds, he picked up the navigation lights of another aircraft which he followed, hoping that it would lead him to a landing ground. However, after 25 min it went down and appeared to hit the sea. He circled at 300 ft and saw some lights on the water, which quickly disappeared.

Keys then followed the golden rule for British aviators lost over the North Sea—keep steering west—and after negotiating more cloud and mist patches he thankfully saw a flarepath. He turned into wind, but when letting down hit the ground, damaging his undercarriage and lower wings. The aerodrome was Kelstern in Lincolnshire, some 500 ft above sea level—and his altimeter was set at zero for Yarmouth, nearly 100 miles away.

Also close at hand when L70 went down were Iron and Owen in a new D.H.9, its compass not yet swung and no navigation lights fitted. Their sortie report suggests that they initially went after the L56 and L63 before sighting L70. Their attempt to pursue L65 and L53 flying further north was abandoned when Iron realized that at 15,500 ft the D.H.9 had reached its ceiling and could make no more than 60 mph. After a long and anxious descent through the clouds they landed at Sedgeford shortly after Cadbury.

Fetherston and Mossop saw three Zeppelins at 21.30 hr, but soon appreciated that they had no chance of keeping them in sight while their ponderous F.2A flying-boat tried to reach combat altitude.

Ironically, while day bombers acting as fighters had an eventful night, the purpose-built Camels from Yarmouth and Burgh Castle were beset by troubles. Three returned early for various reasons, and one of the Burgh Castle aircraft, flown by Lieut G. F. Hodson, was missing.

Kirkpatrick achieved a full but frustrating sortie. He first sighted L.56 and L.63 at 21.20 hr, and as he climbed northwards two more airships came into view. He eventually reached 17,000 ft—still below the enemy—but his Camel would go no higher, nor could he get within combat range. Abandoning the pursuit, he flew west long enough to ensure that he was well over land and put down on the first

Camel N6620, flown by Lieut G. F. Hodson from Burgh Castle, was one of the two No.4 Group aircraft missing on 5/6 August, 1918.

landing ground seen after breaking cloud—Saxthorpe, ten miles southwest of Cromer.

Also missing was the D.H.9 crewed by Jardine and Munday. Jardine had arrived at Yarmouth only that morning and, unfamiliar with local conditions, was making his first sortie from the base on a night when the weather posed problems for the more experienced pilots, causing five to land at aerodromes 25 to 100 miles from base.

Aircrew reports potentially relevant to aircraft crashed or ditched at sea were mostly vague as to the positions, and no wreckage was found. Keys was effectively lost when he saw the possible ditching mentioned earlier, and Cadbury was unable to pin-point what could have been burning petrol on the water, seen through a break in the cloud during his homeward flight. At about 21.50 hr Fetherston saw a bright light falling approximately ten miles from the position of a trawler which later reported that an aircraft had circled, signalling in morse. The fishermen could not read morse and the machine flew off east.

It is unlikely that either of the missing aircraft was shot down by L70 before she was destroyed, since some evidence of the action would have been seen by other nearby British crews.

L65 was lucky to escape the fate of L70 and made an anxious flight home with badly-leaking gas cells, later said to have contained 340 bullet holes. Perhaps this was an exaggeration, since the combat reports of Cadbury and Keys indicate that about 150 rounds would be a generous estimate for the total expenditure of the pair against the airship. This raises the possibility that L65 was also tackled by one of the aircraft which failed to return—though the crew only reported attacks immediately after L70 went down, and thought that these were from a single aircraft.

The other three Zeppelins also saw the destruction of the L70. Misled by their own navigation errors and faulty wireless bearings into believing that they were over land, they abandoned their planned objectives, climbed to heights between 19,400 and 20,700 ft, and claimed to have bombed targets of convenience—King's Lynn, Boston and the Humber area—though their bombs actually fell out to sea at distances up to 65 miles. L56 gave the most determined performance, loitering off the coast until 23.30 hr, when her captain claimed to have flown inland to bomb Norwich at 00.10 hr. In fact the Zeppelin passed over Lowestoft Ness and all her bombs fell in the sea. With so many aircraft down at other aerodromes, and the worsening weather, no sorties against this incursion were attempted from Yarmouth.

The ex-RNAS base at Killingholme, which had become a United States Navy air station, went on standby at 19.30 hr and three hours later despatched an F.2A to patrol between Robin Hood's Bay and the Wash. The American crew saw nothing of the enemy and became lost above the clouds, but with their fuel state becoming desperate, they fortunately reached Tynemouth, about 110 miles north of their base.

As to the activities of No.6 Brigade, the official history boldly asserts that the Zeppelins were fortunate in not coming over land, since it was 'difficult to see how they could have avoided encounter with the many aeroplanes in their path fully capable of attacking them at any height'. Although a comforting note on which to end the story of the German air raids on Britain, it in no way reflected the true situation.

One airship, the L65, which had difficulty in reaching maximum altitude, bombed from 17,500 ft, and the other three from 19,400 to 20,700 ft. Of the meagre 20-strong No.6 Brigade force airborne, only one aircraft—and that surprisingly an F.E.2b—exceeded 19,000 ft, while two B.E.12bs and a Bristol Fighter reached ceilings of only 17–18,000 ft. Prospects of successful combat were clearly remote. The weather generally was bad, with poor visibility in rain low down, and several cloud layers extending from 800 to 15,000 ft in places. Wind at lower levels was blowing at 25 mph, southwesterly. About half the fighters returned early for weather or mechanical reasons.

The inevitable lack of factual reports about Zeppelins over land was counter-balanced by spurious information, originating mainly from strange acoustic effects caused by the weather. Bombs miles out to sea were heard far inland—at Bedford, Weedon and Sheffield—and reported as having dropped near those places. The situation was further confused at 22.30 hr, when Humber garrison telephoned No.33 Squadron headquarters that four Zeppelins were off Yarmouth, and another six miles off Spurn Head. A subsequent 'inquest' by GHQ Great Britain (the new title of Home Forces) established that the original message from the Hull AA defence commander placed the Zeppelin sixty miles east of Spurn.

The high-flying F.E.2b reaching 19,300 ft was flown by Martyn, No.51 Squadron C Flight commander, the only pilot to report a possible Zeppelin sighting. This was at 00.10 hr, when he had been patrolling for more than two hours with little idea of his position—which was almost certainly well north of the L56, the only airship then near the coast. Martyn was too short of petrol to give chase and started descending to the west. On reaching 500 ft he lit a Holt flare and was dismayed to see that he was still over water. He continued west at half throttle and fortunately reached North Coates on the south bank of the Humber and some 65 miles north of his base, Marham, on the dregs in his fuel tank.

Martyn is more likely to have seen a squadron colleague, Drummond of A Flight, Mattishall, who noticed aircraft lights at 00.15 hr, gave chase but was unable to overtake. Drummond lost the machine in cloud at 14,200 ft, then faced the problem of finding a landing ground with his dwindling petrol supply. He put down at Skegness, his F.E.2b turning on to its back, but he escaped injury.

All the nine aircraft of Nos.38, 51 and 75 Squadrons airborne between

21.35 and 21.43 hr encountered extensive cloud, but since no raiders were in their patrol area between Hadleigh and Lincoln this was of little consequence. The weather was subject to much local variation and not all pilots found conditions as bad as Marsden, No.38 Squadron, who spent most of his 126-min sortie without a sight of the ground but, remarkably, still found his way back to Leadenham. Though not specifically stated, weather is the likely reason for the brevity of No.75 Squadron's two Avro sorties, both landing away from the departure bases.

The spurious warning of a Zeppelin off Spurn Head caused No.33 Squadron to despatch two F.Es and two Bristol Fighters between 22.30 and 22.45 hr. An F.E. making an earlier weather reconnaissance had encountered cloud at 800 ft, but conditions improved temporarily, with the main cloud base lifting to about 7,000 ft. Fanstone in a Bristol remained below this height, while Butler took his F.E.2d above, reaching 16,000 ft. Murison's petrol pressure-pump failed early on, but he dutifully hand-pumped his F.E.2d for 90 min before returning.

Benitz in the other Bristol returned with petrol pressure trouble, but was off again 20 min later. He was killed in a landing crash at Atwick, after a 105-min sortie, and Lloyd-Williams, his gunner, was badly injured. The records show no reason for the diversion to Atwick.

In their wanderings over East Anglia and Lincolnshire in search of non-existent Zeppelins, the fighters triggered off more alerts, and aircraft were taking off until five minutes before the all-clear was eventually signalled at 23.50 hr. Before reaching his ceiling of 17,000 ft, Cameron, flying No.33 Squadron's last Bristol Fighter sortie of the night, reported that he was twice apparently fired at by tracer bullets—probably another fighter testing its guns.

The weather again deteriorated, causing anxious moments for several pilots. Rutherford, OC B Flight of No.38 Squadron, entered a patch of cloud immediately after take-off from Buckminster, then spun from 2,500 ft when

An Avro 504K night-fighter with V undercarriage instead of the more familiar 'hockey stick' type. It was not unusual for squadrons to receive small batches of consecutively numbered aircraft, and this machine, D9356, may have belonged to No.75 Squadron, which operated D9355 on 5/6 August, 1918.

B.E.12b C3094 of No.76 Squadron, piloted by Lieut W. E. Watt, patrolled the Humber area on 5/6 August, 1918. The officer in this photograph is Lieut R. McDonald.

peering through driving rain to locate a landmark. He recovered perilously near the ground and thankfully saw the recall signal displayed. Smith, No.33 Squadron, gave up after reaching 4,500 ft with no signs of a break and came down, to emerge conveniently within sight of the aerodrome at Kirton-Lindsey. No.76 Squadron put up three B.E.12bs, Hill reaching 18,000 ft and Watt maintaining an average patrol altitude of 17,600 ft.

The fighters attracted sporadic AA fire, and the gunners claimed that the engine sounds which caused them to open up were different from those of familiar British machines. The B.E.12bs and Bristol Fighters were clearly the prime cause of the gunners' confusion, and Hill, Watt and Fanstone reported gunfire from the Hull, Middlesbrough and Flamborough areas.

One bizarre episode was tactfully omitted from the No.6 Brigade report. Shortly after the first Zeppelin sighting, LADA units were put on readiness, and by some misunderstanding two Camels of No.50 Squadron, Bekesbourne, moved out to take off. One was stopped while still taxi-ing, but the other, flown by Lieut M. Aymard on his first Camel night sortie, got airborne and bored off into the cloud. Aymard climbed through several cloud layers, starting at 500 ft, and was unknowingly blown far beyond the northern limit of the squadron patrol line at Margate. He actually saw the L70 fall in the distance. By that time he was well and truly lost, and with fuel nearing exhaustion, came down through the clouds hoping to find somewhere to land. He was lucky to crash land, with only minor aircraft damage and a broken ankle.

Chapter XXII

Profit and Loss

The ending of aeroplane raids, after the big attack of 19/20 May, and Zeppelin incursions following the destruction of L70 in August, may invite the conclusion that after four years of fluctuating fortunes the defences had finally triumphed, causing Germany to acknowledge that the bomber offensive had become too expensive to continue.

Although the defences had reached new high standards of efficiency—and were further improved during the remainder of the war—such a conclusion would be a misleading over-simplification.

The interception ratio during the final Gotha/Giant raid had not in fact risen significantly—though German air commanders must have noted the extra risks attending operations on clear moonlit nights. There is no evidence that enemy Intelligence was aware that the new R/T control scheme might bring comparable hazards on dark nights.

As for the Zeppelins, Strasser's gross error of judgment on 5/6 August was compounded by an element of chance which exposed his force to one of the most effective defence aircraft airborne that night. Though designed and essentially used as a day bomber, the Rolls-Royce-engined D.H.4 had a performance comparable with the better fighters, and with more imagination it might have become the Mosquito of the First World War. The inadequacies of the majority of aircraft in the Northern Air Defence Area squadrons to deal with Zeppelins flying at 20,000 ft were exposed during their search for the non-existent raiders over land. While the Bristol Fighter had the potential to develop as an effective anti-Zeppelin aircraft, the Avro 504 was hardly more than a token night-fighter. The Avro squadrons could have quickly re-armed with Camels if major raids had demanded such a diversion of front-line fighters from France, but in the event the Government's calculated-risk policy paid off.

Encouraged by several oustandingly successful night attacks on military targets behind the Front in France, Germany decided in May to concentrate her bomber resources in this direction. It was intended to launch the occasional raid against England, but in August politico-military considerations caused the High Command to abandon the offensive altogether. They realized that although direct results were hardly commensurate with the effort required to maintain the campaign, the raids did interrupt British war production and caused an immensely costly diversion of material and manpower from the land fronts. However, they considered that German bomber resources would be better employed against Western Front objectives in a major effort to avert defeat—a prospect which now had to be faced—and that the bombing of England could not affect the final outcome. Furthermore, the build-up of British bomber strength increased the threat of massive retaliation, and Berlin would be within range of the new four-engined Handley Page V/1500 entering production.

L53, commanded by the veteran Kptlt Eduard Prölss, a survivor of the 'silent raid' and the reckless operation of 5/6 August, 1918, was shot down five days later by Lieut S. D. Culley.

Zeppelin raids were halted for other reasons. The loss of Strasser, with its shattering effect on morale in the airship service, was followed on 11 August by the destruction of L53 (Kptlt Prölss), at 18,700 ft off Terschelling, by Lieut S. D. Culley flying a Camel. The Camel was launched from a lighter towed by the destroyer HMS *Redoubt*, a new technique evidently unobserved by the enemy, and the action perhaps implied to the enemy that Britain had very long-range fighters which could gain the upper hand. While limited North Sea reconnaissance activity continued, raids against Britain were suspended until improved Zeppelins could be produced. In fact one—a modified X-class vessel, the L71—was delivered, too late for use during the war.

So the first Battle of Britain petered out, with no clear-cut victory by either side, though imminent developments held the prospect of a marked swing in favour of the defences.

The purpose of this book has been essentially to record the work of the home-defence flying units and the development of combat techniques rather than to analyse in depth the results of the campaign. Nevertheless, the following tables show the main trends which developed as the war progressed and give some of the basic profit-and-loss figures. The latter do not in every case conform with those in the widely-quoted official and semi-official British and German accounts by H. A. Jones and H. von Bülow respectively, and are based on close study of original reports.

A striking feature of the figures is the substantial drop, from 1917, in the number of British aircraft damaged. Apart from a few cases of combat damage, mainly during the Gotha daylight raids, the majority of aircraft in this column suffered flying accidents, mostly at night and with weather a frequent contributory cause. The improvement resulted from greater engine reliability, better ground facilities and training—and partly from the more sensible and realistic attitude towards night flying. By 1918, squadron commanders did not hesitate to cancel flying if conditions were marginal.

German Air Raids					British Fighter Effort		
Year	Raids	Despatched/ Attacked	Destroyed	Damaged	Sorties	Aircrew deaths	Aircraft[1] damaged
Airships							
1915	20	49/39	1 bombed from the air	2 British AA	115	3	15
1916	23	164/123	5 British fighters 2 British AA 1 weather	1 British AA	322	5	49
1917	7	46/29	1 British fighters 2 French AA 4 weather		265	6	14
1918	4	18/11	1 British fighter	2 landing 1 fighters	86	5	8
	Total 54	277/202	17	6	788	19	86
Aeroplanes—Small-scale Nuisance Attacks							
1914 1915	9	12	none	1	43	none	2
1916	19	33	,,	2	225	,,	3
1917	9	16	,,	not known	47	,,	1
	Total 37	61	,,	3	315	,,	6
Gothas—Daylight Phase, May–August 1917							
	8	193/143	6 British fighters 2 British AA 4 weather[2]	16[2]	844	6	18

Gothas/Giants—Night Phase, September 1917–May 1918

19	253/187	7 British fighters 7 British AA 2 Force landed in UK	27	793	3	24
Total 27	446/330	28	43	1,637	9	42

Notes: 1 Additional to aircraft sustaining fatal accidents. Damage ranges from severe, involving write-off, to minor and repairable but excludes minimal bullet holes in fabric.
2 Includes losses/damage on abortive raid of 18 August, 1917.

British Air Raid Casualties* and Damage

	Killed	Injured	Material damage
From airships	557	1,358	£1,527,585
From Gothas/Giants	835	1,973	£1,418,274
From other aeroplanes	22	85	£16,252
	Total 1,414	3,416	£2,962,111

* includes casualties from anti-aircraft shell debris.

Bombs dropped

	British estimate	German figure
From airships	196 tons	Not known—about 30 per cent higher
From aeroplanes	74 tons	113 tons

Home defence personnel

	December 1916	June 1918
Guns, searchlights etc	12,000	6,136
RFC/RAF	2,200	4,614
Others	3,141	2,655 (Balloon barrage)
	Total 17,341	13,405

The figures for the small nuisance raids are revealing. These attacks, mostly against Kent coastal towns, were almost impossible to intercept, and although they caused minimal damage and casualties, could easily have led to a big drain on defence resources. This was probably the enemy's intention, but the British Government firmly resisted the temptation to increase fighter strength substantially despite some public clamour during the first half of 1916, when the defence effort was already showing a certain disproportion. Ironically, one of the only two nuisance raiders known to have been damaged in more than 300 defence sorties was the victim of an aircraft being ferried to France.

The raiding forces predictably lost far more aircraft and crews than the defenders. Against the 28 British fatalities, 158 German navy and army airship crew men lost their lives during sorties against Britain, while 57 Gotha aircrew were killed or missing—excluding any deaths resulting from the 37 landing or approach accidents admitted by the Germans.

As to the logistics of the campaign, regular figures showing actual aircraft strength of the home-defence squadrons are elusive, but units were seldom up to full complement and some never received front-line fighter aircraft. There is little indication that No.6 Brigade exerted any great pressure to bring squadrons up to strength, and they may have considered existing numbers adequate to maintain optimum patrols under the limited control facilities, with any increase being liable to bring confusion and a higher collision risk.

The sixteen home-defence squadrons did not therefore truly represent an equivalent number of active units withheld from the fighting front. At the time of the Armistice the 355 aircraft on the strength of No.6 Brigade—including its nine night-training squadrons—comprised only one hundred and forty-five Camels and fifty-five Bristol Fighters, while there were eighty-two Avros, sixty F.E.2b/ds and thirteen B.E.12s. Discounting the Avros and B.Es, this would have provided perhaps ten full strength fighter squadrons and two or three light night-bomber units. Even so, that was still a sizeable force.

Bristol Fighters had largely replaced the obsolescent F.Es for home defence by the late summer of 1918. C4896 was flown by Lieut L. Latham, No.36 Squadron. (*L. B. Latham*)

Financial costs are a matter for conjecture. The official prices of the various aircraft types used for home defence ranged from £1,406 for a Sopwith Pup to nearly £3,000 (£35,250 at 1980 prices) for a Bristol Fighter. There were many other costs—for maintaining the Brigade's 35 main aerodromes and 139 other landing grounds, the vast expenditure on anti-aircraft guns and ammunition, communications and so on.

The tables also show the commendable British achievement in keeping down the overall home-defence man-power to the minimum consistent with reasonable security, notably for the AA gun network.

It could be argued with some force that the German bomber offensive demanded equally expensive diversions from their own battle-front units, though the airships, Gothas, and Giants, were widely used for operations other than raids against Britain. The cost of the large rigid airships rose from about £50,000 for early models to more than £150,000 for the later types, so the total bill for the 122 Zeppelins and Schütte-Lanz airships built for the German navy and army—assuming a conservative average cost of £100,000—exceeded £12 million (£141 million at 1980 prices). In addition to the seventeen lost on bombing sorties against Britain, another sixty-six were destroyed on other fronts or in accidents. The cost of hangars and ground facilities must have exceeded £5 million.

Based on the prices for comparable British aircraft, a Gotha and a Giant would have cost about £9,000 and £19,000 respectively (£112,500 and £228,000 at 1980 prices).

As regards combat techniques, the fighter successes against the Whit-Sunday raiders indicated that sound night tactics were developing, despite the need for the LADA squadrons to be fully alert and trained to deal with any resumption of daylight raiding. Night-fighting methods were well described by Murlis Green (who retired as a group captain) in an RAF Staff College paper of the early 1920s.

> 'On a dark night with no moon the exhaust flames of a stationary engine machine will usually be seen before the outline of the machine itself, but on a clear moonlight night the outline of the machine is generally first seen.
>
> 'After patrolling for an hour or so in the dark without seeing anything there is a tendency, when a hostile machine is at last seen, to dive straight at it firing both guns. This method seldom leads to success as the flash of the machine-guns, even when shielded, usually impairs the pilot's sight to such an extent that after the first few rounds have been fired he loses the target.
>
> 'The method found most successful up to now is as follows. Once you have seen your objective you must not take your eyes off him until he is destroyed or you wish to break off the fight. Turn your machine quickly into the same direction as he is going and get behind and slightly below him. If you have a 45 deg mounting use it. If your guns fire in line of flight close up until almost colliding, throttle back and open fire.
>
> 'There are two reasons why it is important not to open fire until extremely close range has been reached. Firstly, it is difficult to distinguish friend from foe at night, as of course crosses cannot be distinguished from circles, so that one has to rely entirely upon silhouettes. Secondly, range is very deceptive at night.'

In the same paper, and years ahead of contemporary thinking, Murlis Green postulated a twin-engined night-fighter, armed with ·5-in guns and having 45 deg upward shooting capability.

Major G. W. Murlis Green (the name appears hyphenated only in later RAF records), who flew more home-defence sorties than any other RFC/RAF squadron commander, in his office at Hainault with Lieut C. S. T. Lavers (*left*). No.44 Squadron operated against twenty enemy raids and Murlis Green flew on at least sixteen of those occasions. His work in the Second World War was in areas which attracted little publicity and he retired as a group captain, but his vigorous approach to the early night-bomber problem secures him a lasting place in RAF history. (*R. C. Bowyer*)

Although the validity of upward-firing trials results was strikingly confirmed by Turner and Barwise's competent victory, the single-seat fighter pilots, conditioned to aiming their aircraft with horizontal guns at the target, were, perhaps inevitably unenthusiastic over the stealthy, less dramatic 45 deg approach. During August–September No.151 Squadron in France achieved remarkable success using predominantly conventionally armed Camels against night-bombers, though they were dealing with a more concentrated attack pattern and some of their victories came during bold intruder sorties over the enemy bases.

This may partly explain why specialized night-fighting tactics and techniques received such scant attention in the inter-war years—a strange omission when night-bombers formed a substantial proportion of the RAF home-based strike force. There were occasional reminders from those with personal experience, and Flt Lieut W. M. (later Air Vice-Marshal) Yool, formerly of No.39 Squadron, suggested in a 1929 Staff College paper that fighters be designed to accommodate a detachable upward gun pack for night work. Upward-firing trials were conducted early in the Second World War, but with the decline of the German night offensive after 1941 the method was not developed. It was Germany, forced to devise counters to the massive Bomber Command raids, which rediscovered the benefits of oblique armament, and the 20 mm Schräge Musik (jazz band) installations in Messerschmitt Bf 110s and Junkers Ju 88s from the end of 1943 achieved devastating results.

An unpublished official historical note on No.6 Brigade, produced shortly after the war, claimed that night-fighters, assisted by a well-directed searchlight scheme, were the true counter to the night-bomber. Despite the indifferent searchlight performance during the final aeroplane raid, this was fundamentally true, though clearly the contribution from radio telephony could be equally important.

All the LADA squadrons were fitted with R/T by the end of August, and exercises were held with Handley Pages from the Stonehenge training school, though unfortunately no assessments of these have been traced. The following callsigns were allotted:

Squadron	Base	Aircraft
37	Yukon	Husky
39	Bona	Buffalo
44	Niger	Hippo
50	Bark	Dingo
61	Rockies	Grizzly
78	Cub	Lion
112	Darling	Duckbill
141	Dollars	Rhino
143	Pouch	Kangaroo

Squadron aircraft animal callsigns usually bore some self-evident relationship to the code names for their bases. This principle was necessarily applied loosely because of the need to use words easily recognizable and not liable to be confused with others in the list, an example being Rhino (an almost forgotten slang word for money) representing aircraft from No.141 Sqn's base–Dollars. The collective callsign for all No.6 Brigade aircraft was Menagerie. Patrol areas had geographical designations, *eg*, Brazil, Canada and Mexico. Code words used to precede orders transmitted from the ground included Gulls = the two highest aircraft on patrol, Penguins = all other aircraft, and Rum = recall. An aircraft forced to abandon its patrol signalled its intention with the word Blanket. Height alterations were ordered in thousands of feet, *eg*., 'Step up one' or 'Step down two', meaning climb 1,000 ft or descend 2,000 ft.

No.50 Squadron's R/T call-sign of Dingo was the inspiration for the device worn on their Sopwith Camels at Bekesbourne in the late summer of 1918. It was designed by Capt G. S. M. Insall, VC, then a squadron pilot. (*R. C. Bowyer*)

In favourable conditions, with equipment working well, reception was surprisingly good, and to relieve the tedium of night-training exercises No.50 Squadron sometimes played a portable gramophone in front of the transmitter, regaling pilots with current hit tunes. The almost magical new properties of R/T, difficult to appreciate after more than 60 years, proved irresistible to the bolder spirits attending the Penshurst course, and higher authority was obliged to veto the exchange of ribald limericks over the air, which raised the blushes of young female operators at monitoring stations.

Brig-Gen T. C. R. Higgins, GOC No.6 Brigade, inspecting a No.39 Squadron Bristol Fighter at North Weald during a preliminary round of the Squadron at Arms competition.

R/T procedures formed an important section of a 'squadron at arms' contest organized by the GOC No.6 Brigade to maintain efficiency and enthusiasm during the summer lull in German activity—which was expected to break at any time. This was the prototype of those numerous inter-unit competitions which later became a feature of peace-time RAF life, covering ground smartness and discipline as well as all aspects of flying and weapons proficiency. The final and concours d'élégance at Suttons Farm on 22 September saw No.141 Squadron the winner, with 585 points out of a possible 765. Second and third were No.61 (499 points) and No.50 (475½ points). Adjudged 'Cock Squadron', No.141 became entitled to carry a fighting-cock emblem on its Bristol Fighters—thus anticipating No.43 Squadron and its Gamecock badge by several years.

Although there were no official squadron markings as used on the Western Front, the home-defence units expressed their individuality with unofficial patterns and in the manner of displaying their flight identification numbers or

VIPs listening to the R/T event during the Squadron at Arms contest. In the group are Lord Weir, Secretary of State for the RAF (*seated, right*); Major-General W. S. Brancker, Master-General of Personnel, RAF (*standing, right*); and Lieut-Col M. G. Christie, OC No.49 Wing (*facing right, behind operator*). Brancker, who later became Director of Civil Aviation, was killed in the R101 disaster on 5 October, 1930.

Members of No.141 Squadron at Biggin Hill after winning the title of 'Cock Squadron'. Maj B. E. Baker, the CO, is standing with hands folded, left of centre. Bare-headed behind the rear cockpit is Lieut E. E. Turner.

letters. At one stage No.61 Squadron's S.E.5as were painted in an overall lozenge pattern—probably a piece of private enterprise rather than an official camouflage trial.

The introduction of R/T led to major reorganization and improvements in the LADA control and reporting system which were formally declared operational on 12 September, 1918. The main feature of the central operations room at Spring Gardens, near Admiralty Arch in London, was the large table displaying a squared map, surrounded by ten plotters. A dais provided a grandstand view for Ashmore, Higgins, a police representative, and a few senior operations officers. Plotters received information through telephone head-sets from 26 sub-control centres and transferred it to the map—a disc for a single enemy aircraft and a rectangle for a formation, with arrows indicating courses if known. During a prolonged raid different-coloured symbols were introduced to avoid confusion. Fighters were represented by aircraft-shaped counters. The sub-control centres received their reports from gun and searchlight sites, sound locators and the observation posts. Ashmore had a switchboard enabling him to cut in to plotters' lines should he require further information or to issue instructions to a sub-commander, and Higgins had direct lines to his fighter wings.

One of the ancillary operations rooms in the London Air Defence Area control and reporting centre at Spring Gardens, Admiralty Arch. This one appears to deal with the anti-aircraft gun network. (*Imperial War Museum*)

The gas-operated beacon, or lighthouse, at Hainault—one of the aids which helped to minimize night-flying hazards towards the end of the war.

Ashmore claimed that on average the operations room was now notified of enemy sightings in about 30 seconds, compared with the three minutes or more in September 1917. With R/T to direct the fighters, the prospects for successful interceptions were reckoned to have increased fourfold.

The greater responsibilities which R/T placed on the fighter pilots, and the growing demand for pilots to man new night squadrons in France, led to changes in the training programme. Also there was increasing concern about the number of accidents during training and non-operational flights by No.6 Brigade aircraft, though the accident rate on actual night patrols was remarkably low.

During just under 1,000 sorties flown against aeroplane bombers and Zeppelins in the twenty-six raids since the Gothas began night bombing in September 1917, there were only ten fatal accidents, causing twelve aircrew deaths. Bad weather was a major factor in two and a likely contributory cause of two more, while two aircraft were lost in a collision. Non-operational accident figures have been found for only six months of that period, and those record twenty-four accidents causing twenty-seven deaths in the home-defence squadrons. The total for the full year might well have been double that figure.

Direct comparisons would be misleading since the amount of non-operational flying, which included training sorties, vastly exceeded that spent on patrols—though little would have been undertaken in bad weather. Most accidents were the result of inexperience, a few caused by engine trouble and at least one followed a structural failure. A handful occurred during low aerobatics and 'beat-ups' which were fairly prevalent in those days of more lenient flying discipline. F.E.2b/ds figured in eleven of the accidents, reflecting the bigger training commitments of squadrons flying those machines. The overall RAF flying-accident rate (including training) for August 1918 averaged 2·26 per 100 flying hours, with Camels heading the list at 6·4 and Avro 504s near the bottom with 1·54. The introduction of a two-seater dual-controlled Camel in September considerably reduced the number of Camel training accidents.

Squadron Commanders varied in their methods of instilling flight-safety discipline, and Maj G. Allen's three pages of handling notes on the Bristol Fighter, for the benefit of his new pilots joining No.39 Squadron in March 1918, ended with this exhortation:

> 'Remember you have the best engine in the world. If you are careful of it and observe the few simple rules laid down, it is very unlikely to let you down.
>
> 'Remember you will soon have to take an Observer, if you have not already got one. You must, therefore, be doubly cautious. Observers are singularly confiding, but a "DUD" Pilot will sooner or later reduce his Observer to such a state of terror that he is quite useless.
>
> 'Remember that a crash caused by carelessness is a waste of men, money, and labour. There is no excuse for this kind of crash, and it is especially futile in England.
>
> 'The above hints are not my own. They are a precis of the opinions of experienced overseas Pilots and are meant as a guide to inexperienced Pilots.
>
> 'If you cannot fly a "BRISTOL FIGHTER" you must resign yourself to remaining an indifferent conductor of B.E's, F.E's, D.H.6's etc, for you will never be any kind of a "Pilot".'

No.6 Brigade trained the pilots for its own squadrons, and also for the F.E.2b night-bomber and Camel night-fighter squadrons in France. Pilots were divided into three groups according to preference and temperament—those to man the day and night squadrons of the southern home-defence wings or night-fighter units in France, those for northern night-fighter squadrons with a predominantly anti-Zeppelin role and those for the F.E.2b night-bomber units. Provisional allocations could be modified according to the pupil's aptitude while passing through a three-stage training programme introduced in August 1918. The syllabus for stages 'A' and 'B' was broadly similar for all pupils—except that the day-and-night fighter candidates were required to complete a simulated night cross-country flight wearing dark goggles. Cross-country training flights at night had proved a fruitful source of false air-raid alarms. Stage 'C' provided specialized training for the ultimate roles.

The system was somewhat complex, with the stages completed in different training or operational squadrons according to the category. It was further complicated by introducing two grades of operational pilots for the day-and-night graduates after passing to operational squadrons for their stage 'C' course. On completing this the student had logged at least 25 hours' solo, including four hours' night flying, passed advanced navigation and gunnery tests, landed within 50 yards of a mark from 10,000 ft without using engine, climbed to 19,000 ft in a Camel or Bristol Fighter, and made a 60-mile cross-country flight. He had also received some aerial combat and formation training and covered basic W/T. He was then awarded his 'wings' as a 2nd Class Operations Pilot, and took the R/T course at Penshurst. After more operational training back on his squadron he was upgraded to 1st Class Operations Pilot.

Training was maintained at high pitch during the summer of 1918 while the possibility of resumed air raids existed. Lieut G. F. Hollington, No.37 Squadron, in the cockpit of his Camel, with camera gun installed ready for a mock combat. (*Mrs M. F. Sadler*)

In August, while the possibility of resumed enemy raiding was still thought to exist, the Government agreed that the home-defence force should be raised to twenty squadrons. In fact the number deployed never exceeded sixteen, and by the Armistice on 11 November had fallen to fifteen, the pioneer night-fighter squadron, No.39, having moved to France a few days earlier.

During October the Allied advance forced the Germans to transfer their bombers from the Ghent area to aerodromes further east, and although unaware

This S.E.5a of B Flight No.37 Squadron awaiting an engine change at Stow Maries is a reminder of the vital behind-the-scenes work undertaken by the anonymous air mechanics of the home-defence units. (*Mrs M. F. Sadler*)

of the earlier policy decision to abandon the bombing of English targets, the Air Council considered that this ruled out any likelihood of resumed attacks. It was therefore decided that with enemy resistance crumbling, home-defence squadrons could safely be sent to France to operate as day fighters and help speed the final victory. Three more squadrons had been warned for transfer when the Armistice was agreed, and it had been planned that five others would quickly follow.

At the end of the war the home-defence fighter squadron line-up was:

Southern Group—allotted to London Air Defence Area

Squadron	Station	Aircraft
No.37	Stow Maries (A and B Flights)	Camel
	Goldhanger (C Flight)	,,
No.44	Hainault Farm	Camel
No.50	Bekesbourne	Camel
No.51	Mattishall (A Flight) Tydd St Mary (B Flight) Marham (C Flight)	F.E.2b Camel
No.61	Rochford	Camel
No.75	Hadleigh (A Flight)	Avro 504K
	Elmswell (B and C Flights)	,,
No.78	Suttons Farm	Camel
No.112	Throwley	Camel
No.141	Biggin Hill	Bristol Fighter
No.143	Detling	Camel

Northern Group—allotted to Northern Air Defence Area

Squadron	Station	Aircraft
No.33	Scampton (A Flight)	Avro 504K
	Kirton Lindsey (B Flight)	,,
	Elsham (C Flight)	,,
No.36	Usworth[1] (A Flight) Ashington (B Flight) Seaton Carew (C Flight)	Bristol Fighter, Pup[2]
No.76	Copmanthorpe (A Flight)	Avro 504K
	Helperby (B Flight)	,,
	Catterick (C Flight)	,,
No.77	Whiteburn (A Flight)	Avro 504K
	Penston (B and C Flights)	,,
No.90	Leadenham (A Flight)	Avro 504K
	Buckminster (B Flight)	,,
	Wittering (C Flight)	,,

Notes: 1 formerly named Hylton
2 about to re-arm with Avro 504Ks

This book has traced the growth of one small but vital area of First World War flying activity from the earliest days—when to remain safely airborne throughout a planned sortie was no mean achievement, and provision of some crude armament almost an afterthought—to the closing months when the combat aeroplane had become a reliable and efficient fighting machine. During that time the British air service grew from 270 aeroplanes and 2,073 officers and men to 22,647 aeroplanes and 291,170 officers and men.

In war, as in peace, the greatest acclaim is accorded to the moments of high drama—the outstanding successes and major tragedies. Mere competent completion of an allotted task is considered the norm and therefore of small interest to the public. Thus the best remembered pilots of the First World War are the fighter 'aces'—though the names of those few who achieved spectacular success against the Zeppelins, and to a lesser extent against the Gothas, are kept alive in a trickle of magazine articles and popular books.

But the great majority of the home-defence pilots remain shadowy, unknown figures. Some were engaged on this work at intervals throughout the war, while from 1917 others spent frustrating months, first in aircraft utterly incapable of coming to terms with the Gotha daylight formations, and then, better equipped, in seeking out the elusive enemy in darkness, gradually developing a new category of air combat and destroying for all time the myths surrounding night flying. All too often some technical or weather problem thwarted a well-executed and promising sortie. The courage of the early pilots—when night flying was believed to hold grave intrinsic dangers and the fetish of aircraft stability was akin to holy writ—who took off into fog and cloud knowing that the prospects of a safe return to earth were slender, recalls Bosquet's immortal reflection on the charge of the Light Brigade—'c'est magnifique, mais ce n'est pas la guerre'.

Courage and skill were not, as some contemporary accounts would have people believe, exclusively confined to the British airmen. While deaths of soldiers and sailors in battle were a regrettable but inevitable consequence of war, the bombing of the homeland was a new horror, and it was to be expected that the

Zeppelin crews and senior naval officers at Ahlhorn on 4 September, 1917, to celebrate the Pour le Mérite award to Fregattenkapitän Peter Strasser. Left to right, standing: Kptlts M. von Freudenreich, Hintzmann, L. Bockholt, F. Stabbert, Hptmn K. Manger, Kptlt Martin Dietrich, unidentified, Kptlt R. Schwonder, Adml R. Scheer, Kptn-z-S von Levetzow, Kvtkptn A. Schütze, Fregkptn P. Strasser, Kptlts Kühne, H. K. Gayer, W. Dose, H. Hollender, Oblt Schmidt, Oblt-z-S K. Friemel, Marine Eng Peetz, Marine Sailmaker Meier, Oblt-z-S A. Rothe, Oblt Schmidt, Kptlt P. Wendt, unidentified; seated: Lt-z-S H. von Schiller, Lt-z-S H. Bassenge, Oblt-z-S Gruner, Oblt-z-S R. Frey. Some of the most famous airship commanders had been killed before this photograph was taken, and four in the group later lost their lives on operations.

Gothas of Bogohl 3 at Gontrode—a photograph probably taken after the switch to night operations. The light-coloured aircraft with the undulating serpent decorating its fuselage was operational throughout the daylight campaign. (*Imperial War Museum*).

German bomber crews should be vilified as 'baby killers'. Spiritual guidance for the public varied—from the Bishop of London's condonement of the action of a trawler skipper who left the wrecked L19's crew to drown (on the plea that they might have overpowered his own small crew) to the action of an unnamed RFC chaplain, who had inscribed over the grave of L48's crew the text 'who art thou that judgest another man's servant?'.

The lack of any contemporary appreciation of the German operational achievement is, therefore, hardly surprising. However, no dispassionate observer can fail to admire the courage of the Zeppelin crews, whose fragile craft were not only highly vulnerable to the forces of nature but liable to become flaming infernoes when attacked. Add to this the miseries of sub-zero temperatures, anoxia—then known as 'altitude sickness'—and the anxieties inherent to any 16–20 hr war flying sortie, and the fortitude and devotion of the airship crews can be in no doubt.

The highest degree of professionalism was also displayed by the Gotha crews, whose very versatility is sufficient to refute some of the more absurd, propaganda-inspired assertions—for example that they were drawn from inferior elements of the German army air service. As the situation changed they switched from formation daylight raiding, to individual night sorties, then to intensive tactical operations sometimes demanding two sorties in one night. They were less susceptible than the airship crews to weather hazards, but more exposed to fighter attack, while the failure of an engine virtually ruled out any hope of completing the return sea crossing. And at the end of every sortie they were faced with the lightened bomber's difficult landing characteristics which brought so many to grief.

A remarkable record was established by the Giant crews, who completed 93 per cent of their missions against England—17 per cent better than the Gotha figure—and displayed great tenacity of purpose even after their cumbersome and complex machines had been disabled by the defences or through mechanical causes. That not one was lost to the defences, however, perhaps owed as much to good fortune as to any special features of their design or handling.

Appendix

RAF Home Defence Wings and Squadrons, November 1918

Squadrons are listed under their ultimate parent Wings, though in many cases they existed before the Wings were formed. Dates when aerodromes were occupied by Squadrons and Flights are not given, as official records in this respect are incomplete and sometimes conflicting: the essential facts are self-evident in the operational narrative. The effective formation dates of Squadrons are those given for the appointments of the first commanding officers. Aircraft allotted for assessment are not included.

No.46 Wing

Formed at York, 6 March, 1917. COs: Lieut-Col A. C. E. Marsh, 6 March, 1917; Lieut-Col W. G. Sitwell, 26 October, 1918.

No.36 Squadron.
COs: Capt R. O. Abercromby, 1 February, 1916; Maj C. S. Burnett, 26 April, 1916; Maj A. C. E. Marsh, 26 October, 1916; Maj J. H. S. Tyssen, February 1917; Maj S. W. Price, 1 January, 1918; Maj W. J. Tempest, 26 July, 1918.
Bases: Newcastle (HQ); Ashington, Cramlington, Hylton (renamed Usworth), Seaton Carew.
Aircraft: B.E.2c, B.E.12, Bristol Scout, F.E.2b, F.E.2d, Bristol Fighter, Sopwith Pup.

No.76 Squadron
COs: Maj E. M. Murray, 10 October, 1916; Maj A. C. Wilson, 1 February, 1918.
Bases: Ripon (HQ); Catterick, Copmanthorpe, Helperby.
Aircraft: B.E.2c, B.E.2e, B.E.12, B.E.12a, B.E.12b, Bristol Fighter, Avro 504K.

No.77 Squadron
COs: Maj W. Milne, 10 October, 1916; Maj K. van der Spuy, 13 April, 1917; Maj A. Somervail, 1 September, 1917.
Bases: Turnhouse (HQ); New Haggerston, Penston, Whiteburn.
Aircraft: B.E.2c, B.E.2e, B.E.12, B.E.12b, Avro 504K.

No.47 Wing

Formed at Adastral House, London, 17 October, 1917; Cambridge, 10 November 1917. COs: Lieut-Col A. T. Watson, 6 November, 1917; Lieut-Col H. Wyllie, 10 June, 1918.

No.51 Squadron
COs: Maj H. Wyllie, 18 July, 1916; Maj F. C. Baker, 11 September, 1917; Maj H. Wyllie, 23 March, 1918; Maj H. L. H. Owen, 21 August, 1918.
Bases: Thetford (HQ); Harling Road (formerly Roudham), Hingham, Marham, Mattishall, Tydd St Mary.
Aircraft: F.E.2b, F.E.2d.

No.48 Wing

Formed at Gainsborough, 1 February, 1918. COs: Maj E. M. Murray, 1 February, 1918; Lieut-Col J. C. Halahan, 13 March, 1918; Lieut-Col A. T. Watson, 10 August, 1918.

No.33 Squadron

COs: Maj P. B. Joubert, 15 January, 1916; Capt W. C. K. Birch, June 1916; Maj R. M. Vaughan, October 1916; Maj A. A. B. Thomson, November 1916; Maj C. G. Burge, November 1917; Capt G. M. Turnbull, June 1918.

Bases: Filton, Tadcaster, Gainsborough, Kirton-Lindsey (HQs); Beverley, Bramham Moor, Coal Aston, Elsham, Scampton (formerly Brattlesby).

Aircraft: B.E.2c, B.E.2e, B.E.12, F.E.2b, F.E.2d, Bristol Fighter, Avro 504K.

No.38 Squadron

COs: Capt A. T. Harris, 14 July, 1916; Maj L. J. E. Twisleton-Wykeham-Fiennes, September 1916; Maj C. C. Wigram, July 1917.

Bases: Castle Bromwich, Melton Mowbray (HQs); Buckminster, Leadenham, Stamford.

Aircraft: B.E.2c, B.E.2d, B.E.2e, B.E.12, F.E.2b, F.E.2d.

Note: No.38 Squadron was transferred to France as a night-bomber unit on 31 May, 1918, but a detachment remained on home defence until their commitment was taken over by the newly-formed No.90 Squadron on 22 August, 1918.

No.90 Squadron

CO: Maj W. B. Hargrave, 23 August, 1918.

Bases: Buckminster, Leadenham, Stamford.

Aircraft: Avro 504K.

No.49 Wing

Formed at Upminster, 24 September, 1917. COs: Lieut-Col R. C. Cherry, 24 September, 1917; Lieut-Col M. G. Christie, 8 February, 1918; Lieut-Col A. C. Boddam-Whettam, 26 October, 1918.

No.39 Squadron

COs: Maj T. C. R. Higgins, 1 May, 1916; Maj W. H. C. Mansfield, 13 June, 1916; Capt A. H. Morton, 26 July, 1916; Capt R. G. H. Murray, 20 March, 1917; Maj J. C. Halahan, 7 July, 1917; Maj W. H. D. Acland, 1 August, 1917; Maj G. Allen, 20 November, 1917; Maj W. T. F. Holland, 24 April, 1918.

Bases: Hounslow, Woodford (HQs); Biggin Hill, Hainault Farm, North Weald, Suttons Farm.

Aircraft: B.E.2c, B.E.2e, B.E.12, B.E.12a, Armstrong Whitworth F.K.8, S.E.5, Sopwith Camel, Bristol Fighter.

No.44 Squadron

COs: Maj T. O'B. Hubbard, 24 July, 1917; Capt G. W. M. Green, 29 August, 1917 (Maj from December 1917); Maj A. T. Harris, 11 June, 1918.

Base: Hainault Farm.

Aircraft: Sopwith 1½ Strutter, Sopwith Camel.

No.78 Squadron

COs: Maj H. A. van Ryneveld, 4 November, 1916; Maj J. C. Hallahan, 20 April, 1917; Maj C. R. Rowden, 5 July, 1917; Maj G. Allen, 26 April, 1918; Maj C. J. Truran, 12 August, 1918.

Bases: Hove, Harrietsham (HQs); Telscombe Cliffs, Chiddingstone Causeway (later renamed Penshurst), Gosport, Biggin Hill, Suttons Farm.

Aircraft: B.E.2e, B.E.12, B.E.12a, B.E.12b, Sopwith 1½ Strutter, F.E.2d, Sopwith Camel.

No.141 Squadron

COs: Maj P. Babington, 1 January, 1918; Capt B. E. Baker, 9 February, 1918 (Maj from May 1918).

Bases: Rochford, Biggin Hill.

Aircraft: B.E.12, B.E.12a, B.E.12b, Sopwith Dolphin, Bristol Fighter.

No.50 Wing

Formed at Adastral House, London, 28 August, 1917; Great Baddow, Chelmsford, 26 March, 1918. COs: Lieut-Col J. C. Halahan, 28 August, 1917; Lieut-Col R. C. Cherry, 25 February, 1918; Lieut-Col P. Babington, 20 June, 1918.

No.37 Squadron

COs: Maj W. B. Hargrave, 16 September, 1916; Maj F. W. Honnett, 1 November, 1917.
Bases: Woodham Mortimer (HQ); Goldhanger, Rochford, Stow Maries.
Aircraft: B.E.2d, B.E.2e, B.E.12, B.E.12a, B.E.12b, R.E.7, Sopwith 1½ Strutter, Sopwith Pup, S.E.5a, Sopwith Camel.

No.61 Squadron

COs: Maj E. R. Pretyman, 2 August, 1917; Maj E. M. Murray, 13 March, 1918; Maj E. Henty, 18 April, 1918; Maj E. B. Mason, 25 September, 1918.
Base: Rochford.
Aircraft: Sopwith Pup, S.E.5a, Sopwith Camel.

No.75 Squadron

COs: Maj H. A. Petre, 1 October, 1916; Maj T.O'B. Hubbard, 3 July, 1917; Maj T. F. Rutledge, 28 July, 1917; Maj C. S. Ross, 4 October, 1917; Maj C. A. Ridley, 1 November, 1918.
Bases: Goldington (HQ); Therfield, St Neots, Thrapston, Elmswell, Hadleigh, Harling Road
Aircraft: B.E.2c, B.E.2e, B.E.12, B.E.12b, Avro 504K.

No.53 Wing

Formed at Harrietsham, 11 March, 1918. CO: Lieut-Col A. A. B. Thomson.

No.50 Squadron

COs: Maj M. G. Christie, 15 May, 1916; Maj A. T. Watson, 23 February, 1917; Maj A. de B. Brandon, 16 October, 1917; Maj W. Sowrey, 17 August, 1918.
Bases: Dover, Harrietsham (HQs); Bekesbourne, Detling, Throwley.
Aircraft: B.E.2c, B.E.2e, B.E.12, B.E.12a, B.E.12b, Armstrong Whitworth F.K.8, S.E.5a, Sopwith Camel.

No.112 Squadron

COs: Maj G. Allen, 30 July, 1917; Maj B. F. Moore, 24 November, 1917; Capt C. A. Ridley, 1 December, 1917; Maj C. J. Q. Brand, 15 February, 1918; Maj G. W. M. Green, 9 July, 1918; Maj C. O. Usborne, 6 October, 1918.
Base: Throwley.
Aircraft: Sopwith Pup, Sopwith Camel.

No.143 Squadron

CO: Maj F. Sowrey, 14 February, 1918.
Base: Detling.
Aircraft: Armstrong Whitworth F.K.8, S.E.5a, Sopwith Camel.

General Index

Aircraft

Aeroplanes of RNAS and RFC
[Followed by Aeroplanes, German and Airships, German]

Aeroplanes, German

Airships, German

Aerodromes
RNAS and RFC
[Followed by German]

Aerodromes—RNAS and RFC

German

Service Formations and Units

British
[Followed by German]

Brigades

Groups

Wings

Squadrons, RFC/RAF

Squadrons, RNAS

Reserve Aeroplane Squadrons

Training Squadrons

Aircraft Acceptance Parks

German Units

People